T0366496

DUMBARTON OAKS
MEDIEVAL LIBRARY

Jan M. Ziolkowski, General Editor

ON PLATO'S *TIMAEUS*

CALCIDIUS

DOML 41

On Plato's *Timaeus*

CALCIDIUS

Edited and Translated by

JOHN MAGEE

DUMBARTON OAKS
MEDIEVAL LIBRARY

HARVARD UNIVERSITY PRESS
CAMBRIDGE, MASSACHUSETTS
LONDON, ENGLAND
2016

Library of Congress Cataloging-in-Publication Data
Names: Calcidius. | Magee, John, 1955– editor, translator.
Title: On Plato's Timaeus / Calcidius ; edited and translated by John
Magee.
Other titles: In Platonis Timaeum commentarius. English | Dumbarton
Oaks medieval library ; 41.
Description: Cambridge, Massachusetts : Harvard University Press,
2016. |
    Series: Dumbarton Oaks Medieval Library ; 41 | English translation on
the rectos, with the Latin original on the versos; introductory matter in
English. | Includes bibliographical references.
Identifiers: LCCN 2015037317 | ISBN 9780674599178 (alk. paper)
Subjects: LCSH: Plato. Timaeus. | Cosmology.
Classification: LCC B387 .C3413 2016 | DDC 113—dc23 LC record
available at http://lccn.loc.gov/2015037317

Contents

Introduction

Few works of philosophy have enjoyed the enduring prestige of the *Timaeus,* the dialogue in which Plato (ca. 429–347 BCE) set out to provide a rational account, cast in the form of a cosmological "myth," of the universe and humankind. The first formal exegesis was written by Crantor (ca. 335–ca. 275 BCE), a member of the early Academy, and others followed during the centuries leading up to Porphyry (232/33–ca. 305 CE) and Iamblichus (ca. 240–ca. 325 CE), after whom, in all probability, Calcidius entered the picture. Outside of the Academy, the *Timaeus* prompted immediate reactions from Aristotle (384–322 BCE), Theophrastus (372/69–288/85 BCE), and the Stoics, who absorbed and modified its doctrines before handing them back again to Platonists and Peripatetics of the imperial period.[1] The *Timaeus* formally reached Rome with Cicero's (incomplete) Latin version, which was certainly consulted by Boethius (ca. 480–524/25 CE) but appears not to have been used by Calcidius.[2] Of ancient commentaries, only those of Plutarch (ca. 46–ca. 125 CE),[3] Calcidius, and Proclus (412–485 CE) survive, and since Boethius did not live to translate or comment on any of the Platonic dialogues, it fell to Calcidius to carry the torch in the West until the arrival of Marsilio Ficino in the fifteenth

century.[4] So it happened that Calcidius's influence spanned much of Western Europe over the course of a millennium.

Calcidius himself, however, remains an elusive and enigmatic figure.[5] There is no direct evidence to indicate where he was born, educated, or wrote, and the little that can be gleaned about him derives perforce from conjectures concerning his work and its dedicatee. Even the spelling of his name is uncertain, some manuscripts favoring the aspirated "Chalcidius" over an unaspirated "Cal-"[6] but both suggesting a Latinized Greek derivation of some sort, possibly "Chalkideus." The chronology too is vague except insofar as Calcidius's literary activity obviously postdates the sources he uses or mentions and predates those that use or mention him. Thus an allusion (276) to the Christian theologian Origen sets the earliest possible limit at roughly the mid-third century CE,[7] while a borrowing in Favonius Eulogius sets the latest possible limit at around 400.[8] For further indications, we must turn first to the question of his dedicatee.

Calcidius translated and commented on Plato's *Timaeus* at the invitation of a certain Osius (Hosius), the evidence for whom could in principle point to five or more different individuals.[9] Most prominent among them was:

> Osius 1, the bishop of Cordoba who served as ecclesiastical adviser to Constantine and participated in the Councils of Nicaea and Serdica (325, 343 CE),

after whom comes the following evidence for:

> Osius 2. An undated funerary inscription from Milan points to an Osius who was of Patrician rank and served

as *Comes Rerum Privatarum* and *Comes Sacrarum Largitionum* in the West (*CIL* 5.6253).[10]

OSIUS 3. *Theodosian Code* 6.30.13 mentions a Hosius who served as *Comes Sacrarum Largitionum* in Constantinople in 395 CE.

OSIUS 4. *Theodosian Code* 6.26.6, 6.27.7–9, and 10.22.4 mention a Hosius (or Hosii?) who served as *Magister Officiorum* in Constantinople between 395 and 398 CE.

OSIUS 5. Claudian's *Against Eutropius* (2.342–53) features a Hosius who was allied with Eutropius in the suppression of Tribigild's revolt of 399 CE. He is derided as a former slave and cook of Spanish origin and may have been associated with Theodosius's household.[11]

The evidence is obviously inconclusive, dividing as it does between the first half of the fourth century (OSIUS 1) and the 390s CE (OSIUS 3–5), and between one known Christian (OSIUS 1) and possibly four (or more) court officials whose religious affiliations are unspecified (OSIUS 2–5).

OSIUS 1 was for some time rejected on the grounds of Isidore of Seville's silence regarding Calcidius, and of certain stylistic traits thought to indicate a later date of composition; but distinct echoes in Isidore's *On the Nature of Things* give the lie to the argument from silence,[12] and Calcidius's language is so idiosyncratic that any effort to date his work according to stylistic criteria seems destined only to beg the question. OSIUS 5, by contrast, has been doubted on grounds of the presumed improbability that such a person

would have had the requisite literary, philosophical, or indeed moral credentials for the commissioning of Calcidius's
work; but given the tendentious nature of Claudian's portrait, any such assumption seems equally doomed to mere
circularity. The attractiveness of Osius 1 and 2 has in certain
cases depended upon modern assumptions concerning Calcidius's own religious affiliation, and a related bias is evident
already in those medieval scribes who on the basis of a presumed association with Osius 1 conferred the rank of
(arch-)deacon upon Calcidius himself. Although for each of
the candidates motivations can be conjured up to explain
the commissioning of Calcidius's work, questions remain.
For example, did Osius commission the Latin translation
and commentary to counter deficiencies in his own command of Greek or to meet a perceived need within some
community? If the former, then how plausible are the candi-
dacies of Osius 1 or 3–5?[13] And if the latter, then what, if any,
sensitivities was he likely to have had to philosophical terminology that was acquiring new significance in the context
of fourth-century Trinitarian speculation, or to any indications of metaphysical dualism (295–99) during periods of
mounting anti-Manichean pressures?[14] Moreover, it should
be borne in mind that the evidence is probably incomplete,
in that there almost certainly existed other Osii for whom
no independent testimony survives. In the event, the sole
point of certainty would appear to be that our Osius, to
judge from the manner in which Calcidius expressly addresses him, was a Christian.[15]

Was then Calcidius a Christian as well?[16] He neither pro-
claims himself one nor professes or appeals to any article of
faith such as the Trinity, incarnation, crucifixion, resurrec-

tion, or baptism. Indeed, the very terms "christian," "pagan," and "gentile" are conspicuously absent from his work, most notably from those passages in which he directly addresses Osius.[17] To explain the silence on the grounds that Calcidius's task was to elucidate Platonic cosmology rather than to expound a Judaeo-Christian view of creation is merely to shift the burden of proof back upon those who insist upon his Christianity. And yet we can hardly fail to notice the distancing effect of the transitional phrase ("there is also another recorded tale") Calcidius uses to introduce the tale of the Magi in 126, where the Magi themselves are made to appear alongside an Egyptian Homer and are traced back to Chaldaea. And when he observes that it should not worry "us" that there are wicked angels, since some, "as you [Osius] know perfectly well, [are] minions of the adverse power" (133), he no more identifies himself as a Christian than he lays claim to a linguistic or ethnic identity in pointing out that "we"[18] use the Latin term *competens* whereas the Greeks use *analogia* (16): the one is a rhetorical concession to his dedicatee, the other an aid to his Roman readers. Moreover, a narrowly literal interpretation of the "we" for those passages in which Calcidius explains his Latin terminology with reference to the Greek would in principle mean reading an absurd insinuation of Roman identity into his making Plato's interlocutor Timaeus explain at 36a–b how "the Greeks" speak and write. Finally, a passage in 219 that might be construed as an indication of alignment with the Gospels forms part of an amalgam of Old Testament allusions used to undercut a point of "Hebrew"—and *Empedoclean*—doctrine that Calcidius rejects and evidently anticipates that Osius will reject as well. The chapter, in other words, shows Cal-

cidius uniting the Platonist and Christian in a polemical context.[19]

If Calcidius betrays no express bias in favor of Christianity, then it is equally true that he expresses no hostility toward it, and with that observation certain difficulties of interpretation immediately crop up. Waszink, for example, drew attention to a possible echo of the language of the Nicene Creed in 23 but at the same time noted a Peripatetic thrust in Calcidius's line of thought. Similarly, although some have detected a Christian resonance in Calcidius's reference to god as "preserver" (*conservator*) in 132, allowance clearly has to be made for the ecumenical tone of the passage, especially since its implicit philosophical concern comports with the notion of a Platonic Demiurge who in his ordering of the world ungrudgingly guarantees the conditions upon which its inhabitants must rely for their well-being (29e–30b). Although Plato's "craftsman god" (*deus opifex*) appears throughout the translation and commentary, Calcidius speaks in terms of a "creator" (*creator*) only twice, at 42e (146) and in 132. This is particularly remarkable given his use of the Latin verb *creare* ("to create") in the weaker sense of "giving rise to," as at 49c and 51a (the elements "creating" one another and other things) or in 79 (an astronomical phenomenon "creating" debate) and 215 (atoms "creating" soul), and given his eschewal of *creator* and *creare* in the chapters expressly dedicated to the "Hebrew" doctrine of creation, in which the Demiurge actually makes a surprise appearance (276–78).[20] Calcidius interprets the *Timaeus* metaphorically rather than literally, holding the priority of soul over body to be causal rather than temporal (26, 228) and explaining the Demiurge both as a literary contrivance to help readers past

the apparent contradiction between the notions of generation and eternity and as a force of "stern persuasion" in bringing order to precosmic Matter (138, 270, 300). All the while, he steers a course between the "Hebrew" doctrine of creation, on the one side, and certain Pythagoreans who are taxed with misinterpreting the *Timaeus* (295), on the other. Calcidius makes no explicit attempt either to harmonize the *Timaeus* and Genesis or to make one refute the other; instead, he leaves Plato and Moses to stand more or less independently of one another.

Of course these observations do not prove that Calcidius was not a Christian, but they underscore the challenge involved in extracting the conclusion that he was one from those passages that have most often been adduced in support of the claim. His openness to Christianity, insofar as the latter is actually in evidence in his work, would appear to be an indication of his regarding it, along with "the Hebrews," Moses, Solomon, the Prophets, Scripture, Philo, Orpheus, Homer, Pythagoras, and the Chaldaeans, as forming part of the wisdom tradition that otherwise populates his doxographies with Greek philosophers. In this sense, Calcidius seems a kindred spirit of both the Pythagorean Numenius of Apamea (2nd c. CE), famously reported to have proclaimed Plato an "Atticizing Moses" (fr. 8 des Places), and the Christian Clement of Alexandria (ca. 150–ca. 215 CE), who reflected seriously on the Pythagorean, Platonic, and other related traditions.[21] How, then, are we finally to interpret the apparent signs of impartiality? Is Calcidius's openness to Christianity, assuming he was a pagan, sincere or might it instead (also) reflect a concern to avoid offending his patron? Alternatively, and assuming he was a Chris-

tian, could his Platonism reflect an antiquarian impulse of some sort?[22] And indeed, in what sense does the pagan/Christian disjunction apply in his case?

Calcidius's name, as was mentioned earlier, may be of Greek derivation, and scattered throughout his work are linguistic features that suggest his bilingualism was of the "dominant" rather than "balanced" variety, favoring Greek over Latin.[23] Greek interference can be detected, for example, in his use of *decem et sex* and *decem et octo* for the numbers 16 and 18 (42–43, 46), in his epexegetical coupling of the Latin *origo* ("origin," Greek *archê*) and *arx* ("citadel," 26, 312), in his translating, in an astronomical context, the Greek adjective *polloi* ("many") with the Latin noun *poli* ("poles") rather than *multae* (69), or the Greek preposition *peri* ("around") with the Latin *per* ("through") rather than *circum* (40a, 85, 93),[24] and in his frequent use of the connective *-que et* ("and") in a manner reminiscent of Greek *te kai*.[25] Calcidius periodically refers to Plato with the lone demonstrative *idem* ("the same") or *ipse* ("himself"), as though he were struggling against the interference of Greek *autos*.[26] On one occasion he forgets to adjust for the absence of a Latin definite article and so translates the elliptical phrase, "the [planet] of Venus . . . departing" *(ho de tês Aphroditês . . . aphistamenos)*, with a genitive noun that clashes with a nominative participle (*Veneris . . . discedens,* 70). On another, he evidently writes the Latin *ratio* ("reason") while thinking the Greek *logos* and so forgets to convert the corresponding adjective to the feminine gender (*libidinosus,* 175). Similarly, he shows a certain confusion in the rendering of Greek genitives and datives (35b, 37a/d, 45d, 68, 286), employs the conjunction *ut* as a Greek declarative *hôs,*[27] constructs consecutive clauses with verbs in the infinitive and indicative moods,[28] pens an abla-

tive absolute that shares its subject with the main clause (237), and imports certain Greek constructions and idioms that sit unnaturally in Latin ([26d], 38e, [51a], 211).

Some of these symptoms appear too deeply rooted in Calcidius's language to be the products of later editors or scribes. Such would appear to be the case, for example, with the consecutive clauses mentioned above, two of which are tangled syntactic hybrids involving the subjunctive, indicative, and infinitive moods (215, 224). Surely it would be uneconomical to assume that an editor or scribe forced infinitives and indicatives upon subjunctives that Calcidius himself had correctly penned. Similarly, to explain the genitive *Veneris* in 70, the genitive of comparison *huius ipsius* in 68, or the genitive of difference *carentiae* in 286 as later errors we would have to assume that the putative editor or scribe forced a false Greek syntax upon the Latin while following precisely the same Greek sources as those Calcidius had used. But this too violates any rational principle of economy. Certain symptoms, it will perhaps be objected, demonstrate that Calcidius's command of Greek was in fact *weak*. Might not, for example, the genitive of comparison in 68 indicate a failure to grasp the astronomical phenomenon at issue precisely because of his deficient command of his Greek source, whether Theon of Smyrna or Adrastus of Aphrodisias (both 2nd century CE)?—Possibly, although no such assumption can explain the genitive of difference in 286, where Calcidius paraphrases Aristotle in a viable but *altered* Greek syntax. The latter, along with a multitude of passages in which Calcidius's Latin evidently spins out of control independently of any particular Greek interference, suggests that it was the Latin side of his mind that faltered in 68.

If these considerations support the suggestion that Calcidius essentially thought in Greek rather than Latin, they nevertheless fail to pinpoint a geographical or ethnic point of origin for him. Calcidius's name, for example, has sometimes been thought to suggest a connection with Chalcis in Euboea; but Euboean Chalcidians colonized widely from a very early period, and given that there was in any case more than one ancient city of Chalcis, the name in itself cannot be assumed to point to any particular region.[29] It seems in the end that, barring the emergence of new evidence, we are in no position to know where Calcidius was born or raised, and the same may be said of his education. Homer (93, 125, 154, 183, 266, 280), Hesiod (123, 134), Euripides (153, 183), Alexander "of Miletus" (72), Terence (184), and Virgil (66, 260, [266], 325, 352–53) form the list of (nonphilosopher) poets whom he quotes, paraphrases, or echoes, with Isocrates (E1) and Cicero (266)[30] putting in balanced appearances on behalf of oratory. The longest poetic quotation is unmistakably derivative, consisting of ten verses of Alexander copied from either Theon or Adrastus. Otherwise, Homer and Euripides make two back-to-back showings in contexts that may point to an intermediate source of some sort; Terence looks as though he has been brought in as a Roman school author to balance the Euripides quoted immediately before him; Virgil, obliquely referred to either as "the poet" or with an allusive "the poets," is quoted only once but generates a number of quieter echoes; and Isocrates launches Calcidius's work with an implicit exhortation to virtue, while Cicero is made to cap a brief catalog of Greeks extending from Homer to the Stoics. The fact that Greeks outnumber Romans undoubtedly has something to do with the array of sources employed by Calcidius, on which more will be said

presently; but it may be generally stated that the patterns of citation suggest his grafting of limited quantities of Terence, Cicero, and Virgil onto Greek sources that themselves quoted from a much wider array of philosophical and literary works. Although this may well indicate a rather shallow and narrow Latin literary culture, it should be pointed out that Calcidius nevertheless shows himself capable of composing some respectable iambic and dactylic verse for his Greeks.

The Translation and Commentary

Plato's *Timaeus* consists of four parts, an introduction (17a–29d) followed by accounts of the works of Reason (29d–47e), of Necessity (47e–69a), and of Reason in cooperation with Necessity (69a–92c). Calcidius translated but did not comment on 17a–31b, deliberately restricting attention to those parts of the dialogue that require detailed technical analysis. The extant translation and commentary consist of two matching parts, with the commentary in turn comprising thirteen thematically defined tracts (7):

I. *Timaeus* 31c–39e
   1. On the Generation of the World: 8–25
   2. On the Origin of Soul: 26–39
   3. On Harmonic Modulation: 40–45
   4. On Numbers: 46–55
   5. On the Fixed and Wandering Stars: 56–97
   6. On the Heaven: 98–118
II. *Timaeus* 39e–53c
   7. On the Four Kinds of Living Beings: 119–201
   8. On the Origin of Mankind: 202–7

Calcidius goes on to list fourteen others, which form no part of the extant text. The fact that both the translation and the commentary trail off at precisely the same point in 53c, together with what appears to be the concluding echo, in 355, of an emphasis laid, in 2, upon the four mathematical sciences, suggests that the extension of the transmitted text is not the result of chance survival. Whether the remaining translation and commentary perished or were never written is uncertain, although Calcidius's mention (E8) of sending Osius a "taste" of the first parts of the *Timaeus* indicates that our text was at any rate planned as part of a larger project.[31] Although certain manuscripts favor the disposition, *Timaeus* I–II, Commentary I–II, as in modern editions, most favor the ordering, *Timaeus* I, Commentary I, *Timaeus* II, Commentary II, as was probably intended by Calcidius himself.[32] Particularly significant are the implications of the broader architecture of the work, for in setting the main divide at 39e (119) rather than 47e (268), Calcidius shifts the emphasis away from Reason and Necessity to the universe and our place within it (Macrocosm—Microcosm)[33] while at the same time structuring the first part of the commentary along the lines of what after Boethius would become known as the Quadrivium, or the mathematical disciplines (arithmetic, geometry, music, astronomy), which in 355 are de-

scribed as the foundations of a liberal education and the first stages of a philosophical ascent.

Calcidius's commentary is thus built upon lemmata, or passages excerpted from the *Timaeus* for running commentary, but is at the same time shaped by the series of thirteen tracts mentioned above.[34] Points of articulation within the series remain conjectural insofar as the thirteen titles were evidently missing already in the archetype. Tracts 5, 7, and 13 together compose more than 60 percent of the commentary; tracts 2–5 (or 6) intermittently follow a source that cuts a trajectory across the four (five) discrete themes, while tract 7 exhibits just the opposite pattern in embracing an excursus on demons (127–36) and a subtreatise on fate (142–90), which bring their own sources and methods into play. These contrasting patterns indicate that the division of the commentary into tracts was, in Calcidius's mind, logically prior to the sources he gathered for use, although there must have been considerable interplay between his sources and the structuring principles he devised for the commentary.

Although readers encountering Calcidius for the first time may wonder at his command of the full sweep of Greek philosophy from Thales (280, 325, 332) in the sixth century through Chrysippus (144, 220, 290) in the third century BCE, repeated readings will eventually breed the suspicion that a number of his historico-philosophical wares are not only secondhand but damaged. Pythagoras and Pythagoreans dominate the first part of the commentary largely because of their prominence in his main source (Theon or Adrastus) and because of the general mathematical emphasis. The second part of the commentary displays a more varied pattern of citations and allusions. In some cases phi-

losophers or schools cluster within a chapter, possibly suggesting a doxographical tradition,[35] whereas in others chapters cluster around a philosopher or school, suggesting direct access to the relevant material or perhaps biographical traditions of some sort.[36] Certain chapters that quote from Plato and Aristotle appear to have been translated directly from the relevant works, but others leave room for doubt. In 168, for example, Calcidius discusses a passage of the *Theages* that he goes on to quote in 255, but as from the *Euthydemus*. Did he actually consult the *Theages* twice and mistake its title the second time, or was he copying from a confused intermediary? In the event, we have to reckon, even in the cases of Plato and Aristotle, with the likelihood of Calcidius's periodic reliance upon school traditions that had prepackaged material for him.[37] The point is underscored by 158, which consists of observations loosely based on Aristotle and variously echoed by later sources: Calcidius sets the discussion in motion with a "he says" that has no stated or implied subject, as though he were copying predigested material without remembering to fit it to context.

To judge from the list of figures actually named by Calcidius, Greek philosophy began with Thales, came to a halt with Chrysippus, then resumed with Numenius (295–99) three and a half centuries later. After Numenius, silence descends upon the commentary insofar as Calcidius never mentions Plotinus (ca. 205–270 CE), Porphyry, Iamblichus, or any other later figure. Any argument from silence will of course be undercut by his unacknowledged use of Theon (or Adrastus), Alcinous (2nd c. CE), Pseudo-Plutarch (2nd c. CE), and others, while any attempt to explain the silence on *chronological* grounds would only beg the question. That

leaves us to weigh mere probabilities. Plotinian echoes are faint if at all audible. Porphyry has tended to exert a magnetic effect, attracting attention wherever evidence for known or probable sources leaves a vacuum. Thus Waszink, followed by van Winden and den Boeft, maintained that significant portions of Calcidius's commentary were copied from Porphyry, and their view was brought into sharp relief when Sodano adopted extended passages of Calcidius as evidence for Porphyry's lost *Timaeus* commentary.[38] Others, however, have since expressed caution, if not skepticism.[39] In 301 (and 352) an interpretation of precosmic tumult is traced back to certain unnamed interpreters; Philoponus attributes the same interpretation to Porphyry, thereby securing a date of sometime after circa 305 CE for Calcidius's work. Otherwise, however, the question of Porphyrian influence remains open.

Iamblichus raises further uncertainties. In 272, for example, Calcidius classifies the *Timaeus* as a work of natural philosophy (physics) and the *Parmenides* as an "epoptic" dialogue, which might be thought to reflect Iamblichus's classification of the *Timaeus* as a work of natural philosophy and the *Parmenides* as one of theology or metaphysics.[40] But the *Timaeus*–physics association undoubtedly antedates Iamblichus, who in any case does not appear to have classified the *Parmenides* specifically as "epoptic." A particular interpretation of metempsychosis that is discussed in 198 may however indicate an Iamblichean connection of some sort; if so, then it would also serve to date Calcidius's work to sometime after circa 325 CE.

In the end, chronology does little to explain Calcidius's work, which so obviously falls outside the scope of any

strictly developmental account of "Middle-" and "Neopla-tonism." Calcidius's identification of the Platonic Recep-tacle with Aristotelian Matter and his various Stoicising impulses obviously reflect traditions that had significantly altered ancient perspectives on the *Timaeus,* but it is diffi-cult to ascertain the precise degree to which his philosophi-cal points of reference are Numenius, Alcinous, and Apu-leius in the second century CE, as opposed to Plotinus, Porphyry, and Iamblichus in the third to fourth. This puz-zling sense of anachronism may have contributed to the later fascination with Calcidius, especially during the "re-naissance" of the twelfth century, when his translation and commentary presented themselves as a coalescence of ideas frozen outside of time and space. From Calcidius, twelfth-century readers may have learned how ancient opinions on the World Soul, Fate, and Matter lined up conceptu-ally, but they got from him no reliable means of disentan-gling the historical descent or intersections of those opin-ions. Yet Calcidius proved to be a fundamental source of inspiration for thinkers such as Bernardus Silvestris, Wil-liam of Conches, and Alan of Lille, who set out to make new sense of the world, its architecture, the forces that animate it, and our place within it. His panoramic doxographies and scientific encyclopedism gave them a *Timaeus* that could be interpreted as intimating, in veiled allegories or symbols, the deepest mysteries of the world.[41]

A warm word of thanks is due first to three institutions, for their generous support: Dumbarton Oaks, which hosted me as a Director's Visiting Scholar in May of 2013; the Freiburg Institute for Advanced Studies, Albert-Ludwigs-

Universität, for a Senior External Fellowship held during the 2013–14 academic year; the Council of the Humanities and Department of Classics, Princeton University, for an Old Dominion Fellowship held during the fall term of 2014. The Latin text was initially set up and corrected by Emily Blakelock, Madeleine Getz, and Eduardo Fabbro, who also compiled the Index. Béatrice Bakhouche, Timothy Barnes, Caroline Bynum, Christoph Helmig, Christina Hoenig, Scott Johnson, George Karamanolis, Nino Luraghi, Gretchen Reydams-Schils, Andreas Speer, Brian Stock, Massimiliano Vitiello, Jarrett Welsh, and Kevin Wilkinson commented on sections of the book or on papers that were presented in the course of its preparation. The translation benefitted from insightful readings given it by Coleman Connelly, Justin Stover, Danuta Shanzer, and Winthrop Wetherbee; and Brad Inwood, Robert Kaster, and Christian Wildberg gave focused consideration to a number of particularly troublesome passages. All remaining errors, of course, remain my sole responsibility. My greatest debt is to Raquel Begleiter, Heather Hughes, Danuta Shanzer, and Jan Ziolkowski, for their patient support during the course of this long and difficult project. The book is dedicated to my daughters, Sanjana and Helena.

NOTES

1 See Tarán, "Creation Myth,"388–90; Reydams-Schils, *Demiurge and Providence,* 41–205. *System of references:* Arabic numerals preceded by uppercase "E" refer to the Dedicatory Epistle (E1, E2, E3); those followed by lowercase letters refer to the *Timaeus* (17a, 17b, 17c); those without letters refer to the Commentary (1, 2, 3).

2 Boethius, *On Cicero's Topics* 3.5.27 (1092d); Bakhouche, *Calcidius,* 120–24.

3 *On the Generation of the Soul in the "Timaeus,"* a lemmatized monograph on 35a–36b.

INTRODUCTION

4 No *Timaeus* translation survives from Henricus Aristippus; on William of Moerbeke and Proclus's commentary, see G. Verbeke, "Guillaume de Moerbeke, traducteur de Proclus," *Revue philosophique de Louvain* 51 (1953): 349–73.

5 See *RE* 3.2.2042–43, 8.2.2493; *PLRE* 1.172–73, 1.445, 2.572; Waszink, *Timaeus,* ix–xvii, clxxxvi; Dillon, *Middle Platonists,* 401–8; Gersh, *Middle Platonism and Neoplatonism,* 421–34; Moreschini, *Calcidio,* xii–xvi; Dutton, "Medieval Approaches," 184–88; Bakhouche, *Calcidius,* 7–13.

6 Compare "Chrysippus" (144, 220, 290), "Chaldaeorum" (126), "Acyles" (276).

7 Origen died in 254/55 CE; his Genesis commentary may have dated to the 230s.

8 Dorfbauer, "Favonius Eulogius," 383 n. 16, 394. Macrobius quotes Calcidius's translation of *Timaeus* 50e in the preface to the *Saturnalia* (8). On the later grammarian Calcidius, see R. A. Kaster, *Guardians of Language: The Grammarian and Society in Late Antiquity* (Berkeley, Los Angeles, and London, 1988), 250.

9 To judge from E4/7 (with 20a–b), Osius was senior to Calcidius (assuming he is not a mere fiction, on which see Ratkowitsch, "Die Timaios-Übersetzung," 141; Moreschini, *Calcidio,* xiii n. 9).

10 Dated by *PLRE* (2.572) to the first half of the fifth century CE, and presumed by some to have been a Christian. The titles, at any rate, probably indicate the 340s at the earliest (*PLRE* 1.1062–65).

11 J. Long, *Claudian's "In Eutropium." Or, How, When, and Why to Slander a Eunuch* (Chapel Hill and London, 1996), 41 n. 71 (combining Osius 4–5).

12 Bakhouche, *Calcidius,* 54–55. The underlying assumption was that any known Spanish connection would inevitably have received mention from Isidore.

13 E5 suggests that Osius's command of Greek was not the concern, but account obviously has to be taken of the literary genre in play there. On knowledge of Greek in the Latin West generally, see P. Courcelle, *Later Latin Writers and Their Greek Sources,* trans. H. E. Wedeck (Cambridge, Mass., 1969); A. Cameron, *The Last Pagans of Rome* (Oxford, 2011), 527–66.

14 Manicheism was targeted by Diocletian in the 290s CE but came under increasing pressure from Theodosius in the 380s. In the West, it figures in Philastrius's *Catalogue of Heresies* (61), written circa 383/84, and is repeat-

edly attacked by Augustine during the years following his conversion in 386.

15 Ratkowitsch suggests, however, that he may have been a pagan Neoplatonist leaning toward conversion ("Die Timaios-Übersetzung," 161–62).

16 See generally Reydams-Schils, "Calcidius Christianus?" 204–9; Moreschini, *Calcidio,* xxxi–xxxix; Bakhouche, *Calcidius,* 42–44; Hoenig, "*Timaeus Latinus*," 92–96.

17 Whose Christianity is itself only indirectly acknowledged (126, 133), Origen's as well (276). Occurrences of the Latin *natio,* it may be noted, involve no pejorative sense of the "non-Christian" (19d, 41e [191], 7).

18 *A nobis* ("by us"), 16, is a conjectural supplement to the received text, but undoubtedly correct (compare 123, 268, 273, 346).

19 Compare Reydams-Schils, "Calcidius on God," 252.

20 The quotation of Proverbs in 276 *(Creavit me . . . deus)* is obviously a special case.

21 Note Dronke's portrait of Calcidius as a philosophically uncompromising Christian who declined to "gain points" for the Bible or Christianity (*The Spell of Calcidius,* xiv–xviii).

22 Compare more generally, A. Cameron and A. Cameron, "Christianity and Tradition in the Historiography of the Late Empire," *CQ* n.s. 14 (1964): 316–28.

23 On the "dominant"/"balanced" distinction, see *BLL* 6–8. Waszink already detected a number of revealing Grecisms (on *Timaeus,* 100.3–4, 151.14–15, 232.19–33.13, 234.1, 273.16, 301.6), and Bakhouche raises the main question at the beginning of her monumental edition (*Calcidius,* 8).

24 On further signs of phonetic interference, see Notes to the Translation, 29d.

25 See Notes to the Translation, 23c.

26 See Notes to the Translation, 31.

27 See Notes to the Translation, 27c; and further on *ut - hôs,* 37c, 43a, 299.

28 See Notes to the Translation, 43e.

29 The grammarian Calcidius (above, n. 8), for example, was evidently North African; conversely, Iamblichus hailed from a city of Chalcis in Syria Coele.

30 The reference to Cicero in 27 is a red herring.

31 Note the intimations of 67c–e in 244 and 260. That Calcidius made

more than one attempt at translation, or revised the translation over time, is evident from certain commentary citations (123–24, 139, 273, 325, 329, 332, 354) that do not appear in the continuous version. Bakhouche, moreover, has identified numerous points of difference between the continuous translation and commentary citations. Compare Notes to the Translation, 301.

32 Bakhouche, *Calcidius,* 77.

33 See Notes to the Translation, E1, 119–201.

34 Several passages explicitly signal a shift between general theory and exegesis (91, 137–38, 321). The commentary is in fact a blend of lemmatized exegesis, paraphrase, and thematically defined questions.

35 For example, 203, 215, 220, 246, 266, 279–82.

36 For example, 160–75, 222–26, 283–320.

37 Note his observations on discordant Platonists (301), "the Peripatetics" (223, 238), and certain generational disputes within traditions (243, 246, 252).

38 Waszink, *Timaeus,* xc–xcv; van Winden, *Calcidius on Matter,* 246–47; den Boeft, *Calcidius on Fate,* 132–37; *Calcidius on Demons,* 57–61; A. R. Sodano, ed., *Porphyrii in Platonis Timaeum commentariorum fragmenta* (Naples, 1964).

39 Dillon, *Middle Platonists,* 403–4; Gersh, *Middle Platonism and Neoplatonism,* 431–32; Moreschini, *Calcidio,* xxiv–xxx; Bakhouche, *Calcidius,* 38–39.

40 Waszink, *Timaeus,* xcvi–xcix; J. M. Dillon, ed., *Iamblichi chalcidensis in Platonis dialogos commentariorum fragmenta* (Leiden, 1973), 264–65.

41 On the medieval fortunes of Calcidius, see (among many others) R. Klibansky, *The Continuity of the Platonic Tradition During the Middle Ages* (Munich, 1981²); T. Gregory, *Platonismo Medievale. Studi e Ricerche* (Rome, 1958); C. Ratkowitsch, *Die Cosmographia des Bernardus Silvestris—eine Theodizee* (Cologne, 1995); Dronke, *The Spell of Calcidius.*

DEDICATORY EPISTLE

Osio Suo Calcidius

{E1} Isocrates in exhortationibus suis virtutem laudans, cum omnium bonorum totiusque prosperitatis consistere causam penes eam diceret, addidit solam esse quae res impossibiles redigeret ad possibilem facilitatem. {E2} Praeclare; quid enim generosam magnanimitatem vel aggredi pigeat vel coeptum fatiget, ut tamquam victa difficultatibus temperet a labore? {E3} Eadem est, opinor, vis amicitiae parque impossibilium paene rerum extricatio, cum alter ex amicis iubendi religione, alter parendi voto complaciti operis adminiculentur effectui. {E4} Conceperas animo florente omnibus studiis humanitatis excellentique ingenio tuo dignam spem proventuri operis intemptati ad hoc tempus eiusque usum a Graecis Latio statueras mutuandum. {E5} Et quamquam ipse hoc cum facilius tum commodius facere posses, credo propter admirabilem verecundiam, ei potius malueris iniungere quem te esse alterum iudicares. {E6} Possemne, oro te, quamvis res esset ardua, tanto honore habito de quo

Calcidius, to His Osius

{E1} Isocrates, in the course of praising virtue in his *Exhortations*, and after pointing out that the cause of all good things and of all prosperity depends upon it, added that it alone is capable of bringing impossible conditions back to a state of being possible to manage. {E2} It is a splendid point, for when it comes to a noble magnanimity, what could either cause it to be annoyed by an undertaking or, once the task is underway, exhaust it to the point of its being virtually overcome by the difficulties and refraining from the effort? {E3} Such, I suppose, is the power of friendship, just so its ability to remove the constraints of nearly impossible conditions, when friends support one another in the performance of an agreed-upon task, one of them by the obligation of commanding and the other by a vow of obeying. {E4} You had conceived the hope—one that was worthy of your mind, which blossoms with all forms of liberal education, and of your extraordinary character—of seeing the emergence of a hitherto unattempted work, and had determined that with it Latium should make borrowed usage from the Greeks. {E5} And although capable yourself of completing the work both more easily and to better effect, you preferred instead, no doubt because of your admirable sense of modesty, to enjoin it upon one whom you regarded as your other you. {E6} Although the matter was a difficult one, could I, please tell me, have refused the obligation when you made such a

3

ita senseras iniunctum excusare munus, et qui numquam, ne
in sollemnibus quidem et usitatis voluntatibus, ullum officium recusassem huic tanto tamque honesto desiderio con-
tradicere, in quo declinatio speciosi muneris excusatione
ignorationis callida esset scientiae futura simulatio? {E7} Itaque parui certus non sine divino instinctu id mihi a te munus
iniungi proptereaque alacriore mente speque confirmatiore
primas partes Timaei Platonis aggressus non solum transtuli
sed etiam partis eiusdem commentarium feci putans recon-
ditae rei simulacrum sine interpretationis explanatione aliquanto obscurius ipso exemplo futurum. {E8} Causa vero
in partes dividendi libri fuit operis prolixitas, simul quia
cautius videbatur esse, si tamquam libamen aliquod ad de-
gustandum auribus atque animo tuo mitterem, quod cum
non displicuisse rescriberetur, faceret audendi maiorem fi-
duciam.

display of honor in enjoining it upon me? Could I, who had never refused any duty when it came even to customary or routine wishes, have said no to this desire, one so considerable and honorable, when declining this splendid obligation on a plea of ignorance would have proved a calculated simulation of knowledge? {E7} And so, feeling certain that it was not without divine instigation that the obligation had been enjoined upon me by you, I complied and consequently not only undertook, with quickened intention and a strengthened sense of hope, to translate the first parts of Plato's *Timaeus* but also produced a commentary on the same on the understanding that without an explanatory interpretation the image of a recondite reality would prove even more obscure than the original itself. {E8} As for the rest, the length of the work was my reason for dividing the book into parts, also, because my sending a kind of first sampling, as it were, for your ears and mind to taste seemed the safer course: once the reply came back, indicating that it had not displeased, it would strengthen my resolve to forge ahead.

TIMAEUS

Pars Prima Timaei Platonis

SOCRATES TIMAEUS HERMOCRATES CRITIAS

{17a} *Socrates:* Unus, duo, tres—quartum e numero, Timaee, vestro requiro, ut qui hesterni quidem epuli convivae fueritis, hodierni praebitores invitatoresque ex condicto resideatis.

Timaeus: Languor eum repente, ut fit, ortus moratur. Nec enim sponte se tali coetu tantaeque rei tractatu et communicatione fraudaret.

Socrates: Ergo tui et item horum erit officii complere id quod deest participis absentia?

{17b} *Timaeus:* Aequum postulas. Denique enitemur omnes pro viribus, neque enim fas est laute acceptos heri minoris tibi apparatus repraesentare convivium.

Socrates: Tenetis certe memoria praescriptam vobis a me tractatus normulam?

Timaeus: Partim tenemus; in quibus porro nutabit memoria, praesens ipse in tempore suggeres. Immo, nisi erit molestum, breviter ab exordio dicta demum retexe, quo digestus ordo solidetur.

{17c} *Socrates:* Ita fiet. Cardo, nisi fallor, disputationis hesternae res erat publica, qualis mihi quibusque institutis et moribus civium videretur optima.

The *Timaeus* of Plato, First Part

SOCRATES TIMAEUS HERMOCRATES CRITIAS

{17a} *Socrates:* One, two, three — I'm missing the fourth member of your group, Timaeus, for having been guests at yesterday's banquet, you were by agreement to reconvene as the inviting hosts of today's.

Timaeus: An illness, nothing serious, which has suddenly arisen is detaining him. For not by choice would he have deprived himself of such a gathering, or of the treatment and communication of a matter of such importance.

Socrates: Will it then be your duty and that of the others to complete the part which remains owing to his absence?

{17b} *Timaeus:* Yours is a fair request. In short, we will collectively do what we can, for it is not right that those who were so lavishly entertained yesterday should offer you in return a feast that is any less well prepared.

Socrates: You recall, I assume, the terms for the discussion I set for you?

Timaeus: We do in part; and those points in connection with which our memory falters you yourself will be there to supply as needed. Better still, if you have no objection, simply retrace briefly from the beginning what you said, in order to confirm the order of exposition.

{17c} *Socrates:* Very well. Yesterday's discussion, if I am not mistaken, centered on the state, the sort I considered to be the best, and taking into account its institutions and customs.

Timaeus: Nobis certe qui audiebamus, o Socrate, ad arbitrium probata.

Socrates: Quid illud? Nonne inter initia cultores agrorum ceterarumque artium professores a destinata bellicis negotiis iuventute secrevimus?

Timaeus: Sic factum est.

Socrates: Tributo nempe ceteris quod cuique eximium a natura {17d} datum est, solis his qui pro salute omnium bella tractarent unum hoc munus iniunximus protegendae civitatis vel adversum externos vel adversum intestinos ac domesticos hostes; mitibus quidem iudiciis erga {18a} oboedientes, utpote consanguineos naturaque amicos, asperis autem contra armatas acies in congressionibus Martiis; biformi siquidem natura praeditos, in tutela patriae civiumque ferociores, porro in pacis officiis religione sapientes; proptereaque mites suis, adversum alienigenas feroces.

Timaeus: Memini.

Socrates: Quid? Huius ipsius ancipitis naturae magisterium et quasi quandam nutricationem nonne in exercitio corporum gymnasiorumque luctamine, animorum item placiditatem constituebamus in delinimentis et affabilitate musicae ceterarumque institutionum quas adulescentes ingenuos scire par est?

Timaeus: Ita.

{18b} *Socrates:* At vero hac educatione altis auri argentique

Timaeus: We at any rate who were listening, Socrates, were in ready agreement with you.

Socrates: Well then, did we not in the first stages separate those who cultivate the land and the practitioners of other technical arts from the youth destined to conduct the business of war?

Timaeus: So we did.

Socrates: And of course, after assigning to the rest the task for which each was most naturally {17d} endowed, we enjoined upon those alone who were to conduct wars in the interests of the common safety the single task of protecting the city against its enemies, whether external or internal and domestic. We said that they were to pronounce lenient judgments in the case of those who were {18a} obedient, being related to and by nature amicably disposed toward them, but harsh ones against armed aggressors in periods of martial engagement. For we said that they were to be endowed with a double nature, being more ferocious in their protection of the fatherland and its citizens but wisely guided by a sense of devotion in their management of the affairs of peace; hence, that they were to be gentle toward their own but ferocious in the face of foreigners.

Timaeus: I remember.

Socrates: And what about the education of this twofold nature, its nourishment, as it were? Did we not base it upon bodily exercise and gymnastic contests, and the peaceful disposition of their minds upon the soothing delight of music and the other disciplines which our freeborn youth really ought to know?

Timaeus: We did.

{18b} *Socrates:* But we said that for those who had been

et supellectilis ceterae possessionem cuiusque propriam nullam esse aut existimari licere praediximus sed sola mercede contentos, exhibentibus quorum salutem tuerentur, uti communiter tanta quae satis sit occupatis erga custodiam communis salutis et a cetera functione operis cessantibus.

Timaeus: Dicta haec omnia in istum modum sunt.

{18c} *Socrates:* De feminis quoque opinor habitam mentionem, quod similes eiusdemque naturae maribus conveniat effingi sine ulla morum differentia, quo uterque sexus isdem et communibus institutis regatur. Quid de procreandis suscipiendisque liberis? An vero hoc ita ut cetera, quae praeter opinionem hominum consuetudinemque vitae dici videntur, memorabile vivaciorisque tenacitatis de existimandis communibus nuptiis communique prole, si suos quisque minime internoscat affectus? {18d} Proptereaque omnes omnibus religionem consanguinitatis exhibeant, dum aequales quidem fratrum et sororum caritate benivolentiaque ducantur, maioribus vero parentum religio, eorumque antiquioribus avorum exhibeatur atque atavorum reverentia, infraque filiis et nepotibus debita caritas atque indulgentia convalescat?

raised under this system of education it would not be permitted for any gold, silver, or other instrument of exchange to be, or to be considered, the private possession of a particular individual but that, being content with only the pay furnished by those whose well-being they were responsible for, they would make common use of such possessions as are sufficient for those who are engaged in the oversight of the common weal but refrain from functional tasks of any other kind.

Timaeus: These points were all made just as you have indicated.

{18c} *Socrates:* I suppose that concerning the women too there was discussion to the effect that it would be fitting for them to be molded similarly to the men, the same in nature and without any difference of character, in order that both sexes might be brought under the same, common instructional regime. What about their procreation of and responsibility for children? Or is this another instance of claims that apparently exceed the limits of what people believe and are accustomed to in life? Is our point concerning marriages and offspring being regarded as commonly shared memorable, and indeed more vividly unforgettable, if no individual is in a position to distinguish his own loved ones? {18d} So that all would display the devotion of blood kinship to all—those of like age behaving with the benevolent affection of brothers and sisters, displaying filial devotion toward their elders and the reverence for grandparents and older generations toward *their* elders, and the patient love that is owed to children and grandchildren taking root as concerns those younger than them?

Timaeus: Haec quoque facilia memoratu et a nobis reti-
nentur optime.

Socrates: Quid illud, quod sine odio atque aemulatione
nubentium melioribus procis melius moratae virgines sortito obveniant, inferiores porro inferioribus? Non tenetis
saluberrimam sortis fraudem {18e} curantibus in utroque
sexu praefectis nuptiarum, quo suam quisque fortunam sortis improsperam culpet nec praelationem doleat alterius?

Timaeus: Hoc quoque memoria tenemus.

{19a} *Socrates:* Illud etiam promulgatum puto, lectorum
fetus parentum summa cura, utpote naturale bonitatis pri-
vilegium praeferentes, alendos.

Timaeus: Id ipsum.

Socrates: Ceteros alii cuidam usui patriae futuros, processuque aetatis eorum nihilo remissiore cura notanda pueri-
tiae et item adulescentiae merita, quo tam ex secundi ordinis populo provehantur ad primum ordinem propugnatorum
qui merebuntur quam ex his qui a parentum virtute degene-
raverint ad secundae dignitatis ordinem relegentur. Ecquid
ergo, Timaee, satis videtur factum recepto cunctis partibus
orationis hesternae, strictim licet compendioque decursis,
an aliquid etiam vultis addi?

Timaeus: These points too are easily recalled and remain firmly fixed in our minds.

Socrates: And what about our saying that the young women of better moral conditioning should obtain by lot the better suitors and those of poorer conditioning inferior ones, without there being any enmity or rivalry among those who are marrying? Do you not recall the highly advantageous contrivance {18e} of drawing lots which were to be managed by the members of either sex who have been charged with the oversight of marriages, the point being that an individual should lay blame on the misfortune of his particular lot rather than nurse a feeling of resentment toward the preference shown to another?

Timaeus: This too we hold fixed in memory.

{19a} *Socrates:* I suppose the following point was proposed as well, that the offspring of selected parents were to be raised with the utmost care owing to their projecting the sense of privilege that is naturally associated with their goodness.

Timaeus: Precisely.

Socrates: And that the rest should be destined for some other service to the fatherland: that as they advanced in age the merits they displayed during childhood and adolescence would be noted with no less focused attention, so that those who show themselves worthy may be moved up from the common people or second order to the first order or warriors, and those who fall away from the virtue exhibited by their parents be relegated to the order of the second rank. So, Timaeus, do you think that my promise to rehearse the various points of yesterday's discussion has been satisfied, even if only summarily, or does the group wish anything to be added?

{19b} *Timaeus:* Nihil sane.

Socrates: Scisne igitur quid ego de ista re publica sentiam quodve et quantum animi desiderium feram?

Timaeus: Quid illud?

Socrates: Ut si quis visis eximiae pulchritudinis ac venustatis animalibus pictis vel etiam viventibus quidem sed immobiliter quiescentibus motus actusque et certamen aliquod eorum spectare desideret, {19c} sic ego nunc informatae urbis adumbrataeque sermone populum agentem aliquid cum finitimis civitatibus in pace aut bello dignum tanta fama et educatione magna quadam expectatione deposco. Quippe fateor, o Critia et Hermocrate, {19d} non eum esse me qui tantam indolem digne laudare possim. Nec mirum non posse me, quando ne veteres quidem auctores vel praesentis saeculi poetas posse confidam. Non quo contemnam poeticam nationem sed quod evidens perspicuumque sit imitandi peritos ea demum aemulari posse perfecte quorum ab ineunte aetate habeant usum experientiamque et in quibus propemodum sint educati, at vero incogniti moris peregrinaeque institutionis imitationem, {19e} effictam praesertim oratione seu versibus, praeclaris licet praestantibusque ingeniis esse difficilem. Sophistas quoque verborum agmine atque inundatione sermonis beatos iudico, vereor tamen ne, ut sunt vagi palantesque nec certis propriisque sedibus ac domiciliis, philosophorum mores et instituta civilis

{19b} *Timaeus:* Nothing at all.

Socrates: Do you know, then, my feelings about this state, or the nature and degree of my mind's yearning for it?

Timaeus: Which is that?

Socrates: Just as on seeing exceptionally beautiful and fine living creatures in a painting, or indeed on seeing them alive but at rest, one yearns to witness their movements, activities, and engagement in some contest, {19c} so with a certain great excitement I am in search of the people of the city which has now been outlined and adumbrated by our discussion—of their engagement with neighboring cities in peace or war, their performance of something worthy of their extraordinary reputation and education. For in fact I confess, Critias and Hermocrates, {19d} to being a person who is incapable of delivering praise worthy of a natural ability at a level such as that. My incapability is unsurprising given my lack of confidence in the ability even of the ancient writers, or in the poets of the present age. Not that I hold the race of poets in low esteem. Rather, it is that it is manifestly evident that their skill in imitation renders them fully capable of evoking only those things which they have used and had experience of from an early age, things which they have more or less been educated in, but that, despite their celebrated and superior talent, the imitation, {19e} especially as contrived in prose or verse, of an unknown custom or foreign institution is difficult for them. I count the sophists too as blessed in their ability to marshal words and flood us with speech, and yet fear that because of their wandering from place to place without a fixed seat or abode of their own they are incapable of grasping, even by conjecture, the ways of philosophers and the institutions born of

prudentiae ne coniectura quidem assequi valeant nec demonstrare ceteris, cuius modi esse debeant officia pacata et item in bellis fides provecti ad sapientiam populi. Superest igitur solum vestrae eruditionis ingenium {20a} nutritum cura publica philosophiaeque naturali studio flagrans: siquidem Timaeus iste ex Locris, quae urbs Italiae flos est, nobilitate divitiis rerum gestarum gloria facile princeps idemque ad hoc tempus arcem obtineat amoris sapientiae; Critiam vero, utpote civem, sciamus in studiis humanitatis omnibus apprime vigere; de Hermocratis porro natura educationeque facta et accommodata rebus his de quibus agimus explicandis dubitare nullum puto. {20b} Ideoque iubentibus vobis hesterno die facile parui quaeque mihi visa sunt de publicis disserenda esse impigre sum executus illud cogitans reliquas partes instituti operis a nullo commodius posse explicari. Denique impleto competenter officio finitoque sermone contendi a vobis quoque mutuum fieri {20c} vosque imperatum munus recepistis; et adsum, ut videtis, paratus ad desponsam dapem.

Hermocrates: Nos quoque omnes, ut pollicitus est modo Timaeus, iniunctum nobis a te munus pro viribus exequemur, praesertim cum nulla excusandi competat ratio; namque et praeterito die mox conventu soluto cum ad hospitium rediremus quo suscepti a Critia sumus et ibidem

political wisdom, or of pointing out to others the sort of duties that should obtain in peacetime and, in times of war, the
assurance of protection that should obtain among a population which is advanced in its wisdom. And so that leaves
only the disposition associated with your form of erudition,
{20a} a disposition which has been nourished on concern
for the state and which is by nature passionately devoted to
philosophy: for your Timaeus here comes from Locri, the
splendor of Italian cities, and is easily their leader in nobility, wealth, and the glory of his accomplishments, and he at
present represents the summit of their love of wisdom; as to
Critias, we ought to know, given that he is a citizen here,
that he is held in the highest repute for all forms of liberal
education; and I suppose that none has any doubt about
Hermocrates's character and education, both of which have
been shaped and equipped for exposition of the subjects we
are treating of. {20b} And so I readily complied with your request yesterday and eagerly delivered what I thought needed
to be explained concerning states, in the view that it would
be impossible for the remaining portions of the task we had
fixed upon to be treated by another any more favorably.
Finally, after having duly completed the assignment and
brought the discussion to a close, I sought from you the
same in return, {20c} and you agreed to the task I requested;
and as you see, I am here and prepared for the promised
feast.

Hermocrates: And we for our part will collectively do what
we can to complete the task you have set for us, as Timaeus
has just promised, especially since we have no suitable
grounds for excusing ourselves; for on returning to the guest
chamber in which Critias received us shortly after breaking

postea de ipsa re habuimus tractatum non otiosum. {20d} Hic igitur nobis ex historia vetere narrationem recensuit quam velim, Critia, repetas, ut, cum cognoverit Socrates, aestimet sitne futura utilis ad imperatae remunerationis effectum.

Critias: Sic fieri convenit, si tertio consorti muneris Timaeo non aliter videtur. Audi, o Socrate, miram quidem sed plenam fidei veritatisque rem, ut e numero septem sapientium primarius {20e} Solo recensebat, quem avi mei et consortis in nomine Critiae fuisse aiunt admodum familiarem. Quo referente puer ego accepi res gestas huius urbis memorabiles diuturnitate interituque hominum annullatas evanuisse; inter quas unam prae ceteris illustrem, {21a} cuius fiet commemoratio, quo tam penes te gratia collocetur quam debita deae, cuius hodierna pompa est, instauretur veneratio. Narrabat ergo grandis natu, ut qui ad nonagesimum {21b} iam propinquaret annum, me tunc agente annos decem, publicis caerimoniis celebri die orta causa commemorationis ex Solonis versuum cantilena; erat enim sollemne familiae nostrae festis diebus nos pueros ad certamen memoriae propositis invitare praemiis puerilibus. Multis ergo carminibus tam veterum quam novorum poetarum memoriter pronuntiatis, inter quae Solonis aliquanto pluribus (ut quae novitas commendaret ad gratiam), memini quendam—sive quod ita iudicaret seu quod vellet Critiam

up yesterday we subsequently engaged there in a lively discussion of the very same matter. {20d} He then recounted for us a narrative based on an ancient tale which, Critias, I would ask you to repeat, so that after hearing it Socrates may decide whether it will prove useful for our making good on the stipulated remuneration.

Critias: That works well, assuming Timaeus, our third partner in the endeavor, is in agreement. Listen, Socrates, to something extraordinary and yet fully creditable and true according to {20e} the account of Solon, who was preeminent among the seven wise men and whom people claim to have been a close friend of my grandfather Critias, for whom I was named. As a boy I heard him tell of remarkable deeds of this city, deeds that vanished and were wiped out by the lapse of time and passing of generations; he spoke of one of them as having been particularly illustrious, {21a} and it is the one we will recount, so that our debt of gratitude to you may be paid and the veneration due to the goddess whose feast it is today be celebrated at the same time. Now, he was old when he related it, for he was {21b} already approaching his ninetieth year, and I was then in my tenth: it was during the public ceremonies, on a feast day, and his recollection of the tale was stirred by a sung performance of Solon's verses; for on feast days it was customary for our family to invite us as children to a recitation contest for which prizes suitable to that age had been arranged. I recall, then, that after a number of poems of poets both old and new had been recited from memory, among them a slightly higher proportion of Solon's (for their novelty brought them popular favor), a man proclaimed unequivocally—either because it was his opinion or because he was hoping to impress

promereri—dixisse plane Solonem videri sibi non solum
prudentia ceteris {21c} laude dignis sed etiam carminibus
praestitisse. Igitur senex (valde enim memini) laetatus eximie, "Quid, si non perfunctorie sed dedita opera poeticam
fuisset," inquit, "executus Solo, mi Amynander, vel sermonem quem ab Aegypto reversus instituerat implesset, a
quo quidem seditionibus ceteraque intemperie civilis dis-
sensionis impediente descivit? {21d} Non opinor minorem
Hesiodo vel Homero futurum fuisse." Et ille, "Quinam iste
fuit, o Critia, sermo vel qua de re institutus?" "De maximo,"
inquit, "eximiae virtutis et famosissimo titulo quem gessit
haec civitas, cuius extincta memoria est tam morte eorum
qui gesserunt quam impendio temporis." "Dic, quaeso," inquit, "o Critia, quod illud opus et quatenus actum et a quibus compertum Solo tuus recensebat."

{21e} "Est," inquit, "Aegypti regio Delta, cuius e vertice
Nili scinduntur fluenta, iuxta quam Sais nomine civitas
magna, quam regit mos vetus lex Saitica nuncupatus. Ex hac
urbe Amasis fuit imperator. Conditor vero deus urbis Aegyp-
tia lingua censetur Neuth, Graeca dicitur Athena. Ipsi porro
homines amatores Atheniensium istiusque urbis cognatione
se nobilitari prae se ferunt. Quo Solo profectum se satis hos-
pitaliter honoratum esse referebat {22a} expertumque liquido quod de vetustatis memoria nullus nostrae nationis
vir ne tenuem quidem habeat scientiam. Denique cum in

Critias—that he thought Solon stood above other praise-worthy men not only {21c} for his wisdom but also for his poetry. The old man then smiled broadly (for I remember it very well) and replied, "My dear Amynander, what if Solon had produced the poetry with dedicated effort rather than casually, or had completed the account which he started after his return from Egypt but dropped owing to the factionalism and other political unrest that got in the way? {21d} I suppose he would have been destined to be considered inferior to neither Hesiod nor Homer." To which he said, "Which account do you mean, Critias, what was it about?" "It was," he replied, "about the greatest and most celebrated distinction this city has earned for extraordinary virtue, the memory of which has been extinguished by both the demise of those who accomplished it and the loss exacted by time." "Tell me, please, Critias," he said, "what that deed was, how it was accomplished, and on whose authority your Solon reported it as certain."

{21e} "There is in Egypt," he said, "a region, the Delta, at the apex of which the streams of the Nile separate, and next to it is a great city called Saïs, which is governed by an ancient custom known as the Saïtic Law. The pharaoh Amasis was from this city. The founding deity of the city is claimed to be Nêith, in Egyptian, and Athena, in Greek. Furthermore, the people themselves are admirers of the Athenenians and boast of their being renowned because of their kinship with this city. Solon spoke of his having been honored with a most hospitable reception on arrival there, {22a} and of his having clearly discovered that no man originating from within our stock has even tenuous knowledge when it comes to the recollection of antiquity. And he said that

conventu sacerdotum penes quos praecipua sit memoria
vetustatis eliciendi studio quae scirent verba faceret de anti-
quissimis historiis Athenarum—Phoroneo et Nioba postque inundationem mundi de Pyrrha {22b} et Deucalione—
studioseque prosequi pergeret prosapiam renovatae gentis
humanae usque ad memoriam parentum annorumque numerum recenseret, inrisum se esse a quodam ex sacerdoti-
bus qui diceret: "O Solo, Graeci pueri semper estis nec quisquam e Graecia senex." Cur istud diceret percontatum Solonem, "Quia rudi novellaque estis memoria semper nec
est," inquit, "ulla penes vos cana scientia. {22c} Nec immerito; multae quippe neces hominum partim conflagratione
partim inundationibus vastantibus acciderunt. Denique illa
etiam fama quae vobis quoque comperta est—Phaethontem
quondam, Solis filium, affectantem officium patris currus
ascendisse luciferos nec servatis sollemnibus aurigationis
orbitis exussisse terrena ipsumque flammis caelestibus
conflagrasse—fabulosa quidem putatur sed {22d} est vera.
Fit enim longo intervallo mundi circumactionis exorbitatio,
quam inflammationis vastitas consequatur necesse est. Tunc
igitur hi qui in siccis et editis locis mansitant magis pereunt
quam vicini litoribus et fluviis; nobis porro Nilus cum in plerisque rebus salutaris tum adversum huius modi pericula

once, during an assembly of the priests who maintain special control over the recollection of antiquity, when he approached them in hopes of finding out what they knew of the most ancient tales of Athens—Phoroneus and Niobe and, after the inundation of the world, Pyrrha {22b} and Deucalion—and studiously proceeded to trace the line of descent of the newly founded human race down to the period that was still within memory for his parents, one of the priests finally smiled scornfully and said, "Solon, you Greeks are forever children, and no one who comes from Greece is old." He said that when Solon asked about the reason for his remark the priest replied: "Because you are forever inexperienced and young of memory, and you command no knowledge that has grown gray with the passing of time. {22c} And this is understandable, for the human race has undergone numerous periods of destruction owing to devastations caused by either conflagration or inundation. To put it briefly, even that tale which is familiar also among your people—that Phaethon, son of the Sun, once sought to assume his father's role and mounted the light-bearing chariot, but that by his failure to guide it along the set orbits he set fire to all that was upon the earth and went up in celestial flames himself—is perhaps considered the stuff of myth, and yet {22d} is true. For over the course of a long period of time there occurs a deviation in the world's orbiting, the necessary consequence of which is devastation through conflagration. At that moment, then, those who dwell high up on dry lands perish in greater numbers than do those who dwell along the shores and rivers; and the Nile, which benefits us in so many ways, including acting as a bulwark against this kind of peril, by virtue of its quenching current and

meatu inriguo perennique gurgite obiectus arcet exitium.
Item cum terra erit humore abluenda, pastores quidem ves-
tri montium edita capessentes periculo non continguntur at
vero {22e} civitates in planitie sitae cum populis suis rapiuntur ad maria. Quibus periculis regio ista minime continge-
tur, non enim ut in ceteris regionibus humor in planitiem
superne manat sed ex imo per eandem planitiem tranquillo
reditu stagnis detumescentibus remanat. Quae causa monumentorum publicorum privatorumque perseverantiam nu-
trit studioseque tam nostrae nationis rerum gestarum memoria quam ceterarum gentium, quas vel fama nobis per
cognitionem tradit, descripta templorum custodiis continetur. {23a} Apud vos et ceteros nunc plane et nuper refec-
tae monumentorum aedes ictae caelesti demum liquore
procumbunt involutaeque litteris publicis cum antiquioris
historiae memoria dissipantur, {23b} ut necesse sit novo initio vitae novoque populo novam condi memoriam litterarum. Qua ratione fit ut neque vestras proprias res antiquas
nec aliorum sciatis; eaque ipsa quae recensere memoriter
arbitrabare non multum distant a puerilibus fabulis: principio quod unius modo memineris inundationis, cum infinitae
praecesserint; dehinc quod optimum vestrorum maiorum
genus nesciatis ex quo tu et Athenienses {23c} ceteri estis

perpetual waters prevents our being destroyed. Similarly, when the earth is on the verge of being cleansed by flood waters your shepherds take to the mountainous highlands and are untouched by the peril, whereas {22e} cites situated on the plains are swept away to the seas along with their populations. Our region will be untouched by those perils, for the water does not flow down upon our plains from above, as in other regions, but instead flows back up onto the same plains from below, causing the bodies of standing water to rise in the course of its gradual return. This is what explains the prolonged sustenance of our public and private monuments, and the record of our own nation's deeds, no less than those of other races whose reputation has become known to us through tradition, has been studiously copied down and maintained by our temple guardians. {23a} For you and other peoples, the buildings which are dedicated to the monuments and have only just recently been rebuilt are eventually struck by a celestial torrent and collapse and are destroyed, thereby sweeping away the public documents they contain, along with their record of the older history, {23b} so that it becomes necessary for the documentary record to be established anew with the new start of life under a new people. And that is how it comes to pass that you know neither your own antiquities nor those of others; and those very matters which you supposed yourself to be recounting from past memory hardly differ from children's fables: first, because you recall only one period of inundation, even though an indefinite number of them preceded it; and second, because you are ignorant of that most noble race of your ancestors, from whose tiny seed, which then survived the city's destruction, you and the other {23c} Athenians

exiguo semine facti tunc superstite publicae cladi. Fuit enim
olim Atheniensium civitas longe ceteris praestans morum
bonitate ac potentia virium belloque et pace memoranda
eiusque opera magnifica omnem, sicut nos accepimus,
quamvis praeclarae gloriae illustrationem obumbrantia."

{23d} Tum admiratum Solonem orare atque obsecrare ut
sibi omnia sacerdos de veteribus civibus revelaret, et illum
"Nulla est invidia" respondisse "praesertim cum et tibi sit
mos gerendus et honor debitus amicae civitati referendus et
id me facere cogat veneratio deae quae utramque urbem
condidit educavit instituit, priorem vestram {23e} annis fere
mille ex indigete agro et Vulcanio semine, posteriorem hanc
nostram, octo milibus annis ante, ut sacris delubrorum api-
cibus continetur. De his ergo maioribus vestris audies, o
Solo, qui ante novem milia annorum vixerunt, quibus sint
usi legibus quamque amplis et quam praeclaris facinoribus
nobilitati. Si probationem desiderabis, {24a} post ex otio
sacras litteras recensebimus. Ac primum leges intuere, fors
enim multa reperies indicia germanitatis, vel quod sacerdo-
tiis praediti separatim a cetero populo manent, ne contagione aliqua profana castitas polluatur, vel quod varia opifi-
cum genera ita inter se discreta sint ut promisce nullus
operetur. Pastores vero et item penes quos est venandi
colendique ruris {24b} exercendique scientia disparatas

derive. For the city of the Athenians was once far superior to others in its good morals and military prowess, and in war and peace its magnificent accomplishments, so we are told, overshadowed every other distinction for glory, no matter how remarkable."

{23d} He said that Solon was astonished and eagerly urged the priest to explain everything concerning the ancient cities to him, whereupon the latter replied, "I would not begrudge you that, especially since your wish should be gratified and our respects paid to a city which is our friend, and I am obliged to do it out of veneration for the goddess who founded, raised, and educated both cities, yours first {23e} by nearly a thousand years, from indigenous soil and the seed of Vulcan, and later this city of ours, eight thousand years ago, according to what is contained in the sacred writings of the temples. You will hear, then, about these ancestors of yours, Solon, who lived nine thousand years ago, about the systems of law they enjoyed and the great and noble deeds for which they were renowned. If you desire supporting evidence, {24a} then we will go through the sacred documents at our leisure later on. But first gaze upon their laws, for you will perhaps discover a number of indications of their kinship with your own, whether in the fact that those upon whom priesthoods are bestowed remain apart from the rest of the population in order to prevent the pollution of their purity by any contact with the profane, or that the different classes of craftsmen are separated from one another in such a way that none conducts his work in confusion with another. And the herdsmen and those who understand hunting and the cultivation and working {24b} of the land have dwellings apart from the encampments and equipment of

sedes habent a propugnatorum armataeque iuventutis castris et insignibus ipsorumque insignium idem usus et differentia tam hic quam apud vos etiam nunc habetur: clipeorum tegmen, thoracum indumenta, iaculorum amentata missilia. Prudentiae vero curam ubi maiorem leges habendam sanciunt aut honestas apud quos tantam dignitatem obtinet in vitae muneribus et officiis? {24c} Quid divinatio, quid medela? Nonne ad homines instinctu conditricis deae commeaverunt? Hac quippe exornatione priorem vestram urbem sepsit honestavitque numen quod condidit, electo salubri subtiliumque ingeniorum et prudentiae feraci loco. Utpote enim bellicosa {24d} et sapiens dea regionem eligendam censuit talem, quae sui similes esset viros editura. His ergo legibus vel honestioribus etiam institutis ad omnem virtutem eruditi veteres Athenienses, utpote divinae prosapiae germani, maximis et ultra humanae gloriae captum titulis laudum nobilitati sunt. E quibus {24e} unum eminens et praedecorum facinus in monumentis veteribus invenimus: immanem quondam iniuriis et inexpugnabilem numero manum, quae prope iam cunctam Europam atque Asiam subegisset, a vestris legionibus esse deletam ex Atlantico mari bellum omnibus gentibus et nationibus inferentem. Tunc enim fretum illud erat, opinor, commeabile habens in ore ac vestibulo sinus insulam, quod os a vobis Herculis censetur columnae; quae quidem insula fertur aliquanto maior fuisse quam Libya atque Asia. Simul ergo per eam perque

the soldiers and youth in arms, and of the equipment in particular there is the same deployment and differentiation as is maintained by you even today: shields for defensive coverage, cuirasses to cover the chest, and javelins propelled by thongs. And in what land do the laws decree a greater obligation to foster wisdom, among which people is virtue paid such respect in connection with life's duties and offices? {24c} What about divination, or medicine? Have they not come to mankind at the instigation of the founding goddess? For in founding your city earlier the divinity enclosed it within this ordered system and bestowed honor upon it after having selected an environment which was advantageous and productive of subtle ingenuity and wisdom. For being a lover of war {24d} and wisdom, the goddess thought it necessary to select a region likely to produce men who resembled herself. Having been educated, then, to the full degree of excellence under these laws and more honorable institutions, the ancient Athenians were ennobled by a claim to praise extending beyond the reach of human glory, for theirs was a kinship of divine lineage. In the ancient documents we find among their deeds {24e} one that stands out and shines beyond the others: how an army, vast in the destruction it caused and insuperable by virtue of its numbers, one which had already subjugated nearly the whole of Europe and Asia, was once wiped out by your legions in the course of its making war on all peoples and nations from the Atlantic ocean on. For in those days the straits could be crossed, I suppose, because of their having an island at the mouth, where the land forms an enclosure, held by your people to be the Pillars of Hercules; and the island is said to have been slightly larger than Libya and Asia. Now, at the

contiguas alias insulas iter tunc illud agentibus commeatus patebat usque ad defectum insularum {25a} et initium terrae continentis, vicinae vero mari; quippe hoc intra os sive Herculeas columnas fretum angusto quodam litore, in quo etiam nunc portus veteris apparent vestigia, dividitur a continenti, at vero illud pelagus immensae atque inaestimabilis magnitudinis verum mare. Igitur in hac Atlantide insula maxima et admirabilis potentia extitit regum omnem insulam finitimasque alias obtinentium maximaeque parti continentis dominantium; siquidem tertiae mundi {25b} parti quae Libya dicitur usque ad Aegyptum imperarunt, Europae vero usque ad Tyrrhenum mare. Quae quidem vis potentiaque collecta et armata nostram, o Solo, vestramque regionem, hoc amplius eas gentes quae intra Herculis columnas consistunt adoriri et expugnare gestiit. Tunc ergo vestrae civitatis virtus ultra omnem gloriam enituit, quod pro communi omnium salute ac libertate {25c} desperantibus deserentibusque metu communem custodiam cunctis magnitudine animi bellicisque artibus assecuta est, ut per extrema discrimina erumpens hostes humani generis primo fugaret, dehinc funderet, libertatem subiugatis redderet, intactos in sua genuinaque libertate servaret. Neque ita multo post accidit ut motu terrae et illuvione {25d} diei noctisque iugi praeclara illa vestra militaris iuventus periret et Atlantis insula tota

same time it opened up passageways for those who back then journeyed by way of that island and the others contiguous with it up to the point where the islands ended {25a} and there began the continent which bordered an ocean in the true sense; for on this side of the mouth or Pillars of Hercules the straits are separated from the continent by a certain narrow shoreline on which the vestiges of an ancient port can be seen even today, whereas the outer body of water is incalculably large in magnitude and an ocean in the true sense. Now, on this island of Atlantis an enormous and awe-inspiring power emerged under kings who held the whole of the island along with the others neighboring it, and who ruled. over the greater portion of the continent; for their empire reached across a third of the world, {25b} the portion called Libya and extending to Egypt, and Europe to the Tyrrhenian Sea. And once gathered and armed, Solon, this force or power endeavored to rise up and attack our country and yours and, beyond that, the peoples who dwell this side of the Pillars of Hercules. It was at that moment, then, that the valor of your city outshone every type and degree of glory, in that for the common safety and freedom of all, and while others {25c} despaired and in fear abandoned their share of the defense, it by its boldness of spirit and military prowess managed amid extreme danger to put the enemy of mankind to flight prior to destroying them, and to confer freedom upon those who had suffered subjugation while safeguarding the naturally possessed freedom of those who had been untouched by it. It happened shortly thereafter that that noble military youth of yours perished in an earthquake and inundation {25d} which lasted over the course of a day and night, and that the whole of the island of

sine indicio prioris existentiae submergeretur, nisi quod pelagus illud pigrius quam cetera crasso dehiscentis insulae limo et superne fluctibus concreto habetur."

Haec sunt, o Socrate, quae Critias {25e} vetus a Solone sibi relata et exposita narravit. Sed cum praeterito die de rebus publicis deque pacatis officiis militaribusque tractares, subiit quaedam me ex recordatione miratio non sine deo dici quae diceres, siquidem quam constituebas oratione rem publicam eadem aut certe proximae similitudinis videretur ei quam ex Critiae relatione compereram. Reticui {26a} tamen veritus ne, si quaesitum aliquid a me foret, dehinc oblivionis incommodo minime expedirem, ridiculus essem, maluique apud memet ipsum de memoria prius experiri. Ex quo factum est ut cito consentirem imperio tuo, quod confidebam facile me, si recordatione memoriam exercuissem, posse reminisci. Itaque, ut hic modo dixit, tam hesterno die post digressum protinus ad praesentes {26b} retuli quam nocturnis vigiliis omnia scrutinabundus recuperavi certumque illud expertus sum tenaciorem fore memoriam eorum quae in prima aetate discuntur. Quippe haud confidam quae pridie audierim an referre possim postridie, cum quae puer cognoverim incolumi memoria plane retexam; nisi forte maior in illa aetate cognitionis delectatio altius insignit mentibus

Atlantis sank, leaving no indication of its former existence apart from the fact that the outer body of water is kept more stagnant than others because of the mud that issues from fissures in the island, which thickens and is cemented by the waves that flow over it."

That, Socrates, is the story told by the aged {25e} Critias, as related and explained to him by Solon. But in thinking back on what you said yesterday when treating of states and the duties associated with peace and war, I was suddenly struck by a certain feeling of surprise at the thought that your words were not lacking in divine inspiration, for the state whose constitution you elaborated seemed identical to, or at least a very close approximation of, the one I had come to know from Critias's tale. But {26a} I kept quiet, fearing to make a fool of myself if on being confronted with some question I should then fail to explain because of an embarrassing bout of forgetfulness, and I decided instead to see whether I could summon the memory in my own mind first. The result of this was that I consented straightaway to your assignment, for I was confident that I would easily be able recall it if given the chance to exercise my memory. And so, as he just pointed out, immediately after our departure yesterday {26b} I related it to the group and by going over it during the night I recovered all the details, and I experienced the truth of the saying that our recollection of things learned during the early years is more persistent. To be honest, I am by no means certain of being able to relate on one day what I heard the day before, although I can accurately and with unfailing recall repeat what I learned as a child; perhaps the greater delight which we take in learning at that age causes the knowledge to make a deeper impression on

cognita, {26c} fors etiam quod studiosa senis et assidua relatio meracam quandam et inobsoletam infecerit animo notam. Quare ut id ad quod omnia quae dicta sunt pertinent eloquar dicere sum paratus, non ut narrationem retexam sed ut ostendam rem publicam et populum sermone Socratis hesterna disputatione adumbratum non picturatam effigiem beatae civitatis {26d} sed vere beatam civitatem et vivum populum quondam fuisse propugnatoresque, quos iste instituebat ad tolerantiam laborum virtutemque animi gymnasiis et musica mansuetudine, maiores nostros fuisse, quos ille sacerdos Aegyptius praedicaret, quando facta eorum nutrimentis ab hoc memoratis institutisque conveniant. Imperato quippe nobis a Socrate muneri non aliter satisfieri posse arbitror nisi—consensu omnium participum officii recepti—probabitur illam quam Socrates vario sermone depinxit urbem veteres Athenas fuisse. Quare, mi Socrate, fieri huiusce modi remuneratione contentus aestima<s>?

{26e} *Socrates:* Nullam vero aliam, Critia, magis approbo quam istam ipsam quae est propria praesentium feriarum, magnificum vero illud non fictam commenticiamque fabulam sed veram historiam vitae possibilis fato quodam a me vestris animis intimatam. Quare fortuna prosperante pergite iter institutae orationis; ego, ut probum auditorem decet, {27a} attento silentio mentem atque aures parabo.

Critias: Etiamne consideras, o Socrate, si est commoda dispositio debiti apparatus tibi? Placuit enim nobis

our minds, {26c} and it may also be that the old man's enthusiastic and assiduous rehearsal of it left a pure and indelible mark upon my mind. And so I am ready to address the point which is the focus of the whole conversation, not with the intention of repeating the tale but of showing that the state and people adumbrated by Socrates's contribution to yesterday's discussion were, not the portrait or likeness of a prosperous city, {26d} but a city and people that once lived and were truly prosperous, and that the warriors whom that people through gymnastic training and the gentle effects of music instructed in the endurance of hardship and mental virtue were those ancestors of ours whom the Egyptian priest praised, for what they did matches the education and institutions he mentioned. I suppose, in fact, that the task assigned to us by Socrates can be completed to his satisfaction only if—assuming the consent of all who have agreed to take part in the effort—it is proved that the city depicted by Socrates's wide-ranging account was ancient Athens. And so, Socrates, do you think you will be content with repayment along these lines?

{26e} *Socrates:* I approve of none other, Critias, than the very one you suggest, which is appropriate for today's festival, and it is magnificent to think that by some turn of fate I have had a share in summoning to your minds, not a fictitiously contrived myth, but the true history of a life capable of having existed. And so with fortune's blessing continue along the path of the discussion as planned; I will be of ready mind and ear, {27a} and attentively silent, as befits a good listener.

Critias: Would you please consider as well, Socrates, whether our arrangement of the provisions owed is

Timaeum quidem, utpote in astronomia ceteris eminentem naturaeque rerum arcana rimatum, principe loco dicere orsum a mundi sensibilis constitutione usque ad genus hominum generationemque; me vero susceptis ab hoc hominibus eiusdem oratione formatis, tua porro ad egregiam frugem imbutis et eruditis legum sanctiore moderamine, {27b} iuxta Solonem vero vel sacros Aegyptiorum libros revocare cives clarissimos veteres et ante nos constituere spectaculum venerabile populi quem inundatione submersum profundo maris Aegyptiorum monumentorum fama celebravit; atque ita ut de maioribus nostris sermonem contexere.

Socrates: Ne ego magnifice sum invitatus hodie, ut ex ordinatione apparatus intellegi datur. Ergo age, Timaee, deliba coeptum vocata, ut mos est, in auxilium divinitate.

{27c} *Timaeus:* Vere, mi Socrate, nam cum omnibus mos sit et quasi quaedam religio, qui vel de maximis rebus vel de minimis acturi aliquid sunt, precari ad auxilium divinitatem, quanto nos aequius est, qui universitatis naturae substantiaeque rationem praestaturi sumus, invocare divinam opem—nisi plane saevo quodam furore atque implacabili raptamur amentia. Sit igitur meis precibus comprehensum maxime quidem ut ea dicantur a nobis quae placeant deo {27d} tum ut nobis quoque ipsis consequenter, propositoque

agreeable to you? For we decided that Timaeus, being better versed in astronomy than the rest of us, and having explored the mysteries of the nature of things, should speak first, beginning with the establishment of the sensible world and taking it up to the generation of mankind; and that after taking over from him the human beings as formed by his exposition and as initiated and instructed by yours to full fruition in the more sacred governance prescribed by the laws, {27b} I should conjure up those most illustrious citizens of old, taking my cue from Solon and the sacred books of the Egyptians, and establish in our presence a reverent display of a people who, although submerged deep beneath the sea because of the inundation, are celebrated through the report of the Egyptian documents; and that I should construct the exposition in such a way that it concerns our ancestors.

Socrates: I am indeed being lavishly entertained today, to judge from the order of the provisions. Come then, Timaeus, a libation to the undertaking after invoking the support of the divinity, as is the custom.

{27c} *Timaeus:* Certainly, Socrates, for since it is the custom and a kind of religious observance, as it were, for all who are about to engage in some undertaking to call upon the divinity for support in matters great or small, it is all the more just that we who are about to provide an account of the nature and substance of the universe should invoke divine aid—assuming, of course, that we are not in the grip of some savage rage or implacable madness. Let it be understood from my entreaty, then, that our words should be pleasing above all to god, {27d} and then, that they should consequently be pleasing also to ourselves, and that we

operi decenter profemur, et quatenus vos quidem facile assequamini ego iuxta anticipatam animo speciem orationis expediam.

Est igitur, ut mihi quidem videtur, in primis dividendum quid sit quod semper est, carens generatione, quid item quod gignitur {28a} nec est semper. Alterum intellectu perceptibile ductu et investigatione rationis, semper idem, porro alterum opinione cum inrationabili sensu opinabile proptereaque incertum, nascens et occidens neque umquam in existendi condicione constanti et rata perseverans. Omne autem quod gignitur ex causa aliqua necessario gignitur; nihil enim fit cuius ortum non legitima causa et ratio praecedat. Operi porro fortunam dat opifex suus; quippe ad immortalis quidem et in statu genuino persistentis exempli similitudinem atque aemulationem formans operis effigiem honestum efficiat {28b} simulacrum necesse est; at vero ad nativum respiciens generatumque contemplans minime decorum. Omne igitur caelum vel mundus seu quo alio dignatur nomine—faciendum est enim quod in omni tractatu fieri decet, ut inter initia consideretur quid sit quo de agitur; item mundus fueritne semper citra exordium temporis an sit originem sortitus ex tempore, considerandum. Factus est, utpote corporeus et qui videatur atque tangatur, cuncta siquidem huius modi sensilis corporeaeque naturae,

should speak in a manner befitting the proposed task, and that my treatment should for its part conform to the anticipated plan of exposition, so that you may follow with ease.

Very well. We must first distinguish, I think, between that which forever is and lacks a process of coming to be, and that which is forever coming to be {28a} but is not. The one, being forever the same, is perceptible by intellect under rational guidance and investigation, while the other is opinable by opinion combined with irrational sense perception and as such is uncertain, subject to birth and death, and never enduring in a constant and fixed condition of existence. But everything that comes to be necessarily comes to be because of some cause; for nothing whose birth is not preceded by a legitimate cause and reason comes to be. Now, that which is produced has its particular craftsman to determine its lot; and in fact, if the latter forms the effigy of his product with an eye to its resembling and emulating an immortal model persisting in its natural state, then he inevitably produces {28b} a respectable imitation thereof; but if he directs his gaze to that which is subject to birth, or fixes his contemplation on that which is generated, then he inevitably produces something unseemly. So the whole heaven, or world, or any other name deemed suitable for it—for we must do what it is right to do in every exposition, such that consideration is given first to *what* the subject under discussion is; to put it another way, we must consider whether the world has always been, before the beginning of time, or has acquired its starting point at some point in time. It has come to be, for it is corporeal, being visible and tangible, and by this we are assuming that all such things are of a sensible and corporeal nature, {28c} that sensibles are those

{28c} sensilia porro ea quae opinio sensu aliquo commota praesumit eaque omnia facta sunt habentque ex aliqua generatione substantiam; at vero ea quae fiunt habere auctorem suum constitit. Igitur opificem genitoremque universitatis tam invenire difficile quam inventum impossibile digne profari. Certe dubium non est ad cuius modi exemplum animadverterit mundani operis fundamenta constituens, {29a} utrum ad immutabile perpetuamque obtinens proprietatem an ad factum et elaboratum. Nam si est (ut quidem est) pulchritudine incomparabili mundus, opifexque et fabricator eius optimus, perspicuum est quod iuxta sincerae atque immutabilis proprietatis exemplum mundi sit instituta molitio; sin vero (quod ne cogitari quidem aut mente concipi fas est), ad elaboratum. Quod cum sit rationis alienum, liquet opificem deum venerabilis exempli normam in constituendo mundo secutum, quippe hic generatorum omnium speciosissimus, ille auctor maximus; †operisque sui† ratione prudentiaque his quae semper eadem existunt accommodatus imago est, opinor, alterius. {29b} Et quoniam rationem originis explicare non est facile factu, distinguendae sunt imaginis exemplique naturae. Causae quae cur unaquaeque res sit ostendunt earundem rerum consanguineae sunt. Ita constantis quidem generis stabilisque naturae et intellectui

which opinion apprehends once it has been moved by some sense perception, and that they have all come to be and possess their being because of some process of generation; but it is evident that things that come to be have their particular maker. Now, the difficulty of finding the craftsman and parent of the universe is matched only by the impossibility of making any utterance worthy of him after having found him. There is at any rate no doubt about which type of model he directed his gaze to in establishing the foundations for the work that is the world, {29a} whether it was to one that was immutable and possessed of an everlasting property or to one that had been made and wrought. For if (as must be the case) the world is of incomparable beauty and its craftsman and constructor supremely good, then it is obvious that the construction of the world was effected with an eye to a model of pure and immutable properties; but if not (and even to think or mentally conceive it is unspeakable), then to one that had been wrought. But since the latter proposition is inimical to reason, it is clear that in establishing the world the craftsman god followed a straight edge that served as his venerable model, for the world is the most seemly of all generated things and its craftsman a maker of the highest order; and [having been made] according to reason and wisdom and in conformity with things which are forever the same, it is, I suppose, the image of something else. {29b} And given that it is in practice difficult to develop an account of its origin, we must distinguish between the nature of an image and that of a model. Causal accounts revelatory of *why* each and every thing is are naturally akin to those same things. Thus the causal explanation of a thing that is unchanging in kind, stable in nature, and

prudentiaeque perspicuae rei causa et ratio constans perspicuaque et inexpugnabilis reperitur, {29c} at vero eius quae ad similitudinem constantis perpetuaeque rei facta est ratio—utpote imaginis imaginaria simulacrumque rationis—perfunctoriam similitudinem mutuatur; quantoque est melior essentia generatione tanto fama et opinionis incerto praestantior veritas. Quare praedico iam nunc, Socrate: si dum de natura universae rei disputatur minime inconcussas inexpugnabilesque rationes afferre valuerim, ne miremini; quin potius illud intuere, si nihilo minus quam quivis alius consentaneas assertiones afferam. Memento enim tam me qui loquor quam {29d} vos qui iudicatis homines fore atque in rebus ita sublimibus mediocrem explanationem magni cuiusdam esse onus laboris.

Socrates: Omnes tibi, o Timaee, veniam largimur volentes, et tamen principium orationis admiror; superest ut leges quoque sacri certaminis exequaris.

Timaeus: Dicendum igitur cur rerum conditor fabricatorque geniturae omne hoc instituendum {29e} putaverit. Optimus erat, ab optimo porro invidia longe relegata est. Itaque consequenter cuncta sui similia, prout cuiusque natura capax beatitudinis esse poterat, effici voluit; quam quidem voluntatem dei originem rerum certissimam si quis ponat, recte eum putare consentiam. {30a} Volens siquidem

perspicuous to intellect and wisdom is found to be unchanging, perspicuous, and unassailable, {29c} whereas an explanation of that which has been made in the likeness of an unchanging and perpetual reality borrows—by virtue of its having the status of an image in relation to an image, and being the likeness of an account—a superficial element of likeness; and to the degree that being is superior to becoming, truth is correspondingly higher than conjecture and the incertitude of opinion. And so, Socrates, a preliminary word of warning: if in the course of a disputation that concerns the nature of the universe I should prove incapable of offering unshakeable and unassailable explanations, the group must not be surprised; keep an eye rather on the question whether I offer claims no less plausible than those offered by anyone else. For bear in mind that both I who speak and {29d} you who are acting as judges are human, and that when it comes to realities as sublime as these, even a limited explanation is a burden involving some considerable effort.

Socrates: All of us, Timaeus, readily grant you this concession, and yet I admire the start you have made to the discussion; it remains for you also to go through the rules of this sacred contest.

Timaeus: We should state, then, why the founder of things and constructor of generation thought it necessary to establish this {29e} All. He was supremely good, and from the supremely good jealousy is banished afar. And so it followed that he desired that all things should be made like himself insofar as the nature of each proved capable of a state of happiness; and if anyone should suppose that this desire of god's was a most certain beginning for things, then I would grant that his supposition is right. {30a} For desiring that all

deus bona quidem omnia provenire, mali porro nullius, prout eorum quae nascuntur natura fert, relinqui propaginem, omne visibile corporeumque motu importuno fluctuans neque umquam quiescens ex inordinata iactatione redegit in ordinem sciens ordinatorum fortunam confusis inordinatisque praestare. Nec vero fas erat bonitati praestanti quicquam facere nisi pulchrum {30b} eratque certum tantae divinitati nihil eorum quae sentiuntur, hebes dumtaxat nec intellegens, esse melius intellegente, intellectum porro nisi animae non provenire. Hac igitur reputatione intellectu in anima, porro anima in corpore locata, totum animantis mundi ambitum cum veneranda illustratione composuit. Ex quo apparet sensibilem mundum animal intellegens esse {30c} divinae providentiae sanctione.

Hoc ita posito quae sequuntur expedienda sunt: ad cuius animantis similitudinem constituerit eum suus conditor. Speciali quidem nemini similem — siquidem perfectio in genere est, non in specie, proptereaque mundus imperfectae rei similis minime perfectus esset — at vero eius, in quo omnia genera et quasi quidam fontes continentur animalium intellegibilium — siquidem animalium genera mundus alter complectitur perinde ut {30d} hic nos et cetera subiecta visui et ceteris sensibus. Ergo intellegibili substantiae

that emerged should be good and that, insofar as the nature of things that come to be allows, no room should be left for the propagation of evil, god brought all that was visible and corporeal and forever fluctuating restlessly in agitated movement from a disordered state of agitation back to one of order, knowing that their lot once they had been set in order was superior to being confused and disordered. At the same time, it would not have been right for a superior goodness to produce anything except what is beautiful, {30b} and to a divinity of such stature it was certain that among the things that are sensible none, at least insofar as it was dull and without intelligence, was better than that which had intelligence, and that intellect did not join with anything except soul. On this reasoning, then, after placing intellect in soul and soul in body he constructed the entire sphere of the living world, giving it a venerable splendor. And from this it is clear that the sensible world is a living being endowed with intelligence {30c} because of a decree of divine providence.

With our premises laid down in this way, we may proceed to the points that follow from it: In the likeness of what living being did its founder establish it? Not in the likeness of any at the level of a species—for perfection is in the genus, not the species, hence a world made in the likeness of an imperfect reality would in no way be perfect—but rather of that in which all of the genera and fountainheads, as it were, of intelligible living beings are contained—for the other world embraces the genera of living beings in the way that {30d} this one embraces us and the other things subject to vision and the other sense faculties. Desiring, then, that it should be begotten in the likeness of a superior intelligible

47

praecellenti principalique naturae omnifariam quoque perfectae deus opifex gigni simile volens sensibile animal unum
et visibile constituit, naturae suae convenientia cuncta {31a}
quae vita fruuntur intra conseptum et limitem suum continens. Nunc, utrum recte mundum unum dixerimus an plures
dici oportuerit vel innumerabiles, etiam considerandum.
Unum plane, quoniam iuxta exemplum formatus est, id
enim quod universa continet intellegibilia cum alio secundum esse non poterat; utrum enim ex duobus contineret
omnia non, opinor, liqueret nec esset unum et simplex
initium cuncta continens, sed coniugatio copulata. Ut {31b}
igitur exemplari cuius aemulationem mutuabatur etiam in
numero similis esset, idcirco neque duo nec innumerabiles
mundi sed unicus a deo factus est.

Et quia corpulentus visibilisque et contiguus erat merito
futurus, sine igni porro nihil visibile sentitur, nec vero tangi
quicquam potest sine soliditate, soliditas porro nulla sine
terra, ignem terramque corporis mundi fundamenta iecit
deus. Quoniamque nulla duo sine adiunctione tertii firme et
indissolubiliter cohaerent {31c}—nexu enim medio extrema
nectente opus est, nexus vero firmissimus ille certe est qui et
se ipsum et ea quae secum vinciuntur facit unum, hoc porro
modus et congrua mensura partium efficit. Cum enim ex tribus vel numeris vel molibus {32a} vel ulla alia potentia medietas imo perinde quadrat ut summitas medio, rursumque ut
imum medio sic medietas summo, tunc certe medietas a

being and a nature that is primary and perfect in every way, the craftsman god established it as a single sensible and visible living being, containing all of the things {31a} which in a manner befitting its own nature enjoy life within its confines or boundary. At this point we should also consider whether it was right for us to speak of the world as one or it was necessary that many and indeed innumerable ones should be spoken of. Clearly we should speak of it as one given that it was formed according to a model, for that which contains all intelligible things was incapable of being a second alongside another; for, I suppose, it would not be clear which of the two contained all things, nor would there be a single and simple all-embracing principle but rather a coupled conjunction. In order, {31b} then, that in number too it might be like the model from which it sought a borrowed form of emulation, for that reason there was made by god, not two or innumerable worlds, but a unique one.

And since it was rightly to be corporeal, visible, and tangible, and there is no perception of anything visible in the absence of fire, or of anything tangible in the absence of solidity, and no solidity without earth, god laid down fire and earth as the foundations of the world body. And since no two things cohere firmly and indissolubly without the binding force of a third {31c}—for an intermediate bond is required to connect the extremes, but the firmest bond is that which makes both itself and the things bound with it one, and mode or harmonic measure between parts brings this about. For when of three things, whether numbers, masses, {32a} or any other power, the middle stands to the last as the first does to the middle, and conversely, the last to the middle as the middle to the first, then surely the middle differs

summo et item imo nihil differt; rursumque extimis illis ad
medietatis condicionem atque ad eiusdem parilitatem redactis, cum medietas quoque extimorum vicem suscipit, fit,
opinor, ut tota materia una et eadem ratione societur eoque
pacto eadem sibi erunt universa membra, quippe cum eorum sit una condicio; unis porro effectis membris unum erit
atque idem totum. Quare, si corpus universae rei longitudinem et latitudinem solam, crassitudinem vero nullam habere deberet essetque huius modi, qualis est corporum solidorum superficies, una medietas sufficeret {32b} ad semet
ipsam vinciendam et extimas partes. Nunc quoniam soliditate opus erat mundano corpori, solida porro numquam una
sed duabus medietatibus vinciuntur, idcirco mundi opifex
inter ignem terramque aera et aquam inseruit libratis isdem
elementis salubri modo, ut quae cognatio est inter ignem et
aera eadem foret inter aera et aquam, rursum quae inter aera
et aquam haec eadem in aquae terraeque societate consisteret. Atque ita ex quattuor supra dictis materiis {32c} praecla-
ram istam machinam visibilem contiguamque fabricatus est
amica partium aequilibritatis ratione sociatam, quo immortalis indissolubilisque esset adversum omnem casum ex-
cepta fabricatoris sui voluntate.

Igitur quattuor illa integra corpora et sine ulla deliba-
tione ad mundi continentiam sumpta sunt. Ex omni quippe
igni et item totis illis reliquis, aere aqua terra, constructus
est nulla vel corporis vel potentiae parte derelicta contemp-
taque, {32d} propterea ut perfectum animal esset, utpote ex

in no way from either the first or last; conversely, if the extremes are reduced to the status of the middle and made identical with it, while the middle for its part takes up the role of the extremes, the result, I suppose, is that the whole of the material is united by one and the same relation, and in this way all of the parts will be identical to one another, there being a single status between them; the whole, moreover, will be one and the same in that the parts have been made a unity. And so if the body of the world were required to have only length and width but no solidity and were of the same sort as the surface of fully formed bodies, then one mean would suffice {32b} for the cohesion of it and its extreme parts. But as it is, since the world body required solidity, and the cohesion of solids involves never one but two means, the craftsman of the world accordingly inserted air and water between fire and earth, salubriously balancing the same elements so that the relationship between air and water would be the same as that between fire and air, and conversely, so that the relationship in the binding of water and earth would be the same as that between air and water. And so from the four material elements here named {32c} he fabricated this splendid engine as visible, tangible, and bound together by a harmonious proportion in the equilibrium of its parts, so that it might be immortal and indissoluble as against any contingency except that which its fabricator intended.

Those four types of body, then, were taken up, entirely and without any loss, for the framing of the world. For it was constructed from all of fire and likewise the whole of those other elements, air, water, and earth, with no part, whether of a body or its power, left out or disregarded, {32d} and this with the intention that as a conflation of whole and

integris corporibus perfectisque conflatum, {33a} hoc amplius ut aeternae compos incolumitatis foret. Videbat enim eam esse naturam corporis, ut ei facile importuna caloris accessione vel contra frigoris omniumque huius modi, quae in magna sunt violentaque potentia, noceretur. Quo consilio quaque reputatione unum perfectum ex perfectis omnibus citra senium {33b} dissolutionemque composuit formamque dedit ei congruam, quippe animali cuncta intra suum ambitum animalia et omnes eorum formas regesturo: globosam et rotundam, quae a medietate ad omnem ambitum extimarum partium spatiis aequalibus distat, quo totus sui similis foret, meliorem similitudinem dissimilitudine iudicans. Levem porro globum {33c} undique versum extrinsecus expolivit non otiose, siquidem neque videndi necessarius esset usus, cunctis intra globum visibilibus regestis, nec auditus, nullo extra posito audiendo sono, nec vero respirandi adiumento opus, quippe omnis coercebatur intrinsecus spiritus, nec membris quidem talibus per quae novo admisso cibo vetus liquore posito pelleretur. Neque enim quicquam ex eo recedebat nec erat accedendi facultas cunctis coercitis; sed corruptela partium intra se senescentium vicem quandam obtinebat cibatus {33d} idemque ut ageret et pateretur etiam omnia mundi globus partibus suis intra se agentibus ac perpetientibus. Nec vero manus ei necessarias esse duxit, cum

complete bodies it should be a complete living being, {33a} and so that it might additionally possess an eternal immunity from harm. For he saw that the nature of body was such that it would easily be injured by the onset of an unsuitable degree of heat or, conversely, cold or any such manifestation of great and violent power. And on this plan and reasoning he composed it as a single complete entity consisting of all complete entities, impervious to old age {33b} and dissolution, and for shape he gave it one that was consistent with it, for it was a living being which was to embrace within its periphery living beings in all their shapes: he gave it the shape that was spherical and round, that which is spatially equidistant from the center to every point of the periphery at its outermost parts, so that the world might be wholly like unto itself, for he judged likeness to be superior to its opposite.

And he polished the sphere smooth {33c} and turned round from without on all sides, and not without purpose, for the use of sight was unnecessary, since all visible beings were embraced within its sphere, as was hearing, for there was no externally located sound to be heard, and there was no need of the support provided by respiration, for all breathable air was confined within it, or of organs suitable for expelling old food once the new had been ingested and its juices disposed of. For nothing withdrew from it and there was no possibility of approaching it, since everything was enclosed within it; instead, with the corruption of its internal parts through age the world sphere acquired a kind of successive exchange of nourishment, {33d} such that while remaining the same it at the same time acted and was acted upon in every way as the parts within it acted and were acted upon. And he deemed that it had need neither of hands, since there was

nihil superesset comprehendendum, nec pedes, {34a} quoniam ex septem motibus non locularis ei quisquam sed rationabilis competebat, qui animarum proprius est circuitus neque ullum locum ex loco mutans ideoque in orbem fertur et velut fixo circumvolat cardine; proptereaque rata et inerrabilis eius agitatio est.

Haec igitur aeterni dei prospicientia iuxta nativum et umquam futurum {34b} deum levem eum et aequiremum indeclivemque et a medietate undique versum aequalem exque perfectis universisque totum perfectumque progenuit. Animam vero in medietate eius locavit eandemque per omnem globum aequaliter porrigi iussit, quo tectis interioribus partibus extima quoque totius corporis ambitu animae circumdarentur. Atque ita orbem teretem in orbem atque in suum ambitum voluit converti et moveri solum praecipuum, qui virtutum praestantia sufficeret conciliationi propriae nec extraordinario cuiusquam indigeret auxilio, amicumque semper sibi; ideoque summe beatum, divina potentia praeditum, genuit.

Nec tamen eo quo nos ad praesens loquimur ordine ortum animae deus annuit {34c} iunioremque et posteriorem corporibus eam fecit, neque enim decebat rem antiquiorem a post genita regi; sed hominibus mos est passim praepostereque et sine observatione ordinis fari, at vero deus tam antiquitate quam virtutibus praeire animam naturae

nothing remaining to be grasped, nor of feet, {34a} since of the seven kinds of motion none of the local ones but rather the rational was befitting it, i.e., the rotary motion proper to souls, which by virtue of its involving no change from place to place moves in a circle and revolves as though around a fixed pivot; and this is the reason for its agitation being fixed and nonwandering.

Now, this, the eternal god's foresight on behalf of {34b} the god who was generated and at some point to be, begat him smooth, even, balanced, turned round equally from the center on all sides, whole, complete, and consisting of the universal array of complete entities. And at its center he placed a soul and ordered it to extend equally throughout the whole of the sphere, so that with the interior parts under their cover the outermost regions of the universal body might also be enveloped by soul as their periphery. And so he desired that the well-rounded orb should rotate and move orbitally within its own periphery, alone, and sovereign in that, owing to its superior excellence, it was sufficient unto its own desires and in need of no extraordinary support from another, and forever in friendship with itself; and in these respects he produced it supremely blessed and endowed with divine power.

But god did not assent to the soul's arising in the order in which we are at present discussing it, {34c} so as to make it junior or posterior to bodies, for it was not proper that an elder reality should be ruled by one begotten after it; however, there is everywhere among human beings a custom of speaking preposterously, that is, without regard to order, but god ordered that in both antiquity and excellence soul should precede the nature of body, and he desired that it

corporis iussit dominamque eam et principali iure voluit
esse circa id quod tuetur. {35a} Itaque tertium animae genus
excogitavit hoc pacto: ex individua semperque in suo statu
perseverante substantia itemque alia quae inseparabilis
corporum comes per eadem corpora scindere se putatur
tertium substantiae genus mixtum locavit medium inter
utramque substantiam; eodemque modo ex gemina bifor-
mique natura [quippe] cuius pars idem pars diversum voce-
tur tertium naturae genus commentus est, quod medium
locavit inter individuam et item coniugatione corporea dividuam substantiam; triaque haec omnia in unam speciem
permiscuit diversa illa natura concretioni atque adunationi
generum repugnante. {35b} Quibus cum substantia mixtis et
ex tribus in unum redactis rursum totum hoc unum divisit in
partes competenter quo singulae partes constarent ex substantia, diversi, et item eius quod idem vocatur, [gemina na-
tura] divisionem instaurans hactenus: unam sumpsit ex universo primitus portionem, post quam duplicem eius quam
sumpserat, tertiam vero sescuplam quidem secundae, triplam vero primitus sumptae, at vero quartam sumpsit duplicem secundae, quintam triplam {35c} tertiae, sexta fuit assumptio partibus septem quam prima propensior, septima
sex et viginti partibus quam prima maior. Quibus ita divisis
consequenter {36a} complebat intervalla duplicis et triplicis
quantitatis ex universitate partes secans etiam nunc et ex his
intervallorum spatia complens quo singula intervalla binis
medietatibus fulcirentur. Medietatum porro altera quota

should act as its mistress and hold a right of sovereignty over that which it oversees. {35a} And so he devised a third kind, that of soul, in the following way: from Being which is indivisible and forever persists in its proper state and another form of Being which as the inseparable concomitant of bodies is held to be distributed throughout the same bodies, he placed a third, blended kind of Being midway between the two forms of Being; similarly, from the double or twofold nature a part of which is called the Same and a part the Other he contrived a third kind of nature which he placed midway between Being which is indivisible and Being which is divisible through its conjunction with body; and he blended all three of them into one form despite the resistance of the nature of the Other to the blending and union of kinds. {35b} And once they had been blended with Being and brought back from three into one he then proportionately divided the whole of the one into portions, so that the individual portions consisted of Being, Other, and that which is called the Same, commencing the division thus far: first he took one portion from the whole, after which he took one double that which he had taken, and a third portion one and a half times the second and triple the one taken first; fourth, he took a portion double the second, and fifth, one triple {35c} the third; the sixth portion taken was seven parts greater than the first, and the seventh twenty-six parts greater than the first. When they had been divided thus he then {36a} filled the intervals of the multiples of the double and triple, cutting parts now from the whole and with them filling the spaces between the intervals so that each of the intervals would be braced by two means. Of the means, moreover, one exceeded the one extreme by the same

parte limitis extimi praecellebat unum extimum limitem, tota praecellebatur ab alio extimo limite, altera pari summa et aequali ad numerum modo praecellebat et praecellebatur ab extimis. Natis itaque limitibus sescuplorum et item eorum quibus accedit pars sui tertia, quod genus a Graecis epitritum dicitur, item eorum quibus accedit pars sui octava, qui numerus epogdous ab isdem vocatur, ex his nexibus illa prima spatia, {36b} id est epogdoi spatiis epitritorum omnium intervalla, complebat, ita ut ad perfectam cumulatamque completionem deesset aliquid epitrito, tantum scilicet quantum deest habita comparatione ducentis quadraginta tribus adversus ducentos quinquaginta sex; et iam omne fere commixtum illud genus essentiae consumptum erat huius modi sectionibus partium. Tunc hanc ipsam seriem in longum secuit et ex una serie duas fecit easque mediam mediae in speciem chi Graecae litterae coartavit {36c} curvavitque in orbes quoad coirent inter se capita, orbemque orbi sic inseruit ut alter eorum adverso alter obliquo circuitu rotarentur, et exterioris quidem circuli motum eundem, quod erat eiusdem naturae consanguineus, cognominavit, interioris autem diversum; atque exteriorem quidem circulum, quem eundem cognominatum esse diximus, a regione dextra per sinistrum latus usque ad dextrum inflexit, diversum porro per diametrum in sinistrum latus {36d} eidem et simili illi circumactioni virtute pontificioque rotatus dato. Unam quippe ut erat eam et indivisam reliquit, interiorem vero scidit sexies septemque impares orbes fabricatus est iuxta dupli et tripli spatia orbesque ipsos

portion of the extreme as that by which it was exceeded by the other extreme, while the other exceeded and was exceeded by the extremes in numerically the same and equal measure. And so, there having arisen the terms of the sesquialters and of those on which a third part supervenes, the kind called the epitriton by the Greeks, and of those on which an eighth part supervenes, the number referred to by them as the epogdoon, on the basis of these bonds he filled the first intervals, {36b} i.e., with intervals of an epogdoon he filled the intervals of all the epitrita, such that in relation to the whole and aggregate process of completion something was lacking to the epitriton, namely, the amount lacking when the ratio of 243:256 is formed; and now nearly the whole of that blended form of Being had in this way been consumed by the cutting of parts. Then he cut the series itself lengthwise and from one series made two, and he forced them round, middle to middle, into the shape of the Greek letter chi and {36c} bent them into circles so that their ends joined one another, and he set one circle within the other such that they rotated, one of them in a lateral orbit and the other in an oblique one, and the movement of the outer circle, since it was cognate with the nature of the Same, he called the Same, and that of the inner one he called the Other; and the outer circle, which we have said was called the Same, he bent from the right to the left side and back to the right, and the Other across the diameter to the left side, giving the rotational force and preeminence to the circumlations {36d} of the Same or like. Now, the one series he left undivided, just as it was, but the inner one he cut six times, constructing seven unequal circles according to intervals of the double and triple, and these circles he ordered to move

contraria ferri iussit agitatione, ex quibus septem tres quidem pari velocitate, quattuor vero et sibimet ipsis et ad
comparationem ceterorum impari dissimilique sed cum ratione motu.

Igitur cum pro voluntate patris cuncta rationabilis animae substantia nasceretur, aliquanto post omne corporeum
intra {36e} conseptum eius effinxit mediumque applicans
mediae modulamine apto iugabat; ast illa complectens caeli
ultima circumfusaque eidem exteriore complexu operiensque ambitu suo ipsaque in semet convertens divinam originem auspicata est indefessae sapientisque et sine intermissione vitae. Et corpus quidem caeli sive mundi visibile
factum, ipsa vero invisibilis, rationis tamen et item {37a}
modulaminis compos cunctis intellegibilibus praestantior a
praestantissimo auctore facta. Ut igitur ex eiusdem et diversi natura cum essentia mixtis coagmentata indigete motu
et orbiculata circuitione in se ipsam revertens cum aliquam
vel dissipabilem substantiam offenderit vel individuam, facile recognoscit quid sit eiusdem individuaeque {37b} quid
item diversae dissolubilisque naturae. Causasque omnium
quae proveniunt videt et ex his quae accidunt quae sint futura metitur motusque eius rationabilis sine voce sine sono
cum quid sensile spectat circulusque diversi generis sine errore fertur. Veridico sensu et certa nuntiante cunctae animae, rectae opiniones et dignae credulitate nascuntur, {37c}
porro cum individuum genus semperque idem conspexerit,

in contrary motion, three of the seven with equal velocity and four with unequal or dissimilar velocity in relation both to one another and to the rest, but with measured motion.

And so once the Being of rational soul had arisen in its entirety and in conformity with the desire of its father, the latter shortly thereafter fashioned within {36e} its confines all that is corporeal, and attaching the center of body to that of soul he joined them in suitable harmony; but the soul, embracing the outermost reaches of the heaven and being infused throughout it by virtue of its external embrace and enclosing it within its periphery and itself revolving back upon itself, inaugurated the divine beginning of a life that was untiring and wise and without intermission. And the body of the heaven or world was made visible, whereas soul was invisible and yet possessed of reason and {37a} harmony, being superior to all other intelligibles in having been made by the most superior maker. Having been compounded, then, of the natures of the Same and Other as blended with Being, and revolving back upon itself in its innate orbital movement, when it encounters any Being that is either subject to dissipation or indivisible it easily distinguishes what is of the nature of the Same and indivisible, {37b} and what of the nature of the Other and dissoluble. And it sees the causes of all things that emerge and takes the measure of those which are to be from those which are occurring, and without voice or sound its rational movement, the circling of the nature of the Other, on perceiving anything sensible moves without error. And while its veridical perception announces certitudes to the whole of soul right opinions worthy of belief arise, {37c} whereas on perceiving a nature that is indivisible and forever the Same its

ea quae sunt motu intimo fideliter nuntiante, intellectus et scientia convalescunt. Quae quidem omnia in anima fieri eidemque insigniri palam est.

Quam cum moveri et vivere animadverteret factum a se simulacrum immortalis divinitatis genitor suus, hilaratus impendio multo magis ad exemplum eius aemulae similitudinis aliud specimen censuit excogitandum. {37d} Ut igitur haec immortalis et sempiterna sic mundum quoque sensibilem animal immortale constituit. Sed animal<is> quidem [id quod est generale animal] natura aevo exaequatur, unde facto nativoque operi cum aevo societas congruere minime videbatur. Quapropter imaginem eius mobilem numeroque serpentem factae a se machinae deus sociabat eam quae tempus dicitur, aevo intacto et in singularitate perseverante. {37e} Dies enim et noctes et menses et annos, qui ante caelestem exornationem non erant, tunc nascente mundo iussit existere; quae omnia partes sunt temporis, nosque haec cum aevo assignamus, id est solitariae naturae, non recte partes individuae rei fingimus. Dicimus enim "fuit," "est," "erit," ast illi esse solum competit iuxta {38a} veram sinceramque rationem, fuisse vero et fore deinceps non competit. Haec quippe geniturae temporis proprie, motus enim sunt—unus praetereuntis alter imminentis—non aevi sed temporis; aevi

understanding and knowledge gain strength while an inner impulse faithfully announces the things that are. And it is manifest that it is in and upon soul that all of this occurs and leaves its mark.

When its father observed that the image of immortal divinity which he had made was in motion and alive, he was greatly pleased and decided that a further indication of likeness, one that strove for a much closer approximation of its pattern, should be devised. {37d} And so, as the divinity is immortal and eternal, just so he established the sensible world too as an immortal living being. But the nature of the living being is consistent with eternity, and thus the association with eternity appeared incompatible with a work that had been made and generated. And for this reason god brought a moving image thereof, an image which progresses according to number and is called time, into association with the engine he had made, with eternity left untouched and abiding in unity. {37e} For he ordered that days and nights and months and years, which did not exist prior to the process of celestial adornment, should arise at the same time as the world came into being; and they are all parts of time, and when we speak of them in connection with eternity, i.e., in connection with a nature which is unitary, we incorrectly imagine an indivisible reality as having parts. For we say it "was," "is," or "will be" despite the fact that the only expression compatible with it according to {38a} the true and pure account is that it is, whereas the expression that it was or will later be is incompatible with it. For the latter are processes of becoming which are properly associated with time, for they are movements—in one case of that which is passing away and in the other of that which is imminent—

quippe mansio perpetua et immutabilis. Ergo neque iunior se neque senior nec fuit nec erit nec patietur eorum aliquid quae sensibilis natura patitur {38b} sed sunt haec omnia vices temporis imitantis aevum. Ac de his quidem fors erit aptior deinceps disputandi locus.

Tempus vero caelo aequaevum est, ut una orta una dissolvantur, si modo dissolvi ratio fasque patietur, simul ut aevitatis exemplo similis esset uterque mundus; {38c} archetypus quippe omni aevo semper existens est, hic sensibilis imagoque eius is est qui per omne tempus fuerit, quippe et futurus sit. Hac ergo dei ratione consilioque huius modi genituram temporis volentis creari sol et luna et aliae quinque stellae quae vocantur erraticae factae sunt, quo tam partes temporis notarentur certa dimensione quam reditus anfractusque temporarii sub numeri comprehensionem venirent. Corporaque siderea fabricatus assignavit vitalibus diversae naturae motibus numero septem {38d} totidem corpora: lunae quidem iuxta terram in prima circumactione, solis vero in secunda, tum Luciferi et Mercurii collocat ignes in eo motu qui concurrit quidem solstitiali circuitioni, contraria tamen ab eo circumfertur agitatione, quare fit ut comprehendant se invicem et a se rursum comprehendantur hae stellae.

associated, not with eternity, but with time; for with eternity is associated a perpetual and immutable remaining. Thus it was not and will not be either younger or older than itself, nor will it undergo any of the changes which sensible nature undergoes, {38b} but such changes are all reciprocal alterations associated with time in its imitation of eternity. But there will perhaps be a more suitable opportunity later for discussion of these matters.

Time at any rate is of the same age as the heaven, so that they may come into being together and be dissolved together, assuming reason or divine law ever allows their dissolution, and at the same time, so that each of the two worlds may resemble the model of eternity; {38c} for the archetype is forever existent in all eternity, and this sensible world, its image, is that which has been and indeed will be through all time. In virtue, then, of this reasoning, this kind of plan, on the part of god, who desired that the generation of time should be brought into effect, the Sun, Moon, and five other so-called wandering stars were made so that the parts of time might be recorded according to a fixed method of measurement and the temporal cycles of return and procession might equally well come within the grasp of number. And after having fabricated the celestial bodies he assigned them to the vital movements of the nature of the Other, seven bodies for {38d} seven patterns of movement: that of the Moon in the first orbit, next to Earth, and that of the Sun in the second, then he sets the celestial fires of Venus and Mercury alongside one another in a pattern of movement concurrent with the solar orbit and yet circling with a momentum contrary to it, that being the explanation for these stars' overtaking and in turn being overtaken by one

Ceteros quoque siderum ortus et progressiones divinae rationis ductu digessit in ordinem, cuius exornationis causam explicare si quis velit, {38e} plus erit opere ipso cuius gratia sumitur; verum haec, si erunt ad id quo de agitur utilia, post exequemur. Igitur singulis universisque apto et decenti sibi motu locatis—videlicet his quae consequens erat tempore provenire—, nexibusque vitalibus ubi constricta corpora facta sunt animalia imperatumque didicerunt, ea, quae diversae naturae motus {39a} obliquus per directum eiusdem naturae motum vertens semet (utpote constrictus) circumferebat, partim maiore partim minore curriculo rotabantur, citius quidem dimensum spatium peragentia quae minore tardius vero quae maiore, utpote ambitu circumacta prolixiore. Qua de causa fiebat ut ex uniformi eiusdem naturae conversione quae citius circuirent ab his quae tardius circumferebantur comprehendentia comprehendi viderentur. Omnes quippe circulos eorum uniformis et inerrabilis illa conversio vertens in spiram et velut sinuosum acanthi volumen, quia gemino et {39b} contrario motu ferebantur, tum ipsa etiam cita et volucris ea quae tardius a se recedebant proxima sibi semper ex consecutione faciebat. Atque ut rationabilis et consulta haec motuum varietas et moderatio

another. Under the guidance of divine reason he established an order for the risings and progressions of the other astral bodies as well, and if anyone should wish to explicate the reason for the pattern of adornment, {38e} then it will involve more than the very effort for the sake of which it is undertaken; however, we will pursue these matters later if they prove useful for the task in hand. Now, they—namely, those whose emergence was by definition in time—had individually and in their entirety been placed in a pattern of movement that was apt and befitting them; and once their limbs, under the constraints of the vital bonds, became living beings and learned their appointed task, then the bodies which the movement of the nature of the Other—{39a} which revolved obliquely across the path of the nature of the Same (for it was constrained by it)—conveyed round began to revolve, some along a larger and others along a smaller orbit, with those that moved along a smaller one completing the measured distance more rapidly and those that moved along a larger one doing so more slowly due to their being carried round a longer periphery. And for th!is reason it came about that owing to the uniform rotation of the nature of the Same those which orbited more rapidly appeared to be overtaken by those which orbited more slowly although they were overtaking them. For that uniform and unvarying rotation, turning all of their orbits round in a spiral and, as it were, winding acanthus coil by virtue of their traveling in double or {39b} contrary patterns of movement, and being quick and swift itself, then made the bodies which departed most slowly from it consequently always nearest to it. And in order that this rationally planned variation in and temperament of movements might also be visibly observable

visu quoque notaretur omniumque octo motuum perspicua esset chorea, ignivit lucem clarissimam deus rerum conditor e regione secundi a terra globi, quam lucem solem vocamus, cuius splendore caelum infraque illustrarentur omnia numerusque omnium extaret animantium. {39c} Hinc ergo noctis dieique ortus ex eodem semper et inerrabili motu factus rata alterna lucis atque umbrarum successione, mensis vero proventus, cum lustrato luna circulo suo solem consequitur, anni, cum sol item emensis anfractibus renovat exordia; ceterarum vero stellarum circuitus neque notant neque dinumerant homines exceptis paucis {39d} nec intellegunt discursus erroresque earum temporis esse genituram, in quo sit admiranda varietas proventuum caelestes tramites undique stellis variantibus. Est tamen intellectu facile quod perfectus temporis numerus perfectum annum compleat tunc demum cum omnium octo circumactionum cursus peracti velut ad originem atque exordium circumactionis alterius revertentur, quam semper idem atque uniformis motus dimetietur; quam ob causam cetera quoque nata sunt astra quae per caelum meantia conversiones habent, ut {39e} quam simillimum esset omne hoc perfecto illi quod mente perspicitur animali aevoque exaequatae naturae temporis socia natura nancisceretur imaginem.

and the round of all eight movements perspicuous, god the founder of things ignited a most brilliant light in the region of the sphere second from Earth, which light we call the Sun, so that the heaven and everything beneath it might be illuminated by its light and there might be a form of number belonging to all living beings. {39c} It was from this, then, that night and day came to be born, from the movement that is forever the Same and unvarying and with a fixed alternation in the succession of light and darkness, and a month emerges when after having gone round its own course the Moon catches up with the Sun, and a year, when after having similarly passed through its cycle the Sun renews its commencement; but the circuits of the other stars human beings, with few exceptions, neither observe nor calculate, {39d} nor do they understand that time arises with their courses and wanderings, wherein there is an astonishing variety of phenomena due to ubiquitous variation in stellar movement along the celestial paths. It is nevertheless easy to understand that the perfect number of time should mark the completion of the perfect year at the point when the completed courses of all eight revolutions will return to the origin, as it were, and commencement of a second revolution, which the movement that is forever the Same and uniform will measure; and for this reason there were born as well all of the astral bodies that have reversals in their wanderings through the heaven: so that {39e} this All might resemble in the highest possible degree that perfect living being which is visible to the mind, and so that the associated nature of time might obtain a likeness of the nature that equals eternity.

Pars Secunda Timaei Platonis

Et iam fere cuncta provenerant usque ad genituram temporis ad germanam composita similitudinem exempli et veritatis suae, nisi quod nondum hic mundus cuncta continebat animalia perinde ut intellegibilis, ad cuius aemulationem fiebat. Hoc igitur quod deerat addebat opifex deus; atque ut mens, cuius visus contemplatioque intellectus est, idearum genera contemplatur in intellegibili mundo, quae ideae sunt illic animalia, sic deus in hoc opere suo sensili diversa animalium genera statuit esse debere constituitque quattuor: primum caeleste plenum divinitatis; aliud deinde {40a} praepes aerivagum; tertium aquae liquoribus accommodatum; quartum quod terrena soliditas sustineret. Et divini quidem generis ex parte maxima speciem ignis serena claritudine perpolibat, ut propter eximium splendorem nitoremque videntibus esset visurisque venerabilis, figuram porro eius figurae mundi intellegibilis accommodans indeclinabiliter evenustabat totumque eum posuit in gremio prudentiae caeli undique ineffabilis pulchritudinis ornamentis stipans eum et convegetans ad aeternitatem. Motumque eius circulis convenientem et pro cuiusque natura commentus est: alterum circum se perque eandem orbitam semper obeuntem eademque {40b} semper deliberantem ac de isdem

The *Timaeus* of Plato, Second Part

And now, up to the point when time came to be, nearly everything had emerged constructed as a genuine likeness of the model which expressed what it truly was, except that this world did not yet contain all living beings in the way the intelligible one in whose likeness it was made did. The craftsman god therefore set out to supply what was missing; and just as mind, whose vision or contemplation is intellect, contemplates the range of ideas in the intelligible world, where the ideas are living beings, so god determined that there should be a diverse range of living beings in this sensible product of his workmanship, and established four kinds: first, a celestial one, full of divinity; next after it, {40a} a winged one, wandering through the air; third, one that was adapted to liquid bodies of water; and fourth, that which solid earth was to sustain. And the form of the divine kind he perfected for the most part with the shining luminosity of fire, such that because of its exceptional splendor and brightness it would inspire a feeling of reverence in those who looked or were to look upon it, while in adapting its shape to that of the intelligible world he beautified it with stability, and he placed the whole of it in the bosom of wisdom, filling it all around with the adornments of the ineffable beauty of the heaven and quickening it unto eternity. And he devised a pattern of movement befitting its circles and in consideration of the nature of each: one of them forever moving round itself and through the same orbit and forever {40b} reflecting on and thinking about the same

ratiocinantem; alterum vero talem qui semper ultra procedere gestiens eiusdem atque immutabilis naturae coer-
citione intra obiectum eius rotabundus teneretur; quinque
illis erraticis et contrariis sibi invicem prohibitis motibus ut
uterque circulus esset in optimo beatissimoque agitationis
statu. Qua ex causa facti sunt summa divinitate praediti omnes illi ignes siderei qui nullos errores exorbitationesque patiuntur proptereaque in semet ipsos convertuntur aeterno
circuitu, at vero alii vagi palantesque ignes erroris causam
habent eam cuius in superioribus habita commemoratio est.
Terram vero matrem et altricem omnium terrenorum animantium constrictam {40c} limitibus per omnia vadentis et
cuncta continentis poli diei noctisque custodem locavit, antiquissimam et eximiae dignitatis deam ex eorum numero
qui intra mundi ambitum continentur deorum. Stellarum
vero choreas, et alterius applicationes ad alteram, variosque
gyros quos edunt admirabili venustate iuxta ambitus circulorum, reditusque et anfractus ad eas sedes ex quibus progressae sunt, accessus etiam et recessus, cumque contiguae
sibi invicem fiunt quales ex contagione sua condiciones ac-
cipiant quamque et cuius modi nanciscantur qualitatem ex
varia designatione, cumque, quod aliquanto intervallo temporis fieri solet, certae stellae mersae ac latentes operiuntur,
quae significent et mox aut aliquanto post futura porten-
dant, vel cum insolitis horis curriculisque temporum rursus
emergunt et apparent, quantos denuntient metus {40d} his

things; and the other such that it would be kept under the
constraints of the nature which is the Same and immutable,
revolving within the confines of the latter while forever
straining to move straight forward; and with the five wandering and mutually contrary patterns of movement being
held in check so that each of the two circles might be in the
most perfect and undisturbed state of rotation. And for this
reason there came to be all of those starry fires which are
endowed with the highest divinity and which experience no
wanderings or deviations from their orbits and therefore re-
vert back upon themselves in an eternal revolving, while
other vagrant and erratic fires have for their wandering the
cause which has been mentioned earlier. And Earth, the
mother and nourisher of all earthly living creatures, constrained {40c} by the limits of the pole that traverses and
contains all things, he positioned as the guardian of day and
night, a goddess most ancient and of exceptional dignity
among the array of gods contained within the world sphere.
But as for the stellar rounds, the juxtapositions of one star
with another, the varied circuits which they display with astonishing beauty within the confines of their orbits, the cycles of return and procession to their points of departure,
their advances and retreats, the types of disposition they
obtain from their conjunction and the manner and mode
which determine their achieving a particular type from the
range of configurations when they come into conjunction
with one another; and as for the question of what certain
stars signify and portend for the immediate or more distant future when according to anticipated patterns of occurrence within some fixed interval of time they are concealed,
submerged and hidden, or of the level of fear they betoken

qui rationem motus earum intellegere possunt—cunctaque huius modi ratione atque orationibus persequi nihil agentis ac frustra laborantis est, maxime cum motus earum descriptioque sit a visu atque oculis disputantis remota. Quapropter ea quae de sideribus visibilibusque divinis potestatibus dicta sunt satis superque dicta finem habeant suum.

At vero invisibilium divinarum potestatum quae daemones nuncupantur praestare rationem maius est opus quam ferre valeat hominis ingenium; igitur compendium ex credulitate sumatur. Credamus ergo his qui apud saeculum prius, cum ipsi cognationem propinquitatemque divini generis praeferrent, de natura deorum maiorum atque avorum deque genituris singulorum aeterna monumenta in libris posteritati reliquerunt. Certe deorum {40e} filiis aut nepotibus non credi satis inreligiosum; quamvis incongruis nec necessariis probationibus dicant, tamen, quia de domesticis rebus pronuntiant, credendum esse merito puto. Sit igitur nostra quoque credulitas comes asseverationi priscorum virorum, quod Terrae Caelique filii sint Oceanus et Tethys, horum porro Saturnus et Rhea et Phorcus, {41a} Saturni porro et Rheae proles Iupiter et Iuno et ceteri qui sunt in ore hominum ac mentibus et de quorum fraternitate fama celebratur; atque ex his alii nati sunt qui dii putantur.

{40d} for those who are capable of understanding their pattern of movement when they once again emerge and appear at or within unanticipated hours or temporal cycles: to pursue these and all related phenomena in thought and speech is the mark of one who accomplishes nothing and labors in vain, especially given that stellar movement and a means of describing it are beyond what the eyes of the disputant can see. And for these reasons we may conclude our account of the stars and visible divine powers, for it is more than sufficient.

At the same time, to give an account of the invisible divine powers known as demons is a task greater than our human ability is capable of sustaining; a brief résumé based on trust must therefore be taken as granted. Let us then trust those who in their books long ago, when they themselves revealed their relationship and propinquity to the divine race, left to posterity perennial records of the nature of the gods, their ancestors and forebears, and of the progeny of each. {40e} To mistrust the children and grandchildren of gods would surely be quite sacrilegious; and although their accounts are based on proofs which are inconsistent and lack cogency, I nevertheless think it right that they should be trusted, given that they pronounce upon matters which have to do with their own family histories. Our trust should also go along with the men of old, then, when they assert that Ocean and Tethys are the children of Earth and Heaven, that Saturn, Rhea, and Phorcus are their children, {41a} and that Jupiter, Juno, and all those who occupy the words and thoughts of men and whose kinship is celebrated as a matter of tradition are the offspring of Saturn and Rhea; and from them were born others who are thought to be gods.

His igitur omnibus, qui vel videntur in convexis caelestibus flammanti corpore vel non videntur, natis atque altis divinitatemque obtinentibus conditor universitatis deus observanda iubet sancitque oratione tali: "Dii, deorum quorum opifex idem paterque ego, opera siquidem vos mea dissolubilia natura, me tamen ita volente indissolubilia, omne siquidem quod {41b} iunctum est natura dissolubile, at vero quod bona ratione iunctum atque modulatum est dissolvi velle non est dei. Quapropter, quia facti generatique estis, immortales quidem nequaquam nec omnino indissolubiles, nec tamen umquam dissolvemini nec mortis necessitatem subibitis, quia voluntas mea maior est nexus et vegetatior ad aeternitatis custodiam quam illi nexus vitales ex quibus aeternitas vestra coagmentata atque composita est. Iubendi ergo quod iubeo causa haec est: tria etiam nunc mortalia genera desunt universitati, quibus carens universa res perfectione indigebit, erit porro imperfecta si universa mortalia genera intra {41c} conseptum suum minime continebit; oportet autem, si erit mundus perfectus futurus—proveniet porro hoc idem virtute auctoritatis meae—, esse plenam universi generis substantiam, quo animalibus singulis suppeditato vivendi vigore ea quae sunt meliora proximam divinitati fortunam dignitatemque sortiantur. Quapropter, ut et

Now, once they have all been brought to birth and have developed in the course of acquiring their divinity, both those who with their fiery bodies manifest themselves in the heavenly vault and those who do not, the founding god of the universe orders and sanctions the rules they are to observe, in the following words: "O gods, you gods of whom I am at once the craftsman and father, although insofar as you are my works you are by nature subject to dissolution, you are nevertheless immune to dissolution because of my so willing it, for everything that {41b} has been joined together is indeed by nature subject to dissolution, but it is not for a god to will the dissolution of that which has been joined together and harmonized in good proportion. And so, although insofar as you have been made and generated you are by no means immortal or entirely immune to dissolution, nevertheless you will neither be dissolved nor undergo the necessity of death, for my will is a bond which is greater and, as concerns the guardianship of eternity, more vigorous than the vital bonds from which the eternity you enjoy has been joined together and composed. The reason, then, for enjoining what I now enjoin is this: at present, three kinds of mortal being are lacking to the universe, and if deprived of them the universe will be wanting in completeness and will be incomplete unless it contains the universal array of mortal kinds within {41c} its confines; but if the world is to be complete—and by the power of my authority it will indeed come to pass—, then it is necessary that its substance should be filled with the universal array of kinds so that once the life-giving force has been bestowed upon individual living beings those which are superior may obtain a lot or rank bordering on divinity. And so, in order both that there may

mortalia sint et universa res non indigeat perfectione sed sit tota atque universa vere, iubeo aggrediamini secundum naturam mortalium generum institutionem. Imitantes ergo meam iuxta effectum vestrum sollertiam ita instituite atque extricate mortalia ut, quibus consortium divinitatis et appellationis parilitas competit, divina praeditum firmitate fingatis; erit vero tale quod vobis obsequi iustitiamque colere prospexeritis. Huius ego universi generis sementem faciam {41d} vobisque tradam; vos cetera exequi par est, ita ut immortalem caelestemque naturam mortali textu extrinsecus ambiatis, iubeatisque nasci, cibumque provideatis, et incrementa detis, ac post dissolutionem id faenus quod credideratis facta secessione animi et corporis recipiatis."

Haec dixit et demum reliquias prioris concretionis, ex qua mundi animam commiscuerat, in eiusdem crateris sinum refundens eodem propemodum genere atque eadem ratione miscebat, nec tamen eadem exoriebatur puritas serenitasque proventuum nec tam immutabilis perseverantiae sed secundae ac tertiae dignitatis. Coagmentataque mox universae rei machina delegit animas stellarum numero pares {41e} singulasque singulis comparavit easdemque vehiculis competentibus superimpositas universae rei naturam spectare iussit legesque immutabilis decreti docuit, ostendens quod prima quidem generatio uniformis in omnibus

be mortal beings and that the universe may be, not wanting in completeness, but whole and truly universal, I bid you undertake in accordance with your nature the establishment of mortal kinds. In imitation of my ingenuity in producing you, then, establish and set free the mortals in such a way that you fashion those who are suitable for participation in and assuming the title of divinity as endowed with divine stability; and it is to be such that you will observe its submission to you and its cultivation of justice. I for my part will perform the sowing of this universal array according to kind {41d} and hand it over to you; your repayment is to attend to the rest, in the following way: you are to envelop the immortal and celestial nature with a mortal tissue on its exterior, to bid it come to birth, to provide for its nourishment, to give it growth, and after its dissolution, when the separation of mind and body has been effected, to reap the interest on what you invested on credit."

So he spoke, and pouring the remainder of the mixture from which he had originally blended the world soul together back into the cavity of the same bowl he then set about blending it in more or less the same way and the same proportion, although there did not emerge the same purity and clarity in the results, which were marked by a permanence that was, not immutable as in the case of the original blend, but of the second or third order. And as soon as the engine of the universe had been joined together he selected souls equal in number with the stars {41e} and coupled them one to one, and after mounting them in the appropriate vehicles he bade them gaze upon the nature of the universe and instructed them in the laws of the immutable decree, indicating that the first generation was to be uniform and at

eiusdemque ordinis esset futura ne cui competens iustum aliqua ex parte a se minueretur. Oportebat porro satas eas certis legitimisque temporum vicibus {42a} piae nationis animalium quaeque praeter ceteras animantes deum suspiciant afferre frugem, esse autem naturam hominis geminam, cuius quod melius sit genus censendum fore viri nomine. Cumque necessitate decreti corporibus inserentur corporeaque supellex varie mutabitur quibusdam labentibus et aliis invicem succedentibus membris, primo quidem sensum ex violentis passionibus excitari, post quem mixtam ex voluptate tristitiaque cupidinem nasci, tum vero metum atque iracundiam ceterasque {42b} pedissequas earum perturbationes diverso affectu pro natura sua permoventes; quas quidem si frenarent ac subiugarent, iustam his lenemque vitam fore, sin vincerentur, iniustam et confragosam. Et victricibus quidem ad comparis stellae contubernium sedemque reditum patere acturis deinceps vitam veram et beatam, victas porro mutare sexum atque ad infirmitatem naturae muliebris relegari {42c} secundae generationis tempore; nec a vitiis intemperantiaque desciscentibus [tamen] poenam reiectionemque in deteriora non cessare donec instituto meritisque congruas immanium ferarum induant formas; pausamque malorum non prius fore quam consecuta eas rata et eadem

the same rank in every case, so that none would in any way be deprived by him of its appropriate and just due. And it was necessary that the souls, once sown according to fixed and prescribed seasons, {42a} should bear fruit in the form of a pious race of beings that live and acknowledge god as other living creatures cannot; and he indicated that human nature should be twofold, and that its superior kind was to be assessed at the value associated with the name "man." And he indicated that, once they are implanted in bodies by necessity of the decree and their bodily apparatus experiences varied changes with the slipping away of certain parts and the emergence of others to take their place, in the first instance sensation should be stirred up by the violent passions, and that after it desire blended from pleasure and pain should arise, and then fear and irascibility and the other disturbances {42b} that follow from them, each one initiating change with varying influence depending on its nature; and that if they curbed and subjugated the disturbances their life should be just and smooth, but that if they were overcome by them it should be unjust and rough. And he indicated that for those souls who were victorious the path was open to their returning to inhabit the abode of their consort star and leading a true and blessed life thereafter, whereas those who had been overcome should change their sex and be relegated to the infirmity of the female nature {42c} at the time of the second birth. And that for those who did not free themselves from vice and intemperance the punishment and rejection to inferior states should not cease until they assume the forms of wild beasts, forms congruent with their mode of life and deserts. And that there should be no respite from their hardships before that fixed

semper volucris illa mundi circumactio cuncta earum vitia
ex igni et aqua {42d} terraque et aere contracta omnemque
illuviem deterserit inconsultis et immoderatis erroribus ad
modum rationis temperiemque redactis, quo positis sordi-
bus expiatae purificataeque demum ad antiqui vultus honestatem pertingere mereantur. Quibus cunctis fatalium legum
promulgationibus in istum modum patefactis et expositis,
ne qua penes se deinceps ex reticentia noxae resideret auctoritas, sementem fecit eius modi deus, ut partim in terra
partim in luna generis humani iacerentur exordia partim in
ceteris quae instrumenta sunt temporis. Ea porro officia
quae sementem sequuntur factis a se diis iniunxit, ut dix-
eram, maximeque formandorum corporum curam mortalium; ac si qua pars etiam tunc hominis animae residua
superesset, cuius constitutioni navanda opera {42e} videretur, ceteraque omnia consequenter aggrederentur hortatus
est, quae operis perfectio rerumque ordo deposceret proque
viribus eniterentur ut quam optime mortalis natura regere-
tur exceptis improsperitatibus quarum esset auctoritas et
causa penes ipsos.

Quibus in istum modum digestis omnibus cum in proposito rerum creator maneret, intellegentes iussionem patris
filii iuxta mandatam informationem, immortali sumpto initio mortalis animantis ex mundi materiis igni terraque et
aqua cum spiritu, faenus elementarium mutuati {43a} quod

and forever selfsame circumlation of the winged world overtakes them and wipes away all of the defects and all of the filth they have contracted from fire, water, {42d} earth, and air, bringing their irrational and intemperate errors back to the moderation and temperance of reason, so that after having been expiated and purified by the laying aside of their uncleanliness they may be worthy of attaining the dignity of their original appearance. And after all of the promulgations of the laws of fate had been thus disclosed and expounded, in order that no responsibility for wrongdoing would in future fall to him for keeping silent god performed the sowing such that the first beginnings of mankind were laid partly in the Earth, partly in the Moon, and partly in the other bodies serving as instruments of time. And as I have indicated, he enjoined upon the gods who had been made by him the duties that are ensuant upon his sowing, above all, their oversight of the forming of mortal bodies; and he exhorted them to attend to any part of the human soul that was still left remaining, any part {42e} evidently requiring work for the soul's full construction, and to attend to all other tasks entailed by the completion of their work and by the order of things, and he exhorted them to ensure to the best of their abilities that the mortal nature would be governed in the best way possible, apart from those misfortunes which the mortals were responsible for bringing upon themselves.

And when all of these things had been separated out thus and the creator of things continued to abide by his plan, the sons reflected on their father's command in light of the conception it stipulated, and after drawing upon the world's material elements of fire, earth, water, and air as an immortal starting point for the mortal living creature by borrowing

redderetur cum opus foret, ea quae acceperant conglutinabant non isdem quibus ipsi nexibus sed aliis ob incom-
prehensibilem brevitatem invisibilibus gomphis. Itaque apparata materia circuitus immortalis animae circumligabant
inriguo fluidoque corpori; circuitus porro ut torrenti rapido
defluoque obligati neque tenebant neque tenebantur sed ita
vi ferebant et invicem ferebantur ut {43b} totum quidem animal moveretur, praecipiti tamen et inordinata iactatione,
quippe cum sex sine ratione raptaretur motibus, ultro citro,
dextrorsum sinistrorsum et item sursum deorsumque pergens atque oberrans. Immenso quippe inrigante et immoderate effluente gurgite, ex quo cibus et alimenta comparaban-
tur, multo maior extrinsecus turba conflictatioque vexabat,
cum corpus aliquod in raptatu incurrisset {43c} ignis offen-
sionem vel etiam terrenam complosionem, similiter aquae
lubricas violentasque ventorum procellas hisque interpella-
tionibus omnibus per corpus ad animam commeantibus
stimulata mens aestuaret; qui quidem aestus propterea et
initio et nunc usque sensus cognominantur. Maximos vio-
lentosque motus cientes cum naturali derivatione iugiter et
sine intermissione {43d} effluente, circuitus animae quasi
quibusdam turbinibus simul quatiunt, illum quidem provi-
dum eius consultumque motum (scilicet eiusdem circuli,
cuius est orbiculata circumvolutatio), statuentes et contra

elemental capital {43a} which was to be repaid as needed, they set about cementing together what they had received, not with the same bonds as those by which they themselves were cemented together but with other ones, bolts that were incomprehensibly minute to the point of being invisible. And so once the material had been made ready they confined the circuits of the immortal soul to a body which was subject to ebbs and flows; and being confined by this rapidly flowing torrent the circuits neither restrained nor were restrained but caused and in turn suffered movement with such force that although {43b} the whole living being moved it did so with a violent and disorderly agitation, for it jostled about aimlessly, advancing and shifting direction by a combination of six forms of movement, forward and backward, to the right and left, and up and down. For although the stream from which their food and nourishment was procured flowed in and out without measure or limit, the tumultuous impact of external disturbances was far greater still, whenever in the course of its trajectory an individual body encountered a vexing blockage {43c} of fire, a blow of earth, or blasts of gliding water and violent winds, causing the mind to become agitated under the stimulus of all these incursions wandering through the body to the soul; and that explains why the agitations are called sensations, initially and up until now. In stirring up the most violent commotion in the form of a natural current that flows away continuously and without intermission, {43d} they simultaneously disturb the circuits of the soul as though by whirlwinds of some sort, blocking its provident and deliberative movement (namely, that of the circle of the Same, with its orbital rotation), exerting an effect contrary to its movement, and

quam illa movetur operantes, imperiumque eius respuentes
at vero diversi circuli diversis motibus incertisque famu-
lantes. Usque adeo ut—quia limites duplicis illius et triplicis
quantitatis et item intervalla terna per utrumque latus
epitritorum sescuplorumque et epogdoorum medietatibus
confirmata dissolvi a nullo quam ab eo solo qui iunxerat poterant, omni tamen {43e} iactationis genere divexarent adversis sibi invicem motibus animam, totam eius substantiam
diverse distrahentes—ut una quidem feratur cum confirma-
tionis suae nexibus, verum sine ratione, utpote discordanti-
bus motibus et depravante rectum iter sensuum illecebra.
Propterea varias inclinationes existere, obliquas, contrarias,
et item resupinis casibus similes, ut si quis naturalem membris regionem mutans caput pro pedibus solo figat, pedes in
altum pro capite sustollat: tunc, opinor, tam eius qui patitur
quam eorum qui spectant dextrae quidem partes sinistrae
sinistrae vero dextrae videntur invicem.

Id ipsum animae quoque circuitus patiuntur {44a} proptereaque errant in eiusdem diversique generis contemplatione, cum quod diversum idem et quod est idem diversum
imbecillitate discernendi autumant estque haec eorum
plena erroris et falsitatis opinio orta ex depravatione sensuum, nec habet ullum certum ducem talis peragratio; cumque extra positi sensus pulsaverint animam vehementius

rejecting its commanding authority while serving the varying and uncertain movements of the circle of the Other. And all of this to such an extent that—since the terms associated with the multiples of the double and triple, and the three intervals along either side that were held together by the means associated with the epitritic, hemiolic, and epogdoic ratios, could be dissolved by no one except by him alone who had joined them, and yet by all manner {43e} of agitation they tore the soul asunder with mutually opposed movements, pulling the whole of its substance in different directions—with the bonds that held it together it managed to move as a unity but did so aimlessly, for its movements were discordant and the lure of the senses distorted its movement in a straight line. And so there arose altered inclinations, oblique, contrary, and resembling cases of inversion, as when by changing the regions to which his body parts are naturally assigned someone fixes his head rather than feet to the ground and raises his feet rather than head up high: then, I suppose, in the cases of both the one who experiences the change and those who witness it the right-hand parts appear on the left and the lefthand ones in turn on the right.

The circuits of the soul too experience the very same thing {44a} and consequently err in their contemplation of that which falls under the Same or Other when in their inability to distinguish they proclaim that which is other the same and that which is the same other, and this for them is an opinion full of error and falsity, originating in distortions caused by the senses, and they wander in this way without having any sure guide; and when sensations coming from without assail the soul with particular force and take full

omnemque eam possederint, tunc illa subiugata et serviens pontificium aliquod potestatemque retinere falso putatur eademque passionibus aegra {44b} et initio, cum incorporata est, et quamdiu perinde afficietur amens erit. At postquam incrementi nutricationisque tenui iam rivo meatus effluet animaeque circuitus tranquilliore motu viam suam peragent processuque temporis sedatiores erunt, utpote qui a naturae suae competenti motu minime exorbitent, facile iam diversae naturae vitia bonitatemque et honestatem semper eiusdem cum alterius appetitu, alterius vero detestatione secernent hominemque ita institutum plena et incolumi prudentia tuebuntur. Ac si ad hunc statum accedat auxiliatrix eruditionis honestae moderationisque diligentia, {44c} immunis omni perturbatione atque aegritudine ducet aevum; si negleget, claudum iter vitae serpens cum familiari demum stultitia revocabitur ad inferna.

Sed haec quidem novissime provenient meritis iam vitae locatis; nunc vero divinae providentiae spectari pensum convenit ex membrorum rationabili conformatione, quae suscipiendo vitali vigori caelestis apparabat prospicientia. {44d} Principio figuram capitis divinae potestates, quibus informandi corporis erat officium concreditum, ex mundi figura mutuatae teretem globosamque finxerunt eidemque duos circuitus venerandae divinitatis innexuerunt. Est

possession of it, it is then falsely supposed to retain a certain right or power even though it is subjugated and subservient, and also ailing with affections it will be without intelligence {44b} from the moment of its embodiment and for as long as it is affected thereafter. But once the current of increase and nourishment flows in what becomes a light stream, and the circuits of the soul complete their journey in a more tranquil movement and with the passage of time prove more sedate owing to their not deviating from the orbital movement befitting their nature, at that point they will easily distinguish between the defects of the nature of the Other and the goodness and honor of that which is forever the Same, by attraction in the one case and with aversion in the other, and will safeguard the man thus prepared with full and unimpaired wisdom. And if care in the form of an honorable education and moderation is added as a support to his achieving this state then he will live his life {44c} immune to all disturbance and disease; but if he is negligent then he will ultimately be summoned back to the infernal regions for creeping in habitual foolishness along the crippled path of his life.

But these developments will emerge at the very end, once the merits of the present life have been posited; for the moment it is appropriate that the care taken by divine providence should be viewed in light of the rational configuration of the parts of the body, which the celestial foresight equipped to receive the vital force. {44d} First the divine powers to whom the task of forming the body had been entrusted fashioned the head in a round and spherical shape by borrowing from the shape of the world, and within it they bound the two circuits of venerable divinity. The head,

autem caput praeter ceterum corpus honoratius et optimati quadam eminentia; cui reliqua membra dominanti parent atque obsequuntur iure meritoque subiecta, ne sine sede humiliter in imo plane iacens asperas, cum moveretur, terrenarum lacunarum offensiones {44e} proclivitatis et item declivitatis incurreret, maxime cui esset necesse cuncta motuum genera experiri. Hac igitur de causa vehiculo corporis utpote arx sustinetur. Addita est crurum quoque et brachiorum porrigibilis et flexuosa substantia, ut tenendi omittendi progrediendi resistendique usus ex arbitrio praesto foret {45a} eminente divino capitis gestamine. Progrediendi porro commodius officium quam recedendi rata divina mens ire ulterius mage quam recessim voluit moveri; priores quoque corporis partes meliores posterioribus iudicans in homine primo omnium e regione certa capitis personam subdidit vultus eamque appellavit faciem eidemque instrumenta {45b} quae adminicularentur providis animae motibus assignavit. E quibus primi luciferi oculorum orbes coruscant hac de causa dati. Duae sunt, opinor, virtutes ignis, altera edax et peremptoria altera mulcebris innoxio lumine. Huic igitur ex qua lux diem invehens panditur domesticum et familiare corpus oculorum divinae potestates commentae sunt, intimum siquidem nostri corporis ignem, {45c} utpote germanum ignis perlucidi sereni et defaecati liquoris, per

moreover, stands apart from the rest of the body by virtue of its greater dignity and a certain noble preeminence; the other parts submit to its domination and obediently subject themselves to it as a matter of right or obligation, so that it might not lie abjectly on the open ground, without a seat, and in the course of its movement run into the rough stumbling blocks of the land with its hollows that slope {44e} up and down, and this primarily because it would be necessary for it to experience all forms of movement. This, then, is the reason for its being supported, in the sense that a citadel is, by the body as its vehicle. An extendable and flexible substance was further added in its legs and arms, to promote its free and ready use of the powers of holding on, letting go, advancing, and stopping in consideration of {45a} the preeminent and divine load it carried, its head. And holding the function of forward progression to be more advantageous than that of retrogression the divine mind determined that they should go forward rather than move in reverse; and also considering the front portions of the human body to be superior to those at the back, they added before all else a mask, or countenance, in a fixed area of the head and called it the face and assigned to it organs {45b} to support the provident movements of the soul. And first among them the light-bearing ocular orbs glimmer, which have been provided for the following reason. Fire, I suppose, has two powers, one consuming and destructive and the other soothing due to its harmless light. The divine powers, then, devised an ocular body that was akin and related to the power from which the light that ushers in the day emanates, for they determined that {45c} as the sibling of the brightly shining fire and the unmuddied fluid the fire within our body should

oculos fluere ac demanare voluerunt, ut per leves congestosque et tamquam firmiore soliditate probatos orbes luminum, quorum tamen esset angusta medietas subtilior, serenus ignis per eandem efflueret medietatem. Itaque cum
diurnum iubar applicat se visus fusioni, tunc nimirum incurrentia semet invicem duo similia in unius corporis speciem
cohaerent, quo concurrunt oculorum acies emicantes quoque effluentis intimae fusionis acies contiguae imaginis occursu repercutitur. Totum igitur hoc similem eandemque
sortitum passionem et ob indifferentem similitudinem eiusdem passionis effectum, cum quid aliud {45d} tangit vel ipsum ab alio tangitur, tactuum motu diffundens se per omne
corpus perque corpus usque ad animam porrigens sensum
efficit qui visus vocatur. At postquam in noctem discesserit
cognatus ignis, desertum lucis eius auxilio consortioque velut viduatum hebet, ut quippe ad dissimile procedens proptereaque immutatum extinguitur nullam habens cum proximo tunc aere naturae communicationem, utpote splendore
ignis carenti, videreque desinit factum illecebra somni. Etenim divinae potestates salubre oculis tegmen palpebrarum
machinatae sunt, {45e} quibus obductis vis illa ignis intimi
coniventia tegminis coercetur compressaque fundit se per
membra mollitisque et relaxatis convalescit quies. Quae
cum est vehementior motuum reliquiis, cuius modi erunt et

flow and stream through the eyes such that the bright fire would flow through the smooth, dense orbs of light, which had been tested, as it were, for a higher degree of firm solidity but whose narrow center was nevertheless of a subtler consistency, and such that it would flow through that center. And so when daylight makes contact with the stream of vision, then on encountering one another the two like entities undoubtedly cohere in the form of a single body where the rays emanating from the eyes meet and the ray of the effluent inner stream rebounds after encountering a contiguous image. When this whole, therefore, on receiving a like or identical affection and becoming [assimilated] because of the undifferentiated likeness of an identical affection—when it comes into contact {45d} with another thing or is itself drawn into contact by another, then spreading throughout the body under the stimulus of the contact and extending through the body all the way to the soul, it produces the form of sense perception called vision. But once the cognate fire has departed at nightfall, this body, being deprived of the support of its light and, as it were, bereft of a consort, becomes inert, for by moving toward what is unlike it and being thereby changed it is extinguished, having at that point no natural means of communication with the surrounding air, for the brightness of fire is lacking, and ceases to see, having come to that by the inducement of sleep. For the divine powers contrived the salubrious covering of eyelids for the eyes, {45e} and once the eyelids are drawn shut the power of the internal fire becomes confined by the connivance of the covering and under pressure spreads throughout the limbs, and as the limbs become softened and relaxed rest sets in. And when the rest is stronger than any lingering

quibus in locis reliquiae, {46a} talia pariaque somniorum simulacra nascentur, eorumque expergefactos quoque memoria comitabitur. At vero simulacrorum quae in speculis oboriuntur, umbrarum etiam quae in humida cernuntur superficie, facilis assecutio est, siquidem utriusque ignis tam intimi quam extra positi concursu incidente in tersam aliquam levemque materiae superficiem {46b} formatique in multas et varias figuras simulacra ex levigati corporis conspectu resultant. Dextrae porro partes quae sunt sinistrae videntur in isdem speculis insolito quodam more, propterea quod dextris partibus visus contra sinistram partem speculi, sinistris item contra dextram positis, motu facto corporis ex adverso partis eius unde motus fit gesticulatur motus imago. At vero dextrae corporis partes dextrae ita ut sunt in speculis quoque sinistraeque item sinistrae videntur, cum ex coitu visus et splendoris e speculo corpulentior conglobata imago recidet; {46c} quod fit quotiens teres speculi serenitas hinc inde tumidioribus et provectis in molem lateribus dextram visus partem in laevam speculi, laevam item in dexteriora deiecit. Cuius speculi demum si talis facta erit conversio ut elatiores illae partes altera superior altera inferior locentur, resupini vultus apparebunt videntis splendore luminis e superiore margine cum summis oris partibus et ipso capite

movements, then dream images will arise, {46a} corresponding precisely to the mode and locations in which they linger, and even after waking up a recollection thereof will stay with those who have had them. But of the images that appear in mirrors and the faint traces seen on liquid surfaces the explanation is simple, for when a combination of the two fires, both internal and external, encounters a polished or smooth material surface of some sort {46b} and assumes a variety of different shapes, the images rebound as a function of our directing our gaze toward the smooth body. In the same mirrors, moreover, parts that are on the right appear left, against the usual norm, as it were, and do so because when the visual ray on the right side makes contact with the opposite side of the mirror and that on the left side with the right, the image of any bodily movement that occurs mimics the gesture from the side opposite to that in which the movement originates. However, the right-hand parts of the body appear on the right in the mirror, exactly as in reality, and the left-hand ones on the left when the image rebounds after having become more densely compressed in the shape of a ball because of the convergence of the visual ray and the luminous splendor issuing from the mirror; {46c} and this occurs whenever the smoothly polished brightness of the mirror, with its sides protruding and built up in elevation, drives the visual ray from one direction to the other, the one on the right side to the left side of the mirror and likewise the one on the left side to the right. And if the mirror is then rotated in such a way that one of the raised parts is positioned above and the other below, then the features will appear inverted, with the luminous ray of the onlooker, together with the upper parts of the face and the peak of the

ad inferiora deiectis, simile porro ut mento genisque ad superiora sublatis.

Qui quidem sensus famulantur actibus opificis dei summam optimamque et primariam speciem {46d} molientis; sed vulgo per semet ipsos sentire existimantur et agere aliquid, ut si quis non opifici sed serrae vel asciae tribuat effecti operis auctoritatem, cum a se plurimum distent causae et ea quae causam sequuntur. Licet enim corporea sint fundamenta omnium sensuum, quod tamen sentit, alienum a natura corporis, excipit sensus puro et incorporeo vigore; quippe corpora frigus et calorem, astrictionem et relaxationem recipiunt, non sentiunt nec vero rationem intellectumque in rebus ratione prudentiaque agendis sciunt; sed quod ex omnibus quae sunt intellectum prudentiamque habet, sola anima, hoc porro invisibile, at vero ignis et aqua ceteraeque materiae visibilia sunt corpora. Oportet autem intellectus et disciplinae amatorem prudentissimae naturae principalem causam, non adminicula causae principalis {46e} inquirere, illas vero quae ab aliis motae movent alias, secundas existimandum. Nobis quoque igitur in eundem modum faciendum est et de utroque causarum genere disserendum, sed separatim quidem de optimis quae cum intellectu prudentiaque cuncta honesta et bona moliuntur, seorsum vero de his quae mente prudentiaque cassae temere et ut libet confusa et inordinata quae faciunt relinquunt.

head, driven from the upper margin down to the lower area and likewise the chin and cheeks raised to the upper one.

And these senses serve the activities of the craftsman god in his striving for the highest, noblest, and {46d} primary form; but the run of people suppose that they sense and perform some function on their own accord, as if one were to attribute the responsibility for a completed work, not to a craftsman, but to a saw or ax, when in fact causes and the things that follow from them are fundamentally different from one another. For although the foundations of all sense perception are corporeal, nevertheless that which perceives is, by virtue of its being foreign to the nature of body, recipient of sense perceptions because of a pure and incorporeal power; for bodies are recipient of cold and heat and of constriction and relaxation without having either sensation or knowledge of the reason and understanding involved in performing tasks with reason and wisdom; but of all the things that exist it is soul alone that has understanding and wisdom, and this is an invisible thing, whereas fire, water, and the other material elements are visible bodies. Moreover, it behooves the lover of understanding and knowledge to seek the primary cause belonging to the wisest of natures rather than to seek things auxiliary to {46e} the primary cause, and those causes which are moved by others and set yet others in motion should be regarded as secondary. It is also incumbent upon us, therefore, to proceed accordingly and examine both kinds of cause, only making sure to take the highest ones, which with understanding and wisdom produce all things honorable and good, separately from those which, being destitute of mind and wisdom, thoughtlessly and randomly leave the things they make in a disordered state of confusion.

Et de oculorum quidem ministerii causa, ob quam nacti sunt eam quam habent virtutem, satis dictum, de praecipua tamen utilitate operis eorum {47a} mox erit aptior disserendi locus. Visus enim iuxta meam sententiam causa est maximi commodi plerisque non otiose natis atque institutis ob id ipsum quod nunc agimus, neque enim de universa re quisquam quaereret nisi prius stellis sole caeloque visis. At nunc diei noctisque insinuata nobis alterna vice menses annorumque obitus et anfractus nati sunt eorumque ipsorum dinumeratio, et ex dinumeratione perfectus et absolutus extitit numerus, tum temporis recordatio quae naturam universae rei quaeri docuit curamque investigationis iniecit mentibus quasi quoddam seminarium {47b} philosophiae pangens; quo bono nihil umquam maius ad hominum genus divina munificentia commeavit. Hoc igitur maximum beneficium visus oculorumque esse dico; minora alia praetereo quibus qui a philosophia remoti sunt carentes debiles caecique maestam vitam lugubremque agunt. Nobis vero causa dicenda demonstrandaque videtur divini muneris quod providentia commenta est salubriter hactenus: deum oculos hominibus idcirco dedisse ut mentis providentiaeque circuitus qui fiunt in caelo notantes eorum similes cognatosque in usum redigerent suae mentis, circuitusque animae qui

And although sufficient attention has been given to the underlying cause of the service provided by the eyes, the cause which accounts for their having the capability they have, there is nevertheless further room {47a} for discussion of the particular utility of the work they do. For vision, in my opinion, is the cause of the greatest benefit to those whose birth (as is generally the case) has not proved meaningless and whose education has been directed toward the very activity we are now engaged in, for no one would form a question about the universe without first having seen the stars, the Sun, and the heaven. In fact, however, it is because of our being confronted with the alternating exchange of day and night that the months, the cyclical approaches of years, and our calculation thereof have come to be, and that from the calculation perfect and complete number has arisen, followed by the notion of time, which has informed our inquiry into the nature of the universe and, as though by planting a kind of nursery garden {47b} of philosophy, has instilled in our minds a concern for inquiry; and no good greater than this has ever come to mankind by divine munificence. My point, then, is that this is the greatest benefit of vision and the eyes; I pass over the other minor ones, for the lack of which those who avoid philosophy feebly and blindly lead a grim and mournful life. However, we evidently should articulate and identify the cause of the divine gift which providence has devised for our benefit, and as follows: we should point out that god gave eyes to human beings so that by observing the circuits of mind and providence that occur in the heaven they might to the advantage of their own mind retrieve circuits which are like and akin to them, so that they might make the circuits in their soul

animadversiones seu deliberationes vocantur quam simillimos efficerent divinae mentis providis motibus {47c} placidis tranquillisque perturbatos licet, confirmatoque ingene-
ratae rationis examine dum imitantur aplanem mundi
intellegibilis circumactionem suae mentis motus erraticos
corrigant. Eadem vocis quoque et auditus ratio est ad eosdem usus atque ad plenam vitae hominum instructionem
datorum, siquidem propterea sermonis est ordinata com-
municatio ut praesto forent mutuae voluntatis indicia,
quantumque {47d} per vocem utilitatis capitur ex musica,
totum hoc constat hominum generi propter harmoniam tributum. Harmonia vero, id est modulatio, utpote intentio
modificata, cognatas et velut consanguineas habens commotiones animae nostrae circuitionibus, prudenter utentibus Musarum munere temperantiaeque causa potius quam
oblectationis satis est commoda, quippe quae discrepantes
et inconsonantes animae commotiones ad concentum ex-
ornationemque concordiae Musis auxiliantibus revocet;
rhythmus autem datus ut medela contra illepidam {47e} nu-
merorumque et modorum nesciam gratiaeque expertem in
plerisque naturam.

Nunc quoniam cuncta exceptis admodum paucis executi
sumus quae providae mentis intellectus instituit, oportet de
illis etiam quae necessitas invehit dicere, mixta {48a} siquidem mundi sensilis ex necessitatis intellegentiaeque coetu
constitit generatio dominante intellectu et salubri persuasione rigorem necessitatis assidue trahente ad optimos
actus. Itaque victa et parente providis auctoritatibus

which are called considerations and deliberations as like as possible, despite their disturbances, to the provident, {47c} calm, and tranquil movements of the divine mind, and so that with the strengthened consideration of ungenerated reason they may correct the erratic movements of their mind while imitating the nonwandering circumlation of the intelligible world. The same account holds also for voice and hearing, which have been given for the same purposes and for the full instruction of human life, since communication through speech was arranged so that there might be a ready means of indicating our intentions to one another, and it is clear that as much of {47d} the vocal utility as is captured in connection with music has been conferred upon mankind entirely for the sake of harmony. And harmony, i.e., modulation, being a regulated tension and having agitations that are cognate with and, as it were, akin to the circumlations of our soul, is quite beneficial for those who use the gift of the Muses wisely and for the sake of moderation rather than pleasure, for with the help of the Muses it recalls the soul's discordant and unharmonious agitations back into attunement and ordered concord; and rhythm has been given as the remedy for a nature which is for the most part unruly, {47e} ignorant of number and limit, and devoid of grace.

Since with very few exceptions we have treated of all that the intellect of the provident mind established, it is necessary now to speak also about the things for which necessity is responsible, for the generation of the sensible world consisted of a blended {48a} union of necessity and intelligence, with intellect dominating and salubrious persuasion assiduously drawing the recalcitrance of necessity toward the highest acts. And so once necessity had been subdued

necessitate prima rerum mundique exordia constiterunt. Si quis ergo vere iuxtaque meram fidem mundi huius institutionem insinuaturus erit, hunc oportet erraticae quoque causae speciem demonstrare. Quod ita demum commode fiet si ad eorum quae erroribus implicant originem {48b} facto recursu, perinde ut in his quae ex mente sunt fecimus, genituram substantiamque eorum ab exordio retexamus—naturamque ignis et terrae, ceterarum item materiarum ex quibus mundi sensilis coagmentata molitio est consideremus nec naturam modo veram illam veterem quae fuit ante concretionem sed antiquas etiam ipsorum elementorum perpessiones. Nullus quippe ad hoc usque tempus genituram eorum indicavit sed tamquam scientibus quid sit ignis et cetera sic loquimur et dicimus initia universitatis constituentes ea quae ne syllabarum {48c} quidem locum vicemque pro veri examinis ratione obtinent. Nostra igitur haec est professio, nihil ad praesens de universitatis vel initio vel initiis, ut quidam putant, esse dicendum, non quo sit ullum impedimentum praeter inextricabilem difficultatem sed quod ita instituto sermone sit impossibile admodum perveniri ad explanationem rei. Neque igitur vos id expectetis nec ego mihi persuadeam posse me {48d} tantum et tanti oneris sustinere. Atque illud potius observabo quod initio sermonis precario petivi: in rebus imaginariis proclivibusque ad

and was obedient to the authority of providence, the first beginnings of things and of the world came to be. If, then, one is going to explain the establishment of this world truly and with pure intention, then it is necessary for him also to identify a form of errant cause. And in the end this will turn out favorably if {48b} by retracing our steps back to the origin of the things that are entangled in errant motion we reconstruct their generation and substance from the beginning, just as we did in the case of the things that originate in mind—and also if we were to consider the nature of fire, earth, and the other material elements from which the construction of the sensible world was cemented together, not only the true and ancient nature that existed before the process of assembling but also the ancient transformations of the elements themselves. For no one up to the present time has given an indication of their generation, but we speak as though to people who knew what fire and the other things are, and refer to "first beginnings" of the universe when positing things which, if the comparison is to be true, hold the place and position not even {48c} of syllables. Our affirmation is therefore the following: that for the moment there will be no discussion of, as some fancy, the "first beginning" or "beginnings" of the universe, and this not to add any further impediment to the inextricable difficulty already before us but because it is virtually impossible, given the limits of our proposed discussion, to arrive at an explanation of the matter. So you should not expect that of me, nor should I persuade myself of my ability {48d} to sustain such an enormous burden. Instead, I will observe the point in connection with which I sought your approval at the beginning of our discussion: that in speculating on the first beginnings

fallendum rationibus rerum earundem verisimilibus asser-
tionibus imaginariisque contentus sim initia singulorum et
universorum originem pandens. Deum ergo etiam nunc
auxiliatorem {48e} invocabimus ante auspicium dictionis,
liberatorem ex turbida et procellosa coepti sermonis iactatione.

Erit ergo initium tale demum universae imaginariae rei
eademque magnificentius dividetur, etenim tunc duae modo
species veniebant in divisionem at nunc tertium quoque
aliud oborietur genus. Quippe in prioribus duo nobis satis abunde sufficere videbantur, unum perpetuum carens
generatione exemplaris eminentiae, alterum simulacrum et
imago eius, {49a} aeternitati propagata secundae, generationis, idque visibile. At vero tertium tunc quidem minime
divisimus, at nunc imposita nobis necessitatem ratio videtur ire obviam manumque conserere adversum inexpugnabilem omni ratione et omni eloquio fraudem crassis tenebris
involutam. Quam igitur eius vim quamve esse naturam putandum est? Opinor, omnium quae gignuntur receptaculum
est, quasi quaedam nutricula. Atque hoc quod de ea dicitur
verum est quidem sed dicendum videtur paulo apertius;
{49b} est tamen arduum eo magis, quod praeconfundi mentis aciem necesse est et aestuare tam de igni quam de ceteris
materiis, qui magis aquam iure aquam dici putarique

and origin of things singularly and universally, and as concerns realities which have the status of images and tend to mislead us, I should be content with explanations and claims that are based upon probability and what can be gathered from images. Once again, then, {48e} we will invoke god at the outset as our supporter, as guidance for our language, and as liberator from the turbulent and stormy agitations of the discussion we have embarked upon.

Such, then, is to be the "first beginning" of the universe as known ultimately from images, and it will form part of a broader division, for then only two forms fell under the division, whereas now another kind, a third one, will spring up as well. For in our earlier discussion two things appeared to us to be quite sufficient, one of them eternal, lacking becoming, and having the status of a preeminent exemplar, and the other its likeness or image, {49a} an image propagated eternally in the secondary sense, that of becoming, and a thing visible in kind. And whereas we then made no third division, the argument appears poised now to impose upon us the necessity of going into the fray and joining forces against an element of deception which is impregnable by reason and speech of every kind and which is enshrouded in dense obscurity. What, then, should we suppose it to have by way of force, what by way of a nature? It is, I suppose, the Receptacle of all that comes to be, a kind of nurse, as it were. And although this point is truly stated of it, still it should evidently be stated a little more plainly; {49b} and yet the task proves the more difficult because of an inevitable confusion and fluctuation in our mental acuity when it comes to fire and the other material elements: given that the bodies possess no certain and stable property to

oporteat quam terram, cum nulla sit certa et stabilis proprietas corporum quae cuiusque indicet naturalem germanitatem. Principio ut de aqua, cuius modo fecimus mentionem, ordiamur: cum astringitur in glaciem, certe saxum terrenaeque soliditatis corpus {49c} et minime fusile apparet; eadem haec ignita et diffluens discretaque varie in humorem spiritum et aereas auras dissolvitur; aer porro exustus ignem creat rursumque extinctus ignis aera corpulentior factus instituit; aer item crassior factus in nubes nebulasque concrescit, quibus elisis et expressis pluviae stagnorumque et fontium largitas; demumque ex aqua terrenae moles aggerantur. Atque ita circuitu quodam vires fomentaque generationis corporibus invicem sibi mutuantibus {49d} nec in una eademque forma perseverantibus quae tandem erit certa eorum et a cunctatione semota comprehensio? Nulla certe. Quapropter de cunctis huius modi mutabilibus ita est habendum: hoc quod saepe alias aliter formatum nobis videtur et plerumque iuxta ignis effigiem non est, opinor, ignis sed igneum quiddam, nec aer sed aereum, nec omnino quicquam velut habens ullam stabilitatem. Denique ne pronominibus quidem ullis signanda sunt quibus in demonstratione uti solemus, {49e} cum dicimus "hoc" vel "illud," fugiunt enim nec expectant eam appellationem, quae de his tamquam existentibus habetur.

Igitur ignem quoque eum esse vere putandum qui semper

provide indications of the natural origins of each, in what sense is it necessary that water should by right be called and thought of as water rather than earth? To begin first with what we have just now referred to as water: when it hardens into ice it appears, so we think, to be stone, a body of earthen solidity {49c} and not at all liquid; but under the influence of fire this same water dissolves, flowing and expanding variously into vapor, wind, and airy breezes; under combustion air for its part creates fire; and when extinguished and made denser the fire in turn gives rise to air; while air when made thicker coalesces in clouds and vapors, and when they collide under pressure showers and an abundance of pools and springs appear; and finally from the water earthen masses accumulate. But if the bodies thus borrow the powers and kindling of generation from one another in a kind of cycle {49d} and do not remain in one and the same form, what certain and unwavering comprehension of them will there be in the end? Surely none. And so in connection with all such mutable things our procedure should be the following: that which is regularly presenting itself to us in different forms at different times but on balance projects the appearance of fire is, I suppose, not fire but a fiery something, not air but an airy something, and in general nothing should be regarded as possessed of any stability. In the final analysis, they should not even be indicated by any of the pronouns we conventionally use for pointing things out, {49e} expressions such as "this" or "that," for they slip away without awaiting the appellative, which is applied on the assumption that they exist.

We should also suppose, therefore, that the fire which is forever the same exists in the true sense, and so too in the

idem est, et omne cuius proprietas manet. At vero id in quo
fieri singula haec videntur et demum dissolvi pereuntiaque
ad alias inde transire formas {50a} solum illud appellandum
puto certo pronomine recteque de eo dici posse "hoc" vel
"illud," porro quod recipit qualitatem vel etiam verti potest
in contrarias qualitates calidum dici vel candidum, proprioque et certo nomine appellari quod sit incertum et mutabile minime convenire. Sed, opinor, apertius etiam nunc
de eodem erit dissertare conandum. Si quis enim cunctas
formas figurasque ex una eademque auri materia fictas iugiter et sine intermissione in alias atque alias reformet, tunc,
si quis electa qualibet una figura quaerat {50b} quae sit,
opinor posse firme et diligenter ac sine reprehensione responderi aurum illud esse nec addere trianguli cylindri ve<l>
cuiusvis alterius <quod> videbitur. Eadem et consimilis ratio
difficultasque in ea natura quae cuncta recipit corpora reperitur, haec quippe minime recedit ex condicione propria; recipit enim cuncta {50c} nec ullam ex isdem formam trahit, et
cum velut intra gremium eius formentur quae recipiuntur,
ipsa informis manet estque usus eius similis molli cedentique materiae in quam imprimuntur varia signacula, move-
turque et conformatur omnimode ab introeuntibus, ipsa
nec formam nec motum habens ex natura sua. Quae vero in-
grediuntur, formas mutant aliasque alia et diversa cernuntur,

case of everything that is possessed of a permanent property. But I suppose that that in which each of these things appears to arise and subsequently dissolve and by its perishing to shift from one form to another {50a} is alone to be indicated by a fixed pronoun, and that "this" or "that" can rightly be predicated of it but that it is inappropriate for that which is recipient of quality and is also capable of transforming to contrary qualities to be called "hot" or "white" or for that which is unstable and mutable to be indicated by a proper and fixed name. But this, I suppose, is precisely the point at which an effort will be required to explain the matter more plainly. For suppose someone were constantly and continuously to reshape all of the forms and figures that had been molded from one and the same material, gold, shaping it into one figure after another: if one were to select any one figure and ask {50b} what it is, then I suppose a reply could reliably, sincerely, and uncontroversially be given to the effect that it is gold, and given without adding that it is that of a triangle, cylinder, or anything else that is bound to appear. Precisely the same explanation and difficulty is encountered in connection with the nature that is recipient of all bodies, since it in no way recedes from the condition proper to it; for it receives all things {50c} without extracting any form from them, and although the things received take on form within its womb, as it were, it remains formless in itself, and its behavior is like that of the soft and supple material upon which different seal impressions are stamped, and it is in every way moved and given form by the things that enter it despite having in itself and of its own nature neither form nor movement. The things that enter, by contrast, change forms and at different times appear other or different, and

eademque quae introeunt et egrediuntur simulacra sunt
vere existentium rerum miro quodam vixque explicabili
modo formata ab isdem vere existentibus rebus, quem ad
modum mox demonstrare nitemur pro viribus.

At vero nunc trinum genus animo sumendum est: quod
{50d} gignitur; item aliud in quo gignitur; praeterea tertium
ex quo similitudinem trahit mutuaturque quod gignitur. Decet ergo facere comparationem similitudinemque impertiri:
illi quidem quod suscipit, matris; at vero unde obvenit, patris; illi autem naturae quae inter haec duo est, prolis. Simul
ita intellegendum fieri non posse ut una existat facies quae
omnes rerum omnium formas vultusque contineat variaque
corporis undique ora demonstret, nisi subiecto prius informi aliquo corporum gremio, perinde ut quae in picturis
substernitur infectio decolor ad colorum lumina subvehenda. {50e} Etenim si erit alicuius eorum quae in se recipit simile receptaculum, cum quid obveniet dissimile his
quibus simile est, discordabit, opinor, vultus eius cum introgressi corporis vultu nullamque exprimet similitudinem. Ex
quo fit ut receptaculi sinus nullam propriam naturaliterque
expressam habeat figuram proptereaque informis intellegatur omni quippe forma carens. Ut qui odora pigmenta conficiunt ante omnia curant ut nullius sint odoris proprii quae
condientur, susceptura videlicet humidos sucos odoraminum; et qui materiis mollibus impressionique cedentibus
insignire formas aliquas volunt pure levigatas apparant nec

these things that enter and exit are images of the truly existent realities and are in some mysterious and barely explica-
ble manner given form by the same truly existent realities,
as we will later attempt to show to the best of our abilities.

For the moment, however, we must assume in our minds
three kinds of thing: that which {50d} becomes; secondly,
that in which it becomes; and thirdly, that from which that
which becomes draws or obtains its element of likeness. It
behooves us, then, to form a comparison and note the points
of similarity: in the case of that which takes in, it is to a
mother; in the case of that from which it emerges, to a father; and in the case of the nature which is between the two,
to their offspring. At the same time, we should understand
that it is thereby impossible for there to be a single aspect to
capture all of the forms and appearances of all things and to
display the various bodily appearances throughout if a kind
of formless womb has not first been provided as a substrate
for bodies, like the neutral base which is laid down to support the luminous colors in paintings. {50e} For if ever the
Receptacle is like any of the things it receives within itself,
then, I suppose, whenever anything unlike the things it is
like appears, its appearance will be out of accord with that
of the incoming body and express no likeness to it. So it happens that the Receptacle or bosom has no proper or naturally expressed shape and is therefore conceived of as formless and indeed deprived of all form. As those who are
preparing scented lotions ensure at the start that the materials which are to be worked with have no scent of their own,
namely, if they are to receive the moist scented fluids; and as
those who plan to stamp shapes of some sort upon soft materials that yield supplely to impressions prepare those ma-

ullam omnino formam in apparata levigatione apparere patiuntur: {51a} sic ei quod omnibus rerum omnium formis et
figuris aeternae vitae mansurisque per saecula recte in-
signietur, nulla omnino propria species falsa opinione tri-
buenda est. Ideoque facti generati visibilis animalis matrem
corporeaeque substantiae receptaculum neque terram neque aquam nec vero ignem vel aera nec quicquam aliud quod
ex his creatum est nec vero ex quibus haec ipsa subsistunt
appellandum sed invisibilem potius speciem quandam et informem capacitatem {51b} mira quadam et incomprehensibili ratione inter nullam et aliquam substantiam, nec plane
intellegibilem nec plane sensibilem positam sed quae ex his
quae in ea commutantur intellegi tamen posse videatur.
Ignis quidem pars eius ignita, humectata vero pars eiusdem
aqua, si modo expertis rei pars ulla dici potest; terra quoque
et aer ratione illa, si forte qua simulacra eorum recipit in se.
De quibus singulis huius modi tractatus instituendus videtur: Estne aliquis ignis seorsum positus et incommunicabilis? Item ceterae species quas concipientes mente dicimus
{51c} semper separatas a coetu corporearum specierum fore
archetypa exemplaria rei sensilis, an haec sola sunt quae videntur quaeque corporis intentione sentimus, nec praeter
haec ulla sunt uspiam sed frustra praesumitur esse intellegibiles species quarum sint imagines sensiles easque nihil

terials by making them pure and smooth, allowing no shape whatsoever to appear in the smoothing process: {51a} so no intrinsic form whatsoever is by false opinion to be ascribed to that which is duly to receive the stamp of all the forms and shapes of all realities and eternal life, forms and shapes which are destined to endure through all time. And so the mother of the made, generated, and visible living being, the Receptacle of corporeal being, must not be called earth, water, fire, air, or any other thing either created from them or from which they themselves come to be, but it must instead be referred to as a certain invisible form and formless capacity, situated {51b} in some mysterious and incomprehensible way between nonbeing and some sort of being, clearly neither intelligible nor sensible but a form or capacity which nevertheless can evidently be understood from the things that undergo change within it. Fire is the part of it that has become fiery and water the part that has become moist, assuming we can speak of any "part" of a thing that has none; and earth and air according to the same reasoning, assuming it receives some likenesses thereof within itself. And our treatment of them individually should evidently be approached along the following lines: Is there some fire which is set apart and incommunicable? And is it the same with the other forms of which we form a mental conception and {51c} in consideration of their permanent separation from interaction with corporeal forms describe as the archetypal exemplars of sensible reality, or do only visible things and things which we perceive because of the body's attention exist? Are there no others beyond them anywhere? Is it idle to suppose the existence of intelligible forms that have sensible ones as their images? Are we to suppose that they are

aliud esse quam verba? Quod quidem neque inexaminatum relinqui placet nec ad prolixum natura sua tractatum minime pertinens ad rem verborum agmen addendum; {51d} at vero si quis amplae rei finis disceptationem compendio dirimet, hunc certe asciscere operae pretium facientis est. Ipse igitur, quid de hac re sentiam, dicam.

Si intellectus itemque vera opinio duae res sunt, necesse est haec ipsa per semet esse, intellectu potius quam sensibus assequenda; sin vero, ut quibusdam videtur, vera opinio ab intellectu nihil differt, omnia quae corpore[a] sentimus certa habenda sunt. Sed opinor {51e} duo esse dicendum, propterea quod utraque magna differentia distant; quippe quorum alterum doctrina nobis insinuet, alterum persuasionis assumptio, et alterum quidem semper cum ratione vera, porro sine ulla ratione alterum, item alterum nulla persuasione transducibile, alterum nutans incertum semper et derivabile. Quid quod rectae opinionis omnis vir particeps, intellectus vero dei proprius et paucorum admodum lectorum hominum? Quod cum ita sit, {52a} fatendum est esse eius modi speciem: semotam a sensibus in semet locatam, sine ortu sine occasu, quae neque in se recipit quicquam aliunde neque ipsa procedit ad aliud quicquam, invisibilem insensilem soli mentis intentioni animadversionique perspicuam; porro quod ab hoc secundum est, nativum sensile sustentabile, consistens aliquo in loco et rursum cum immutatione

nothing other than words? Now, it does not seem right either that this question should be left unexamined or that an irrelevant abundance of words should be added to an inquiry which by its very nature tends toward prolixity; {51d} but if some distinction of ample substance will settle the matter in short order, then it is certainly worthwhile for the one conducting the discussion to adopt it. And so I will state my own view of the matter.

If intellect and true opinion are two things, then it is necessary that they should exist as those very things in themselves, perceptible by intellect rather than the senses; but if true opinion is no different from intellect, as some think, then all of the things which we perceive through the body must be considered certain. But I suppose {51e} we should maintain that they are two, in that both are separated by a wide range of difference; for instruction instills one of them in us while the acceptance of persuasion instills the other, one is always combined with a true account while the other has none, and one is not misled by any persuasion while the other is vacillating, always uncertain, and susceptible to diversion. And what about the fact that every man has a share in right opinion whereas intellect is proper to god and a few very select human beings? This being so, {52a} we must acknowledge the existence of a form of the following sort: removed from the senses and situated within itself, without birth or death, which neither receives anything external within itself nor itself proceeds toward anything else, which is invisible, imperceptible, and evident only to the mind's attention and awareness; and second to it, that which is born, perceptible, and sustained, which comes to be in some place and recedes again with its transformation and passing away,

et interitu recedens, sensibus et opinione noscendum; tertium genus est loci, quod ne ad interitum quidem pertinet {52b} sedem porro praebet his quae generantur sed ipsum sine sensu tangentis tangitur, adulterina quadam ratione opinabile. Denique cum id animo intuemur, patimur quod somniantes, putamus enim necesse esse ut omne quod est in aliquo sit loco positum regionemque obtineat ullam, porro quod neque in terra neque in caelo sit minime existere. Ob quam depravationem itemque alias consanguineas ne in reputatione quidem et consideratione vere existentis vereque pervigilis naturae {52c} mente consistimus propter huius modi somnia, cum ne imaginari quidem ullam huius lubricae <rei> speciem formamque valeamus; propriam quippe nullam habet et habere omnes videtur cum intra gremium eius conversione ad aliud ex alio formae transfigurantur. Idemque hoc in altero, inter aliquam et nullam substantiam positum, invenitur, suam nullam habet nec tamen nihil est; at enim vere existentium rerum assertio perspicua rationis luce firmatur docens, dum quidem erit hoc aliud itemque illud aliud, neutrum in neutro posse consistere {52d} nec simul idem unum et duo fieri.

Haec est meae quidem sententiae mens: esse et ante mundi quoque sensilis exornationem fuisse tria haec, existens locum generationem; igitur generationis nutriculam humectatam modo modo ignitam terraeque item et aeris

and which is knowable by the senses and opinion; the third kind is that of Place, a kind which is immune to passing away {52b} even while providing a seat for the things that are generated, but is itself tangible independently of any sensory experience on the part of the one who comes into contact with it, and opinable by a certain illegitimate form of reasoning. Finally, when gazing upon it in our mind we experience what those who are dreaming do, for we suppose that everything that exists must necessarily be situated in some place and occupy some region, and that what is neither on earth nor in heaven does not exist. And because of this and other related distorting effects arising from such dream states {52c} we become mentally unsteady in our reflection on and consideration of the truly existent and truly waking nature, being incapable even of imagining any form or shape for this slippery reality; for it has no form or shape of its own and yet when shapes are transfigured through conversion from one thing to another within its womb it appears to have them all. And this same thing, situated between some sort of being and nonbeing, emerges in something else and has no being of its own yet is not nothing; our affirmation of the truly existent realities, on the other hand, is confirmed by the clear light of reason and states that, so long as this is one thing and that another, it is impossible for either to come to be in the other {52d} or for them to become at once one and the same, and two.

The thinking behind my view is then the following: That there are and were even before the adornment of the sensible world these three things, Being, Place, and Becoming. And that the nurse of Becoming is therefore moistened one moment and made fiery another, and in taking up the shapes

formas suscipientem ceterasque pedissequas {52e} passiones
perpetientem omniformem visu videri; quod tamen privatim neque similibus viribus neque exaequatis potentiis instruatur nihil esse eius aequale sed undique vergentem et in
pronum vel absonum praeponderantem agitari quidem materiis agitantibus invicemque reciproco pulsu pulsare atque
agitare materias; ex quo fluctu turbatas materias in diversa
raptari discernique a se; perinde ut quae in frumenti purgatione pistoriis instrumentis motu et excussione discerni videmus, {53a} gravia quidem et solida seorsum tenuia vero et
levia in aliam partem, sic illa quattuor velut in Euripo fluctuante iactari vel machina quadam facta ad motus ciendos,
dissimillima quaeque a dissimillimis plurimum aliqua vero
similitudine sociata nequaquam disparari proptereaque sedibus fuisse divisa ante mundi scilicet exornationem. Ac
tunc quidem erat huius modi rationis expers rerum inordinata confusio, {53b} sed ubi cuncta redigi ad modum placuit,
ignem primo terramque et aera atque aquam continuavit
opifex deus, non talia ut nunc sunt sed quae praeferrent elementorum vestigia in eo squalore ac deformitate quae apparet in his quibus divina deest prospicientia; nunc vero singulis luce ac specie tributa numerus quoque illustratorum
omnium genituram sequebatur pulchris omnibus ex non

of earth and air and undergoing all of their attendant {52e} modifications projects a multiform appearance to sight. But that since on her own she is equipped with powers which are neither alike nor evenly balanced, no part of her is in a state of equilibrium, but leaning this way and that and inclining downward or out of kilter she is agitated by the agitations of the material elements and with a reciprocal jolting jolts and agitates them in return. And that once thrown into confusion because of this fluctuation the material elements are tossed in different directions and sorted from one another. And that as with the things we see being sorted by the moving and shaking of winnowing tools in the cleansing of grain, {53a} where the heavy and dense ones move downward and the rare and light ones move to another area, so the four things are jostled about as though in the fluctuating Euripus or by some engine designed to stir up movement, those which are most unlike being in each case the farthest removed from one another, and those which are associated by some element of likeness being the least separated and, consequently, divided by regions, namely, before the adornment of the world. At that point there was a disordered confusion of things, a confusion devoid of any such element of reason, {53b} but after taking the decision to bring everything back within measure the craftsman god first gave binding unity to fire, earth, air, and water, not in their present states but such that they exhibited the traces of elements despite the squalor and deformity manifested by things that lack divine foresight; and once light and form had been bestowed upon each of them, number too proceeded to follow the generation of all the things thus illuminated, with the result that they were all established in a state of beauty such as they

talibus quondam institutis. Nunc iam ordinationem genituramque eorum singillatim demonstrari convenit {53c} novo
quidem et inusitato genere demonstrationis verum vobis,
qui omnes eruditionis ingenuae vias peragraveritis, neque
incognito et ex levi admonitione perspicuo.

had not previously enjoyed. It is appropriate now to demonstrate their arrangement and generation individually, {53c} and to do so with a mode of demonstration which although new and unfamiliar is not unknown to you, who have traveled all the paths of liberal erudition, and which will become clear with gentle reminding.

COMMENTARY

Commentarii Pars Prima

Timaeus Platonis et a veteribus difficilis habitus atque existimatus est ad intellegendum, non ex imbecillitate sermonis obscuritate nata (quid enim illo viro promptius?) sed quia legentes artificiosae rationis quae operatur in explicandis rerum quaestionibus usum non habebant stili genere sic instituto ut non alienigenis sed propriis quaestionum probationibus id quod in tractatum venerat ostenderetur. Illa enim demum certa est probatio quae congruis accommodatisque rationibus quaestiones revelat. Ut si de motu stellarum oriatur aliqua cunctatio ex ea disciplina quae astronomia dicitur demanet assertio; si de fidium varietate et de eo qui ex diversis vocibus sonisque nascitur concentu tractatus habeatur; musicae remediis cunctatio sopiatur; et prorsus teneatur id institutum quod a peritissimis medicis usque quaque observari solet, cum pro natura vulnerum auxilia medicamentorum adhibent in medendo.

2. In hoc porro libro cum de statu agatur universae rei omniumque eorum quae mundus complectitur causa et ratio praestetur, necesse fuit multas et varias existere quaestiones, de planis figuris, de solidis corporibus, de incorporatione animae vivificantis sensibilem mundum, de

Commentary, First Part

Even the ancients considered Plato's *Timaeus* difficult, not because of a fault arising from the obscurity of its language (for what is more accessible than Plato?), but because readers were unaccustomed to the technical reasoning at work in its explication of questions concerning the nature of things; for his style of writing was developed so that what arose for discussion might be demonstrated through proofs which are, not foreign, but proper to the questions at issue. For ultimately that proof is certain which reveals the answers to questions by corresponding and suitable methods of reasoning. For example, if some uncertainty should arise concerning stellar movement, the answer would be derived from the discipline called astronomy; if there should be a treatment of the variety of strings and the consonance that results from different sounds and tones, the uncertainty would be put to rest by the remedy of the discipline of music; and in general, that precept of instruction traditionally observed by the most skilled physicians everywhere should be adhered to, when in therapy they apply the aid of medication in accordance with the nature of the wounds.

2. Now, since this book concerns the constitution of the universe and provides a causal explanation of all that the world embraces, it was inevitable that there should be many questions of various types, concerning plane figures, solid bodies, the incorporation of the soul that vivifies the sensi-

motu eius et agitatione perpetua, de stellarum discursibus
ratis et errantibus; cunctis certarum disciplinarum artificialibus remediis occurrendum erat—arithmeticis astronomi-
cis geometricis musicis—, quo singulae res domesticis et
consanguineis rationibus explicarentur. Ideoque his qui in
artificialium usu non fuerant tamquam alienigenum sermonem ignorantibus minime probabantur, porro aliis qui
unam aliquam ex disciplinis perceperant id solum quod
sciebant recognoscentibus probabatur, cetera ignorationis
obscuro latebant.

3. Ex quo apparet hoc opus illis propemodum solis elaboratum esse ac videri qui in omnium fuerant huius modi
scientiarum usu atque exercitatione versati. Quos cum
oporteret tantam scientiae claritudinem communicare cum
ceteris, infelicis invidiae detestabili restrictione largae beatitudinis fusionem incommunicabilem penes se retinue-
runt.

4. Itaque quia iubentibus vobis mos erat gerendus (licet
ea quae iubebantur potiora essent quam sustinere mediocre
ingenium valeret), sola translatione contentus non fui ratus
obscuri minimeque illustris exempli simulacrum sine inter-
pretatione translatum in eiusdem aut etiam maioris obscuritatis vitio futurum, et ea quae mihi visa sunt in aliqua diffi-
cultate sic interpretatus sum ut ea sola explanarem quae
incognitarum artium disciplinarumque ignoratione tege-
rentur; erat enim arrogantis et velut ingeniis legentium

ble world, concerning its movement and perpetual rotation, concerning the courses of the fixed and errant stars; and recourse to all of the technical remedies of the sciences—to arithmetic, astronomy, geometry, and music—was required, so that the various subjects might be explained by cognate and related methods of reasoning. And so for those who had no familiarity with the technical disciplines and were ignorant of the language, as though it were foreign, matters remained unproved, while for others who had gained a grasp of some one of the disciplines only that which they knew was proved, once they came to recognize it, but the rest lay buried in the obscurity of their ignorance.

3. From this it is clear that this work has been, and is perceived to have been, devised almost exclusively for those who are versed in the use and application of all such sciences. Although they had an obligation to share with others the extraordinary light of their knowledge, acting under the detestable restraints of an infelicitous ill will they kept back for themselves the outpouring of bountiful happiness.

4. And so, given that it was necessary to satisfy your request (although what you requested was more than a mediocre talent could sustain), I was not content with a translation alone, thinking that without interpretation the translated image of an obscure and opaque original would prove subject to the same or an even greater charge of obscurity, and I interpreted the passages which struck me as particularly difficult in such a way that my commentary was restricted to points that lay hidden because of our ignorance of unfamiliar arts and disciplines; for it would have been the mark of arrogance and, as it were, despair as to my readers'

diffidentis ea quae communi omnium intellegentiae pa-
terent superstitiosa interrogatione frustra retexere. Denique de principio libri, quo simplex narratio continebatur rerum ante gestarum et historiae veteris recensitio, nihil dixi,
rationem tamen totius operis et scriptoris propositum et
ordinationem libri declaranda esse duxi.

5. Nam cum pridie Socrates decem libris omnibus de re
publica disputasset, ad quem tractatum non ex principali
causa sed ex consequenti descenderat (siquidem cum de iustitia quaeri coeptum fuisset quam definierat Thrasymachus
orator eam esse quae huic prodesset qui plurimum posset,
Socrates contra docuisset immo eam potius quae his prodesset qui minimum possent), ut illustriore uteretur exemplo, si eam non in unius hominis ingenio sed in urbis alicuius
populosae frequentia populari scrutaretur, imaginem quandam depinxit urbis quae iustis moribus institutisque regere-
tur et convenienti legibus felicitate frueretur, contraque si
quando degenerasset ab institutis quam improspera esset ei
civitati quamque exitiabilis mutatio morum futura.

6. Igitur cum in illis libris quaesita atque inventa videretur esse iustitia quae versaretur in rebus humanis, superesset
autem ut naturalis aequitatis fieret investigatio, huius tanti
operis effectum quod ingenio suo diceret onerosum Socrates, Timaeo et Critiae et Hermocrati delegandum putavit atque illi munus iniunctum receperunt. Ex quo apparet
in hoc libro principaliter illud agi, contemplationem
considerationemque institui non positivae sed naturalis

abilities if to no good purpose I were to repeat by a blindly pedantic line of inquiry what was evident to the common understanding of all. Hence I have said nothing about the first part of the work, where there is a straightforward narrative of past events, a recounting of ancient history, but I have thought it necessary to indicate the plan of the work as a whole, its author's intention and the structure of the book.

5. For since on the previous day Socrates had given a disputation on the state, in ten complete books, which he came to treat of incidentally rather than by design (for when the question of justice was taken up and the orator Thrasymachus defined it as that which benefits the one who has the most power, Socrates countered with the doctrine that justice is rather that which benefits those who have the least), in order to employ a more illustrious example by examining justice in the whole citizenry of a certain populous city rather than in the character of a single human being, he depicted the image, as it were, of a city ruled by just customs and institutions and reaping the benefits of the happiness provided for by its laws, and by contrast, how devastating and fatal a change in customs would result if ever the city were to abandon its institutions.

6. Now, since in those books the question of the justice pertaining to human affairs had obviously been raised and identified but there remained a need for an inquiry into the equity of nature, Socrates decided that its completion should be delegated to Timaeus, Critias, and Hermocrates, declaring such an endeavor more than his own abilities could sustain; and they accepted the task enjoined upon them. And from this it is clear that in this work the primary task is to initiate contemplation and consideration of justice

illius iustitiae atque aequitatis, quae inscripta instituendis legibus describendisque formulis tribuit ex genuina moderatione substantiam. Perindeque ut Socrates, cum de iustitia dissereret qua homines utuntur, induxit effigiem civilis rei publicae ita Timaeus Locrensis ex Pythagorae magisterio astronomiae quoque disciplinae perfecte peritus eam iustitiam qua divinum genus adversum se utitur in mundi huius sensilis veluti quadam communi urbe ac re publica voluit inquiri.

7. Nunc ordinationes libri et species revelanda est:

- i. Quaeritur primo de genitura mundi;
- ii. Dehinc de ortu animae;
- iii. Tunc de modulatione sive harmonia;
- iv. De numeris;
- v. De stellis ratis et errantibus, in quarum numero sol etiam constituitur et luna;
- vi. De caelo;
- vii. De quattuor generibus animalium, hoc est caelestium praepetum nantium terrenorum;
- viii. De ortu generis humani;
- ix. Causae cur hominum plerique sint sapientes, alii insipientes;
- x. De visu;
- xi. De imaginibus;
- xii. Laus videndi;
- xiii. De silva;
- xiv. De tempore;

and equity, not the positive kind but the natural, which, although unwritten, owing to its innate moderation gives substance to the establishment of laws and the writing down of legal formulas. And just as Socrates in discussing the justice enjoyed by human beings introduced the pattern for a republic of citizens, so Timaeus of Locri, a follower of Pythagoras's teaching and fully versed as well in the science of astronomy, thought there should be an inquiry into the justice enjoyed by the divine race within the common city or republic, as it were, of this sensible world.

7. It is time now to reveal the order or pattern of the book:

1. The question raised first, on the generation of the world.
2. Thereafter, on the origin of soul.
3. Then, on harmonic modulation.
4. On numbers.
5. On the fixed and wandering stars, among which are included the Sun and Moon.
6. On the heaven.
7. On the four kinds of living beings, i.e., the celestial, winged, aquatic, and terrestrial.
8. On the origin of mankind.
9. The reasons why a good many human beings are wise and the rest unwise.
10. On vision.
11. On images.
12. In praise of vision.
13. On matter.
14. On time.

Quorum omnium singillatim secundum ordinem libri expositio fiet.

1. De Genitura Mundi

8. Iam ut doceat mundi corpus perfectum esse—perfecta porro corpora sunt solida quae ex tribus constant, longitudine latitudine crassitudine—prius epipedas, hoc est planas figuras, quae longitudinem modo et latitudinem, nullam vero profunditatem habent, exponit. Quibus ait unam sufficere medietatem, quippe duo distantia una media interiectione continuari habente aliquam inter duo illa distantia cognationem, sic dicens: Cum enim ex tribus vel numeris vel molibus vel potentiis medietas imo perinde quadrat ut

Our exposition of the book will treat of each of these subjects in order.

I. On the Generation of the World

8. With the aim now of explaining the perfection of the world body—and perfect bodies are solids consisting of three things, length, width, and depth—he first expounds the *epipeda,* i.e., plane figures, which have only length and width but no depth. He says that a single mean is sufficient for them, in that two extremes are made continuous by the interjection of a single mean possessed of some natural affinity with both. Here are his words [31c–32a]: *For when of three things, whether numbers, masses, or powers, the middle stands*

summitas medio rursumque ut imum medio sic medietas summo, tunc certe medietas a summo et item imo nihil differt; rursumque extimis illis ad medietatis condicionem atque ad eiusdem parilitatem redactis cum medietas quoque extimorum vicem suscipit, fit, opinor, ut tota materia una et eadem ratione societur eoque pacto eadem sibi erunt universa membra, quippe quorum sit una condicio; unis porro effectis membris unum erit atque idem totum.

9. Utitur probatione arithmetica. Sit ergo descripta trigemina figura quae ostendat quatenus, si duo distent a se, una media continuentur cognata interiectione. Quadrati quod principe loco descriptum est sit unum latus in momentis verbi causa duobus, aliud latus in momentis tribus; hoc supputatum facit aream totius perfecti quadrati momentorum sex, bis enim tria sex sunt. Ultimi vero quadrati et distantis primo sit demum latus unum momentorum quattuor, aliud latus momentorum sex; hoc supputatum facit aream integri quadrati momentorum viginti quattuor, quater enim sex viginti et quattuor sunt. Haec autem medietas quae est in duodecim et ita adhaeret, ut impulsa extima quadrata continuatura videatur, cognata est extimis, siquidem quota parte minor est imo, id est dimidia, tota maior est summo, siquidem duodecim viginti et quattuor dimidia pars sit. Summa rursum viginti quattuor posita in imo sit duodecim, quae est in medio dupla; summa item media summae superioris dupla, bis sex enim duodecim.

10. Ita dimidietatis et dupli ratione sociantur et fit extimorum limitum et medietatis una eademque condicio. Quid

to the last as the first does to the middle, and conversely, the last to
the middle as the middle to the first, then surely the middle differs
in no way from either the first or last; conversely, if the extremes
are reduced to the status of the middle and made identical with it
while the middle for its part takes up the role of the extremes, the
result, I suppose, is that the whole of the material is united by one
and the same relation, and in this way all of the parts will be iden-
tical to one another; there being a single status between them; the
whole, moreover, will be one and the same in that the parts have
been made a unity.

9. He employs an arithmetical proof. Let, then, a tripartite figure be drawn so as to demonstrate how two of the
parts, if different from one another, may be connected by
the intercalation of a single cognate mean. Let one side of a
quadrilateral drawn in the first position be of (say) 2 units
and the other side of 3; this produces in total an area of 6
units for the whole quadrilateral, since twice 3 is 6. Then let
one side of a quadrilateral positioned farthest from the first
be of 4 units and the other side of 6; this produces in total an
area of 24 units for the whole quadrilateral, since 6 times 4 is
24. But the mean, being in 12 units and adjoined such that by
its intercalation it appears to give continuity to the outer
quadrilaterals, is cognate with them, since it is smaller than
the last by the same proportion, i.e., by half, as it is greater
than the first, 12 being half of 24. Conversely, let the sum 24
be placed in the last, double the 12 which is in the middle; at
the same time, the middle sum will be double the first, since
twice 6 is 12. (See Diagram 1.)

10. They are thus united by the ratio of the half and double, and there results one and the same status of mean and
extremes. What of the fact that the mean derives from the

quod medietas de extimis nascitur? Sive enim summi limitis minorem summam cum imi limitis maiore summa multiplicavero seu contra summi limitis maiorem summam cum imi limitis minore summa contulero multiplicans, utraque hac via nascitur duodecim numerus, tam enim bis sex quam ter quaterni duodecim fient.

11. Haec eadem distantium a se duum continuatio unius interiectu medietatis geometricis etiam probationibus revelatur. Sint ergo etiam nunc descriptae figurae. Duas ex adverso positas lineas parallelogrammas geometrici appellant, consequenter etiam planas quadraturas parallelogramma. Propositum est probare quem ad modum duum parallelogrammorum similium unum medium inveniatur quod ratione non careat. Sint igitur duo similia parallelogramma, quibus assistunt Graecae litterae ΑΓΘ, habentia aequales angulos, unum qui est sub ΒΓΔ ei qui est sub ΗΓΖ. Porro ubi aequales anguli, latera pro competenti erunt, ut enim est ΒΓ latus iuxta ΓΖ latus ita ΔΓ latus iuxta ΓΗ latus. Dico duum horum similium parallelogrammorum inveniri medium aliud rationabile: sit quippe directum ΒΓ latus ΓΖ lateri; erit igitur etiam ΔΓ latus ΓΗ lateri directum; et directis lineis ΑΔ et ΘΖ agantur extimae lineae ΔΕ et ΖΕ compleaturque hoc pacto omnis figura. Ut igitur ΒΓ latus iuxta ΓΖ latus ita ΒΔ parallelogrammum iuxta ΔΖ parallelogrammum, sunt enim in eadem quadratura ΑΕΒΖ; rursumque ut ΔΓ latus iuxta ΓΗ latus sic et parallelogrammum ΓΕ iuxta ΖΗ parallelogrammum, sunt enim haec quoque in quadratura ΔΗΕΘ; ut ergo ΒΔ parallelogrammum iuxta ΔΖ parallelogrammum sic item ΔΖ parallelogrammum iuxta id quod subter est ΓΘ parallelogrammum. Inventum

extremes? For whether I multiply the smaller sum of the first term by the larger one of the last or, conversely, through multiplication I bring the larger sum of the first term into relation with the smaller one of the last, either way the number 12 emerges, for from both 2 × 6 and 3 × 4 there will result 12.

11. This same continuous binding of two mutually discrete terms by the intercalation of a single mean is also revealed by geometrical proofs. Let, then, figures be drawn once again. Geometers call two lines which are placed opposite one another parallel, and consequently two-dimensional quadrilaterals parallelograms. The intention is to demonstrate how for two similar parallelograms a single mean can be found which is not disproportional. Let there be two similar parallelograms, then, framed by the Greek letters ΑΓΘ and having equal angles, one of them ΒΓΔ and the other ΗΓΖ. Moreover, where the angles are equal the sides will be analogously proportioned, for as ΒΓ is to ΓΖ so ΔΓ is to ΓΗ. My point is that for these two similar parallelograms another is found to be their proportional mean: let ΒΓ be extended to ΓΖ; ΔΓ will consequently be extended to ΓΗ; to ΑΔ and ΘΖ the outer segments ΔΕ and ΖΕ will be extended so that the whole figure will thus be completed. As, then, side ΒΓ is to ΓΖ so the parallelogram ΒΔ is to ΔΖ, for they are in the same quadrilateral, ΑΕΒΖ; and as ΔΓ is to ΓΗ so the parallelogram ΓΕ is to ΖΗ, for they too are in a quadrilateral, ΔΗΕΘ; as, then, the parallelogram ΒΔ is to ΔΖ so too ΔΖ is to the parallelogram ΓΘ beneath it.

est ergo unum medium, id est ΔZ parallelogrammum, inter duo similia parallelogramma, quod fieri debuit.

12. Nihilo minus etiam in triangularibus formis medietatis insertio consideratur in huius modi forma. Propositum est probare quem ad modum duum triangulorum similium unum medium competens inveniatur. Sint duo similia triangula limitata Graecis litteris, unum ΑΒΓΑ alterum ΔΒΕΔ aequis angulis, uno qui est sub ΑΒΓ altero qui est sub ΔΒΕ. Ubi autem aequales anguli, etiam latera pro competenti erunt, ut enim est AB latus iuxta BE latus sic ΓΒ latus iuxta BΔ latus. Dico horum duum similium triangulorum unum medium competens inveniri: sit enim concessum directum esse AB latus BE lateri; erit etiam ΓΒ latus directum BΔ lateri, et coniungat ducta linea in directum latus quod est AΔ. Ergo ut est AB latus iuxta BE latus sic BΔEB triangulum iuxta ΔΒΑΔ triangulum, sub eadem quippe altitudine sunt Δ litterae; ut autem ΓΒ latus iuxta BΔ latus sic ΔΒΑΔ triangulum iuxta ΑΒΓΑ triangulum, sunt enim sub eadem haec quoque altitudine A litterae; erit ergo, ut ΔΒΕΔ triangulum iuxta ΔΒΑΔ triangulum sic item ΔΒΑΔ triangulum iuxta ΑΒΓΑ triangulum. Duum ergo similium triangulorum, id est ΑΒΓΑ et ΔΒΕΔ, factum est tertium, id est ΔΒΑΔ, quod faciendum erat.

13. Igitur, inquit, si mundi corpus longitudinem et latitudinem solam, soliditatem vero nullam habere deberet essetque huius modi qualis est perfectorum corporum superficies, una medietas sufficeret ad semet ipsam vinciendam et extimas partes. Nunc quoniam soliditate opus erat mundano corpori, solida porro numquam una sed duabus medietatibus vinciuntur, idcirco mundi opifex inter ignem terramque aera et aquam inseruit libratis isdem elementis

Thus a single mean, the parallelogram ΔZ, has been found between similar parallelograms, as was supposed to happen. (See Diagram 2.)

12. Likewise, in the case of triangular shapes the insertion of a mean of the same shape comes under consideration. The intention is to demonstrate how for two similar triangles a single proportional mean is found. Let there be two congruent triangles defined by the Greek letters ABΓA and ΔBEΔ, with equal angles ABΓ and ΔBE. Moreover, where the angles are equal the sides too will be analogously proportioned, for as AB is to BE so ΓB is to BΔ. My point is that for these two congruent triangles a single proportional mean is found: let it be granted that AB be extended to BE; ΓB will similarly be extended to BΔ, and let a line be extended to form the side AΔ. As, then, side AB is to BE so the triangle BΔEB is to ΔBAΔ, for they are at the same height, that of the letter Δ; moreover, as side ΓB is to BΔ so triangle ΔBAΔ is to ABΓA, for they too are at the same height, that of the letter A; hence as triangle ΔBEΔ will be to ΔBAΔ so too triangle ΔBAΔ will be to ABΓA. Thus for the two similar triangles, i.e., ABΓA and ΔBEΔ, a third has been produced, i.e., ΔBAΔ, as was supposed to happen. (See Diagram 3.)

13. *Thus,* he says [32a–b], *if the body of the world were required to have only length and width but no solidity and were of the same sort as the surface of fully formed bodies, then one mean would suffice for the cohesion of it and its extreme parts. But as it is, since the world body required solidity, and the cohesion of solids involves never one but two means, the craftsman of the world accordingly inserted air and water between fire and earth, salubriously balancing the same elements so that the relationship between*

salubri modo, ut quae cognatio est inter ignem et aera, eadem foret inter aera et aquam, rursum quae inter aera et
aquam, haec eadem in aquae terraeque societate consisteret. Mundi corpus solidum esse dicit et globosum; huius
modi autem corpora duabus medietatibus vinciuntur, quatenus ut in effigie pilae et in illo ambitu: est quippe aliqua longitudo, est etiam latitudo, quas dimetimur impresso puncto
in medietate summitatis, ad quam medietatem undique ab
ambitu aequales lineae porriguntur. Una igitur haec medietas in superficie sita est, altera in profundo, ad quam punctum illud pervenit, si deprimatur usque ad altitudinem
mediam.

14. Qua de causa geminis existentibus medietatibus non,
ut in planis figuris, semel est facienda multiplicatio sed bis.
Quippe illic duo latera describebamus, quorum alterum in
duobus momentis, alterum in tribus constituebamus duoque ad tria multiplicantes inveniebamus nasci senarium
numerum; at in his solidis formis propter geminam medietatem geminabitur multiplicatio; ut, cum ex duobus et tribus multiplicatis natus erit idem senarius iuxta unius interim medietatis rationem, iuxta alterius quoque medietatis
(quae forte erit in numero quattuor) quater sex supputemus
atque ita summa omnis sive numeri sive molis seu qualitatis
in viginti et quattuor partibus inveniatur, et, quoniam mundi
summitas, id est ignis, solidum corpus existens habet illa
tria, longitudinem latitudinem soliditatem sed non peraeque, siquidem in illo igni plus est claritudinis, aliquanto
minus moderati caloris, exiguum vero soliditatis, in terrae
autem globo plus sit soliditatis, aliquantum vero humoris,
perexiguum lucis, aeris et aquae duae medietates quam habeant cognationem cum supra memoratis elementis intelle-
gamus.

air and water would be the same as that between fire and air, and conversely, so that the relationship in the binding of water and earth would be the same as that between air and water. He says that the body is solid and spherical; but the cohesion of such bodies involves two means, in that the circumference is analogous to the surface of a ball: there is without doubt a certain length, but there is also width, and we measure them by way of a point embedded midway between the outer extremes: equal lines extend from all around the circumference to the middle point. Thus the one mean is situated on the surface and the other deep within: the surface point reaches it if pressed to precisely half the depth.

14. For this reason, there being two means, the multiplication must be performed, not once, as in the case of plane figures, but twice. For in the previous case we drew two sides, one of which we made 2 units and the other 3, and in multiplying 2 × 3 we discovered that the number 6 resulted; but in the case of these solid figures, the multiplication will be doubled because of the double mean. The result is that, since from the multiplication of 2 × 3 there results this same 6 according to the ratio currently based on a single mean, we calculate, according to the ratio based on a second mean (which happens to be the number 4), 4 × 6 and the sum of every *number, mass* [31c], or quality is thus found to be of 24 units, and we comprehend the relationship which the two means of air and water have with the elements mentioned earlier, since the highest point of the world, i.e., fire, being a solid body, has the three qualities of length, width, and solidity, although not equally, for fire has more luminosity, slightly less in the way of moderate heat, and little solidity, whereas the terrestrial sphere has more solidity, a little moisture, and very little light. (See Diagram 4.)

15. Harum solidarum formarum cognatio numerorum indicatur consortio, siquidem primi limitis summa dimidia pars sit secundi limitis summae (nam viginti quattuor numerus quadraginta octo numeri dimidia pars est); secunda item tertiae et haec quarti limitis summae dimidietas; aeque retrorsum quoque: postrema tertiae dupla, tertia item secundae dupla, et primae secunda. Atque his mediis duabus, quae inter duas extimas formas inseruntur, genitura est de isdem extimis; est enim primi limitis medietas in potiore numero, id est senario, qui nascitur ex multiplicatis summis minoribus, bis tribus; est item novissimi limitis in minore numero medietas, id est octo. Igitur primi limitis maiorem medietatem cum postremi limitis minore medietate multiplicans creo secundi limitis totam in quadraginta et octo numero positam substantiam. At vero si primi limitis minorem medietatem, quae est quattuor, cum postremi limitis maiore medietate, quae est in viginti et quattuor summa nata ex quater senis, comparavero, creabitur omnis substantia tertii limitis, quae est posita in nonaginta sex. Sic duo extimi solidorum corporum duabus medietatibus vinciuntur, ut certa minimeque infitiabilis arithmeticae disciplinae confirmat auctoritas testimonium praebens Platoni.

16. Haec eadem solidorum duum corporum distantiva seu duplex medietas coniungere distantia corpora geometricis etiam rationibus pro competenti modo sic ostenditur. Sed prius, quia est e re accommodatumque tractatui, quid sit hoc quod competens appellatur a nobis, analogia vero a Graecis, explicabo. Geminum est competens, unum continuum alterum distans; continuum competens est quod

15. The relationship between these solid figures is indicated by the corresponding numbers, since the sum corresponding to the first term is half that of the second (for the number 24 is half of the number 48); similarly, the second is half the third sum, and the third half the sum of the fourth term; and it is the same in reverse: the last is double the third, the third double the second, and the second double the first. And the two middle figures, those inserted between the two outer ones, originate from the same outer ones; for there is a mean in the higher number of the first term, i.e., 6, which is the product of the smaller sums (2 × 3); likewise, there is a mean in the lower number of the last term, i.e., 8. Thus by multiplying the larger mean of the first term with the smaller mean of the last term I generate the whole substance of the second term, positioned above in the number 48. But if I bring the smaller mean of the first term, i.e., 4, into conjunction with the larger mean of the last term, i.e., 24 (the sum arising from 4 × 6), then there will be generated the whole substance of the third term, which is positioned in 96. Thus the two extremes among the solid bodies are bound by two means, as the certain and incontestable authority of arithmetic confirms in support of Plato.

16. This same discrete or double mean between two solid bodies is analogously shown to conjoin discrete bodies also by geometric ratios, in the following way. But first, since it arises from the matter at hand and is pertinent to the discussion, I will explain what that is which we call a proportion and the Greeks an *analogia*. There are two types of proportion, the continuous and the discrete; a continuous proportion is that which conjoins extremes by a common

communi medio fine coniungit extima, distans quod duobus mediis finibus separat extima. Ratio vero est duorum finium iuxta semet ipsos habitus et quasi quaedam conventio, itaque competens ex complurium rationum comparatione subsistit Et continuum quidem competens in tribus ut parum finibus invenitur: sicut primus iuxta secundum sic secundus iuxta tertium, hoc est ut octo iuxta quattuor sic quattuor iuxta duo; quorum quidem finium is qui est medius in se replicatus aequalis est ei qui de multiplicatione nascitur extimorum [quadrato], bis octoni siquidem sedecim et quaterni quater totidem. Distans autem competens in quattuor minimum limitibus reperitur: sicut primus iuxta secundum sic tertius iuxta quartum, id est ut octo iuxta quattuor ita sex iuxta tria; non enim possumus repetentes dicere, "sic quattuor iuxta sex." In quibus aeque ut in continui competentis finibus is qui confit ab extimis aequalis est ei qui nascitur ex supputatione mediorum, ter enim octo viginti quattuor summam faciunt, aeque sexies quattuor eandem summam creant.

17. Utitur ergo nunc ratione ac remedio continui competentis propterea quod natura eius coniugabilis est et adunatrix distantium limitum similisque eius rationis, qua deus mundi sensilis fabricator usus est, cum extimis mundi limitibus, igni atque terrae, aeris et aquae insereret medietatem.

18. Quatenus ergo haec descriptio demonstrat, duo solida corpora, quae parallelepipeda geometrici vocant, insertis aliis similibus solidis duobus continuari iuxta rationem continui competentis tam ex coagmentatione quam ex dissolutione fiet palam. Describitur parallelogrammum, id est quadratura, quam limitant Graecae litterae quattuor hae

intermediate term, and a discrete proportion is that which separates extremes by two intermediate terms. A ratio, by contrast, is a reciprocal relation—a kind of convergence, as it were—between two terms, such that a proportion consists of the comparison between a number of ratios. A *continuous* proportion emerges with a minimum of three terms: as the first is to the second so the second is to the third, i.e., 8:4=4:2; of these three terms the middle one when multiplied by itself is equal to the one which results from the multiplication of the extremes, since 2 × 8 = 16 and 4 × 4 just as many. A *discrete* proportion, on the other hand, emerges with a minimum of four terms: as the first is to the second so the third is to the fourth, i.e., 8:4=6:3; for we cannot backtrack and say "=4:6." With these, as with the terms of a continuous proportion, the one which results from the extremes is equal to the one which results from multiplication of the means, for 3 × 8 makes a sum of 24 just as 6 × 4 generates the same sum. (See Diagram 5.)

17. Here, then, he uses the ratio or remedy of a continuous proportion, since it is by its nature a unifier capable of conjoining discrete terms and is akin to the ratio which god used in fabricating the sensible world, since he inserted the means of air and water between the extreme limits of the world, fire and earth. (See Diagram 6.)

18. The extent, then, to which this diagram demonstrates that two solid bodies, which the geometers call parallelepipeds, are bound by the insertion of two other similar solids according to the ratio of a continuous proportion will be made evident on the basis of both their coalescence and their separation. There is drawn a parallelogram, i.e., a quadrilateral, which the four Greek letters ΑΒΓΔ delimit;

ΛΒΓΔ; et huic quadraturae superimponitur aliud quadra-
tum quod continetur litteris EZHΘ, et conectuntur EA,
item ZB, item ΘΔ, item HΓ, et hoc facto completur unum
solidum sive parallelepipedum. Huic aliud simile describitur
hoc modo: per EΘ lineam eicitur ΘΛ et item per ΔΘ eicitur linea ΘΞ et per HΘ crescit linea ΘK et ex nota K eicitur linea KM, item ex nota M deducitur linea MΛ, ex nota
item Ξ eicitur linea ΞΟ, et ex isdem ΞΟ notis aguntur in directum duae lineae, una ΞN altera ΟΠ. Et sint aequales EΘ
quidem lineae ΘΛ linea, ΔΘ vero lineae ΘΞ linea, HΘ lineae ΘK linea, item aequalia parallelogramma KΘΛM,
NΞΟΠ, et conectantur NK, ΠM, ΟΛ, ΞΘ. Erit hoc pacto
solidum natum aliud ex hac descriptione. Dico igitur inter
haec duo similia solida duo alia similia solida iuxta rationem
continui competentis inveniri. Deduco enim per NΞ lineam
ΞΥ lineam, per ΠΟ lineam ΟΦ lineam, per MΛ vero li-
neam ΛT lineam, per AΔ lineam item ΔΣ lineam, per BΓ
lineam ΓP lineam. Et sint aequales NΞ linea ΞΥ lineae, ΠΟ
linea ΟΦ lineae, MΛ linea ΛT lineae, AΔ linea ΔΣ lineae,
BΓ linea ΓP lineae; parallelogramma item sint aequalia quae
in isdem sunt quadraturis, et conectantur ΥH, ΣΛ, ΦT, TP
et si qua alia latera. Eruntque expresse conexa quattuor solida.

19. Quatenus hoc probatur? Ut est EΘ latus iuxta ΘΛ latus ita in longum erit EZΘH parallelogrammum iuxta
ΘHTΛ parallelogrammum, erit ergo etiam ΛΒΓΔEZHΘ
solidum iuxta ΔΓPΣΘHTΛ solidum. At enim latera supra
comprehensa habent adversum se competentem modum,
utpote quae sub isdem quadraturis sint, quadraturae item
sibi competunt, quia sunt sub eadem altitudine; et solida

superimposed on this is another quadrilateral, delimited by
the letters EZHΘ, and EA are connected, as are ZB, ΘΔ,
and HΓ, and thereby is completed one solid or parallelepiped. A second one, similar to it, is drawn as follows: the line
EΘ is extended to ΘΛ, and ΔΘ is likewise extended to ΘΞ,
and ΘK extends from HΘ, and from point K the line KM is
drawn, as MΛ is from point M and ΞO from point Ξ, and
from these same points ΞO two upright lines are drawn, one
ΞN, the other OΠ. And let them be equal, line ΘΛ to line
EΘ, line ΘΞ to line ΔΘ, line ΘK to line HΘ, and likewise
the parallelograms KΘΛM and NΞOΠ equal, and let NK,
ΠM, OΛ, and ΞΘ be connected. In this way another solid
will have arisen out this diagram. My point, then, is that between these two similar solids two other similar ones are
discovered according to the ratio of a continuous proportion. For I draw a line ΞΥ down through line NΞ, a line OΦ
through line ΠO, and a line ΛT through line MΛ, likewise a
line ΔΣ through line AΔ, and a line ΓP through line BΓ.
And let them be equal, line NΞ to line ΞΥ, line ΠO to line
OΦ, line MΛ to line ΛT, line AΔ to line ΔΣ, line BΓ to line
ΓP; likewise, let the parallelograms which are in the same
quadrilaterals be equal, and let ΥH, ΣΛ, ΦT, TP and any
other sides be connected. And there will be four visibly connected solids.

19. To what extent is this proved? As side EΘ is to side
ΘΛ so, as to its length, will parallelogram EZΘH be to parallelogram ΘHTΛ, and thus, the solid ABΓΔEZHΘ to the
solid ΔΓPΣΘHTΛ. But the sides considered above have a
proportional measure to one another, being in the same
quadrilaterals, and the quadrilaterals are likewise proportional to one another, being of the same height; thus the

ergo supra dicta habebunt adversum se competentem parilitatem. Rursum ut est ΔΘ latus iuxta ΘΞ latus in altitudine ita erit ΘΔΓΗ parallelogrammum iuxta ΘΞΥΗ parallelogrammum, erit ergo etiam ΔΓΡΣΘΗΤΛ solidum iuxta ΘΗΤΛΞΥΦΟ solidum. At enim latera supra comprehensa habent adversum se competentem modum, utpote quae sub isdem quadraturis sint, quadraturae quoque sibi competunt, quia sunt sub eadem altitudine; et solida ergo supra dicta habebunt adversum se competentem parilitatem. Rursum ut est ΗΘ latus iuxta ΘΚ latus in altitudine ita erit ΘΗΤΛ parallelogrammum iuxta ΚΘΛΜ parallelogrammum; erit ergo etiam ΘΗΤΛΞΥΦΟ solidum iuxta ΚΘΛΜΝΞΟΠ solidum. At enim latera supra comprehensa habent inter se analogiam, utpote quae sub isdem quadraturis sint, quadraturae quoque sibi competunt, quia sunt sub eadem altitudine; et solida ergo supra dicta habebunt inter se analogiam sive competentiam. Ut ergo ΑΒΓΔΕΖΗΘ solidum iuxta ΔΓΡΣΘΗΤΛ sic hoc ipsum solidum iuxta ΘΗΤΛΞΥΦΟ solidum et item hoc ipsum iuxta ΚΘΛΜΝΞΟΠ solidum. Quo pacto ostensum est duum solidorum parallelepipedorum similium duo media similia solida parallelepipeda iuxta rationem continui competentis inveniri, quod oportebat ostendi.

20. Dicet aliquis duo quidem solida corpora intervallo longiore distantia coniungi duabus interiectis medietatibus iuxta rationem continui competentis sufficienter probari sibi, sed inter ignem et terram, quae sunt solida corpora, nullam apparere similitudinem. Quando iuxta ipsum Platonem ignis quidem forma et figura pyramoides esse dicatur, id est in modum pyramidis excrescat, terra vero cubus sit,

solids considered above will also have a proportional equality to one another. Again, as side ΔΘ is to side ΘΞ in height so will parallelogram ΘΔΓΗ be to ΘΞΥΗ, and thus, the solid ΔΓΡΣΘΗΤΛ to ΘΗΤΛΞΥΦΟ. But the sides considered above have a proportional measure to one another, being in the same quadrilaterals, and the quadrilaterals too are proportional to one another, being of the same height; thus the solids considered above will also have a proportional equality to one another. Again, as side ΗΘ is to side ΘΚ in height so will parallelogram ΘΗΤΛ be to parallelogram ΚΘΛΜ, and thus, the solid ΘΗΤΛΞΥΦΟ to the solid ΚΘΛΜΝΞΟΠ. But the sides considered above have between them an *analogia,* being in the same quadrilaterals, and the quadrilaterals too are proportional to one another, being of the same height; thus the solids considered above will also have an *analogia* or proportion to one another other. As, then, the solid ΑΒΓΔΕΖΗΘ is to ΔΓΡΣΘΗΤΛ so the latter solid is to the solid ΘΗΤΛΞΥΦΟ, and likewise, the latter to the solid ΚΘΛΜΝΞΟΠ. And in this way it is shown that of two similar parallelepiped solids two similar intermediate parallelepiped solids are found according to the ratio of a continuous proportion, which was what needed to be shown.

20. Someone will say that, although he is satisfied with the proof that two solid bodies separated by an extended interval are conjoined by two intermediates intercalated according to the ratio of a continuous proportion, nevertheless there is no apparent similitude between fire and earth, which are solid bodies. For according to Plato himself, fire is claimed to be pyramidical in form and shape, i.e., its extension is in the manner of a pyramid, whereas earth is a cube,

hae porro formae nullam ex se similitudinem mutuentur,
quia non sint aequalibus angulis (quippe cubus omnis rectis
est angulis, ergo, quia terra in cubica est figura, rectos angulos habeat necesse est, at vero pyramidis anguli productiores
sunt in acumine); ubi autem non sunt aequales anguli, ne latera quidem erunt pro competenti proptereaque similia sui
non erunt. Quae distantia corpora si alia duo solida interiecta continuabunt, impedietur hoc pacto continuatio, siquidem inter duo non quaelibet sed quae similia sunt invicem sibi solida corpora inseri debent.

21. Cui respondebitur hactenus: memores nos esse debere
eorum quibus Plato hanc ipsam difficultatem multo ante
praevidens eos qui ita sensuri sint ab errore revocaverit.
Dixit enim, si meminimus, similitudinem non solum in formis et figuris sed etiam in potentiis et qualitatibus quaeri
oportere, cum ita dixit: Cum in tribus sive numeris seu molibus seu potentiis perinde erit medietas imo quem ad modum summitas medio. Quare si inter ignem et terram nulla
est in specie et velut in vultu similitudo, quaerenda erit in
naturis ac qualitatibus ipsorum elementorum iuxta quas faciunt aliquid aut patiuntur et in his proprietatibus ex quibus
utriusque elementi vis et germanitas apprime designatur.
Sunt igitur tam ignis quam terrae multae quidem et aliae
proprietates sed quae vel maxime vim earum proprietatemque declarent nimirum hae: ignis quidem acumen, quod
est acutus et penetrans, deinde quod est tener et delicata

and these shapes share no likeness with one another, since they do not consist of equal angles (for every cube consists of right angles, and so earth, being cubic in shape, necessarily has right angles, whereas the angles of a pyramid are more acute at the tip); and wherever the angles are not equal neither will the sides be proportional, and hence they will not be similar to one another. If two other solids are to bind the discrete bodies by their intercalation, then on the current supposition the continuous bond will be impeded, since they should not be inserted between any two solid bodies whatsoever, but between ones which are similar to one another.

21. The response to this will be as follows: We must bear in mind the points by which Plato, who foresaw this difficulty well in advance, drew those inclined to take such a view away from their mistake. For he indicated, as we recall, that similitude is to be sought not only in forms and shapes but also in potencies and qualities. Here are his words [31c–32a]: *whenever* among *three things, whether numbers, masses, or powers, the middle* is *to the last as the first to the middle.* Hence if between fire and earth there is no similitude in form and, as it were, appearance, then it will have to be sought in the natures and qualities of the elements themselves, those in accordance with which they act upon something or are acted upon, and in the properties on the basis of which the power or relationship of each of the two elements is in the first instance made evident. Thus although fire and earth possess numerous other properties, those which most fully express their power and property are undoubtedly the following: of fire, the acuteness, that it is sharp and capable of penetrating, and that it is light and of a certain delicate fineness, and

quadam subtilitate, tum quod est mobilis et semper in motu; terrae vero <obtunsitas,> quod est retunsa, quod corpulenta, quod semper immobilis. Hae vero naturae licet sint contrariae, habent tamen aliquam ex ipsa contrarietate parilitatem (tam enim similia similibus quam dissimilia dissimilibus comparantur) et haec est analogia, id est ratio continui competentis: quod enim est acumen adversum obtunsitatem hoc subtilitas iuxta corpulentiam, et quod subtilitas iuxta corpulentiam hoc mobilitas adversus immobilitatem; et si verteris ut id quod medium est extimum fiat, quae vero sunt extima singillatim in medio locentur, servabitur analogiae norma.

22. Quatenus igitur inter haec duo solida corpora, quorum est talis similitudo qualem demonstravimus, alia duo solida interiecta facient continuationem iuxta rationem continui competentis, docet arithmetica disciplina. Si enim vicinum igni elementum quid sit et ex quibus conflatum voluerimus inquirere, sumemus ignis quidem de proximo duas virtutes, subtilitatem et mobilitatem, unam vero terrae, id est obtunsitatem, et invenietur genitura secundi elementi quod est subter ignem, id est aeris; est enim aer obtunsus subtilis mobilis. Rursumque si eius elementi quod est vicinum terrae, id est aquae, genituram consideremus, sumemus duas quidem terrae virtutes, id est obtunsitatem et corpulentiam, unam vero ignis, id est motum, et exorietur aquae substantia, quae est corpus obtunsum corpulentum mobile. Atque ita inter ignem et terram aer et aqua de extimorum concretione nascentur, ex quibus constat mundi continuatio. Conservatur autem hoc pacto analogia quoque geometrica iuxta rationem continui competentis, ut enim ignis adversum aera sic aer adversum aquam et demum aqua

again, that it is mobile and always in motion; of earth, the compactness, that it is blunt, that it is corporeal, that it is always immobile. Now although these natures are indeed contrary, they nevertheless have a certain likeness deriving from their very contrariety (for like is compared to like no more than unlike to unlike), and this is their *analogia,* i.e., their ratio of continuous proportion: for acuteness is to compactness what fineness is to corporeality, and fineness is to corporeality what mobility is to immobility; and if you change them such that the middle becomes an extreme and the extremes are by turns placed in the middle, then the rule of *analogia* will be preserved.

22. Thus the science of arithmetic explains the extent to which between these two solid bodies, whose similitude is as we have demonstrated, two other solids will by their intercalation produce a continuous bond according to the ratio of a continuous proportion. For if we wish to inquire into the nature and constituent parts of the element bordering on fire, we will isolate first two powers of fire, its fineness and mobility, and one of earth, i.e., its compactness, and the origins of the element immediately below fire, i.e., air, will be found; for air is compact, fine, and mobile. Again, if we reflect on the origins of the element neighboring on earth, i.e., water, we will isolate two powers of earth, i.e., its compactness and corporeality, and one of fire, i.e., its movement, and the substance of water will emerge, that being a body compact, corporeal, and mobile. And thus between fire and earth from the coalescence of extremes air and water will arise, giving binding continuity to the world. And in this way is preserved as well the geometric *analogia* according to the ratio of a continuous proportion: as fire is to air so

iuxta terram, retrorsumque ut terra adversum aquam sic aqua adversum aera et aer adversus ignem.

23. Hactenus de constitutione mundani corporis et de materiarum ex quibus constat germanitate disseritur. Quem cum factum esse, quia sit corporeus, affirmet et eundem indissolubilem, cum quae fiunt quaeque nascuntur facta dissolvantur nata occidant, ut huic quod est praeter opinionem hominum medeatur, dicit a quo factus sit, ex quibus constet, ad quod exemplum institutus, qua de causa, quatenus aeternitati propagatus. Omnia enim quae sunt vel dei opera sunt vel naturae vel naturam imitantis hominis artificis. Operum naturalium origo et initium semina sunt, quae facta comprehenduntur vel terrae visceribus ad frugis arboreae cerealisve proventum vel genitalium membrorum fecunditate conceptum animalium germen adolentium. Quorum omnium ortus in tempore, par enim et aequaevum natale naturae ac temporis; ita naturae opera, quia ortum habent ex eo quo esse coeperunt tempore, finem quoque et occasum intra seriem continuationemque eius sortita sunt. At vero dei operum origo et initium incomprehensibile, nulla est enim certa nota, nullum indicium temporis ex quo esse coeperunt; sola—si forte—causa—et haec ipsa vix intelligitur—cur eorum quid quamve ob causam existat certum est, siquidem nihil a deo factum esse sine causa. Ut igitur illis quae lege naturae procreantur fundamenta sunt semina ita eorum

air is to water and, finally, water to earth; and conversely, as earth is to water so water is to air and air to fire.

23. So much for the constitution of the world body and the relationship between the material elements of which it consists. In consideration of his claim that the world, by virtue of its being corporeal, was made and is at the same time *indissoluble* [32c], and since that which is made and comes to be dissolves and passes away after being made and coming to be, he states who it was made by, what it consists of, the pattern after which it is formed, for what reason, and the extent to which it is propagated to eternity in order to remedy this challenge to normal human expectations. For everything that exists is a work of god, nature, or man acting as an artisan in imitation of nature. The origin and beginning of natural works are seeds which once formed are taken up either in the bowels of the earth for the production of crops and grain or in the fertility of the genital organs for the conception and germination of living beings endowed with the power of growth. The birth of all such things occurs in time, for the birth of nature is the same as and coeval with that of time; thus the works of nature, since they have their birth from the time when they begin to exist, are also allotted their end and death within its series or continuum. But the origin or beginning of the works of god is incomprehensible, for there is no fixed mark to serve as an indication of the time from which they began to be; only the reason why, the cause in virtue of which, any of them comes to be is certain, in that nothing is created by god without cause [reason]— but this only possibly, as the reason [cause] is barely intelligible in itself. Now, as seeds are the foundation for all that is procreated according to the law of nature, so the causes

quae deus instituit fundamenta sunt causae quae sunt perspicuae divinae providentiae; deus autem ante institutionem temporis et per aevum, simulacrum est enim tempus aevi; causae igitur operum omnium dei tempore antiquiores, et sicut deus per aevum sic etiam causae per aevum. Quod sequitur ut quicquid a deo fit temporarium non sit, quod temporarium non sit, nulla temporis lege teneatur; et tempus immutationem aetatis—morbos, senectutem, occasum—invehit; his ergo omnibus quod a deo instituitur immune est origoque eius causativa est, non temporaria; et mundus sensilis opus dei; origo igitur eius causativa, non temporaria. Sic mundus sensilis, licet et corporeus, a deo tamen factus atque institutus, aeternus est.

24. Constat porro ex materiis illibatis atque integris, ex omni, inquit, igni et ex universo spiritu et ex ceteris sine ullius partis imminutione. Ita fit ut nulla ne minima quidem pars cuiuslibet corporis extra ambitum mundi relicta sit. Quae quia omnia corpora partim frigida partim calida sunt, nulla importuna frigoris calorisve extrinsecus accessione moveant aegritudinem mundo; igitur extra necessitatem incommodi positus aeternus est.—Sed natura corporis fluida est et mundus constat ex corpore.—Sed et detrimentum et interitus partium non in fluxu est sed in effluendo, id est extra fluendo (amittitur quippe id quod ex universitate defecerit), intra mundum vero regestis omnibus nihil certe extra mundi ambitum est. Ita quod secundum naturam corporis

envisioned by divine providence are the foundation for all that god establishes; but god is prior to the establishment of time and is through eternity, for time is an *image* [37d] of eternity; thus the causes of all god's works are prior to time, and as god is through eternity, so the causes are through eternity as well. And it follows that everything made by god is atemporal, and that that which is atemporal is subject to no law of time; and time introduces the changes associated with aging—sickness, old age, and death; to all of these, then, that which is established by god is immune, and the origin of the latter is causative, not temporal; and the sensible world is the work of god; its origin is therefore causative, not temporal. And so the sensible world, although corporeal, is nevertheless eternal in having been made and established by god.

24. Moreover, the world consists of material elements which are undiminished and complete, *from all of fire,* he says [32c], and the whole of air and so on, *without* diminution of *any* part. So it is that not even the smallest part of any body is left outside the enclosure of the world. And since all of these bodies are variously divided between cold and hot, none can bring disease to the world by importing from without a destructive element of coldness or heat; thus the world, placed beyond the necessity of harm, is eternal.—But body is by its nature in a state of flux, and the world consists of body.—Yes, but the corruption and dissolution of the parts is not in their fluctuation but in their *effluence,* i.e., their flowing *out* (for only that which has passed away from the whole is lost), but since they are all retained within the world, clearly nothing is outside the enclosure of the world. So that which, by virtue of its being corporeal in nature, is in

fluit quo effluat non habet; influit ergo, non effluit, et ad summam universitatis iactura demum recurrens fatigatarum diuturnitate partium recreatio est.

25. Quid quod institutus est ad exemplum alterius intellegibilis et immutabilis perennitatis ? Iam illud nemo dubitat, quae ad similitudinem instituuntur exempli sempiterni habere similitudinem perpetuitatis. Et perpetuitas in aevo, quare exemplum, id est intellegibilis mundus, per aevum, id vero quod ad exemplum institutum est, sensilis scilicet mundus, per tempora. Et temporis quidem proprium progredi, aevi propria mansio semperque in idem perseveratio; temporis item partes, dies et noctes, menses et anni, aevi partes nullae; temporis item species praeteritum praesens futurum, aevi substantia uniformis in solo perpetuoque praesenti. Mundus igitur intellegibilis semper est; hic simulacrum eius semper fuit, est, erit.

2. De Ortu Animae

26. Hinc ad animae mundi tractatum pergens Plato prius illud curat, quod praepostere de corporis eius constitutione ante quam de inspiratione animae disputatum sit, cum animam corpore omni constet antiquiorem. Nec recedit ab instituto ut, quia mundum a deo factum asseruit, animam quoque eius factam esse a deo dicat. Quod in hoc solo libro

flux has no place to flow out to; as a result, it flows within rather than out, and with respect to the whole of the universe the recurrent loss is in the end a re-formation of parts which are exhausted over time.

25. What of the fact that the world is fashioned after the pattern of another one, an intelligible and immutable eternity? No one now doubts the point that things fashioned in the likeness of a sempiternal pattern have the likeness of perpetuity. And perpetuity is within eternity, and so the pattern, i.e., the intelligible world, is through eternity, whereas that which is fashioned after a pattern, namely, the sensible world, is through periods of time. And whereas the defining property of time is progression, that of eternity is its proper abiding and forever holding to the same; similarly, time has parts, days and nights and months and years, but eternity has none; again, time takes the forms of past, present, and future, but the substance of eternity is uniform, in a unique and perpetual present. Thus the intelligible world forever is; this one, its image, forever has been, is, and will be.

2. On the Origin of Soul

26. Moving from these considerations to treatment of the world soul Plato first attends to the fact that treatment of the fashioning of the world body comes *out of order* [34c] or prior to that on the insufflation of soul, although it is clear that soul is prior to body of every kind. Nor does he deviate from his intention and end up claiming that, since he asserted that the world was made by god, its soul too was made by god. The procedure of contriving processes of generation for eternal things, which he adopts in this book alone, is, I

facere animadvertitur, aeternarum rerum genituras comminisci, credo propterea ne, si audiant homines esse quaedam
quae fuerint ex origine nata numquam, principatui summi
dei derogari putent si pari atque eadem sint qua deus anti-
quitatis praestantia, nescientes longe aliter dici originem rerum aeternarum et item caducarum; siquidem mortalium
auctoritas et origo illa est quae praecedit ortum ceterorum,
ut origo est pater filii et populorum atque urbium condi-
tores eorum, at vero divinorum generum aeternarumque
gentium origo et arx non in anticipatione temporis sed dignitatis eminentia consideratur; vel quod effecti operis pontificium et auctoritatem manibus magis quam dispositioni
mentis soleamus ascribere, vel quod plerique ex mortali natura sua divinam naturam aestimantes nasci omnia neque
esse quicquam quod non natum sit existimant. Quorum animis sic institutis difficile persuadeatur mundi esse auctorem
deum, nisi eum tamquam opifex aliquis manibus ceterorumque artuum molitione construxerit. Certe propositum
scriptoris considerandum puto, nam si id ageret in hoc libro
principaliter ut immortalem esse animam probaret, non
conveniret animae genituram comminisci propterea quod
cuncta quae gignuntur intereunt; at vero cum de mundi, hoc
est universae rei, constitutione tractetur, ad praesens e re
fuit nascentem et velut in lucem proditam inducere animam
eius, quo audientes imaginarentur animae formam aliquam,
perinde ut eorum omnium quae nascuntur vident.

believe, to avert the possibility of people supposing, on hearing that there are certain things which have existed from the beginning and never came into being, that it detracts from the primacy of the highest god for those things to be of one and the same preeminence in antiquity as he is. They would not know that "origin" is applied in very different ways to eternal and perishable realities. In the case of mortal beings the authority and origin is that which precedes the birth of others, as in the case of a father's being the origin of a son or that of the founders of peoples and their cities, but in the case of divine kinds and eternal races the origin and pinnacle is a consideration of preeminence in dignity rather than preexistence in time. They would not know that we generally ascribe the power or authority over created work to our hands rather than to a disposition of the mind, or that in measuring the divine according to their own mortal nature most people suppose that all things are subject to birth and that there is nothing which is not born. It would be difficult to persuade minds so conditioned that god is the author of the world unless a kind of craftsman, as it were, constructed it by his hands and the exertion of his other limbs. At any rate, I think we must take the writer's intention into consideration, for if in this book his primary concern were to prove that the soul is immortal, then to contrive for it a process of generation would be inappropriate, since everything that is generated passes away; but since the discussion concerns the constitution of the world, i.e., the universe, it was for present purposes relevant to present its soul as being born and, as it were, brought to the light of day, so that those who heard it might imagine soul as having a form of some sort, precisely as they see in the case of all the things that are born.

27. Itaque deus, inquit, tertium animae genus excogitavit hoc pacto: ex individua semperque in suo statu perseverante substantia itemque alia quae inseparabilis corporum comes per eadem corpora scindere se putatur tertium substantiae genus mixtum locavit medium inter utramque substantiam et cetera. Quid est quod ait? Docet nos substantiam sive, ut Cicero dicit, essentiam duplicem esse, unam individuam, alteram per corpora dividuam. Et individuam quidem esse eam, cuius generis sunt omnia aeterna et sine corpore, quae intellegibilia dicuntur, dividuam vero, quae corporibus existendi causa est. Unumquodque enim corpus est certe, quod vero est, habet essentiam; et corpora multa sunt, una vero dividua essentia, quae in cunctis corporibus invenitur; quae igitur una in multis simul invenitur, recte scindere se putatur recteque dividua. Igitur ex his duabus ait opificem deum tertium genus essentiae miscuisse idque medium locasse inter essentiam utramque.

28. Similiter docet naturam quoque non esse simplicem sed bimembrem, et ex his duabus facit opificis iussu tertium naturae genus extitisse quod aeque medium positum esset inter utramque essentiam, individuam videlicet atque dividuam. Quatenus ergo bimembris est natura? Omnia, inquit, naturalia vel eadem sibi vel diversa sunt: eadem genere, diversa specie, ut puta homo et item equus idem sunt (nam et hoc et illud animal est), at vero specie diversa sunt (alterum enim eorum rationabile animal est, alterum inrationabile et mutum, et alterum bipes, alterum quadrupes). Haec igitur omnia existentia, idem et essentiam et diversum, in unam,

27. *And so,* he says [35a], god *devised a third kind, that of soul, in the following way: from Being which is indivisible and forever persists in its proper state and another form of Being which as the inseparable concomitant of bodies is held to be distributed throughout the same bodies he placed a third, blended kind of Being midway between the two forms of Being,* etc. What does he mean by this? He is showing us that Substance [*substantia*] or, as Cicero says, Being [*essentia*] is twofold, one of them indivisible and the other divisible throughout bodies, and that the indivisible is of the same kind as all eternal and incorporeal things, which are called intelligibles, whereas the divisible is that which is the cause of existence in bodies. For each and every body undoubtedly exists, but that which exists has Being; and bodies are many, whereas the divisible Being found in them all is one; thus the one Being simultaneously found in many things is rightly *thought to be distributed* and divisible. And that is why he says that the craftsman god *blended a third kind* of Being *from* the two and *placed it midway between* them both.

28. Similarly, he explains that nature too is not simple but twofold, and from the two he by order of the craftsman has a third kind of nature come to be, which would likewise be placed midway between the two forms of Being, namely, the indivisible and divisible. In what sense, then, is nature twofold? All natural beings, he says [35a–b], are either the *same* as or *different* from one another: the same in genus, different in species, as, e.g., man and horse are the same (for each is an animal) but different in species (for one of them is a rational animal and the other irrational and mute, one two-footed and the other four-footed). Thus, he says, god *blended all of these* existent entities, Same, Being, and Other, *into one form,*

inquit, speciem commiscuit deus et effecit ex tribus unum, [idem diversum dividuum] diversa illa natura difficile se commodante concretioni atque adunationi generum. Rursumque unum illud ex tribus concretum divisit in partes ita ut singulae partes tres illas potentias obtinerent, hoc est, ut idem non solum idem esset sed etiam substantia et haberet aliquid ex diversitate, essentia quoque et essentia esset et idem et diversum, diversum quoque et diversum esset et essentia et haberet aliquid ex eo quod idem vocatur.

29. Disceptatum tamen est a veteribus quae sit quae a Platone dicitur individua quae item dividua substantia ex quibus mundi sensilis fabricator deus tertium substantiae genus quamve ob causam conflaverit. Num speciem intellegibilis mundi ad cuius similitudinem formas mente conceptas ad corpora transferebat individuam substantiam nuncupaverit, dividuam vero silvam quae velut exordium et fons est corporum, ita ut tertium illud mixtum substantiae genus formam esse intellegendum sit qua informata sint, tam mundi quam cetera quae mundus complectitur, corpora? An potius individuam Plato substantiam censeat eminentiorem animam quae nulli sit incorporationi obnoxia cuiusque veneranda puritas nulla corporis contagione violetur, dividuam vero substantiam illam animam dicat quae non solum cunctis animalibus sed etiam stirpibus et arboribus dat vitalem vigorem, ut sit ex his duabus conflatum tertium animae genus rationabile, idcirco ne omnia muta essent et ratione carerent quae vitam sortirentur corpora, videlicet animalia, sed esset praeterea genus animantium huius modi quod rationis disciplinaeque et intellectus capax divini operis admirandam rationem dispositionemque intellegens veneraretur mundani operis auctorem?

and out of three made *one, the nature of the Other* adapting itself with difficulty *to the blending and union of kinds. And* that *one* which was a coalescence *of the three he then divided into portions,* such that the *individual portions* received those three powers, i.e., such that the Same was not only Same but also Being and had something of Otherness, and Being too was Being and Same and Other, and the Other too was Other and Being and had something of that which is *called the Same.*

29. Yet there was among the ancients disagreement concerning what Plato meant by the indivisible and divisible Being from the blending of which god the maker of the sensible world fabricated the third kind of Being, and disagreement concerning the reason why. Is it that by "indivisible" Being he indicated the form of the intelligible world after whose likeness [the craftsman god] transferred to bodies the forms conceived in his mind, and by "divisible" Being matter, which is the beginning, as it were, and fountainhead of bodies, so that the *third, blended kind of Being* [35a] should be understood to be the form by which bodies, that of the world and all those it embraces, acquire form? Or by "indivisible" Being does Plato instead mean a higher level of soul which is subject to no embodiment and whose venerable purity is inviolable by any bodily contagion, and by "divisible" Being the soul that provides vital force not only to all forms of animal but to plants and trees, so that a third, rational kind of soul might be blended from the two, to prevent the bodies, namely, living beings, that received life from being completely mute and without reason, and there might additionally be a kind of living being which in its capacity for reason, learning, and intellect would venerate its author in contemplating the wondrous plan and disposition of the divine work that is the world?

30. [Quod] Itaque hi qui speciem intellegibilis mundi, quod semper eadem sit nec immutetur umquam, putabant a Platone individuam substantiam dici, dividuam porro silvam, negabant habere rationem, cum mundi esset instituta generatio animantique quasi mox futuro quaereretur competens anima, illam animam quae tam mutis animalibus quam stirpibus et arboribus vitam daret, esse uspiam dici a Platone nondum natis animalibus nec vero arboribus et ceteris quibus datura vitas foret. Proptereaque individuam quidem substantiam mundi intellegibilis speciem ad cuius similitudinem formatus sit sensilis mundus Platonem cognominasse dicebant, dividuam porro silvam.

31. At vero hi qui ex individua substantia (id est immuni ab incorporatione anima) item alia inseparabili corporum comite (id est stirpea) conflatum tertiae animae genus asserebant (id est rationabile) sic assistebant sententiae propriae. Primo omnium praeposterum esse, cum de constitutione mundani corporis in superioribus tractatum esset finitoque eo tractatu perventum foret ad animae genituram, quae vivificaret sensilem mundum, rursum ad priorem tractatum retrorsum iri, ut de silva et corporibus mundi formaque eorum tractatus de integro fieret et a genitura animae recederetur. Deinde frustra dici animam stirpeam nondum esse posse propterea, quia quae vivificatura erat animalia nondum essent: fuisse enim semper tam animae quam corporis vim nec deum ex his quae non erant fecisse

30. Those, then, who maintained that by "indivisible" Being Plato meant the form of the intelligible world, that which is forever the same and unchanging, and by "divisible" Being matter, claimed that, once the generation of the world had been established and a soul suitable for a living being which in some sense had yet to appear was being sought, it made no sense that the soul which was to give life to mute animals, plants, and trees should be said by Plato to exist anywhere, since neither the animals nor the trees and other things to which it was to give life had yet been born. And for that reason they claimed that by "indivisible" Being Plato meant the form of the intelligible world in whose likeness the sensible world was formed, and by "divisible" Being matter.

31. But those who maintained that from indivisible Being (i.e., soul which is immune to embodiment) and another form of Being which is the inseparable concomitant of body (i.e., vegetative soul) a third kind of soul (i.e., the rational) was formed supported their view as follows. First, they held that it would be utterly preposterous if, after the treatment earlier of the constitution of the world body and the shift thereafter to the generation of the soul which was to vivify the sensible world, there should be a return to the first treatment, resulting in a renewed treatment of matter, the bodies that make up the world, and their form, and a movement away from the generation of soul. Further, they held that the claim that the vegetative soul cannot yet exist since the living beings it was to vivify did not yet exist would be idle; for they held that there always existed the potentiality of both soul and body, and that god did not make the world from things that did not exist but rather gave order to things

mundum sed ea quae erant sine ordine ac modo ordinasse, itaque potius ea quae existebant exornasse quam generasse quae non erant, inordinatos quippe animi errores et agitationem fluctibus similem intellectu assignato ex inordinata iactatione ad ordinem redegisse, corporis etiam motum instabilem salubri moderataque agitatione frenasse et eidem formam et figuram congruam et convenientem ornatum dedisse, ut ipse in superioribus dixit: meliorem ordinatorum fortunam inordinatis ratus. Quare, cum sensili mundo conveniens anima instituatur, ortum eius ex individua una quae mens intellectusque est et alia quae per universa corpora dividitur et scinditur, provenire eamque mediam inter individuam et dividuam animas locatam, scilicet ut immunis quidem ab incorporatione in mundo esset intellegibili semper, stirpea mutis et item nihil sentientibus opitularetur. Haec vero media quia necesse erat in mundo fore genus animalium quod ratione uteretur, huic eidem generi vitam et spiritum ministraret interque duas posita naturas, eandem diversamque, modo eiusdem naturae contemplaretur divinitatem attollens aciem ad sublimia modo ad ima sedemque diversae naturae vergens haec etiam iuxta opificis scita dispensaret terrenisque impertiret providentiam.

32. Deinde progrediens ultra Plato demonstrat ipsam partitionem: unam sumpsit ex universo primitus portionem, post quam duplicem eius quam sumpserat, tertiam vero sescuplam quidem secundae, triplam vero primitus sumptae; at

that existed without order or limit, and hence that he conferred order on things that existed rather than generated things that did not, and that by conferring intellect he brought the disordered wanderings of the mind, its agitation resembling that of waves, from a disordered tossing about to order, and that he reined in the unstable movement of body too by a healthy and tempered agitation and conferred upon body suitable form, shape, and order, as he indicated earlier [30a]: *he considered the fortune of ordered things* preferable *to that of disordered ones.* They held that this, the establishment of a soul suitable for the sensible world, explains why its origin stems from the indivisible Being which is mind or intellect and another form of Being which is universally divided and distributed throughout bodies, and why it is situated intermediate between the indivisible and divisible souls, namely, so as to be forever in the intelligible world, immune to embodiment, while the vegetative soul sustains both dumb and nonsentient beings. And since it was necessary that there should be in the world a class of living beings which would employ reason, the intermediate soul was to administer life and spirit to the same, and being situated between the two natures, Same and Other, would by turns contemplate the divinity of the nature of the Same by raising its gaze on high and in turning down toward the realm of the nature of the Other provide dispensation for earthly things according to the decrees of their maker and confer providential order upon them.

32. Continuing, Plato then describes the actual partitioning [35b–c]: *first he took one portion from the whole, after which he took one double that which he had taken, and a third portion one and a half times the second and triple the one taken first; fourth, he*

vero quartam sumpsit duplicem secundae, quintam triplam tertiae; sexta fuit assumptio partibus septem quam prima propensior, septima sex et viginti partibus quam prima maior. In hac forma virium animae tamquam e speculo simulacrum resultat. Partitio quippe consideratio est virium ordinatioque veluti membrorum actuum eius officiorumque et omnium munerum designat congruentiam tribus hoc asserentibus praecipuis disciplinis, geometrica arithmetica harmonica, ex quibus geometrica vicem obtinet fundamentorum, ceterae vero superstructionis. Etenim quod nullas partes habet proptereaque sub nullos sensus venit est tamen et animo cernitur geometrae notam appellant, lineam vero sine latitudine prolixitatem quae in notas suas desinit, porro eam in qua est aliqua latitudo superficiem vocant ut sit superficies nacta latitudinem longitudo, quod vero ex tribus constat, id est longitudine latitudine profunditate, solidum corpus cognominant.

33. Ista ergo descriptio quae partium ex quibus anima constare dicitur genituram seu coagmentationem deliniat, ostendit rationem animae corporisque coniugii. Quippe corpus animalium, quod inspiratur animae vigore, habet certe superficiem, habet etiam soliditatem. Quae igitur cum vitali vigore penetratura erat tam superficiem quam soliditatem, similes soliditati, similes etiam superficiei vires habere debuit, siquidem paria paribus congregantur. Unam igitur primitus sumpsit, inquit, ex universo portionem. Quo universo? Quod ex tribus in unam speciem redactum, sicut supra demonstravit, essentia videlicet et eodem et diverso, dividebat. Portionis quoque elocutio notanda est, non enim

took a portion double the second, and fifth, one triple the third; the sixth portion taken was seven parts greater than the first, and the seventh twenty-six parts greater than the first. The figure above reflects as in a mirror an image of the powers of the soul. For the partitioning offers an ordered theoretical perspective on its powers and activities, as though on its parts, and it points to the congruence of all its tasks and functions as asserted by three disciplines in particular, geometry, arithmetic, and harmonic theory, of which geometry serves as a foundation and the others as a superstructure. For geometers refer to that which has no parts and is consequently imperceptible to any sensory faculties and yet exists and is discernible to the mind as a point, and to line as length which has no width and terminates at the points, and they call that a plane surface in which there is some width, such that a plane surface is length that has acquired width, and that which consists of three things, i.e., length, width, and depth, they refer to as a solid body. (See Diagram 7.)

33. Thus this diagram delineating the generation or coalescence of the parts from which soul is said to consist reveals the principle underlying the union of soul and body. The body possessed by living beings, which has the force of soul breathed into it, certainly has surface area and it has solidity. Since, then, soul was to permeate both surface area and solidity with its life force, it had to be endowed with powers resembling both solidity and surface area, since like joins with like. Hence he says, *first he took one portion from the whole* [35b–c]. Which whole? That which, as he explained earlier, he carved out of the three things, namely, Being, Same, and Other, and brought into unified form. The word "portion" should be noted as well, for he did not speak of the

partem (quippe simplicis et incorporeae rei) sed portionem, id est partis instar, dixit esse sublatum, quod est geometricae illius notae simile. Postea duplicem eius sumpsit quam sumpserat, hoc est duo, quae subter unum posita sunt in laeva parte formulae. Tertio sescuplam quidem secundae, triplam vero primitus sumptae. Merito; tria enim adversum duo sescupli ratione praecellunt, constant enim tria ex duobus et item uno, quod duum dimidia pars est. Quarto duplicem secundae, ideo quia bis duo quattuor. Quinto triplam tertiae, id est novem, ter enim tria novem sunt. Sexta fuit sumptio partibus septem quam prima propensior, id est in numero octonario, qui est ultimus in eo latere quod ex paribus numeris est ordinatum. Septima sex et viginti partibus quam prima maior, hoc est viginti septem, qui numerus tantum valet quantum octonarius, ut docebo. Apex ergo numerorum singularitas sine ullis partibus, ut geometrica nota; cuius duplum linea, sine latitudine longitudo; lineae duplum superficies, quae est prolixitas cum latitudine; cuius duplum cubus, corpus per longum latum profundumque divisum, bis duo bis, quod est octo. Eodemque modo iuxta rationem tripli in altero latere numerorum germanitas reperitur, cubusque qui est in summa viginti et septem primus est imparis numeri cubus, ter enim tria ter conficiunt summam supra dictam. Igitur secundum rationem continui competentis, quae est ratio geometrica, quod valet octo adversum quattuor, hoc quattuor adversum duo et duo adversum unum, rursus quod valet viginti septem numerus adversum novem, hoc novem adversum tria et tria adversum unum.

34. Quaeritur hoc loco primo quidem cur in tantum produxerit divisionem ut septem constitueret limites, terna autem in utrisque lateribus intervalla, tam in eo quod ex

thing removed, what approximates the geometrical point, as a part (namely, of a simple and incorporeal reality) but rather as a *portion,* i.e., something resembling a part. *After which he took another portion double that which he had taken,* i.e., 2, placed under 1 on the left of the diagram. *Third, a portion one and a half times the second and triple the one first taken.* Rightly so, for 3 exceeds 2 by the ratio of the sesquilater [3:2], for 3 = 2 + 1, which is half of 2. *Fourth, a portion double the second,* because 2 × 2 = 4. *Fifth, a portion triple the third,* i.e., 9, for 3 × 3 = 9. *The sixth portion taken was seven parts greater than the first,* i.e., the number 8, which is last on the side ordered according to even numbers. *The seventh twenty-six parts greater than the first,* i.e., 27, the number which corresponds precisely to 8, as I will explain. Now, the apex of these numerical series is a unity which like the geometrical point lacks parts of any kind; the double of which is a line, length without width; the double of the line is a plane surface, or length with width; the double of that is the cube, a body divisible into length, width, and depth, 2 × 2 × 2 [2^3], i.e., 8. Similarly, there is found on the other side an affinity between numbers in the ratio of the triple: the cube, in the sum of 27, is the first cubic power among odd numbers, for 3 × 3 × 3 [3^3] produces the sum indicated. Hence, according to the ratio of a continuous proportion, i.e., a geometric ratio, 8:4 = 4:2 = 2:1, and conversely, 27:9 = 9:3 = 3:1.

34. There arises, first, the question of why he extended the division up to the point of establishing seven terms and on either side three intervals based on ordered series of

duplicibus et paribus numeris est ordinatum quam in eo
quod ex triplicibus et imparibus; deinde quos oporteat numeros imponere partibus, si enim primam partem singulari-
tatem semper posuerimus et deinceps ceteras secundum
descriptionem, inter hos numeros duos alios qui compleant
universam intervallorum continuationem, sicut iubet fieri,
minime inveniemus; tertio qualis debeat esse forma descriptionis.

35. Quod igitur ex tribus principe loco diximus quaeri so-
lere, hoc primum demonstrandum erit, rationabiliter septem limites esse digestos quibus intervalla sex continentur.
Erit autem probatio auctoritatibus nixa. Etenim septem numerus laudatur a Pythagoreis ut optimus et naturalissimus
et sufficientissimus. Nam perfectus quidem numerus est
decem ideo, quod a singularitate orsi usque ad decem numerum numeramus, residua vero numeratio non tam numeratio est quam eorundem numerorum quibus ante usi sumus
in numerando replicatio; undecim enim et duodecim et
ceteri tales nascuntur ex praecedentium replicatione. Quem
quidem decimanum numerum Pythagorici appellant primam quadraturam propterea quod ex primis quattuor
numeris confit, uno duobus tribus quattuor. Symphoniae
quoque ratio ex eorundem numerorum qui decimanum numerum complent quasi quodam fonte demanat, siquidem ex
his epitriti et sescuplares et duplices et triplices et quadruplices numeri sonique nascuntur: epitriti quidem ut quattuor adversum tres, habent enim totum numerum trientem
et eius tertiam partem, id est unum; sescuplares vero ut tres
adversum duo, habent enim tres totum numerum dualem et
eius partem dimidiam, id est unum; duplices vero ut sunt
duo adversus unum; triplices porro ut sunt tres adversus

numbers, the multiples of 2 (and even) and those of 3 (and odd); second, the question of the numbers which we should assign to the parts, for if we consistently posit unity, as the first part and with additional instances thereafter, as in the diagram, then between these numbers we will not find the two others to complete a full continuity of intervals as he instructs us to do; third, the question of which shape the diagram ought to take.

35. In answer, then, to the first of the three questions we mentioned as traditionally having been raised, it should be demonstrated first that seven terms embracing six intervals are set out on the basis of ratios. The proof will be based on authorities. 7 is extolled by the Pythagoreans as the most noble, natural, and self-sufficient number. The number 10 is perfect in the sense that beginning with unity we count up to 10, whereas thereafter it is not so much counting as a replication of numbers previously employed in the process of counting, since 11, 12, and the others like them result from replication of previous numbers. The Pythagoreans refer to the number 10 as the primary square on the grounds that it is the composite of the first four numbers, 1, 2, 3, 4. Harmonic ratio as well flows from a sort of fountainhead, as it were, of the same four numbers which make up 10, since from them arise numbers and musical intervals in the ratios of the *epitriton,* sesquialter, double, triple, and quadruple: the *epitriton,* as in 4:3, comprising the whole of 3 and a third thereof, i.e., 1; the sesquialter, as in 3:2, comprising the whole of 2 and a half thereof, i.e., 1; the double, as in 2:1; the triple,

unum; et quadruplices ut sunt quattuor adversus unum. Epitritus autem in calculando idem est qui diatessaron dicitur in canendo, sescuplaris vero idem est qui diapente dicitur in canendo, duplex vero qui diapason dicitur in canendo, quadruplex qui disdiapason dicitur in canendo.

36. Deinde alia quoque septenarii numeri proprietas consideratur, quam ceteri numeri non habent, siquidem, cum alii numeri, qui finibus decimani numeri continentur, partim ipsi alios pariant, partim ab aliis pariantur, partim et pariant alios et pariantur ab aliis, solus septenarius numerus neque gignat ex se alium numerum infra decimanum limitem neque a quoquam ipse nascatur. Etenim duo duplicati pariunt quattuor numerum; tria nullo duplicato nascuntur, ipsa autem duplicata pariunt senarium numerum; quattuor numerus et paritur et parit—paritur quidem a bis duobus parit autem duplicatus octonarium numerum; rursum quinque numerus a nullo nascitur bis supputato, ipse autem bis supputatus parit decem; item sex numerus nascitur quidem ex duplicato triente parit autem infra decimanum limitem neminem; octavus nascitur ex bis supputatis quattuor, ipse neminem parit; nonus nascitur ex ter tribus, ipse autem neminem parit; decimus nascitur ex duplicato numero quinque, ipse porro neminem parit. Itaque omnibus partim nascentibus, partim parientibus, partim et nascentibus et parientibus solus septenarius numerus neque ex duplicatione alterius nascitur nec infra decimanum limitem parit quemquam proptereaque Minerva est a veteribus cognominatus: item ut illa sine matre perpetuoque virgo.

37. Naturalis vero atque optimus habetur idcirco quia multa eorum quae naturae lege proveniunt iuxta hunc

as in 3:1; and the quadruple, as in 4:1. Now, for purposes of calculation the *epitriton* is the same as that which in harmonic terms is called the *diatessaron* [fourth], while the sesquialter is the same as the *diapente* [fifth], the double the same as the *diapason* [octave], and the quadruple the same as the *disdiapason* [double octave].

36. Next, a further property of the number 7 which the other numbers lack comes under consideration; for although the other numbers 10 and below by turns generate other numbers, are generated by them, or both generate and are generated by them, only the number 7 neither generates from itself nor is itself generated by any other number within the limit 10. For when doubled 2 generates the number 4; 3 is not generated by doubling any other but when doubled itself generates the number 6; the number 4 both is generated and generates—is generated by the doubling of 2 and generates the number 8 when doubled; again, the number 5 is not generated by doubling any other but when doubled itself generates 10; likewise, the number 6 is generated from the doubling of 3 but generates no number within the limit 10; 8 is generated from the doubling of 4 but itself generates none; 9 is generated from the tripling 3 but generates none; 10 is generated from the doubling of 5 but itself generates none. And so, whereas all of the numbers are either generated, generative, or both, the number 7 alone neither is generated by the doubling of another nor generates any at all within the limit 10, and for that reason the ancients named it Minerva: like her, motherless and forever a maiden.

37. The number 7 is considered natural and the most noble owing to the fact that many of the things which occur according to the law of nature are seen to emerge in

numerum fieri notantur. Principio septimani partus ante ceteros legitimi sunt in generis humani fetibus; deinde quod post partum septimo mense dentes aguntur septimo deinceps anno mutantur. Idem quoque secunda hebdomade pubertatem affert utrique sexui gignendique et pariendi maturitatem. Tertia vero hebdomade ostentat se flos et lanugo circa genas. Quarta vero hebdomade definiuntur incrementa staturae, quinta plenam iuvenilis aetatis affert perfectionem. In aegritudinibus quoque iuxta eundem numerum motus fieri usus experientiaque docuit et Hippocrates cum saepe alias in plerisque libris suis tum etiam in his evidenter quos de hebdomadibus instituit. Dinumerantur quoque sensuum omnium qui sunt in capite septem meatus (oculorum aurium narium atque oris), vitalia quoque paris numeri (lingua pulmo cor lien hepar duo renes). Vocalium quoque litterarum numerus idem ex quibus consonantium confragositas levigatur. Lunae quoque crescentis et senescentis multiformis illa transfiguratio in eodem numero notatur, siquidem de obscura crescente lumine fit bicornis, dehinc sectilis, dehinc dimidiato maior, dehinc plena retrorsumque maior dimidiato sectilis bicornis. Quid quod in mundo septem sunt planetes distantes a se musico modulamine, sicut ipse testatur cum dicit deum sexies scidisse diversae naturae circulum septemque orbes impares esse fabricatum, qui contrariis motibus agitationibusque vertantur iuxta dupli et tripli spatia, in quibus solem et lunam et ceteros erraticos ignes collocat.

connection with this number. First, seven-month births, those occurring prior to others, are legitimate for human offspring; then again, there is the fact that teeth are produced in the seventh month after birth and then replaced in the seventh year. In the second seven-year period the same number produces puberty and the maturity required for each sex to reproduce and procreate. In the third seven-year period the first hints of a beard reveal themselves on the cheeks, while in the fourth full bodily height is achieved, and the fifth brings full completion of the stage of life associated with youth. Practice and experience have shown that developments in diseases too occur in accordance with patterns which reflect the same number, as Hippocrates repeatedly taught in numerous works, most obviously those in which he treated of seven-day cycles. Again, the sensory channels in the head total seven in number (eyes, ears, nostrils, and mouth), and the vital organs the same (tongue, lung, heart, spleen, liver, two kidneys). Also, the vowels, which smooth the harsh gaps between consonants, are the same in number. The manifold transformations of the Moon as it waxes and wanes are observed to be the same in number, since from its obscure phase it becomes crescent as its light increases, then quarter, then greater than half, then full, and then back: greater than half, quarter, crescent. What of the fact that the world has seven planets, each different from the others in its harmonic modulation? He himself testifies to this when he says [36d] that god *cut* the circle derived from the nature of the other *six ways* and *fashioned seven disparate spheres,* which in contrary patterns of movement revolve *according to the intervals of the double and triple,* and in those orbits he places the Sun, Moon, and other wandering luminaries.

38. Et limitum quidem septem sic ratio praestatur; intervallorum vero ternorum hanc dicunt esse rationem: Rursus enim tria numerus alio quodam genere habetur optimus. Primus enim et ante omnes perfectus est habens initium finem medietatem quibus crescunt corpora et iuxta quae corporea incrementa progrediuntur, quippe cum intervallum unum lineam faciat, duo superficiem, tria corpus indivisum atque individuum, quo nihil est perfectius; tria enim haec intervalla corpus absolvunt, longitudo latitudo soliditas. Certe tria primitus dicta sunt omnia, quod de duobus dici non potest, utrumque enim dicitur de duobus. Haec igitur terna intervalla in utroque latere descriptionis sita sex intervalla conficiunt, et senarius numerus plenus et perfectus merito habetur, quippe qui sit aequalis his partibus ex quibus ipse constat; habet enim dimidietatem in tribus, habet tertiam portionem in duobus, habet sextam in uno, quae simul atque in unum collecta complent eundem. Denique qui ab eo quadratus nascitur, id est triginta et sex numerus, secunda dicitur quadratura constans ex quattuor quidem imparibus numeris, hoc est uno tribus quinque septem, et ex aliis paribus numeris quattuor aeque, id est duobus quattuor sex octo. Rursum quinquaginta et quattuor numerus qui nascitur ex triangulo supra descripto tertia quadratura cognominatur, quia continet quattuor quidem limites in duplici latere, hoc est unum duos quattuor octo, quattuor vero alios in eo latere quod ex triplicibus compositum est, uno tribus novem viginti septem, communi videlicet accepta singularitate, quae est utriusque lateris caput ideoque singularitas par atque impar habetur. Iure igitur septem quidem limites constituuntur, terna vero per utrumque latus intervalla cernuntur, nam singularitas initium est numerorum

38. Thus the explanation offered for the seven terms; as to the three intervals, they claim that the explanation is as follows: The number 3 is in turn considered most noble, in another sense. It is first and before all others in perfection, having a beginning, end, and middle, the stages through which bodies grow and according to which corporeal growth progresses: a single interval produces the line, two the plane figure, and three the indivisible or individual body which nothing exceeds in perfection, for the three intervals that make a body complete are these: length, width, and solidity. To be sure, all things are said in the first instance to be three, which cannot be said of duality, for of duality one thing or the other is said. Now, the three intervals situated on either side of the diagram bring the total up to six, and the number 6 too is rightly considered to be a full and perfect number, being equal to the parts of which it consists; for its half is 3, its third 2, and its sixth 1, and these three when added together make the very same number. Then, the square produced by it, i.e., 36 [6^2], is called the secondary square, consisting of four odd numbers (1, 3, 5, 7) and four even ones as well (2, 4, 6, 8). Again, the number 54 that arises from the triangular diagram above is called the tertiary square, containing four terms on the side of the double multiples (1, 2, 4, 8) and four others on the side of the triple ones (1, 3, 9, 27), namely, with 1 taken in common, since as the apex of each side it is held to be both equal and odd. It is right, then, that seven terms are established and three intervals discernible on either side, for unity is the beginning point of numbers

paris et imparis, proptereaque par et impar habetur et omnes in se formas numerorum creditur continere, epipedam
triangularem cubum. Quae singula persequi longum est; suf-
ficiat igitur demonstrasse rationem nascentis animae, quae
incorporationi erat destinata, quod orsa a singularitate
individua atque incorporea re gradatim per lineam et superficiem increverit usque ad perfectum corpus prolixitatis latitudinis profunditatisque intervallis proptereaque tam sub-
tilia quam solida penetret mundi sensilis corpora.

39. Nunc praestanda est ratio formae istius triangularis,
in qua sunt limites septem et sex intervalla duplicis et triplicis quantitatis. Nullam dico esse aptiorem figuram quam est
haec, in qua singularitas cacumini superimposita summitatem atque arcem obtinere consideratur, ut per eam velut
emissaculum quoddam tamquam e sinu fontis perennis providae intellegentiae quasi quidam largus amnis efflueret
ipsaque singularitas mens sive intellegentia vel ipse deus
opifex intellegatur esse. Cum enim sit origo numerorum
omnibusque ex se substantiam subministret rationesque
eorum tam simplices quam multiplicatas ipsa contineat, ceteris numeris incrementis imminutionibusque mutatis atque ex propria natura recedentibus, sola inconcusso iure est
atque in statu suo perseverat semper eadem, semper immutabilis et singularitas semper, quem ad modum divina omnia
quae nulla temporis progressione mutantur suntque semper
impetibili felicitate.

even and odd, and is for that reason considered to be both, and is held to contain within itself all of the shapes, plane, triangular, and cubic, associated with numbers. To go through them all would be a long task; let it therefore suffice as an account of the origins of the soul that was destined for embodiment to have shown that, arising from an indivisible unity and incorporeal reality, it increased in stages, through the line and plane surface to body replete with the intervals associated with length, width, and depth, thus permeating the bodies both fine and dense in the sensible world.

39. An explanation should now be offered for the triangular shape in which are the seven terms and six *intervals of the multiples of the double and triple* [35c–36a]. The point I am making is that no shape is more suitable than this one, in which the unity placed at the top is seen to hold the place of the summit or pinnacle, so that through it as a kind of conduit, so to speak, a certain bountiful river, as it were, might flow as if from the depths of the perennial fount of provident intelligence and the unity itself be understood to be mind, intelligence, or the craftsman god himself. For as the origin of numbers, providing from itself being for all things and itself embracing both the simple and manifold rational principles that determine them, it is alone in its inviolable sovereignty and perseveres, forever the same in its proper state, forever immutable, forever a unity, like all things divine, which are unaltered by any temporal progression and exist forever in a state of impassible felicity; all this, while through increase and decrease the other numbers undergo change and recede from their proper nature.

3. De Modulatione sive Harmonia

40. Deinde prosequitur Plato: Quibus ita divisis consequenter complebat intervalla duplicis et triplicis quantitatis ex universitate partes secans etiam nunc et ex his intervallorum spatia complens, quo singula intervalla binis medietatibus fulcirentur. Medietatum porro altera quota parte limitis extimi praecellebat unum extimum limitem, tota praecellebatur ab alio extimo limite, altera pari summa et aequali ad numerum modo praecellebat et praecellebatur ab extimis. Ut harmonici modulantes organa inter duos extimarum fidium limites, gravissimae hypates et acutissimae netes, alias internectunt medias dispari strepitu tinnituque chordas, quae mediae sunt acutiores quidem primo limite graviores autem ultimo, atque ita per accentum ad acuminis postremi sonum pervenitur, qua pererrat digitorum et pectinis pulsus, sic deus animam mundi modulans inducitur sex illa intervalla duplicis et triplicis quantitatis singula binis medietatibus stipans, ita ut una ex duabus medietas potior sit minore limite tertia eius parte, maiore autem limite inferior eadem tertia parte maioris limitis. Describenda est itaque figura similis eius, quae paulo superius exscripta est, solis ab ea numeris distans ita ut maiores numeri contineantur quorum intervalla binum medietatum capiant interiectionem.

41. Quia sex numerus facit unum limitem et item duodecim secundum efficit limitem iuxta rationem duplicis quantitatis et a se distant, interponuntur duae medietates, una octonarii numeri altera novenarii. Ergo octo numerus adversum sex limitem comparatus praecedit eum tertia eiusdem

3. ON HARMONIC MODULATION

40. Plato goes on to say [35c–36a]: *When they had been divided thus he then filled the intervals of the multiples of the double and triple, cutting parts now from the whole and with them filling the spaces between the intervals so that each of the intervals would be braced by two means. Of the means, moreover, one exceeded the one extreme by the same portion of the extreme as that by which it was exceeded by the other extreme,* while *the other exceeded and was exceeded by the extremes in the same and equal numerical measure.* As when musicians in tuning instruments within the two extremes set by the outer strings, the lowest being the *hypate* and the highest the *nete,* insert other intermediate ones of varying tone and pitch, ones higher than the lowest but lower than the highest, and by way of the attunement work their way up to the tone associated with the final pitch, like the plucking by fingers or plectrum up and down the scale, so god is represented as attuning the world soul, filling each of the six *intervals of the multiples of the double and triple by two means,* such that that of the two means one is greater than the smaller term by a third of it but smaller than the greater term by the same proportion, a third, of it. So a diagram similar to the one sketched out a while back must be drawn, differing only in the numbers, such that larger numbers whose intervals capture the intercalation of two means are contained therein.

41. Given that the number 6 constitutes one term and 12 a second, and that the difference between them is in the ratio of the double, two means are intercalated, one of them being the number 8 and the other 9. Now, the number 8 relative to the term 6 exceeds the same term 6 by a third, i.e., by

senarii limitis portione, id est duobus, ipse autem praeceditur tertia portione duodecim limitis, id est quattuor; sic una
medietas octo numeri quota parte praecedit senarium limitem, tota praeceditur a duodecim limite. Rursum novem
medietas altera praecedit sex limitem tribus numeris et
praeceditur a duodecim limite isdem aeque tribus. Nec immerito; octo enim adversum sex comparata epitrito potiora
sunt, epitritum autem dicunt intervallum quotiens numero
ad numerum comparato maior minorem totum in se continet et eius tertiam portionem; aeque duodecim limes adversum novem, unam ex medietatibus, comparatus epitritus
eius esse invenitur, continet enim totum novem et eius tertiam portionem. Rursumque duum medietatum intervallum
epogdoum est; novenarius enim numerus totum octonarium
in se continet et eius octavam portionem, id est unum. Sic
duae medietates praecellunt limites et a limitibus praecel-
luntur duplici diversaque ratione, altera partibus altera numeris, sicut ostensum est.

42. Haec eadem ratio etiam in triplicibus numeris invenitur. Sex enim limes unus distans a decem et octo altero
limite intervallum quod interiacet triplum esse demonstrat
in altero formulae latere. Sunt hic quoque duae medietates,
una in novem altera in duodecim numeris: novem medietas
adversum sex limitem comparata sescuplo superat, habet
enim totum sex et eius dimidiam portionem, id est tres; eadem adversum decem et octo limitem comparata duplo
praeceditur, bis enim novem decem et octo sunt. Rursum
alia medietas, id est duodecim, si adversum sex limitem
comparetur, duplo praecellit, si vero adversum alium qui
maior est, id est decem et octo, sex numeris minor invenitur,
qui sex numeris aeque potior erat senario limite. Haec

2 [8:6 = 4:3], but is itself exceeded by a third of the term 12, i.e., by 4 [12/3 = 4 + 8 = 12]; so the one mean, the number 8, exceeds the limit 6 *by the same portion as that by which* it is exceeded by the limit 12. Again, the other mean, 9, exceeds the term 6 by the number 3 and is equally exceeded by the term 12 by *the same* 3 [12 − 9 = 9 − 6 = 3]. And rightly so, for 8 relative to 6 is greater by an *epitriton* [8:6 = 4:3], and they refer to the *epitriton* as the interval that obtains whenever of two proportionately related numbers the greater contains within itself the whole of the smaller and a third thereof; the limit 12 relative to 9 (one of the means) is found equally to be its *epitriton*, for it contains the whole of 9 and a third thereof [12:9 = 4:3]. And again, the interval between the two means is the *epogdoon*, for the number 9 contains within itself the whole of 8 and an eighth thereof, i.e., 1 [9:8]. In this way the two means exceed and are exceeded by the terms according to two distinct ratios, one proportional and the other numerical, as has been shown. (See Diagram 8.)

42. This same ratio is found also among the numerical multiples of 3. For on the other side of the diagram the limit 6 shows, in its distance from the other limit, 18, that the intervening interval is the triple. Here too there are two means, one the number 9 and the other the number 12. Relative to the limit 6 the mean 9 exceeds by the sesquialter, for it has the whole of 6 and a half thereof, i.e., 3 [9:6 = 3:2]; relative to the limit 18 the same mean is exceeded by the ratio of the double, for 2 × 9 = 18. Again, when compared with the limit 6 the other mean, i.e., 12, exceeds by the double, whereas if compared with the other, greater one, i.e., 18, it is found to be smaller by the number 6, and it was greater than the limit 6 in equal measure, by the number 6 [18 − 6 = 12 − 6

eadem ratio invenitur inter alios quoque duos limites dupli ratione distantes, id est duodecim et viginti quattuor, nam et hic medietas sedecim duodecim limitem epitriti ratione praecedit, viginti quattuor quoque limes decem et octo medietatem epitriti ratione praecellit. Et rursum viginti quattuor limes adversum quadraginta et octo dupli ratione distat et medietates habet, unam triginta et duo aliam triginta et sex: triginta et duo medietas adversum viginti et quattuor limitem comparata facit intervallum epitritae quantitatis, habet enim totum viginti quattuor et eius tertiam portionem, id est octo; quadraginta et octo vero limes triginta et sex numeri, quae medietas est altera, epitritus est, continet enim in se totum triginta et sex numerum et eius tertiam portionem, id est duodecim, triginta et sex enim et duodecim complent numerum quadraginta et octo.

43. Haec eadem ratio invenitur etiam in eo latere quod ex triplicibus numeris est ordinatum. Quia igitur novem et octo epogdoum faciunt spatium et ex his duo limites dupli ratione distantes, id est sex et duodecim, complentur, recte dixit epogdoi spatio epitritorum omnium intervalla compleri. Rursum enim decem et octo numerus adversum decem et sex numerum epogdoi rationem obtinet, ex quibus duabus medietatibus epogdoum spatium habentibus duodecim limitis et viginti quattuor aeque limitis intervallum completur. Rursum viginti et quattuor limitis et quadraginta octo spatium complent duae medietates epogdoae, id est triginta sex et triginta duo. Evidenter itaque epogdoi spatio epitritorum intervalla complentur.

44. Deinde prosequitur: ita ut ad perfectam cumulatamque perfectionem deesset aliquid epitrito, tantum scilicet quantum deest habita comparatione ducentis quadra-

= 6]. This same ratio is found also between two other limits separated by the ratio of the double, i.e., 12 and 24, for here too the mean 16 exceeds the limit 12 by the ratio of an *epitriton* [16:12 = 4:3], and the limit 24 exceeds the mean 18 by the ratio of an *epitriton* as well [24:18 = 4:3]. And again, relative to 48 the limit 24 differs by the ratio of the double and has one mean in 32 and the other in 36: relative to the limit 24 the mean 32 produces an interval measuring an *epitriton,* for it has the whole of 24 and a third thereof, i.e., 8 [32:24 = 4:3]; and the limit 48 is the *epitriton* of the number 36, the other mean, for it contains within itself the whole of the number 36 and a third thereof, i.e., 12, for 36 + 12 = 48 [48:36 = 4:3].

43. This same ratio is found also on the side ordered according to multiples of 3. Thus, given that 9 and 8 produce the interval of an *epogdoon* [9:8] and that they fill the two limits separated by the ratio of the double, i.e., 6 and 12, he rightly said that *the intervals of all the epitrita are filled by that of an epogdoon* [36b]. Again, the number 18 relative to the number 16 brings the ratio of an *epogdoon* [18:16 = 9:8], and these two means separated by the interval of an *epogdoon* fill the interval between the limits 12 and 24. Again, two epogdoic means, i.e., 36 and 32, fill the interval between the limits 24 and 48 [36:32 = 9:8]. Thus the evidence for *the intervals of the epitrita being filled by that of an epogdoon.*

44. He goes on to say [36b]: *such that in relation to the whole and aggregate process of completion something was lacking to the epitriton, namely, the amount lacking when the ratio of 243:256 is formed.* What does he intend to be understood? I will get to that after explaining the points that have to be made first. Just as the principal and maximal parts of articulated spoken sound are nouns and verbs, and their parts syllables, and the

ginta tribus adversum ducentos quinquaginta sex. Quid est
quod vult intellegi? Dicam, sed quae ante dicenda sunt prius
explicabo. Etenim quem ad modum articulatae vocis principales sunt et maximae partes nomina et verba, horum autem
syllabae, syllabarum litterae, quae sunt primae voces individuae atque elementariae (ex his enim totius orationis constituitur continentia et ad postremas easdem litteras disso-
lutio pervenit orationis), ita etiam canorae vocis, quae a
Graecis emmeles dicitur et est modis numerisque composita, principales quidem partes sunt hae quae a musicis appellantur systemata. Haec autem ipsa constant ex <partibus
quae existunt ex> certo <con>tractu pronuntiationis quae
dicuntur diastemata, diastematum porro ipsorum partes
sunt pthongi, qui a nobis vocantur soni; hi autem soni prima
sunt fundamenta cantus. Est autem in sonis differentia iuxta
chordarum intentionem, siquidem acuti soni vehementius
et citius percusso aere excitantur, graviores autem quotiens
leniores et tardiores pulsus erunt. Et accentus quidem existunt ex nimio incitatoque pulsu, succentus vero leni et tar-
diore, ex accentibus porro et succentibus variata ratione
musicae cantilena symphonia dicitur. Prima igitur symphonia in quattuor primis modulis invenitur quae diatessaron
dicitur, secunda vero quae ex quinque primis modulis constat diapente cognominata est, quibus compositis in ordinem nascitur ea cantilena quae epogdous, et diapason,
vocatur. Propterea epogdous quia veteres musici octo solis
chordis utebantur, quarum princeps erat hypate edens gra-
vissimum sonum, ultima vero nete acutum edens sonum, qui
duo diversi soni habent inter se miro quodam genere concentum et consonantiam. Post vero aucta musica est as-
sumptis in utramque partem pluribus fidibus, priores tamen

parts of syllables letters, which are the primary, indivisible, and elemental spoken sounds (for from them the structure of the whole of speech is built up, and into them as well speech is finally resolved), so too of musical sound, which is called *emmelês* by the Greeks and consists of numerical measures, the principal parts are those which are called *systêmata* [systems] by musicians. And these in turn consist of parts which result from a fixed contraction in pronunciation and are called *diastêmata* [intervals], and the parts of the *diastêmata* are in turn *phthongi,* which we call sounds; and these sounds are the primary foundations of song. Now, there is a difference between musical sounds depending on the tension of the strings, for acute sounds are generated when air is the more intensely and rapidly set in vibration, and lower ones whenever the impulses are less intense and slower. Rises in pitch result from the intense and rapid impulse, and drops in pitch from the calm and slower one, and the musical accord resulting from variation in the relation between rises and drops is called a *symphonia* [consonance]. The first consonance, then, is found in the first four unit notes, and it is called the *diatessaron* [fourth], while the second, which consists of the first five notes, is called the *diapente* [fifth], and when they have been arranged in order there arises the musical accord called the *epogdoon* [whole tone], and that called the *diapason* [octave]. The *epogdoon,* because ancient musicians employed only eight strings, the first of which was the *hypatê,* which produces the lowest pitch, and the last the *nêtê,* which produces the high one, and together these two different pitches produce a harmony and consonance of a certain wonderous kind. With time the musical range increased as numerous strings were added on either side, but

symphoniae perseverant in suo nomine et ex his hae, quae addebantur, componebantur, ut diapason: adiuncta sibi ea quae diatessaron dicitur, adiuncta quoque alia diapente, accepit duplicem perfectionem proptereaque disdiapason vocatur.

45. Hos igitur concinentes sibi invicem sonos primus dicitur Pythagoras notasse et intellexisse habere aliquam cum numeris germanitatem. Itaque diatessaron cantilenam dixit eandem habere rationem quam habet epitritus in numeris, rursum diapente symphoniam habere rationem similem eius quantitatis quae est sescuplaris in numeris, diapason vero vim obtinere duplicis quantitatis. Itaque comparationem fecit huius modi ut diapason et diatessaron symphonias tantam habere differentiam diceret quantam habent inter se octo et tria, octo enim <adversum tria> et duplex est et [bis] epitritus trium numeri. Rursum diapason et diapente rationem obtinere dixit tripli, at vero disdiapason quadrupli, tonon vero epogdoi dixit habere rationem. Hemitonium quod dicitur, a veteribus autem dihesis appellabatur, limma cognominavit; limma vero est cum aliquid deest integritati, hoc ipsum quod deest, id est hemitonium sive limma, dixit [hanc] habere rationem quam habent inter se numeri comparati, id est ducentorum quinquaginta sex summa adversum summam ducentorum quadraginta trium. Experiendo ad disciplinam harum rerum atque intellectum vocatus suspendit, [enim] opinor, momenta ponderum certa chordis aequalibus tam in prolixitate quam in crassitudine et invenit eum qui tonos dicitur in octo esse momentis.

the original consonances preserve their nomenclature and from them were composed those that were added, as in the case of the *diapason:* when the consonance called the *diatessaron* is joined to it and a further *diapente* is joined as well, it obtains a full doubling and is for that reason called a *disdiapason.*

45. Pythagoras, then, is said to have been the first to remark these mutually concordant pitches and to grasp that they have a particular affinity with numbers. Thus he said that the *diatessaron* accord [fourth] has the same ratio as the numerical *epitriton* [4:3], further, that the *diapente* consonance [fifth] has a ratio comparable to the quantity of the numerical sesquialter [3:2], and that the *diapason* [octave] has the force of a doubling in quantity [2:1]. Thus he formed the comparison in such a way as to say that *diapason* + *diatessaron* consonances [octave + fourth] have the same difference as 8 and 3 have relative to one another, for 8:3 combines the double and the *epitriton* of the number 3 [2:1 × 4:3]. Again, he said that the *diapason* + *diapente* [octave + fifth] has the ratio of 3:1 [2:1 × 3:2] and the *disdiapason* [double octave] that of 4:1 [2:1 × 2:1], and that the whole tone has the ratio of an *epogdoon* [9:8]. That which is called a semitone but was called a *diesis* by the ancients, he named a *leimma;* there is a *leimma* when the whole lacks something, and he said that in this case the lacking element, i.e., the semitone or *leimma,* has the ratio which [two] numbers have relative to one another, i.e., the sum of 256:243. Being drawn to a scientific understanding of these matters by a process of experimentation, I suppose, he suspended fixed units of weight from strings that were equal in both length and density and discovered that the so-called whole tone was of eight units.

4. De Numeris

46. Ita symphonia musicae symphoniae numerorum concinere invenitur. Quia igitur diapason ex duabus primigenis cantilenis diatessaron et diapente constat, ratio autem diapason quidem in duplici quantitate posita invenitur, diatessaron vero in epitrito, diapente autem in sescuplo, etiam is numerus, quem in duplici quantitate diximus inveniri, constet necesse est ex epitrito et sescuplo. Etenim octo numerus sex numeri epitritus est, octo vero numeri duodecim numerus sescuplaris. Duodecim igitur numerus sex numeri duplex, qui dividitur in epitritam rationem, duodecim adversum novem, et aliam sescuplarem, novem adversum sex. Rursum diapente adversum diatessaron symphoniam praecellit uno tono, quippe diapente constat ex tribus tonis et hemitonio, diatessaron vero ex duobus tonis et hemitonio, id est dimidio tono, ex quo apparet tonon in epogdoa ratione inveniri et sescuplum modum epitrito modo potiorem esse ratione epogdoa; siquidem ex sescuplo, ut puta novem adversum sex, sublato epitrito octo adversum sex, superest epogdous modus, id est novem adversum octo. Item quia diapason symphonia in duplici modo posita invenitur, diatessaron autem in epitrito, quod ex his confit in ea ratione positum dinoscitur in qua est octo numerus adversum tria numerum; etenim trium epitrita sunt quattuor, horum duplicia octo. Diapason autem et diapente in ratione tripla, sescuplaris enim et duplex simul compositi efficiunt hunc eundem, id est decem et octo, quippe novem adversum sex comparatus sescuplaris invenitur, cuius decem et octo numerus duplex est, triplex vero adversum sex comparatus. Similiter etiam ea symphonia, quae disdiapason appellatur,

4. ON NUMBERS

46. Thus musical concordance is found to harmonize with numerical concordance. Since, then, the *diapason* consists of two primary consonances, the *diatessaron* and *diapente,* and its ratio is found to consist in the quantity of the double, while the *diatessaron* is in the *epitriton* and the *diapente* in the *sesquialter,* that number too which we said is found in the quantity of the double [2:1] necessarily consists of the *epitriton* + *sesquialter* [4:3 × 3:2]. For the number 8 is the *epitriton* of the number 6, and the number 12 is the *sesquialter* of the number 8. The number 12, then, is double the number 6, and this pair breaks down into the ratio of an *epitriton,* 12:9, as also into that of a *sesquialter,* 9:6. Again, the *diapente* exceeds the concordance of the *diatessaron* by a whole tone, since it consists of three tones and a semitone, and the *diatessaron* of two tones and a semitone, i.e., half a whole tone, and from this it is evident that the whole tone is found in the epogdoic ratio and that the measure of the *sesquialter* exceeds the measure of the *epitriton* by the ratio of the *epogdoon;* for of the *sesquialter,* e.g., 9:6, there remains, once the *epitriton* 8:6 has been removed, the measure of the *epogdoon,* i.e., 9:8. Likewise, since the concordance of the *diapason* is found to consist in the measure of the double and the *diatessaron* in the *epitriton,* what results from them can be seen to consist in the ratio of 8:3, for 4 is the *epitriton* of 3 and 8 the double of 4. The *diapason* + *diapente,* however, is in the ratio of 3:1, for when combined the *sesquialter* and double together produce this same triple number, i.e., 18, for 9 relative to 6 is found to be a *sesquialter* and its double is the number 18, or 3 × 6. Similarly, the concordance known as the *disdiapason* is

rationem obtinet quadrupli; additus enim triplex numerus epitrito numero complet quadruplam quantitatem, et diapente symphonia addita diapason symphoniae triplam efficit quantitatem, diatessaron vero symphonia epitrita ratio est, ut saepe iam diximus. Ex his autem disdiapason constat symphonia, etenim decem et octo numerus sex numerum triplo anteit, hunc ipsum autem decem et octo numerum epitriti ratione praecellit viginti et quattuor numerus, viginti et quattuor autem numerus adversum sex comparatus quater tantus est. Rursumque sex numeri epitritus est octonarius numerus, huius autem ipsius triplus est is qui in viginti quattuor momentis invenitur; idem autem viginti quattuor numerus sex numeri quadruplus invenitur.

47. His igitur in hunc modum peragratis ad ordinationis ipsius considerationem revertamur. Natis itaque limitibus sescuplorum et item eorum quibus accedit pars sui tertia, quod genus a Graecis epitritum dicitur, et item eorum quibus accedit pars sui octava, qui numerus epogdous ab isdem vocatur, ex his nexibus illa prima spatia, id est epogdoi spatiis epitritorum omnia intervalla complebat. Quae sunt igitur illa prima spatia? Illa scilicet quae continentur primitus descripta forma, quae ex duplicibus numeris est ordinata, in qua nascuntur sescuplares et epitriti, in hac vero quae secundo loco descripta est inveniuntur nasci epogdoi numeri qui toni sunt. Deinde ait epogdoi spatiis epitrita omnia compleri, hoc est etiam illa epitrita quae sunt in sescuplaribus numeris, nam et in his epitrita ratio continetur, propterea quod epogdoa supputatione maior est sescuplaris numerus epitrito numero, id est uno tono. Eadem epitriti

in the ratio of 4:1; for when added to the numerical *epitriton* the triple makes up a quadruple value [3:1 × 4:3], and when added to the *diapason* concordance the *diapente* concordance produces a triple value, whereas the *diatessaron* concordance is the ratio of an *epitriton,* as we have repeatedly indicated. And the *disdiapason* concordance consists of these, for the number 18 is three times greater than the number 6, but the number 24 exceeds the number 18 by the ratio of an *epitriton,* whereas relative to 6 the number 24 is four times greater. Again, the number 8 is the *epitriton* of the number 6, while its triple is found to be of 24 units, and the same number 24 is found to be 4 × 6.

47. Now that these points have been reviewed thus, let us return to consideration of the next section in the text [36a–b]: *And so, there having arisen thus the terms of the sesquialters and of those on which a third part supervenes, the kind called the epitriton by the Greeks, and of those on which an eighth part supervenes, the number referred to by them as the epogdoon, on the basis of these bonds he filled the first intervals, i.e., with intervals of an epogdoon he filled all the intervals of the epitrita.* What, then, are the *first intervals?* Obviously those which are contained in the figure drawn first [Diagram 7], the one ordered according to a double set of numbers among which the numerical *sesquialters* and *epitrita* emerge, whereas in the one drawn second [Diagram 8] the numerical *epogdoa* or tones are found to emerge. Then he says that *all* of the *epitrita* were filled with the *intervals of an epogdoon,* i.e., even those *epitrita* which are within numerical *sesquialters,* for within the latter is also contained the ratio of an *epitriton* in that the numerical *sesquialter* exceeds the numerical *epitriton* by the value of an *epogdoon,* i.e., by one whole tone. The same ratio of the

ratio etiam in duplici et triplici quantitate contineatur necesse est; nec immerito, prima enim symphonia est haec
ipsa quae appellatur diatessaron, in epitrito modo posita. Et
quia epitritus non solum ex duobus epogdois constat sed
etiam ex alio quoque, aliquantulo scilicet, sicut diatessaron
non ex solis duobus tonis constat sed ex hemitonio quod veteres limma appellabant, huius quoque rationis tractatum
habens dixit singulorum epitritorum esse quandam porti-
unculam reliquam, hanc ipsam scilicet rationem hemitonii
designans, quod ait tantum esse quantum desit ducentis
quadraginta tribus adversum ducentos quinquaginta sex,
quo minus sit plenus epogdous numerus.

48. Quare rursum tertia est facienda descriptio quae subest, ut non solum intellegendo sed videndo etiam assequa-
mur, quid sit et quantum illud quod epitritis deest epogdoa
ratione dimensis. Sumentur itaque maiores numeri, ut totius vocis densitas et omnis quasi quaedam constipatio procedat admittente id fieri maiorum summarum capacitate.

49. Quis igitur primae portionis numerus conveniet institutae ratiocinationi? Nimirum centum nonaginta duo,
quem sic invenio: sumo eum, qui ante omnes numeros ex
tribus partibus constat, id est trientem; hunc octies [sibi]
complico, nascetur viginti quattuor numerus; hunc ipsum
viginti quattuor numerum octies supputo, invenitur is qui
quaeritur numerus centum nonaginta duo, cuius tertia pars
est sexaginta quattuor, dimidia vero nonaginta sex. Sed quia
epogdoi rationem discutere instituimus, adhibeo alium limitem distantem ab eo, duplicem eius qui est in summa, trecentorum octoginta quattuor. Dico numerum ducentos

epitriton is necessarily contained within the quantity of the double [octave] and the triple [octave + fifth] as well; and rightly so, for the primary concordance is precisely this one called the *diatessaron* [fourth], and it sits within the limits of an *epitriton*. And since the *epitriton* consists not only of two *epogdoa* but also of another, namely, minimal, amount as well, precisely as the *diatessaron* consists not only of two whole tones but of the semitone which the ancients called a *leimma,* in treating of this ratio too he said that each of the *epitrita* has a certain small portion left over, namely, indicating precisely this ratio of the semitone, which he says is the same as the amount lacking to 243 in relation to 256, the amount by which the numerical *epogdoon* is less than complete.

48. Hence we must again produce a diagram, our third one, provided below, so that not only by mentally conceptualizing but by visualizing we may grasp what and how large an amount is lacking when *epitrita* are measured by the ratio of an *epogdoon.* Let, then, larger numbers be assumed, in order that the density of the full sound, its full packing in, as it were, may proceed, the accomplishment of which is made possible by the capacity of larger numbers. (See Diagram 9.)

49. Which number, then, for the first section will suit the method of demonstration selected? Undoubtedly 192, which I derive as follows: I select the first of all numbers to consist of three parts, i.e., 3; I multiply it by 8, and the number 24 will appear; this same number 24 I multiply by 8, and the number sought after is found, 192, a third of which is 64, and a half 96. But since we set out to isolate the ratio of the *epogdoon,* I supply another term, one separated from and double that which is at the top: 384. My point is that the number

quinquaginta sex epitritum esse eius numeri quem constituimus limitem summum, id est centum nonaginta duo, habet enim hunc ipsum numerum centum nonaginta duo et tertiam partem eius, sexaginta quattuor. Cuius limitis centum nonaginta duum epogdous numerus est ducenti sedecim, habet enim in se totum limitem centum nonaginta duum et eius octavam partem, viginti quattuor. Huius ipsius ducentorum sedecim numeri epogdous est is, qui est in summa ducentorum quadraginta trium, continet enim ducentos sedecim et eorum partem octavam, id est viginti septem. At vero ducentorum quinquaginta sex, quem epitritum diximus esse centum nonaginta duum numeri, epogdous est qui summam complet ducentorum octoginta octo, habet enim eundem et octavam partem eius, hoc est triginta duo. Huius ipsius numeri qui est in ducentis octoginta octo epogdous numerus est trecentorum viginti quattuor, habens ipsum et octavam partem eius, id est triginta sex. Rursum huius ipsius numeri trecentorum viginti quattuor epogdous est numerus is qui habet summam trecentorum sexaginta quattuor semis, habet enim ipsum et eius octavam portionem, quadraginta semis.

50. Supersunt duae summae, una quae est in ducentis quinquaginta sex, alia quae est in ducentis quadraginta tribus. Non possumus dicere ducentos quinquaginta sex ducentorum quadraginta trium epogdoum esse, non enim in numero ducentorum quinquaginta sex numerus ducentorum quadraginta trium totus continetur et eius octava pars, est etenim octava pars ducentorum quadraginta trium triginta et prope semis, at inter ducentos quinquaginta sex et item ducentos quadraginta tres soli intersunt tredecim numeri; non igitur epogdoi ratio inter hos numeros conservari

256 is the *epitriton* of the number which we have established as the highest term, i.e., 192, for it has this same number 192 and a third thereof, 64. And the numerical *epogdoon* of the term 192 is 216, for it has within it the whole of the term 192 and an eighth thereof, 24. The *epogdoon* of this number 216 is in turn in the sum of 243, for it contains 216 and an eighth thereof, i.e., 27. But the *epogdoon* of 256, which we said was the *epitriton* of the number 192, is that which comprises the sum of 288, for it has that same number and an eighth thereof, i.e., 32. The numerical *epogdoon* of this number 288 is in turn 324, having it and an eighth thereof, i.e., 36. Again, the numerical *epogdoon* of this number 324 is in turn that which has the sum of 364½, for it has that same number and an eighth thereof, 40½.

50. Two sums remain, one of which is 256 and the other 243. We cannot say that 256 is the epogdoon of 243, for in the number 256 is not contained the whole of 243 and an eighth thereof, since an eighth of 243 is approximately 30½, whereas between 256 and 243 only thirteen numbers intervene; hence, between these numbers the ratio of the

potest. Et quoniam epogdous in numeris idem est qui est in musica tonos, perspicuum est quantum ad complendum tonum desit supra dictis inter se numeris comparatis. Nec vero integrum hemitonium conservari potest, unde recte addidit: ita ut ad perfectam cumulatamque perfectionem deesset aliquid epitrito, tantum scilicet quantum deest habita comparatione ducentis quadraginta tribus adversum ducentos quinquaginta sex, quae ratio invenitur etiam in ceteris numeris qui sunt in formula. Certe conveniens oratio disputanti, iste enim Timaeus qui in hoc libro tractat ex Pythagorae magisterio fuit, quem rationabiliter inducit Plato domesticis et familiaribus sibi probationibus utentem docere animae naturam congruere numeris, concinere etiam modulationibus musicae.

51. Nunc quoniam ex quibus constet anima mundi virtutibus, velut ex partibus membrisque coagmentata isdem virtutibus, et quem ad modum natura eius numeris modisque conveniat palam factum est, quod illud propositum exequens ad hunc tractatum descenderit Plato, manifestandum est, ut rationabili ductu ad destinatum operis effectum ratione ac via pervenerimus. Vult igitur animam sensibilis mundi tamquam permissa usurpandi licentia nasci, cognitricem tamen rerum omnium, quae sunt tam intellegibiles quam sensiles. Est porro Pythagoricum dogma similia non nisi a similibus suis comprehendi. Quod etiam Empedocles sequens ait in suis versibus:

Terram terreno comprendimus, aethera flammis,

epogdoon cannot be preserved. And since the numerical *epogdoon* is the same as the musical whole tone, it is clear how much is lacking to complete the whole tone in the numerical ratio mentioned above. But neither can a full semitone be preserved, and so he rightly added [36b], *such that in relation to the whole and aggregate process of completion something was lacking to the epitriton, namely, the amount lacking when the ratio of 243:256 is formed,* which ratio is found also between other numbers in the figure. To be sure, the mode of speech suits its exponent, for the Timaeus who conducts the exposition in this book was a follower of Pythagoras's teaching, and with good reason Plato has him teach, employing cognate and familiar proofs, that the soul has both a natural correspondence with number and a harmony with musical accords.

51. Since it is clear from which powers the world soul consists, being constructed from those same powers as though from parts or members, and it has been made evident how its nature is in accord with numerical proportions, it must now be made manifest that Plato comes to treat of the present subject in the course of pursuing his proposed intention, so that through the guidance of reason we may by rational method reach the appointed goal of the work. Now, he maintains by a kind of right of appropriation that the soul of the sensible world is born yet knows all realities, the intelligible as well as sensible. There is, moreover, the Pythagorean doctrine that "like is comprehended only by like," which Empedocles too follows, when he says in his poem:

Earth we grasp by what is earthy, ether by flames,

humorem liquido, nostro spirabile flatu,
pacem tranquillo, litem quoque litigioso.

Haec quippe constituebat elementa et initia universitatis,
ex quibus animae quoque censebat constare substantiam
proptereaque penes eam omnium rerum esse plenam scientiam simili suo similitudinem habentia comprehendentem.

52. Atque ipse etiam Plato hoc ipsum asserens animam ex
omnibus initiis conflat, ut et ipsorum initiorum et quae initia sequuntur et prorsus omnium rerum existentium scia esset ac de omnibus iudicaret. Denique postquam commiscuit
eam ex his virtutibus, ex quibus componendam putavit, et
compositam divisit in partes iuxta quasdam geometricas et
arithmeticas et musicas rationes, hoc addidit: Tunc hanc ipsam unamque eius seriem secuit in longum et ex una duas
fecit easque mediam mediae in speciem chi Graecae litterae
coartavit curvavitque in orbes quoad coirent inter se capita,
orbemque orbi sic inseruit ut alter eorum adverso alter
obliquo circuitu rotarentur. Hoc etiam addidit quibusdam
interpositis: Itaque ut ex eiusdem diversique natura cum
essentia mixtis coagmentata indigete motu et orbiculata circuitione in se ipsam revertens cum aliquam vel dissipabilem
substantiam offenderit vel individuam, facile recognoscit
quid sit eiusdem individuaeque quid item diversae dissolubilisque naturae causasque omnium quae proveniunt videt et
ex his quae accidunt quae sint futura metitur.

the humid by what is liquid, breathable air by the wind in
us,

peace by what is tranquil, and strife by what is litigious.

These, of course, he established as the elements and first beginnings of all reality, from which he held the substance of
soul to consist as well; and thus he held that soul possesses
full knowledge of all realities, grasping likeness by the likeness within itself.

52. And Plato himself asserts this very point as well, that
soul is a conflation of all the primary elements, so that it
might know the primary elements themselves, their deriva-
tives, and of course all existent realities, and might form
judgments about them all. Then, after having blended it
from these powers, which he thought necessary for its composition, and having divided it into parts according to certain geometric, arithmetic, and musical ratios, he added
[36b–c], *Then he cut this,* its unified *series, itself lengthwise and
from one made two, and he forced them round, middle to middle,
into the shape of the Greek letter chi and bent them into circles so
that their ends joined one another, and he set one circle within the
other such that they rotated, one of them in a lateral orbit and the
other in an oblique one.* And a few lines further on he added
[37a–b], *And so, having been compounded of the natures of the
Same and Other as blended with Being, and revolving back upon
itself in its innate orbital movement, when it encounters any Being
that is either subject to dissipation or indivisible it easily distinguishes what is of the nature of the Same and indivisible, and what
of the nature of the Other and dissoluble. And it sees the causes of
all things that emerge and takes the measure of those which are yet
to be from those which are occurring.*

53. Ex quo perspicuum est, cum sint antiquissima initia rerum essentia sive substantia et haec duplex (altera individua dividua altera) naturaeque gemina diversitas longe vetustissima, conflatam animam ex utraque substantia (eademque et item diversa natura) constare ex omnibus originibus ideoque naturam eius numerorum naturae maxime convenire; quos constet antiquiores esse etiam ipsis geometricae formis, quae in aliquo numero inveniantur necesse est, ut trium et quattuor et item plurium laterum figurae, rursum quae vocantur hexahedra et octahedra: haec quippe sine numeris esse non possunt, numeros vero sine his formis esse nihil impedit. Sic igitur antiquissima numerorum natio esse invenitur omnibus rationibus, ipsorum porro numerorum initia et principia sunt singularitas et item duitas, siquidem has duas ceterorum numerorum origines esse constat. Qua ratione concluditur animam ex duplici concretam substantia geminaque natura numerorum potentiae concinentem vivificantemque caelestia corpora animaliaque, in quibus sit ratio et disciplina, habere omnium rerum conscientiam ex quarum potentiis ipsa constet.

54. Haec est illa rationabilis mundi anima quae gemina <natura praedita> iuxta meliorem naturam <mundi auctorem contemplatur magna> veneratione <et iuxta inferiorem naturam> tutelam praebet inferioribus, divinis dispositionibus obsequens, providentiam nativis impertiens,

53. And so, since the most ancient beginnings of things are Being [*essentia*], or Substance [*substantia*], and since in both of its manifestations (indivisible and divisible) this twofold diversity of nature is by far the oldest, it is clear that soul, being a conflation of each type of Being (the natures of the Same and Other), consists of all the original elements and that its nature therefore comports in the highest degree with the nature of numbers; and the latter are clearly more ancient even than geometrical forms themselves, which necessarily are found to depend upon number in some sense, as in the case of figures of three, four, or even more sides, or again, those which are called hexahedra and octahedra: these forms obviously cannot exist without numbers, but there is nothing to prevent numbers from existing without them. By all accounts, then, the origin of numbers is found to be the most ancient, while the beginnings or principles of numbers themselves are unity and duality, since they are clearly the origins of other numbers. By this line of reasoning we reach the conclusion that soul, being composed of a double Being and twofold nature, in harmony with the potency of numbers, and vivifying the celestial bodies and living beings that possess the faculty of reason and scientific knowledge, has the capacity to know all the things from the combination of whose potencies it itself consists.

54. This is the rational world soul which by virtue of its being endowed with a double nature contemplates with great veneration the author of the world according to its higher nature while offering guidance to lower things according to its lower nature, complying with the divine commands, imparting its provident care to the things that come

aeternorum similitudine propter cognationem beata, disso-
lubilium rerum auxiliatrix et patrona. Cuius in consulendo
ratiocinandoque virtutis in moribus hominis apparent in-
signia, qui cultor eximius dei diligentiam mansuetis impertit
animalibus; isdem quippe virtutibus animae quibus sensilis
mundus fovetur, quando ad ceteros vitales vigores qui sunt
communes hominibus et bestiis, stirpibus etiam, id est cres-
cendi movendi semet appetendique et imaginandi, accedens
ratio propriam hominis animam perficit ut non solum vitae
compos sit sed etiam bene vivendi non desit optio. Atque ita
naturalis et rationabilis item animae contubernio vita hominum temperatur.

55. Quod quidem verum esse testatur eminens quaedam
doctrina sectae sanctioris et in comprehensione divinae rei
prudentioris. Quae perhibet deum absoluto illustratoque
sensili mundo genus hominum instituentem corpus quidem
eius parte humi sumpta iuxta hanc effigiem aedificasse
formasseque, vitam vero eidem ex convexis accersisse caelestibus postque intimis eius inspirationem proprio flatu
intimasse, inspirationem hanc dei consilium animae rationemque significans. Et ratio dei deus est humanis rebus
consulens, quae causa est hominibus bene beateque vivendi
si non concessum sibi munus summo a deo neglegant. Ac de
anima quidem mundi ex duabus essentiis, eiusdemque et
item diversae naturae concretione, conflata deque divisione

to be, blessed by its likeness to eternal things based on its natural affinity to them, an aid and protectress to things subject to dissolution. The signs of this power of forethought and reasoning are apparent in the behavior of man, who in uniquely worshipping god bestows vigilant care upon domestic animals; and indeed, they are apparent in the same powers of the soul as those by which the sensible world is fostered, since in supervening upon all of the vital capacities shared by human beings, beasts, and plants, i.e., those of growth, self-movement, appetite, and forming mental images, reason perfects the soul that is proper to human beings such that it not only possesses the capacity for life but is not without the capacity for choosing to live well. And so human life is tempered by the cohabitation of the natural and rational soul.

55. A certain eminent doctrine of a sect which is more holy and wise in its comprehension of divine reality attests that this is indeed true. The doctrine states that God, in fashioning humankind after His completion and illumination of the sensible world, constructed and formed the human bodily element after the pattern of the sensible world by taking a portion from earth, but derived its vital element from the celestial vault and then with His own breath imparted the insufflation deep within it; and by divine "insufflation" the soul's deliberation and reason is here indicated. And the divine reason is god's deliberation over human affairs, and it is the cause of their living well and happily insofar as they do not neglect the gift granted them by the supreme god. But enough has been said concerning the world soul that consists of the coalescence of two forms of Being, the nature of the Same and Other, and concerning the divi-

eius iuxta rationes harmonicam arithmeticam geometricam
facta quove modo natura eius numeris sonisque conveniat,
satis dictum.

5. De Stellis Ratis et Errantibus

56. Nunc quem ad modum animae sectio sectioni caelestium membrorum inflexionique conveniat circulorum, quorum motibus concurrat animae conversio, prosequemur.
Artificialiter quippe satis agit ut ostendat animam pari qua
caelestia ratione institutam facile cognationem suam recog-
noscere, vel (quia dogma eius huius modi est) universi motus
initium penes id esse quod ex se ipso movetur; nec est quicquam nisi anima quod ex se movetur, unde perspicuum est
eandem fore mundi quoque motus originem et causam. Fertur porro mundus in gyrum, prius igitur animae motus gyris
circuit <et> anfractibus ut omne caelestis convexi corporeum isdem orbitis circumferatur. Quod autem ex semet
ipsa moveatur anima, declarat idem, cum differentiam faciens opinionum et scientiae dicit haec: Ut igitur ex eiusdem et diversi natura cum essentia mixtis coagmentata indigete motu et orbiculata circumfertur agitatione in se ipsam
revertens cum aliquam vel dissipabilem substantiam offenderit vel individuam, facile recognoscit quid sit eiusdem
individuaeque quid item diversae dissolubilisque naturae.
Causasque omnium quae proveniunt videt et ex his quae accidunt quae sint futura metitur motusque eius rationabilis
sine voce sine sono cum quid sensile spectat circulusque

sion of it that has been drawn according to the harmonic, arithmetic, and geometrical ratios, and how its nature comports with number and sound.

5. On the Fixed and Wandering Stars

56. We will now turn to the question of how the division of soul comports with that of the heavenly bodies and the course of their orbits, with whose motion its own conversion runs concurrent. His procedure is, to be sure, technically sufficient to show that the soul, fashioned after the same pattern as the celestial bodies, immediately recognizes its own natural affinity to them, or that (for such is the nature of his doctrine) the origin of the world's motion is in that which is self-moving; and since there is nothing except soul that is self-moving, it is clear that it is the origin and cause also of the world's motion. Now, the world moves in a circle, and so by virtue of its priority the movement of the soul circles in curved orbits so that the whole corporeal element of the celestial vault may revolve in identical orbits. And that soul is self-moving he declares by drawing the distinction between opinion and knowledge, as follows [37a–c]: *Having been compounded, then, of the natures of the Same and Other as blended with Being it moves in circles, revolving back upon itself in its innate orbital movement, and when it encounters any Being that is either subject to dissipation or indivisible it easily distinguishes what is of the nature of the Same and indivisible, and what of the nature of the Other and dissoluble. And it sees the causes of all things that emerge and takes the measure of those which are to be from those which are occurring, and without voice or sound its rational movement, the circling of the nature of the*

diversi generis sine errore fertur. Veridico sensu et certa nuntiante cunctae animae, rectae opiniones et dignae credulitate nascuntur, porro cum individuum genus semperque idem conspexerit, ea quae sunt motu intimo fideliter nuntiante, intellectus et scientia convalescunt. Quae quidem omnia in anima fieri eidemque insigniri palam est.

57. Hoc idem aliquanto apertius significat in Phaedro dicens ita: Omnis anima immortalis. Quia quod semper movetur semper in vita est; at vero quod aliud movet aliunde sumpta virtute motus, pausam movendi patiens pausam quoque vivendi patiatur necesse est. Solum ergo quod se ipsum movet, ut<pote> quod numquam motum suum deserat, numquam movere se desinit; quin ceteris etiam quae motum ex natura sua non habent fons et initium motus fit. Initium porro sine ortu, quando quae gignuntur ex initio creantur ipsum porro ex nullo initio; nam si ex aliquo initium, non erit initium, quando cuncta quae gignuntur ex initio sint oportet. Et quia caret generatione, caret etiam morte; quippe initio sepulto neque ipsum ex aliquo reparabitur nec quicquam ex eo; nimirum enim ex initio cuncta quae sunt in generatione subsistunt. Sic ergo motus quidem initium quod intimo et genuino motu movetur; hoc porro nec nasci nec emori fas est aut [vero] omne caelum omnemque genituram labefactatam consistere nec ullum remedium fore

Other, on perceiving anything sensible moves without error. And while its veridical perception announces certitudes to the whole of soul right opinions worthy of belief arise, whereas on its perceiving a nature that is indivisible and forever the Same its understanding and knowledge gain strength while an inner impulse faithfully announces the things that are. And it is manifest that it is in and upon soul that all of this occurs and leaves its mark.

57. He makes the same point rather more explicitly in the *Phaedrus,* when he says: "The whole of soul is immortal. For that which is always in motion is always in life; but that which moves another while being moved by an external force is, by virtue of its being subject to cessation of movement, necessarily subject to a cessation of life as well. Hence that which moves *itself* is unique in never ceasing from self-movement, since it never abandons its movement; indeed, it becomes the source and principle of movement also for all that of its own nature lacks it. And the principle is ungenerated, for things subject to birth are created from a principle whereas it arises out of no principle; for if the principle arises out of something then it will not be a principle, for all things subject to birth necessarily arise out of a principle. And since it lacks generation, it also lacks death; for if the origin perishes then neither will it be restored from anything nor will anything be restored from it; for all things subject to generation certainly come to subsist from a principle. So then, the principle of movement is that which moves according to an internal and innate motion; but it is not right that this should either be born or die, or for the whole heaven and all of generation to collapse and come to a halt and there be no means by which those things whose movement is required for the sake of preserving other

213

quo demum quae moveri conservationis rerum exigat causa recreentur. Quare ostensa immortalitate eius quod ex se movetur animae mentisque immortalitas revelata est. Omne enim corpus quod quidem habet intra se motivum vigorem cum anima est, quod vero extra, sine anima, siquidem haec animae natura sit. Quod cum ita sit, apparet animam solam fore quae ex se ipsa moveatur proptereaque positam extra ortus interitusque necessitatem.

58. Hanc igitur, inquit, constitutionem deus tamquam seriem in longum scidit et ex una duas fecit easque mediam mediae in speciem chi Graecae litterae coartavit curvavitque in orbes, quoad coirent inter se capita, orbemque orbi sic inseruit ut alter adverso alter obliquo circuitu rotarentur, et exterioris quidem circuli motum eundem, quod erat eiusdem naturae consanguineus, cognominavit, interioris autem diversum; et exteriorem quidem circulum, quem eundem cognominatum esse diximus, a regione dextra per sinistrum latus usque ad dextrum inflexit, diversum vero per diametrum in sinistrum latus eidem et simili illi circumactioni virtute pontificioque rotatus dato. Unam quippe, ut erat, eam et indivisam reliquit, interiorem vero scidit sexies septemque impares orbes fabricatus est iuxta dupli et tripli spatia orbesque ipsos contraria ferri iussit agitatione, ex quibus septem tres quidem pari velocitate, quattuor vero et sibimet ipsis et ad comparationem ceterorum dispari dissimilique sed cum ratione motu.

59. Rursum quo etiam expertibus astronomiae assecutio tradatur aliquatenus, ea quae ad praesentem tractatum pertinent breviter dilucideque prout natura eorum est

things may finally be replenished. In this sense, then, once the immortality of that which is self-moving has been demonstrated, the immortality of soul and mind has been revealed. For every body that has motive force within itself is conjoined with soul, whereas that which has it from without is separate from soul, that being the nature of soul. Given that this is so, it is evident that soul alone is self-moving and therefore situated beyond the necessity of birth and destruction."

58. He says [36b–d]: *This structure, then, god divided lengthwise as if in a series and from one made two, and he forced them round, middle to middle, into the shape of the Greek letter chi and bent them into circles so that their ends joined one another, and he set one circle within the other such that they rotated, one in a lateral orbit and the other in an oblique one, and the movement of the outer circle, since it was cognate with the nature of the Same, he called the Same, and that of the inner one he called the Other; and the outer circle, which we have said was called the Same, he bent from the right to the left side and back to the right, and the Other across the diameter to the left side, giving the rotational force and preeminence to the circumlations of the Same or like. Now, the one series he left undivided, just as it was, but the inner one he cut six times, constructing seven unequal circles according to intervals of the double and triple, and these circles he ordered to move in contrary motion, three of the seven with equal velocity and four with unequal or dissimilar velocity in relation both to one another and to the rest, but with measured motion.*

59. Again, in order that a means of understanding may be passed along also to those who are inexperienced in astronomy, those subjects which pertain to the present discussion will be briefly and clearly explained according to their

explicabuntur. Ait Plato mundi formam rotundam esse et globosam, terram item globosam in medietate mundi sitam eamque puncti quidem instar obtinere, quod ad positionem pertinet, quod vero ad exiguitatem, notae cum universae rei magnitudine comparatam. Sed, opinor, dixisse hoc eum non sufficit nisi hoc ita esse evidentibus ostendatur rationibus. Quatenus igitur est mundi forma teres et globosa? Principio caelestium ignium ortus velut emergentium ex imo peragrationesque cum certis exaltationibus et deinceps descensionibus usque ad occasuum submersionem eorumque rursum ipsorum ortus ex eodem loco et item occasus in occiduum mare testantur ambire se diebus ac noctibus caeli extimam superficiem. Dehinc quod ex qualibet regione terrae dimidia et in summitate posita mundi pars videatur a nobis, inferior vero non videatur nisi dierum et noctium vicibus et successione superior reddita, obiecta et visui nostro obsistente terra. Tum quod ex omni visu omnes lineae undique versum porrectae usque ad extimos ambitus caeli aequales videantur, similiter ut circuli cuius a puncto radii pervenientes usque ad extimam circumactionem aequali mensura sunt. Praeterea quod signifer circulus, obliqua vertigine levans in ortum signa certa, ex adverso consistentia diametroque distantia signa alia signis orientibus condat et premat in occasum item ut in rotae vertigine, cuius cum certa pars ascendat descendit eius adversa, quod in alia forma nisi in sola rotunditate non provenit.

nature. Plato says that the world is round and spherical in shape, that the Earth is spherical and situated at the center of the world, that in its position the Earth is the equivalent of the center, but that in size it is the equivalent of a mere point when compared with the magnitude of the universe. But his having said this is, I suppose, insufficient unless it is shown to be so by means of evident lines of reasoning. In what sense, then, is the world round and spherical in shape? First, the rising of the celestial luminaries as they emerge, as it were, from the deep, and their paths, with fixed ascents and then descents down into the ocean, followed by their rising once again from the same place and then falling again into the Western ocean: these phenomena bear witness to the fact that through the course of days and nights they circle round the outermost surface of the sky. Second, there is the fact that from any region of the Earth half of the world, its pinnacle, is visible to us, whereas, given the Earth's obstruction and blocking of our line of sight, the lower part is visible only by becoming the upper part through the interchange and succession of days and nights. Then there is the fact that from every vantage point all lines extending in all directions to the outermost revolutions of the sky appear equal, as with a circle from whose center the radii in extending to the outermost circumference are equal in measure. Moreover, there is the fact that with its oblique revolutions the zodiacal belt lifts certain signs up into a rising position and, as they rise, buries other signs that stand diametrically opposite them, thereby forcing them into descent, as with the spinning of a wheel: as a certain part of it ascends the part opposite it descends, and the only shape in connection with which this occurs is the spherical one.

60. Sphaerae autem similitudo in effigie terrae multi-
mode comprehenditur. Vel quod non isdem momentis temporum dies ubique illucescit noxque succedens umbras facit
sed tam ortus quam occasus in eois quidem citius fiunt in
occiduis vero regionibus tardius, ut perspicuum sit esse aliquam elatiorem eminentiam inter utramque caeli plagam
quae obiecta, priusquam sol fiat excelsior, teneat noctis umbras. Vel quod lunae defectus idem ubique eodemque momento accidens diversis temporibus notatur, orienti quidem
vicinis regionibus tardius, ceteris vero pro locorum diversitate, propter anfractus metasque et naturales eminentias
terrae non isdem ubique curriculis illustrante sole terrae
plagas, ideoque luci eius e diverso terrenis umbris etiam
nunc obstantibus, et a lunae illustratione prohibentibus
cum lunae labor nocturna tempestate fiat. Quid quod globo-
sitas terrae liquido apparet inter aquiloni septentrionique et
item austro meridieique subiecta? Cum ex utraque regione
huc atque illuc nocturnis itineribus commeantes incognitas
sibi stellas spectant cum admiratione novitatis, cum sit evidens non regionum stellas esse proprias sed homines impediri quo minus omnes videant sciantque terrae molibus atque exaggerationibus visui obiectis. Ex quo concluditur
terram sphaerae globo similem esse, cuius ex omnibus regionibus crescere in molem superficies comprehendatur.

61. Idem hoc etiam naturaliter intellegi et comprehendi
potest, siquidem omnia quae in aliquo sunt pondere undique

60. The likeness in the Earth's surface to a sphere is grasped in a number of ways. For example, in the fact that the day does not appear everywhere at the same points in time, or night that produces darkness as it follows, but both risings and settings occur earlier in Eastern regions and later in Western ones, so that it is clear that between each celestial zone there is a certain slightly higher projection which by its obstruction holds the nocturnal darkness prior to the Sun's rising. Or there is the fact that despite its occurring everywhere at one and the same moment the same lunar eclipse is observed at different times, later in regions to the East, and in other regions according to the differences in their location: given the natural contours of the Earth, its bends and limits, the Sun does not illuminate its regions according to the identical circuits everywhere, and so at fixed moments shadows cast by the Earth obstruct the sunlight, or they shield it from illumination by the Moon when a lunar eclipse occurs at night. And what about the fact that the Earth's roundness is clearly evident between the regions exposed to the North Wind in the North and the South Wind in the South? People traveling between them by night gaze in wonder upon stars that are unfamiliar to them even though it is evident, not that the stars are peculiar to the regions, but that the people are prevented from seeing and knowing all of them because the heaping up of the Earth's mass blocks their line of sight. From these considerations we may conclude that the Earth resembles a rounded sphere, from any given point of which the surface is understood to increase in its curvature.

61. This same point can be understood and grasped also from the standpoint of physics, in that all things of any

et ex qualibet parte directo tenore descendentia ad unum punctum medietatis commeent. Omnia descensusque rigidi tractus faciant in modum et speciem linearum a latiore exordio profectarum et angustiore semper tramite usque ad puncti sedem pervenientium eandem puncti sedem aequalibus undique circumsistentibus angulis; quae est imago rotunditatis. Porro quod omnia in qualicumque pondere festinent ad medium sic probatur, quod etiam vi extrinsecus adhibita sibi pleraque pondera, ubi primum vis recesserit, secundum naturam prona in terram ferantur, ut in iaculorum tormentis, quae quamdiu viget pulsus suspensa volitare et secare auram videntur, ubi porro vis illa quae impellebat defecerit converso mucrone descendunt ad terram, quae medietas mundi est, festinantia.

62. Maris etiam et totius aquae, cum est in tranquillitate stabili, forma et species apparet globosa. Quae enim stantes in litore videmus ultra fretum, ut arborem turrimve aut etiam in eodem freto navim, haec iacentes exaequata facie visuque cum dorso et superficie maris aut omnino non videmus aut multo certe minora quam prius videbantur, obsistente videlicet contemplantibus marina incurvitate. Atque etiam in navigando saepe numero cum de navi terra nondum videretur, ascensa arbore videre nautae, scilicet ut praetexto oppositae molis emenso libero iam ex altiore despectu subiecta undique considerentur. Artificialiter quoque considerantes invenimus aquae placidae et quiescentis globositatem, siquidem natura tributum sit ut ex superioribus locis humor in depressiora defluat. Sunt porro celsiora

weight move from every possible direction in a straight line of descent to a single point, the center. They all cut trajectories of direct descent, like lines that originate from broadly spaced points and with increasing narrowness arrive at the center point, with equal angles converging from all sides on the same center point; and that is the shape of a sphere. Moreover, that all things of any weight rush to the center is proved by the fact that weighted bodies under an externally applied force will, once the force is removed, naturally move down toward the Earth, as with the ballistas used to hurl missiles: so long as the force impels them, they can be seen to make their way through the air, suspended on high, but once the driving force lets up they descend toward the Earth, the center of the world, with their tips pointing downward.

62. And the form and shape of the sea and of all water in a tranquil state is clearly spherical. For while standing on the shore we see objects beyond the sea, such as a tree, tower, or even a ship on the same sea; lying down with our face and line of sight aligned with the sea's surface we either do not see the objects at all or at the very least they appear much shorter than before, and that because the sea's curvature blocks our vision. And often also in navigating when land was not yet visible from the ship, by climbing the mast sailors have seen it, such that owing now to the unhindered view from above the things below are seen all around, namely, once the barrier of the intervening mass is removed. In considering the point from a technical perspective as well we discover the sphericity of a calm and placid body of water, in that the flow of liquid from higher points down to lower ones is a natural attribute. Now, the higher points are

quidem ea quae a puncto terrae plurimum distant, humiliora
vero quae minimum; quare si ponamus aquae superficiem
planam et in directa linea positam, ut est ABΓ, dehinc a
puncto terrae, ut puta K, sursum versum ducatur linea KB,
coniungantur autem extimae superficiei partes duabus lineis
his, KA et KΓ, maiores erunt utraeque hae lineae KB lineae
comparatae; quam si exaequare voluerimus, perveniet incrementum usque ad BH et erit vera superficies in AHΓ; itaque ex superioribus partibus tam A quam Γ fluet aqua in
humiliorem B usque eo quoad completo vase a fundo K
contegatur incremento aquae etiam B et perveniatur usque
ad H, quo aequabiliter se per omnia membra fundat aqua
cum ambitu cumuli. Ex quo perspicuum est marinam quoque et totius aquae superficiem globosam esse, siquidem
una eademque sit ratio universitatis et partium.

63. Quod si quis ad cacumina montium prolixitatemque
et saxosam asperitatem aspiciens similem dicet esse ad
tornum levigatae pilae deformitatem asperiorum montium,
non recte sentit; non enim nos terram globum esse dicimus
sed globosam, nec pilam sed similem pilae. Certe totius terrae magnitudinem animo rationabiliter concipientes veritatem non visu et sensibus investigamus sed ad rationis
intellegentiaeque remedia potius examinationemque dedu-
cimus.

64. Nunc iam quo pacto mediam mundi sedem obtineat
considerabitur. Opinor, si media non est atque a medietatis
rigore deflectit, non ex omni et qualibet sui parte dimidietatem caeli supra se, dimidietatem vero alteram infra se

those situated farthest from the Earth's center, and the lower ones those least removed; hence if we suppose the water's surface as being flatly situated along a straight line, as with ABΓ, and then from the Earth's center K line KB is drawn straight upward and the outer parts of the surface are conjoined by the two lines KA and KΓ, the latter two will both be longer when compared with line KB; and if we want to make it equal to them, we will extend it from B to H and get the correct surface line in AHΓ; and so from the upper points A and Γ water will flow down to B until, as the vessel is filled from the bottom K, owing to the rising water B is then reached, and finally H, so that the water is equally suffused throughout and forms a curvature as it accumulates. From these considerations it is clear that even the surface of the sea or of any body of water is spherical, since what holds for the whole holds also for the parts. (See Diagram 10.)

63. If, however, in gazing upon the craggy, rocky height of mountain peaks someone claims that the deformity of the jagged mountains resembles a ball that has been made smooth on the lathe, his perception is wrong; for we do not claim that the Earth is a sphere, but that it is spherical, not that it is a ball, but that it resembles one. To be sure, if in our minds we form a rational conception of the magnitude of the Earth as a whole, it is not through sight or the senses that we conduct the investigation, but rather we form deductions aiming at the solutions and evaluation offered by reason and intelligence.

64. We will now consider the question of the sense in which the Earth is the center point of the world. If, I suppose, it is not at the center but is offset from the radius leading to the center, then it will not have half of the heaven above and the other half below it at every and any given

habebit nec lineas porrectas ex qualibet nota et usque ad extremum ambitum mundi pervenientes aequales invicem; at aequalia spatia linearum non esse nullus docet; minime ergo a medietate deflectit. Quod vero cum amplitudine universae rei comparata notae obtineat modum declaratur acie verutorum, qui gnomones appellantur a mechanicis, ad faciendam solariis umbram qua declarantur horae; quippe mechanici horologia instituentes per omnes provincias omnesque etiam plagas habitabiles sumunt sibi promisce atque indifferenter horum ipsorum gnomonum mucrones pro puncto et medietate solstitialis pilae, nec errant. Ergo si est una vera et certa medietas solstitialis pilae, omnes autem notae atque omnia puncta ex omni regione terrarum assequuntur veram istam solis medietatem, perspicuum est quod omnis terra puncti vicem habeat adversum solis globum comparata. Sed de forma quidem totius mundi, terrae etiam, hoc amplius de eiusdem media positione, comparatione quoque adversum universi corporis immensitatem hactenus dictum.

65. Sed enim caelite sphaera vertente semet circa fixos et manentes semper polos continuantemque eosdem polos axem, cui adhaeret medio media tellus, comitatur vertiginem caelitis sphaerae stellarum omnium populus et promisce signa caelestia, gyris aequabiliter ex propria conversione distantibus depingentia circulos adversos atque obvios axi. Quorum multitudo vincit dinumerationem, pauci tamen nobili celebres appellatione, quos scire utile est ad spectaculum caelestis choreae. Unus qui excelso cognitoque nobis et perspicuo polo vicinus est, septentrionalis

point, or have lines of equal length extending from a fixed point out to the world's outermost circumference; but no one maintains that their linear extensions are unequal; thus the Earth is not offset from the center point. That in comparison with the vastness of the universe the Earth has the proportions of a point is shown by the tip of the spears, called gnomons by engineers, used for sundials to produce the shadow that tells the hours; for in setting up devices for measuring time throughout the provinces and inhabitable zones, engineers randomly and indifferently take the tips of the gnomons as the center point of the solar sphere, and they do not err. So if there is a single true and fixed center of the solar sphere and all the markers and points in every region of the Earth converge on the Sun's true center, then it is clear that in comparison with the solar sphere the whole of the Earth holds the place of a point. But enough has been said about the shape of the world as a whole, about that of the Earth, also about its central position and its size as compared with the immensity of the body of the universe.

65. But as the heavenly sphere revolves around the fixed and forever abiding poles and the axis that binds them, the axis to whose center the center of the Earth adheres, the population of all the stars and the celestial constellations conjointly accompany the spinning of the heavenly sphere while displaying, in measured circumlations that differ because of individual patterns of rotation, circuits that are opposite to and facing the axis. And although their number is beyond count, a few are nevertheless well known by name, and a knowledge of them is useful for observation of the celestial chorus. The one located near the uppermost pole, which is known and visible to us, is called the septentrional

appellatur ob constellatum sibi sidus septentrionis. Alter adversus aequalis huic iuxta submersum latentemque semper polum ipse etiam latens, antarcticus. Medius et maximus omnium bis dividens sphaeram aequidialis, quem isemerinon appellant propterea quod subiectis sibi regionibus terrae noctes omnes diebus omnibus aequales exhibet; nihiloque minus in aliis quoque minime subiectis sibi regionibus quae solis ortus et occasus vident, cum idem sol ad hunc se applicuerit circulum pares horas diei noctisque metitur.

66. Inter hunc porro et arctoos hac atque illac duo tropici, aestivus et brumalis, hic e regione nostra vicinus aquiloni, brumalis austro propinquus. Per quos obliquus curvatur signifer, et ipse maximus circulus, contingens tropicos singulis signis, aestivum quidem Cancro brumalem autem Capricorno; idemque aequidialem bis secat circulum et ipse ab eo totiens secatur per Chelas et Arietem, sub quem luna et sol feruntur ceterique ignes qui vocantur planetae, Phaenon idemque Saturni, et Phaethon Iovis, Pyrois quoque Martius, item Lucifer Veneris (qui alio quoque censetur Hesperus nomine), praeterea Stilbon Mercuriale sidus. Dicitur etiam circulus finalis quem noster visus imaginatur horizon Graeco nomine, limitans mundum dividensque in duas partes iuxta hominum visum, quando obiectu terrae solum id hemisphaerium quod superne fuerit videtur, alterum interim latet sub australi polo, quem ut ait poeta:

Sub pedibus Styx atra videt Manesque profundi,

[Arctic] because the constellations of Ursa Major and Minor [*sidus septentrionis*] are in the same region as it. A second, equal but opposite it, is itself hidden because the pole is always submerged and hidden: the Antarctic. The middle one and largest of all divides the equinoctial sphere, and they call it the *isêmerinos* owing to the fact that it displays for the regions of the Earth beneath it nights that are in every instance equal to the days; nonetheless, even in other regions which are not beneath it but which look upon the risings and settings of the Sun, the same Sun measures out equal hours of day and night as it moves along this circuit.

66. Now, between this circle and those of the arctics are on either side the two tropics, those of the summer and winter solstices, the summer to the North of our region, the winter to the South. The zodiac bends its way obliquely through these, being the largest circle and intersecting the tropics at their respective signs, the summer solstice at Cancer and the winter at Capricorn; it cuts across the tropical belt twice and is itself cut across as many times by it, through Libra and Aries, under which there run the Moon, Sun, and other luminaries called planets, Phaenon being that of Saturn, Phaethon that of Jupiter, Pyrois being Mars, Lucifer that of Venus (also called Hesperus), and Stilbon the star of Mercury. And the final circle, which we picture in our mind's eye, is called the *horizôn* in Greek, for it limits the world by dividing it into two parts from the perspective of human vision: due to the Earth's interposition the upper hemisphere alone is visible, while the other hemisphere lies hidden beneath the Southern pole, which, as the poet says:

Beneath our feet dark Styx and the deep Manes see,

magnus et ipse et maximos secans gemina sectione aequidialem atque zodiacum, unde fit ut signorum diametro a se distantium alterum quidem in ortu alterum appareat in occasu. Hunc autem ipsum bifariam dividit meridialis, qui meshemerinos dicitur; maximus hic quoque per ambos curvatus polos sed qui rectus intellegatur adversum finalem, quem urget; meridialis appellatur quia medio die per eum sol excelso itineris elatior terram directo despicit nutu.

67. Sed aequidialis quidem et qui latera eius circumsistunt tam magnitudine quam positione fixi confirmatique, zodiacus autem, magnitudine quidem fixus et firmo cardine positione etiam iuxta caleum rata, iuxta nos tamen praeponderat pro obliquitate varie nutans aliterque nobis atque aliter insistens. Meridialis quoque et item finalis, quod ad magnitudinem spectat, vigorati sunt, quippe maximi, sed positione nutant per diversas terrae plagas his et item aliis se applicantes. At vero vicini polis, id est septentrionalis et huic diversus antarcticus, neque magnitudine neque positione solidati sunt sed pro differentia regionum aquilentanae itemque australis apud quosdam maiores apud alios minores putantur. Contra meditullium tamen terrae, id est ubi sub meridialem circulum zona se porrigit exusta ardore flammanti proptereaque inhabitabilis, <uterque invisibilis> est, utrisque polis illic visibilibus et perspicuis per quos limes it partes mundi determinans.

68. Etiam illud addendum: ceteros circulos id ipsum esse circulos iuxta definitionem quae docet circulum esse planam figuram quam una linea circumducta contineat, itaque

and being large itself, the horizon cuts across the broadest circles, the tropic and zodiac, at two points, which is why of two diametrically opposed signs one ascends as the other is seen to descend. And this limiting circle is itself divided in two by the meridian, which is called the *mesêmerios;* this, the broadest one, also bends its way through both poles but when conceived at right angles intersects the final circle, on which it presses; it is called the meridian because at midday the Sun, at its zenith, looks directly down along it at Earth.

67. But whereas the equinoctial circle and those flanking it are firmly fixed in both magnitude and position, the zodiac, although fixed in its magnitude, steady axis of rotation, and constant position relative to the heavens, nevertheless moves along an oblique course relative to us, approaching and receding from us by turns. As to their magnitude, the meridian and final circle are firmly set, being the largest, but as to their position they descend through different zones of the Earth, approaching one and then another. But the circles bordering on the poles, i.e., the Arctic and the Antarctic opposite it, are fixed in neither magnitude nor position but, depending on the Northern or Southern regional differences, are considered larger by some but smaller by others. But toward the central region of the Earth, i.e., where the sun-scorched and thus uninhabitable zone extends beneath the equatorial belt, neither is visible, although each of the poles is clearly visible at the points where the limit intersects them and demarcates the parts of the world. (See Diagram 11.)

68. The following point should be added as well: that each of the other circles is a true circle according to the definition which states that a circle is a plane figure circumscribed by a single curved line, so that individual circles are

singulos singulis lineis circumductis contineri; signiferum
vero ex multis constare, in speciem circuli tympanorum in
cuius latitudine signorum adumbrantur figurae. Secat porro
latitudinem eius circulus qui inter signa medius appellatur,
existens maximus, contingens utrumque tropicum, et aequidialem bis secans; reliqui extimi duo signiferae latitudinis
circuli huius ipsius qui inter signa medius vocatur breviores
sunt.

69. Igitur fixae quidem stellae nec errantes et item poli
cum maxima cunctaque amplexu proprio continente
sphaera, quae aplanes vocatur, circumferuntur una simpli-
cique [circa illam] agitatione adhaerentes ei quaque circum-
egerit circumactae, unam et eandem semper positionem
obtinentes ordinemque immutabili tenore servantes neque
umquam vel in conformatione vel in ortu vel in quantitate
vel etiam in colore admittentes ullam mutationem. Sol vero
et luna et ceteri quinque, id est planetes, una quidem maioris globi conversione rapiuntur ab oriente in occidentem per
dies singulos item ut illae ratae atque inerrabiles stellae, varias tamen alias agitationes facere videntur, cum vel in praetereuntis signi locum migrant tamquam universi globi motui
contrarios motus agentes, vel cum ab aquilentanis ad austra-
lia et contra latiore deflexione oberrant atque ab aestivo ad
brumalem tropicum et inde demum ad aestivum revertuntur. Cuius quidem causa esse signiferi orbis latitudo aesti-
matur. Atque etiam in ipsius zodiaci latitudine obliqua
modo ad aquilonem modo ad austrum vertentes, cum quidem aquiloni se applicant elatiores cum vero austro humiles
cognominantur, idque ipsum non omnes peraeque sed alii
magis quidam minus. Videtur etiam non nulla intuentibus in
quantitate diversitas, siquidem e longinquo minores, de

circumscribed by individual curved lines; and that the zodiac consists of many lines, projecting the shape of the circle along the breadth of which the figures of zodiacal signs are depicted on tympana. Now, the so-called midzodiacal circle cuts across its belt, being the largest, touching on both tropics, and bisecting the equinox; the two remaining circles outside the zodiacal belt are smaller than this so-called midzodiacal circle.

69. The fixed and nonwandering stars, then, and the poles along with the largest sphere, which embraces all things and is called the *aplanês,* are borne round in a unified and constant movement, adhering to it as it leads them round, always maintaining one and the same position and preserving their order in an unvarying pattern, never admitting any change in position, ascent, size, or even color. And although the Sun, Moon, and five others, i.e., the planets speed day by day from East to West along with the rotation of the outer sphere as the fixed and nonwandering stars do, they are nevertheless seen to make other, varying patterns of movement, as when they enter the position occupied by a passing sign and engage in movement that gives the appearance of being contrary to that of the universal sphere, or when they move with broadened compass from North to South and back again, from the summer to the winter tropic and then back to the summer. The zodiacal belt is considered to be the explanation for this. And as they orbit obliquely along the zodiacal belt, alternating between North and South, they are said to be higher as they move to the North and lower as they move to the South, and not all equally, but some more and others less. There is even evident to viewers a certain variation in size, in that they necessarily appear smaller

proximo, cum ad ima vergunt, maiores videantur necesse est. Proptereaque etiam in motu non aequa velocitas, quod aequa signorum dimensa non aequis videantur conficere temporibus sed citius quidem tunc cum ex proximitate maiores apparent, tardius vero cum longius a terra remoti minores videntur.

70. Evagatio tamen in latum quae fit in zodiaco non aequa est omnium, quippe solis minor quam ceterorum ignium, tota enim evagatio sub unius portionis aestimationem venit, lunae vero et Luciferi iuxta opinionem veterum virorum longe maior ad duodecim fere portiones, Mercurii fere ad octo partes, Pyrois et Phaethontis ad quinque, Saturni ad tres portiones. Obeunt porro signiferi orbis circulos in longum, id est qua finis exordiique confinium est. Luna quidem dierum et noctium spatiis XXVII et tertia parte diurni nocturnique spatii dimetitur, sol item anno, id est CCCLXV diebus et propemodum quarta diurni et nocturni spatii; Lucifer et Stilbon imparibus quidem gressibus, isdem tamen paene temporibus quibus sol cursus conficiunt, modo incitato volatu comprehendentes eum modo pigro tractu demum ab eodem comprehensi; Pyrois paene biennio, Phaethon prope annis duodecim, Phaenon triginta annis modico minus; proptereaque solis peragrationibus effulsionibusque et obscurationibus, quas ortus et occasus vocamus, minime concurrunt. Quippe luna quidem post conventum coitumque solis, quia prior convenit ad destinatum, prior vesperi semper apparens et exoriens, matutina conditur in occasum.

from afar but larger from shorter distances, when they are in descent. And that explains the disparity in their movement as well, since they appear, not to traverse equal stretches of the zodiac in equal temporal periods, but to do so more rapidly when they appear larger because of their proximity and more slowly when they appear smaller because of their greater distance from the Earth.

70. But not all celestial bodies share a course of equal expanse across the zodiac: the Sun's is smaller than that of the other celestial luminaries, for its entire course is calculated at a single degree, whereas those of the Moon and Venus are, according to the opinion of the ancients, much larger, at approximately twelve degrees, that of Mercury at approximately eight degrees, of Mars and Jupiter at five, and that of Saturn at three degrees. Moreover, they complete the full lengths of their zodiacal circuits, i.e., returning to the point in the zodiac that marks both the beginning and end of their cycle. The Moon measures its cycle over the period of twenty-seven and a third days and nights, and the Sun over a year, i.e., 365 days and the equivalent of a quarter day and night; although Venus and Mercury move at varying rates, they complete their courses in nearly the same period of time as the Sun does, overtaking it with quickened flight at one time, moving more slowly at another, and finally being overtaken by it; Mars orbits in nearly two years, Jupiter in twelve, and Saturn in just under thirty; and this is the reason for their not coinciding with the cycles of the Sun or its phases of brightness and darkness, which we call its risings and settings. In fact, after its meeting and conjunction with the Sun the Moon, since it completes its cycle first, is always the first to appear or rise in the evening, setting to the West

Contra Phaenon et Phaethon et Pyrois, quia tardius quam sol signorum spatia peragunt, tamquam ab eo comprehensi et praeteriti semper vespere occidentes exoriuntur matutinae lucis auspicio. Lucifer porro et Stilbon concurrentes soli iuxtaque eum plerumque comitantes, comprehendentes etiam et ab eo invicem comprehensi; si quidem vespere orientur, condentur in aliam vesperam, si matutino illucescent, in aliud mane mergentur. Etenim ceteris erraticis stellis a sole longo intervallo recedentibus ut plerumque diametro distent, Stilbon et Lucifer circa solem semper videntur: Stilbon quidem viginti momentis non amplius, id est duabus unius signi partibus vel ad aquilonem vel non numquam ad austrum propensior, Veneris vero prope quinquaginta momentis ad orientem occidentemque discedens.

71. Ortus autem varie dicitur: proprie quidem prima stellarum et solis effulsio et ultra finalem circulum elatio; promisce vero primus splendor inuehentis solis diem—hunc poetae iubar et interdum auroram cognominant; tertia quae appellatur acronychos, cum sole occidente astrum diametro distans in parte orientis videtur. Similiter occasus: proprie quidem primus descensus infra circulum limitantem; aliter tamen etiam prima stellae alicuius obscuratio sole obumbrante; tertia acronychos, cum sole oriente diametro distans mergitur stella. Ortuum vero et occasuum quorum sol auctor est, hoc est effulsionum et occultationum, quidam matutini quidam vespertini sunt. Matutinus ortus dicitur quotiens solis splendore praevento stella quaepiam ante ortum

in the morning. Saturn, Jupiter, and Mars, on the other hand, since they traverse the expanse of the zodiac more slowly than the Sun, as though having been caught up with and overtaken by it, always set in the evening and rise at the first portent of morning light. Venus and Mercury move concurrently with the Sun and regularly accompany it, overtaking it and in turn being overtaken by it; if they rise in the evening, then they will set on the next evening, but if their light becomes visible in the morning, then they will set on the next morning. For whereas the other wandering stars recede far away from the Sun so as at regular intervals to stand diametrically opposite it, Mercury and Venus always appear in the vicinity of the Sun: Mercury moving toward the North or sometimes South at a distance of no more than twenty degrees, i.e., two degrees of a single sign, and Venus departing approximately fifty degrees to the East and West.

71. Now, the term "rising" has various senses: in the strict sense, it is the first light of the Sun and stars or their emergence above the horizon; in the general sense, it is the first light of the Sun as it ushers in the day—the poets call it daybreak or sometimes dawn; *akronychos* gives the third sense, when as the Sun sets an astral body appears diametrically opposite it to the East. Similarly, "setting": in the strict sense, the first point of descent below the horizon; second, the first point of a star's disappearance as the Sun's light obscures it; the *akronychos* is third, when as the Sun rises a star sets diametrically opposite it. Of risings and settings, i.e., appearances and occultations, which are caused by the Sun, some occur in the morning and others in the evening. We speak of a morning rising whenever in the wake of first sunlight a particular star appears prior to its rising, as in the

eius apparet, ut Canicula; vespertinus, cum post occasum solis primitus exoriens astrum videtur, ut lunam novam dicimus exoriri. Similiter occasus matutinus quidem quotiens stella quae pridie ante solem orta erat proximante sibi sole splendore eius obumbrata obscuratur et latet, ut lunam videmus; vespertinus vero cum in occasu positam stellam aliquam sol consecutus primam eam corusco splendore condit.

72. Positionem vero atque ordinem collocationis globorum vel etiam orbium quibus collocati feruntur planetes quidam ex Pythagoreis hanc esse dixerunt: citimum quidem terrae praecipue esse lunae globum, post quem Mercurii secundo loco, supra quos Luciferi, superque eum solis, ultra quos globum Martium, ulterius Iovium, ultimum vero et vicinum aplani stellisque adhaerentibus ei Saturnium sidus, scilicet ut inter planetas sol medius locatus cordis, immo vitalium omnium praestantiam obtinere intellegatur. Consentit his Alexander Milesius ita dicens:

Sortitos celsis replicant anfractibus orbes:
vicinum terris circumvolat aurea luna,
quam super invehitur Cyllenius. Alma superne
nectareum ridens late splendet Cytherea.
Quadriiugis invectus equis sol igneus ambit
quartus et aethereas metas, quem deinde superne

case of the Dog Star; and of an evening rising when after sunset an astral body is first seen to rise, as when we speak of a new Moon's rising. Similarly, we speak of a morning setting whenever a star which on the previous day rose before the Sun is obscured and hidden because its light is overshadowed by the Sun as it approaches that star, as we see in the case of the Moon; and of an evening setting when the Sun, in proximity to a star that is in the process of setting, first buries the star with its shimmering rays.

72. Certain Pythagoreans have indicated that the position and order of collocation of the spheres or orbits along which the planets are placed and move is as follows: closest to Earth and most conspicuously is the sphere of the Moon, after which is that of Mercury in second position, and beyond them that of Venus, further beyond it that of the Sun, beyond them the globe of Mars, further still that of Jupiter, and furthest out but closest to the *aplanês* and stars that adhere to it, the star Saturn: so that the Sun by virtue of its occupying the middle position among the planets is understood to obtain the preeminence analogous to that of the heart, or indeed of the vital organs as a whole. Alexander of Miletus supports this with the following verses:

In lofty revolutions they repeat the orbits assigned them:
close to Earth the golden Moon wheels round,
above which the Cyllenian travels. The gentle Cytherean
sweetly smiling from on high broadcasts her light.
Fourth, the fiery Sun borne by his team of four horses
circles the ethereal boundaries, upon which from above

despicit Armipotens. Sextus Phaethontius ardor
suspicit excelsum brumali frigore sidus.
Plectricanae citharae septem discriminibus quos
assimilans genitor concordi examine iunxit.

73. Pythagoreum dogma est ratione harmonica constare
mundum caelestiaque distantia congruis et consonis sibi invicem intervallis impetu nimio et velocitate raptatus edere
sonos musicos. Quem secutus Eratosthenes motu quidem
stellarum sonos musicos edi consentit sed ordinem collocationis non eundem esse dicit. Statim quippe post lunam secundam altitudinem a terra soli dat memorans fabulose
Mercurium commenta recens a se lyra, cum caelum ascen-
deret, primitus transeuntem per ea quae motu planetum ad
organicum modum personabant a se inventae lyrae similem
miratum—quod imago a se inventi operis in caelo quoque
reperiretur stellarum collocatione—quae causa esset conci-
nentiae recensere: primum se a terra transmisisse lunae globum, post quem superasse solis, dehinc Mercurii (Stilbontis) et ceterorum cum aplani summa et excelsa. Mathematici
tamen neque hanc neque unam omnes ordinationem stellarum errantium ponunt sed solem quidem post lunam, ultra
hunc autem quidam Mercurium, quidam alium aliquem ex

the Mighty in Arms looks next. Sixth, Phaethon's light
gazes up in frozen cold to the lofty star.
The Father joined them in harmonious accord,
attuning them as with the seven tones of a plucked
    cithara.

73. The Pythagorean doctrine is that the world consists
of harmonic ratio and that the celestial bodies, separated by
intervals which are congruent and consonant with one another, produce musical sounds owing to the extremely rapid
impulse of their flight. Although Eratosthenes follows Pythagoras in agreeing that musical sounds are produced by
stellar movement, he does not affirm the same order of collocation. For he assigns the Sun the second position above
Earth, immediately after the Moon, and tells the tale of how
Mercury had just invented the lyre and, when he was ascending the heavens and first passed those bodies which in
their planetary movement produced sound as though on an
instrument, was struck by the fact that their manner of producing it resembled that of the lyre he had invented—that
even in the heavens there was found, in the stellar collocation, an image of the work he had invented—and recounted
his deduction as to the cause of the harmony: that from
Earth he had first passed the sphere of the Moon, that after
that he had passed that of the Sun, and thereafter those of
Mercury (Stilbon), and the rest, including the highest and
lofty *aplanês*. Not all astronomers, however, posit either this
or one and the same order of planets but some, although
placing the Sun after the Moon, place Mercury after the Sun
while others place another one of the remaining planets

residuis collocant. Plato etiam in hoc ipso Timaeo primam altitudinem a terra usque ad lunarem circulum, secundam usque ad solem liquido dimensus est, etiam in Politia non ordinationem modo commemorans planetum sed singulorum magnitudines velocitates, etiam colores, hoc est splendores ac serenitates, notans, axem caelitem fuso circulosque axem ambientes—tam extimos et vicinos polis quam medios tres—verticillis comparans.

74. Superest ut tractatui qui est habitus de stellis errantibus illud addatur, quasdam earum sequaces esse, quas appellant hypolipticas mathematici, ut sol et luna sunt, hi quippe ignes numquam ad praecedentia signa transitum faciunt sed ad ea semper quae sequuntur proptereaque nec subsistunt in motu nec regradantur umquam; alias vero stellas nonnumquam praeire nonnumquam deseri, ut ceterae, quae interdum stare interdum redire pro spisso motu videntur. Est quippe sequacitas visum imaginatioque stellae velut ad sequentia signa pergentis atque ad orientem transeuntis, ut a Cancro ad Leonem; statio vero visum et imaginatio stellae diu manentis in eodem loco iuxta aliam fixam stellam nec errantem; porro regradatio visum et imaginatio stellae propter stationem, quasi ad contrarium iter prioris itineris provectio. Quae omnia ita fieri nobis videntur sed reapse non ita fiunt ut videntur. Causa vero erroris in contemplando ea est, quod, cum per proprios orbes ferantur seu globos idem planetes infraque aplanos orbis excelsa, nobis e regione ter-

there. And here in the *Timaeus* too Plato lucidly measured out the distance from Earth to the lunar orbit as the first celestial height, and the second as that up to the Sun, and in the *Republic* he observes not only the order of the planets but their individual magnitudes, velocities, and colors, i.e., their brightness and purity, likening the celestial axis to a spindle and the orbits revolving around it—the outermost ones, those nearest the poles, and the three in between—to its flywheels. (See Diagram 12.)

74. It remains to add the following point to our treatment of the wandering stars: that some of them are followers, which the astronomers call hypoliptic, the Sun and Moon being examples, for these celestial luminaries never advance to signs that lie ahead but always to ones that follow and as such never cease from or reverse their movement; but that others alternate between advancing and being left behind, as with the rest, which depending on the sluggishness of their movement alternate between appearing to stand still and to move in reverse. Now, movement in reverse is the visual phenomenon of a star's progressing as though to signs that follow and advancing to the East, as from Cancer to Leo; standing still is the visual phenomenon of a star's remaining over time in the same place, alongside another that is fixed and nonwandering; and retrogradation is the visual phenomenon produced by a star in consequence of its standing still, its advancing as though in a direction contrary to the previous one. To us all of these phenomena appear to occur as described, although in reality they do not occur in the way they appear. The cause of the error in our contemplation of these matters is that, although the planets move consistently through their proper orbits or spheres below

rae videntibus obiectu aerei corporis impediente aspectum zodiacum exteriorem orbem peragrare videantur. Faciendum ergo ut expositis demonstratisque errorum causis falsa opinio conquiescat.

75. Est igitur totius mundi talis constitutio ex corporibus materiisque integris, providentiae gubernaculis ad motum aeternitati convenientem directa motuique proprio similem formam praeferens globeam. Verum ad dinumerationem conversionesque temporum immutationesque et diversitatem terrenorum stellarum errantium varius motus necessarius omnibus qui nunc accidunt proventibus auctoritatem dedit. Quippe simplex atque uniformis aplanus, utpote eiusdem naturae, rata atque eadem semper conversio aequalis et ordinata, errantium vero orbiculata quidem et ipsa sed neque aequalis et inordinata variaque, nec una sed multiformis.

76. At vero sub luna usque ad nos omne genus motuum omne etiam mutationum, prorsus ut est in vetere versu [Naevii]:

<N>ex ubi vis rabies furiarum examina mille.

Namque generatio et item mors in isto loco incrementa quoque et imminutiones et omnifaria commutatio transitioque ex locis ad loca, quae cunctae passiones originem trahunt ex motu planetum. Quod tamen hac ratione hactenus dicitur, ne quis putet illa aeterna et beata generatorum et

the heights of the nonwandering sphere, to us, whose view originates from Earth's region such that the interposition of the aerial element impedes it, they appear to progress along the outer sphere of the zodiac. Our task, then, is to ensure that false opinion acquiesces once the causes of errors have been laid out and demonstrated.

75. Such, then, is the constitution of the world in its entirety: consisting of bodies and material elements which are complete in themselves, directed by the rudder of providence to a form of movement suited to eternity, and in conformity with its proper movement bearing spherical form. For the computation and revolutions of time, however, and for the changes and diversity between earthly things the varied movement of the wandering stars was necessary and conferred authority upon all the developments that now occur. So the circumlation of the *aplanês,* being of the nature of the Same, is simple and uniform, fixed and forever the same, constant and ordered, whereas that of the wandering bodies, although orbital in itself, is inconstant, disordered, and variable, manifold rather than unified.

76. But from the Moon down to us there is every kind of movement and change, as indeed in the ancient verse:

Where are murder, violence, madness, and a thousand
    hosts of furies.

For birth and death are in this region, also increase and diminution, every kind of transformation, and transposition from place to place, and all these and the other affects originate in planetary movement. And yet this sort of claim is sustained only up to a point: one should not suppose that those eternal and blessed beings are disposed thus for the

occiduorum causa sic esse disposita, quin potius illa quidem
habere congruum felicitati suae cursum, haec vero ex accidenti quodam et aliquatenus consentienti cum illis consortio imitari quoad possunt divinam felicitatem. Ut enim universae rei motus similis esset semperque in orbem rotaretur
ipsa haec agitatio, [vita] actus atque operatio mundi existens et vita divina, necesse fuit terram mediam manere, circa
quam quae per medium ferrentur irent; terra porro manente
ignem diversam regionem capessere levem altivagam, quae
materiam sequebatur; hisque late distantibus ratio poscebat
ceteras quoque aeris et item aquae materias inseri medias
continuandi totius corporis causa. His porro ad unam veluti
seriem continuatis demum erat necesse fore aliquam ex alio
ad aliud elementum transfusionem, cum eorum silva sit
utrobique mutabilis, ipsarum autem materiarum vis et natura contraria.

77. Causa itaque mutationum ex vario motu planetum,
nam si una eademque esset perinde ut fixarum stellarum circumvectio, unum semper eundemque modum observanti-
bus omnibus stellis, ne ista quidem ulla proveniret diversitas. At nunc conversiones et aequinoctia processusque et
regradationes per latitudinem perque altum, maxime quidem solis et lunae tum ceterorum quoque siderum, vices
temporum mutant et omnem istam important commuta-
tionem atque inconstantiam. Quae quidem inconstantia

sake of the things that come to be and perish, but rather that the course of their movement is consistent with their state of imperturbability while these below imitate insofar as they can the divine imperturbability owing to a certain incidental quality and limited communion comporting with those above. For in order that the movement of the universe might be consistent and this very force engage in endless orbital rotation as the activity, existent operation, and divine life of the world, it was necessary that Earth should abide at the center and that the things that move in the middle region should revolve around it; and that while Earth abided fire should occupy the opposite region, which in consequence of its material element floats on high; and with these standing at farthest removes, reason demanded as well that the other material elements, air and water, should be placed in the middle for purposes of binding the whole corporeal continuum. And once they had been bound together in a kind of unified series, it was then necessary that there should be a certain flowing between one element and the other, since their matter is mutable both ways and the natural potency of the material elements themselves one of contrariety.

77. Thus the cause of such changes originates in the varied movement of the planets. For if as in the case of the fixed stars theirs were a unified and invariable rotation, with all of the stars constantly adhering to the same disposition, then there would no diversity, certainly not of the sort down here. But in fact the solstices and equinoxes, the advances and retrogradations in latitude and altitude, those especially of the Sun and Moon but also of the other celestial bodies, produce the ordered succession of times and account for every form of change and variability down here. Now, the

non ita ut nobis videtur provenit, nulla enim in divinis actibus inconstantia; sed ut ita videatur fit ex eo quod, illis positis et immobiliter adhaerentibus propriis circulis per quos
feruntur aequali semper ordinatoque gressu, noster visus
ferri ea per altiora convexa signiferi orbis imaginetur ex
ordinatione rati et aequabilis motus, nascente motu prae-
postero iuxta visum hominum. Consequenter; est enim aequalis quidem motus qui aequalia spatia aequalibus curriculis temporum conficit sine pigritia vel incitatione, ordinatus
vero in quo neque resistitur nec retrorsum reditur sed ad
proxima quaeque moderato incessu pervenitur, videntur tamen nobis omnes quidem planetes non aequali motu quidam tamen inordinata quoque agitatione ferri.

78. Quam igitur causam dicemus huius erroris praesump-
tionisque? Supra memoratam a Pythagora intellectam: quod
cum in globis suis consistentes ferantur per zodiacum ferri
languente visus acie putentur. Id adeo in aliquo ex errantibus, immo in eo per quem videntur omnia, sole, consideretur. Sit enim zodiacus circulus per ABΓΔ notas circumactus;
cuius et universi mundi in medietate posita, iuxta quam sti-
patam manere dicimus terram, littera sit Θ; per quam lineae
duae dirigantur bis secantes circulum in aequalia dimensa
quattuor hae AΓ et BΔ, diametros utraque; intellegaturque
A in exordio Arietis locatum, B in exordio Cancri, item Γ in
regione Librae, Δ Capricorni. Ergo sol accedens ad A facere

variability does not occur precisely as appears to us, for in the divine activities there is no variability; but that it should appear so results from the fact that, although the planets are immovably fixed and adherent to the individual orbits through which they move in constantly stable and ordered progression, our vision forms an impression of their moving through the outer vaults of the zodiac, so that from our perspective there occurs a movement in reverse. This is inevitable, for although there is an unvarying movement which without deceleration or acceleration covers fixed distances within fixed temporal intervals, an ordered movement in which there is no stopping or reversal of direction but regulated progress through successive points, to us all of the planets nevertheless appear to move at different rates, and certain ones in disordered patterns.

78. What, then, will we say is the cause of this persistent error? The one mentioned earlier, and as understood by Pythagoras: that, although they move consistently with their individual orbits, because of a failure in our visual acuity they are thought to move through the zodiac. Let this be considered in connection with one of the planets, indeed, the one because of which all things are visible, the Sun. Let the zodiacal circle be drawn around through the points ΑΒΓΔ; positioned at the center of this and of the universe let there be the letter Θ, at which we maintain that the Earth sits motionless and dense; let two lines, each one a diameter, be drawn through it, ΑΓ and ΒΔ, bisecting the circle twice, into four equally measured sections; and let A be conceived as positioned at the beginning of Aries, B at the beginning of Cancer, Γ similarly in the region of Libra, and Δ in that of Capricorn. Now, on reaching A the Sun is seen

videtur aequinoctium vernum, ad B autem aestivam conversionem, item ad Γ autumnale aequinoctium, ad Δ hiema-
lem conversionem. Aequales ergo partes mundi quattuor
has AB, BΓ, ΓΔ, ΔA iniquis et imparibus temporibus videtur circumire, siquidem ex aequinoctio verno usque ad aestivam conversionem spatium caeli quod interiacet nonaginta fere et quattuor semis diebus et noctibus conficit, ex
conversione vero aestiva usque ad autumnale aequinoctium
nonaginta et duobus semis diebus et noctibus pervenit, ab
autumnali porro aequinoctio pergens ad brumalem conversionem octoginta et octo diebus pervenit et octava parte
unius diei, residuum item spatium quod inter brumalem
conversionem et vernum aequinoctium interiacet nonaginta fere diebus et parte octua diei conficit; proptereaque
omnem circuli meatum trecentis sexaginta et quinque diebus ac noctibus et parte quarta diei propemodum obire consensu omnium creditur: e regione Geminorum tardissimus,
e finibus Sagittarii volucer, medius in transitione tam Virgi-
nis quam etiam Piscium. Fieri tamen non potest ut contra
naturam suam divinitate praeditam faciant aliquid vel patiantur inordinatum; ex quo apparet per suum circulum et
solem et ceteras stellas meantes aequabiliter et ordinate nobis e regione terrae spectantibus videri per ABΓΔ circulum,
qui est non solstitialis sed zodiacus, meare.

79. Quia igitur non per hunc zodiacum circulum sol, sed
per alium solstitialem qui est eius proprius incedit, siquidem
utriusque circuli punctum unum et idem esset in Θ, eadem
ratione divisus solstitialis, qua zodiacus, in isdem vitiis et
iniquitatibus inveniretur eodemque modo ABΓΔ circuli
partes aequales quattuor pluribus has, paucioribus alias

to produce the vernal equinox, and on reaching B, the summer solstice, and Γ, the autumnal equinox, and Δ, the winter
solstice. It is seen, then, to circle these four equal parts of
the world, AB, BΓ, ΓΔ, ΔA, in unequal or differing periods
of time, since from the vernal equinox to the summer solstice it covers the intervening stretch of the sky in approximately 94½ days and nights, and it moves from the summer
solstice to the autumnal equinox in 92½ days and nights,
journeying from the autumnal equinox to the winter solstice
in 88⅛ days, and the stretch that remains between the winter solstice and vernal equinox it covers in approximately
90⅛ days; so that by universal consent it is held to traverse
the full course of its orbit in approximately 365¼ days and
nights: most slowly from the region of Gemini, swiftly from
the edge of Sagittarius, at an intermediate pace in the transition from both Virgo and Pisces. And yet it is impossible
that they act or are acted upon in a disorderly way, against
their divinely endowed nature; and for this reason it appears
to us, who gaze out from the region of Earth, that the Sun
and other wandering stars, although moving through their
individual orbits at a constant and ordered pace, travel
through the orbit ABΓΔ, i.e., not the solar one but the zodiacal. (See Diagram 13.)

79. Since, then, the Sun passes, not through this zodiacal
orbit, but through another, the solar orbit which is proper
to it: given that the center at Θ is for each circle one and the
same, the solar orbit should turn out to be divided in the
same way as the zodiac, with the same defects and irregular-
ities, and should lead through the four equal parts of the
circle ABΓΔ in the same manner: through some parts over
the course of more days, through others over the course of

obiret diebus. Sed si haec contra naturam siderum falso putare homines ratio monstraverit, certe perspicuum erit illius
globi per quem sol movetur punctum in Θ non esse. Ergo
circulus solis vel intra se continebit Θ, sed non ut punctum
vel medietatem, vel per idem Θ transiet vel excludet omnino a gremio suo. At enim per Θ, id est terram, ire solem
impossible est, conflagrabunt enim terrena solis ardoribus
semperque solis globo superiore existente dies erit perpetua
nec ei succedet nox, numquam scilicet mergente sole.
Superest igitur ut Θ vel intra ambitum solstitialis circuli sit
vel extra, utrumque enim assumptum rationem habere
monstrabitur. Quae quidem res inter mathematicos disceptationem creavit, siquidem alii sphaeris eccentris, id est
quae terram intra se contineant quidem sed non ut punctum
suum, vehi planetas asserunt, alii epicyclis potius, hoc est a
terra separativis nec imminentibus ei globis.

80. Sit igitur solstitialis eccentrus circulus EZHK et habeat punctum sub EZ ambitu in medietate, scilicet ubi est
M. Hoc igitur circulo in trecentas sexaginta quinque partes
et partem quartam unius portionis diviso ad earundem partium exaequationem EZ quidem ambitus nonaginta quattuor semis portionibus continebitur, ZH vero nonaginta
duum semis erit partium, item HK octoginta et octo partes
habebit et unius partis octavam, residuus ambitus KE ex
nonaginta constabit partibus et octava unius partis. Necesse
est itaque ut cum sol accedat ad eam partem in qua est E
nobis in puncto agentibus mundi totius Θ, id est terra, et
inde quoad possumus intuentibus super A tunc ferri videatur, cum illa regio non solstitialis circuli sed zodiaci sit multo

fewer. But if reason demonstrates that humans hold these views falsely, against what the nature of the heavenly bodies allows, then it will surely be clear that the center of the sphere through which the sun moves is not at Θ. The solar orbit, then, will either contain Θ within itself, but not as its center point, or it will pass through the same Θ, or it will exclude it altogether from its inner recess. But it is impossible for the Sun to pass through Θ, i.e., Earth, since terrestrial things will burn up because of the heat of the Sun, and if the Sun's sphere is always hovering overhead then the day will be endless, with no night to replace it, namely, since the Sun would never set. It remains, then, that Θ is either within or outside the circumference of the solar orbit, for each assumption will be shown to be rationally defensible. This matter has in fact created debate among astronomers, for some assert that the planets move through eccentric spheres, i.e., ones that contain the Earth but not as their center, and others that it moves through epicycles, i.e., spheres offset from the Earth and not directly above it. (See Diagram 14.)

80. Let, then, the solar orbit be the eccentric circle EZHK and have its center in the middle, under the arc EZ, namely, where M is. Once this circle is divided into 365¼ sections such that they are equal, the arc EZ will comprise 94½ sections, ZH will be 92½ sections, and HK will have 88⅛ sections, and the remaining arc, KE, will consist of 90⅛ sections. Hence when the Sun approaches the section in which E lies, it is necessary that to us, who operate at the center of the whole world, Θ, i.e., Earth, and gaze out as far as possible from there, it should then appear to hover above A, although that region marks the zenith, not of the solar

altioris summitas, ad quam visus noster non potest pervenire. Atque ita per EZ ambitum means aequabiliter, qui ambitus tribus ceteris maior est, pluribus ut necesse est diebus
maiorem ambitum conficiens, ubi ad Z pervenerit ad B pervenisse videbitur, et tamquam AB peragrato ambitu aequalem quartam partem zodiaci circuli pluribus quam ratio
aequabilitatis exigit diebus obisse creditur. Rursumque ZH
ambitu sui circuli secundae magnitudinis peragrato aequabiliter diebus nonaginta duobus semis (tot enim partium est
idem ambitus), ubi ad H pervenerit videbitur nobis ad Γ
pervenisse et BΓ ambitum velut aequalem priori paucioribus diebus emensus. Eodemque modo HK minimum ambitum lustrans, utpote qui sit in octoginta octo partibus et
octava, ubi totidem diebus obierit perveneritque ad K, e
regione Θ spectantibus videbitur quidem ferri supra Δ, putabitur autem ΓΔ ambitum aequalem ceteris paucioribus
diebus obisse. Similique erroris perseverantia KE ambitu
emenso nonaginta diebus et octava parte iuxta numerum
portionum repraesentatusque demum in E finito anniversa-
rio anfractu ΔA ambitum putatur emensus aequalem ceteris
iniquo et impari gressu nec in E exordium sui circuli repraesentatus sed in A alieni, id est zodiaci, circuli summitatem.
Quod si duum circulorum, id est maioris zodiaci et minoris
solstitialis eccentri, duo puncta coniungantur et fiat MΘ,

orbit, but of the zodiac much higher up, and our vision is incapable of reaching that region. And so, moving at a constant rate of speed through the arc EZ, which is longer than the other three, and inevitably covering the larger arc over the course of a greater number of days, on reaching Z it will appear to have reached B, and once the arc AB has apparently been traversed, the Sun is believed to have passed through an equal section, a fourth, of the zodiacal belt in a greater number of days than is required by a ratio derived on the assumption of constant velocity and distance. Again, once the arc ZH, the second largest in the orbit, over the course of 92½ days (corresponding to the number of degrees comprised by the arc) has been traversed at a constant rate of speed, on reaching H it will appear to us to have reached Γ and to have traversed an arc, BΓ, apparently equal to the previous one over the course of fewer days. Similarly, in moving through HK, the smallest arc insofar as it consists of 88⅛ degrees, after traveling for as many days and reaching K, although to those observing from region Θ it will appear to hover above Δ, it will be reckoned to have traversed an arc, ΓΔ, equal to the others over the course of fewer days. And to continue with this deceptive phenomenon, once the arc KE has been traversed over the course of 90⅛ days, corresponding to the number of degrees, and the Sun finally appears in E as its yearly orbit is brought to an end, it is reckoned to have traversed an arc, ΔA, equal to the others at an unequal or different velocity, since it appears to be, not at the starting point, E, of its own orbit, but at A, the zenith of another one, i.e., the zodiac. But if the respective center points of these two circles, i.e., the larger (zodiac) and the smaller (solar eccentric) one, were to be connected and MΘ

deinde per hanc ducta perexeat NΞ linea: quia EZHK circuli punctum et medietas est M et Θ ΑΒΓΔ circuli punctum et medietas est, aequales erunt lineae NM, MΞ; maior igitur est NM linea quam ΞΘ, multo ergo maior NΘ quam ΘΞ. Cum ergo sol per N feretur longius a terra remotus, id est a Θ, minor nobis videbitur e longinquo, etiam tardior, quod fit iuxta quintam semis fere partem Geminorum; cum vero per Ξ feretur proximus terrae, maior putabitur velociorque intuentibus, quod demum fit iuxta quintam semis partem Sagittarii; mediae vero tam staturae quam velocitatis, cum aut Pisces aut Virginem transiet.

81. Et quoniam solis motus intemperiem falso putari demonstravimus in eccentris circulis, nunc si, ut quidam putant, per epicyclos globos fertur, nihilo minus moderatis eum gressibus temperatisque conficere annuos cursus exposita epicyclorum forma docebimus. Epicyclus dicitur globus qui per aliquem circulum fertur. Sit igitur etiam nunc zodiacus circulus quem limitant notae ΑΒΓΔ, solstitialis vero excludens zodiaci circuli punctum, id est EZHK, habens ipse proprium punctum M; et a puncto quidem Θ intervallo autem M describatur circulus MONΞ; et EZHK epicyclus intellegatur cum universi mundi vertigine rapi similiter ut ceteri ignes ab oriente in occidentem raptatu cotidiano, ferri tamen naturaliter adversum totius mundi volatum; solque rursus in eodem epicyclo constitutus iuxta totius mundi conversionem moveri. Ergo EZHK epicyclus per

produced, and then a line NΞ were to be drawn extending through it and beyond: since M is the center point of the circle EZHK and Θ the center point of circle ABΓΔ, lines NM and MΞ will be equal; line NM is therefore greater than ΞΘ, and consequently NΘ much greater than ΘΞ. And so as the Sun moves farther away from the Earth, i.e., Θ, through N, it will at a distance appear smaller from our perspective, slower as well, as proves to be the case in connection with the fifth and a half degree of Gemini; but as it moves through Ξ, closest to Earth, to observers it will appear to be larger and more rapid, as ultimately proves to be the case in connection with the fifth and a half degree of Sagittarius; and of medium size as well as velocity when it passes through either Pisces or Virgo.

81. And given that we have demonstrated the falseness of supposing that the movement of the Sun is erratic, we will now show, after laying out the pattern of its epicycles, that if it moves through epicyclical spheres, as some suppose, it nevertheless completes its annual course in moderated and ordered stages. By epicycle we mean a sphere that moves along a certain orbit. Let, then, the zodiacal circle now be defined by the points ABΓΔ and the solar one, i.e., EZHK, exclude the center point of the zodiacal circle while having M as its center point; and at the interval from point Θ to M let a circle MONΞ be drawn; and as in the case of the other luminaries, let the epicycle EZHK be understood to be carried along by the rotation of the universe in its daily course from East to West but naturally to move contrary to the course of the whole world; conversely, let the Sun, fixed in the same epicycle, be understood to move according to the rotation of the whole world. Thus while moving through the

descriptum MONΞ circulum naturali motu means contra quam movetur totius mundi raptatio moderate et aequabiliter anni spatio cursum istum conficiat solque item in hoc eodem epicyclo constitutus epicycli quidem sui motui contrarium motum moliatur, mundi vero totius comitatum sequatur. Ibit ergo EZHK epicyclus per MONΞ circulum gradiens et, cum pervenerit ad O litteram, quartam mundi partem obibit; tunc sol ab E ad K perget; erit ergo sol ubi est O littera, nobis tamen a terra, id est Θ, spectantibus directa visus acie videbitur esse apud notam B; ita cum quartam confecerit mundi partem, minorem quartam confecisse videbitur. Ac rursum idem epicyclus a regione O litterae profectus perveniat ad N, et sol a K ad H perget; erit ubi est N, nobis tamen directo visu intuentibus videbitur esse ubi est Γ littera; ita cum aequalem quartam mundi partem confecerit a littera B usque ad Γ litteram, maiorem quartam citius et incitatius videbitur peragrasse. Rursum idem epicyclus conficiat aliam mundi aequalem partem, id est NΞ, sol quoque item ut in prioribus ab H ad Z pergat; erit ubi est Ξ, nobis autem videbitur ubi est Δ littera; ita cum aequalem quartam mundi partem peragraverit, maiorem peragrasse putabitur ΓΔ zodiaci circuli. Residuum demum quadrantem ΞM idem obeat epicyclus; cum pervenerit ad E repraesentatus post annum loco suo, videbitur esse tunc sol ubi est A et putabitur zodiaci circuli obrepsisse semitam ΔA.

82. Qua ratione palam fit etiam secundum epicycli

depicted circle MONΞ in a motion that is naturally contrary to that of the whole world, the epicycle EZHK moder-
ately and without variation completes this course in the
space of a year, and the Sun, established in this same epicycle, forces a movement contrary to that of its own epicycle
even as it follows in the train of the whole world. Thus the
epicycle EZHK will make its way through the circle
MONΞ and on reaching the letter O cover a fourth part of
the world; the Sun will then proceed from E to K; hence the
Sun will be where the letter O is but will appear to us, observing with a direct line of sight from Earth, i.e., Θ, to be at
point B; and so on completing a fourth part of the world it
will appear to have completed a smaller fourth. And again,
let the same epicycle proceed from the region of the letter
O and reach N while the Sun proceeds from K to H; it will
be where N is but will appear to us, gazing with a direct line
of sight, to be where the letter Γ is; and so on completing an
equal, fourth part of the world, from letter B to the letter Γ,
it will appear to have covered a larger quarter at a more rapid
and accelerated pace. Again, let the same epicycle complete
another equal part of the world, i.e., NΞ, and the Sun proceed from H to Z, as in the previous stages; it will be where
Ξ is but will appear to us to be where the letter Δ is; and so
on covering an equal, fourth part of the world, it will be supposed to have covered a greater part of the zodiacal belt,
ΓΔ. Finally, let the same epicycle move through the remaining quarter, ΞM; on reaching E and reappearing in its proper
place after a year, the Sun will then appear to be where A is
and be thought to have crept along path ΔA of the zodiacal
belt. (See Diagram 15.)

82. And by this line of reasoning, following the move-

motum ea quae videntur nobis aliter quam reapse fiunt
videri; tardior enim et minor visu videtur sol cum velut in
Geminis erit, maximus vero et incitatissimus cum velut in
Sagittario. Nec immerito; quippe EZHK epicyclo moto per
MONΞ circulum sol ab E ad K pergens contra quam fertur
epicyclus suus moram faciens tardius ad O deferetur tardiusque MO obibit ambitum multoque tardius zodiaci circuli
AB regionem obisse existimatur. Et rursum epicyclo supra
dicto moto ad ON ambitum sol demum a K ad H pergens
concurrere videbitur mundi circumactioni et adiutus ab ea
propere et citius obire zodiaci quadrantem. Eodemque
modo epicyclo moto per NΞ ambitum sol demum ab H ad
Z pergens tamquam praecurrens epicycli sui motum praeci-
pitare cursum per zodiacum videtur. Rursumque eodem epicyclo moto per ΞM ambitum sol a Z ad E pergens contra
quam fertur epicyclus suus moram faciens tardius ad M deferetur tardiusque ΞM obibit quadrantem multoque putatur tardius ΔA zodiaci circuli quadrantem peragrasse. Sic et
epicyclus anno vertente conficiet cursum suum et sol naturalem estque in solis circuitu maximum intervallum a Θ ad
E, id est, a terra ad summum limitem solstitialis epicycli,
minimum vero ad eiusdem infimum limitem.

83. Eodem modo ceteri planetae cum in globis consistentes ferantur per zodiacum ferri nobis ob supra demonstratas

ment of the epicycle, it becomes clear that phenomena appear differently to us than how they occur in reality; for as to what we see, the Sun appears slower and smaller when approaching Gemini but at its largest and most rapid when approaching Sagittarius. And rightly so, since as the epicycle EZHK moves through the orbit MONΞ the Sun, in moving contrary to its epicycle from E to K and producing a retarding effect, will the more slowly arrive at O and move through the arc MO and be reckoned to have moved much more slowly through region AB of the zodiacal belt. And again, as the aforesaid epicycle moves through to the end of the arc ON the Sun, proceeding then from K to H, will appear to run in tandem with the revolution of the world and, being hastened by it, to move increasingly rapidly through a quarter of the zodiac. In the same way, as the epicycle moves through the arc NΞ the Sun, proceeding then from H to Z and by all appearances outstripping the movement of its own epicycle, appears to hasten its course through the zodiac. And again, as the same epicycle moves through the arc ΞM the Sun, in moving contrary to its epicycle from Z to E and producing a retarding effect, will the more slowly arrive at M and move through the quarter ΞM and be supposed to have covered much more slowly the quarter ΔA of the zodiacal belt. Thus as the year comes around to completion the epicycle and Sun will each complete its natural course, and there is in the solar orbit a largest distance, from Θ to E, i.e., from Earth to the outermost limit of the solar epicycle, and a smallest one, to the innermost limit of the same.

83. In the same way, although the other planets move fixed in their spheres, for the reasons demonstrated above they appear to us to move through the zodiac, and the same

causas videntur, tarditatisque et celeritatis idem intellectus in omnibus erraticis rationem assequetur, licet diversis temporibus ceteri nec isdem quibus sol cursus suos peragant usque adeo ut quidam eorum propter nimiam tarditatem interdum consistere interdum repedare videantur. Sol enim minorem, utpote anniversarium, circulum lustrans minores evagationes, vel cum exaltatur vel cum humiliatur vel cum a medietate ad diversas caeli plagas discedit, incurrere nobis videtur eamque omnem intemperiem anni vertentis termino claudit. Ceteri planetae, quia singillatim uniuscuiusque eorum pro magnitudine circulorum quos obeunt et prolixitate temporum quibus confecto cursu ad exordia revertuntur fit reditus ad exordia, varias et multiformes motuum condiciones pati non immerito putantur; quippe unus biennio alter duodecim annis tertius prope triginta orbes suos obeunt. Ex quo fit ut visus noster motum stellarum notans sine intellectu et recordatione alterius stellae compendii ex brevitate circuli provenientis, aliarum item tarditatis quae provenit ex amplissimorum orbium peragrationibus, praeire alios planetas alios subsistere alios regradari, id est ferri retrorsum, imaginetur. Quod in circuitu solis Luciferique et Stilbontis minime apparet, propter brevitatem circulorum angustiasque temporis intra quod conficiunt cursus suos, multoque etiam magis in lunae motibus; quippe in horum motibus vel statio vel regradatio nulla cernitur sed in

interpretation will suffice to account for both the slowness and rapidity in all of the wandering bodies, although the others complete their various courses within periods diverse and different from those of the Sun, to the point that some of them appear intermittently to stop and reverse direction owing to their extreme slowness. For in covering its smaller orbit, the one that defines the year, the Sun appears to us to undergo smaller deviations in its ascent, descent, or departure from the center to one celestial zone or the other, and it confines all of that variation within the limit of its yearly cycle. As to the other planets, since for each of them individually there is a return to the starting point, a return determined by the magnitude of the orbits they complete and the length of time required to bring each course back to its starting point, they are understandably thought to undergo varying and manifold changes of movement; for one completes its orbit in two years, another in twelve, and another in nearly thirty. The result of this is that in its observations of stellar movement our vision forms the impression that planets variously advance, stop, and retrace their steps, i.e., move in reverse, for it ignorantly misapprehends the gain one star makes owing to the brevity of the orbit it travels, and the falling behind of others that results from their traversing the most enormous orbits. There is no such phenomenon in connection with the orbit of the Sun, Lucifer, or Mercury, because of the brevity of their orbits and the restricted time within which they complete their various courses, and much more so in connection with the movements of the Moon; for there is no observed stopping or retrogradation in connection with the movements of these bodies, but only in connection with those whose larger

illis solis quorum maiores ambitus competenti temporis
prolixitate peragrantur.

84. Aristoteles tamen contra opinionem omnium neque
quiescente corpore aethereo ferri stellas veluti soluto ac libero motu, nec secundum universae rei motum vel contra
moveri docet, quin potius omnes eas trahi una et eadem naturali mundi circumactione. Idemque et eccentrorum et
epicyclorum tollit opinionem propterea quod circulis, hoc
est lineis picturatis et carentibus corpore, vehi stellarum
vera et solida corpora non posse dicat. Quatenus enim corpus incorporeae rei nexu vinciri possit? Sed sphaeras esse
quasdam quinti illius corporis naturae congruentes easdemque per omne caelum ferri vario diversoque motu, earum
alias esse maximas alias minimas, quasdam ex alto moveri
quasdam ad ima esse depressas, iamque alias cassas solidas
item alias stellarum corpora continentes, easdemque omnes
perinde ut ceteras stellas minime errantes infixas esse caelo
atque ex diversis regionibus depressisque et elatioribus locis
ad occidentem meare; eamque esse causam cur circulorum
effigies depingatur, quia concursus ad unum locum ex diversis caeli plagis tamquam vestigia variorum deliniet tra-
mitum, ut si naves ex omnibus maris regionibus ad unum
eundemque portum variis temporibus deferantur. Ac de
stellarum quidem errantium inconstanti discursione dictum
satis.

85. Sequitur ut, quoniam videntur quaedam nobis earum

orbits are traversed over a proportionately long period of time.

84. But against universally received opinion Aristotle teaches that the stars do not move in uncontrolled, as it were, and free patterns while the body of ether remains motionless, or that they move in conformity with or contrary to the universe, but that they are instead drawn by the unified and constant natural revolution of the world. And he also refutes the received opinion concerning both the eccentrics and epicycles, on the grounds that stellar bodies which are truly solid cannot be conveyed along circles, i.e., along lines that have been drawn and lack corporeality. For to what extent can a body be bound by a connection with an incorporeal thing? But he claims that certain spheres are congruent with the nature of that fifth corporeal element and travel through the whole heaven with varying and diverse movement: some of them are extremely large and others extremely small; certain ones move on high while others are pressed down toward the lower areas; and now some are hollow and others solid, containing the stellar bodies; and all of them, like the other nonwandering stars, are fixed in the heaven and from their different regions and lower and higher locations move toward the West. And he says that the reason why the image depicted is one of circles is that the convergence on a single location from different zones of the heaven produces an image of the traces, as it were, of various paths, as if ships from all regions of the sea were at various times to move toward one and the same port. But enough has been said about the variable course of the wandering stars.

85. Since some of them appear from our perspective to

modo stare in progressu, modo regradari et interdum praecurrere certa signa zodiaci circuli, interdum remanere ac relinqui, quae causa sit huius imaginis consideretur. Sit ergo
zodiacus circulus ABΓΔ cuius punctum in medietate Θ, epicyclus autem erraticae cuiuslibet stellae EZH cuius item
punctum in medietate sit littera M; per quam medietatem
velut axem proprium feratur idem epicyclus cum stella in
semet locata zodiaci circuli pari motu, hoc est ab oriente in
occidentem. Agantur etiam e regione Θ obliquae duae lineae, stringentes utrimque extremos ambitus epicycli, ΘZB
ΘHΔ, perque epicycli punctum M ducatur in altum linea
ΘMA. Ergo stella cum erit in Z, nobis e terra directo visu
spectantibus videbitur consistere in regione zodiaci in qua
est B, et cum ZE lustraverit ambitum, putabitur zodiaci BA
ambitum peragrasse et ad praecedentia signa versum pro-
gressa esse. Similiter EH ambitu lustrato videbitur AΔ zodiaci ambitum obisse et ad praecedentia versum signa nunc
festinasse. Rursum HZ regione peragrata videbitur nobis
per ΔA ad B demum repedasse obvia facta signis sequacibus
proptereaque esse regradata. Cumque non multum spatii a
Z recedet, etiam nunc tamquam in B diu in eodem loco mo-
rari putabitur; at vero cum recesserit longius transitoque E
limite ad H pervenerit, rursum consistere in Δ et praecedentia signa existimabitur praecurrisse recedensque ab H
longius per HZ ad B repedasse.

come to halt their progress at one time then move in reverse at another, and sometimes to move in advance of certain signs along the zodiacal belt and sometimes to keep pace with them or to be left behind, the next step is to consider the reason for this visual impression. So let there be a zodiacal circle ABΓΔ whose center point is Θ and an epicycle EZH of some wandering star, with, similarly, the letter M as its center point; and around this center as its proper axis let the same epicycle, along with the star situated on it, proceed in a movement that is the same as that of the zodiacal belt, that is, from East to West. Let as well two angled lines ΘZB and ΘHΔ be drawn from point Θ, tangent on either side to the periphery of the epicycle, and through point M of the epicycle let line ΘMA be drawn vertically. So then, when the star reaches Z, to us, looking directly out from Earth, it will appear to be in the region of the zodiac where B is, and on having traversed the arc ZE it will be thought to have completed the zodiacal arc BA and to have moved in reverse toward the preceding signs. Similarly, on having traversed the arc EH it will appear to have moved through the zodiacal arc AΔ and now to have hastened in reverse toward the preceding signs. Again, on having completed the region HZ it will appear to us to have retraced its course through ΔA and finally to B—will appear by virtue of its being in the path of the stars behind it to have moved in reverse. And on receding a slight distance from Z it will still be thought to remain motionless in the fixed point B for a period; but on having receded further and reaching H after passing point E it will once again be supposed to be in Δ and to have moved in advance of the signs ahead of it and, on receding further from H, to have retraced its course through HZ to B. (See Diagram 16.)

86. Mathematicorum tamen non eadem est opinio quae philosophorum, qui non ad ea quae videntur sed ad naturalem stellarum motum animadvertunt; nullam quippe stellam diverso contrariove motu moveri contra universae rei motum circumactionemque asserunt sed omnes uniformiter ferri secundum naturam suam. Faciam ergo ut etiam iuxta mathematicos EZH epicyclus contra totius mundi motum feratur: ergo stella cum erit in H videbitur esse penes Δ; et cum EH lustraverit ambitum AΔ zodiaci orbis ambitum obisse credetur iuxta signorum sequentium ordinem pergens; EZ autem ambitu lustrato similiter etiam nunc ad sequentia signa putabitur progredi; ZH porro ambitum emensa rursum consistere putabitur in Δ, per BA ambitum ad Δ retrorsum reversa proptereaque regradata. Atque ita tam physicorum quam mathematicorum rationibus stationum praecessionumque et regradationum visa patefiunt.

87. Longum est demonstrando persequi quae sit et quatenus accidat maxima stellarum errantium altitudo quaeve media quae minima, seu per eccentros ferantur seu per epicyclos circulos. Itaque veniemus ad demonstrationem coetuum quos alio etiam nomine concursus solemus vocare, item obstaculorum effulsionumque et repentinarum obscurationum. Erit porro dissertationis initium tale: Quia naturaliter visus noster in directum porrigitur, est porro longe excelsa et eminens sphaera quae aplanes dicitur, subter quam sunt positae sphaerae planetum ita, ut supra demonstravimus, ordinatae, perspicuum est lunae globum, qui est

86. But astronomers are not of the same opinion as philosophers, who reason, not from the visible phenomena, but from the natural movement of the stars; for they assert that no star moves in a divergent or contrary pattern against the movement and circumlation of the universe but that in accordance with their inherent nature they all move in uniformity. I will suppose, then, as astronomers too do, that the epicycle EZH moves contrary to the world as a whole: thus on reaching H the star will appear to be under Δ; and on completing the arc EH it will be believed to have traversed the arc AΔ of the zodiacal belt, progressing through the ordered sequence of signs; and on having traversed the arc EZ it will similarly be thought then to proceed to the following signs; and on having traversed the arc ZH it will be thought to stand once again in Δ, having reversed its course through the arc BA back to Δ and therefore moving backward. And so the phenomena of stopping, forward motion, and retrogradation surface in the explanations of natural philosophers as well as astronomers.

87. It would be a long task to demonstrate in detail the nature and extent of the maximum, intermediate, and minimum altitude of the wandering stars, and whether they move along eccentric orbits or epicycles. Hence we will move on to a demonstration of convergences, which we generally call by another name, "conjunctions," and of occultations, effulgences, and sudden eclipses. And the explanation will begin as follows: Given that our vision naturally extends in a direct line, and there is far above us and on high the sphere that is called the *aplanês,* below which are situated the spheres of the planets, ordered in the way we have demonstrated, it is clear that the lunar sphere, which is the

infimus proximusque terrae, ceteris ultra se locatis obstare
sideribus omniaque tam rata quam errantia, cum inter visum
nostrum et aliquod ex sideribus ad directam lineam se obiecerit, obumbrare. Sol autem, cui luna nonnumquam obstat,
alias stellas superiores diversa ratione condit, vel cum proximus factus lucis suae claritudine ceterorum luces tegit vel
cum obiectu suo visui nostro resultat. Stilbon vero et Lucifer et superiores a visu nostro stellas interpositi removent et
plerumque sibi invicem obsistunt propter mensuras non ae-
quas obliquationesque orbium et positionum diversitatem
superiores invicem humilioresque facti; mera enim prehen-
sio difficilis est in ipsis propter inseparabilem prope con-
cursum comitatumque. Solus quoque Mercurius minimo
corpore exiguoque igni soli magis proximus adhaerensque
eiusdem inflammatione obumbratur. Mars duos supra se
planetas plerumque condit. Phaenon quoque summus ab
obsistente sibi occultatur Phaethonte et omnes planetes
imminentes sibi ad directam lineam ratas stellas obumbrant.
Luna item diametro a sole distans et incurrens umbram terrae obscuratur nec tamen omnibus mensibus, sicut ne omni
quidem coetu, hoc est omni nova luna, solis obscuratio
intervenit aut omni plena perfectaque luna lunae labor fit
atque obscuratio, propterea quod circuli eorum nimia obliquitate a se invicem differant.

88. Quippe sol sub ipsam libram medietatis signiferi omnis modico dicatur ferri deflexior, ad dimidium fere momentum declinans vel in austrum vel in aquilonem, at vero luna,

lowest and closest to Earth, eclipses the other celestial bodies which are located above it, and that when it intrudes upon the direct line leading between our point of sight and any of the celestial bodies it conceals them all, the fixed as well as errant. And the Sun, which the Moon periodically eclipses, conceals other higher stars in various ways, either when in its proximity it buries the lights of the others because of the brightness of its own light, or when it blocks our line of vision by its interposition. Mercury and Venus, on the other hand, both remove the higher stars from our sight by their interposition and frequently block one another because of their disparate sizes, the obliquity of their orbits, and their respective positions, shifting between being higher and lower; in their case, unconfused perception is complicated by the fact that they are nearly always converging or moving in tandem. And Mercury alone, with its minimal size, weak light, and greater proximity or adherence to the Sun, is obscured owing to the brightness of the latter. Mars frequently conceals the two planets above it. And Saturn, the highest, is concealed by Jupiter's interposition, while all planets obscure the fixed stars located directly above them. Similarly, the Moon when standing diametrically opposite the Sun and encountering Earth's shadow is obscured, and yet not in all months, just as an eclipse of the Sun does not occur at every conjunction either, i.e., at every new moon, or a lunar eclipse or occultation at every full and complete moon, since their orbits differ significantly from one another in their obliquity. (See Diagram 17.)

88. For just below the mid-elevation of the whole zodiac the Sun can be said to move with a slight deviation, diverging by approximately half a degree to either the South or

ut asseverat Hipparchus, decem utrimque momentis devia
reperitur. Igitur si utrosque orbes epipedos—id est planos
et sine ulla soliditate—tam solis quam lunae consideremus
animo positos adversum se ita directa positione ut una per
medios orbes ducta linea spinam duobus planis orbibus in-
signiat, erit diametrus amborum eadem linea et eius summa
pars scindens proximum circulum catabibazon appellatur,
ima vero secans aeque sursum versum maiorem orbem ana-
bibazon. Quare si coetus solis et lunae fiet directus et velut
ad perpendiculi destinationem, utpote proximis sibi factis
ex concursu corporibus, obiciet se ante visum nostrum et
obstabit angustum videndi obsidens tramitem luna lucem-
que solis a nobis arcet, minor licet multo maiorem obcae-
cans ob directum proptereaque angustum oculorum nostrorum tramitem. Si vero non ad perpendiculum coetus eorum
factus erit sed prolixitas quidem intervalli <eadem> erit, latera porro a rigore declinabunt aliquatenus ita ut alter ignium ad aquilonem alter vero ad austrum vergat, obscuratio
nulla fiet.

89. Lunae vero labor sive defectio sic demonstratur.
Quod quidem cum incurrerit umbram terrae deficere videatur constat apud omnes, sed cur non semper aut omnibus
mensibus, hoc dicendum. Ignium lucem praebentium radii
directi feruntur umbras obiectorum corporum formantes in
varias figuras. Ergo cum ignis lucem praebens aequalis erit

North, while the Moon, as Hipparchus maintains, is found to deviate by ten degrees both ways. Hence, if we mentally conceive of the two orbital planes—i.e., of flat ones, and lacking any solidity—of the Sun and Moon as placed directly opposite one another so that a single line drawn through the center of each marks out the spine for the two orbital planes, there will be the same line for the diameter of each, and its upper part, which splits the proximate circle, is called the *katabibazôn* [descending node] and the lower one, which cuts the larger orb equally from the bottom up, the *anabibazôn* [ascending node]. And so whenever the conjunction of the Sun and Moon proves to be direct and, as it were, perpendicular because of the mutual proximity resulting from the convergence of the bodies, then the Moon will intrude upon and block our line of sight, obstructing the narrow trajectory of our vision, and will cut the Sun's light off from us, making, despite its smaller size, the much larger body invisible because of the direct and hence narrow trajectory of our eyesight. But whenever their conjunction has not proved to be perpendicular but the extent of the intervening distance is the same and their latitudes incline slightly away from the direct line such that one of the astral luminaries verges to the North and the other to the South, then no eclipse will result.

89. And the lunar eclipse or disappearance is demonstrated as follows. All agree that it is seen to be eclipsed as it encounters Earth's shadow, but what needs to be explained is why it is not so always or in all months. The rays of the luminescent celestial fires travel in straight lines, shaping variously the shadows cast by the intervening bodies. Thus whenever the luminescent celestial fire is equal to the body

corpori ex quo emicant umbrae, si tam ignis quam corporis globosa erit forma, umbrae nascentur in modum cylindri. Ut puta sit lucem afferens et luminans AB, quod vero illuminatur ΓΔ, haec vero aequalia sint et globosa utraque: perspicuum est radios, unum AΓ alterum BΔ, in directum exaltatos iuxta se esse dispositos aequali distantia; merito; quia circuli AB diametrus circuli ΓΔ diametro aequalis est. Idem radii crescant in altum: erit AΓE radius radio BΔZ distans aequali rigore, hoc est sine inclinatione; et ΓE ergo adversum ΔZ radium sine inclinatione distabit et uterque radius in immensum licet auctus aequali crescet rigore nec eorum cacumina coniungentur umquam vel contingent se invicem. Quod cum ita sit, dubium non est ΓΔ sphaerae umbram in effigiem cylindri formari crescentem per immensum licet.

90. Si tamen quod illuminat brevius erit, ut HΘ, quod vero illuminatur maius, ut KΛ, manifestum est umbram orbis KΛ, quae est KMΛN, in formam quidem effigiari calathi nec tamen hanc speciem mutari etiamsi crescat umbra in immensum; nam cum sit maior KΛ diametrus HΘ diametro, profecto tam HKM radius quam ΘΛN in immensum porrecti latiorem quo plus crescent effigiant opacitatem. Ergo sive umbra cylindroides seu calathoides erit, contingat necesse est ut multae stellae quae supra nos imminebunt per noctem non videantur a nobis hac aut illa<c> [alia] umbris obiectis et obstantibus. Sed hoc rationem non habet. Oportet igitur semper maiorem esse illustrantem globum his

from which the shadows emanate and both the fire and body are of spherical shape, then shadows in the form of a cylinder will result. For example, let AB be what produces light and illuminates, and ΓΔ be the thing illuminated, and let the two be equal and spherical: it is clear that both rays, AΓ and BΔ, as they extend directly upward are equidistant in their relative juxtaposition; rightly so, since the diameter of the circle AB is equal to that of ΓΔ. Let the same rays extend upward: ray AΓE will be unbendingly equidistant from ray BΔZ, i.e., without any obliquity; thus ΓE too will stand opposite ray ΔZ without any obliquity, and even if increased indefinitely both rays will extend with unbending equidistance, and their end points will never come into conjunction or contact with one another. But if that is so, then there is no doubt that the shadow cast by the sphere ΓΔ is formed in the shape of a cylinder even if it extends indefinitely. (See Diagram 18.)

90. But whenever that which illuminates is smaller and that which is illuminated larger, as with HΘ and KΛ, then it is manifest that, although the shadow cast by sphere KΛ, the shadow KMΛN, makes the form of a basket, this shape is nevertheless unchanged even if the shadow should extend indefinitely; for since the diameter KΛ is larger than the diameter HΘ, surely the rays HKM as well as ΘΛN would, if extended indefinitely, make the opacity broaden out in shape as they increase. Thus whether the shadow is cylindrical or in the form of a basket, it necessarily results that many stars located overhead will be unseen by us at night, since shadows intruding on one side or the other block them from view. But this is in need of explanation. Now, it is always necessary that the illuminating sphere should be larger than

quae illuminantur. Itaque si lucem advehens praestabit magnitudine, ut ΞO, minus vero erit quod illustratur, ut ΠP, utraque autem globosa, ΠP circuli umbra quae est ΠPΣ nascitur in modum coni, desinens in acumen ibidemque finita, ΞΠ et OP radiis porrectis in altum et contingentibus se invicem apud notam Σ. Quod fit ex eodem, quia ΠP diametrus minor est diametro ΞO, proptereaque umbrae species conoides erit.

91. Quia igitur Hipparchus in eo opere quod inscribitur De secessibus atque intervallis solis et lunae docet magnitudinem solis mille octingentis octoginta partibus potiorem esse quam terram, terram demum viginti septem partibus potiorem esse quam lunam multoque solem altiorem esse quam luna sit, apparet umbram terrae coni similem effici. Quippe radii solis ΞΠ et item OP angustant se iuxta diametrum terrae ΠP et dextra laevaque omnia illuminant; terra vero obiecta lumini solis circumfluente se lumine umbram efficit a diametri sui latitudine in angustiam provectam et usque ad finem ultimum angustiarum attenuatam. Quam cum inciderit nocturna luna diametro a terra et sole distans, ut<pote> quae propria luce indigeat atque a sole semper mutuetur et sit minor quam terra, obsistente sibi ea in tenebras conditur. Porro cum non ad directum rigorem solis terraeque et lunae positio conveniet ut per puncta medietatum transeat diametra linea sed sol in aquilonem luna in austrum vergat vel contra, evasa terrena umbra nullam patitur

those that are illuminated. Thus whenever the sphere radiating light has the greater magnitude and the illuminated one the smaller, as with ΞO and ΠP, and both are spherical, then the shadow ΠPΣ cast by the circle ΠP arises in the form of a cone: it ends in a point and is there finished, the rays ΞΠ and OP extending upward and touching one another at point Σ. And this happens for the same reason, that since the diameter ΠP is smaller than the diameter ΞO the shape of the shadow will therefore be conical. (See Diagram 19.)

91. Now since in the work entitled *On the Secessions and Distances Between the Sun and Moon* Hipparchus explains that the Sun's magnitude is 1,880 times greater than the Earth and the Earth only twenty-seven times greater than the Moon, and the Sun is much higher than the Moon, it is clear that the shadow cast by the Earth is produced in the shape of a cone. For the Sun's rays, ΞΠ and OP, narrow at the Earth's diameter, ΠP, and illuminate everything to the right and left; but when the Earth obstructs the Sun's light, the latter then flowing around it, it produces a shadow that narrows, starting from the width that is the Earth's diameter, down to the final point of convergence. And when the nocturnal Moon crosses this shadow by standing diametrically opposite the Earth and Sun, since it lacks any light of its own but is forever borrowing it from the Sun, and since it is smaller than the Earth, it is buried in the darkness caused by the Earth's obstruction. And whenever it is not the case that the Sun, Earth, and Moon are in a position of direct alignment such that the line of diameter passes through their center points but the Sun verges to the North and the Moon to the South or vice versa, the Moon escapes the Earth's

obscurationem. Ac de his quidem hactenus; nunc vero iam peragratis omnibus veniamus ad orationem.

92. Et iam omne fere commixtum illud genus essentiae consumptum erat huius modi sectionibus partium. Tunc hanc ipsam seriem in longum secuit et ex una serie duas fecit easque mediam mediae in speciem chi Graecae litterae coartavit curvavitque in orbes quoad coirent inter se capita. Ex tribus his, essentia scilicet et eodem et diverso miscuerat animam et eam secuerat in numeros partim duplices usque ad cubum, qui primus ex duplicibus nascitur, partim triplices usque ad cubum, qui primus ex triplicibus nascitur. Horum numerorum intervalla numeris aliis contexi volebat, ut esset in animae textu corporis similitudo. Itaque limitibus constitutis, uno sex altero duodecim, qui est duplex, duabus medietatibus, octo et novem, sex et duodecim limitum intervallum continuavit epitrita item sescuplari potentia. Perindeque ut inter ignis limitem terraeque alterum limitem insertis aeris et aquae materiis mundi corpus continuatum est ita numerorum potentiis insertis, <ut> tamquam elementis materiisque membra animae intellegibilia conecterentur essetque aliqua inter animam corpusque similitudo. Hanc igitur seriem, non materiam neque corpus, secuit, inquit, deus, ut si quis AB rectam lineam in longum findat et de segminibus duobus chi faciat, ΓΔ EZ, id ipsum incurvet demum et duos innexos sibi invicem circulos faciat, ΗΘΚΛ et ΗΜΚΝ, hosque ipsos exteriore alio circulo cuius motus conversioque idem semper et uniformis sit

shadow and undergoes no eclipse. So much for these matters; having gone through them all, let us now come to the text.

92. [36b–c] *And now nearly the whole of that blended form of Being had in this way been consumed by the cutting of parts. Then he cut the series itself lengthwise and from one series made two, and he forced them round, middle to middle, into the shape of the Greek letter chi and bent them into circles so that their ends joined one another.* From these three things, namely, Being, Same, and Other, he had blended soul and cut it, partly into the numerical multiples of 2 up to the third power, as arising first from the double, partly into multiples of 3 up to the third power, as arising first from the triple. His intention was that the intervals between these numbers should be interwoven by means of other numbers, so that in the soul's tissue there might be a likeness to that of body. The limits thus established, one being 6 and the other 12, its double, he gave continuity to the interval between the limits 6 and 12 with two means, 8 and 9, the ratio of an *epitriton* and sesquialter. And just as the body of the world is given continuity by the insertion of the material elements of air and water between the limit that is fire and the other that is earth, so with the insertion of numerical ratios, so that by the material elements, as it were, the intelligible members of the soul might be connected and there be a certain likeness between soul and body. Thus, he says, god *cut this series,* which is neither matter nor body, as if someone should split a straight line AB lengthwise and from the two segments make a chi, ΓΔ EZ, and then by bending that around make two interconnected circles, HΘKΛ and HMKN, and encircle these with another outer circle, i.e., the *aplanês,* whose movement or cir-

circumliget, id est aplani. Huius quippe orbiculata est agitatio semper eadem semper aequali velocitate ne locum quidem ullum desiderans extra consueti ambitus semitam. Et exterior quidem circulus quem dicit eundem is est qui in aplani globo summus est, quem meridialem nos, Graeci mesembrinon appellant, utrumque complectentem polum cumque isdem vertilabundum aplanus effigiem globi deliniare; interior vero circulus intellegi debet is in quo signorum circumfertur ordo subter quem planetes feruntur. Ideoque exteriorem motum eundem cognominavit quia idem semper minimeque differens est aplanus volatus; interiorem vero diversum, cuncti enim qui subter zodiacum oberrant planetes, licet in orbem ferantur singuli, diversas tamen variis de causis et compugnanter accidentibus casibus faciunt agitationes vel facere potius videntur dum exaltantur et humiliantur, tardius interdum interdum incitatius pergunt proptereaque rapiuntur ab universae rei motu et tamen ut possunt renituntur; interdum etiam latius evagantur, saepe etiam praecurrere signa saepe remanere saepe subsistere putantur saepe repedare.

93. Quod autem de nullis aliis sed de his ipsis sentiat ac loquatur, ipse manifestat cum ita dicit: et exteriorem quidem circulum, quem eundem cognominatum esse diximus, a regione dextra per sinistrum latus usque ad dextrum inflexit, diversum porro per diametrum in sinistrum latus. Eadem quippe semper et constans sibi circumvectio, id est aplanes, per quam meridialis circulus volvitur dextra parte

cumlation is always the same and uniform. The orbital rotation of the latter is always the same, always of a constant velocity, and does not so much as consider any place outside the path of its habitual spinning. And the outer circle which he calls the Same is that which is highest in the nonwandering sphere, which we call the meridian and the Greeks the *mesêmbrinos,* and which we say embraces either pole and by its whirling around with them delineates the shape of the nonwandering sphere; the inner circle, on the other hand, is to be understood as that in which the signs rotate in ordered series and below which the planets move. And the reason for his calling the outer movement that of the Same is that the flight of the *aplanês* is always the same and unchanging; the inner one, on the other hand, he called that of the Other, for although all of the planets traveling below the zodiac move orbitally along their individual paths, they nevertheless produce, or rather, owing to variable causes and conflicting incidental concurrences appear to produce, diverse patterns of movement as they ascend and descend, as they advance more slowly at one moment and more rapidly at another, and are thereby drawn by the movement of the universe while resisting it insofar as they can; at times they even stray rather widely, often they are thought to move in advance of the signs, often to lag behind them, often to stop, and often to reverse direction. (See Diagram 20.)

93. And he makes it clear that he means and is discussing precisely these points and no others, when he says [36c]: *and the outer circle, which we have said was called the Same, he bent around from the right to the left side and back to the right, and the Other across the diameter to the left side.* For the ever constant and selfsame rotation, i.e., the *aplanês,* around which the cir-

mundi movetur; dextra porro mundi pars oriens esse do-
cebitur. Diversum porro, inquit, per diametrum, id est
interiorem motum, quo subter obliquitatem orbis signiferi
planetes moventur. Latera vero, cum sit mundi corpus
sphaerae simile et globosum et undique versum simile nec
differens. Itemque dextrae laevaeque partes mundi non
recte dici videntur sphaeram cogitantibus et ad solam eius
speciem respicientibus; quia tamen idem mundus animal est
et animal intellegens, dextras partes habebit profecto eas in
quibus est initium motus et ex qua parte perinde ut cetera
animalia moventur primitus. Haec porro mundi pars in eois
est proptereaque Homerum puto lapsum alitis augurantem
dixisse:

Dexter ad eoum volitans solemque diemque.

Nec vero summum quid aut imum erit in effigie pilae sed in
vivente atque animali pila vere dici haec nihil impedit. Demus enim corpori nostro quaedam extrinsecus ex luto ce-
rave additamenta usque ad tumorem globi: certe mutata
forma erit, ac undique versum membris omnibus similibus
effectis et ad indeclivem rotunditatem redactis nullum dextrum nullum sinistrum videtur latus nec imi pedes nec summum caput, cum sint membra condita involucris. Vitalis
vero substantiae ratio imas summas dextrasque et sinistras
partes scit intus latere; sic mundi partium diversa interstities

cle of the meridian revolves moves from the right side of the world; and the part of the world to the right, it will be explained, is the East. *And the Other,* he says, *across the diameter,* i.e., the inner movement, along which the planets move below the oblique sphere of the zodiac. And *sides,* because the world body is like a sphere, rounded and the same from every side, without any element of difference. At the same time, to speak in terms of *right* and *left* parts of the world seems inappropriate if you think of a sphere and focus on its shape alone; but since the same world is a living being and one endowed with intelligence, it will in fact have on the right those parts in which movement originates, the part from which, exactly as in the case of other living beings, movement primarily derives. And this part of the world is to the East, which no doubt is why Homer said of the bird's flight consulted for augury:

Flying on the right toward the dawn, the Sun, and day.

In the case of a ball's shape, nothing will be either the top or bottom, but in the case of a living and animate ball there is nothing to prevent these determinations from being truly predicated. For suppose we apply to our body some extrinsic additions composed of clay or wax, ballooning it up into the shape of a sphere: the form will certainly have been altered, and once all its parts have been made the same all around and reduced to a balanced rotundity, no right or left side is discernible, no feet below or head above, since the parts are concealed within the enveloping structure. But the reason possessed by the living substance knows that the lower, upper, right, and left parts lie hidden within; thus the differentiated space between the parts of the world,

quamvis indifferenti membrorum similitudine occultatur in superficie, motu tamen et spirabili proditur convegetatione ut corpus animalque formatum.

94. Deinde prosequitur: eidem et simili illi circumactioni virtute pontificioque rotatus dato. Unam quippe, ut erat, eam et indivisam reliquit. Merito; nam sphaera una quae aplanes dicitur multas et innumerabiles stellas circumagit, cum planetas singulos multae sphaerae circumferant. Potest tamen et alio genere virtus eius, quam obtinet adversum motum omnium planetum, intellegi, quod eadem semper atque indifferens eius conversio tam ipsos planetas quam ceteras stellas cohaerentes sibi curriculo noctis dieique circumagat ab oriente in occidentem. Ex quo aiunt planetas mutabilis illius naturae quae diversa cognominatur esse participes, utpote qui rapti vertigine universae rei ab eois ad occidua referantur demum ab occiduis ad eoa; ut in navigando, cum ad destinata venti pulsu navi volante e regione prorae quidam ex navigantibus ad puppim recurrunt.

95. Deinde ait: interiorem vero scidit sexies — interiorem, id est diversum circulum — septemque impares orbes fabricatus est iuxta dupli et tripli spatia. Tenemus memoria primam psychogoniae descriptionem sic esse formatam, ut unum quidem latus ex duplicibus alterum vero ex triplicibus numeris sit ordinatum, septemque utrimque limites factos, quorum per singula latera sint intervalla terna. Huic ergo adumbrationi qua depinxit animam imaginem similitudinis

although superficially hidden by an undifferentiated likeness between the members, is nevertheless revealed as a
body and a living being informed by movement and the
quickening principle of breath.

94. He then resumes [36c–d]: *giving the rotational force and
preeminence to the circumlations of the Same or like. Now, the one
series he left undivided, just as it was.* Rightly so, for the single
sphere called the *aplanês* drives the orbits of many, indeed
innumerable, stars, whereas multiple spheres drive the orbits of the individual planets. But the force it has relative to
the movement of all planets can be understood in another
way, in that its ever constant and unchanging rotation drives
the orbits of the very planets as well as those of the other
stars which adhere to its East-West rotation over the course
of a night and day. That is why they say that the planets partake of the mutable nature that is called the Other, for the
planets are caught up in the spinning of the universe and
driven from East to West and then West to East; it is as in
navigation, when as the ship flies, driven by the wind to its
destination, some of those on board move backward, from
the area of the prow to the stern.

95. Then he says [36d]: *but the inner one he cut six times*—the
inner one, i.e., the circle of the Other—*constructing seven unequal circles according to intervals of the double and triple.* We recall that the first diagram of the psychogony was formed in
such a way that one side was ordered according to multiples
of two and the other according to multiples of three, and
that seven terms resulted for the two sides together, with
three intervals to separate them on either [Diagram 7]. He
traces, then, an image or shape of the world which strives to
approximate this sketch for his depiction of the soul, and he

aemulae speciemque mundi deliniat septemque circulos instituit planetum eosdemque adversum se distare facit intervallis musicis, ut iuxta Pythagoram motu harmonico stellae
rotatae musicos in vertigine modos edant; similiter ut in
Politia Sirenas singulis insistere circulis dicens, quas rotatas
cum circulis unam ciere mellifluam cantilenam atque ex
imparibus octo sonis unum concordem concentum excitari.
Erit ergo animae aplanes ratio, planetes ut iracundia et cupiditas ceterique huius modi motus quorum concentu fit totius mundi vita modificata.

96. Sectioni quoque partium ex quibus animam constituit positio planetum conveniens videtur, cum unam ab universo facit sumptam primitus portionem, id est minimam, a
terra ad lunam; cuius duplicem secundam, id est quae inter
lunam solemque interiacet; cuius triplam tertiam, scilicet
Veneris; quartam duplicem secundae, id est quadruplam primae, Mercurii; octuplam vero Martis, quae quinta sectio
est; sextam triplam tertiae, id est regionem seu circulum
Iovis; septem porro et viginti partium Saturni novissimam
sectionem.

97. Quod vero dicit deum septem illos circulos contraria
ferri agitatione iussisse, plerique sic intellegunt ut omnes
contra mundi totius moveantur agitationem: quando quidem semper eiusdem motus conversio a dextro latere
incipiat moveri, ut hae septem conversiones uni rapienti
semet intellegantur occurrere. Alii non ita sed ut ipsorum

establishes the seven planetary orbits and sets them apart from one another by musical intervals such that the stars, as according to Pythagoras, in harmonized movement produce musical modes as they rotate in their spinning; this is consistent with his claim in the *Republic* that the Sirens, each positioned on its own orbit, set a single mellifluous song into motion as they rotate along with the orbits, and that from the eight different sounds one harmonious consonance is stirred up. The *aplanês,* then, will be the rational part within the soul, and the planets will be analogous to the spirited and appetitive parts and to the other associated movements through whose attunement the life of the entire world is tempered.

96. The position of the planets is in evident accord also with the cutting of the parts from which he constituted the soul, since he has: first, one portion, i.e., the smallest, drawn from the whole, from Earth to the Moon; second, its double, i.e., the one lying between the Moon and Sun; third, its triple, namely, that of Venus; fourth, double the second, i.e., quadruple the first, that of Mercury; and the octuple portion, that of Mars, which is the fifth cut; sixth, triple the third, i.e., the region or orbit of Jupiter; and the last cut, that of Saturn, of 27 parts. (See Diagram 21.)

97. And most understand his claim that god *ordered these* seven *circles to move in contrary motion* [36d] to mean that they all move *contrary* to the *motion* of the entire world: that insofar as the rotation of the movement that is forever the Same begins to move from the right side, the seven rotations are understood to run against the unified movement that carries them along. Others disagree and understand him to mean that the planets themselves have different and

planetum sit diversa contrariaque conversio idemque sibi
invicem occursus obvios faciant; propterea quod in anfractibus eorum varia et multiformis inveniatur diversitas, siquidem solis et lunae conversiones, comites universitatis motus
eccentri sui vel etiam epicycli, quatenus possunt ab instituto
naturalique cursu remorentur progressionem, aliorum vero
quinque naturalis motus is esse comprehendatur, qui totius
mundi conversioni resistat licet eum praepotens illa vertigo
corripiat. Ex quo fit ut subsistere nonnumquam etiam repedare videantur, hoc amplius quod quaedam ex stellis errantibus vesperi semper occidunt, interdiu sub claritudine solis
latentes et exacta demum nocte ante solis ortum appares-
centes, ut Saturni stella et Martis et Iovis. Contra autem
luna, cum vespere ante omnes stellas appareat, mane conditur in occasum, Lucifer vero et Stilbon utroque genere et
oriuntur et occidunt. Quid quod ceteri planetes longius a
sole discedunt usque adeo ut certis temporibus diametro
distent? Stilbon porro et Lucifer numquam diametro distant a solis orbitis, ex utraque regione mundi eois aut oc-
cidentalibus satis proximi facti, sed soli semper proximi
cursus suos peragunt, proptereaque dixisse videtur Plato
tres quidem pari atque eadem velocitate illos vero alios
quattuor et sibimet invicem et his tribus dissimiliter ince-
dere. Quos tamen omnes diversos motus contrariasque agitationes planetum ratione subnixos esse dicit, ea videlicet,
quam iugi tractatu manifestare curavit.

contrary patterns of rotation and produce conjunctions against one another; they base their claim on the fact that a varied and manifold diversity is observed in their orbits, for the rotations of the Sun and Moon, and their eccentrics or epicycles that accompany the movement of the universe, retard their progress insofar as they can, deviating from the naturally established course, while the natural movement of the five others is understood to be that which resists the rotation of the entire world even though the spinning of the latter overpowers and carries it along. And the result of this is that they appear to stop and sometimes even to reverse direction, even more, that certain wandering stars such as Saturn, Mars, and Jupiter always set in the evening then, after lying hidden for a period beneath the Sun's brightness, begin to appear before sunrise, as night finally comes to an end. The Moon, by contrast, although appearing before any stars in the evening, disappears in the morning with its setting, whereas Venus and Mercury both rise and set in either way. And what about the fact that the other planets move farther away from the Sun to the point that they at fixed times stand diametrically opposite it? Mercury and Venus, however, never stand diametrically opposite the Sun's orbits, being sufficiently close to both regions of the world, East and West, but they always complete their orbits near the Sun, which evidently underlies Plato's claim that *three* move with *equal* and constant *velocity while* those *four* others move *differently from* both *one another* and these three. He says, however, that all of these different and contrary patterns of planetary movement and rotation are based on a rational pattern, namely, the one he has undertaken to reveal through his continuous exposition.

6. DE CAELO

98. Idem inde prosequitur: Igitur cum pro voluntate patris cuncta rationabilis animae substantia nasceretur, aliquanto post omne corporeum intra conseptum eius effinxit mediumque applicans mediae modulamine apto iugabat; ast illa complectens caeli ultima circumfusaque eidem exteriore complexu operiensque ambitu suo ipsaque convertens in semet divinam originem auspicata est indefessae sapientisque et sine intermissione vitae. Caelum diverse et dicitur et accipitur: partim mundi superficies quam uranon Graeci appellant, velut visus nostri limitem ultra quem porrigi nequeat, quasi oranon; partim sphaera quae aplanes vocatur; proprie vero omne hoc quod a lunari globo surgit; communiter autem quidquid supra nos est, in qua regione nubila concrescunt et aliquanto superius, ubi astra sunt. Nam et pluvias ex caelo dicimus demanare, et stellas in caelo apparere quae appellantur cometae, et cetera quae apparent infra lunae globum, caelum quoque usurpantes mundum omnem vocamus.

99. Animam ergo mundi dicit orsam ex medietate usque ad extremitatem mundani corporis et inde usque ad aliam extremitatem circumfusam omni globo corporis operuisse universum eius ambitum, ex quo apparet a vitalibus mundi per extimas partes complexum esse circumdatum, hoc est ut intra atque extra vitali vigore foveatur; neque enim

6. ON THE HEAVEN

98. He then continues [36d–e]: *And so once the Being of rational soul had arisen in its entirety and in conformity with the desire of its father, the latter shortly thereafter fashioned within its confines all that is corporeal, and attaching the center of body to that of soul he joined them in suitable harmony; but the soul, embracing the outermost reaches of the heaven and being infused throughout it by virtue of its external embrace and enclosing it within its periphery and itself revolving back upon itself, inaugurated the divine beginning of a life that was untiring and wise and without intermission.* "Heaven" is said and understood in different ways: in some cases, as the outer surface of the world which the Greeks call *ouranos,* the limit, as it were, beyond which our vision cannot extend, as though it were *oranos;* in others, as the sphere called the *aplanês;* in the strict sense, as all that which rises beyond the lunar sphere; and in the general sense, as anything that is above us, the region in which clouds form and just above, where the astral bodies are. For we say that rain falls "from the heaven," that the stars called comets appear "in heaven," and so on for the other sublunary phenomena, and by false appropriation we refer to the entire world as the "heaven."

99. Now, he says that the world soul, extending from the center up to one outermost point of the corporeal world and *broadcast* [36d] from there throughout the whole corporeal sphere up to another outermost point, *enclosed* the whole of its *circumference,* from which it is apparent that the corporeal sphere is *embraced* and enveloped by vital principles extending to the outermost parts of the world, i.e., so as to be sustained within and without by a vital force; for the universal

universum corpus alterius corporis (quod nullum supererat) auxilio complexuque indigebat sed incorporeae naturae viribus totus vitali complebatur substantia.

100. Illud vero, quod a meditullio porrecta anima esse dicitur, quidam dici sic putant ut non tamquam a medietate totius corporis facta dimensione porrecta sit sed ex ea parte membrorum vitalium in quibus pontificium vivendi situm est, ideoque vitalia nuncupantur. Non ergo a medietate corporis, quae terra est, sed a regione vitalium, id est sole, animae vigorem infusum esse mundano corpori potius intellegendum pronuntiant; siquidem terra immobilis, sol vero semper in motu, itemque uteri medietas immobilis, cor[dis] semper in motu, quando etiam recens extinctorum animalium corda superstites etiam tunc motus agant. Ideoque solem cordis obtinere rationem et vitalia mundi totius in hoc igni posita esse dicunt.

101. Ipsam vero animam in semet convertere non utique corporali conversione facta intellegendum sed cogitationis recordationisque gyris et anfractibus, parente sibi corpore sicut quoque nostrae animae motibus corpus obsequitur, idque mundo fuisse initium, inde auspicium indefessae ac sine intermissione vitae. Praeclare; quando quidem indefessa et sine intermissione vita tempori curriculisque eius propagata sit, aevi tamen alia quaedam est et in sublimiore maiestate perseverantia; temporis enim partes anni menses dies horae,

body required no support or embrace of another body (there was no body left over), but owing to the forces of the incorporeal nature the entire world was filled with the vital substance.

100. Some suppose that by the soul's being said to extend out from the center is meant, not some sort of measured extension from the center point of the entire body, but an extension from the part of the vital members in which the principle of life is situated, that being the reason for their being called vital. Thus they claim that the soul's life force should be thought of as being suffused throughout the world body, not from the center point of its corporeality, the Earth, but rather from the region of the vital elements, the Sun; for the Earth is stationary but the Sun always in motion, and the center point of the abdomen is similarly stationary but the heart always in motion, for the hearts of animals that have just died generate residual movement even then. And that is why they say that the Sun is analogous to the heart and that the vital elements of the entire world are located in this its fire.

101. And soul's *revolving back upon itself* [36e] is not to be understood as the emergence of corporeal revolution but as the curved spinning of thought and intellection, with which the body complies even as it also obeys the movements of our soul, and it is to be understood that *that* was the beginning of the world, that from that point there was an *inauguration of life unflagging and without pause.* Obviously so, for the *life unflagging and without pause* is propagated through time and its cycles but eternity possesses a certain perseverance of a different sort, in its more sublime majesty; for years, months, days, and hours are the parts of time, but eternity

at vero aevi neque initium neque finis ullus proptereaque indeterminatum et perpetuum. Cum ergo mundum generatum intro daret, consequenter temporis quoque generationem mundo aequaevam commentus est.

102. Atque haec quidem mox ipse latius explicabit, nunc tamen animam docet esse incorpoream cum dicit: Et corpus quidem caeli sive mundi visibile factum, ipsa vero invisibilis, rationis tamen et item modulaminis compos cunctis intellegibilibus praestantior, a praestantissimo auctore facta. Cum enim dicit invisibilem sensui minime subiacere pronuntiat; et quod nec visu nec ceteris percipitur sensibus, hoc corpus esse minime potest. Rationis tamen compos, ut declaret naturam rationabilem carentem corpore, quae quidem est animae rationabilis propria et conveniens adumbratio. Porro quod eandem modulatam esse asserit, originem eius et quasi quaedam elementa ex quibus eandem inter initia constituit recordatur et repetit, ut ex ternis originibus, id est individuae dividuaeque substantiae itemque eadem diversaque naturis coagmentata, similitudinem dissimilitudinemque rerum, bonitatisque et malitiae diversitatem, optandaeque et execrandae naturae disparilitatem facile ipsis in rebus recognoscat; utpote quae divisa sit numeris, composita analogiis, stipata medietatibus, ordinata rationibus musicis scissaque a deo sexies, et rursum devincta immortalibus vinculis convenientibus diverso varioque totius mundani corporis motui, omnia sciat et omnia iuxta naturam propriam assequatur.

has neither a beginning nor any end and is in that sense unlimited and perpetual. In view, then, of his having introduced the world as *generated*, he consequently established that the generation of time is coeval with the world.

102. And although he will presently explain these matters in greater detail, for now he shows that the soul is incorporeal, when he says [36e–37a]: *And the body of the heaven or world was made visible, whereas soul was invisible and yet possessed of reason and harmony, being superior to all other intelligibles in having been made by the most superior maker.* For in saying *invisible* he indicates that it is in no way subject to sense perception; and that which is perceptible to neither sight nor the other senses is in no way capable of being a body. *And yet possessed of reason,* so as to declare its rational nature, one lacking body, which is indeed the description properly suited to the rational soul. And with the assertion that the same soul is possessed of *harmony* he recalls and harkens back to its origin and the elements, as it were, from which he constructed it in the initial stages, such that by virtue of its threefold origins, i.e., its *being compounded* of the *natures* of indivisible and divisible *Being* and of the Same and Other, it easily *distinguishes* the similarity and dissimilarity of things, the difference between goodness and evil, the inequality of natures worthy of pursuit or avoidance—all in the things themselves; for being divisible by numbers, composed of proportions, tightly packed with mathematical means, ordered according to musical ratios, divided six ways by god and then bound by immortal linkages which comport with the diverse and varied movement of the whole world body, soul knows and understands all things according to their proper nature.

103. Denique addit: Ut ergo ex eiusdem et diversi natura cum essentia mixtis coagmentata indigete motu et orbiculata circuitione in se ipsam revertens cum aliquam vel dissipabilem substantiam offenderit vel individuam, facile recognoscit quid sit eiusdem individuaeque quid item diversae dissolubilisque naturae. Causasque omnium quae proveniunt videt et ex his quae accidunt quae sint futura metitur. In his enim clare manifestat nihil esse quod animam lateat eiusdemque intellegentiam manifeste revelat cum dicit: motus eius rationabilis sine voce sine sono cum quid sensile spectat circulusque diversi generis sine errore fertur. Veridico sensu et certa nuntiante cunctae animae, rectae opiniones et dignae credulitate nascuntur, porro cum individuum genus semperque idem conspexerit, ea quae sunt motu intimo fideliter nuntiante, intellectus et scientia convalescunt.

104. Sine voce ac sono motus ratio est in intimis mentis penetralibus residens. Haec autem differt ab oratione, est enim oratio interpres animo conceptae rationis. Quae ratio cum se exerit in his quae nascuntur et occidunt vel manu fiunt et prorsus omnibus quae sentiuntur, et recte tamen movetur idem hic motus intimae mentis, nascuntur verae opiniones et credulitate dignae. Nec tamen satis certa provenit et firma cognitio, siquidem inter scientiam et opinionem sit ampla distantia; cum autem constituerit se spectatricem rerum immutabilium quae sunt eaedem semper intellegibilemque naturam suspexerit et in isdem spectaculis

103. Thereafter he adds [37a–c]: *Having been compounded, then, of the natures of the Same and Other as blended with Being, and revolving back upon itself in its innate orbital movement, when it encounters any Being that is either subject to dissipation or indivisible it easily distinguishes what is of the nature of the Same and indivisible, and what of the nature of the Other and dissoluble. And it sees the causes of all things that emerge and takes the measure of those which are to be from those which are occurring.* For with these words he makes *manifestly* clear that there is nothing that escapes soul and *manifestly* reveals its form of understanding, when he says: *and without voice or sound its rational movement, the circling of the nature of the Other, on perceiving anything sensible moves without error. And while its veridical perception announces certitudes to the whole of soul right opinions worthy of belief arise, whereas on perceiving a nature that is indivisible and forever the Same its understanding and knowledge gain strength while an inner impulse faithfully announces the things that are.*

104. A *movement without voice or sound* [37b] is reason residing in the innermost recesses of the mind. And this differs from speech in that speech is the interpreter of the reasoning conceived within the mind. And when this rational activity exerts itself in connection with things that come to be and pass away or that are manufactured, and in connection generally with all sensible things, and when this same motion of the innermost mind nevertheless moves *rightly, opinions* true *and worthy of belief arise.* But sufficiently certain and firm cognition does not emerge, since the gap between knowledge and opinion is considerable; once, however, the rational activity establishes itself as an observer of the immutable realities that are forever the same, and casts its gaze

perspicacem mentis contemplationem convegetaverit, tunc motus similis eius globi motui qui aplanes vocatur sine errore circumactus veram menti cognitionem divini generis creat.

105. Nunc venit ad aevi temporisque discretionem et docet: quia mundus intellegibilis exemplum est mundi sensilis, utpote principatum obtinens animal inter ceteras intellegibilis divinitatis animantes, per omne aevum manet inconcussa stabilitate. Imago quoque eius hic sensilis simulacro aevi facto atque instituto iungetur; imago enim demum aevi tempus est manentis in suo statu, tempus porro minime manens, immo progrediens semper et replicabile. [Imago] Itaque ut intellegibilis mundus per aevum sic sensilis per omne tempus, alia quippe exemplorum alia imaginum vita, recteque uno eodemque momento mundus exaedificabatur sensilis et dierum noctiumque instituebantur vices, elementa seriesque temporis ex quibus menses et anni, partes eius, ratione ac supputatione dividuae.

106. Nosque haec cum aevo assignamus, inquit, id est solitariae naturae, non recte partes individuae rei fingimus. Dicimus enim "fuit," "est," "erit," ast illi esse solum competit. Propter eos qui addubitant num tempus quod dicitur esse nullum sit, haec processit assertio. Dicunt enim praeterita quidem omnia iam esse desisse, si quid porro

up to the intelligible nature and in the actual processes of reflection quickens the focused contemplation of the mind, then a motion resembling that of the sphere called the *aplanês* in revolving *without error* generates for the mind true cognition of the divine sort.

105. He comes now to the distinction between eternity and time, and explains: since the intelligible world, as the living being holding the position of primacy among other living beings begotten of the intelligible divinity, is the model for the sensible world, it abides in unshaken stability through all eternity. Its image too, this sensible world, will be conjoined with the image of eternity once it has been created and established; for time is ultimately the image of eternity abiding in its proper state, and time in no way abides but is forever progressing and unfolding in cycles. Hence, as the intelligible world is through eternity so the sensible one is through all time, for the life of models is one thing and that of images another, and it is right that at one and the same moment the edifice of the sensible world should have been completed and that there should have been established the alternation between days and nights, the elements and succession of time from which come months and years, its parts, which are divisible conceptually and through calculation.

106. *And when we ascribe them to eternity,* he says [37e], *i.e., to a nature which is unitary, we incorrectly imagine an indivisible reality as having parts. For we say it "was," "is," or "will be" despite the fact that the only suitable expression for it is that it is.* This point emerged because of those who raise the doubt whether there is no time which can be said to "be." For they say that everything past has already ceased to be, that any-

immineat hoc nondum esse, praesentia vero neque plane
esse neque omnino non esse—propter instabile atque inre-
frenabile momentorum agmen, fluere enim et transire omnia ostendit. Ergo praeteritam quidem temporis partem sic
dicit esse ut intellegatur fuisse non ut ad praesens existere,
ut cum Homerum esse dicimus divinum poetam; futurum
vero sic esse dicit ut non iam existat atque ad praesens habeatur, ut cum dicimus ad annum proximum lustri esse conclusionem vel certamen esse Olympiacum; porro quod ad
praesens fiat ita esse non ut per aliquam diuturnitatem man-
surum esse videatur sed ut tamquam fluat atque praetereat,
ut cum dicimus Compitalia esse hodie ullamve aliam publicam privatamque celebritatem, quippe cum eiusdem diei
quaedam iam exacta momenta sint aliquanta vero adhuc
maneant, eodemque modo mensem nunc esse Ianuarium vel
alium quemquam vel sacrum certamen agi cum puerorum
certamine exacto adulescentes citantur et post eos deinceps
perfectae aetatis iuvenes manus conserunt.

107. Quid quod etiam illa quae non sunt esse dicimus cum
eadem non esse volumus ostendere? Ut cum dicimus quadrati latus esse dispar lateribus ceteris vel diametrum lateribus esse maiorem, ita enim dicentes probamus minime esse
aequalem lateribus proptereaque absonum. Vel cum idem
Plato silvam esse dicit in nulla substantia propterea quod
nulla silvestria habeant ullam perfectionem; dum enim sunt
adhuc silvestria, informia sunt ac sine ordine ac specie. Ut

thing imminent is not yet, and that the present neither fully is nor altogether is not—all because of the unstable and un-restrainable stream of moments, for it shows that every-thing is in flux and transitory. His point, then, is that the past portion of time *is* in the sense that it is understood to have been but not to be at present, as when we say that Ho-mer "is" a divine poet; and that the future *is* in the sense that it does not yet exist and is not presently in hand, as when we say that next year "is" the end of the census period or "is" that of the Olympic contest; and that what occurs at pres-ent *is,* not in the sense that it projects the impression of be-ing likely to abide through any period of time, but that it is in flux, as it were, and passing away, as when we say that the Compitalia or any other public or private function "is" to-day, when in fact certain moments of a single day have al-ready transpired and a certain number still remain, similarly, that January or any other month "is" or that a sacred contest "is" being conducted when adolescents are summoned after the children's contest and mature youths engage one an-other after them.

107. And what about our even saying that things which are not "are" when our focus is on showing their nonbeing? For example, when we say that the side of a quadrilateral is incommensurate with the other sides, or that the diagonal is larger than the sides, for in speaking thus we point to the fact that it is not commensurate with the sides and there-fore is not in accord with them. Or when Plato says, in con-sideration of the fact that material objects possess no de-gree of perfection, that matter is in no substance; for while still in their raw material state the objects are shapeless, lacking order and form. For example, stones: even if they

saxa, quorum tamen est naturalis possibilitas ut accedente artificio simulacrum fiat vel quid aliud huius modi, quod vero sola possibilitate et sine effectu videtur esse minime est, utpote carens perfectione. Verum haec disputatio quia nihil pertinet ad naturalem tractatum, cum sit rationabilis, differetur.

108. Genituram vero temporis necessario dicit esse institutam, ut tam eadem tempora sub dimensionem venirent quam dierum mensiumque et annorum dinumerari spatia possent, proptereaque solis lunaeque illustrationes et occasus necessarios fuisse ceterasque erraticas stellas superimpositas esse gyris circulorum iussasque agere motum septemplicem diversis et dissimilibus maeandris in ea regione quae sub zodiaci orbis circumflexum iacet: lunae quidem iuxta terram in prima circumactione, solis vero in secunda diametro a luna distantis, tunc Luciferi et Mercurii collocat ignes, inquit, in eo motu qui concurrit solstitiali circuitioni, contraria tamen ab eo circumfertur agitatione, quare fit ut comprehendant se invicem et a se rursum comprehendantur hae stellae. Cur has stellas pari esse dicat velocitate manifestat ipse, cum asserit anni vertentis spatio cursus ab omnibus peragi sed ita ut modo tardius modo incitatius euntes comprehendant subinde solem et subinde a sole comprehendantur.

109. Ait tamen hos ignes contrariam quoque habere vim,

possess a natural potentiality such that through the application of artistry a statue or some other such thing were to result, that which evidently is in mere potentiality and lacks actuality is not insofar as it is deprived of perfection. But since this level of explanation is irrelevant to our discussion of the natural order, it should be postponed despite its relevance to the rational one.

108. And he says that the generation of time was established as a matter of necessity, so that temporal periods might be subject to the process of reckoning in precise conformity with the possibility of the intervals between days, months, and years being calculated, and says that for that reason the risings and settings of the Sun and Moon were necessary and that the other errant stars were superimposed on the orbital cycles and constrained to conduct their sevenfold pattern of movement by way of their diverse and disparate meanderings in the region that lies beneath the vault of the zodiacal belt [38d]: *that of the Moon in the first orbit, next to Earth, and that of the Sun* diametrically opposite the Moon *in the second, then,* he says, *he sets the celestial fires of Venus and Mercury alongside one another in a pattern of movement concurrent with the solar orbit and yet circling with a momentum contrary to it, that being the explanation for these stars' overtaking and in turn being overtaken by one another.* He indicates why he says that these stars are possessed of equal velocity when he explains that the courses are completed by them all in the interval of a yearly cycle but in such a way that they alternately *overtake* the Sun and *are overtaken* by it, moving more slowly at one moment and more rapidly at another.

109. And yet he says [38d] that these celestial fires also have *contrary* force, a point which different people interpret

quam rem alii aliter accipiunt. Quidam enim contrarietatem hanc nasci putant ex eo quod sol quidem, cum naturaliter ab eois ad occidua semper feratur, perinde ut omnis mundus movetur, epicyclum tamen suum peragat anni spatio; cuius epicycli contraria est conversio mundi conversioni, Lucifer vero et Mercurius contrarios semper motus exerant mundi circumactioni. Quidam vero putant contrariam vim esse in his stellis propterea quod comprehendant solis incessum Mercurius et Lucifer et interdum remorantes eos sol comprehendat—cum ortus et item occasus effulsionesque et obumbrationes, interdum mane interdum vesperascente patiantur, praecedentes modo modo relicti, sic enim fere semper iuxta solem comitari videntur. Quod his usu accidit ex eo quod una medietas atque punctum unum est tam solstitialis circuli quam cuiuslibet alterius stellarum harum.

110. Denique Heraclides Ponticus, cum circulum Luciferi describeret item solis et unum punctum atque unam medietatem duobus daret circulis, demonstravit ut interdum Lucifer superior interdum inferior sole fiat. Ait enim et solem et lunam et Luciferum et omnes planetas, ubi eorum quisque sit, una linea a puncto terrae per punctum stellae exeunte demonstrari. Erit ergo una linea directa ex terrae medietate solem demonstrans, duae vero aliae dextra laevaque nihilo minus directae lineae a sole quidem distantes quinquaginta momentis, a se autem invicem centum. Quarum altera linea orienti proxima demonstrat Luciferum, cum Lucifer plurimum a sole distabit factus vicinus

differently. For some suppose that this contrariety arises from the fact that although the Sun's natural movement is always from East to West, as with the world as a whole, it nevertheless completes its epicycle in the course of a year, and the rotation of this epicycle is contrary to the rotation of the world, whereas Venus and Mercury display patterns of movement that are always contrary to the circumlations of the world as a whole. Others, however, suppose that there is a contrary force within the stars, and this on the grounds that Mercury and Venus overtake the Sun's progress and the Sun meanwhile overtakes them as they hold back—all the while they undergo risings and then settings, shining forth and fading, alternating between dawn and dusk, leading at one moment, following at another, for thus they are almost always seen to accompany the sun, alongside it. And this regularly occurs with them because of the fact that the center point of both the solar orbit and the orbit of any of these stars whatsoever is one.

110. Finally, in describing the orbit of Venus and the Sun and in assigning one center point to the two orbits, Heraclides of Pontus showed that Venus sometimes appears above and sometimes below the Sun. For he says that the location of the Sun, Moon, Venus, and all planets, each and every one, is indicated if a single line is drawn extending out from the center of the Earth through that of the star. So there will be a single straight line out from the center of the Earth and pointing toward the Sun, and two other equally straight lines on the right and left, standing at a distance of fifty degrees from the Sun and a hundred degrees from one another. One of the lines, that to the East, indicates Venus when it stands farthest from the Sun toward the Eastern

orientalibus plagis proptereaque idem Hesperi nomen accipiens, quod in eois vespere postque occasum solis appareat; altera vero occidenti proxima, cum plurimum distabit idem Lucifer a sole factus vicinus occiduis proptereaque Lucifer nominatus. Etenim perspicuum est Hesperum quidem dici tunc, cum in partibus orientis videtur sequens solis occasum, Luciferum vero, cum ante solem mergitur et rursus exacta propemodum nocte oritur ante solem.

III. Sit igitur punctum terrae caelique ubi est littera X, zodiacus vero circulus super quem sunt ABΓ notae; et sit AB ambitus momentorum quinquaginta, item BΓ ambitus totidem momentorum; et per XB lineam punctum sit solis in littera K. Erit ergo linea XKB quae solem demonstrat, id est litteram B. Tantum autem moveatur haec eadem linea quantum sol movetur prope cotidiana momenta singula, similiter ceterae lineae XA et XΓ dividantur in quinquaginta momenta; sit porro XA linea in parte orientis, XΓ vero linea in parte occidentis, haec quidem, id est XΓ linea, prius occidens et prius oriens quam sol, illa vero alia XA posterius occidens et posterius exoriens. Necesse est igitur ut haec quidem, id est XA linea, demonstret Luciferum in littera A Hesperum eo videlicet tempore quo eadem stella longius a sole discesserit, illa vero alia linea, id est XΓ, eandem stellam demonstret esse Luciferum temporibus matutinis in signo litterae Γ. Hoc autem fiet apertius si per XKB lineam circumducatur circulus qui contingat duas a se distantes lineas, id est XA et XΓ, quae demonstrant modum discessionis a sole Luciferi.

zones and assumes, while remaining the same, the name "Hesperus" [Evening Star] due to the fact that in the evening it appears after sunset in the East; and the other line, that to the West, indicates when Venus, the same planet, stands farthest from the Sun toward the Western zones and is consequently called "Lucifer" [Morning Star]. For it is evident that it is called "Hesperus" when it appears in the regions of the East following sunset but "Lucifer" when it sets before the Sun and then in turn rises before the Sun once night has nearly passed.

III. Let, then, the center point of the Earth and heaven be where the letter X is, and the zodiacal circle be that on which there are the points ABΓ; and let the arc AB be fifty degrees and BΓ as many; and intersecting the line XB let the center point of the Sun be at letter K. Thus the line XKB will be that which indicates the Sun, i.e., letter B. Now, let this same line move in tandem with the Sun's movement at approximately one degree per day, and the other lines, XA and XΓ, be similarly divided into fifty degrees; and let line XA be in the Eastern region and line XΓ in the Western, the latter, i.e., line XΓ, setting and rising before the Sun, and the other one, the former, XA, setting and rising after it. The necessary result, therefore, is that the latter, i.e., line XA, indicates Venus as Hesperus at letter A, namely, at the time when the same star has moved farther from the Sun, while the other (former) line, i.e., XΓ, indicates that at the point that is letter Γ the same star is Venus in its morning periods. This will be made clearer if a circle intersecting line XKB is drawn so as to be tangent with the two lines that stand apart from one another, i.e., XA and XΓ, which indicate Venus's degree of separation from the Sun. (See Diagram 22.)

COMMENTARY

112. At vero Plato quique huius indaginis diligentius examen habuerunt affirmant aliquanto quam solis esse elatiorem Luciferi globum qui limitatur notis ΔEZH contingens ΚΑ quidem lineam per E litteram, ΚΓ vero per H. Quare cum Lucifer lustrans circulum proprium perveniet ad E videbitur in A locatus a sole plurimum, utpote momentis quinquaginta omnibus, separatus et ad orientem ac diem vergens; quippe sol non nisi ubi est B littera indifferenter videtur. Porro cum in H erit Lucifer videbitur in excelsitate Γ consistere isdem quinquaginta demum momentis a sole et ad occidua semotior; cum vero vel penes Δ vel penes Z consistet dubium non est proximum soli factum visum iri concursumque fecisse unum excelsiorem procul a regione terrae penes Δ, alterum citimum terraeque proximum in Z. Iam illud observatione diligentiore perceptum: stellam ipsam in maxima secessione, sive orientalis seu occidua erit illa secessio, diebus fere quingentis octoginta et quattuor ad id in quo pridem fuerat vel E vel H remeare; ut sit perspicuum totum obire circulum suum, qui est ΔEZH, memoratam stellam memorato numero dierurn, ita ut maiorem quidem discessionis ambitum, qui est ab eois ad occidua, hoc est HΔE, quadringentis quadraginta octo peragret diebus, minorem vero depressioremque, id est EZH, reliquis centum triginta et sex, maximae siquidem discessionis ab occiduis ad eoa prolapsio hoc dierum numero revocatur, ut frequens veterum virorum observatio palam fecit.

113. Rursum subtexit haec: Igitur singulis universisque apto et decenti sibi motu locatis—videlicet his quae consequens erat tempore provenire—nexibus vitalibus ubi constricta corpora facta sunt animalia imperatumque

306

112. Plato, on the other hand, and those who have more diligently tested this inquiry, affirm that Venus's sphere is slightly above that of the Sun and delimited by points ΔEZH, tangent with line KA at the intersection of letter E and with KΓ at the intersection of H. So once Venus arrives at E on its way around its proper orbit it will appear to be located in A, at its farthest remove from the Sun, namely, fifty degrees in all, and moving toward the East and daylight; for the Sun appears as before, being only where the letter B is. And once Venus is at H it will appear to be at elevation Γ, removed farther to the West, and ultimately at the same fifty degrees from the Sun; but once it is at Δ or Z there is no doubt about its appearing to pass in close proximity to the Sun after having made a first, higher conjunction far from the Earth's region at Δ and a second one of nearest proximity to the Earth at Z. On closer observation the following is now perceived: that at its farthest point of removal, whether to the East or to the West, within approximately 584 days this very star returns to the point where it was, whether E or H; so that it is clear that the star under consideration completes its whole orbit, ΔEZH, in the number of days mentioned, such that it traverses the larger section of arc in its East-West journey, the arc HΔE, in 448 days, and the smaller, lower one, EZH, in the remaining 136, since its West-East journey elapses over the latter number of days, as repeated observation on the part of the ancients made manifest.

113. Coming back now to our text, he introduces the following [38e]: *Now, they—namely, those whose emergence was by definition in time—had individually and in their entirety been placed in a pattern of movement that was apt and befitting them;*

didicerunt. Caelestia corpora constricta vitalibus nexibus, id est stellas, animalia facta esse asserit et cognovisse quae a deo iubebantur, scilicet ut planetes quoque in globos proprios redacti non solum anima vitaque fruerentur sed cum isdem omnibus etiam mundus et anima uteretur et rationis particeps esset. Quatenus enim carens quid ratione poterit intellegere quae iubentur?

114. Ea, quae diversae naturae motus obliquus per directum eiusdem naturae motum vertens semet (utpote constrictus) circumferebat, partim maiore partim minore circulo rotabantur, citius quidem dimensum spatium peragentia quae minore tardius vero quae maiore, utpote ambitu circumacta prolixiore. Diversa natura quae sit, saepe iam ostensum est in superioribus, quodque motus eius ab occidente ad orientem feratur. Haec ergo cum sit interior contineatur necesse est ab exteriore orbe qui aplanes dicitur; tardaque ipsa in progrediendo ab aplanis velociore rapitur ad contrarium motum, et comprehensa sequi sequentem comprehendere etiam comprehendentem videtur. Planetum vero quidam citius alii tardius cursus suos peragunt. Merito; circulorum enim minorum compendia adversum maiorum anfractus comparata modicis temporum impendiis curriculorum spatia complent, ut luna quae iuxta cubicum numerum viginti et septem diebus circulum suum

and once their bodies, under the constraints of the vital bonds, be-came living beings and learned their appointed task. He asserts that *under the constraints of the vital bonds* the celestial *bodies,* i.e., stars, *became living beings* and became cognizant of the tasks enjoined by god, namely, not only so that even the planets, once brought into their proper orbits, might enjoy soul and life but also so that the world might benefit from soul and participate in reason along with them all. For to what extent will anything which is deprived of reason be ca-pable of understanding the tasks enjoined?

114. *Then the bodies which the movement of the nature of the Other—which revolved obliquely across the path of the nature of the Same (for it was constrained by it)—conveyed round began to revolve, some along a larger and others along a smaller orbit, with those that moved along a smaller one completing the measured dis-tance more rapidly and those that moved along a larger one doing so more slowly due to their being carried round a longer periphery* [38e–39a]. What the nature of the Other is has already been pointed out repeatedly in earlier sections, also, that its movement is from West to East. Given, then, that this is the inner nature, it inevitably is embraced by the outer sphere, called the *aplanês;* and because of its advancing slowly it is in fact overtaken by the more rapid course of the *aplanês,* pro-ducing the contrary motion: in being overtaken it appears both to follow the one following it and to overtake the one overtaking it. Some planets complete their orbits more rap-idly, others more slowly. Rightly so, for by comparison with the circumferences of the larger orbits the short paths of the smaller ones allow completion of the orbital distances in small expenditures of time, as in the case of the Moon, which traverses its orbit in twenty-seven days, in confor-

lustrat, cum Saturnium sidus triginta prope annis redeat ad pristinum exordium.

115. Qua de causa fiebat, inquit, ut ex uniformi eiusdem naturae conversione quae citius circumibant ab his quae tardius circumferebantur comprehendentia comprehendi viderentur. Uniformis eiusdem naturae conversio rapit stellas motu nitentes contrario ad volatum suum cotidianis diebus, illae autem naturaliter incedunt per suos circulos quorum motus atque agitatio dissentit rapientis se motui. Itaque quoniam planetes partim minores partim maiores circulos obeunt, qui minores circulos, obeunt in illa diei noctisque vertigine consequuntur eos qui pigrius progrediuntur; quia per prolixiores orbes feruntur proptereaque comprehendentes et transeuntes comprehendi ab his quos praeterierint putantur. Comitata enim verbi gratia iuxta primum momentum Arietis luna cum sole diebus viginti et novem totum circulum transit octavoque et vicesimo momento eiusdem signi solem comprehendens, quia transit eum atque progreditur, velut fugere eum et comprehendi ab eo videtur. Eadem ista ratio etiam in ceteris astris quorum dispar cursus est invenitur.

116. Deinde prosequitur: Omnes quippe circulos eorum uniformis et inerrabilis illa conversio vertens in spiram et velut sinuosum acanthi volumen. Cum fixo cardine circini casu vel etiam voluntate nostra oppresso aut relaxato circino describuntur circuli tales ut postremitas circumductae lineae non solum non perveniat ad exordium sed deflectens a competenti rigore infra vel supra circumducta linea

mity with the cubic number, while the star Saturn travels back around to its original starting point in nearly thirty years.

115. *And for this reason,* he says [39a], *it came about that owing to the uniform rotation of the nature of the Same those which orbited more rapidly appeared to be overtaken by those which orbited more slowly although they were overtaking them.* Day by day the unvarying circumlation of the nature of the Same carries along in its flight the stars that strain under a contrary form of movement, while those whose movement or trajectory departs from that of the one carrying them along naturally proceed along their own orbits. Thus, given that some planets travel along smaller orbits and others along larger ones, those traveling along the smaller ones pursue within the cycle of a day and night those that proceed more slowly; for they move along more extended orbits and for that reason are supposed, *although overtaking* and surpassing, *to be overtaken by those* they have passed. For the Moon (to take that example), though conjoined with the Sun in the first degree of Aries, passes through its entire orbit in twenty-nine days, and in overtaking the Sun in the twenty-eighth degree of the same sign it appears, because it surpasses the Sun and moves on, to flee from it, as it were, and to be overtaken by it. This same account obtains also in connection with other astral bodies with disparate orbits.

116. He then continues [39a]: *For that uniform and unvarying rotation, turning all of their orbits round in a spiral and, as it were, winding acanthus coil.* When the fixed pivot of a compass is inadvertently or deliberately closed or widened and curves are drawn not only such that the end of the traced line misses the beginning but, in deviating below or above the intended course, the traced line produces curves that

saepius artiores laxioresve circulos faciat, hoc genus circulorum spiram solemus vocare vel acanthi volumen. Igitur quia
planetas sic aplanes rapit cotidiana vertigine ut non patiatur
eos in eundem locum et velut sedem ex qua progressi fuerant repraesentari sed vel transire cogat vel leniore progressione minime occurrere ad destinata, recte dixit errantes
stellas in spiram et velut sinuosum acanthi volumen rotari
ob inconstantem atque inaequabilem circumvectionem. Ut
si stella forte Veneris sit in Arietis signo deinde rapiat eam
mundi conversio ita ut eam longius a pridiana progressione
protrahat, certe tunc aliqua fiet ab Ariete discessio; quantoque plures conversiones fient tanto longius ab Ariete ad
praecedentia signa discedet et ad postremum ad Pisces atque inde ad Aquarium provehetur. Contra si remissior erit
raptatio, ab Ariete ad Taurum versus recedet et ad Geminos
atque Cancrum iniquis semper gyris et deflectentibus ab
exordiis atque aberrantibus a convenienti rigore. Quos quidem gyros Graeci helicas appellant, quorum incrementa ab
imminutionibus, imminutiones porro ab incrementis notantur. Suntque similes eius formulae quae subter ascripta
est.

117. Deinde ait: Atque ut rationabilis et consulta haec motuum varietas et moderatio visu quoque notaretur omniumque octo motuum perspicua esset chorea, ignivit lucem
clarissimam deus rerum conditor e regione secundi a terra
globi, quam lucem solem vocamus. Cum propter ceteras
ineffabiles utilitates quas universo mundo sol invehit tum
etiam propterea ignis huius dicit extitisse genituram ut

become increasingly narrow or wide, we customarily refer to such a curve as a "spiral" or "acanthus coil." In consideration of the fact, then, that the *aplanês* carries the planets along in its daily rotation in a way that it does not allow them to re-appear at the same place—their abode, as it were—from which they departed but compels them to shift course or to miss their destinations with slackened trajectory, he said that the errant stars revolve in a *spiral and, as it were, winding acanthus coil;* and rightly so, given their inconstant and un-even circumlation. For example, if the star Venus happens to be in the sign of Aries and the rotation of the world then carries it along in such a way as to pull it farther off its previ-ous trajectory, at that point a certain movement away from Aries will inevitably result; and with an increase in the num-ber of rotations it will correspondingly move farther away from Aries in the direction of the antecedent signs and be conveyed finally to Pisces and from there to Aquarius. If, on the other hand, the conveyance is slower, then it will with-draw from Aries in the direction of Taurus, Gemini, and Cancer in increasingly uneven circles that deviate from the starting points and stray from the fixed course. The Greeks call these circles *helikes,* the expansions of which are marked as departures from their constrictions, and their constric-tions as departures from their expansion. And its shapes re-semble the one drawn below. (See Diagram 23.)

117. He then says [39b–c]: *And in order that this rationally planned variation in and temperament of movements might also be visibly observable and the round of all eight movements be perspic-uous, god the founder of things ignited a most brilliant light in the region of the sphere second from Earth, which light we call the Sun.* He indicates that this fire came into being not only for the sake of the other ineffable advantages which the Sun con-

tanta rerum designatio nulla tegeretur obscuritate, ut cum idem rebus colorem daret tum etiam numeri quo temporis spatia notantur commoditas proveniret, atque ut dierum et noctium vicissitudo succederet. Mensis vero designavit esse genituram cum luna peragrato circulo suo solem convenit, anni quoque cum sol ad idem signum ex quo progressus erat revertitur numero dierum trecentorum sexaginta quinque et parte quarta. Quare factum ut a prudentissimis viris et iuxta caelestium rerum observationem exercitatissimis quarta illa portio quarto post anno in unum collecta et ac-corporata spatium diei noctisque compleret.

118. Est tamen intellectu facile quod perfectus temporis numerus perfectum annum compleat tum demum cum om-nium octo circumactionum cursus peracti velut ad originem atque exordium circumactionis alterius revertentur, quam semper idem atque uniformis motus dimetietur. Perfectum temporis numerum qui perfectum complet annum appellat eum, quo tam septem planetae quam ceterae stellae, quae dicuntur ratae, repraesentatae originalibus sedibus eandem, quae fuit initio rerum principioque mundi constitutionis, efficiunt designationem, ita ut et prolixitas prolixitati et in-tervallorum pristinorum altitudini altitudo et profunditati profunditas quadret. Hoc autem tempus continet annorum innumerabilem seriem, quippe cum stellarum errantium circuitus impares sint necessarioque diversis temporibus cursus suos compleant. Praeterea latius aliae a medietate mundi evagentur, angustius vero aliae ad austri septentrio-

fers upon the entire world but also so that such an extraordinary configuration of things might not be concealed by any obscurity, that it came into being not only so that the Sun might bestow color upon things but so that the advantages of the *numerical reckoning* used for observation of temporal intervals might *emerge,* and so that there might be an alternating *succession* of days and nights. And he pointed out that a *month* comes to be when after having traversed *its own course the Moon* comes into conjunction with *the Sun, and a year, when the Sun* returns to the same sign as that from which it set out, the days numbering 365¼. And so it came about that, once consolidated and incorporated at the end of the fourth year by men most wise and skilled in the observation of celestial phenomena, the fraction of a fourth completed the interval of a *day and night.*

118. [39d] *It is nevertheless easy to understand that the perfect number of time should mark the completion of the perfect year at the point when the completed courses of all eight revolutions will return to the origin, as it were, and commencement of a second revolution, which the movement that is forever the Same and uniform will measure.* He refers to it as the *perfect number of time* which *marks the completion of the perfect year,* wherein the seven planets and the other stars, the so-called fixed ones, on reappearing in their original abodes project the same configuration as obtained at the start of things, that is, at the beginning of the world, such that the longitude, latitude, and depth square with the longitude, latitude, and depth of the original intervals. This period of time, moreover, contains an innumerable series of years, in that the orbits of the wandering stars are unequal and necessarily complete their individual courses within different time periods. Moreover, some stars wander farther from the center of the world

nisve convexa, celsiores aliae a terra sint, aliae non adeo longo altitudinis intervallo distent a regione terrae. Diversos quoque inter se motus agant, ut citae tardius progredientibus, ultra progredientes retrorsum recedentibus, humilibus excelsae, dextrae sinistris, sinisteriores dexterioribus occurrant. In unum nihilque omnino sit quod in designatione differat a ceterorum astrorum habitu specie figuris. Atque ut omnes omnibus aequis diametris distent unumque nutum atque unam efficiant stellarum omnium conformationem cum sit necesse, si unus aliquis ex ignibus repraesentatus fuerit in antiquae constellationis statum iuxta rationem forte altitudinis, latitudini tamen non sit repraesentatus antiquae, vel si perfecte per omnia momenta unus revocatus ad antiquum statum fuerit ceterorum tamen quorum est diversa condicio perfecta repraesentatio minime provenerit, necesse sit etiam eius stellae quae in repraesentatione perfecta invenietur rursum fieri aliam mutationem, quoad opportunitas illa proveniat quae unam faciem atque eandem repraesentet quae fuit ab initio mundi. Quem quidem motum et quam designationem non est putandum labem dissolutionemque afferre mundo quin potius recreationem et quasi novellam viriditatem positam in auspicio motus novi. Haud sciam an in quibusdam regionibus terrae proventura sit ulla ex innovatione iactura. Hactenus de mundi sensilis constitutione tractavit.

while others adhere more closely to the heavenly vaults South or North, and some are higher above the Earth while others stand separated from its region by a moderate latitudinal interval. The movements they conduct differ from one another as well, such that the rapid stars converge on the more slowly moving ones, those that are advancing on those that are receding, the high on the low, those to the right on those to the left, and those farther to the left on those farther to the right. In configuration, it is unified: there is absolutely no point of divergence in disposition, form, or shape from one astral body to another. And given the requirements of their all being diametrically separated from all at equal distances and of their effecting a single pull and a single configuration across all stars, if any one of the celestial fires reappears at the position of its original constellation as regards, say, the calculation of its latitude but does not reappear at the original longitude, or if through the course of all its degrees one is fully recalled to its original position but due to their being differently situated the complete reappearance of the others does not occur, then it is necessary for the star found to be in full reappearance to undergo yet further permutation until there arises that occasion which again projects one and the same appearance as obtained at the beginning of the world. And we must suppose that this movement and this configuration imply, not a defect or process of dissolution for the world, but rather regeneration, tender new youth, as it were, located within the first impulse of new movement. Whether in certain regions of the Earth the process of renewal results in any loss, I would not know. This is as far as he took the discussion of the establishment of the sensible world.

Commentarii Pars Secunda

119. Mundi totius perfectionem ab opifice absolutam deo praeteriti operis textu secrevimus Platonicis dogmatibus, quoad mediocritas ingenii passa est, inhaerentes iuxta naturae contemplationem artificiosasque rationes. Deinde ante omnes res primam pertractat caelestium orbium qui sunt infixi tergo ratae atque inerrabilis conversionis generationem, eorum etiam quae mundus complectitur, quo sit plena perfectaque universa res animalque sensilis mundi proximam similitudinem nanciscatur perfecto intellegibilique et exemplari ex se genito mundo. Quattuorque sensilium animalium species tam caelestium quam terrenorum naturali contemplatione dinumerat: caelestium quidem stellas; terrenorum vero volatilia et item nantia quaeque per terram feruntur, iure dicta terrena, quippe quae terra nutriantur et in eiusdem terrae gremio quiescant, quodque corpora eorum ex maiore parte terrena ex obtinentis materiae vocabulo cognominantur; perinde ut caelestia, quae ex maiore parte ignis puri liquidique concreta aeterni appellantur ignes.

120. Nec contentus supra dictorum animalium demonstratione porrigit diligentiam usque ad angelicae naturae

Commentary, Second Part

7. ON THE FOUR KINDS OF LIVING BEINGS

119. In the text of the previous part of this work we have given a separate treatment of the completion of the entire world as effected by the craftsman god, adhering insofar as our modest capability permitted to Platonic doctrines as concerns the contemplation of nature and the technical modes of reasoning. Next, and prior to all other matters, he discusses the first generation of the celestial spheres that are fixed on the arched surface of constant and immutable revolution, and of the things the world contains, so that the universe might be full and complete and the living being that is the sensible world might attain the strictest likeness to the perfect intelligible world, the pattern for the world generated from it. And in his contemplation of nature he distinguishes four kinds of sentient living beings, celestial as well as terrestrial: of the celestial, the stars; and of the terrestrial, those that fly, live in water, and move on land. The latter are rightly called terrestrial in that they draw nourishment from the earth [*terra*] and take their rest in the bosom of the same earth, and because their bodies, which consist primarily of earth, draw their name from the matter that obtains in them; similarly, the celestial bodies, which, being composed primarily of pure and liquid fire, are referred to as eternal fires.

120. Not confining himself to treatment of the aforementioned living beings, he extends his attention to unraveling the question of the angelic nature, the beings he refers to as

quos daemonas vocat extricationem. Quorum quod est purius in aethere sedes habet, alterum in aere, tertium in ea regione quae humecta essentia nominatur, quo interna mundi congesta sint animalibus ratione utentibus nec sit ulla eius regio deserta. Quem quidem tractatum, quod sit elatior et ultra naturae contemplationem, necessario differt et ait deum post generationem stellarum ratarum, cum unaquaeque earum divinum animal esset utens corpore mixto ex sincerissimis materiis quattuor et ex maiore parte ignis sereni, coruscum quoddam animal et formatum in modum sphaerae infixisse summo cum modulamine aplani globo eumque omnem huius modi luminibus exornasse. Ubi vero movendi usus est necessarius visus, ex omnibus motibus duos hos tribuisse praecipuos: unum ex accidenti, quo rapit stellas aplanes ad occidua, quem motum nunc vocat in antecedentia, alterum vero principalem, qui est circumactio circaque semet vertitur, similem deliberativo animae motui quinque ceteris cessantibus motibus.

121. Etenim loculares motus septem sunt, opinor: duo quidem iuxta longitudinem, id est ante et post, duo item alii per latitudinem, in dextram et sinistram, duoque alii iuxta profunditatem, sursum et deorsum, et ultimus supra memoratae circumactioni similis, qui fixo circumuolat cardine. Quia ergo ex his septem motibus duum tantummodo singulis ratis stellis usum tribuit deus, principalem quidem circumactionem, ex accidenti vero qui fertur in dextram, recte

demons. Of these, the purer type has its abode in the ether, the second in the air, the third in the region named the moist substance, such that the internal parts of the world are filled with living beings endowed with reason and no region of it is deserted. And this treatment he necessarily postpones, since it is of a higher order and beyond the contemplation of nature, and says that after the generation of the fixed stars, since each and every one of them was a divine living being employing a body blended of the four purest material elements, especially that of limpid fire, god attached each particular radiant living being shaped in the form of a sphere to the nonwandering sphere, with the highest degree of harmony, and adorned the whole of it with celestial lights of this kind. And when their employment of the ability to move presented itself as necessary, he assigned the following two from among all the types of motion: one of them incidental, by which the *aplanês* carries the stars along toward the West, which he now calls movement ahead, and the other primary—which is a form of rotation and revolves back upon itself—, resembling the deliberative motion of the soul. The other five types of motion remain in the background.

121. For the types of locomotion are, I suppose, seven: two measured in longitude, i.e., forward and backward, likewise two measured in latitude, to the right and left, and two others measured in depth, upward and downward, the final one resembling the rotation mentioned above, movement that wings its way around a fixed axis. Given, then, that he assigns the use of only two of these seven forms of motion, the primary rotation and the incidental (which moves to the right), to the individual fixed stars, he rightly stated that the

dixit quinque praeterea motus alios vacare. Deinde concludit commemorans de motibus se stellarum errantium in superioribus disputasse. Et caelum quidem ita exornatum est
sapientibus et aeternis animalibus inquilinis.

122. Quod vero consequens videretur mortalium quoque
et obnoxiorum passionibus animalium demonstrari genituram, haec sunt porro terrena, iure meritoque prius quae de
terra ipsa dicenda existimabat exponit. Dicit autem quod
hanc quoque deus constrictam limitibus per omnia vadentis
et cuncta continentis poli constituerit noctis dieique custodem. Sed polum nuncupat eum, qui omne mundi corpus
pervadit, axem. Constrictam vero dupliciter intellegendum,
vel iuxta Pythagoram ignem vertentem se circum axem, placet quippe Pythagoreis ignem quidem utpote materiarum
omnium principem medietatem mundi obtinere, quem Iovis custodem appellant; per hunc porro moveri circumactas
in gyrum tamquam stellas terram et anticthona. Quare vel
sic intellegendum vel aliquanto verisimilius medietati mundi
adhaerentem quiescere terram proptereaque et a Platone et
a multis aliis Vestam cognominari. Denique in Phaedro
idem ait, "manet enim Vesta in divino domicilio sola."

123. Custodem vero et opificem diei et noctis propterea
dicit esse, quia per eandem, id est terram, vectus sol partes
eius subiectas sibimet illustrans diem facit. Cum vero
obiecerit se ex aliqua parte solis anfractibus terra ipsa

five other forms of motion beyond them are absent. He then concludes by pointing out that he discussed the movements of the errant stars in previous sections. And in this way the heaven was adorned with wise and eternal living beings as its inhabitants.

122. And since this evidently entailed treating also of the generation of mortal living beings which are subject to passions, they being the *earthly* ones, he rightly and with good reason expounds what he thought should be said first about Earth itself. And he says [40b–c] that this too, *constrained by the limits of the pole that traverses and contains all things*, god established *as the guardian of night and day*. But with the *pole* he refers to the axis that *passes through* the entire body of the world. *Constrained*, on the other hand, is to be understood in one of two ways: Either, with Pythagoras, as indicating a fire revolving around an axis, for the Pythagoreans maintain that fire, being preeminent among all material realities, occupies the center of the world, and they call it the *guardian* of Jupiter; furthermore, they hold that the Earth and Counter-Earth move around this fire, driven round in an orbit like the stars. And so it is to be understood either in this way or, with slightly greater probability, as indicating that the Earth is at rest, adhering to the center of the world, and is for that reason called Vesta by both Plato and many others. Finally, he says in the *Phaedrus*, "for Vesta alone remains in the divine domicile."

123. But he says [40c] that it is the *guardian and craftsman of day and night* because in its conveyance across the same — i.e., Earth — the Sun produces day by illuminating the parts of it that lie beneath itself. When, however, it partially blocks the Sun as it moves along the ecliptic, the Earth itself

obumbratur; itaque ex umbris crassa noctis caligo succedit.
Simul quia immobilis terra est, significanter eam custodem
noctis et diei cognominavit. Neque enim pereunte die nox
nascitur vel noctis amissione dies oritur, sed utraque salva
succedit altera. Quia vero hoc fit per eam indefesse ipsa manente semper in sua sede, spectatrix est, opinor, eorum quae
velut ante conspectum suum geruntur meritoque custos.
Antiquissimam vero deorum dicit, opinor, vel quia locus est
animalium capax, regio porro et locus praecogitetur his quae
in loco sunt necesse est, vel quia puncti rationem obtinet
hoc porro antiquius esse omni magnitudine atque omnibus
quantitatibus naturali quadam mentis conceptione praenos-
citur, velut ait Hesiodus:

> Prima quidem haec caligo, dehinc post terra creata est,
> spirantum sedes firmissima pectore vasto.

Post enim chaos, quam Graeci hylen, nos silvam vocamus,
substitisse terram docet in medietate mundani ambitus ut
fundamenta fixam et immobilem. Nobis autem natura tributum est id quod stat prius his quae moventur mente perci-
pere; omnis quippe motus post stationem sumit exordium.

124. Stellarum vero errantium opera quae propter modulatam et consonam celebrantur agitationem, quam idem

is brought under shadows in one or another region, and because of the shadows the dense darkness of night thus takes over. At the same time, given that the Earth is immobile, there is significance in his having referred to it as the *guardian of night and day,* in the sense that night does not emerge with the perishing of day or day arise with the destruction of night, but one takes over from the other, both of them remaining intact. And since this occurs in relation to the Earth, which for its part always indefatigably remains in its seat, it is, I suppose, the observer and, rightly, *guardian* of all things conducted, as it were, before its gaze. And he says that it is the *most ancient among the gods* either, I suppose, because it is a place suitable for living beings—and it is necessary that a region or place should be planned for those things that are in it—or because it is analogous to a point; and by a certain natural mental preconception the latter is known to be more ancient than all magnitude and quantities, just as Hesiod says:

Indeed, this darkness was created first, then Earth,
in its vast bosom a seat most firm for creatures that draw
breath.

For he explains that after chaos, which the Greeks call *hylê* and we call *silva,* the Earth, fixed and immobile, came into being as a foundation at the center of the world's circumference. Moreover, we have been naturally endowed with the power of mentally perceiving that which is stationary before perceiving things that are in motion; for every motion takes its start after a stationary state.

124. The activities of the errant stars, celebrated for the harmonious and constant movement which Plato refers to

appellat choream, in progressibus et anfractibus earundem
stellarum perspicue videntur, ut cum apparent nimio quodam incitatoque motu progressae longius vel cum diu stare
in uno atque eodem loco et item cum retrorsum ferri putantur, tum in coetibus quoque et effulsionibus et absconsioni-
bus vel in eois vel in occiduis, conversionibus quoque et ae-
quinoctiis omnibusque transfigurationibus, hoc amplius in
defectionibus et reparatis illustrationibus, denique ceteris
huius modi. <De quibus> si quis dedita opera disputet, hunc
frustra dicit terere supervacuum laborem proptereaque ex-
cusat ratus tractatum istum ad astronomiam potius quam
physiologiam pertinere. Parabolas enim quasdam appellat,
qui comitatus sunt siderum, ut iuxta solem individui semper
Mercurius et Lucifer, reciprocos circuitus, quos astrologi
regradationes vocant, progressus item ad praecedentia pro-
fectionem, etiam coniugationem; duplex vero est coniugatio, altera per cathetum, altera per diametrum, atque ea
quae per cathetum fit significat, cuius modi stellae qualibus
coeant quaeve sit earum coetus significatio, per diametrum
vero contra distantium a se stellarum positionem vult intellegi, cum ex medietate stellae ad alterius contra positae
stellae medietatem directa linea conectit et continuat
utramque. Quos vero defectus mathematici vocant, Plato
obstacula appellat proprie magis et aliquanto significantius,
non quo sibi invicem obsistant sed quod nobis a terra

as a *round* [40c], are clearly evident in the forward and cyclical patterns of movement of the same stars, as when they are seen progressing through the longer courses at some highly accelerated rate of movement, or when they are thought to stand in one and the same place for a period and to move again in reverse; then again, in their conjunctions, in the phases of resplendence and obscurity, in the East or West, also in their conversions, equinoxes, and manifold transfigurations, all the more in their eclipses and phases of restored resplendence—and in short, in all other manifestations of this sort. And as concerns these, he says that it would be an idle waste of effort for one to dispute their assigned activities and so excuses himself on the assumption that a treatment of that type pertains to astronomy rather than natural philosophy. For the concomitant movement of stars he refers to as certain *juxtapositions,* as in the case of Mercury and Lucifer, which are always inseparably in the Sun's vicinity; what the astronomers refer to as retrogradations he refers to as *reciprocal conversions,* and forward advancement as *progression,* also *conjunction.* Conjunction, however, is of two types, one perpendicular, the other diametrical, and that which proves to be perpendicular indicates the mode of conjunction between stars, which kinds they conjoin with and what their conjunction indicates, while by the diametrical is meant the relative position of stars that stand opposite one another, when a straight line forms a connection between the center of a star to the center of a star positioned opposite it and brings the two into continuity. And what the astronomers call eclipses Plato refers to as *obstacles* in a stricter and slightly more meaningful sense—not that they stand in one another's way, but that

spectantibus inferioris subiectu visus arceatur stellae superioris proptereaque deficere ac laborare propter obiectum
inferioris superior existimatur.

125. Item inquit: Quae longo intervallo rursus apparent,
metus et quaedam portenta significant vel mox futura vel
serius, significationem vero pertinere ad eos qui de his rebus
ratiocinari possunt putat; ex quo intellegi datur non stellas
facere quae proveniunt sed futura praenuntiare. Quam rationem secutus etiam vates Homerus ortum Caniculae Ca-
nem Orionis appellat—cum hanc eandem stellam Astrocy-
non quidam, Aegyptii vero Sothin vocent—cuius completur
annus qui Cynicus vocatur annis mille quadringentis sexaginta. Dicit autem Homerus de hoc sidere hactenus:

Iste quidem clarus, sed tristia fata minatur

—tunc, opinor, cum fuerit intervallo temporis visus. Videtur
porro interposito quadriennio sed non in isdem locis; quater
porro trecentis sexaginta quinque <annis sive trecentis sexaginta quinque> quadrienniis completur Cynicus Annus.

126. Aegyptiorum quoque prophetae stellam quandam
aliquot annis non visam verentur, quam vocant Ach, porro
sidus hoc exoriens morbos populorum multorumque opti-
matium mortes denuntiat. Homerus denique, qui idem fuerit Aegyptius, siquidem Thebanus fertur, quae civitas est
apud Aegyptum nobilissima, id ipsum latenter exequitur in
Iliadis exordio, cum dicit propter iram Achillis, cuius pater
Peleus, mater vero maritima fuerit dea, morbum atque

relative to our perspective on Earth the line of sight leading to the higher star is cut off owing to the lower one's position below it, so that owing to the interposition of the lower one the higher one is thought to grow dim.

125. He says as well [40c–d]: And those that *once again appear* after a long *interval* signify *fear* and certain *portents* for either the *immediate future* or later. And he holds that their signification is relevant to those *who are capable* of calculating the phenomena, from which it may be understood that the stars do not cause future events but give advance warning of them. Following this line of reasoning the poet Homer too refers to the rising of Canicula [Sirius] as Orion's Dog—although some call the star Astrocynos [*astrokuôn*, Dog Star], and the Egyptians, Sothis—and its Year is completed in 1,460 years and referred to as that of the Dog. Here is how Homer speaks of the star:

Though shining bright yet it threatens grim fates

—at the point, I suppose, *when* it appears *within the interval of time.* Now, it appears at four-year intervals but in different locations; the Year of the Dog, however, is completed in 4 × 365 years, or 365 four-year cycles.

126. The prophets of the Egyptians also fear a certain star called Ach, which appears only every so many years, and in its rising the star portends disease and death among the people and many of the nobility. In the event, Homer, who was Egyptian too according to the tradition of his being from Thebes, the noblest city in Egypt, implicitly rehearses this very point at the beginning of the *Iliad,* when he says that because of the wrath of Achilles, whose father was Peleus and mother a sea goddess, disease and death

interitum non modo clarorum virorum sed aliorum quoque
animalium et pecorum bello necessariorum extitisse; quo
quidem sumpto exordio cetera poetica licentia finxit. Est
quoque alia sanctior et venerabilior historia quae perhibet
ortu stellae cuiusdam non morbos mortesque denuntiatas
sed descensum dei venerabilis ad humanae conservationis
rerumque mortalium gratiam. Quam stellam cum nocturno
itinere suspexissent Chaldaeorum profecto sapientes viri et
in consideratione rerum caelestium satis exercitati, quae-
sisse dicuntur recentem ortum dei repertaque illa maiestate
puerili veneratos esse et vota tanto deo convenientia nuncu-
passe. Quae tibi multo melius sunt comperta quam ceteris.

127. At vero naturae daemonum praestare rationem maius
esse opus dicit quam ferre valeat hominis ingenium, non
quo disputatio haec a philosophis aliena sit (quibus enim
aliis magis competat?) sed quod inquisitio istius rei prima-
riae superuectaeque contemplationis sit, quae appellatur
epoptica, altior aliquanto quam physica, proptereaque nobis, qui de rerum natura nunc disputamus, nequaquam
conveniens esse videatur. Idem tamen breviter et strictim
de his potestatibus quae dii putantur locutus, credo propterea, ne mundi constitutio imperfecta relinqueretur ex
quotacumque parte si sileret de huius modi rebus, credule
mage quam persuadenter et probabiliter ostendit oportere

appeared not only among the noblemen but even among other living beings, including the beasts required for the war; with that once assumed as his starting point, poetic license contrived the rest. There is also another recorded tale, one more holy and venerable, according to which with the rising of a certain star there was portended, not disease and death, but the descent of a venerable God to bestow the grace of salvation upon mankind and mortal beings. Men from among the Chaldaeans who were undoubtedly wise and skilled in the observation of celestial phenomena are said, on having observed the star during a night journey, to have gone in search of the new birth of God and, on discovering the child in that state of majesty, to have venerated Him and offered prayers befitting a God of such greatness. These matters are much better known to you than to others.

127. *At the same time,* he says [40d–e] that *to give an account* of the nature *of demons is a task greater than our human ability is naturally capable of sustaining,* not in the sense that a disputation of this type is alien to philosophers (for to whom else would it be better suited?), but because inquiry into this matter is the concern of the first and highest order of contemplation, which is called the *epoptic:* somewhat higher than natural philosophy, and for that reason appearing quite unsuited to our task now, which is to engage in disputation about the nature of things. Yet he spoke briefly and pointedly about these powers which are *thought to be gods,* and, I believe, for the following reason: in order to avoid the world's formation being left somehow incomplete because of silence about such matters, in proceeding on trust rather than by persuasion or probability he showed that it is neces-

credulitatem omnes doctrinas praecedere—maxime cum non quorumlibet sed magnorum et prope divinorum virorum sit assertio—denique non frustra de Pythagora dictum "ipsum dicere" proptereaque ultra quaeri non oportere. Ergo, inquit, neque probationes semper adhibendae nec persuadens assertio his quae dicuntur a priscis divina quadam sapientia praeditis. Simul exponit ea quae Orpheus et Linus et Musaeus de divinis potestatibus vaticinati sunt, non quo delectaretur aut crederet sed quod tanta esset auctoritas vaticinantium ut his asseverantibus parcius credi non oporteret.

128. At vero in eo libro qui Philosophus inscribitur summa diligentia praecipuaque cura omnes exequitur huius modi quaestiones: priscorum hominum genus omnia quae ad usum hominum vitaeque agendae facultatem divino consilio providentiaque demanant auxiliantibus atque operantibus tam potentiis quam rationibus, haec ipsa quae auxiliantur deos existimasse, propterea quod rudibus animis nondum insedisset veri dei sciscitatio. Erant enim pastores et silvicaedi ceterique huius modi sine studiis humanitatis, quos cladis publicae superstites fecerat opportuna habitatio ex tempestatum atque illuvionis incommodo. Quae poetae postea blandientes humanis passionibus propter cupiditatem lucri versibus suis formata membratimque effigiata amplis et reconditis nominibus exornaverunt usque adeo ut

sary for *trust* to take precedence over all teaching—especially given that an *assertion* pertains, not to any men whatsoever, but to the great and nearly divine—and in effect showed that the tradition of Pythagoras's "having pronounced" and thereby removed the need for further inquiry was not pointless. Now, he says, neither *proofs* nor persuasive assertion need always to be offered for the sayings of the *men of old* who were endowed with a certain divine wisdom. He expounds at the same time Orpheus's, Linus's, and Musaeus's divine pronouncements concerning the divine powers, not for the sake of his own pleasure or trust but because the authority of those who made the pronouncements was such that it would have been wrong for them to be trusted with any degree of restriction.

128. But in the book entitled *The Philosopher* he pursues with the greatest diligence and special care all points of the following sort: that all of the things that flow down from divine counsel and providence for the benefit of men, and for their capacity to conduct life with the aid and cooperation of the powers and of reason, that these very sources of aid were considered by the race of men past to be gods, the reason being that knowledge of the true god had not yet taken root in their crude minds. For they were shepherds, woodsmen, and others of the same sort, all deprived of a liberal education, whose advantageous habitat had enabled them to survive the general destruction wrought by the misfortunes of storm and flood. And poets, who play on human emotions out of a desire for profit, later dressed these matters up, shaping them in their verses and through long, recondite names creating effigies limb by limb, to the point that they even passed the vicious allurements and the most

etiam vitiosas hominum illecebras turpissimosque actus
deos cognominarent obnoxios passioni. Itaque factum ut
pro gratia, quae ab hominibus debetur divinae providentiae,
origo et ortus sacrilegio panderetur; cuius erroris opinio
crevit inconsultorum hominum vanitate.

129. Haec ad praesens Plato quidem de daemonum genere disseruit, nos tamen oportet, etsi non usque quaque,
veram eorum breviter explicare rationem, quae est huius
modi. Quinque regiones vel locos idem Plato esse dicit in
mundo capaces animalium habentes aliquam inter se differentiam positionum ob differentiam corporum quae inha-
bitent eosdem locos. Summum enim esse locum ait ignis
sereni, huic proximum aethereum, cuius corpus esse ignem
aeque sed aliquanto crassiorem quam est altior ille caelestis,
dehinc aeris, post humectae substantiae quam Graeci
hygran usian appellant, quae humecta substantia aer est
crassior, ut sit aer iste quem homines spirant, imus vero atque ultimus locus terrae. Quae porro in locis differentia est,
eadem etiam in magnitudinibus invenitur: caelestis maximus, quippe qui omnia intra complexum suum redigat, bre-
vissimus terrae, quia ceteris omnibus corporibus ambitur,
iuxtaque rationem continui competentis ceteri medii.

130. Cum igitur extimi limites [id est summus atque imus]
celebrentur convenientibus animalibus naturae suae, [scili-
cet ratione utentibus] caelestis quidem stellis terrestris autem hominibus, consequens est etiam ceteros locos regio-
nesque interiectas plenas esse rationabilibus animalibus
existimari, ne quis mundi locus desertus relinquatur. Etenim

lurid human acts off as those of gods in the grip of passion. And so it came to pass that sacrilege rather than the thanks owed by men to divine providence found its point of origin, its birth; and belief in this error grew, thanks to the vain arrogance of foolish men.

129. These, for the moment, are the points laid out by Plato concerning the race of demons; our task, however, is briefly to furnish a true account of them, although not down to the level of every detail. It is as follows. Plato says that there are in the world five regions or places suitable for living beings, and that they exhibit mutual differences in position owing to the difference in the bodies that inhabit those same places. For he says that the highest region is that of pure fire, that next to it is the ethereal region, the corporeal aspect of which is also fire only somewhat denser than that higher celestial fire is, that next is the region of air, that after it is the region of the moist substance the Greeks call *hygra ousia,* which moist substance is air in its denser state, giving us the air that men breathe; and the lowest and final region is that of earth. The difference obtaining between regions is found to be the same as between magnitudes as well: the heavenly region is the largest, bringing all things within its embrace, the smallest is that of earth, surrounded by all other bodies, and the rest are intermediate, according to the ratio of a continuous proportion.

130. Given, then, that the extreme limits are filled with living beings befitting their nature, the celestial region with stars and the terrestrial one with human beings, it follows that the other places and regions should be considered to be full of rational living beings as well, to prevent any place in the world being left deserted. For it is absurd to suppose

est absurdum homines quidem imam mundi regionem inha-
bitantes fragili corpore, animo cum amentia et sine sinceritate pleno paenitudinis ob inconstantiam commotionum
suarum, alias aliis atque aliis placentibus, rationabiles animantes putari, stellas vero prudentis naturae ob aeternam
actuum suorum constantiam nulli paenitudini obnoxias,
puro minimeque dissolubili corpore, utpote quae extimas
ignis cuncta ambientis regiones incolant, sine anima fore,
carere etiam vita putare. Cui quidem rei Hebraeorum quoque sententia concinit, qui perhibent exornatorem mundi
deum mandasse provinciam soli quidem ut diem regeret lunae vero ut noctem tueretur, ceteras quoque stellas dispo-
suisse tamquam limites temporum annorumque signa, indicia quoque futurorum proventuum. Quae cuncta certe tam
moderate, tam prudenter, tam iugiter continueque agi sine
rationabili quin potius sine sapientissimo rectore non possent.

131. Quare cum sit divinum quidem et immortale genus
animalium caeleste sidereum, temporarium vero et occiduum passionique obnoxium terrenum, necesse est esse
inter haec duo medietatem aliquam conectentem extimos
limites, sicut in harmonia videmus et in ipso mundo. Ut
enim sunt in ipsis materiis medietates quae interpositae totius mundi corpus continuant iugiter; suntque inter ignem
et terram duae medietates aeris et aquae quae mediae tan-
gunt conectuntque extimos limites: sic, cum sit immortale

both at once: that human beings—who are fragile of body in virtue of their inhabiting the lowest region of the world, and whose minds are foolish, impure, and full of regret owing to the emotional inconstancy entailed by their ever-shifting desires—are rational ensouled (living) beings; but that the stars—which are by nature wise and owing to the eternal constancy of their actions subject to no regret, and which are pure and indissoluble of body in virtue of their inhabiting the outermost regions of the all-embracing fire—lack soul and even life. The view held by the Hebrews is in accord with this as well, for they claim that the God who conferred order upon the world bade that the Sun's province should be to rule over the day, and the Moon's to keep watch over the night, and that he also disposed the other stars as the limits, as it were, between temporal periods and as the signs of years, as indications also of future events. At the very least, in the absence of a rational and indeed supremely wise ruler none of these things would be able to be accomplished with such order, wisdom, and enduring continuity.

131. Given, then, that the divine and immortal race of living beings is celestial, associated with the stars, while the temporary, perishable one subject to passion is associated with earth, it is necessary that there should be between these two some intermediate to connect the extreme limits, just as we see in the cases of musical harmony and the world itself. For as among the material elements themselves there are intermediates which by their interposition give binding continuity to the body of the entire world; and as between fire and earth there are air and water as two intermediates which by their mediating contact connect the extreme limits: so it is necessary, given the existence of a living being

animal et impatibile idemque rationabile, quod caeleste dicitur, existente item alio mortali passionibusque obnoxio,
genere nostro, necesse est aliquod genus medium fore quod
tam caelestis quam terrenae naturae sit particeps idque et
immortale esse et obnoxium passioni. Talis porro natura
daemonum est, opinor, habens cum divinitate consortium
propter immortalitatem, habens etiam cum occiduis cognationem, quia est patibile nec immune a passionibus, cuius
affectus nobis quoque consulit.

132. Huius porro generis est illud aethereum, quod in secundo loco commemoravimus positum, quos Hebraei vocant sanctos angelos stareque eos dicunt ante dei venerabilis
contemplationem, summa <prudentia> atque acri intellegentia, mira etiam memoriae tenacitate, rebus quidem divinis obsequium navantes summa sapientia, humanis vero
prudenter opitulantes idemque speculatores et executores,
daemones, opinor, tamquam daemones dicti, daemonas
porro Graeci scios rerum omnium nuncupant. Quos quidem
praefectos sensili mundo primo quidem vicem imitari aliquam putandum (ut enim deus iuxta angelum sic angelus
iuxta hominem), dehinc quod usui nobis sint interpretantes
et nuntiantes deo nostras preces et item hominibus dei
voluntatem intimantes, illi nostram indigentiam, porro ad
nos divinam opem deferentes; quam ob causam appellati
angeli ob assiduum officium nuntiandi. Testis est huius
beneficii cuncta Graecia omne Latium omnisque Barbaria

which is immortal, impassible, and rational (that which is called the celestial) and another which is mortal and subject to passions (*our* race), that there should be some intermediate race to participate in the celestial as well as terrestrial nature, and that it should be both immortal and subject to passion. And such, I suppose, is the nature of demons, having a close connection with divinity by virtue of its immortality, and having a close relation with perishable beings in that it is passible, not immune to passions, and whose sense of empathy even looks after us.

132. And to this class belongs that ethereal one which we mentioned as being placed at the second level. The Hebrews call them holy "angels" and say that they stand in the presence of the venerable God's contemplation, with the highest degree of prudence and acute intelligence, also a wondrous tenacity of memory, devoting themselves with the highest degree of wisdom in their service to divine concerns while prudently aiding human ones—at once observers and executors, and called "demons" [*daimones*], I suppose, as though it were *daêmones* [knowers]: the Greeks refer to those who are all-knowing as *daêmones*. And we should hold, first, that these beings who have been given responsibility for the sensible world imitate in a sense the one whose place they hold (for as god is to an angel, so the angel is to a human being), and second, that they perform for us the service of interpreting and reporting our prayers to god and likewise of interpreting and reporting god's will to humans, revealing to him our needs and bringing divine aid down to us, the assiduous task of reporting being the reason for their being called "angels." The whole of Greece, all of Latium, all of the barbarian world, and the expressions of thanks offered up

gratulationesque populorum libris conditis ad memoriam perpetuitatis. Indiget quippe natura generis humani nimium imbecilla suffragio melioris praestantiorisque naturae; quam ob causam creator omnium et conservator deus volens esse hominum genus praefecit his, per quos recte regerentur, angelos sive daemonas.

133. Nec nos terreat nomen promisce bonis et improbis positum, quoniam nec angelorum quidem terret cum angeli partim dei sint ministri (qui ita sunt, sancti vocantur) partim adversae potestatis satellites, ut optime nosti; igitur iuxta usurpatam penes Graecos loquendi consuetudinem tam sancti sunt daemones quam polluti et infecti. De quibus mox erit aptior disputandi locus, nunc de eo genere sit sermo quod ait Plato admirabili quadam esse prudentia memoriaque et docilitate felici, quod omnia sciat cogitationesque hominum introspiciat et bonis quidem eximie delectetur, improbos oderit contingente se tristitia quae nascitur ex odio displicentis; solus quippe deus, utpote plenae perfectaeque divinitatis, neque tristitia neque voluptate contingitur.

134. Cunctis ergo caeli regionibus sortitis daemonas inquilinos agi mutuos commeatus mediam mundi sedem incolentibus potestatibus obsequium caelo praebentibus etiam terrena curantibus; quae potestates aetherei aereique sunt

by peoples in the books preserved to perpetuate their memory are testimony to this benefit. For the nature of the human race, being exceedingly fragile, is in need of support from a better and superior nature, which is why god, the creator and preserver of all things, in willing that there should be a race of men gave the "angels," or "demons," responsibility for them, so that through them the men might be rightly guided.

133. Nor should the name by virtue of its being imposed indifferently upon good and evil beings be for us a cause for concern, for the name "angels" occasions no concern even though some angels are God's servants (and those who are, are called holy) but others minions of the adverse power, as you know perfectly well; hence according to the custom of speaking adopted by the Greeks "demons" are as likely to be holy as polluted or tainted. Concerning the latter there will presently be a more suitable opportunity to explain, but for the moment our discussion should concern the class which Plato describes as characterized by a certain wondrous wisdom and a felicitous memory and docility, in that it is all-knowing, sees into the thoughts of men, and while taking special pleasure in good ones is repelled by those who are wicked, being affected by a pain that arises from a repulsion to that which causes displeasure; for god alone, being of full and perfect divinity, is unaffected by either pain or pleasure.

134. Now, in that all regions of the heaven have been allotted demons as their inhabitants and the powers that inhabit the world's intermediate abode provide obedient service to the heaven while also looking after the interests of terrestrial beings, communications are said to be conducted back and forth; and the powers that are ethereal or aerial

daemones, remoti a visu nostro et ceteris sensibus, quia corpora eorum neque tantum ignis habent, ut sint perspicua, neque tantum terrae, ut soliditas eorum tactui renitatur, totaque eorum compago ex aetheris serenitate et aeris liquore conexa indissolubilem coagmentavit superficiem; ex quo non nulli regionem hanc nostram Ἅιδην merito, quod sit aides, hoc est obscura, cognominatam putant. Multos porro esse daemonas etiam Hesiodo placet, ait enim ter esse eorum decem milia eosque esse tam in obsequio dei quam in tutela mortalium, non certam summam conficiens numeri eorum sed iuxta vim pleni numeri trium multiplicans decem milia.

135. Erit ergo definitio daemonis talis: "daemon est animal rationabile immortale patibile aethereum diligentiam hominibus impertiens." "Animal" quidem quia est anima corpore utens; "rationabile" vero quia prudens; "immortale" porro quia non mutat corpus aliud ex alio sed eodem semper utitur; "patibile" vero propterea quia consulit, neque enim dilectus haberi potest sine affectus perpessione; "aethereum" item ex loco vel ex qualitate corporis cognominatum; "diligentiam" vero "hominibus impertiens" propter dei voluntatem qui custodes dedit. Eadem haec erit definitio aerei quoque daemonis, nisi quod hic in aere mansitat et, quanto est terrae propinquior, eo passioni affectus accommodatior. Reliqui daemones neque ita probabiles neque ita commodi nec invisibiles semper, sed interdum contemplabiles, cum in diversas convertuntur figuras. Exsanguium quoque simulacrorum umbraticas formas induuntur obesi corporis illuviem trahentes, saepe etiam scelerum et impietatis ultores

demons are removed from our vision and other senses, since their bodies have neither fire sufficient to make them visible nor earth sufficient to make their solidity resistant to touch, and the whole of their structure, compounded as it is of pure ether and limpid air, has given cohesion to an indissoluble surface. In consideration of this, some suppose that this region of ours is for good reason named "Hades" because it is *aidês,* i.e., obscure. And Hesiod too is of the opinion that demons are numerous, for he says that there are 3 × 10,000 of them and that they are engaged in both obedient service to god and caring for mortals; he was not contriving a fixed sum for their numbers but multiplying 10,000 by the power of the whole number 3.

135. The definition of a demon, then, will be as follows: "A demon is a rational, immortal, passible, ethereal living being engaged in the care of human beings." "Living being," because it is a soul using a body; "rational," because wise; "immortal," because it does not shift from one body to another but always uses the same one; "passible," because of the fact that it deliberates, for a choice cannot be made without experiencing a passion; and called "ethereal" owing to its location and type of body; "engaged in the care of human beings," on account of the will of god, who provided them as guardians. This same definition will apply also to an aerial demon, except that the latter type frequents the air and is the more disposed to experiencing passion the closer it comes to Earth. The other types are by comparison neither praiseworthy nor beneficial, nor are they always invisible but can sometimes be seen, shifting from shape to shape. They also don the shadowy forms of bloodless images, taking on the filth of corporeal density, often serving even as

iuxta iustitiae divinae sanctionem. Ultro etiam plerumque laedunt; tanguntur enim ex vicinia terrae terrena libidine habentque nimiam cum silva communionem, quam malignam animam veteres vocabant. Hos quidam et huius modi daemonas proprie vocant desertores angelos, quibus nulla quaestio referenda est super nomine.

136. Plerique tamen ex Platonis magisterio daemonas putant animas corporeo munere liberatas, laudabilium quoque virorum aethereos daemonas, improborum vero nocentes, easdemque animas anno demum millesimo terrenum corpus resumere, Empedoclesque non aliter longaevos daemonas fieri has animas putat, Pythagoras etiam in suis Aureis Versibus:

> Corpore deposito cum liber ad aethera perges,
> evades hominem factus deus aetheris almi.

Quibus Plato consentire minime videtur cum in Politia tyranni animam facit excruciari post mortem ab ultoribus, ex quo apparet aliam esse animam alium daemonem (siquidem quod cruciatur et item quod cruciat diversa esse necesse sit), quodque opifex deus ante daemonas instituit quam nostras animas creavit, quodque has indigere auxilio daemonum, illos his voluerit praebere tutelam. Quasdam tamen animas quae vitam eximie per trinam incorporationem egerint

avengers of crimes and impiety by sanction of divine justice. They are also the cause of gratuitous and frequent suffering, for owing to their proximity to the Earth they are affected by earthly lust and have an excessively high level of communion with matter, which the ancients referred to as the malign soul. Some refer to these demons or demons of this type as, strictly speaking, "deserter angels," and we should bring no case against them over the expression.

136. Many followers of Plato' teaching think, however, that demons are souls that have been set free from corporeal service, the ethereal demons being those precisely of praiseworthy men and the malicious ones those of the wicked, and that the same souls take on a new earthly body only in the thousandth year; and Empedocles similarly thinks that these souls become demons that survive for very long periods, so too Pythagoras, in his *Golden Verses:*

> When you set out for ether, free, with your body laid
> aside,
> you will escape being human by being made a god of gra-
> cious ether.

Plato is evidently in disagreement with these words when in the *Republic* he has the tyrant's soul tormented by avengers after death, from which it is apparent that a soul is one thing and a demon another (for that which is tormented and that which torments are necessarily different things), that the craftsman god established the demons prior to creating our souls, and that his intention was that the latter should require the aid of demons while the former should watch over the latter. At the same time, he thinks that certain souls which have conducted their life exceptionally through the

virtutis merito aereis vel etiam aethereis plagis consecrari
putat a necessitate incorporationis immunes.

137. Hactenus de natura daemonum. Deinde de mortalium
genere disserit ac primo de hominibus eorumque ipsorum
sexu virili, rationabilem partem animae duplici virtute praeditam docens: alteram quae contemplatur eandem semper
immutabilemque naturam, ex qua intentione mentis convalescit sapientia, alteram item quae mutabilium generato-
rumque opinatrix est, cui prudentiae vocabulum congruit.
Utramque porro hanc animae potentiam a summo et intellegibili deo dicit universi corporis, mundi sensilis videlicet,
animae datam, ceteras ratione carentes et occiduas animae
portiones, id est appetitum sensuum locularem motum
quaque corpora nutriuntur totumque corpus, iussu et ordinatione architecti dei a generatis ab ipso potestatibus as-
signata esse mortalibus; propterea ne, si haec etiam ab opifice et intellegibili deo forent, unius essent fortunae omnia
immortalibusque existentibus cunctis nullo existente mortali semine claudicaret universitatis perfectio, cum in exemplari, hoc est intellegibili mundo, inferioris naturae semina
intellegibiliter extent.

138. Videamus nunc sermonis textum. Di, deorum quorum opifex idem paterque ego. Dramatica est dialogi, quod
ad dispositionem pertinet, adumbratio, sermo vero speciei

third incarnation are by merit of their virtue raised to the aerial or even ethereal zones, protected from the necessity of incarnation.

137. So much for the nature of demons. He treats next the race of mortals, and first human beings; and of those the male sex, explaining that the rational part of the soul is endowed with a double capacity: one that contemplates the nature that is the Same and forever immutable, the state of mental concentration from which wisdom gathers its strength; and the other, that which forms opinions about mutable and generated things, which the term "prudence" fits. He says, furthermore, that each of the two powers of soul was bestowed by the highest, intelligible god upon the soul of the corporeal universe, namely, of the sensible world, and that in lacking reason and being subject to corruption the other parts of soul—i.e., the appetitive one associated with the senses, spatial movement, that by which bodies derive nourishment, and the body as a whole—were assigned to mortals on the command and order of the architect god through the agency of the powers generated by him. The purpose of this was to prevent everything from sharing in a single lot by virtue of common descent from an intelligible craftsman god, and to prevent the perfection of the universe from being rendered defective by having all that exists be immortal—by the *nonexistence* of any mortal seeds, for the seeds of a lower nature exist within the exemplar, i.e., within the intelligible world.

138. Let us look now at the language of the text [41a]: *O gods, you gods of whom I am at once the craftsman and father.* The conceit of the dialogue is that of a drama, which addresses the question of its literary form, but its language is of a more

augustioris. Decet denique hoc in genere orationis arcanorum interpretatio fabulosa. Nihil ergo inconvenienter facit auctor, quod opificem deum inducit contionantem sancientemque a se genitis quae observari vellet, multis rationibus: primo recreationis legentium causa, quippe res difficilis lepido sermone condita facilius ad intima mentis admittitur; deinde inopinatae allocutionis varietas mixta religioni raptis animis ad imaginem contionantis praesentem laborem sentiri non sinit; tum immutatio magisterii novo instituto operis exordio novas vires excitat audientis, siquidem et deficit omnis auditor adversum molestiam uniformis eloquii, porro attentior fit, cum novae spes dispositionis ostenditur. Hoc in loco dogmata etiam sua studiose asserit, ut non tam a se inventa quam a deo praedicta videantur— praedicta autem non illo sermone qui est positus in sono vocis ad declarandos motus intimos propter humanae mentis involucra (deus enim nullo obstaculo prohiberi potest ab intellectu scientiaque omnium rerum) <sed> lege divina, quam Plato inevitabilem appellat promulgationem.

139. Quid ergo dicit deus? Di, deorum quorum idem opifex paterque ego. Praeclare; facit enim regem optimatibus sancientem, ut lex illis data etiam ad ceteras potestates

august variety. With this kind of speech the mythic interpretation of hidden mysteries is unquestionably suitable. For several reasons, then, the author is in no way acting inappropriately in introducing the craftsman god as speaking before an assembly and *sanctioning* the tasks he wished to be *observed* by those who had been *begotten* by him. For one thing, it allows readers to relax, for difficult subject matter is the more readily admitted to the mind's inner recesses if it is seasoned with agreeable language. Again, once their minds have been drawn into imagining his speaking before an assembly, the shift to an unanticipated style of address combined with a religious sensibility prevents the present difficulty from being perceived. Then too, as a work establishes a new start a change in the mode of instruction stirs up renewed strength in the listener, for every listener fades when confronted with the annoyance of a uniform style of speech and becomes more attentive once hopes for a new literary form are raised. In this passage he studiously asserts doctrines that are indeed his own but in such a way that they have the appearance, not of having been invented by him, but of having been proclaimed by the god—not proclaimed, however, in speech which owing to the concealments of the human mind employs vocal sound in order to declare the inner processes (for god is incapable of being prevented by any obstacle from understanding and knowing all things), but by the divine law which Plato refers to as an "inevitable decree."

139. What, then, does god say? [41a–d] *O gods, you gods of whom I am at once the craftsman and father.* This is done with perfect clarity; for he produces a king *sanctioning* for his nobles that the law given them should make its way down to

atque animas commearet. Opificem se et parentem eorum
esse commemorat, opificem quidem, utpote a quo facti sint,
patrem vero, ut qui consulat provide, quatenus aeterni ac
beati sint. Opera siquidem vos mea, quia pater est et opifex
non substantiae sed generationis; illi enim optimates, id est
stellae, non sunt intellegibiles sed sensiles, at vero fabricator
eorum intellegibilis apprime. Deinde docet eos cuius naturae sint quodque ex compositione subsistant; porro quae ex
compositione subsistunt dissolubilia sunt isdem rationibus
quibus subsisterent; ipsi tamen indissolubiles; merito, non
enim sunt ex ullo ortu temporario sed ex voluntate summi
dei emensa omnem temporum antiquitatem. Qui vero indissolubiles eos esse confitetur, sine ullo quoque ortu conce-
dat necesse est; quod vero initium non habet, sine fine certe
est, et quod finem non habet, sine ortu est. Divinum autem
et immortale cognomentum vocat rationis potentiam, id est
rationem, mortalia porro et associata—immo, ut ipse ait,
attexta—quae sunt, opinor, in vitiis, iram videlicet et voluptatem.

140. Deinde genituram humanarum prosequitur animarum, ut natura eius liquido comprehendatur, et perseverat
in fabula quam interposuit, propterea ut quae dicuntur manifesta sint. Rursus enim cratera proponit et mixturam
concretionemque earum potentiarum ex quibus mundi
anima concreverat exque reliquiis earum nostras machina-
tur, videlicet ex illa duplici natura eiusdem et item diversi

the other powers and souls as well. He mentions that he is their *craftsman* and parent: *craftsman,* meaning the one by whom they were made, and *father,* as the one who assumes providential care over their being eternal and blessed. *Insofar as you are my works,* because he is the *father* and *craftsman,* not of their being, but of their coming to be; for those nobles, i.e., stars, are not intelligible but sensible, whereas their maker is supremely intelligible. Then he explains to them of what nature they are and that they subsist by virtue of composition; and things that subsist by virtue of composition are *subject to dissolution* for the same reasons as those that explain their subsistence; *nevertheless* they themselves are *immune to dissolution;* rightly so, in that they do not exist by virtue of any process of birth in time but because of the *wish* of the highest god, which traverses the whole of time from its origins. But he who grants that they are immune to dissolution must concede that they are also without any process of birth; but what has no beginning is surely without an end, and what has no end is without a process of birth. *Divine,* moreover, and *immortal* are the names by which he says the *rational power,* i.e., reason, is called, whereas *mortal* and conjoined—rather, *woven together,* as he himself says— are the things which, I suppose, exist defectively, namely, irascibility and pleasure.

140. He turns next to the generation of human souls, to make its nature clearly understood, and he persists with the myth which he inserted, his purpose being to clarify the words spoken. For once again he introduces mixing bowls and the mixture and formation of the powers from which the world soul had been formed, and from what remains of these he devises our souls, namely, *from the* twofold *nature of*

<nec non individuae> dividuaeque substantiae, quae non ut antea sincerae puritatis erant. Neque enim anima quae ex sincerissimis excuderetur in tanta silvae vitia posset incidere nec congruere cum mortalis corporis fragilitate. Miscebat autem, inquit, eodem propemodum genere, nec tamen eadem exoriebatur puritas serenitasque proventuum. Merito, quoniam in his animis quae vivificant morti obnoxia genera animalium non pura ratio intellectusve sincerus sed aliquantum tam iracundiae quam libidinis invenitur. Mixta igitur, inquit, anima ipsa etiam in longum secatur eiusque una pars integra relinquitur iuxta naturae, quae vocatur eadem, circumactionem, ex quo intellegunt divina omnia sapientesque fiunt qui intellegunt, diversae vero naturae partem secat sexies iuxta motum rationabilem planetum harmonicis et arithmeticis et geometricis medietatibus, ut supra demonstratum est; haec est animae virtus quae opinio dicitur, qua duce quae nascuntur et occidunt noscimus. Quae constitutio animae propterea facta est ut esset, opinor, eadem anima scia tam intellegibilium quam substantiae sensilis, utpote quae rationes utriusque naturae habeat in semet ipsa. Haec est animae rationabilis institutio a venerabili deo facta in hominis innexa vultum, cum occasiones vitiorum percipit aeternae legis provida moderatione.

141. Deinde ait delegisse animas stellarum numero pares singulasque singulis comparasse easdemque vehiculis

the Same and Other [37a] and of indivisible and divisible Being, which were not of the same unalloyed *purity* [41d] as before. For soul, which was forged out of the purest materials, was incapable of descending to union with the enormous defects of matter or of conforming with the fragility of the mortal body. But *he set about blending it,* he says [41d], *in more or less the same way, although there did not emerge the same purity and clarity of results.* Rightly so, for in the souls that give life to the kinds of living beings which are subject to death there is found, not *pure* reason and unalloyed intellect, but some measure of irascibility as well as desire. Thus the blended soul *itself,* he says, is also *cut lengthwise* [36b], and one part of it is left whole to account for the circumlation of the nature called the Same, from which all divine beings *understand,* and those who understand become wise, but the part that is of the nature of the Other he cuts *six ways* [36d], by harmonic, arithmetic, and geometrical means, to account for the rationally proportioned movement of the planets, as demonstrated earlier. This is the power of the soul called *opinion* [37b], under whose guidance we gain knowledge of the things that come to be and pass away. And the reason why this constitution of the soul was effected was, I suppose, so that the same soul might be capable of knowing both the intelligibles and sensible being, in other words, so that it might have within itself the rational capacities corresponding to both natures. This is the establishment of the rational soul as effected by the venerable god and *fixed* [44d] within the countenance of man, when within the providentially established limits of the eternal law it perceives the opportunities for vice.

141. Next he says [41c–e] that he *selected souls equal in number with the stars and coupled them one to one, and after mounting*

competentibus superimpositas universae rei naturam spectare iussisse. Antequam sementem faceret animarum, superimposuit stellis singulis singulas animas, quo isdem vehiculis usae in circuitu stellarum cunctam mundi naturam considerarent, illud docens, quod sine divinitatis adminiculo ipsa per se anima nihil valeat spectare atque intellegere divinum.

142. Legesque immutabilis decreti docuit. Hic iam magnam et difficilem rationem commovet, de qua multa disceptatio habita inter veteres perseverat etiam nunc. Perfunctorium ergo tractatum haberi nunc convenit iuxta Platonicum dogma; longum est enim persequi ceterorum, quorum plerique nihil putant fato fieri, alii omnia (nec quicquam arbitrio ac voluntate), quidam alia esse quae fato nihiloque minus alia esse quae voluntate fiant.

143. Igitur iuxta Platonem praecedit providentia, sequitur fatum; ait enim deum post mundi constitutionem divisisse animas stellarum numero pares singulasque singulis comparasse universique mundi monstrasse naturam atque universam fatorum seriem revelasse. Horum enim quae prima sunt providentiam indicant, secunda leges fatales, proptereaque iuxta Platonem praenascitur providentia, ideoque fatum quidem dicimus ex providentia fore, non tamen providentiam ex fato. Fatum ergo iuxta Platonem dupliciter intellegitur et dicitur: unum, cum substantiam eius

them in the appropriate vehicles he bade them gaze upon the nature of the universe. Before *producing the seed for the sowing* of souls he *mounted* souls on stars, *one to one,* so that by employing the same stars as *vehicles* they might contemplate the entire *nature* of the world in the course of the stellar orbit, the point of his explanation being that without the aid of divinity the soul on its own is incapable of *gazing upon* and understanding anything divine.

142. *And he instructed them in the laws of the immutable decree* [41e]. At this point he now sets a great and difficult account in motion, one in connection with which the frequent disagreement that obtained among the ancients persists even today. For the moment, then, it is appropriate that a perfunctory treatment should be conducted in conformity with Platonic doctrine, since it would take too long to pursue those of others, many of whom think that nothing happens by fate, others that everything does (and nothing by free choice or the will), and some that there are some things which happen by fate and others which nonetheless happen because of the will.

143. Now, according to Plato providence precedes and fate follows; for he says [41d–e] that after the establishment of the world god divided it into *souls equal in number with the stars and coupled them one to one* and pointed to the nature of the universe and revealed the universal series of fates. For the first phrase refers to providence and the second to the laws of fate, and for this reason providence, according to Plato, comes into being first, and so although we do indeed say that fate is from providence, nevertheless we do not say that providence is from fate. According to Plato, then, fate is understood and predicated in two ways: one, when we

355

animo intuemur; alterum, cum ex his quae agit et esse id et cuius modi vim habeat recognoscimus. Idem fatum in Phaedro quidem scitum inevitabile, in Timaeo leges quas deus de universae rei natura dixerit caelestibus animis, porro in Politia Lacheseos appellat orationem, non tragice sed more theologorum.

144. Possumus ergo inevitabile quidem scitum interpretari legem minime mutabilem ex inevitabili causa, leges vero, quas de universa natura dixit animis deus, legem quae mundi naturam sequitur et qua reguntur mundana omnia, Lacheseos vero, hoc est Necessitatis <filiae,> orationem divinam legem qua praeteritis et item praesentibus conectuntur futura. At vero in substantia positum fatum mundi anima est tripertita in aplane sphaeram inque eam quae putatur erratica et in sublunarem tertiam; quarum elatam quidem ad superna dici Atropon, mediam Clotho, imam Lachesin: Atropon, quod aplanes in nulla sit deflexione; Clotho, propter varie perplexam tortuosamque vertiginem, qua proveniunt ea quae diversae naturae devius motus importat; Lachesin vero tamquam sortitam id munus, ut omnia praedictarum opera effectusque suscipiat. Itaque non nulli putant praesumi differentiam providentiae fatique, cum reapse una sit, quippe providentiam dei fore voluntatem, voluntatem porro eius seriem esse causarum, et ex eo quidem quia voluntas providentia est, <providentiam,> porro quia eadem series causarum est, fatum cognominatam, ex

gaze mentally upon its substance; the other, when we come to recognize from its effects both its being and the kind of power it has. Plato also in the *Phaedrus* refers to fate as an "inevitable decree," and in the *Timaeus* as *laws* which god proclaimed to the celestial souls *concerning the nature of the universe,* and in the *Republic* as the speech of Lachesis, not in the tragic style but in the manner of the theologians.

144. Thus we can indeed interpret the "inevitable decree" as an immovable *law* originating from an "inevitable" cause, and the laws that god proclaimed to the souls *concerning the nature of the universe* [41e] as the law which is consequent upon the nature of the world and by which all things in the world are ruled, and the speech of Lachesis, i.e., of the daughter of Necessity, as the divine law by which future events are linked with past and present ones. As understood with respect to its substance, however, fate is the world soul divided into its three parts, the nonwandering sphere, the one held to be wandering, and, third, the sublunary one, and of these the one raised to the heights he says is called Atropos, the middle one Clotho, the lowest Lachesis: Atropos, because the *aplanês* admits of no deviation; Clotho, because of the varying complexities in its spiraling whorl, by virtue of which there come to pass the things which the deviant movement of the nature of the Other introduces; and Lachesis, as though having been allotted the task of taking up all of the works and effects of those just mentioned. Some, then, suppose that a difference between providence and fate is presumed, when in fact it is one reality: for providence is the will of god, and his will is a series of causes, and it is called providence because his will *is* foresight [*providentia*] but fate because it is also a series of causes, from which

quo fieri ut quae secundum fatum sunt etiam ex providentia
sint, eodemque modo quae secundum providentiam ex fato,
ut putat Chrysippus. Alii vero, quae quidem ex providentiae
auctoritate fataliter quoque provenire, nec tamen quae fataliter ex providentia, ut Cleanthes.

145. Sed Platoni placet neque omnia ex providentia fore,
neque enim uniformem naturam esse rerum quae dispensantur; ita quaedam ex providentia tantum, quaedam ex
decreto, non nulla ex voluntate nostra, non nulla etiam ex
varietate fortunae, pleraque casu, quae ut libet accidunt. Et
divina quidem atque intellegibilia quaeque his proxima sunt
secundum providentiam solam, naturalia vero et corporea
iuxta fatum; ea porro, quae nostri arbitrii nostrique iuris
sunt, sponte nostra; porro quae extra nos posita sine ratione
atque inopinate accidunt: si quidem ex nostro disposito
coepta erunt, fortuita, si sine nostra institutione, casu provenire dicuntur.

146. Quae cuncta manifestius in Timaeo digerit ita dicens: Quibus ita ordinatis cum in proposito rerum creator
maneret. Quaenam ordinaverat? Scilicet quod universae rei
animam corpusque omne modulamine apto iugaverat. Intellegentes, inquit, iussionem patris filii iuxta mandatam informationem, immortali sumpto initio mortalis animantis
ex mundi materiis igni terraque et aqua cum spiritu, faenus
elementarium mutuati quod redderetur cum opus foret, ea

it results that the things which are according to fate are also from providence and likewise that the things which are according to providence are from fate, as Chrysippus supposes. But others, such as Cleanthes, suppose that, although the things which occur from the authority of providence are also fated, those which are fated nevertheless do not occur from providence.

145. But according to Plato things are not wholly from providence, for the nature of things that come under a dispensation is not uniform; thus some things are from providence only, others by decree, some from our will, some also from the variability of fortune, and many by chance and occurring as chance has it. And the divine and intelligible things and those nearest them are according to providence alone, whereas the natural and corporeal ones are according to fate; and those that come under our choice and jurisdiction are according to our will; and those situated beyond our control occur independently of reason and unexpectedly: they are said to be fortuitous if initiated on the basis of what we dispose but to occur by chance if they are independent of what we arrange.

146. He articulates all of these points with greater clarity when in the *Timaeus* he says [42e–43a]: *And when these things* had been set in order thus *and the creator of things continued to abide by his plan.* What things had he set in order? There is of course the fact that he had yoked the soul of the universe and the universal body together in fitting harmony. *The sons,* he says, *reflected on their father's command in light of the conception it stipulated, and after drawing upon the world's material elements of fire, earth, water, and air as an immortal starting point for the mortal living creature by borrowing elemental capital*

quae acceperant conglutinabant non indissolubilibus illis nexibus ex quibus ipsi cohaeserant. Etenim iussum dei cui parent dii secundi ratio est, opinor, continens ordinationem perpetuam quae fatum vocatur, idque trahit originem ex providentia.

147. Quid cum dicit: Coagmentataque mox universae rei machina delegit animas stellarum numero pares singulasque singulis comparavit easdemque vehiculis competentibus superimpositas universae rei naturam spectare iussit legesque immutabilis decreti docuit. Mundi quippe machinam absolvere, deligere animas stellarum numero pares, vehiculis aptis superimponere, universae rei monstrare naturam, leges immutabilis decreti docere—cuncta haec officia providentiae sunt. Ipsae vero leges quae dictae sunt fatum est idque divina lex est mundi animae insinuata, salubre rerum omnium regimen. Sic fatum quidem ex providentia est nec tamen ex fato providentia.

148. Nunc iam de fato quod in munere atque actu positum est loquemur, quippe de hoc plurimae disceptationes habentur morales naturales logicae. Nam cum omnia quae fiunt infinita sint et ex infinito per immensum tempus infinitumque proveniant, cuncta undique complectens fatum ipsum tamen finitum est ac determinatum—neque enim lex neque ratio neque quid omnino divinitate praeditum indeterminatum—idque ipsum manifestatur ex statu et conformatione caeli sub id tempus, quod perfectum annum

which was to be repaid as needed, they set about cementing together what they had received, not with the indissoluble bonds by which they themselves had acquired coherence. For the command of god with which the secondary gods comply is, I suppose, reason as containing the perpetual ordinance which is called fate, and it derives its origin from providence.

147. What about his saying [41d–e], *And as soon as the engine of the universe had been joined together he selected souls equal in number with the stars and coupled them one to one, and after mounting them in the appropriate vehicles he bade them gaze upon the nature of the universe and instructed them in the laws of the immutable decree?* Surely all of these points — to complete the *engine* of the world, to *select souls equal in number with the stars,* to *mount* them on suitable *vehicles,* to point to the *nature of the universe,* and to *instruct them in the laws of the immutable decree* — are the tasks of providence. Fate, however, is precisely the laws proclaimed, and it is the divine law permeating the world soul, the salubrious guidance of all things. And in this sense fate is indeed from providence, but providence is not from fate.

148. We will now speak about fate as understood with respect to its function and act, since concerning this point the number of moral, natural, and logical disputes is considerable. For although taken together the things that come to pass are infinite and emerge out of the infinite through an immense and infinite span of time, nevertheless the fate actually embracing them on all sides is finite and determinate — for neither law, nor reason, nor anything at all endowed with divinity is indeterminate — and this very fact is made manifest by the disposition and configuration of the heaven over the course of the temporal period they call the

vocant. De quo Plato sic ait: Est tamen intellectu facile
quod perfectus temporis numerus perfectum annum compleat tunc demum cum omnium octo circumactionum cursus peracti velut ad originem et caput circumactionis alterius revertentur, quam semper idem atque uniformis motus
dimetietur. Hoc quippe omni tempore finito ut cuius deter-
minatio certi circuitus spatio consideretur, omnia quae vel
in caelo vel in terris proveniunt rursum de integro ad prae-
teritas condiciones redeant necesse est. Ut puta qui nunc est
habitus constellationis post prolixam temporis seriem in-
staurabitur eodemque modo qui sequitur deinceps est hoc
semper.

149. Ex quo apparet in actu positum fatum infinita varietate accidentium et ex infinito in infinitum tempus quae accidunt, ipsum tamen esse determinatum et immutabili semperque eadem proprietate. Ut enim circularis motus et item
quod dimetitur eum tempus utraque sunt circuli, sic ea
omnia quae in gyros circumferuntur circuli sint necesse
est. Ergo scitum inevitabile vocat ille fatum, inevitabilem
vim potentiamque intellegens principalem causam omnium
quae in mundo consequenter continueque fiunt. Haec porro
anima est mundi tripertita, quod in substantia positum fatum in superioribus diximus. Scitum porro dei lex est, quam
inexcusabilem fore asseruimus ob inevitabilem causam.

150. Haec porro lex et oratio est et sanctio, quam sanxit
deus animae mundi ad perpetuam rerum omnium gubernationem, neque enim ut esset mundus modo, sed ut aeternus
et indissolubilis esset, curaverat. Quae sanctio cum cuncta

Perfect Year, about which Plato says the following [39d]: *It is nevertheless easy to understand that the perfect number of time should mark the completion of the perfect year at the point when the completed courses of all eight revolutions will return to the origin, as it were, and head of a second revolution, which the movement that is forever the Same and uniform will measure.* For when the whole of this period of time is completed such that its determination is observable within the span of a known cycle, then all of the things that occur in heaven or on Earth necessarily return once again to their past conditions. For example, the current disposition of a configuration will be renewed after a long period of time, and in this sense the disposition that follows next is always *this*.

149. And from this it is apparent that, despite the infinite variety of occurrences occurring out of the infinite for an infinite span of time, fate itself, as understood with respect to its act, is nevertheless determinate and characterized by an immutable and constant sameness. For as both circular motion and the period of time that measures it are cycles, so all of the things that are borne round in circular motion necessarily are cycles. Now, he refers to fate as an "inevitable decree," thereby meaning an inevitable force or potency, the principal cause of all that occurs in the world, in sequence and continuously. This is the tripartite world soul which we earlier said is fate as understood with respect to its substance, and the "decree" is the law of god which we declared inexorable by virtue of its being an "inevitable" cause.

150. This law, moreover, is both the speech and the sanction that god sanctioned for the world soul for its perpetual governance of all things, for he had ensured not only that the world should be but that it should be eternal and indissoluble. And given that this sanction contains all things

intra se contineat, alia ex aliqua praecessione fiunt, quaedam secundum praecessionem, scilicet ut in geometrica
initia ex praecessione sunt, theoremata vero secundum
praecessionem; concessis quippe initiis, ut notae et item
lineae ceterorumque huius modi velut originibus elemen-
tisque, theoremata secundum praecessionem aperiuntur,
quasi quae habeant consequentiam concessae praecessionis.
Sic etiam sanctio ordinatio existens et lex omnia complexa
causas praecedentes ex meritis nostris habet ut initia
quaedam; quae porro necessitatibus constricta proveniunt,
iuxta praecessionem necessitatemque eius consequenter
eveniunt.

151. Ergo initium divinae legis, id est fati, providentia, fatum vero quod et parendi sibi obsequium et non parendi
contumaciam velut edicto complectitur. Animadversiones
porro vel praemia exoriuntur secundum collocati meriti
praecessionem; collocati autem in alterutram partem meriti
praecessio animarum nostrarum motus est iudiciumque et
consensus earum et appetitus vel declinatio, quae sunt in
nobis posita, quoniam tam horum quam eorum quae his
contraria sunt optio penes nos est. Igitur in hac rerum ordinatione atque lege antiquissima quaeque ex praecessione
dicuntur fore et sunt nostrae potestatis, quae vero post illa
sunt, secundum praecessionem et necessitate constricta.
Atque ut aliud lex, aliud quod legem sequitur, id est legiti-
mum, sic aliud fatum et alia quae fatum sequuntur ex inevitabili necessitate, <id est> fatalia.

152. Est igitur universae rei anima fatum in substantia

within itself, some arise from some premise and others according to a premise, namely, as in geometry: the axioms are from a premise, whereas the theorems are according to a premise. For once the axioms—e.g., the point, line, and so on for the rest—have been granted as starting points or elements, then the theorems are revealed in accordance with the premise, as though possessing the consequence of the premise once granted. In the same way the sanction too, being an ordinance and all-embracing law, has as certain "axioms" the causes premised on the basis of our merits, and the things that issue forth under the constraint of necessity result in accordance with the premise and as a consequence of the necessity it enjoins.

151. The "axiom," then, of the divine law, i.e., of fate, is providence, while fate is what embraces as though by an edict both the compliance of submitting to it and the stubborn defiance of not submitting. Punishments, moreover, or rewards arise in accordance with what is premised by the merit once posited; but the premise of the merit as posited one way or the other is a movement of our souls, their judgment, consent, and desire for or against, and these are situated *in* us in the sense that the choice, whether for these possibilities or for those contrary to them, is within our control. Thus under this ordering of realities, this law, all of the most ancient things are said to be from a premise and are within our power, while those after them are according to a premise and constrained by necessity. And as the law is one thing and what follows from the law—i.e., the lawful—another, so fate is one thing and the things that of inevitable necessity follow from fate—i.e., the fated—another.

152. The world soul, then, is fate as understood with

positum, est item data huic informatio rem omnem recte gerendi lex, quae in munere atque actu positum fatum continet <et> habet textum et consequentiam talem: "si hoc erit, sequetur illud." Ergo quod ex his praecedit, in nobis est, quod sequitur, secundum fatum, quod alio nomine fatale dicitur, a fato plurimum differens, ut sint tria: quod in nobis positum est et ipsum fatum et quod secundum fati legem pro meritis imminet. Deinde ipsius legis verba ponit: Quae se comitem deo fecerit anima eorumque aliquid viderit quae vere sunt, usque ad alterius circuitus tempus erit incolumis, ac si semper hoc faciet, semper incolumis manebit. Est igitur totum hoc: lex et edictum, quod fatum proprie vocatur, secutum vero Socratem legis edictum deo se comitem praebuisse proprium Socratis opus; porro quod, cum ita viveret Socrates, anima eius "usque ad alterius circuitus tempus incolumis" perseverat, iuxta fatale decretum provenit: "ac si semper hoc faciat"—quod est in Socrate—"semper incolumis" erit—iuxta fatum.

153. Hac ratione Laio praedictum est ab Apolline:

Cave vetatos liberum sulcos seras:
generatus ille te mactabit impie
et omnis aula respergetur sanguine.

His quippe oraculis ostendit penes Laium fuisse, ne sereret,

respect to its substance; it is likewise the instruction given to it, the law of managing everything correctly, which contains fate as understood with respect to its function or act and possesses an interweaving, an entailment, of the following sort: "if this obtains, then that will follow." Of these, then, that which is premised is within our control, and that which follows is according to fate, which under another name is referred to as the fated and differs widely from fate. There are as a result three things: that which is placed within our control; fate itself; and that which according to the law of fate follows in conformity with our merits. Therefore he lays down the words of the actual law: "The soul that makes itself a companion of god and beholds any of the things that truly are will be unharmed up until the time of the next revolution, and if it always does this, then it will always remain unharmed." The point, then, is this: the law or edict is what is called fate in the proper sense, whereas Socrates's having shown himself to be a companion of the god by following the edict of the law is the work proper to Socrates; also, the fact that because of his having lived as he did Socrates's soul continues "unharmed up until the time of the next revolution" results according to the decree of fate: "and if he should always do this"—which is within Socrates's control—"then he will always be unharmed"—according to fate.

153. In conformity with this reasoning the prediction was given by Apollo to Laius:

> Beware of sowing the forbidden furrows of offspring:
> that one, if begotten, will slay you impiously,
> and the whole court will be spattered with blood.

For with this oracle he showed that it had been within

quae praecessio est; quod porro insecutum est, iam non in potestate Laii sed potius in necessitate fatali iuxta meritum praecessionis. Quod si necesse esset Laio sortem illam incurrere aut iam dudum immineret clades illa ex inevitabili necessitate, vacaret sciscitatio, vacaret etiam praedictio. Sed ille quidem, utpote praescius quae sequerentur, sementem iuxta fatum fieri vetabat sciens in potestate eius positum, si abstinere vellet, Laius vero, ut homo nescius futurorum, ab eo qui sciret, quid agendum sibi esset sciscitabatur, sevit autem non fato eliciente sed victus intemperantia.

154. Eodemque modo Thetis praedixerat filio, si bellaret apud Troiam, amicitia sibi paratura necem, maturum exitium cum ingenti fama futurum, si rediret ad patriam, longa vitae spatia portendi sine gloria. Bellavit tamen nulla fati cogente violentia, nulla quippe in optione ancipiti, sed tamquam bilis violentia, sed propenso iuxta gloriam favore. Quibus concinit etiam illud Platonis: causa penes optantem, deus extra culpam, item liberam esse virtutem nec ulli obnoxiam necessitati vel cum ait animis Lachesis nullam earum sortito sub dicionem daemonibus esse venturam, sed ipsas sponte lecturas sibi daemonem quem quaeque putaverit deligendum. Iuxtaque Moysea deus primigenis interdixit ne edulibus arborum, ex quibus notitia boni malique animis

Laius's power not to sow, which is the premise; and that which followed was no longer within Laius's power but instead came under fatal necessity according to the merit associated with the premise. But if Laius's incurring that lot were necessary or the disaster had long since been threatening because of an inevitable necessity, then the inquiry would be in vain, as would the prediction. But knowing in advance what would follow, Apollo forbade according to fate that the sowing should occur, knowing that it was placed within Laius's power to abstain if he wished, whereas Laius, being a man ignorant of the future, inquired of one who knew what he was supposed to do and yet sowed, not because fate induced him, but because he was overcome by intemperance.

154. Thetis had similarly predicted to her son that if he fought at Troy the friendship would bring him death, his end would be premature, accompanied by immense fame, but that if he returned home a long lifespan without glory lay in store. And yet he fought, although no compulsion of fate forced him to, none, that is, in the uncertain choice but rather under the compulsion, we might say, of his bile, out of a preference that leaned toward glory. And the following passage of Plato comports with this: "Blame rests with the one who chooses, god is beyond fault," and, "virtue is free and liable to no necessity," or when Lachesis addresses the souls, "none of them is by lot to come under the authority of demons, but they will freely choose for themselves the demon whom each one considers it suitable to choose." And according to Moses, God ordered the firstborn people not to eat the edible fruits of the trees from which the knowledge of good and evil would creep into their souls, for, since

eorum obreperet, vescerentur, quia, cum et abstinendi et non abstinendi potestas penes eos esset, qui consultum his vellet deus quid cavendum esset ostendit, non prohibiturus frustra si id fieri esset necesse.

155. Nunc iam de his agemus quae in hominis potestate sunt. Omnia quae sunt in tres partes a veteribus divisa sunt, possibile necessarium ambiguum: possibile ut genus, necessarium et dubium ut species; ergo omne possibile vel dubium vel necessarium est. Necessarium porro dicitur quod necessitate constrictum est, et quia possibilium pleraque obstari, quo minus proveniant, non possunt, quaedam prohibentur declinanturque consiliis, definitionibus adumbrantur huius modi: necessarium est possibile cuius contrarium est impossibile, ut est omnia orta occidere et aucta senescere; necesse est enim omne quod sit natum emori, et quod usque ad senectutem provectum senescere, nec est contrarietati locus, scilicet, quod ortum sit non occidere. Dubiorum vero definitio talis est: dubium est possibile cuius etiam contrarium possibile, ut hodie post occasum solis pluviam futuram; hoc enim possibile, aeque etiam contrarium eius possibile, ut post occasum solis omnino non pluat.

156. Iam vero dubiorum proventuum plures differentiae, quaedam enim frequentia sunt, quaedam peraeque frequentia, ut barbire utque scire litteras vel agere causas; adversantur porro frequentibus quae quidem rari exempli sunt, his

the power of abstaining or not abstaining was within their control, in wishing to provide them counsel god showed what was to be cautioned against and would not have issued a pointless prohibition if the event was necessarily to occur.

155. Now we will address the matters that are within human power. All existing things were divided by the ancients into three parts, the possible, necessary, and contingent: the possible as genus, and the necessary and contingent as species; thus every possible thing is either contingent or necessary. But that which is constrained by necessity is said to be necessary, and since of possible things most are incapable of being prevented from coming about, while some are prevented and diverted by deliberation, they are outlined by definitions of the following sort: the necessary is the possible the contrary of which is impossible, as in the proposition that all things that have been born die, and that they grow old after reaching maturity; for it is necessary that everything that has been born should die and that that which advances to old age should grow old: there is no room for contrariety, namely, that that which has been born should not die. The definition of contingent things, on the other hand, is as follows: the contingent is the possible the contrary of which is possible as well, as in the prospect of there being rain after sunset today; for this is possible, but its contrary, that it does not rain at all after sunset, is equally possible as well.

156. Now, there are several distinctions pertaining to contingent events, for some are frequent but others equally disposed as to their frequency, as in having a beard, being literate, or pleading cases; but those which are of rare occurrence are opposed to the frequent ones, and those which are not

porro quae peraeque proveniunt quae non sunt peraeque. Erit ergo eorum quae peraeque dubia sunt optio penes hominem, qui, utpote rationabile animal, cuncta revocat ad rationem atque consilium. Ratio porro et consilium motus est intimus eius, quod est in anima principale; hoc vero ex se movetur motusque eius assensus est vel appetitus. Igitur assensus et appetitus ex se moventur nec tamen sine imaginatione, quam phantasian Graeci vocant. Ex quo fit ut persaepe fallente imagine motus ille principalis animae potestatis vel consensus depravetur et eligat vitiosa pro optimis. Cuius rei multiplex causa est, vel agrestis in consultando inelegantia vel ignoratio vel nimium dedita mens importuno favori vel falsae opinionis anticipatio vel consuetudo prava, certe alicuius vitii tyrannica quaedam dominatio; propatereaque vi aut violentis delinimentis potius quam voluntate peccare dicimur.

157. Quae cum ita sint, salva est, opinor, divinatio, ne praesagio derogetur auctoritas; potest quippe praescius tali facta informatione fati consilium dare aggrediendi vel non aggrediendi recteque et rationabiliter mathematicus originem captabit instituendi actus ex prosperitate siderum atque signorum, ut, si hoc factum erit, proveniat illud. Haec porro et huius modi remedia sunt dubiorum proventuum, in quibus consilii salubritas medicina est. Habent etiam disciplinae locum maximeque legum latio; quid est enim lex nisi

equally disposed to those whose occurrence is equally disposed. The choice, then, between equally disposed uncertainties will be within the control of man, who, being a rational animal, summons all matters back to reason and deliberation. But reason or deliberation is an inner movement of that which is the ruling principle within the soul; and the latter is self-moving, its movement being assent or impulse. Assent and impulse, then, are self-moving, although not in the absence of imagination, which the Greeks call *phantasia*. So it happens that the movement of the soul's ruling power, its consent, is very often depraved because of a deceptive image and chooses vice over that which is best. There are many reasons for this: an uncultivated coarseness in deliberating, ignorance, a mind excessively devoted to importune adulation, the prejudice of false opinion, habituation to depravity—at all events, a certain tyrannical domination on the part of one or another vice, that being the reason for our being said to sin owing to compulsion or compulsive allurements rather than our will.

157. Given that these things are so, divination is, I suppose, saved from having its authority to make predictions impugned. One who possesses foreknowledge can certainly, when so informed by fate, provide advice concerning undertaking something or not, and an astrologer will rightly and reasonably seek out the point at which to undertake an act based on a propitious disposition of the stars and constellations such that if one thing happens another occurs. These and the like are the remedies for contingent outcomes, where the salutary effect of deliberation serves as the medical knowledge. The sciences and above all legislation have their place as well, for what is law other than a command

iussum sciscens honesta, prohibens contraria? Idcirco, quia
horum electio in potestate nostra est, laudisque honor et
vituperationis nota praemiique gratia et suppliciorum animadversio, cetera item exhortamenta virtutis malitiaeque
retinacula iure prospecta.

158. Nunc, quoniam quid rerum sit providentia quidve fatum in substantia positum et item quod in munere atque
actu invenitur quidve in hominis potestate sit, quid item
quod iuxta fati decretum provenit, prosecuti sumus, de fortuna deque his quae casu proveniunt disseremus. Fortunae
potestatem omnem in rebus hominum dicit esse, casus
aliam quandam iurisdictionem; quae enim vel rebus vita carentibus vel sine ratione viventibus animalibus accidunt non
ex natura vel arte, haec omnia casu facta dicuntur, quae vero
hominibus accidunt vel faventia negotiis eorum vel adver-
santia, fortuita et ex fortunae arbitrio putantur. Causarum
vero altera principalis est, altera accidens; principalis causa
est itineris faciendi vel negotiatio vel ruris inspectatio vel
aliqua generis huius, accidens, ut cum iter ingressos sol atque aestus adurunt, quae sequitur infectio vultus et colora-
tio, quippe non infectionis causa iter fuerat institutum.
Communiter ergo tam fortunam quam casum principali
causae accidentes causas esse dicemus, ut sit causa quidem
principalis in fato, in fortuna vero et casibus causa accidens.
Et quia quae fiunt partim ex necessitate habent auctoritatem, partim usitati et frequentis exempli sunt, partim ex
raro accidunt, et fortuna et casus in his inveniuntur quae

that ordains virtue and forbids its contrary? Given that the choice between these is within our power, the honor of praise and stigma of blame, the gift of reward and censure of punishment, and other inducements of virtue and restraints of vice have rightly been provided for.

158. Since we have pursued the questions of what providence is, what fate is—as understood with respect to its substance and also that which arises with respect to its function or act—, what is within human power, and what happens according to the decree of fate, we will now treat of fortune and the things that happen by chance. He says that the power of fortune resides entirely in human affairs and that chance has a certain other jurisdiction; for events that affect lifeless things or irrational animals independently of nature or art are all said to happen by chance, whereas those that affect human beings are, whether favorable or adverse to their undertakings, considered fortuitous or subject to the arbitration of fortune. And among causes one is primary and the other incidental: the primary cause in making a journey is perhaps a business dealing, whether the inspection of land or some similar cause; an incidental cause would be the sun and heat burning those who have set out on the journey, resulting in the face becoming dark and tanned, for the journey was not undertaken for the sake of the tanning. In general, then, we will say that both fortune and chance are causes incidental to the primary cause, so that the primary cause is in fate and the incidental cause in fortune and chance occurrences. And given that some of the things that happen have their warrant from necessity while others are in accordance with a usual or frequent pattern and others occur rarely, both fortune and chance are found among

raro accidunt; et fortunae quidem inrationabilis et cum
admiratione proventus inopinus ex hominum proposito
sumit originem, casus vero citra propositum hominis fit,
siquidem quod casu accidit vel in rebus vita carentibus vel in
mutis animalibus invenitur.

159. Breviter ergo, cum duae causae initium habentes ex
proposito nostro ita concurrunt, ut non quod propositum
est, at longe secus praeterque opinionem accidat, fortunae
ludus est, ut si quis occulte thesaurum terrae mandet, dehinc agricola propositum habens vitem aliamve quamlibet
stirpem propagare thesaurum illum, dum scrobem molitur,
inveniat; certe neque qui condidit, ut alius inveniret, sed ut
ipse, cum prolato opus esset, reportaret, nec agricola ut
thesaurum inveniret, sed ut scrobem faceret, laboraverat, et
tamen uterque usus fortuna est inopina. Quare sic etiam
fortuna recte definiri potest: Fortuna est concursus simul
cadentium causarum duarum originem ex proposito trahen-
tium, ex quo concursu provenit aliquid praeter spem cum
admiratione, ut si creditor ob diu frustra repetitum debitum
procedat ad forum instruendorum gratia patronorum, eodem etiam debitor mercandi causa, dehinc conventus debitor arbitris patronis diu tractum debitum depraesentet;
diversa quippe causa utrisque procedendi fuit, et est illud
potius actum quod propositum non erat quam quod iam
paene agebatur. Erit ergo etiam casus concursus simul atque

those that occur rarely; and an occurrence of fortune, being irrational, unanticipated, and occasioning surprise, originates in human intention, whereas a chance occurrence arises outside the scope of human intention, since that which occurs by chance arises in connection with either lifeless things or dumb animals.

159. Briefly, then, when two causes deriving their starting point from our intention come together in such a way that what was intended does not occur, but instead something quite different and independent of what was anticipated, it is the trick of fortune. For example, if someone secretly consigns a treasure to the earth, and a farmer who intends to propagate a vine or other plant thereafter finds that treasure while furrowing, the one who buried the treasure surely toiled with the intention, not that another should find it, but that he himself should retrieve it when there was a need of getting it out, while the farmer toiled, not with the intention of finding treasure, but of furrowing; and yet each one experienced a fortune he had not foreseen. And so fortune too can be correctly defined, as follows: fortune is the concurrence of two simultaneously occurring causes that draw their origin from an intention, from which concurrence something happens that occasions surprise independently of what was hoped for. Suppose a creditor goes to the forum in order to retain advocates because of a long sought after but unrecovered debt, and the debtor goes there in order to make a purchase but on encountering him pays the protracted debt, with the advocates as witnesses: the cause of going there was undoubtedly different for each, and that which had not been intended was done rather than what was then on the point of being done. Chance too, then, will

una accidentium sine ratione causarum in vita carentibus vel mutis animalibus, ut cum clausae ferae stabulis evasis rursum ad eadem stabula revertuntur ultro cumque ultro dicimus saxum concidisse. Ac de fato quidem deque his quae in hominis potestate sunt fortuna quoque et casibus satis dictum.

160. Sed quia sunt aliquanta quae contra haec e diverso dicuntur, proponenda sunt et diluenda; tunc demum enim firmis erit fundamentis locata Platonis sententia. Aiunt: "Ergo, si deus cuncta ex initio scit, antequam fiant, nec sola caelestia, quae felici necessitate perpetuae beatitudinis quasi quodam fato tenentur, sed illas etiam nostras cogitationes et voluntates, scit quoque dubiam illam naturam tenetque et praeterita et praesentia et futura, et hoc ex initio, nec potest falli deus, omnia certe ex initio disposita atque decreta sunt, tam ea quae in nostra potestate posita esse dicuntur quam fortuita nec non subiecta casibus." Porro cum haec omnia iam dudum decreta sint, cuncta quae proveniunt ex fato provenire concludunt, leges etiam et exhortationes et obiurgationes et disciplinas—quaeque huius modi sunt omnia teneri fatalibus condicionibus, quando si cui quid accidere decretum est, una etiam illud decretum sit cuius ope vel beneficio debeat provenire. Ut si cui salus proventura erit in navigando, proveniat ei non alio quoquam sed illo gubernatore navim regente; vel si cui civitati

be the concurrence of simultaneously occurring irrational causes affecting lifeless things or dumb animals, as when beasts that have been enclosed within stables escape and of their own accord return to them again, and when we speak of a rock having fallen of its own accord. But enough has been said about fate, things that are within human power, fortune, and chance occurrences.

160. But since there are certain points which have been raised contrary to these, they should be laid out and answered, for only then will Plato's view be set upon a firm foundation. "Now," they say, "if god knows all things from the start and prior to their happening, not only the celestial phenomena, which are held in the happy necessity of perpetual beatitude as if by a certain fate, but also those thoughts and acts of will of ours, i.e., if he also knows this contingent nature and holds things past, present, and future—and that from the start—and, as god, cannot be deceived, then surely all things are disposed and decreed from the start, those which are said to be placed within our power as well as the ones that are fortuitous and subject to chance." And on the grounds that all these things have long since been decreed, they conclude that all that happens happens because of fate, even laws, moral exhortation and reproach, instruction—all such things are held by the stipulations of fate, for if it is decreed that something should happen to someone, then that by means of which or by whose aid it is bound to happen is simultaneously decreed as well. For example, if safety is to result for someone in connection with the act of navigating, then it should result, not with just anyone steering the ship, but with the *pilot* doing it; or if it is to result for some city that it should enjoy good institutions

proventurum erit ut bonis utatur institutis et moribus, ut Spartae, Lycurgi legibus hoc debeat provenire; item si quis erit iustus futurus, ut Aristides, huic educatio parentum adiumento sit in iustitiae atque aequitatis obtentu.

161. Artes quoque sub fati decretum cadere manifestum esse aiunt, nam et hinc iam dudum esse ordinatum, quis aeger quo medente revalescat; denique fieri frequenter ut non a medico sed ab imperito curetur aeger, cum talis erit condicio decreti. Similis ratio est laudum vituperationum animadversionum praemiorum; fit enim frequenter ut adversante fato quae recte gesta sunt non modo nullam laudem sed contra reprehensionem suppliciaque afferant. At vero divinationem dicunt clare demonstrare proventus iam dudum esse decretos; neque enim, nisi decretum praecederet, ad rationem eius accedere potuisse praesagos. Animorum vero nostrorum motus nihil aliud esse quam ministeria decretorum fatalium, siquidem necesse sit agi per nos agente fato. Ita homines vicem obtinere eorum quae dicuntur "sine quibus agi non potest," sicut sine loco esse non potest motus aut statio.

162. Adversum quae tam pugnaciter et ipso fato violentius instituta quid respondebimus? Quod deus sciat quidem omnia sed unumquidque pro natura sua [ipsorum] sciat: necessitati quidem subiugatum ut necessitati obnoxium, anceps vero ut quod ea sit natura praeditum, cui consilium viam pandat; neque enim ita scit ambigui naturam deus ut quod

and customs, then, as in the case of Sparta, it should be bound to result through the laws of a Lycurgus; and if someone is destined to be just, as in the case of Aristides, then the education provided by his parents should assist him in obtaining justice and equity.

161. They claim that it is obvious that the arts too fall under the decree of fate: for by fate too it has long since been ordained which patient will become better through whose medical assistance; indeed, that it frequently happens that the patient is cured, not by a physician, but by a layman, whenever the stipulation of the decree is such. Their explanation of praise, blame, punishment, and reward is along the same lines: it frequently happens that, when fate prevents it, deeds rightly done not only fail to bring praise but actually bring censure and punishment. And they claim that divination clearly demonstrates that events have long since been decreed: unless the decree came first, those who have foretold it would not have been able to arrive at an account of it. And that the movements of our minds are mere functions of the decrees of fate insofar as it is necessary for them to be conducted with fate acting *through* us: hence human beings are in the position of those things that come under the description, "in the absence of which it cannot be done," just as in the absence of place there cannot be motion or rest.

162. What will we say in reply to points established so contentiously, indeed, with more violence than that of fate itself? That god does indeed know all things, but that he knows each and every thing in virtue of its proper nature: as subject to necessity insofar as it is liable to necessity, and as contingent insofar as it is endowed with a nature for which deliberation opens up a path. For god does not know the

certum et necessitate constrictum (sic enim falletur et nesciet) sed ita ut pro natura sua vere dubium sciat. Quid ergo dicimus? Deum scire omnia scientiamque eius ex aeternitate solidari; porro quae sciuntur partim divina esse et immortalia, partim occidua et ad tempus; immortalium rerum substantiam stabilem et fixam fore, mortalium mutabilem et dubiam aliasque aliter se habentem ob naturae inconstantiam. Ergo etiam dei scientia de divinis quidem, quorum est certa et necessitate perpetua munita felicitas, certa et necessaria scientia est tam propter ipsius scientiae certam comprehensionem quam pro eorum quae sciuntur substantia. At vero incertorum necessaria quidem scientia, quod incerta sint et in eventu ambiguo posita (nec enim possunt aliter esse quam est natura eorum), ipsa tamen in utramque partem possibilia sunt potius quam necessitatibus subiugata.

163. Non ergo etiam dubia ex initio rigide disposita atque decreta sunt, nisi forte id ipsum quod incerta esse et ex ancipiti eventu pendere debeant. Quare quod animae quoque hominis natura talis sit ut interdum ad virtutem se applicet interdum ad malitiam praeponderet, perinde ut corpus modo sospitati modo aegritudini proximum, fixum plane est et decretum ex origine. Quis porro malus sit futurus aut bonus, neque decretum neque imperatum, proptereaque leges magisteria deliberationes exhortationes revocationes institutiones nutrimentorum certa observatio laus vituperatio

contingent as something certain and constrained by necessity (for in that case he will be deceived and *not* know) but in such a way as to know it in virtue of its proper nature, as truly contingent. What, then, do we say? That god knows all things and that his knowledge is confirmed from eternity; but that some of the objects of his knowledge are divine and immortal and others mortal and temporal; that the substance of immortal things is stable and fixed, and that of mortal ones mutable and contingent, being differently disposed through time owing to the inconstancy of its nature. Hence too god's knowledge of divine things, whose good fortune is certain and secured by perpetual necessity, is certain and necessary knowledge both because of the certain comprehension in the knowledge itself and by virtue of the substance of the objects known. But, although his knowledge that uncertain things are uncertain and by disposition contingent as to their outcome is necessary (for they cannot be other than their nature is), they themselves are nevertheless capable of opposite determinations rather than subjugated to necessity.

163. Contingent events, then, are not also rigidly disposed and decreed from the start, except perhaps for the very fact of their having to be uncertain and dependent upon an outcome one way or the other. And so the fact that the nature of the human soul is such as in one instance to apply itself to virtue but in another to lean toward malice, as with the body's wavering between health and sickness, is obviously fixed and decreed from the beginning as well. Moreover, it is neither decreed nor ordained who is destined to be evil or good; hence our laws, instructions, deliberations, exhortations, warnings, education, steady attention to nourish-

quaeque his simulantur, quia recte vivendi optio penes nos est.

164. Si igitur eorum quae sunt pleraque iuris nostri sunt alia extra nostram potestatem—nostra quidem appetitus iudicium voluntas consensus praeparatio electio declinatio, aliena vero divitiae gloria species fortitudo ceteraque quae potius optare possumus quam vindicare—, recte dicitur si quis forte velit quae non sunt in potestate nostra nostri iuris esse praesumere nihil sapere, consequenter ergo etiam is qui quae nostra propria sunt praesumit aliena nihil, opinor, sapit. Denique nullus laudatur ob adeptionem secundorum quae in hominis potestate non sunt, nisi forte putatur beatus, prosperitas enim non est in eius arbitrio; at vero in iustitiae contractibus temperantiaeque negotiis et in ceterarum virtutum observantia iure laudamur, siquidem virtus libera est, contraque agentes reprehendimur, quod dare operam ut peccemus existimamur.

165. Dicunt porro non spontanea esse delicta, ideo quod omnis anima particeps divinitatis naturali appetitu bonum quidem semper expetit, errat tamen aliquando in iudicio bonorum et malorum; namque alii nostrum summum bonum voluptatem putant, divitias alii, plerique gloriam et omnia magis quam ipsum verum bonum. Est erroris causa multiplex: prima, quam Stoici duplicem perversionem vocant; haec autem nascitur tam ex rebus ipsis quam ex divulgatione famae. Quippe mox natis exque materno viscere decidentibus provenit ortus cum aliquanto dolore, propterea

ment, praise, blame, and all such things. For the choice of living rightly is within our control.

164. If, then, of the things that are, many are under our jurisdiction but others beyond our power—ours being desire, judgment, will, consent, preparation, choice for and against, and not ours, wealth, glory, beauty, strength, and other things that we can hope for but not lay claim to—, then anyone who may aim to presume that things not within our power are under our jurisdiction is rightly said to be foolish, from which it follows also that one who presumes that things proper to us are *not* ours is, I suppose, foolish. Finally, apart, perhaps, from one's having a reputation for being fortunate no one is praised for acquiring the secondary things that are not within human power, for prosperity is not within one's power of choice; but since virtue is freely chosen, we are justly praised for agreements, undertakings, and commitments that are based on justice, moderation, and the other virtues, and blamed for doing the opposite, since we are held to make a goal of wrongdoing.

165. They claim, however, that our failings are not freely chosen, on the grounds that, although every soul, as participating in divinity, by virtue of its natural desire always pursues the good, it nevertheless errs sometimes in its judgment of goods and evils; for some consider pleasure to be our highest good, others wealth, many glory and anything but the true good. There are numerous reasons for this error, the primary one being that which the Stoics call the double perversion; and this arises both from things in themselves and from the promulgation of what people say. For the moment children separate from the mother's womb, the birth takes place accompanied by a certain amount of pain

quod ex calida atque humida sede ad frigus et siccitatem aeris circumfusi migrent; adversum quem dolorem frigusque
puerorum opposita est medicinae loco artificiosa obstetri-
cum provisio, ut aqua calida confoveantur recens nati adhi-
beanturque vices et similitudo materni gremii ex calefac-
tione atque fotu, quo laxatum corpus tenerum delectatur et
quiescit. Ergo ex utroque sensu tam doloris quam delecta-
tionis opinio quaedam naturalis exoritur omne suave ac de-
lectabile bonum, contraque quod dolorem afferat malum
esse atque vitandum.

166. Par atque eadem habetur sententia de indigentia
quoque et exsaturatione, blanditiis et obiurgationibus, cum
aetatis fuerint auctioris, proptereaque confirmata eadem
aetate in anticipata sententia permanent omne blandum
bonum, etiam si sit inutile, omne etiam laboriosum, etiam si
commoditatem afferat, malum existimantes. Consequenter
divitias, quod praestantissimum sit in his instrumentum voluptatis, eximie diligunt gloriamque pro honore amplexan-
tur. Natura quippe omnis homo laudis atque honoris est ap-
petens, est enim honor virtutis testimonium; sed prudentes
quidem versatique in sciscitatione sapientiae viri sciunt
quam et cuius modi debeant excolere virtutem, vulgus vero
imperitum pro ignoratione rerum pro honore gloriam popu-
laremque existimationem colunt, pro virtute vero vitam
consectantur voluptatibus delibutam, potestatem faciendi
quae velint regiam quandam esse eminentiam existimantes.
Natura siquidem regium animal est homo et quia regnum
semper comitatur potestas, potestati quoque regnum

because of the fact that they move from a warm and moist environment to the cold and dryness of the ambient air. To counteract this pain and cold experienced by babies the specialized care provided by midwives is enlisted in place of medicine, such that the newborns are warmed with warm water and changes in condition are applied, i.e., a simulation of the mother's womb through a warmth and heat conducive to the tender body's feeling pleasure and resting relaxedly. Thus from both sensations equally, pain and pleasure, a kind of natural opinion emerges to the effect that everything soothing and pleasurable is good and, conversely, that what causes pain is bad and to be avoided.

166. As they reach a more mature age, a similar, indeed identical, opinion is maintained with respect to need and satiety, their blandishments and rebukes, which is why once confirmed in that age they persist in an opinion formed earlier, thinking that everything pleasing is good, even if it is of no utility, and everything painful bad, even if it is advantageous. Consequently, they are excessively devoted to wealth, in which they perceive the primary means to pleasure, and embrace glory instead of honor. To be sure, every human being is by nature desirous of praise and honor, for honor is evidence of virtue; but whereas wise men and those skilled in the inquiry into wisdom know which and which kind of virtue they should cultivate, in its ignorance of things the inexperienced mob cultivate glory and popular esteem instead of honor and pursue a life drowning in pleasures instead of virtue, thinking that the power to do what they want is a kind of regal distinction. And on the grounds that man is by nature a royal animal and power always accompanies kingship, they draw the further inference that kingship entails

obsequi suspica<n>tur, cum regnum iusta sit tutela paren-
tium. Simul quia beatum necesse est libenter vivere, putant
etiam eos qui cum voluptate vivant beatos fore. Talis error
est, opinor, qui ex rebus ortus hominum animos possidet.

167. Ex divulgatione autem succedit errori supra dicto ex
matrum et nutricum votis de divitiis gloriaque et ceteris
falso putatis bonis insusurratio <in> terriculis etiam quibus
tenera aetas vehementius commovetur nec non in solaciis et
omnibus huius modi perturbatio. Quin etiam corroborata-
rum mentium delinitrix poetica et cetera scriptorum et auc-
torum opera magnifica quantam animis rudibus invehunt
iuxta voluptatem laboremque inclinationem favoris? Quid
pictores quoque et fictores? Nonne rapiunt animos ad suavi-
tatem ab industria? Maxima vero vitiorum excitatio est in
corporis [atque] humorum concretione, quorum abundan-
tia vel indigentia propensiores ad libidinem aut iracundiam
sumus. His accedunt vitae ipsius agendae sortisque discrimina: aegritudo servitium inopia rerum necessariarum—
quibus occupati ab studiis honestis ad consentanea vitae
institutae officia deducimur atque a cognitione revocamur
veri boni.

168. Opus est ergo futuris sapientibus tam educatione li-
berali praeceptisque ad honestatem ducentibus quam erudi-
tione a vulgo separata videndaque eis et spectanda sunt lecta

power, although kingship is a just form of guardianship of the obedient. At the same time, on the grounds that the happy man necessarily lives as he pleases, they make the further supposition that those who live according to their pleasure are happy. Such, I suppose, is the experience-based error that takes hold of human minds.

167. From a promulgation of opinion originating in the hopes cherished by mothers and nurses, by contrast, an intimation concerning wealth, glory, and the other falsely supposed goods takes the place of the aforementioned error, an anxiety even in the form of the incipient terrors by which the tender age is all the more intensely disturbed, also in solaces and all such things. But as measured in terms of pleasure or pain, how great an inclination toward courting favor do the poetry, which seduces even sturdy minds, and other grand works of writers and authors instill in inexperienced minds? What of painters and sculptors? Do they not seize minds away from hard work, for pleasure? But the greatest stirring up of the vices occurs in connection with the concretion of bodily humors, by the abundance or lack of which we are the more prone to the appetitive or irascible instinct. To these considerations are added the hardships of simply conducting our lives, and of chance: sickness, servitude, the want of real necessities—in our preoccupation with these we are dragged down from virtuous pursuits to the obligations comporting with life as it is, and distracted from recognition of the true good.

168. Thus those who would be wise require a liberal education and precepts leading to virtue as well as an erudition which is foreign to the mob, and they must see and contemplate all that has been selected to drive them toward

omnia quae protelent ad sapientiam. Ante omnia divino praesidio opus est ad perceptionem bonorum maximorum quae, cum sint propria divinitatis, cum hominibus tamen communicantur. Corporis quoque obsequium sufficiens animae viribus esse debet ad tolerandum exercitii laborem. Oportet item sufficere praeceptores bonos propositumque id quod sortiti sumus singuli numen. Quippe Socrati dicitur a pueris comes daemon rerum agendarum praeceptor fuisse, non ut hortaretur eum ad aliquem actum sed ut prohiberet quae fieri non expediret. Propterea quoque quae in hominis potestate sunt, si per imprudentiam agantur, cum agi ea sit inutile, cladem afferant, quod a Socrate arcebat benivolum numen.

169. Divinatio vero necessitati quidem subiectarum rerum, ambiguarum etiam sed quarum iam fatalis completus sit, exitus vera est et complexibilis si modo divinatio dicenda est, quippe quae semel acciderunt infecta esse non possunt; ambiguarum vero quarum exitus adhuc pendent nondum praecedentibus meritis ambigua est et obliqua, ut est illa Apollinis:

Perdet Croesus Halyn transgressus maxima regna.

Istic enim tria erant, nisi fallor, ambigua: unum utrum Cyri et Persarum regnum esset periturum; alterum an ipsius Croesi potius et Lydium; tertium utrum condicionibus

wisdom. Above all, they require divine aid for perception of the highest goods, which, although proper to divinity, are nevertheless made common to human beings. Also, the body's obedience to the faculties of the soul must be at a level sufficient for its tolerating the labor entailed by the exercise. Likewise, good teachers must be available, and the mode of conduct that each is allotted in the form of his tutelary genius. For Socrates is said to have been "accompanied from childhood by a demon," an instructor in what was to be done, not one such as to urge him to any particular course of action, but such as to warn against those whose fulfillment would not be beneficial, the reason being that, if the things that are within human power should be enacted through imprudence when it is not beneficial for them to be enacted, they would bring ruin, which the benevolent genius kept away from Socrates.

169. But the divination of things which are subject to necessity, including the contingent ones whose fated outcome has already been brought to completion, is true and comprehensive if it is to be called divination at all, for once the things have happened they cannot be undone; the divination of contingent things whose outcomes depend upon merits not yet premised is by contrast ambiguous and oblique, as in the case of Apollo's:

> In crossing the Halys Croesus will destroy mighty kingdoms.

For unless I am mistaken, there were three contingencies therein: first, whether the kingdom of Cyrus and the Persians would perish; second, whether that of Croesus, the Lydian one, would instead; third, whether war would be

iustis bellum deponeretur. Hoc quippe fieri poterat et depositorum bellorum aliquot exempla praecesserant, sed quia voluntas utriusque adversabatur armorum depositioni, cum et Cyrus fera quadam esset et gloriosa natura, Croesus quoque confidens potentiaeque praecupidus. Decretum quod sequebatur ratum erat factum ex utriusque proposito pacem inter eos minime futuram, supererat igitur ex reliquis alterutrum idque erat dubium cuiusnam regnum extingueretur. Proptereaque dubia sors dubiique intellectus processit oraculum, ut quodcumque accidisset id praedictum ab Apolline videretur.

170. Sunt aliae praedictiones consiliorum examini similes, quia, cum sit in nostra potestate deligere ex incertis alterum, ne in delectu peccetur ex ignoratione, suadet hominibus quid sit optandum propitia divinitas, ut Argivis per oraculum quaerentibus, an adversum Persas bellum suscipi conveniret, responsum est:

Vicinis offensa, deo carissima plebes,
armorum cohibe munimina: corporis omne
discrimen sola capitis tutabitur umbra.

Sciebat enim quid esset eligendum quodque optio penes hominem, id vero quod sequitur optionem penes fatum.

171. Hebraeis quoque consilium datum est a deo cum praedictione rerum futurarum in istum modum: si praeceptis meis parebitis, bona "terrarum" omnia penes vos erunt,

forestalled on the basis of just conditions for peace. For the latter was possible, there having been a number of precedents for forestalling wars, but the will of each was opposed to the laying down of arms: Cyrus was by nature vainglorious and in some sense wild, while Croesus was arrogant and very hungry for power. The subsequent decree came to be ratified based on the intention of each that there should be no peace between them, leaving as a result one or the other of the remaining possibilities, the issue in doubt being whose kingdom would be extinguished. And a doubtful lot, an oracle of doubtful meaning, came forth, so that no matter what happened it would appear to have been predicted by Apollo.

170. There are other forms of prediction which resemble the weighing of counsels. For although it is within our power to choose one or another from among uncertain courses of action, the divinity propitiously persuades men as to what should be chosen in order to prevent their sinning through a choice based on ignorance, as in the response given the Argives when they asked the oracle whether war should be taken up against the Persians:

> O people, hated by its neighbors, most dear to god,
> hold close the defense work of your arms: all danger
> to the body will be averted by the mere shadow of the
> head.

For he knew what should be chosen and that the choice is in the hands of man, but that which follows from the choice is in the hands of fate.

171. Counsel was given by God to the Hebrews, too, with a prediction of future things along the following lines: if you obey my commands, all goods of "the earth" will be within

"lac" itaque "et melliflui fluctus" non deerunt; si contempse-
ritis, poenarum imminentium seriem divina vox prosecuta
est, quippe quod esset dubium id quod erat positum in hominis potestate, parere vel contemnere iussa caelestia.
Quod si optionem eorum praecederet decretum inevitabile
necessarioque contemnendum esset, abundaret praedictio,
abundarent etiam promissa et minae. Est igitur aliquid in
hominis potestate nec sunt homines, ita ut a contra sentientibus asserebatur, materiae, rerum earum quae aguntur, per
quas aguntur sed causa praecedens quam sequitur id quod
ex fato est.

172.—Sed praeter spem aiunt aliquanta provenire.—
Scimus, et horum omnium duplex genus: unum eorum quae
perraro accidunt, quae vel forte proveniunt vel casu aliquo
importantur, ut ex hominibus portenta nasci; alterum quod
frequentius quidem provenit sed originem sumit ex humani
iudicii depravatione, cum vel a potentibus iratis vel ab ini-
micis res iudicantur, ut accidit Socrati, eiusdemque populi
iudicio cum vir iustissimus condemnatus est Aristides, vel
cum prophetae a consceleratis unus membratim sectus, alter obrutus saxis. Numquid etiam horum causa est penes fatum? Nec intellegunt diversas se contrariasque potentias, id
est virtutem et item vitia simul, quod fieri non potest,

your control, and so "milk and rivers of flowing honey" will not be lacking; but if you disobey, then the divine pronouncement has explained in advance the series of imminent punishments—the point being that that which had been placed within human power, the obeying or disobeying of celestial commands, was contingent. But if an "inevitable decree" were to establish in advance the choice between them and the command were to be disobeyed as a matter of *necessity,* then the prediction would be superfluous, as would promises and threats. There is, then, something within human power, and human beings are not, in the manner asserted by those who held the opposite view, the means through which the things that are enacted are enacted, but a preestablished cause which the element extending from fate follows.

172.—But they claim that a certain number of things occur beyond anticipation.—We know, and the class under which they all fall divides in two: one is that of the things that happen very rarely, which either occur fortuitously or are brought about by some element of chance, as in monsters being born from human beings; the other is what occurs with greater frequency but originates in a depravation of human judgment, when matters are judged either by enraged potentates or by one's enemies, as happened to Socrates, or when Aristides, the most just of men, was condemned by a judgment from the same people, or the Prophets, when one was torn limb from limb by wicked men, and another buried under rocks. Is the cause of these too really in the hands of fate? They do not understand that in claiming that crimes of this sort are proper to fate they are assigning diverse and contrary powers, i.e., virtue and vices simultane-

assignare decreto, cum huius modi crimina fati propria esse
dicunt. Constituant denique, quid esse fatum velint. Virtu-
temne divinam? Sed non esset causa malorum. An vero animam malignam? Sed demum a malitia nihil boni fieri potest
et fato dicuntur etiam bona provenire. Dicent fortasse mixtam quandam esse substantiam? Et qui fieri potest ut unum
et idem quid malitia simul et bonitate sit praeditum intem-
perantiamque et castitatem creet ceteramque virtutum vi-
tiorumque importet contrarietatem?

173. Quae porro erit de fato existimatio? Quod velit certe
omnia esse bona nec tamen possit? Erit igitur imbecillum
quiddam et sine viribus. An potest quidem nec tamen vult?
Haec vero iam fera est quaedam et immanis invidia. An vero
neque vult neque potest? At hoc dicere de fato praesertim
flagitiosum. An et potest et vult? Erit ergo causa bonorum
omnium, nec malorum auctoritas pertinebit ad fatum.

174. Unde ergo mala? Motum stellarum causantur. Sed
ipse motus unde? Et utrum volentibus stellis motus ipse talis fit, ut ex eodem motu et mala proveniant et bona, an invitis? Si volentibus, animalia sunt stellae et iuxta propositum
moventur; si invitis, nullus est earum actus. Certe aut omnes
stellae divinae sunt et bonae nec quicquam faciunt mali aut
quaedam maleficae. Sed maleficas esse in illo sancto et pleno
bonitatis loco quatenus convenit, cumque omnia sidera
plena sint caelestis sapientiae, malitiam porro sciamus ex

ously, to its decree, which is impossible. Let them determine, finally, what they mean fate to be. A divine power? But it would not be the cause of *evils*. Or if not, then a malign soul? But then no *good* can be wrought by evil, and yet good things too are said to occur in accordance with fate. Perhaps they will claim that it is some kind of blended substance? And yet how is it possible for one and the same thing to be endowed with evil and goodness simultaneously, to breed both intemperance and chasteness and to trigger all manner of contrariety between virtues and vices?

173. And what will their assessment of fate be?—That it surely desires all things to be good but is nevertheless incapable?—Then it will be something ineffective and powerless.—That although capable it nevertheless lacks the desire?—But then this is a wild and brutal ill will of some kind.—That it neither has the desire nor is capable?—But to say this of fate is outrageous in the extreme.—That it both is capable and has the desire?—Then it will be the cause of all *goods,* and the responsibility for evils will have no bearing on fate.

174. What, then, is the origin of evil? They indict stellar movement. But what is the origin of the *movement?* Does the movement proper occur such that, while it remains the same, both goods and evils issue from it, and if so, then with the stars willing it or not willing it? If with them willing it, then the stars are living beings and move according to purpose; if with them not willing it, then theirs is no capacity for action. To be sure, either all stars are divine, good, and productive of no evil or certain ones are maleficent. But given that all heavenly bodies are full of celestial wisdom, and we know that evil arises from mindlessness, to what

dementia nasci, quatenus convenit maleficas stellas esse
dicere? Nisi forte, id quod fas non est, interdum easdem bo-
nas interdum malignas esse, existimandum, proptereaque
promisce beneficia et maleficia praebere. Sed hoc absurdum
est, putare caelestem substantiam una eademque natura
praeditam non in omnibus stellis eandem esse sed plerasque
tamquam a propria degenerare natura.—Sed nimirum hoc
invitae stellae patiuntur.—Et quaenam erit illa tanta necessitas quae invitas cogat delinquere? Et haec ipsa utrum divina erit anima an maligna?

175. An vero ratio quaedam est, ut aiunt, qua omnia fiunt
quae ad praesens aguntur quaeque futura erunt provenient?
Sed nimirum monstri simile est dicere ratione fieri mala
quae multo verius dicentur nulla ratione: iniquus es<se>t vel
etiam libidinosus. Series vero illa causarum inevitabilis unde
accipiet exordium nisi prius merita nostra in quamcumque
partem locentur? Illud vero quis ferre possit quod praeter
cetera quae inreligiose dicuntur atque existimantur, providentia quoque dei tollitur hac eorum assertione simulque
omnis divinitas exterminatur? Quid enim faciet deus si omnia secundum hanc versutorum hominum affirmationem
fient atque impulsu rapido ferantur pro necessitatis instinctu? Facit tamen haec vana praesumptio faciliorem causam nocentibus, quibus licebit non animi sui perversitatem
condemnare sed de fatali violentia conqueri, facit bonorum
vota iuxta vitam laudabilem et impetus prudentiae pigriores;

extent is it appropriate to speak of the stars—in *that* place, so holy and full of goodness—as being maleficent? Unless perhaps we are to imagine the unspeakable, that the same stars alternate between being good and malign and therefore bestow benefits and harm indiscriminately. But this is absurd, to suppose, not that the celestial substance endowed with one and the same nature is the same in all stars, but that many of them degenerate, as it were, from their proper nature.—But surely the stars endure this against their will?—And what will be that necessity so great as to compel them to do wrong against their will? And this soul itself, will it be divine or malign?

175. Or is there, as they claim, a kind of Reason through which all of the things now being done come about and those yet to be will occur? But surely it borders on monstrosity to say that evils come about through reason when they will far more truly be said to come about through *no* reason: [otherwise, their principle of Reason] would be iniquitous and indeed libidinous. But if our merits are not first posited one way or the other, where will that inevitable series of causes derive its starting point? But quite apart from the other blasphemous claims and opinions, who can endure god's providence too being torn down by this assertion of theirs, and all divinity being exterminated along with it? For what will *god* do if all things are to happen in the way these clever men affirm and things are violently tossed about at the instigation of necessity? Yet this vain presumption eases the case for those who do wrong: the door will be open to their complaining about the violence of fate as opposed to condemning the perversity of their own mind; it thwarts the vows of the good to live a praiseworthy life and

quare missum faciendum est genus hominum ex versutia et vanitate concretum qui, ut ipsi putant, adverso fato nati sunt, quibus haec et talia opinari fato provenerit.

176. Nos vero divinam legem sequentes repetemus ab exordio digesto ordine quae de fato Plato veritatis ipsius, ut mihi quidem videtur, instinctu locutus est. Principio cuncta quae sunt et ipsum mundum contineri regique principaliter quidem a summo deo qui est summum bonum ultra omnem substantiam omnemque naturam, aestimatione intellectuque melior, quem cuncta expetunt cum ipse sit plenae perfectionis et nullius societatis indiguus, de quo plura dici nunc exorbitare est. Deinde a providentia quae est post illum summum secundae eminentiae quem noyn Graeci vocant; est autem intellegibilis essentia aemula[e] bonitatis propter indefessam ad summum deum conversionem, estque ei ex illo bonitatis haustus quo tam ipsa ornatur quam cetera quae ipso auctore honestantur. Hanc igitur dei voluntatem, tamquam sapientem tutelam rerum omnium, providentiam homines vocant, non, ut plerique aestimant, ideo dictam quia praecurrit in videndo atque intellegendo proventus futuros sed quia proprium divinae mentis intellegere, qui est proprius mentis actus; et est mens dei aeterna; est igitur mens dei intellegendi aeternus actus.

177. Sequitur hanc providentiam fatum, lex divina promulgata intellegentiae sapienti modulamine ad rerum omnium gubernationem. Huic obsequitur ea quae secunda mens dicitur, id est anima mundi tripertita, ut supra

pursue wisdom. And so we must dismiss this class of men so hardened in their clever vanity, who by their own reckoning have been born with fate against them, and who in the end have been fated to hold these and similar opinions.

176. But following the divine law we will repeat from the beginning and in order what Plato at the instigation of truth itself, as it seems to me anyway, said about fate. First, all things that are, including the world itself, are embraced and ruled principally by the Supreme God who is the Supreme Good "beyond all being" and all nature, who is superior to thought and Intellect, whom all things seek because of His being of complete perfection and requiring no fellowship, and about whom to say anything further in the present context would be to digress. Then they are embraced and ruled by the Providence which is second in preeminence to that Supreme God which the Greeks call *Nous;* it is, moreover, intelligible being that emulates Goodness in virtue of its tireless conversion toward the Supreme God, and from the latter it possesses a draft of the Goodness by which it is itself adorned and other things, thanks to His authority, are no less ennobled. And so men refer to this divine Will, this wise guardianship, as it were, of all things, as "*Pro*vidence" [*fore*sight], so called not, as many suppose, because it is a *pre*-cursor in *seeing* and understanding events to come but because understanding, which is the act *pro*per to mind, is a *pro*perty of the divine Mind; and the Mind of God is eternal; hence the Mind of God is the eternal act of understanding.

177. Fate, the divine law promulgated by the wise harmony of intelligence for the governance of all things, follows this Providence. That which is called the Second Mind, i.e., the tripartite World Soul, obeys it, as has been explained

comprehensum est; ut si quis periti legum latoris animam legem vocet. Iuxta hanc legem, id est fatum, omnia reguntur, secundum propriam quaeque naturam, beata quidem necessitate incommutabilique constantia cuncta caelestia, quippe quae sint providentiae vicina atque contigua, frequenter vero accidentia naturalia, propterea quia oriuntur et occidunt omnia quae naturae lege proveniunt; simul, quia imitatur naturam ars et disciplina, etiam haec quae artibus efficiuntur sunt frequentia proventusque crebri. Quae vero reguntur hac lege, ratione ordine ac sine vi reguntur, nihil enim ratione et ordine carens non violentum; quod vero tale est, non diu perseverat, utpote quod contra naturam suam distrahatur.

178. Sequuntur ergo deum proprium singula et, ut ait Plato, regem imperatoremque caeli, principem agminis et ducem sublimem volucri curru dispensantem omnia et moderantem, legiones caelestium et angelicarum potestatum in undecim partes distributae. Solam siquidem Vestam ait manere in sua sede, Vestam scilicet animam corporis universi mentemque eius animae moderantem caeli stellantis habenas iuxta legem a providentia sanctam. Quam legem saepe diximus esse fatum serie quadam consequentiarum atque ordinum sancientem; "volucris" vero "currus" imperatoris dei aplanes intellegenda est, quia et prima est ordine et agilior ceteris omnibus motibus, sicut ostensum est. "Undecim" vero "partes" exercitus dinumerat hactenus: primam aplanem;

above; it is as if one were to refer to the soul of a skilled legislator as the law. In conformity with this law, i.e., Fate, all things are ruled, each according to its proper nature: all celestial beings by virtue of their neighboring on and their contact with Providence are so ruled according to a blessed necessity and unchanging constancy; and those occurring in the natural order are so ruled regularly, owing to the fact that all of the things that occur according to the law of nature come into being and pass away, also that art and knowledge imitate nature, and the things produced by the arts are regular and of frequent occurrence. But all of the things that are ruled by this law are ruled by reason, order, and without compulsion—for nothing that lacks reason and order can fail to be violent: that which is of such a nature does not endure for long, being pulled apart, as against its own nature.

178. Now, things singly follow their proper god, and as Plato says, "legions of celestial and angelic powers, distributed in eleven columns, follow the king and commander of heaven, first among the host, a sublime leader dispensing and controlling all things from his winged chariot." For he says that "Vesta alone remains in her abode," namely, that Vesta, the soul of the universal body and the mind of that soul, controls the reins of the starry heaven in conformity with the law sanctioned by providence. And we have said repeatedly that this law, whose sanction is according to a series, as it were, of consequences and ranks, is fate; the "winged chariot" of the commander god, on the other hand, is to be understood as the *aplanês,* since it is both first in rank and swifter than all other forms of motion, as has been shown. And he enumerates the "eleven columns" of the army as follows: first, the *aplanês;* thereafter, the abodes of the seven

deinde septem planetum, nonam aetheris sedem, quam in-
colunt aetherei daemones; decimam aeream; undecimam
humectae substantiae; duodecimam terram, quae immobilis
ex conversione mundi manet. Verum hoc fortassis extra propositum, quamvis instituto sermoni concinat, quod fatum
sine vi ac sine ulla necessitate inextricabili modo salubri atque ordine administretur.

179. Ex hoc ordine rerum demanant illa quae rari exempli
sunt, quorum partim fortuna potestatem habet, partim im-
provisa et sua sponte proveniunt, quibus omnibus casus dicitur imperare. Quae fatalia quidem sunt, continentur enim
edictis fatalibus, nec tamen sunt necessitate violenta, perinde ut quae a nobis fiunt; continentur quippe legibus nostris, nec tamen secundum leges proveniunt quibus utimur.
Ut puta iubet lex interfici patriae proditorem. Quid ergo?
Quia proditorem vocat eum cui poenam statuit, necesse est,
ut lex faciat proditorem? Non, opinor, nam proditor quidem
sua mala mente—quin potius amentia—prorumpit ad facinus, punitur vero iuxta legem. Rursumque lex est ut qui for-
titer bellaverit praemio afficiatur; haec lex iubet, non tamen
victorem aut victoriam lex facit—et tamen praemium lex
dat. Proptereaque lex generaliter iubet omnibus quae facienda sint prohibetque omnes ab inconvenientibus; sed
non omnes obtemperant nec omnes faciunt quae iubentur.
Quae res ostendit optionem quidem esse in hominibus nec

planets, and ninth, that of ether, which the ethereal demons inhabit; tenth, that of air; eleventh, that of the moist substance; twelfth, Earth, which remains immobile, outside the circumlation of the world. But this perhaps goes beyond what was intended, although it is consistent with what was set for discussion, in that fate is administered in an inextricable manner and according to a salvific order, without compulsion or any necessity.

179. From this ordered ranking of realities descend those things that are of rare occurrence. Sometimes fortune has control over them, sometimes they occur unexpectedly and spontaneously, and over all of the latter cases chance is said to dominate. And although they are fated insofar as they are embraced by the edicts of fate, yet they are not under violent necessity. Precisely as in the case of the things done by us: they are of course embraced by our laws, yet they do not *occur* according to the laws that we live by. For example, the law orders that a traitor to the fatherland be killed. Well then, does the law necessarily make the one for whom it determines the punishment a traitor by virtue of the fact that it pronounces him a traitor? I suppose not, for the traitor leaps at the deed because of his own evil mind—or better, because of his being *out of* his mind—but is punished in conformity with the law. Conversely, the law is that he who fights bravely should be rewarded; the law orders these things, yet the law does not *make* the victor or victory—and yet the law confers the reward. Thus the law orders generally, for all, what things are to be done, and it prohibits all from unsuitable actions; but not all obey, nor do all do what they are ordered to. This fact shows that although choice rests with human beings the *same* choice does not rest with

eandem in omnibus; ea vero quae sequuntur, id est legitima, id est animadversiones vel praemia, ex lege sancta.

180. Talis est, opinor, etiam lex illa caelestis, quae fatum vocatur, sciscens hominibus honesta, prohibens contraria. Sequi porro nostrum est et a fati iugo liberum, laudari vero bene agentem tam iuxta legem quam iuxta commune iudicium, similiter ergo etiam contraria: mentiri quidem et pessime agere vitam continetur edicto et est in hominis arbitrio ut praecedens; male porro vitam disponere proprium hominis proptereaque puniri plane est ex necessitate fatali, utpote quod legem sequatur. Haec porro omnia sedem habent in animis hominum, quae anima libera est et agit ex arbitrio suo. Optima porro pars animae ea est quam descripsit Plato duplicem habere virtutem, unam in comprehensione divinarum rerum, quae sapientia est, alteram in dispositione rerum mortalium, quae prudentia nominatur.

181. Quod si quis ad humores corporis naturalemque illam concretionem respiciens plerosque intemperantes, alios porro moderatos homines esse non sine fato putat, et intemperantes quidem ex humorum intemperie laborare, moderatos autem ex felicitate concretionis levari eaque omnia decreto fieri putat, vera sentit quidem. Est enim natura tributum, ut imbecilla hominum natio vel laboret improspera concretione vel adiuvetur moderata in obtentu honestatis; ideoque adversum huius modi vitia rationis consiliique

all; but the things that follow from it, i.e., the lawful, i.e., punishments and rewards, are sanctioned by the law.

180. Of such a sort too, I suppose, is that celestial law which is called fate, ordaining virtue for men and forbidding its contrary. And to follow it is our task, one that is free from the yoke of fate; and being praised for acting rightly is in conformity with both the law and common judgment, and so also as concerns the contrary: lying and conducting one's life in the worst way falls, as in the prior case, under the edict and belongs to human free choice; moreover, to dispose one's life badly is a human prerogative, and to be punished on that account clearly originates in a fated necessity in that it *follows* from the law. And all of these things are seated within the souls of men, and the soul is free and acts according to its capacity for choice. And the noblest part of the soul is that which Plato described as having a double capacity: one in its comprehension of divine realities, which is wisdom, the other in its disposition of mortal affairs, which is called prudence.

181. But if in consideration of the bodily humors and the natural temperament associated with them one supposes that it is not without fate that a good many human beings are intemperate and the rest temperate, and that the intemperate suffer from an intemperance in the humors whereas the temperate gain relief from the happy possession of temperament, and that all of this happens by decree, then he is in a sense right. For as concerns the acquisition of virtue, it is a natural attribute that the feeble race of humans should either suffer because of an unpropitious temperament or be aided by a temperate one; and thus by the law of providence the sound influence of reason and deliberation has been set

salubritas opposita est providentiae lege, siquidem avaritia libido crudelitas ceteraeque huius modi pestes nihil in pueritia grande designent sed sint confirmata iam aetate noxia: tunc, opinor, cum etiam consilii salubritas confirmatur cui auxiliatur decus studiorum honestiorum, prodest benivolorum reprehensio, medetur animadversio, contraque adversis rebus obtunditur pravitas mentis atque insolescit.

182. Ideoque ob consortium corporis est inter homines bestiasque et cetera vita carentia societas communioque corporeorum proventuum, siquidem nasci nutriri crescere commune est hominibus cum ceteris, sentire vero et appetere commune demum hominibus et mutis tantum ac ratione carentibus animalibus. Cupiditas porro atque iracundia vel agrestium vel mansuetorum appetitus inrationabilis est, hominis vero cuius est proprium rationi mentem applicare rationabilis. Ratiocinandi tamen atque intellegendi sciendique verum appetitus proprius est hominis, qui a cupiditate atque iracundia plurimum distat; illa quippe etiam in mutis animalibus, et multo quidem acriora, cernuntur, rationis autem perfectio et intellectus propria dei et hominis tantum.

183. Atque inter ipsos homines non peraeque, compugnant quippe se in hominum commotionibus invicem cupiditas iracundiaque et item ratio obtinentque adversum se vicissim: ratio, ut apud Homerum cum Laertius iuvenis:

in opposition to the corresponding vices, for greed, lust, cruelty and all such diseases signify nothing serious in childhood but at an age well confirmed are noxious: all, I suppose, at the point when the soundness of deliberation too is confirmed, a process which the distinction of virtuous pursuits aids, reprehension from well-wishers benefits, their punishment remedies, and when, by contrast, mental perversion becomes obtuse and insolent in the face of adverse circumstances.

182. And so by virtue of their association with body there is between humans, beasts, and other, lifeless things the fellowship and communion of corporeal experiences, since humans have birth, nourishment, and growth in common with the others, whereas they have sense perception and appetite in common only with animals that are dumb and lack reason. Moreover, the irrational appetite in creatures either wild or tame is cupidity, also irascibility, whereas the rational is in man, whose proper characteristic is the application of mind to reason; but proper to man, who stands at the farthest remove from cupidity and irascibility, is the appetite for reasoning, understanding, and knowing the truth. For the former are discerned also in dumb animals, and indeed with much greater intensity, whereas intellect and the perfection of reason are characteristics proper only to god and man.

183. And even between men, in differing degrees; for among the emotional disturbances that afflict human beings cupidity, irascibility, and also reason conflict with one another, by turns gaining the upper hand against one another. Reason, as in Homer, when the son of Laertes:

Pectore pulsato mentem castigat acerbe:
"Quin toleras, mea mens? Etenim graviora tulisti,"

quippe in illius animo ratio tunc iracundiam subiugabat. Apud Euripidem contra in Medeae mente saeva iracundia rationis lumen extinxerat, ait enim:

Nec me latet nunc, quam cruenta cogitem,
sed vincit ira sanitatem pectoris;

usque adeo salubri consilio viam clauserat immoderatus dolor pelicatus.

184. Ergo in animo continentis viri semper plus consilium potest, intemperantis imbecillitas adversum rationem vitiosis animi partibus suffragatur. Saepe etiam haec ipsa vitia se invicem impugnant, ut in adulescente Terentiano, qui adversum acerrimas amoris flammas resistens honesta iracundia nititur, cum negat iturum se ad conspectum amicae "ultro accersentis" ut "exclusum" indigne "revocet" lenocinio blanditiisque "meretriciis." Ergo haec, de quibus intra arcana pectoris disceptamus quaeque utrum facienda necne sint deliberamus et ad postremum tamquam lata sententia decernimus, quatenus non sunt propria nostra? Nisi forte ideo, quia commoti vel depravati libidine disceptatores idonei non sumus, cum aequum iudicium carere tam odii quam gratiae misericordiaeque anticipationibus debeat.

After beating his breast castigates his mind bitterly:
"Why do you not tolerate this, my mind? For you have
    endured worse."

For at that moment reason was subjugating the irascibility
within his mind. In Euripides, by contrast, a savage irascibility within the mind of Medea had extinguished the light of
reason. For she says:

The bloodiness now of my designs does not escape me,
but rage conquers the sanity of my heart.

To such an extent had immoderate grief over a rival closed
the way to healthy counsel.

184. In the mind of the morally continent man, then, deliberation always prevails; the weakness of the intemperate
one receives support against reason from the defective parts
of the mind. Often these defects themselves even attack
one another, as in the case of the young man in Terence who
in resisting the most intense flames of love falls back on a
virtuous form of irascibility, when he says that he will not go
to see the courtesan who "summons him away" in order after "shutting him out" to "call him back" insultingly with her
pandering and "courtesan's" blandishments. Now, these
matters, over which we debate within the hidden chambers
of the heart, deliberating in each case whether or not they
should be acted upon, and which in the end we decide as
though by passing a motion: to what extent are they not
proper to us, or *ours?* Unless perhaps it is in the sense that in
being emotionally disturbed or depraved because of our lust
we are unfit as debaters, since an equitable judgment must
be free of preconceptions based on either malice or indul-
gence and pity.

185.—Sed praedictio, inquiunt, futurorum cuncta iam dudum disposita atque ordinata esse testatur; haec porro dispositio atque ordinatio fatum vocatur.—Immo haec ipsa praedictio fatalem necessitatem dominari negat usque quaque, siquidem praedictio rationabilis sit aestimatio sortis futurae, quae non in rebus certis et necessitate constrictis sed in incertis atque in ambiguis praevalet. Quis enim consulat praesagum de recens nato, utrum mortalis an immortalis futurus sit? Sed illud potius, quod est dubium, quaeri solet, quam prolixa vitae spatia sortitus esse videatur et utrum dives an pauper elataque an plebeia sit atque humili fortuna futurus. Quae cuncta observatione scientia, artificiosa quoque sollertia colliguntur: aut enim alitum volatu aut extis aut oraculis homines praemonentur praedicente aliquo propitio daemone, qui sit eorum omnium quae deinceps sequuntur scius, perinde ut si medicus iuxta disciplinam medendi praedicat vel exitium vel sanitatem aut etiam gubernator caeli condicionum non ignarus ex aliqua nubecula praenuntiet tempestatem futuram; quae cuncta non fato sed artificiosis rationibus usuque et experientia comprehenduntur.

186. Aeque cum ex motu siderum praedictio habetur, signa obseruari solent ortusque et obitus stellarum et conformationes ad rationem redactae iuxta quam fertilitas sterilitasque provenit; omnisque huius modi ratio nihil est

185. But the prediction of future events, they say, is witness to the fact that all things have long since been disposed and ordained, and this disposition and ordaining is called fate. In fact, however, this very prediction in every way undercuts the domination of a fated necessity, in that the prediction is a rational assessment of what has been allotted for the future, an assessment whose prevalence concerns, not things that are certain and constrained by necessity, but ones that are uncertain and contingent. For who would consult a soothsayer on the question of whether a newborn son is destined to be mortal or immortal? Rather, the question generally concerns that which is contingent: how long a lifespan he appears to have been allotted, and whether he is destined to be rich or poor, of high or of common and humble station. And all such inferences are drawn on the basis of observation, knowledge, and technical skill; for through the flight of birds, entrails, or oracles human beings are advised in advance, at the prediction of some propitious demon who is knowledgeable about the ordered sequence of all things, exactly as when on the strength of his knowledge of medicine a physician predicts either death or health, or again, when on the basis of a small cloud a helmsman who understands the sky announces in advance the coming of a storm. And all of these come under the grasp, not of fate, but of technical reasoning and practice and experience.

186. So too when a prediction is derived from the movement of constellations: observations of the signs are customarily made, and the risings and settings of the stars and their formations are reduced to a rational calculation on the basis of which fertility or sterility comes to light; and every such rational calculation is nothing other than a conjecture

aliud quam coniectura rerum earum quae vel ad corpus pertinent vel ad ea quae corporis propria sunt vel ad animam satis corpori servientem. Unde opinor Platonem animarum quidem exaedificationi deum opificem praefuisse dicere, eorum vero quae animis subtexuntur aliis divinis potestatibus inferioribus munus atque officium esse mandatum, ita ut purae quidem animae sinceraeque et vigentes florentesque rationibus a deo factae sint, vitiosarum vero partium eius auctores habeantur hae potestates quibus ab opifice deo talis cura mandata sit.

187. Vitiosae porro partes animi quae subtexuntur, <id> est ira et cupiditas, satis idonea vitae agendae instrumenta. Multa quippe sunt quae per virilem animi commotionem recte in hac vita fiunt et vindicantur, quotiens iusta iracundia comitem se et auxiliatricem rationi praebet, multa etiam ex cupiditate honesta vel mediocri praeter libidinum sordes. Sicut ergo purae mundi animae regnum in perpetua mundi agitatione permissum est, ita his animis quae homines inspirant opus fuit ratione iracundia et cupiditatibus interpolata, ut cum quidem se ad rationem totum animal convertisset curaret intueretur etiam caelestia, cum vero ad terrena despiceret despectus aeque ne esset otiosus sed ex eadem inclinatione cura rerum terrestrium nasceretur.

188. Ut igitur brevi multa complectar, istius rei dispositio talis mente concipienda est: originem quidem rerum ex qua

concerning the things that pertain to the body, to those that are proper to the body, or to the soul in its satisfying the demands of the body. Whence I suppose Plato's claim [41c–d] that the craftsman god oversaw the construction of souls whereas the task of or responsibility for the things interwoven in souls was assigned to divine powers of inferior rank, so that as a result souls pure, unadulterated, thriving, and flourishing in their rational activity were made by god whereas these powers to whom such a responsibility was assigned by the craftsman god are held responsible for the parts of the soul which are defective.

187. And the defective parts of the mind which are interwoven, i.e., irascibility and cupidity, are instruments adequately suited to the conduct of life. For many are the things which owing to a virile emotion within the mind are rightly done and vindicated in this life, whenever a just irascibility shows itself as reason's companion and supporter; many also those that stem from a virtuous or restrained cupidity, one free from sordid lust. As, then, sovereignty over the perpetual movement of the world was granted to the pure world soul, so for these souls that animate human beings there was need of reason's having irascibility and cupidity blended in, so that after its conversion toward reason the whole living creature would also show a concern for and gaze upon celestial things, and so that in looking down upon earthly ones the downward glance would at the same time not be indifferent but a concern for earthly affairs would be born out of the same inclination.

188. In order, then, to summarize briefly these many points, we must mentally conceive of the arrangement of this matter as follows: that the origin of things from which

ceteris omnibus quae sunt substantia ministratur esse summum et ineffabilem deum; post quem providentiam eius
secundum deum, latorem legis utriusque vitae tam aeternae
quam temporariae; tertiam porro esse substantiam quae
secunda mens intellectusque dicitur, quasi quaedam custos
legis aeternae; his subiectas fore rationabiles animas legi
obsequentes, ministras vero potestates naturam fortunam
casum et daemones inspectatores speculatoresque meritorum. Ergo summus deus iubet, secundus ordinat, tertius in-
timat, animae vero lege agunt.

189. Lex porro ipsum fatum est, ut saepe diximus. Cui legi
qui pareat sequaturque principis dei veneranda vestigia,
beatam semper vitam agit iuxta legis perpetuae sanctionem,
quod est iuxta fatum; at vero quae dei comitatum animae
neglexerint, rursum et ipsae alio quodam contrarioque genere secundum fatum vitam exigunt, donec paeniteat eas
delictorum suorum expiatisque criminibus deinceps ad immortalis dei et aeternarum divinarum potestatum choros
revertantur et ille legis rigor ex deteriore fortuna transitum
fieri sinat ad beatam, quod fieri certe non posset si omnia
constricta essent uniformi quadam et rigida atque inrevoca-
bili necessitate. Ex quo apparet providentiam quidem omnia
intra se circumplexam tenere, quippe omnia quae secundum
eandem recte administrantur; at vero fatum providentiae
scitum est, continet autem ea quae sunt in nostra potestate
ut praecedentia, continet etiam meritorum collocationem.
Sequuntur animadversio et approbatio, quae sunt fatalia,
eaque omnia quae casu fortunave fiunt.

being is administered to all things that are is the Supreme
and ineffable God; that the Second God after him is his
Providence, the legislator for both kinds of life, the eternal
and temporal; and that third is the substance called the Second Mind or Intellect, a kind of guardian, as it were, of the
eternal law; that subject to these are the rational Souls that
obey the law, and the administering powers of Nature, Fortune, Chance, and the Demons who inspect and observe
merits. Thus the Supreme God commands, the Second one
ordains, the Third communicates, and Souls act according
to the law.

189. And the law is fate itself, as we have repeatedly said.
And the one who obeys this law and follows in the venerable
path of the First God always leads a happy life in conformity
with the sanction of the perpetual law, that is, in conformity
with Fate; but the Souls that have neglected God's retinue
lead for their part a life in accordance with Fate as well, although in a different and, in a sense, contrary pattern, until
they repent of their faults and upon expiating their wrongs
eventually return to the choruses of the immortal God and
eternal divine powers, and until that rigor of the law permits
the transition from a more abject to a happy state to occur,
which would certainly could not occur if all things were constrained by a uniform, rigid, and irrevocable necessity of
some kind. And from this it is evident that Providence holds
all things within its embrace, for all things are rightly administered by being in accordance with it; but Fate is the decree
of Providence, and it embraces as premised the things that
are within our power, and embraces the positing of merits as
well. Punishment and approbation, the fated elements, follow, and all of the things that happen according to Chance
or Fortune.

190. Quid igitur sibi voluit tractatus huius tam larga prolixitas? Quia multi nulla cura veri sciendi, sed potius veris
rationibus renitendi et ipsi falluntur et ceteros in erroris
ineluctabilis implicant lubrico, quippe qui ad unam aliquam
partem mundanae administrationis respicientes tamquam
de solida atque universa dispensatione pronuntient, quodque in una parte invenerint, id esse in omnibus quoque
mundi partibus asseverant. Proptereaque cum aliquid verum dicunt veri similes habentur quamvis compugnantia invicem dicant, cum autem de parte sentientes perinde habent
tamquam de solido universoque sentiant redarguuntur invicem. Namque fato quaedam agi verum est, et quod quaedam
in nostra potestate sint, hoc quoque verum esse monstratum
est. Quare qui omnia fato fieri dicunt, merito reprehendun-
tur ab his qui probant esse aliquid in nostra potestate, demum qui omnia in nostra potestate constituunt nec quicquam fato relinquunt, falli deteguntur; quis enim ignoret
esse aliquid in fato et extra nostrum ius? Sola igitur vera illa
ratio est fixaque et stabilis sententia, quae docet quaedam
fato fieri, alia porro ex hominum arbitrio et voluntate profi-
cisci.

191. Deinde subnectit leges ipsas et iura fatalia: principalem quidem legem, qua cunctis animis ob uniformem naturam ad virtutis vindicationem aequabilis fato tribuitur facultas sine cuiusquam praeclaratione. Addit secundam legem,

190. What, then, has been the point of such prolixity in this treatment? That many out of a concern, not for knowing the truth, but rather for resisting true reasoning are both themselves deceived and implicate others in the trap of an inescapable error, in that while gazing upon one particular part, as it were, of the world's administration they make pronouncements that appear to concern the dispensation of the entire universe and asseverate that what they have discovered in connection with one part holds also in connection with *all* parts of the world. Hence when they make a true claim they are thought to have probability on their side even though their claims conflict with one another, and when while holding a view concerning a part they behave as though it concerned the entire universe they are refuted by one another. For that certain things are enacted by fate is true, and that certain things are within our power has also been shown to be true. And so those who claim that all things are brought about by fate are rightly reprehended by those who prove that there is something that is within our power and, finally, those who place all things within our power and leave nothing to fate are exposed as being deceived—for who could ignore the fact that there is something within the control of fate and beyond our jurisdiction? Thus that reasoning alone is true, the opinion fixed and stable, which teaches that certain things are brought about by fate while others proceed from human choice and will.

191. He then includes the actual laws or rights of fate, the principal law being that according to which the capacity for the possession of virtue is distributed by fate in equal measure among all souls without prejudice to any one. He adds as the second law that according to which it is sanctioned

qua sanctum est omnes animas, quae comitatae divinum agmen spectaverint aeternarum vereque existentium rerum naturam, formam hominis induere ad tuenda terrena, piae nationis animal hominem significans ideo, quod in mutis animalibus nulla sit cognitio de deo. Porro ex his quae ratione instructa sint praestantissimum quidem animal id esse quod ceteris caelestibus animalibus substantiam ex se largiatur, colat autem aliud multo praestantius in quo sit origo rerum; sequi vero quasi per ordinem quendam inferioris eminentiae potestates, quae singulae potiora quaeque venerentur numina. Quia igitur ultimus est homo ex his quae ratione utuntur animalibus cunctaque meliora et elatiora veneratur, iure praecipua religione praeditum esse dixit. Cumque duplex sit natura hominis, altera melior altera inferior, lege opus fuit tertia quae meliora distingueret. Est porro melior sexus virilis, muliebris inferior, non quo sit aliqua in animis differentia (una est quippe natura) sed diversitas tamen in sexu esse debuit caduca mortalitate partus substitutionesque desiderante. Denique cum una eademque virtus sit maris et feminae, corporum tamen ipsorum diversae vires sunt, cum eorum alterum calidius densiusque, alterum sit frigidius et rarius.

192. Sequitur alia lex, quam designat his verbis: Cumque necessitate decreti corporibus inserentur corporeaque supellex varie mutabitur quibusdam labentibus et aliis invicem succedentibus membris. Necessitatem nunc vocat usum

that all of the souls which in the company of the divine host
have gazed upon the nature of eternal and truly existent realities assume human form for purposes of overseeing
earthly concerns, signifying man with *living being of pious
breed* [42a], since in dumb animals there is no knowledge of
god. And his point is that among those which have been
equipped with reason the most eminent living being is that
which of itself bestows being upon all other celestial ones
while also cultivating another far more eminent one in
whom the origin of things resides; and that as if in a kind of
order there follow powers of inferior eminence which singly
venerate the various more potent divinities. Given, then,
that man is last among these living beings that enjoy the use
of reason, and that he venerates all of the superior and loft-
ier beings, he rightly said that man is endowed with a heightened religious sensibility. And since *human nature* is double,
one *superior,* the other inferior, there was need of a third law
to distinguish the superior beings. The superior sex, moreover, is the male and the inferior the female, not so that
there is any difference between their souls (for their nature
is one), but there nevertheless had to be a distinction in sex,
since their perishing mortality longs for replenishment in
the form of offspring. Finally, although the psychic capacity
of man and woman is one and the same, the powers of their
bodies nevertheless differ, in that one of them is warmer
and denser, the other cooler and more rarefied.

192. There follows another law, which he indicates with
the following words [42a]: *And once they are implanted in bodies by necessity of the decree and their bodily apparatus undergoes
varied changes with the slipping away of certain parts and the
emergence of others to take their place.* By *necessity* he refers here

inexcusabilem munusque incorporationis, neque enim aliter poterant regi terrena rationabili anima regente nisi corporis adhibita coniunctione. Corpus porro terrenum hoc non diu constat, sed torrentis more praecipitis et ipsum effluit et ab effluentibus inundatur; sunt quippe in eo multi meatus multaque item emissacula tam in promptu et visibilia quam latentia et caeca, per quae fertur humor et spiritus aliaeque superfluae reliquiae cibi et potus, quibus egressus conseruationis animalium causa natura commenta est et adversum detrimenta egestionis pro competenti modo vicem reparat ex humido et sicco cibatu atque extrinsecus circumfusi aeris respiratione. Meatus igitur ingredientibus omnibus pro modo proque magnitudine eorum natura fabricata est, idque ipsum est quod dicit idem Plato: quibusdam labentibus et aliis invicem succedentibus membris.

193. Haec ergo lex illud effecit ante omnia: sensum ex violentis passionibus excitari. Merito; vita quippe sine sensu esse non potest, siquidem inter ea quae vivunt et quae vita carent haec sit, opinor, differentia, ut sentiant haec, illa sine sensu sint nascentiaque simul cum vita sensum auspicentur et in diiugio corporis et animae sentire desinant. Certe sive passio sive potentia sive aliquis affectus est, sensus hic animantis est proprius ex corporis animaeque copulatione conflatus. Ex violentis vero passionibus recte, nam eadem ac

to the inescapable use or obligation of embodiment, for earthly things were incapable of being ruled by a ruling rational soul in any way other than by its availing itself of union with the body. Moreover, this earthly body does not remain constant for any length of time, but like a torrent that rushes headlong it both flows away on its own and is inundated by those things that are flowing away; for in it there are many channels and many small effluents, evident and visible as well as hidden and invisible, through which there flows bodily fluid and air and other superfluous remains of food and drink; and nature has devised outlets for them with an eye to the preservation of the living beings, and to counteract damage caused by depletion it supplies replenishment in suitable measure from food, moist and dry, and respiration of the extrinsic ambient air. Thus for all of the things that enter nature has fabricated channels proportionate to their size and magnitude, and that is precisely what Plato means by *with the slipping away of certain parts and the emergence of others to take their place.*

193. This law, then, effected the following before everything else: *that sensation should be stirred up by the violent passions* [42a]. And rightly so, in that without sensation life is incapable of being. For the difference between things that have life and those that are deprived of it is, I suppose, that the one group has sensation while the other exists without it, and things that are subject to birth have their first experience of sensation as soon as they have life, and cease to have it when body and soul are separated. Whether passion, potency, or some form of feeling, this sensation, brought together by virtue of the joining of body and soul, is proper to the living being. And rightly *by violent passions,* for the soul

simili facilitate anima contemplatur—contemplatio quippe facilis intentio est—, sensus vero nascitur ex consortio corporis atque animae passionum; et sunt multae corporis pulsationes eius modi, ut neque contingant animam et sensim latenterque vanescant, qualis est lapsus in videndo vel audiendo, quidam tamen pulsus corporis violentiores sunt, qui ad animam usque permanant.

194. Est ergo sensus passio corporis quibusdam extra positis et pulsantibus varie, eadem passione usque ad animae sedem commeante. Quae passio cum est lenis molliterque palpando potius quam pulsando corpus movet, consentit anima corporis titillationi; atque hoc genus sensus voluptas cognominatur, porro si erit asperitate quadam praedita passio doloris nomen accipiet, ut sit perspicuum voluptatem ac dolorem species esse sensus, sensum vero ipsum genus. Omnis porro talis cupiditas mixta est cum voluptatis et doloris affectu consequenterque amor huius modi rerum inter dolorem voluptatemque positus invenitur; spes quippe fruendi voluptatem creat, dilatio tristitiam et dolorem. Quare sequitur sentiendi legem lex amandi; amor vero conservationi corporis plurimum confert idemque est auctor successionum. Idem hoc in ira quoque reperitur quotiens sine ratione ac sine modo commovemur agresti quodam ardore mentis; adversum quem instruitur anima cautionis salubritate, quae nimia facta transit ad formidinis vitium. Itaque cum animi

engages in contemplation with constant and stable ease, in that contemplation is an unhindered state of attention, whereas sensation arises out of the coupling of the passions of body and soul. And there are many bodily impulses of the sort that do not impinge upon the soul but fade away by degrees and imperceptibly, as when there is a lapse in sight or hearing; but certain bodily impulses are more violent, and they stream all the way through to the soul.

194. *Sensation* [42a], then, is a bodily passion caused by certain objects that are externally situated and variously produce impulses, the passion in question traveling all the way to the seat of the soul. And when the passion is moderate and moves the body by gently stroking rather than striking it, the soul consents to the bodily stimulation, and this kind of sensation is called *pleasure,* whereas if the passion is characterized by some degree of intensity it will be called *pain,* so that it is clear that pleasure and pain are species of sensation and sensation their proper genus. Now, every *desire* of this sort is *blended* with a feeling of pleasure and pain, and as a result the desire for such objects is found situated between pain and pleasure; for hope gives rise to the pleasure of enjoying and postponement to pain and grief. And so the law governing desire follows the law governing sensation; and desire contributes greatly to the preservation of the body and is also the motive force behind the continuation of the species. This same quality is found in *irascibility* as well, whenever without reason or moderation we are moved by a wild ardor, as it were, of the mind, in defense against which the soul is equipped with a healthy state of watchfulness which when excessive converts to the vice of *fear.* And so as the mental force grows increasingly

vigor qui factus immoderatior progressus est ad iracundiae limitem et item cautio [sit] animae data ob tutelam corporis immoderate crescentia perturbant animum potius quam regunt.

195. Ceterasque, inquit, pedissequas earum perturbationes diverso affectu pro natura sua permoventes; quas quidem si frenarent ac subiugarent, iustam his lenemque vitam fore, sin vincerentur, iniustam et confragosam. Et victricibus quidem ad comparis stellae contubernium sedemque reditum patere acturis deinceps vitam veram et beatam, victas porro mutare sexum atque ad infirmitatem naturae muliebris relegari secundae generationis tempore; nec a vitiis intemperantiaque discedentibus [tamen] poenam reiectionemque in deteriora non cessare donec instituto meritisque congruas immanium ferarum induant formas. Pedissequas quidem cupiditati dolorique cognatas et consentaneas passiones aemulationem dicit invidiam obtrectationem et cetera huius modi, voluptati vero in alienis malis gaudium iactantiam gloriae vanitatem, metui porro fugam formidinem, iracundiae nihilo minus saevitiam feritatem calorem quaeque his sunt proxima. Diverso, inquit, affectu pro natura sua permoventes, ea videlicet quae sunt his ipsis contraria virtutum ornamenta quae virtutibus fiunt. Quae quidem vitia si frenarent, inquit, iustam his lenemque vitam fore. Aperte et ita ut dubitare nequeamus, sui iuris esse animas docet in delectu atque optione.

intemperate in verging on the border of irascibility, and the watchfulness of soul that has been provided for the care of the body does so too, they disturb rather than guide the mind because of the increase in intemperance.

195. *And,* he says [42a–c], *the other disturbances that follow from them, each one initiating change with varying influence depending on its nature; and that if they curbed and subjugated the disturbances their life should be just and smooth, but that if they were overcome by them it should be unjust and rough. And he indicated that for those souls who were victorious the path was open to their returning to inhabit the abode of their consort star and leading a true and blessed life thereafter, whereas those who had been overcome should change their sex and be relegated to the infirmity of the female nature at the time of their second birth. And that for those who did not depart from vice and intemperance the punishment and rejection to inferior states should not cease until they assume the forms of wild beasts, forms congruent with their mode of life and deserts.* His point is that jealousy, envy, malice, and the like are passions that *follow from* and are cognate and consistent with *desire and pain,* as joy over others' misfortunes, arrogance, and vainglory follow from *pleasure,* desertion and timidity from *fear,* and similarly savageness, ferocity, excitability and their most closely associated states from *irascibility. Initiating change with varying influence,* he says, *depending on its nature,* namely, those states which adorn the virtues contrary to their actual effects and which arise with the virtues. *And if they curbed* the vices, he says, *their life should be just and smooth.* He explains openly, and so as to leave us in no doubt, that the souls are autonomous in their selecting and choosing.

196. Horum omnium praemia etiam constituit, victricibus vitiorum animis reditum ad caelestem sedem perpetuamque immunitatem, quae vero libidine se commaculave-
rint, in munere vitae secundae asperiorem congruamque
moribus et instituto vitam futuram, siquidem ex virili sexu
transeant in feminae formam, non quo ipsa anima sexum
mutet, sed quod deterioris sexus corpus accipiat. Quae vitam meliorem temperantemque delegerit ad meliorem fortunam revocabitur, porro si deterior facta erit deteriusque
vivet, propter nimiam corporis amplexationem vitae desti-
nabitur infeliciori quoad usque ad ferae naturae perveniat
immanitatem.

197. Empedocles tamen Pythagoram secutus ait eas non
naturam modo agrestem et feram sortiri, sed etiam formas
varias, cum ita dicit:

Namque ego iamdudum vixi puer et solida arbos,
ales et ex undis animal, tum lactea virgo,

non <tantum> iuxta sexus silvestrem conversionem sed in
diversorum animantium <formas transeuntes,> ut ipse aliis
testatur versibus quibus abstineri oportere censet animalibus:

Mutatos subolis mactat pater impius artus

196. He lays out as well the rewards enjoyed by all of the latter [42b–c]: a *return* to the celestial *abode* and perpetual immunity for souls that are *victorious* over vices, but for those that have defiled themselves with lust a life that will, by way of an obligation attaching to their second life, be harsher and *congruent* with their character and *desert,* in that they pass from the male sex to female form, not so that the soul itself changes sex but that it acquires the body possessed by the inferior sex. The soul that chooses a better, temperate life will be summoned back to a better lot, but if it *deteriorates* and conducts its life accordingly, then in consideration of its excessive attachment to the body it will be destined to a life of increasing misfortune until it attains the *wildness* of a *beastly* nature.

197. But following Pythagoras Empedocles claims that the souls are allotted not only the *wild* and beastly nature but the various bodily *forms* [42c] as well, when he says the following:

> For I now have long since lived as a boy and as a solid
> tree,
> as a bird, and as a beast from the waters, then as a milky-
> white maiden,

meaning not only a change of sex at the material level but their transmigration to the forms associated with different animals, as he himself indicates in other verses, in which he expresses his view concerning the necessity of abstaining from animal flesh:

> An impious father sacrifices the limbs of his child, limbs
> that have changed their form,

dis epulum libans. Saeva prece territa mente
hostia, luctifica funestatur dape mensa.
Natus item ut pecudes caedit matremque patremque
nec sentit caros mandens sub dentibus artus.

Item alio loco:

Comprimite, o gentes, homicidia! Nonne videtis
mandere vos proprios artus ac viscera vestra?

198. Sed Plato non putat rationabilem animam vultum atque os ratione carentis animalis induere sed ad vitiorum reliquias accedente corpore incorporationem auctis animae
vitiis efferari ex instituto vitae prioris; et iracundum quidem
hominem eundemque fortem provehi usque ad feritatem
leonis, ferum vero et eundem rapacem ad proximam lupo-
rum naturae similitudinem pervenire, ceterorum item. Sed
cum sit reditus animis ad fortunam priorem (hoc vero fieri
non potest nisi prius reditus factus erit purus ad clemens et
homine dignum institutum), rationabilis porro consilii correctio quae paenitudo est non proveniat in his quae sine ratione vivunt, anima quondam hominis nequaquam transit
ad bestias iuxta Platonem.

199. Deinde ait: Pausamque malorum non prius fore
quam consecuta eas similis eademque semper volucris illa

and offers a libation to the gods. Terrified of mind by the
savage prayer
is the victim, the table stained by the blood of a dire
meal.
A son likewise slaughters both mother and father as cat-
tle,
unaware that the limbs he crushes with his teeth are dear
to him,

and in another passage:

Nations, put an end to the murder! Surely you see
that the limbs you are chewing belong to your kind, that
the flesh is your own?

198. Plato, however, does not think that the rational soul
assumes [42c] the countenance or appearance of an irrational
animal, but that as the body succumbs to its lingering defects the embodiment becomes beastly, with vices increasing in the soul according to the conduct of its prior life; and
that the irascible but also brave human being shifts fully to
the savageness of a lion, while the savage but also rapacious
one attains the nearest likeness to the nature of wolves, and
so on in other cases. Given, however, that the return to a
prior lot is available to souls (and can occur only if a pure return to the civilized conduct worthy of a human being has
first been effected), but that the correction or repentance of
rational deliberation does not arise in beings that live without reason, the soul of what was once a human being is, according to Plato, in no way transferrable to beasts.

199. Then he says [42c–d]: *And that there should be no respite from their hardships before that forever like and selfsame*

mundi circumactio cuncta earum vitia ex igni et aqua terraque et aere contracta omnemque illuviem deterserit inconsultis et immoderatis erroribus ad modum rationis temperiemque redactis. Eandem semper circumactionem motus
intellegentis animae significans, similem vero eius, cum
deliberat ut intellegat; hae quippe virtutes sunt animae rationabilis. Inconsultos porro et immoderatos errores animae
dicit esse qui ex igni terraque et ceteris corporeis elementis
oboriuntur, adversum quos obtinens anima revertitur ad antiquam divinitatem suam et habebit naturam bonis meritis
competentem. Has leges ait a magno opifice deo animis esse
intimatas causamque intimationis ostendit: ne qua penes se
deinceps ex reticentia noxae resideret auctoritas, volens
ostendere malitiam non ex decreto ac voluntate dei provenire hominibus sed ipsorum vel imprudentia vel depravatione.

200. Deinde post expositionem legum fatalium sementem fecit animarum nostrarum deus partim in terra partim
in luna partim in ceteris, quae instrumenta temporis esse
dicit, iuxta Pythagoram quidem, quod ita ut in terra sic
etiam in lunari globo consistant homines et etiam in ceteris
errantibus stellis, iuxta se vero, quod in aliis libris idem asserat alterna vice fungi munere animas quibus rerum terrenarum tutela mandatur, ita ut quae iam iamque fungentur munere primae serantur in terra, quae post has in lunari globo
ac deinceps in aliis globis.

circumlation of the winged world overtakes them and wipes away all of the defects and all of the filth they have contracted from fire, water, earth, and air, bringing their irrational and intemperate errors back to the moderation and temperance of reason. Forever self-*same circumlation* signifies the movements of soul in its act of understanding, a circumlation *like* that which occurs when it deliberates in order to understand; for these are the powers of the rational soul. And he speaks of the *irrational and intemperate errors* of the soul as being those that arise *from fire and earth* and the other corporeal elements, by holding out against which the soul reverts to its ancient divinity and will possess a nature comporting with its good merits. He says that these *laws* were communicated to the souls by the great craftsman god, and indicates the reason for his communicating them: *in order that no responsibility for wrongdoing would in future fall to him for keeping silent,* his intention being to show that human beings experience evil, not because of the decree or will of god, but because of an imprudence and depravity all their own.

200. Then, after *expounding the laws of fate, god performed the sowing* of our souls *partly in the Earth, partly in the Moon, and partly in the other bodies which* he describes [42d] as being the *instruments of time;* this is in accordance with Pythagoras, since human beings also come to be on the lunar sphere and other errant stars just as they do on Earth, and it is in accordance with his own view, since in other books he asserts that souls who are charged with the oversight of earthly concerns perform the task in an alternating pattern, such that those who are immediately to assume the task are sown first on Earth and those after them on the lunar and then other spheres.

201. Consequenter deinde iubet factis a se diis, id est stellis, fingere humana corpora animarum competentium receptacula isdemque adhibere cuncta adminicula vitalis substantiae: principio appetitum, qui dividitur in iracundiam et cupiditatem, sine quibus corpus mortalis animantis neque esse neque vero administrari potest, deinde artes, quae victum necessarium largiuntur, ceteraque omnia iuxta vires ut quam optime mortalis natura regatur—iuxta vires videlicet non efficientium sed eorum quae efficiebantur, propterea quod homines tam ad bonitatem quam ad malitiam inclinationes habent, ex quo fit, ut saepe ipsi sint sibi auctores malorum. Talis ergo fuit ordinatio summi opificis dei, ut quod erat in corpore mortali minime mortale, sed divinum potius et sempiternum, ipse construeret, porro quae dissolubilia umquam essent futura minoribus efficienda mandaret. Denique completa dispositione in suo, inquit, affectu manebat. Quid est? Nimirum ut providentia sua cunctis tam ex aeternitate quam nativis generatisque consuleret, divinis quidem et aeternis immortalitatem propagans temporariis vero perennitatem, non iugem et integram sed ex successione.

201. After which he then orders *the gods who had been made by him* [42d–e], i.e., the stars, to fashion human *bodies* as receptacles of the corresponding souls and to equip them with all of the support mechanisms of a living substance: in the first instance, appetite, which divides into irascibility and desire, and without which the body of a mortal living creature is incapable of existing or administering to its own needs; then the skills for their procuring sustenance and so on *according to the best of their abilities, so that the mortal nature may be governed in the best way possible — according to the best of their abilities,* namely, not of those doing the producing but of the things that were being produced, since human beings have inclinations that are equally balanced as to goodness and evil, often to the point of their actually inflicting evils on themselves. The ordinance, then, of the supreme craftsman god was such that he himself would construct the element of the *mortal body* that was, not mortal, but rather divine and sempiternal while handing over to the minor divinities the production of elements that were destined for dissolution at some point in time. Finally, once their disposition had been brought to completion he *continued to abide in his* mental state. And what was that? No doubt, a state which was such that his providence watched over all things, those wrought from eternity as well as those subject to birth and generation, and propagated immortality among the divine and eternal ones, and perpetuity among those which are subject to time, not a continuous and whole perpetuity but one involving succession.

8. De Ortu Generis Humani

202. Deinde docet ipsam humani corporis aedificationem sentiendique causam et cetera quae sensum sequuntur. Ex mundi, inquit, materiis igni terraque et aqua cum spiritu, faenus elementarium mutuati quod redderetur cum opus foret, et cetera. Corpora nostra ex quattuor materiis esse composita in promptu est. Est enim quiddam in his contiguum quod tactui resistit, idque sine terrena soliditate non est; est etiam calidum aliud idemque visibile, porro quae talia sunt sine igni esse non possunt; est praeterea plenum spiritus, ut sunt hae venae quae arteriae nuncupantur; est etiam humor, ut sanguis et cetera quae manant ex corpore. Sed neque humor sine aqua neque spiritus sine aere consistet umquam; est igitur in corporibus nostris aquae portio et item aeris nec non ignis et terrae. Unde opinor hominem mundum brevem a veteribus appellatum; nec immerito, quia totus mundus et item totus homo ex isdem sunt omnibus, corpore quidem easdem materias habente, anima quoque unius eiusdemque naturae.

203. Invisibiles porro coniunctiones gomphos appellat, vel minorum corpusculorum coacervationem, ut Diodorus, vel eorundem similium inter se conglobationem formabilem, ut Anaxagoras, vel supra dictorum multiformem implicationem, ut Democritus et Leucippus, vel interdum concretionem interdum discretionem, ut Empedocles, concretionem quidem amicitiam discretionem porro et

8. On the Origin of Mankind

202. Next he explains the precise construction of the human body, the cause of sensation, and other particulars consequent upon sensation. *Borrowing,* he says [42e–43a], *from the world's material elements of fire, earth, water and air elemental capital which was to be repaid as needed,* etc. That our bodies are composed of the four material elements is obvious. For there is in them something tangible and resistant to touch, and that does not occur in the absence of the solidity of earth; there is also another quality, a warm and at the same time visible one, and there can be no such things in the absence of fire; there is, moreover, that quality which is filled with breath, as, e.g., are the veins that are called arteries; and there is moisture, e.g., blood and the other things that emanate from the body. But moisture will never exist in the absence of water, nor breath in the absence of air; hence there is within our bodies a portion that is water, and others that are air, fire, and earth. Whence I suppose man's being called the world in miniature by the ancients; and rightly so, in that the world and man, each in its entirety, consist of all the same things, the body in each case possessing the same material elements, the soul too being of one and the same nature.

203. He refers to the *invisible* linkages as *gomphoi* [43a], or a heaping up of tiny corpuscles according to Diodorus, a formable conglomeration of identical homogeneous things according to Anaxagoras, a multiform network of the above-mentioned according to Democritus and Leucippus, an alternation between concretion and discretion according to Empedocles, who refers to concretion as Friendship and

separationem inimicitiam vocans, vel, ut Stoici, corporum diversorum usque quaque concretionem. Quorum omnium quendam nodum concatenationemque dicit esse in minutis solidisque corpusculis, quae gomphos cognominat. Tali igitur humani corporis exaedificatione aeternae animae duos circuitus addidisse dicit deum; qui circuitus animae opera sunt, quorum alter intellegentia est, alter opinio; porro omne quod operatur sit necesse est; substantia ergo animae minime est otiosa. Undique igitur corpus humanum duabus immortalis animae circumactionibus obligatum totum atque ex omnibus regionibus vitali sustentatur vigore. Inriguum porro fluidumque corpus vocat ob praedictas egestionis et exsaturationis vices.

204. Circuitus porro, inquit, ut torrenti rapido defluoque obligati. Torrentem vocat silvam corpoream propterea quod fluere non desinat neque umquam maneat in certa et in stabili constantia nec teneatur. Animas ait corpora non tenuisse nec vero ipsas a corporibus potuisse cohiberi. Quare animae corpora non regebant? Quia nutui suo et velut refrenationi pro arbitrio corpora tunc non obsequebantur. Animae porro a corporibus demum non tenebantur, quippe cum ipsa corpora ambitu animae circumtenerentur et sine complexu eius mox dissiparentur. Sed vi ferebant, inquit, et invicem vi ferebantur: ferebantur quidem ad vitia cogente indigentia corporis, ferebant vero eadem corpora vitam salutemque isdem procurando, quod est proprium munus

discretion or separation as Strife, or a universal coalescence of diverse bodies according to the Stoics. And he says that there is a kind of bond or linking of all these in the minute and solid corpuscles that he calls *gomphoi*. Now, he says that god added the two *circuits* of the eternal soul once the human body had been so constructed, and these orbits are the functions performed by the soul, one of them being intelligence and the other opinion; but every function it performs necessarily is; thus the substance of soul is in no way otiose. The human body, then, being bound throughout by the rotations of the immortal soul, is sustained wholly and in every part by the vital power. And with an eye to the aforementioned cycles of evacuation and repletion he speaks of the *body's* being *subject to ebbs and flows*.

204. *And the circuits,* he says [43a], *being confined by this rapidly flowing torrent.* He is referring to the corporeal matter as a *torrent* on the understanding that it does not cease to flow and never remains still or restrains itself in a certain and stable state of constancy. He says that the souls *neither restrained* the bodies *nor* were themselves able to *be restrained* by them. What was the reason for the souls' not controlling the bodies? That the bodies were at that point in arbitrary disobedience of their will and the reining in, as it were. But the souls were not ultimately restrained by the bodies, since the bodies themselves were restrained within the soul's compass and would suffer immediate dissipation if deprived of its embrace. *But,* he says, *they caused movement with force and in turn suffered movement with force:* they suffered movement in that the indigence of the body drove them toward defects, but caused the very same bodies to move by procuring life and well-being for them, which is the task proper to souls.

animarum. Hoc autem utrumque non est sine violentia, quoniam nec animae voluntate propria in vitia recidebant nec corporibus placebat naturales indigentias ferre ac sustinere patienter, utpote quae naturae suae dissolutionem dissipationemque ferrent.

205. Contingebat ergo ut totum animal moveretur, praecipiti tamen et inordinata iactatione. Praeclare; neque enim quod movet sine eo quod movetur motum potest edere neque demum quod movetur sine movente, sed utrique opus est alterius praesentia. Et est, opinor, quod quidem movet anima, quod vero movetur corpus, ex quibus et animalia constant et motus eorum; et prorsus haec omnia spectant eo, ut concipiatur animae [vitae] puerilis amentia quoque modo sensus excitetur omnibus animalibus secundum naturam eorum. Sex illi motus familiares sunt: est quippe in his ignis, cuius natura summa et alta semper capessit; est etiam terrae aliquantum, quae mediam mundi sedem obtinet; est aereum quiddam et humectum, quae duo huc atque illuc late et prorsus ad omnia natura sua feruntur; quorum motuum compos est animal.

206. Mobilior porro anima puerilis et inquieta maxime quidem ob inrationabilem mentis imbecillitatem nondum ratione firmata, deinde ob nimium calorem humoremque in illa aetate abundantem, sicut ipse ait in Legibus pueros

But one way or the other, this does not obtain without an element of compulsion, for neither did the souls lapse into defects of their own volition nor did the bodies have an interest in passively enduring and withstanding the needs of nature, which of course threatened dissolution and dissipation for *their* nature.

205. It came about, therefore, *that the whole living being moved, but did so with a violent and disorderly agitation* [43a–b]. Clearly, for that which moves cannot generate movement without that which is moved, nor finally can that which is moved move without a mover, but each requires the presence of the other. And soul, I suppose, is that which moves and body that which is moved, and it is from these components that both living beings and their movements consist; and indeed, all of these observations point to the want of mental capacity in the infant soul at conception, and to the manner in which sense perception is aroused in all living beings according to their nature. The *six forms of movement* are intimately connected with them: for in living beings there is fire, the nature of which unceasingly moves toward the loftiest heights; there is as well an element of earth, which cleaves to the center of the world as its seat; there is a certain portion of air and of water, the two elements that by nature move in one direction and the other, far and wide; and these are the forms of movement over which a living being has command.

206. Moreover, the soul of a child is very changeable and particularly restless, its rational part not yet having been firmly established because of an irrational mental weakness and the excessive heat and abundant moisture associated with that age of life, as he points out in the *Laws:* children

nimio ignis luctari calore proptereaque inordinate sine iudicio improbeque omnino motus naturales in pueris celebrari.
Unde ait: Immenso quippe gurgite inrigante et immoderate
effluente, inrigante quidem cum nimio calore cito confectus
cibus resumitur saepius, effluente vero iuxta necessitatem
egestionis. Testatur Hippocrates cibo nimio recreanda esse
puerilia sanciens corpora, ne consumantur damnis egestionis. Sed adhibito cibo tenera aetas delectatur, imminuto aut
denegato dolet; ex quo fit ut voluptatem quidem amplexetur
tamquam bonum, offendatur autem dolore tamquam malo.

207. Etiam quae extrinsecus accidunt, frigus et siccitas,
asperior et durior tactus; quae omnia sensus excitant aspe-
ros, quaeque his contraria sunt iucundos et voluptarios in
tactu odoratione gustatu. Quos quidem sensus ait et initio
et nunc usque maximos et violentos motus ciere, quippe
sensus auxiliante silva nimio inordinatoque fluxu totam animam actusque eius omnes violenta concussione turbare.
Cumque sit animae pars altera sanctior diviniorque, quae
mens atque intellectus est, numquam exorbitans neque ullis
erroribus falsisque opinionibus derivabilis, huius quidem
motum cohibuerunt dominationemque eius in tota anima
compescuerunt contrarios motus agentes, ut esset quidem
intellectus in anima sed nihil ageret impedientibus sensibus.
At vero illam alteram partem animae quae est opinio perdere

struggle with the excessive heat deriving from fire, and the movements naturally obtaining in children therefore teem with an inordinate and completely unbridled deficiency of judgment. And so he says, [43b] *for although the stream flowed in and out without measure or moderation:* it flowed in in the sense that the food, being broken down rapidly by the excessive heat, is replenished at fairly frequent intervals, and flowed out according to the need for evacuation. Hippocrates confirms this in recommending that the bodies of infants be replenished by large quantities of food in order to prevent their being consumed by loss through evacuation. But the tender age of life experiences pleasure in the food offered to it and pain when the food is reduced or withheld, to the point of embracing pleasure as a good and being repelled by pain as an evil.

207. So too the things that impinge upon it *externally* [43c–d], cold and dryness, the harsher and harder form of contact; and all of these arouse harsh sensations, those contrary to them pleasing and pleasurable ones, in what we touch, smell, taste. And he says that these *sensations initially and up to now arouse the most violent commotion,* for with the support of matter, its excessive disordered flux, the senses disturb the whole of the soul and all of its activities with a violent shaking. And although one part of the soul, i.e., mind and intellect, is more holy and divine in its never going off course or being diverted by errors or false opinions of any kind, they inhibited its movement and suppressed its mastery over the whole of the soul by stirring up contrary movements, so that there was indeed intellect within the soul, but it performed no activity while the senses impeded it. At the same time, although they were unable completely to

443

quidem omnino non poterant, nam haec quoque erat praedita divina potentia nec solvi nisi ab eo solo qui conexuerat
valebat ante fatale animae corporisque diiugium, coegerunt
tamen adversum naturam suam niti atque agere actus incon-
gruos, cogentes falsis opinionibus credere.

9. Causae cur Hominum Plerique sint Sapientes, Alii Insipientes

208. Deinde admonens eorum quae in psychogonia docue-
rat medietates illas ait et analogias tamquam regione sua et
loco pulsas, quae consentaneos motus animae caelestibus
tramitibus dirigebant, illud significans, quod in pueris mens
quidem intellectusque eius omnino sit otiosus et velut
constrictus vinculis motum eius prohibentibus, ratio tamen
agat aliquid cum vel appetit quid tenera aetas vel iudicat vel
imaginatur, non recte licet, ad haec trahentibus eam sensibus atque eo genere circumscribentibus ob supra dictas
causas rerumque ignorationem. In quo etiam Aristoteles
consentit dicens initio pueros etiamnum lactentis aetatis
omnes quidem viros putare patres omnes autem feminas
matres, aetatis tamen accessu discernere et non numquam
in discretione falli, saepe etiam falsis captos imaginibus por-
rigere ad imaginem manus. Easque omnes opiniones supi-
nas vocat, cum ea quae laedunt commoda quaeque prosunt
noxia esse arbitrantur, id est cum ad voluptatem pernicio-
sam feruntur, offenduntur autem salubri labore. Quod

impair the other part, opinion, for this too was endowed with the divine potency and could not *be dissolved* prior to the fated decoupling of soul and body except *by him alone who* had bound it together, they nevertheless compelled it to struggle against its own nature and perform activities incongruent with it, that is, to trust in false opinions.

9. THE REASONS WHY A GOOD MANY HUMAN BEINGS ARE WISE AND THE REST UNWISE

208. Then, casting back to what he explained in the psychogony, he says that the means and proportions that were guiding its movements consistently with the celestial courses were, as it were, driven out of their proper region and place, his point being that, although in children the mind and its intellect may be altogether sluggish or constrained by shackles, so to speak, that prohibit its movement, yet its reason performs some activity when the tender age of life either desires something or forms a judgment or mental impression (wrong though it may be), the senses drawing it in these directions and thereby laying constraints upon it for the reasons indicated above, and because of its ignorance of things. Aristotle too expresses agreement with this observation when he says that children not yet weaned initially look upon all men as fathers and all women as mothers but with age distinguish, and that they occasionally slip, and often even reach out to one of the false impressions they have been taken in by. Plato refers to all such opinions as *inverted* [43e]: when they suppose that harmful things are beneficial and beneficial ones harmful, i.e., when they are drawn to a pernicious pleasure and repelled by a healthy

profecto numquam contingeret, nisi nimium sensibus cre-
derent, qui natura plurimum in decipiendo vigent.

209. Atque ut totam rem plane expediret, exemplo quoque utitur perspicuae claritudinis. Summa dementia est,
cum quis non solum ignoret sed id ipsum quod ignoret nesciat proptereaque falsis consentiat imaginibus quaeque
vera sunt falsa esse praesumat, ut cum malitiam quidem
prodesse virtutem vero obesse perniciemque afferre arbitrantur; quae quidem opinio usque ad novissimam aetatem
plerosque comitatur, qui facere iniuriam commodissimum,
recte damnosum putant proptereaque execrantur. Hos Aristoteles senes pueros vocat, quod mens eorum a mente puerili minime differat.

210. Exemplum quod diximus tale est: ex adverso stantes
in laeva nostra certe habemus contra stantium dextras partes, item illi similiter nostras rursumque laevas partes in
dextra. Si igitur, inquit, alter ex duobus recte et secundum
naturam stet, alter vero ita ut caput solo figat, pedes pro capite sustollat et sint ex adverso, tunc se inspicientes invicem
opinabuntur dextras partes sinistras, sinistras dextras invicem. Tale aliquid pati dicit animas quoque iuxta rerum
contemplationem inter initia et recens incorporatas. Cum
igitur ita se habebit et audiet intellegibilem esse naturam et
sine corpore quae sola vere perpetuoque eadem sit, rursum

pain. And this would certainly never occur without the excessive trust they place in the senses, which by nature thrive on deception.

209. And to bring the whole matter to a pointed conclusion, he further employs an illustration of absolute clarity. The height of foolishness is, not simply one's being ignorant, but one's being unaware of the very fact that one is ignorant and so consenting to false mental impressions, assuming things which are true to be false, as when they suppose that evil is beneficial and virtue a pernicious impediment; and indeed, the opinion stays with most people late into life, people who consider the committing of injustice a supreme benefit and acting rightly a detriment, and for that reason abhorring it. These Aristotle refers to as aged children, because their mind differs minimally from that of a child.

210. The illustration we referred to is the following: When standing across from one another we without question have the right-hand parts of those standing opposite us on our left, and they in turn similarly have our left-hand parts on their right. *If,* then, he says [43e–44a], one of two people should stand upright and as nature has it but the other *in such a way as to fix his head to the ground and raise his feet up rather than his head,* and if they should be situated across from one another, *then* while looking at one another they will form the opinion that the *right-hand parts are on the left and the left-hand ones in turn on the right.* His point is that souls newly and recently embodied have some such experience as well in their contemplation of things. Thus once the soul of a child is so disposed and hears that there is an intelligible and incorporeal nature which is uniquely, truly, and perpetually the same but that as concerns the things that

447

de his quae nascuntur et occidunt, id est de corporeis atque
sensilibus, quod fluida sint et mutabilia, opinor, tunc ad-
vocatis sensibus puerilis anima testimoniis eorum facile
credens intellegibilem quidem naturam nullam esse con-
fidit, utpote quam sensus ne somniet quidem; sola autem
sensilia pro vero certoque esse praesumit quae videri tangi
ceterisque sensibus percipi queant, itaque praesumens non,
opinor, mentis intellectusque compos erit. Ideoque addidit:
nec habet ullum certum ducem talis peragratio. Neque enim
intellectus ducem se praebet ceteris animae partibus, ut si
quis sit tunc otiosus, neque illa alia pars animae, in qua sunt
opinationes, quam subegerint atque in servitium redegerint
sensus usque adeo ut cum serviat dominari se putet et aliquid ex pristino splendore ac dignitate retinere.

211. Ac ne quis eum putaret de anima cuiuslibet animalis
haec dicere, addidit: crescente vero homine postquam incrementi nutricationisque tenui iam rivo meatus effluet animaeque circuitus tranquilliore motu viam suam peragent
processuque temporis sedatiores erunt. Merito; fit enim
melior in dies quanto fit perfectior et in cognitione rerum
exercitatior; tunc quippe nuntii sensus minoris erunt auctoritatis minorisque apud animam fidei deprehensa fallendi
consuetudine. Maxime si sit studiis, inquit, elegantioribus
erudita, immunis omni perturbatione atque aegritudine de-
get aevum; si negleget, claudum iter vitae serpens cum familiari demum stultitia revocabitur ad inferna. Consequenter

are born and die, i.e., corporeals and sensibles, they are in flux and mutable, then, I suppose, by summoning the senses and trusting naively in their testimony it confidently concludes that there is no intelligible nature, which of course sense perception does not even dream of; and in presuming as true and certain the existence only of sensibles that can be seen, touched, and perceived by the other senses it will not, I suppose, be in command of its mind and intellect. And so he added, *without having any sure guide.* For neither does the intellect prove itself for the other parts of the soul a leader, one that just happens at that moment to be inactive, nor does that other part of the soul in which opinions are formed do so: the senses have driven and reduced it to such a state of servitude that despite its *subservience* it *thinks* it rules and *retains* something of its original splendor and dignity.

211. And so that no one should suppose that these remarks of his have concerned the soul of just any animal, he added [44b–c]: but as the human being grows, and *once the current of increase and nourishment flows in what becomes a light stream, and the circuits of the soul complete their journey in a more tranquil movement and with the passage of time prove more sedate.* Rightly so, for the human soul improves with each day as it becomes more complete and more skilled in its understanding of things; for once their habit of deceiving has been detected, the senses will have less sway as messengers and command less credence from the soul. Above all, he says, if the soul is educated in the more refined studies *then it will live its life immune to all disturbance and disease; but if it is negligent then it will ultimately be summoned back to the infernal regions for creeping in habitual foolishness along the crippled path of its life.* This is a consistent inference, for it makes the human

449

<sibi;> namque [sibi] hominem componit ex anima et corpore. Quotus quisque igitur utrumque curabit, erit incolumis et fortis, qui neutrum, mancus et debilis, qui alterum ex duobus, claudus. <Quod> ergo indocilis et corpori tantum diligentiam impertiens claudam habebit vitam, procul dubio, claudam quoque etiam illius animam fore cuius rectae quidem sint opiniones sed nequaquam sacris intellegibilium arcanorum sit initiatus.

212. Simul quia de totius hominis constitutione disseruit integre per partes, nunc membratim, sicut in mundani corporis constitutione fecerat, utilitatem cuiusque membri revelat causasque reddit visus nostri et auditus. Sensuum quoque utilitatem persequitur et eorum membrorum quae sensum adiuvant. Dicit etiam de memoria, dicit de somniis. Eorum quoque causas reddit quae in speculis simulacra cernuntur et eorum omnium causas rationesque subdividit. Demonstrat etiam quae principales causae sint, quae item principalibus accidant, quae item sint ipsa quidem immobilia, moveant tamen alia, quae demum ab his ipsis moventur ex aliqua necessitate quaeque cum ratione movent ad effectum rei utilis alicuius, quaeque sine ratione et ut libet.

213. Orditur denique a capite, quam partem corporis principali quadam esse eminentia dicit proptereaque oportuisse in excelso atque eminenti loco tamquam arcem totius corporis collocari, ut domicilium esset partis animae principalis, quod hegemonicon a philosophis dicitur, id est ratio.

being a composite of soul and body. To the extent, then, that he attends to both, each individual will be unharmed and strong, whereas he who attends to neither will be maimed and feeble, and he who attends to one of the two will be *crippled*. That the one who resists instruction and devotes his attention only to the body will have a *crippled life* is therefore beyond doubt, and also, that the soul of the one who possesses right opinions but is completely uninitiated in the sacred rites of the intelligible mysteries will be *crippled*.

212. At the same time, since he has treated of the constitution of the human being in its entirety, *across its parts* [44c], he now reveals the utility of each and every member, one at a time, as he did in connection with the constitution of the world body, and explains the *reasons* for our having sight and hearing. He treats of the utility of the senses too, and of the organs that support sense perception. He speaks also of memory and of dreams. And he explains the causes of the images seen in mirrors, and subdivides the causes and reasons for them all. He demonstrates as well which are the principal causes and which the ones incidental to them, and which are the things which despite being immobile themselves nevertheless move others, and finally, which ones are by these very things moved according to some necessity, which move with reason for purposes of effecting something useful, and which do so without reason and as chance has it.

213. He begins with the *head* [44d–e], the part of the body which he says is characterized by *a certain* principal *preeminence* and had to be situated in a high and prominent place as the *citadel,* so to speak, of the whole body in order to serve as the domicile of the principal part of the soul, which is called the *hêgemonikon* by the philosophers, i.e., its reason. And its

Cuius duplex virtus, altera intellegens opinatrix altera, iuxta quas sapientia cum disciplina et item prudentia cum rectis opinionibus convalescunt. Quas duas divinas circumactiones animae idem auctor appellat iuxtaque eas divinas potestates quae fingebant corpora hominum ad similitudinem mundani corporis formasse dicit caput rotundum et globosum eique ita informato conexuisse rationabilem motum, qui rationabilis motus principalis animae potestas est; proptereaque principalem animae potestatem asserit in capite sedes habere.

214. Sed quoniam de hoc diversae opiniones philosophorum tam veterum quam novorum extiterunt, recensendae nobis singulae sunt, ut habita comparatione quanto ceteris ad veritatem praestet Platonis fiat palam. Qui dividuam fore silvae substantiam censuerunt interponentes immenso inani modo expertia modo partes quidem sed indifferentes sui similes tum atomos vel solidas moles, nullum locum certum definitumque principali animae parti dederunt. Spiritus quippe, ut ipsi asseverant, per fauces ad pulmonem commeans in respiratione attenuatus ad cordis sedem facit transitum, deinde per arterias quae sunt a corde porrectae pervenit ad caroticas ita appellatas venas, quod eaedem vulneratae mortem afferant soporiferam; per quas idem spiritus ad caput fertur per tenues neruorum et angustos meatus, atque ibi primum nasci dicunt initium sentiendi et intermanare ad ceterum corpus. Isque communis sensus est tactus,

faculty is twofold, one being engaged in intelligence and the other in opinion, and in accordance with these, wisdom acquires strength by being combined with education and prudence does so by being combined with right opinions. And our author refers to these as the *two* divine *circumlations* of the soul and says that in conformity with them the *divine powers* that fashioned human bodies formed the head round *and spherical* in imitation of the world body and *bound* rational movement to it once it was thus formed, which rational movement is the principal power of soul; and these are the reasons for his asserting that the principal power of the soul has its *seat* in the head.

214. But since the opinions of ancient as well as recent philosophers have differed on this point, we should go through them individually, so that through comparison the degree to which Plato's outstrips the others in truth may be made clear. Whether they situated partless entities, or indeed [entities with] parts but ones indistinct from and similar to one another, or atoms, or solid masses in the immense void, those who held that the substance of matter is discrete allowed no certain or definite place for the principal part of the soul. For breath, as they themselves asseverate, flowing through the jaws to the lung and becoming attenuated in the course of respiration, makes its way to the seat of the heart then passes through the arteries extending out from the heart to the carotid veins, so called because of their occasioning a soporific death when opened. Through the latter the same spirit moves to the head by way of the slender and narrow passages of the nerves, and they claim that there the initial process of sensation first arises and flows throughout the rest of the body. And the form of sensation common

sed fit proprius ob diversitatem membrorum quibus sentimus. Qualia enim fuerint organa sentiendi, talis sensus existit, ut per oculos visus, auditus per aures, atque in eundem
modum ceteri; unus tamen est spiritus, qui in multis defor-
matur.

215. Aut enim moles quaedam sunt leves et globosae eae-
demque admodum delicatae ex quibus anima subsistit, quod
totum spiritus est, ut Asclepiades putat; aut ignitae atomi
iuxta Democritum, qui ex isdem corporibus et ignem et animam censet excudi; vel id ipsum atomi casu quodam et sine
ratione concurrentes in unum et animam creantes, ut Epicuro placet, ob similitudinem atomorum, quarum una commota omnem spiritum, id est animam, moveri simul. Unde
plerumque audita nive candorem simul et frigus homines
recordari, vel cum quis edit acerba quaedam qui hoc vident
assidue spuunt incremento salivae, et cum oscitantibus simul oscitant alii, inque consonis rhythmis moveri nos iuxta
sonos.

216. Quae cum ita sint, quaerunt qui magis capite quam
pedibus sapiamus, quando scientiae disciplinaeque assiduo
sensus exercitio corroborentur prudentiaeque initium ex
aliquo temperamento orsum usuque assiduo promotum
perveniat ad perfectionem, dum frequens obseruatio rudimenta creat, rudimenta item artem, quae tempore atque usu

throughout is touch, although it is differentiated because of the diverse range of bodily members by means of which we engage in sensation; for the form of sensation is a function of the organs of sense perception, e.g., vision as through the eyes, hearing as through the ears, and so on for the rest, and yet the spirit that takes on different forms across many such organs is one.

215. For either certain smooth, spherical, and at the same time extremely fine molecules are the things of which soul consists, which taken as a whole is breath, as Asclepiades supposes; or fiery atoms are, as according to Democritus, who holds that both fire and soul are forged from these same bodies; or, as Epicurus thinks, atoms pure and simple are, in their colliding by a certain patternless chance and into unity and creating soul on account of the likeness between them, whereby if one of them moves the breath as a whole, i.e., soul, moves simultaneously. So it happens that when snow is mentioned people are in most cases put in mind of a combination of whiteness and cold, or that when someone eats something bitter onlookers generally spit because of an increase in their saliva, and that as one group yawns others do so simultaneously, and that in experiencing consonant rhythms we move in time with the sounds.

216. In light of these considerations they ask how we think with the head rather than feet, when the scientific disciplines are strengthened through the assiduous exercise of sense perception, and the starting point for wisdom, arising out of a certain temperament and developing through assiduous use, attains perfection through frequent observation's engendering the rudiments and the rudiments in turn engendering technical skill, which once confirmed through

confirmata fit disciplina. Idem negant principalem animae vim consistere in capite propterea quod pleraque animalia capite secto vivant ad tempus et agant solita tamquam nullo damno allato corporis universitati, ut apes et item fuci, quae licet capitibus abscisis ad momentum vivunt et volant aculeisque secundum naturam suam se defendunt. quae non facerent, si in capite consisteret quod est in anima principale. <Illud> etiam in corde negant, crocodilos enim avulsis cordibus aliquamdiu vivere et resistere adversum violentiam, hoc idem etiam in testudinibus observatum marinis et terrestribus capris.

217. Adversum quae respondetur ab aliis nihil esse mirum, si, cum initia et quasi quaedam fundamenta dogmatis imbecilla et minus idonea iacta sint, totum eorum dogma nutet. Quae est enim eorum de anima opinio? Nempe quod ex minutis corpusculis constet. Ergo corpus initium est animae et erit animae propria nulla substantia sed potius corporis; corpus enim animam creat iuxta ipsos vitamque animae. Contingit ergo secundum hanc eorum opinionem ut numquam sit eadem anima sed diversa habeatur atque mutabilis. Cum enim dicant corpus esse antiquius anima, dant corpori principatum. Id porro semper fluit atque immutatur; et anima igitur, quae secundae condicionis est, eadem patietur quae corpus; mutabitur ergo tempore et senio, ceteris item, quae fert natura corporis, attemptabitur. Atque ita male fundata sententia honestum invenire non potest exitum.

prolonged use becomes a discipline. They say in addition that the principal power of the soul is not in the head, on the grounds that when the head has been cut off many animals live for a time and perform their usual functions as though no loss had been inflicted upon the integrity of the body as a whole, as in the case of bees and drones, which despite their heads having been cut off live momentarily and fly and defend themselves with their stings in accordance with their nature; but they would not do these things if that which is the principal element in the soul were in the head. They say that it is not in the heart either, pointing out that when their hearts have been torn out crocodiles live for a while and resist attack, and that this same phenomenon is observable also in the turtles in the sea and goats on land.

217. Against these points it is argued by others that it is unsurprising if their doctrine as a whole falters once its first principles and, as it were, foundations have been rejected as weak and inapposite. For what is their opinion concerning the soul? Why, clearly, that it consists of minute corpuscles. Body, then, is the first principle of soul and of soul there will be no proper substance but instead there will be one of body, for on their own view body gives rise to soul and its life. According to this opinion of theirs, then, it turns out that the soul is never the same but is held to be differentiated and mutable. For in claiming that the body is prior to the soul they hand the primacy over to body. Moreover, the body is always in flux and changing; thus the soul too, being of a secondary condition, will suffer the same things as the body does; hence it will change over time and be assailed by a debilitating old age and other conditions which the body naturally endures. And so their poorly founded opinion is incapable of reaching a worthy conclusion.

218. At vero ex illis qui iugem putant esse silvam et aduna-
tione quadam sibi continuatam Empedocles quidem principalem animae vim constituit in corde sic dicens:

Sanguine cordis enim noster viget intellectus,

siquidem intimis sensibus nostris sentiamus ea quae sunt
extra nos propter cognationem. Ideoque ait:

Terram terreno sentimus, at aethera flammis,
humorem humecto, nostro spirabile flatu.

Sed de his omnibus, qualia sint quantamve inter se habeant
differentiam, cordis sanguine diiudicamus.

219. Hebraei quoque videntur secundum hunc opinari de
animae principali cum dicunt, "clamat a[pu]d me sanguis
fratris tui" et item alio loco "non edetis carnem cum sanguine quia" omnium animalium "sanguis anima est." Quae si
ita intelleguntur ut debent, animam esse animalium sanguinem, quia sit vehiculum inrationabilis animae cuius partes
sunt importuni appetitus, habet plane rationem talis assertio. Si autem confitentur animam hominis rationabilem
fore, credant sibi quod deus a se hominibus factis "inspira-
verit" divinum "spiritum" quo ratiocinamur quoque intelle-
gimus et quo veneramur pie deum estque nobis cum divinitate cognatio "diique" esse dicimur "et filii" summi "dei."
Quam cognationem cum deo et omnino rationem qua

218. But among those who hold that matter is uninterrupted and made continuous with itself by a certain principle of unity, Empedocles placed the principal power of the soul in the heart, with the following words:

For our understanding thrives on the blood of the heart

—assuming that by our internal senses we perceive, because of their affinity, the things that are external to us. And so he says:

Earth we perceive by what is earthy, ether by flames,
the humid by what is damp, breathable air by the wind in us.

But by the blood of the heart we distinguish what sort of things these all are and the degree of difference between them.

219. The Hebrews too evidently follow his opinion concerning the principal element of the soul, when they say, "the blood of your brother cries out to me," and in other passages, "you will not eat flesh with blood, for" in all animals "blood is the soul." And if these words are understood as they ought to be, such that soul in animals is the blood *qua* vehicle of the *irrational* soul, whose parts are its relentless desires, then such an assertion makes perfectly good sense. But if they confess to the human soul's being rational, then they should believe their own claim, that after having made human beings God "breathed" into them his divine "breath," by which we employ reason and intellect, and by which we piously venerate God and possess a natural affinity with his divinity and are said to be "gods and sons of" the highest "god." And to suppose that this natural affinity with

ratiocinamur sanguinem putare esse non recte opinantis est. Quae omnia nobis adversum Empedoclea quoque dicta sint.

220. Stoici vero cor quidem sedem esse principalis animae partis consentiunt nec tamen sanguinem qui cum corpore nascitur. Spiritum quippe Zeno quaerit hactenus: Quo recedente a corpore moritur animal, hoc certe anima est; naturali porro spiritu recedente moritur animal, naturalis igitur spiritus anima est. Item Chrysippus: una et eadem, inquit, certe re spiramus et vivimus; spiramus autem naturali spiritu, ergo etiam vivimus eodem spiritu; vivimus autem anima, naturalis igitur spiritus anima esse invenitur. Haec igitur, inquit, octo in partes divisa invenitur; constat enim e principali et quinque sensibus, etiam vocali substantia et serendi procreandique potentia. Porro partes animae velut ex capite fontis cordis sede manantes per universum corpus porriguntur omniaque membra usque quaque vitali spiritu complent, reguntque et moderantur innumerabilibus diversisque virtutibus, nutriendo, adolendo, movendo motibus localibus, instruendo sensibus, compellendo ad operandum. Totaque anima sensus, qui sunt eius officia, velut ramos ex principali parte illa tamquam trabe pandit futuros eorum quae sentiunt nuntios; ipsa de his quae nuntiaverint iudicat ut rex. Ea porro quae sentiuntur composita sunt utpote corpora singulique item sensus unum quiddam

god and the rational capacity in general by which we employ reason are *blood* is the mark of one who forms his opinions incorrectly. And all that we have said should hold also as against Empedocles.

220. By contrast, the Stoics agree that the heart is the seat of the principal part of the soul, but not that blood is, which comes into being along with the body. Indeed, Zeno raises the question of breath, in this way: that thing on the occasion of whose departure from the body the living being dies is without doubt soul; but when the natural breath departs, the living being dies; therefore, the soul is natural breath. Likewise, Chrysippus. Without doubt, he says, we breathe and live by virtue of one and the same thing; but we breathe by virtue of the natural breath and so live by virtue of the same breath as well; but we live by virtue of soul; therefore, the soul is found to be natural breath. Consequently, he says, the latter is found to be divided into eight parts. For it consists of the principal one and the five senses, also the substance associated with vocal sound, and the potency for sowing and procreating. Now, the parts of the soul, flowing from the seat of the heart as from a fountainhead, extend throughout the whole body and fill all its parts in every quarter with the vital breath; they regulate and control them with innumerable and diverse powers: nourishment, growth, locomotion, sensory equipment, and the impulse to action. And the soul as a whole deploys the senses, which are its functional organs, like branches extending out from the principal part or trunk, as it were, to serve as messengers of the things they sense; it for its part passes judgment, like a king, on what they have reported. And the things perceived by sense are composite, being bodies, and the senses

461

sentiunt, hic colores, sonos alius, ast ille sucorum sapores discernit, hic vapores odoraminum, ille asperum levigatio- nemque tactu; atque haec omnia ad praesens, neque enim praeteritorum meminit sensus ullus nec suspicatur futura. Intimae vero deliberationis et considerationis proprium cuiusque sensus intellegere passionem et ex his quae nun- tiant colligere quid sit illud et praesens quidem accipere, absentis autem meminisse, futurum item providere. Definit idem intimam mentis deliberationem sic: intimus est motus animae vis rationabilis. Habent quippe etiam muta vim animae principalem, qua discernunt cibos, imaginantur, de- clinant insidias, praerupta et praecipitia supersiliunt, neces- situdinem recognoscunt, non tamen rationabilem, quin po- tius naturalem; solus vero homo ex mortalibus principali mentis bono, hoc est ratione, utitur, ut ait idem Chrysippus: sicut aranea in medietate cassis omnia filorum tenet pedi- bus exordia, ut, cum quid ex bestiolis plagas incurrerit ex quacumque parte, de proximo sentiat sic animae principale positum in media sede cordis sensuum exordia retinere, ut, cum quid nuntiabunt, de proximo recognoscat. Vocem quo- que dicunt e penetrali pectoris, id est corde, mitti, gremio cordis nitente spiritu qua nervis obsitus limes interiectus cor a pulmone secernit utroque et vitalibus ceteris; quo faucium angustias arietante formanteque lingua et ceteris

likewise perceive singly one determinate thing: this one discerns colors, another sounds, that one the flavors carried by juices, this one the vapors that convey smells, that one what is harsh or smooth to the touch; and all of these pertain to the present, for no sense recalls past things or augurs future ones. And the defining property of inner deliberation and consideration is to understand what each and every sense passively experiences, and on the basis of what they report to infer what the thing is, and to accept it as present, remember it as absent, or foresee it as future. And he defines the mind's inner deliberation as follows: the inner movement of the soul is its rational power. To be sure, dumb creatures too have a principal power of soul by means of which they discern their sources of nourishment, form mental images, avoid hidden dangers, leap over precipitous drops, and acknowledge that which they have need of; they have no rational power, however, but rather a natural one: among mortal beings man alone enjoys the use of the principal good of mind, i.e., reason, as Chrysippus says: as a spider at the center of the web holds on to all of the outermost points with its legs so that it may sense immediately whenever some tiny creature is intercepted at any point, so the soul's principal part situated at the center of the seat of the heart keeps hold of the outermost points of the senses so that whenever they report something it may acknowledge it. They say that the voice too is emitted from the innermost part of the chest, i.e., the heart, the breath forcing its way out from the interior hollow of the heart where a barrier enveloped by sinews is interjected and separates the heart from the two lungs and other vital organs; and as the breath strikes against the narrow passageways of the jaws, with the tongue and other

vocalibus organis articulatos edi sonos, sermonis elementa, quo quidem interprete mentis arcani motus aperiantur. Id porro principale animae vocat.

221. Ergo spiritum animam esse dicentes corpus esse animam plane fatentur. Quod si ita est, corpus corpori sociatum est; societas porro vel ex applicatione fit vel ex permixtione vel ex concretione. Si applicita sint corpus et anima, quid ex applicatione compositum horum duum, quatenus totum erit vivum? Vita enim secundum ipsos in solo spiritu, qui applicitus non permanat ad corpus intimum (nihil enim penetrat applicitum); et totum animal vivere aiunt: non igitur anima et corpus applicatione sociantur. Si vero permixta sunt, anima unum aliquid non erit, sed permixta multa; Stoici spiritum, id est animam, unum quid esse profitentur: non ergo permixta sunt. Superest ut ex concretione manent; ergo et per se invicem transeunt duo corpora et locus unus quo corpus continetur duobus corporibus praebebit capacitatem—cum vas quod aquam recipit vinum et aquam simul capere non possit. Neque igitur ex applicatione neque permixtione neque vero concretione corpus et anima sociantur; ex quo confit animam non esse corpus. Est igitur virtus et potentia carens corpore, quodque est in ea principale competentem naturae suae sedem habeat necesse est.

222. At vero Aristoteles animam definit hactenus: "Anima est prima perfectio corporis naturalis organici possibilitate vitam habentis," "perfectionem" nunc appellans specialem

vocal organs giving form to the process, articulate sounds, the elements of speech, are brought forth so as to reveal through their function as interpreter the mind's arcane movements. And he calls it the principal part of the soul.

221. In claiming, then, that the soul is breath they plainly maintain that the soul is a body. But if it is so, then body is associated with body; and the association arises out of juxtaposition, intermixture, or aggregation. If body and soul are juxtaposed, then what is the composite resulting from the juxtaposition of these two things such that the whole will have life? For on their own view life is in the breath alone, which, if juxtaposed, does not flow through to the innermost body, since nothing penetrates by being juxtaposed; and they claim that the whole body has life: therefore soul and body are not associated through juxtaposition. If, on the other hand, they are intermixed, then the soul will not be a determinate unity but a number of things intermixed; the Stoics profess that breath, i.e., soul, is a determinate unity: thus they are not intermixed. It remains that they derive from aggregation; in which case the two bodies will pass through one another and the one place in which a body is contained will have the capacity for *two* bodies—even though a vessel holding water cannot receive wine *and* the water together. Therefore body and soul are not associated by virtue of juxtaposition, intermixture, or aggregation; and so it turns out that the soul is not a body. It is, then, an incorporeal power and potency, and the principal element in it must needs have a seat analogous to its nature.

222. Aristotle for his part defines the soul as follows: "Soul is the first perfection of a natural body possessed of organs and having the capacity for life," indicating here by

essentiam quae est in effigie. Essentia enim trifariam intellegitur: una quae constat ex corpore, velut animalia vel quae
arte fiunt, essentia dicta, quia haec ipsa est et cetera quae
sunt facit esse; altera qua materiam informem et adhuc silvam mente consideramus, haec quippe possibilitate omnia
est quae ex se fieri possunt, effectu autem nondum quicquam, ut massa aeris et intractata ligna; tertia cui accidens
effectus perficit eam exornatque impressione formae, ex
qua forma, quam insignivit ars, id quod perfectum est nomen accepit, ut statua, quae ex similitudine formae cuius est
statua simulacrum vocatur. Similiter, inquit, homo animal
certe est et est ut silvestris et materialis essentia, et haec
composita ex materia formaque, quippe ex corpore constat
et anima; ergo corpus eius materia est, anima vero species
sive forma, iuxta quam speciem, id est animam, animal est
cognominatum. Hanc ergo speciem qua formantur singula
generaliter Aristoteles "entelechiam," id est absolutam "perfectionem," vocat, hac enim obveniente silvae quae olim
fuerant in sola possibilitate perveniunt ad effectum. Item
quod vivit duplex est, anima et corpus, opinor. Ut quae discuntur duabus rebus sociantur, doctrina et anima, sed
"prius" doctrina qua ipsa anima eruditur; item salvi sumus
salute et corpore sed "prius" salute per quam corpus incolume est: sic etiam vivimus prius anima quam corpore

"perfection" the specific substance that is in the form. For substance is understood in three ways: first, that which consists of body, as in the case of living beings or things produced by art, and called substance [*essentia*] because it in itself is [*est*] and causes other things that are to be [*esse*]; second, that in virtue of which we mentally conceive of a material that is formless or still matter, for this is potentially all of the things that are capable of being made from it but not yet any of them actually, as in the case of a mass of bronze or untreated wood; and third, that to which an actuality by its accession brings perfection or brings it order through the impression of a form, from which form, as impressed by an art, the thing brought to perfection takes its name, as in the case of a statue, which is called a likeness [*simulacrum*] in virtue of its formal similitude to the object of which it is the statue. Similarly, he says, man is certainly an animal, and is so as a material substance, and this as composed of matter and form, inasmuch as it consists of body and soul; the body, then, is its matter and the soul its specific form, and in respect of this form, i.e., the soul [*anima*], it is called an *animal*. Thus Aristotle refers in a general way to the form by which singular entities receive form as an "*entelechy*," i.e., an absolute "*perfection*," for it is by its coming to matter that things which were previously in a state of mere potentiality attain actuality. Again, that which lives is, I suppose, twofold, soul and body. And just as that which is learned is a combination of two things, knowledge and the soul, but "*first*" is the knowledge in which the soul is actually instructed; and just we are healthy owing to health and the body, but "first" is the health by which the body is sound: so too our living is a function of soul before body (for the life of

(siquidem vita corporis in anima locata est) proptereaque anima "entelechia" est "corporis." Quodque corpora partim dicuntur mathematica (ut sphaera et cubus), partim artificiosa (ut navis et statua), pleraque naturalia (quae motus originem intra se habent, vita videlicet utentia), "naturalis" anima "corporis entelechia" sit necesse est. Competit alia etiam divisio, nam corporum quaedam simplicia, ut elementa, quaedam composita, ut quae ex simplicibus coagmentantur; compositorum partim "organica" nuncupantur, partim sine nomine, ut aurum, aes, gemmae, cetera immobili natura minime organica. Animalium vero et stirpium et omnino qualiumcumque vita utentium organica sunt; quippe modulata et habent membrorum per quae agant aliquid aut patiantur opportunitatem, ut ad sumendos cibos et generandam prolem paris eiusdemque naturae, tum ad sentiendum et translativum ex loco ad locum motum, ut cuncta gradientia, tum ad faciendum impetum iuxta desideria et appetitus, ut animalium quae sunt firmiora. Ex quibus concludit Aristoteles "entelechiam" animam esse "corporis naturalis organici." Tale porro est quod corpus recipere oportet, et est, inquit, nam sunt quaedam sola possibilitate animalia, ut ova vel semina, quaedam cum effectu et operatione, ut quae adhibito fotu: ex isdem excuduntur animalia. Ex quo apparet entelechiam fore animam non cuiuslibet

the body is within the domain of soul), and soul is the "entel-echy *of a body*" in that sense. And insofar as bodies are said to be either mathematical (e.g., a sphere or cube), artificial (e.g., a ship or statue), or, as in most cases, natural (which have the first beginnings of movement within themselves, namely, by their partaking of life), soul necessarily is the "en-telechy of a *natural* body." A further division also applies, for of bodies some are simple, as with the elements, and others composite, as with those that are composed of simple ones; of the composite ones, some come under the heading "or-ganic," while others have no named heading, as in the case of gold, bronze, gems, and other things which, being mo-tionless by nature, are nonorganic. And the organic ones are those that pertain to animals, plants, and, in general, any-thing that partakes of life; indeed, in being harmoniously at-tuned they also have the use of bodily members through which they perform something or undergo change, e.g., for purposes of ingesting food or generating offspring of like or identical nature, in some cases for sensing and transitive movement from place to place, as with all of those that walk, and in others for producing an impulse according to their desires and appetites, as with those possessed by animals of higher capacity. And from these points Aristotle concludes that soul is the "entelechy of a natural body *possessed of or-gans*." Of such a sort, moreover, is that which is suited to re-ceive body, and such, he says, is it, for some living beings are possessed of mere potentiality, as in the case of eggs or seeds, while others are in act and possessed of an actuality, as in the case of those that have been exposed to warmth: from these things living beings are shaped. And from this it is clear that the soul is the entelechy, not of just any body,

corporis sed eius quod potest animam sumere, iuxta eiusdem vivere patrocinium, motusque vitales exercere in
agendo, vitae quoque passiones experiri; proptereaque defi-
nitioni additum "possibilitate vitam habentis."

223. Et definitio quidem animae Peripateticis auctoribus
talis est. Quae tamen ex ea confiunt, manifestant principio
animam neque corporeum quicquam esse vel sensile sed intellegibile potius et sine corpore, quae tamen recipiatur a
corpore, quippe corpori perfectionem det ipsa sitque eius
entelechia, res per semet ipsam immobilis, sicut sunt artes
et disciplinae, ex accidenti vero aliquo mobilis propterea
quod sit in animalibus quae, dum vivunt, moventur. Dum
enim naturales motus edit anima, moventur animalia, vel
cum agunt aliquid vel cum patiuntur. Quae cum sit intellegibilis et sine corpore, consequenter etiam sine quantitate
esse invenitur, quippe cuius neque prolixitas ulla neque latitudo nec profunditas extet, non enim est ut linea vel superficies nec vero figuram habet ullam nec est dividua, ut quae
constant ex partibus; dividitur tamen alio quodam genere,
sic ut ex eadem divisione non magis partes eius ullae quam
virtutes et potentiae considerentur. Nec vero species eius
ullae sunt, ut generis alicuius species dici solet, ut rhetoricae
disciplinae, quae est intellegibilis res et sine corpore, species
tamen eius esse dicitur ea oratio quae facta est ad doctrinae
ostentationem et item species contionabilis vel species orationis forensis. Sic ergo, cum anima quoque res sit sine corpore et sine magnitudine, nihil interest dicere partes animae

but of one that is capable of receiving soul, of living under its protection, of exercising the vital movements in the course of its activity, and of undergoing the passive experiences associated with living; hence the addition to the definition, *"and having the capacity for life."*

223. And such is the definition of the soul among the Peripatetic authorities. The considerations that result from it, however, make manifest from the start that soul is not anything corporeal or sensible but rather something intelligible and incorporeal; it is however received by body, since it confers perfection on the body and is its entelechy: a thing immobile in itself, as are the arts and sciences, but mobile in a particular incidental sense insofar as it is situated in living beings which are in movement for as long as they are alive. For, so long as the soul produces the movements natural to them, living beings move in some sense either active or passive. And since it is intelligible and incorporeal, it is consequently found to be without quantity as well, since with it there is no length, width, or depth; for it is not comparable to a line or plane surface, and neither does it have any shape, nor is it divisible as things that consist of parts are; and yet it is divisible in a different way, such that from the division in question not so much any of its parts as its faculties and powers are brought under consideration. Nor are there any species of it in the usual sense according to which there are said to be species of some genus, as in the case of the discipline of rhetoric, which is an intelligible thing and incorporeal and yet the form of speech fashioned for the display of learning is said to be a species of it, likewise speech for public assemblies or law courts—both species. In this way, then, since the soul too is incorporeal and without magnitude,

471

et item potentias animae, vel cum dividimus eam, cum sit illa naturae individuae, in speciem naturalem, iuxta quam nutritur omne animal et crescit et subolem creat, vel in speciem sensilem, iuxta quam differunt inter se quae animam habent et item quae sola vita fruuntur, id est animalia et stirpes, item in eam speciem quae locum ex loco mutat, ut serpentia omnia vel quae habent appetitum qui in perfectioribus invenitur animalibus, in quibus est cupiditas et iracundia, et item in eam speciem, quae est perfectior ceteris, ratione utentium, quae in natura hominis tantum invenitur.

224. Est igitur tota, inquit, anima in totis partibus viventis animalis. Et naturalis quidem eius species per omne se dividit corpus, sensus vero tactus quidem per omne corpus, visus autem vel auditus et ceteri in ceteris membris quae sunt organa sentiendi. Principalis vero animae pars sive potentia, ad quam feruntur quae nuntiant sensus singuli et quae de his quae sentiuntur iudicium facit examinatque, cuius modi sint ea quae occurrunt sensibus varie, hanc vero Aristoteles asserit locatam esse in penetralibus cordis, ubi aliae quoque species animae sunt locatae, id est imaginatio memoria appetitus excursio. Quippe omnium animae virium initia et quasi quaedam radices e sede cordis emanant, quando confecti cibi sucus per venas cordis ceterum corpus

there is no difference between speaking of the soul's parts or powers, or when we divide it, even though it is of an indivisible nature, into a natural species according to which each living being draws nourishment and grows and generates offspring, or into a sentient species according to which things that possess souls and those that benefit from the mere capacity for life, i.e., animals and plants, differ from one another, similarly, into a species that shifts from place to place, as with all things that creep or have the appetitive impulse found in higher-order animals in which there is desire and irascibility, and again, into a species that is of a higher order than the rest, belonging to the beings that employ reason, which is found only in the nature associated with man.

224. The soul, then, he says, is wholly present in all parts of the living animal. That is, whereas the natural form of the soul is distributed throughout the whole body, in the case of sensation although touch is distributed throughout the whole body, vision, hearing, and so on are confined to the various parts that serve as their sense organs. But the principal part or power of the soul, to which are conveyed the messages sent by the separate sense faculties, also what judgment makes of and examines in the sense impressions, among which are included the things that variously present themselves to the senses—Aristotle asserts that *this* part is located within the innermost part of the heart, where other forms of soul are located as well, i.e., imagination, memory, appetite, the outwardly directed impulse. To be sure, the first beginnings and, as it were, roots of all of the soul's faculties emanate from the seat of the heart, in that the juice extracted from digested food irrigates the whole body as it

inrigat et motus corporeus, qui locularis est, a corde initium sumit; namque venarum et nervorum initium et quidam nodus ipsum cor est, iuxta quod intellectus agitatus et rationabiliter ignitus ibidem coacervare se creditur, possibilitate quidem illic habitans, effectu vero extra conseptum cordis atque viciniam commeans. Haec et multa alia huius modi probationum genera asseruntur a supra memorato viro ad probandum quod principalis animae vis in corde sit; quae usque adeo sit animantium propria ut cetera ex vitalibus vim pulsusque patiantur sine animantis interitu, cordis vero sedem ne minimas quidem pulsationes sine interitu animalium sustinere. (Quod si quis nominis praesumptione inductus cardiacam passionem dicat frequenter esse curatam, errat in nomine, quippe cum constet illam passionem non cordis esse sed stomachi.)

225. Adversum quae ita respondetur: Alia quidem fere omnia recte et prout fert natura rerum Platonicisque dogmatibus consentanee dicta sed de animae substantia erratum videri. Non enim specialem essentiam fore animam quam appellat Aristoteles entelechiam, haec quippe forma est corporibus accidens [ut censet Plato] quam hic specialem essentiam nuncupat et est, <ut censet Plato,> imago speciei purae a corpore et intellegibilis, penes quam est dignitas exemplaris. Igitur iuxta hanc formam qua formantur corpora nomina esse imposita rebus verum est, animam tamen esse formabilem hanc speciem nemo ei concedit; hoc quippe formabile fit <corporibus nascentibus> et

passes through the veins originating in the heart, and the body's movement, which is associated with place, originates in the heart. For the heart itself is the point of origin, a sort of node, for the veins and nerves; and the intellect is believed to concentrate itself in proximity to it, being stirred and ignited there by reason, residing there potentially but in act straying beyond the confines and vicinity of the heart. These and many other sorts of related proofs are asserted by the above-mentioned philosopher in order to prove that the principal power of the soul is in the heart; and it is proper to living beings to such an extent that the other vital parts undergo violent shocks without the destruction of the living being but the seat of the heart tolerates not even the slightest shocks without the destruction of the living beings. (If, however, without thinking about the word one is induced to say that a "cardiac" condition is generally curable, his usage is incorrect, in that the condition in question pertains, not to the heart, but to the stomach.)

225. The response to which is as follows. Nearly all other points are indeed correctly articulated, precisely as the nature of things has them and in agreement with the Platonic doctrines, but as concerns the substance of the soul there is evidently an error. For the soul is not the formal essence that Aristotle refers to as an entelechy: the particular form which he calls a formal essence is incidental to bodies and is, as Plato holds, an image of form that is purely incorporeal and intelligible, which possesses the dignified status of an exemplar. It is true, then, that names are imposed upon things according to the particular form by which bodies are informed, but that soul is a particular informing form no one concedes to him; for the informing particular comes

corrumpitur corporibus solutis, anima vero omni est corpore antiquior habens olim et ante coniugationem corporis
substantiam propriam extinctisque animalibus separatur
sine perpetuitatis incommodo, ut quam constet in aeterno
esse motu, quia habet internum domesticumque ex natura
sua motum. Aliud est igitur anima et item aliud specialis essentia. Itemque haec entelechia in rebus quoque cernitur
quae sunt sine anima. Si enim est plena cuiusque seminis
conceptusque perfectio, qui magis animalia quam stirpes et
arbores legitimo tempore accipiunt perfectionem? At vero
anima in solis animalibus. Deinde perfectio adultis iam
[quae in conceptu sunt] adhibetur et cum isdem crescit. At
vero anima sine ortu et ex aeternitate; non sine motu quem
ad modum entelechiam Aristoteles fore confitetur sed in
motu perpetuo, utpote cuius naturaliter motiva vis sit. Proptereaque dividitur primitus in duas species, rationabilem et
eam ex qua sunt appetitus, deinde subdividitur in opinionem intellectumque et demum in iracundiam et cupiditatem; atque his ex divisione speciebus singulis apta membra
tamquam organa sunt distributa.

226. Sed ne praecurrere et delibare videamur quicquam
ex Platonis sententia, ponemus ipsam quae illustrabit
cuncta quae in aliqua obscuritate versantur. Est igitur anima
iuxta Platonem substantia carens corpore semet ipsam
movens rationabilis. Et esse animam rem aliquam nullus
ambigit, movet enim corpus praecedente impetu quodam

into being with the emergence of bodies and passes away with their dissolution, whereas soul, being prior to body in every sense and possessing its proper substance previously, prior to its union with the body, without suffering any harm to its perpetuity separates itself when the living beings are extinguished. So that it is evident that it is in eternal movement, since of its own nature it possesses a movement that is intrinsic and innate. Soul, then, is one thing and the formal essence another. Again, this entelechy is evident even in things that are without soul. For if of each and every insemination and conception there is a full state of perfection, then how do animals any more than plants and trees achieve their state of perfection at an appointed time? But soul is restricted to animals. Furthermore, the perfection is a state achieved by things fully grown and develops along with them. But the soul is without birth and is from eternity; it is not motionless, as Aristotle professes the entelechy to be, but is in perpetual movement since its power is by nature a motive one. And so it is divisible in the first instance into two species, the rational and that from which the appetites derive, then further divisible into opinion and intellect and finally into irascibility and cupidity; and bodily members or "organs" are correspondingly distributed among each of the species resulting from the division.

226. But so that we may not appear to go beyond or curtail anything in Plato's thought, we will lay out that aspect which will illuminate all that is enshrouded in a certain obscurity. According to Plato, then, soul is an incorporeal self-moving rational substance. And that soul is a particular unto itself no one doubts, for when stirred up by the senses it moves the body pursuant to a particular impulse; but since

sensibus excitato; sed quia cuncta quae sunt dividuntur in decem genera, quod cuiusque generis suscipiet proprietatem eidem generi sociabitur. Constat porro inter omnes ex omnibus categoriis proprium essentiae fore suscipere contrarias passiones vicissim et esse antiquissimam praenoscique generibus ceteris. Ut igitur corpus, ut puta hominis, essentia est sine ulla dubitatione propterea quod contrarias passiones vicissim suscipit, ut aegritudinem et sospitatem, turpitudinem et item decentiam, sic animam essentiam fore aperte probatur, quia haec quoque contrarias passiones vicissim suscipit, ut iustitiam (competit porro haec corporeae sospitati), et item iniquitatem (quae demum congruit corporis morbis), sicut pulchritudini quidem temperantia, turpitudini libido, item fortitudini quidem magnanimitas, imbecillitati porro timiditas et ignavia, et omnino bona quidem corporis valetudo comparatur animae bonae valetudini, quae virtus est, mala vero corporis valetudo vitiositati. Deinde anima, sicut in superioribus constitit, modulata est positaque in motu suo habetque cum numeris cognationem. Quae cuncta essentiae quidem non sunt, sed iuxta ea quae sunt habentque essentiam versantur. Si igitur proprium est essentiae vicissim contraria sustinere, idem autem hoc etiam animae commune est, procul dubio nihil est aliud anima quam essentia; certe ridiculum id quod paret atque obsequitur essentiam esse concedere, scilicet corpus, quod vero dominatur et regit negare in substantia positum, cum

all things that exist are divided among the ten Genera of Being, when a thing assumes the property of one or another genus it becomes associated with the same genus. Moreover, all agree that the attribute proper to Substance, among all the Categories, is to be susceptible of change between contrary affects and to be significantly prior to and more immediately known than the other genera. As, then, a body—say, that of a human being—is known certainly to be a substance by virtue of its being susceptible of change between contrary affects such as sickness and health or unsightliness and comeliness, so the soul is manifestly shown to be a substance on the grounds that it too is susceptible of change between contrary affects such as justice (the analogue of bodily health) and iniquity (ultimately, the analogue of bodily diseases)—think of moderation in relation to beauty, lust in relation to unsightliness, magnanimity in relation to strength, timidity or faintheartedness in relation to weakness, and in general, of the good health of the body as compared with the good health of the soul, i.e., virtue, and the poor health of the body as compared with vice. Again, soul, as was indicated earlier, is in a state of attunement and is situated within its own movement and possesses a natural affinity with numbers. Now, although all of these qualities fail to qualify as substances, they are implicated in the things that are and have substance. If, then, the attribute proper to substance is to admit of change between contraries, and this same property is common also to the soul, then the soul is undoubtedly nothing other than a substance. It is at any rate absurd, given Plato's claims in support of soul's venerability in both dignity and preeminence in powers, and in support of its obvious sovereignty over body, to concede that that

Plato tam dignitate quam virtutum praestantia venerabilem dicit esse animam et plane corporis dominam.

227. Et essentiam quidem fore animam sic probatur eandemque antiquiorem esse corpore nec ut entelechiam crescere cum conceptis seminibus cumque isdem maturari et ad perfectionem venire. Sed quia duplex essentia est, altera corporea, altera carens corpore, consequenter docebimus, quod sit anima essentia carens corpore. Principio, quod omne corpus penetret idque vivificet; proprium vero est hoc eius naturae quae est sine corpore, ut dulcedinis quae peruadit melleum corpus, ut lucis quae corpus aereum penetrat. Nam si haec corpora essent, vel applicata corpori vel mixta vel concreta invenirentur; sed applicata non sunt haec nec anima corpori—nec enim ex applicatione eius vita corpori provenit, sed quia anima per omnes se diffundit artus—, nec vero ex permixtione—non enim esset unum quiddam anima sed multa commixta—, sed nec ex concretione—nullum quippe corpus aliud corpus penetrare valet usque quaque. Non ergo anima corpus est vel corporeum aliquid, ut quidam putant: sine corpore igitur. Deinde omne corpus vel intimo vel externo motu movetur; quae externo, sine anima sunt, quae interno, cum anima. Itaque, si corpus esset, vel anima aliunde sumpta uteretur vel sine anima esset; neutrum porro horum rationem habet: est ergo sine corpore. Probatum quoque in superioribus, quod motu intimo

which submits and obeys, namely, body, is a substance but to insist that that which commands and rules does not qualify as a substance.

227. And in this way it is demonstrated that the soul is indeed a substance and that it is also prior to body, that unlike an entelechy it does not develop in conjunction with the inseminations once conceived, or mature and attain a state of perfection along with them. But since substance is twofold, one type being corporeal and the other incorporeal, we will show that the soul is an *incorporeal* substance. First, because it penetrates the entire body and gives it life; but this is a property of the type of nature that is incorporeal, e.g., of the sweetness that pervades the body that is honey, of the light that penetrates the body that is air. For if sweetness and light were bodies, then they would be found to be in a state of juxtaposition, intermixture, or aggregation with body. But they are not juxtaposed, and neither is the soul with body; for it is not by virtue of the soul's juxtaposition that life obtains in body, but because of its diffusion throughout all the limbs; nor is it by virtue of its intermixture, for the soul would not be a unified entity but many things intermingled; nor is it by virtue of its aggregation, since no body is capable of fully penetrating another one. The soul, then, is not a body or corporeal entity, as some suppose: it is therefore incorporeal. Second, each body moves according to a motion that is either extrinsic or intrinsic; the extrinsically moved ones lack soul, the intrinsically moved ones possess it. So if the soul were a body, it would either employ a soul drawn from some other source or be inanimate, and neither of these possibilities makes sense: it is therefore incorporeal. And it has been demonstrated above that it moves

genuinoque moveatur et ex semet ipsa; sequitur ergo, ut etiam immortalis sit et sine ulla generatione, simplex etiam nec ex ulla compositione.

228. Hoc loco calumniari solent homines quibus veri indagandi cura nulla est. Dicunt enim Platonem in Phaedro quidem asserere animam esse sine ulla compositione proptereaque indissolubilem, in Timaeo tamen compositam rem confiteri, siquidem faciat eam constare ex individua dividuaque substantia et item diversa eademque [alia] natura conflante eam et velut coagmentante [ab] opifice deo; male ac miserabiliter nescientes compositum id esse quod ex aliquo initio temporis factum sit, ut navim et domum, quiddam vero quod compositum quidem non sit habeat tamen rationem compositionis, ut in musica symphonia quae diatessaron vocatur et item geometrica theoremata; similiter ergo etiam generatum quidem quod ex aliquo temporis initio natum factumve sit, ut statuam; porro aliud esse longeque diversum quod habeat rationem generationis intellegibilis, ut sphaeram. Igitur cum dicit Plato natam animam et ab opifice deo factam compositamque, nec ex certo tempore initium substantiae dicit trahere nec ut quae non fuerit ante post esse coeperit sed quod habeat rationem ortus et compositionis; cum vero sine genitura et sine compositione dicit, aperte nullum ei dat initium nec ullam originem compositionis.

according to an intrinsic and innate motion, in virtue of *itself*; it follows, then, that it is also immortal and altogether ungenerated, also simple, deriving from no process of composition.

228. On this point people who have no concern for the pursuit of truth generally raise an objection. For they say that, whereas in the *Phaedrus* Plato asserts that the soul is altogether noncomposite and consequently indissoluble, in the *Timaeus* he professes it to be a composite entity in that he makes it consist of indivisible and divisible Being and also of the nature of the Other and the Same, with the craftsman god conflating and, as it were, fitting it together. Poor fools, not knowing that a composite is that the making of which commences at a fixed point in time, as in the case of a ship or house, but that there is a type of thing which, although noncomposite, nevertheless has a structure analogous to that associated with a process of composition, as with the musical consonance known as the *diatessaron* and geometrical theorems; so too, that that is likewise generated, the coming-to-be or making of which commences at a fixed point in time, as in the case of a statue; and that that which, as in the case of a sphere, has a structure originating in intelligible generation is something else and very different again. So when Plato says that soul came into being and was made and put together by the craftsman god, he does not mean that it takes the starting point for its being from a fixed point in time, or that a previously nonexistent soul subsequently began to be, but that it has a structure analogous to that associated with coming-to-be and a process of composition; and when he says that it is without a process of generation or composition, he explicitly denies it any beginning point or any origin in a process of composition.

229. Alia igitur significatione diversaque res generata et item alia diversaque sine generatione anima esse dicitur a Platone, cuius diversissimae vires sint. Est enim quaedam virtus eius in ratiocinando et item alia quae dicitur vigor iracundiae et item quae cupit, quae species sunt appetitus, quae tamen rationi naturaliter pareant. Erit igitur optima virtus eius quae ratiocinatur, ceterae secundae ac tertiae potestatis. Haec Plato de anima sentit, quae strictim breviterque a nobis decursa sunt.

230. Censet vero eam per omnes artus ac totum corpus meare et per singula membra velut organa vim suam ostentare; proinde et in sentiendo ad eam quidem referri omnia quae sensibus occurrant, ea vero quae sensus referant esse diversa. Quia igitur principales vires animae duae sunt, una deliberativa, altera quae ad appetendum quid impellit, et est deliberativa quidem virtus propria rationabilis animantis, illa vero alia id ipsum animantis, consequenter competentia viribus et apta membra dimensa sunt.

231. Rationabili velut arx corporis et regia, utpote virtuti quae regali quadam eminentia praestet, id est domicilium capitis, in quo habitet animae principale, quod ad similitudinem mundi sit exaedificatum, teres et globosum, purum separatumque ab ea quae cibo alimentisque nascatur illuvie. In quo quidem domicilio sensus quoque habitent, qui sunt tamquam comites rationis et signif<eri,> scilicet ut de

229. In one sense, then, the soul is said by Plato to be a generated reality, and in another to be without a process of generation; and its powers vary widely. For it has a particular power in its reasoning, another that is called the irascible power, and again one that desires; and the latter are species of appetite, which, however, are by nature submissive to reason. Thus its most noble power will be that which reasons; the others are of a second- and third-order capability. These are Plato's views concerning the soul, which we have gone over to the letter and briefly.

230. And he thinks that it permeates each of the limbs and the body as a whole and that it manifests its power throughout the individual members, the "organs"; moreover, that everything that confronts the senses in the course of its sensing is reported to it despite differences between what the senses report. Since, then, the principal powers of the soul are two, one deliberative and the other the one that impels it to seek something, and the deliberative one is the power proper to a rational living being while the other is essential to its *being* a living being, the bodily members are consequently assigned analogously and in a manner suited to the powers.

231. The *citadel* [44d–e], as it were, and palace of the body is assigned to the rational power *in the sense that* it stands out with *a certain* regal *preeminence,* i.e., as the domicile that is the head, which the principal part of the soul inhabits and which was constructed so as to resemble the world, *round and spherical,* pure and free from the filth that arises from food and nourishment. And the senses inhabit this domicile as well, acting as the retainers, so to speak, and standard-bearers of reason, namely, so that through their interven-

proximo sensibus interpellantibus statuatur super his quae sentientur, atque etiam intellectus a <delibe>ratione advocatus facile [habeat] commonefiat eorum omnium quae quondam vidit et imaginum recordatione ad veri spectaculi commemorationem retractus <sit.> Quis enim nesciat quod, quam rationem habet sensus adversus deliberationem, hanc deliberatio iuxta intellectum? Ex coniectura siquidem nascitur opinio, ex opinione intellectus, ut idem Plato docuit in Politia. Facile est assequi naturalia arcana ex his quae frequenter accidunt, omnes quippe corporeae passiones quae mentem deliberationemque eius impediunt non nisi in capite proveniunt: phrenesis, oblivio, lapsus epilepticus, furor atque atri fellis incendia ex arce capitis trahunt initia—non quo mens deliberatioque eius laedatur proptereaque fiat obtunsior sed quod organum morbo impeditum officium suum iuxta naturam implere non possit nec animae iussis occurrere. Cerebrique sedes nullam, opinor, fert passionem, provenit enim passionis sensu hominis interitus. Quod si et ratio his quae videntur et quae videntur rationi testimonium invicem praebent, utroque genere verum sincerae fidei esse dogma Platonis probatur, quod animae vis principalis in cerebri locata sit sede.

232. Illud vero aliud principale, quod secundae dignitatis esse praediximus, non rationabilis animantis, sed id ipsum animantis. Commune ergo ut animalis in corde ac medietate, ut vero rationabilis animantis in cerebro. Unde cetera quidem animalia uno utuntur principali quod in corde est, at

tion judgment concerning the things sensed may be passed from close up, and so that after being summoned by deliberation intellect may readily be made mindful of all it has ever seen and be drawn back through its recollection of mental images to remembering the vision of truth. For who does not know that, what sense perception is in relation to deliberation, deliberation is in relation to understanding? For from conjecture arises opinion and from opinion understanding, as Plato explained in the *Republic*. It is easy to grasp the hidden forces of nature on the basis of recurrent phenomena, in the sense that all of the bodily disturbances that impede the mind and its deliberation arise uniquely in the head: derangement, amnesia, the epileptic seizure, rage and inflammations of the black bile start from within the citadel of the head—not so that the mind and its deliberation should be damaged and thereby be made duller but because an organ that is impeded by illness is incapable of fulfilling its natural function or of carrying out the soul's commands. And the seat of the cerebrum is, I suppose, intolerant of disturbance, for the destruction of the human being follows its perception of the disturbance. But on the assumption that reason supports perceived phenomena and that perceived phenomena in turn support reason: either way, Plato's doctrine that the principal power of the soul is located in the *seat* of the cerebrum is proved to be true, of untainted reliability.

232. That other principal part, however, which we said earlier is of secondary rank, defines, not the rational living being, but the element essential to its being a living being. It is therefore the common part, situated in the heart or midsection of the thing *qua* living being but in its cerebrum *qua* rational living being. And so while other animals have the

487

vero homo duobus, uno in corde altero in capite. Certe hominis membra sequuntur ordinationem mundani corporis;
quare si mundus animaque mundi huius sunt ordinationis,
ut summitas quidem sit dimensa caelestibus hisque subiecta
divinis potestatibus quae appellantur angeli et daemones,
[in] terra vero terrestribus, et imperant quidem caelestia,
exequuntur vero angelicae potestates, reguntur porro terrena, prima summum locum obtinentia, secunda medietatem, ea vero quae subiecta sunt imum, consequenter etiam
in natura hominis est quiddam regale, est aliud quoque in
medio positum, est tertium in imo, summum quod imperat,
medium quod agit, tertium quod regitur et administratur.
Imperat igitur anima, exequitur vigor eius in pectore constitutus, reguntur et dispensantur cetera pube tenus et infra.

233. Atque hanc eandem ordinationem invenimus etiam
in libris Politiae. In quibus cum ea iustitia quaereretur qua
homines adversum se utuntur, haec porro tunc convalescit,
cum animae potestates opificia sua recognoscunt nec aliena
appetunt, ex unius hominis ingenio ad illustre civitatis et
populi confugit exemplum et de gentium disputat iustitia.
Principales quidem urbis illius viros ut prudentissimos sa-
pientissimosque editiores urbis locos habitare iussit, post
hos militarem atque in armis positam iuventutem, quibus

use of a single principal part that is in the heart, man has the use of two, one in the heart and the other in the cerebrum. To be sure, the members constitutive of a human being follow the ordered disposition of the body of the world; and so, if the world and world soul are ordered such that the summit is assigned to celestial beings and the regions beneath them to the divine powers called angels and demons whereas earth is assigned to terrestrial beings, and the celestial beings command whereas angelic powers execute and terrestrial things are ruled, the first of these obtaining the highest place, the second the middle position, and those situated beneath them the bottom, then it follows that in the nature of man as well there is a certain regal element and another thing located in the middle and a third at the bottom, the highest being that which commands, the middle that which acts, and the third that which is ruled and administered. The soul, then, rules, the power of the soul situated in the chest executes, the rest, down to and below the genitals, are ruled and regulated.

233. And we have come upon this same ordering also in the books of the *Republic*. And when in that work the justice employed by men in their dealings with one another came under investigation, and this justice gains strength as the powers of the soul come to recognize their individual tasks and cease pursuing ones foreign to them, then he shifts from the innate temperament of the individual human being to the illustrative example of a city and people, and pursues the question of the justice of nations. The men ranking first in that city, being the most prudent and wise, he ordered to inhabit its higher areas; after them he ordered the positioning of the military youth in arms, to whom he made the common

subiecit sellularios atque vulgares, ut illi quidem ut sapientes praecepta dent, militares agant atque exequantur, vulgares vero competens et utile praebeant ministerium. Sic animam quoque ordinatam videmus: rationabilem quidem partem eius ut sapientissimam principem partem obtinentem tamquam totius corporis capitolium; vigorem vero qui est iracundiae similis ut militarem iuventutem in cordis castris manentem; vulgare et sellularium, quod est cupiditas seu libido, inferioribus abditum occultatumque natura.

234. Cum igitur, inquit, horum omnium consensus talis erit et quasi quaedam conspiratio, ut quod oportet praecipere recte officium suum compleat, huic pareat quod est dignitatis secundae, postremum vero atque ultimum morem gerat melioribus, tunc non solum hominum vita sed etiam civitatum et gentium erit laudabilis et apprime beata. Ex quibus ostendit Plato veram hominis proprietatem in capite consistere, cuius species sit mundi formae simillima, et quod germana sustentetur anima vivificantis animae corpus universae rei, cuique cuncta cognitionis rerum instrumenta, sensus videlicet, adiuncta sint, quo quae aguntur extra indicio vicinorum sensuum mens assequatur. Quibus quidem sensibus minime fuit opus mundo—quippe nihil extra ambitum mundi est aut agitur—, at vero perfectae hominis instructioni sunt sensus admodum necessarii, quia initium et quasi quaedam intellegendi sapiendique semina sunt in sentiendo.

sedentary workers subject, on the view that the first ones should in consideration of their wisdom give the orders, that the military men should act and execute, and that the commoners should provide beneficial service in proportion to their ability. The soul too we see ordered in this way: its rational part, as the wisest, obtaining the highest part, the Capitol, as it were, of the whole body; the power manifested as irascibility abiding, as the military youth, in the encampment of the heart; and the common sedentary element, i.e., its desire or lust, naturally hidden away and concealed in the lower regions.

234. Thus, he says, when the consensus and concord, so to speak, between them all will be such that the element entitled to issue commands rightly fulfills its task and that which is of secondary rank obeys it while the final and last one acts in compliance with the wishes of its superiors, then the life not only of individual human beings but of cities and nations will be praiseworthy and supremely blessed. And with this Plato shows that the thing truly characteristic of man is located in the *head:* the shape of which most closely resembles that of the world, and which is sustained by a soul directly related to the one that gives life to the body of the universe, and to which are adjoined all of the organs, namely, sense faculties, instrumental to the cognition of things, so that on the basis of the information supplied by the neighboring senses the mind may grasp external phenomena. And although the world had no need of these sense faculties — for there is nothing, no phenomenon, external to the periphery of the world—yet for the complete formation of the human being the senses are necessary in the highest degree, since the starting point and the seeds, so to speak, of intelligence and wisdom are in sensation.

235. Deinde causam demonstrat cur capiti cetera membra subiecta sint. Oportebat, inquit, animal terrenis negotiis praefici, terrae autem superficies iniqua ex parte maxima declivibus et item acclivibus impedimentis. Erat igitur impossibile motu capitis naturali, hoc est globosa decursione, terras obiri proptereaque divinae potestates vehiculum consimilis eiusdemque naturae capiti ceterum corpus et quae motui futura erant necessaria membra subtexuerunt, quo rationis domicilium ceteris emineret. Quodque ex translativis motibus quaedam est praecedendi coniugatio, retro quidem unde est exordium motus, ante autem ad quod fit impetus; praecedendi officium commodius, inquit, visum est quam recedendi, opinor ideo, quia mundi quoque motus agitur in antecedentia naturaeque animalium congruentius progredi quam recessim moveri. Totius denique corporis conformatio provida naturae sollertia sic ordinata est ore vultuque ad praecedentia versum locata, ducibus quoque ad spatiandum sensibus prorsum spectantibus.

10. De Visu

236. Dehinc subtexit de sensibus et organis sentiendi et incipit ab optimo praeclarissimoque sensuum omnium visu, causas quibus videmus edisserens. Sed quoniam de hoc

235. He then indicates the reason for the *other members* being subject *to the head* [44d–45a]. It was necessary, he says, that the living being should be in control of its earthly activities; but the earth's surface is for the most part uneven, with impediments *that slope down and up*. Thus it was impossible for it to move along the earth with the form of movement natural to the head, i.e., the rolling of a sphere, and the *divine powers* for that reason attached, beneath the head, the rest of the body—including the members that would prove *necessary* for its movement—as a *vehicle* of like or identical nature, so that the domicile of reason might stand above the rest. And given that in forward motion there is a certain interconnection between forms of transitive movement, that which lies behind is the point from which movement originates, whereas that which lies ahead is the point toward which the impetus is directed; and the *function of forward progression,* he says, was deemed *more advantageous than that of retrogression,* the reason, I suppose, being that the world's movement too is in the direction of what lies ahead and that forward movement is better suited to the nature of living beings than movement in reverse. Finally, the configuration of the body as a whole was ordered accordingly by the provident skill of nature: the face and gaze directed toward what lies ahead, also the senses gazing ahead to guide the act of walking.

10. On Vision

236. He next adds material concerning the senses and organs of sensation, and he begins with vision, the highest and noblest of all the senses, explaining the causes of our seeing.

plerique alii post ipsum opiniones varias libris conditis sunt
executi, eas quae sunt in honore perstringam quo perfectior
propositae rei tractatus habeatur. Omnes qui rerum initia
corpora censuerunt vel coetu innumerabilium minutorum
congesto inani vel perpetuorum continuata proceritate, dicunt videre nos simulacrorum incursionibus; fluidam quippe
materiem formatas iuxta sui similitudinem exudare subtiles
corporum fusiones, quae sunt visibilium simulacra rerum,
eaque cum visus noster incurrerit, hausta et recepta meati-
bus transmittat ad eum per quem sentimus spiritum; cumque delicatior simulacri moles erit, separatur panditurque
visus, opinor, et candida tunc quae sentiuntur videntur, si
corpulentior, confundunt aciem et videntur atra, atque ad
eundem modum cetera formata et colorata pro formarum et
colorum cognatione. Multaque ab his dicuntur alia in eundem modum, quibus singulis immorandum non erit.

237. At vero Heraclitus intimum motum qui est intentio
animi sive animadversio porrigi dicit per oculorum meatus
atque ita tangere tractareque visenda. Stoici vero videndi
causam in nativi spiritus intentione constituunt cuius effigiem coni similem volunt: hoc quippe progresso ex oculorum penetrali quae appellatur pupula et ab exordio tenui
quo magis porrigitur in soliditatem opimato, [exordio]

But since many others after him have in their written works pursued various opinions on this, I will summarize those that carry particular weight, so that our treatment of the subject to hand may be deemed the more complete. All of those who have held the first beginnings of things to be bodies, whether by virtue of the void's being filled as a result of the aggregation of innumerable minute particles or by virtue of a continuous extension of perpetual elements, say that our seeing results from an influx of images; for they say that matter, being in a fluid state, exudes subtle effluences of bodies that behave as it does. And these are the images of visible things, and on having encountered them our sight transmits through channels what it has absorbed and received to the breath through which we engage in sensation; and when the density of the image is more rarefied, our vision broadens out and expands, I suppose, and the sense objects then appear bright; if it is more densely corporeal, they block our sight and appear dark, and similarly for the rest, having their shapes and colors according to the natural link with shapes and colors. And many other claims are similarly made by them, although it will be unnecessary to linger on them individually.

237. Heraclitus, by contrast, says that an internal movement which is a tension of the mind or mental attention makes its way through the channels of the eyes and in that way comes into contact with and takes hold of the objects of vision. The Stoics, however, locate the cause of seeing in a tension of the innate breath, the shape of which they would liken to a cone: for they say that the breath, after progressing beyond the inner part of the eyes called the pupil and gaining in solidity the farther it moves from the narrow

penes id quod videtur locatum fundi omnifariam dilatarique visus illustratione; quodque omnis natura modo mensuraque moveatur, spatii quoque magnitudinisque coni modum fore; eaque quae neque valde applicata visui nec nimium distantia visibilia clare videri; certe conum ipsum pro modo mensuraque intentionis augeri. Et prout basis eius vel directa vel inflexa erit incidetque in contemplabilem speciem ita apparebunt quae videntur; oneraria quippe navis eminus visa perexigua apparet deficiente contemplationis vigore nec se per omnia navis membra fundente spiritu; turris item quadrata rotunditatem simulat cylindri, atque etiam ex obliquo visa porticus in exile deficit oculorum depravatione; sic etiam stellarum ignis exiguus apparet atque ipse sol multis partibus quam terra maior intra bipedalis diametri ambitum cernitur. Sentire porro mentem putant perinde ut eam pepulerit spiritus, qui id quod ipse patitur ex visibilium specierum concretione mentis intimis tradit: porrectus siquidem et veluti patefactus candida esse denuntiat quae videntur, confusus porro et confaecatior atra et tenebrosa significat; similisque eius passio est eorum, qui marini piscis contagione torpent, siquidem per linum et harundinem perque manus serpat virus illud penetretque intimum sensum.

238. Geometrae cum Peripateticis concinentes radii effusione visum operari putant, cum per fulgidam lucidamque

starting point, once located within the sphere of the visible object flows in all directions and is broadcast in the luminosity of the visual ray; and that since every nature is moveable as to its extent and measure, the extent of the cone's spatial magnitude is as well; and that visible objects which are neither too near to nor too far from the source of vision are clearly seen; and that the cone itself obviously increases according to the extent and measure of the tension. And the appearance of visible objects will be a function of the orientation, straight or angled, of the base of the cone relative to the visible form; for a transport ship viewed from afar appears very small because of a tapering off in the power of the vision and the breath's not flowing to all parts of the ship; similarly, a square tower gives the impression of cylindrical roundness, and a colonnade viewed obliquely tapers off ever smaller because of a distortion in the eyes; so too the fiery light of the stars appears small, and although it is many times greater than Earth the Sun itself looks confined within a diameter of two feet. And they think that the mind senses in response to the stimulus of the breath, which transmits its own experience of the aggregation of visible forms to the innermost parts of the mind: when extended straight and, we might say, opened up it reports the visible objects as being bright, but when confused and muddied it indicates them as dark and shadowy; and its experience is like that of men numbed through contact with a torpedo fish, for in that case poison steals through the line, rod, and hands and penetrates to the inner sense faculty.

238. The geometers, along with the Peripatetics, reckon that sight becomes active through the effusion of a visual ray, when the ray, shining directly through the bright and

pupulae stolam in directum emicans radius serenam porrigit
lineam, quae gyris oculorum circumuecta motibus dispergat
undique lucem contemplationis; quippe teres et levis oculi
globus et humori lubrico velut innatans sequacem lineam
visus utrobique facile contorquet. Ergo notae geometricae
comparant quod videtur et illuc versum ferri censent visus
intentionem, sed ob nimiam repentinamque conversionem
omnia videri per illustrem contuentis superficiem putant, ut
cum in theatro aliove quolibet conventu popularis multi-
tudinis decursis strictim vultuum partibus totum populum
videre nobis videmur.

239. Idem aiunt videre nos vel tuitione, quam phasin
vocant, vel intuitione, quam emphasin appellant, vel detui-
tione, quam paraphasin nominant. Tuitione quidem ut quae
simpliciter et prompte videntur quaeque clementer visum
recipientia minime eum a se repellunt, ut flexus quin immo
fractus rursum ad oculos redeat. Intuitione vero ut quae
fragmento radii recurrente ad oculorum aciem videntur;
qualia sunt quae in speculis et aqua considerantur ceteris
item quorum tersa est quidem superficies sed ob nimiam
densitatem idoneus vigor ad repellendum quod offenderit.
Ergo etiam radius in quo est vis videndi fractus in speculo
facit angulum quem contineant duae lineae, una quae ab
oculo profecta pervenit ad speculum altera quae a speculo
recurrit ad vultum; qui quidem angulus cum erit acutus imaginem vultuum nostrorum facit in speculo videri remeante

luminous outer layer of the pupil, emits a clear line which, on being broadcast by the orbital movements of the eyes, disperses the visual light in all directions; for the eyeball is round and smooth, and swimming, as it were, in its viscous fluid it easily directs the line of sight by leading it one way and the other. Thus they liken the visual object to a geometrical point and think that the tension associated with vision moves toward it but reckon that because of the constant and sudden rotation everything is viewed through the bright outer surface of that which does the seeing, as when in a theater or some other gathering of a large number of people we think we see the whole populace after rapidly surveying the faces piecemeal.

239. They also say that we see either by direct vision, which they call *phasis,* or by reflection, which they call *emphasis,* or by transparent vision, which they call *paraphasis.* Direct vision has to do with things that are seen simply and openly and that owing to their ready reception of sight do not repel it from themselves, so that it returns to the eyes through reflection, or rather, refraction. And reflection has to do with things that become visible owing to a refracted portion of the visual ray's returning to the line of sight within the eyes; such are the objects viewed in mirrors, water, and other objects possessed of a smooth surface but a resistance which by virtue of its extreme density is able to repel the incoming ray. On being refracted in a mirror, then, the actual ray in which the power of seeing resides produces an angle contained within two lines, one reaching the mirror after having left the eye and the other returning from the mirror to the face; and when the angle is acute, it makes the image of our faces visible in the mirror because of the line of

ad vultum acie atque inde occulte praecipitante simulacrum
in speculi sinum, ex quo fit ut vultus noster transisse ad speculum putetur. Quomodoque simulacrum e speculo resul-
tans e diverso videtur consistere, perinde ac si duo contra
stantes dextras partes sinistris sinistras item dextris obvias
habeant sic adversum nos imagines nostrae dextras et sinistras partes cum immutatione demonstrant. Idem angulus
acutus si ex aliqua conversione vel immutata qualitate posi-
tionis erit acutior et procerior factus, longius evagatus
cuncta quae retro nos sunt in speculo videri facit; quod si
non acutus sed rectus erit angulus, tunc ea quae supra nos
erunt ad directum rigorem videbuntur; sin vero hebes et latior, ea quae contra nos excelsiora sunt apparebunt.

240. Nullo porro angulo facto nec fracto radio nulla in
speculis dumtaxat imago proveniet ut in globosis et sphaerae similibus vasis. At vero si talis erit speculi figura ut sit
eius concava superficies et tornata in modum scapii [qua-
drati] vel imbricis, dehinc intueamur hoc idem speculum ita
conversum ut rectus cernatur imbrex margines porro eius
seu supercilia hinc illinc pro lateribus assistant, tunc, opinor, radius incidens et infractus ob levem speculi rigidamque
soliditatem in proximum latus eius delabitur in decimani
apicis effigiem. Ita dextri lateris imagine in sinistrum, sinis-
tri etiam in dextrum ob eminentiam marginis utriusque
deiecta dextrae partes nostrae etiam in speculo dextrae sinistraeque item sinistrae videbuntur et erit imaginis falsae
remedium imago falsa. Hoc idem speculum si demum ita

vision's turning back around toward the face and impercep-tibly driving the image from there to a point within the mir-ror, thereby creating the sense that our face has moved to the mirror. And just as the image on rebounding from the mirror appears to stand opposite us, precisely as two people if standing opposite one another have their right hands aligned with the left and the left similarly aligned with the right, so our own images facing us exhibit a reversal of the right- and left-hand sides. If the same acute angle by some rotation or qualitative alteration in the mirror's position be-comes more acute and further extended, then as it travels farther it makes all of the objects situated behind us visible in the mirror; if however the angle is not acute but right, then objects above us will appear in direct line of sight; but if it is obtuse and wider, then objects facing us at a higher elevation will appear.

240. And if no angle is produced and the visual ray is un-refracted, then in mirrors at any rate no image will appear, as also in spherical or nearly spherical vessels. If, however, the mirror's shape is such that its surface is concave, made round in the manner of a bowl or semicylindrical tile, and we then gaze at this same mirror turned such that the semi-cylinder is viewed directly and its edges or protrusions are standing on either side, then, I suppose, each visual ray, on making contact and being refracted because of the smooth, rigid density of the mirror, will glide crosswise to the neigh-boring side. The image of the right-hand side being pushed thus to the left and that of the left-hand side to the right because of the protrusion of either edge, our right-hand parts will appear right and the left-hand ones left in the mir-ror as well, and a false image will correct a false image. If this

erit adversum nos locatum ut eminentium marginum alter superior sit alter inferior, nec rectus sed obliquus cernatur imbrex, resupinas ostentat imagines et simulacra praepostera ob similem lapsum fracti radii per acclivia; directus quippe visus ad speculi supercilia cum quidem superiorem conspexerit eminentiam, deicitur simulacrum ad ima resupinum, cum vero inferiorem, facit saltum vultus ad marginem superiorem.

241. Indicat porro causam pravae intuitionis fore in radii fragmine commentum tale. Etenim si duo specula sic collocentur, ut unum sit ante vultum, alterum a tergo, obliquatum, ne impediatur obiectu corporis visus radii commeantis, tunc occipitium nostrum videmus in speculo quod habetur a tergo; quod non fieret, nisi radius visualis applicans se ad speculum adversum fractusque eius obiectu faceret angulum, ex quo rursum recurrens in posterius se speculum arietaret rursumque illic angulo facto desineret in occipitii sedem. Atque ita quod vero visu non sentitur, discursantis aciei lumine proditur. Similiter cum in modum sectae concavae sphaerae formatum erit speculum, maiores veris vultus apparent ideo quod undique se fundente radii lumine velut exaestuans imago porrigitur.

242. Quae autem paraphasis ab his appellatur, provenit quotiens non in cute speculi sed introrsum et tamquam in penetralibus simulacrum invenitur obumbrante aliqua nigredine, ut in pellucidi quidem sed fusci vitri lamina vel

same mirror is then placed facing us such that one of the protruding edges is above and the other below, and the semicylinder is viewed, not directly, but obliquely, then it displays inverted images, figures reversed because of the same gliding of the refracted ray across the curvature; for when a line of vision that is directed at the mirror's protrusions looks at the upper one, the figure is inverted and pushed to the bottom, and when it looks at the lower one, it causes the face to leap to the upper edge.

241. The following test shows that the cause of a distorted reflection is in a fracturing of the visual ray. For if two mirrors are placed such that one is in front of the face and the other behind, angled so that the line of sight associated with the ray is not blocked along the way by an obstruction of the body, then we see the back of our head reflected in the mirror held behind; but this would not happen if the visual ray did not produce an angle by making contact with the mirror and being refracted by its obstruction, and if in making its way back it did not strike the mirror behind and, after another angle had been produced there, come to a stop at the back of the head. And so that which is imperceptible by real vision is revealed by the light of a line of sight running this way and that. Similarly, when a mirror has been given the shape of a bisected concave sphere, the faces appear larger than in reality, because the image is extended and flares up, so to speak, as the light of the ray streams in all directions.

242. That which is by them called *paraphasis,* however, obtains whenever the image is found, not on the outer surface of the mirror, but within it, in its inner depths, as it were, with some darkness casting a shadow over it, as if it were on the metal laminated to transparent but tinted glass or in

stagnis atris ex alto profundo; tunc quippe visus ingreditur
non adeo densam cutem et videt interiora sed non adeo
clare. Infringitur tamen radius ob tersam pellucidae materiae superficiem et obumbrationem atri coloris usque adeo,
ut ipsi etiam nosmet videntes intra speculum nosmet putemus consistere nec os nostrum e speculo sed intra speculum
videre. Quae causa est ut, cum accedimus ad speculum,
imago etiam proximare et, cum redimus, illa etiam videatur
una recedere.

243. Idem unum esse radium qui ex utroque oculo porrigitur argumentantur ex ea passione quae hypochysis dicitur
et ex visu eorum qui duplicia videre creduntur et habere pu-
pulas binas. Etenim cum crassus humor ita oculos obsederit,
ut non omnem eorum occupaverit et obtexerit ambitum,
sed in medietate constiterit liberis hinc inde partibus visus,
tunc scisso radio dividitur bifariam visus et qui hoc vitio la-
borant duplicia videre se censent. Ergo etiam in geminis pu-
pulis idem vitium medicorum detegit experientia; namque
bicori naturali quidem pupula recte quae sunt vident, illa
vero alia simulacra rerum. Quapropter medici quod plus est
quam natura desiderat tollunt et illam praeter naturam pu-
pulam interimunt imposita cicatrice; quo facto revocatur
visus naturalis integritas. Hae sunt de visu probatae sententiae veterum, qui mihi videntur acceptis occasionibus a

pools made dark because of their great depth; for then the line of vision works its way into the outer surface to the extent allowed by its density, and sees what lies within, although with restricted clarity. The visual ray is nevertheless refracted because of the smooth surface of the transparent material and the shadowing effect of the dark coloring, to such an extent that in gazing at ourselves we actually think that we are standing inside the mirror and seeing our face within rather than projected by it. And this explains why our image appears to move toward us as we approach the mirror and also to recede along with our moving away from it.

243. They also maintain, on the basis of the affliction called *hypochysis* [cataracts] and the vision of those believed to see double and to have double pupils, that there is a single visual ray extending from each eye. For when a concentrated moisture takes hold in the eyes such that it does not occupy and cover the whole of their sphere but settles in the center, leaving the portions of the vision on either side unimpeded, then the vision is divided in two because of a splitting of the ray, and those who suffer from this defect think they are seeing double. Now, the experience of physicians reveals the same defect also in twin pupils, for those with double pupils directly view existent objects via the natural pupil but see images of them with the other. And that is why physicians remove what is superfluous to the requirements of nature and destroy the unnatural pupil through surgical intervention, in consequence of which the natural integrity of the vision is restored. These are the approved opinions concerning vision among the ancients, who seem to me to have availed themselves of the opportunity to appropriate their

Platone suum proprium fecisse dogma. Nam cum ille perfectam rationem attulerit docueritque tam ipsam causam
videndi quam cetera quae causam sequuntur atque adiuvant
et sine quibus non potest visus existere, iuniores sumptis ex
plena sententia partibus de isdem partibus tamquam de universitate senserunt; proptereaque ut qui vera dicant merito
movent, sed quia nulla partis perfectio est aliquatenus succi-
dunt ut exposita Platonis sententia res ipsa monstrabit.

244. Censet enim Plato lumen ex oculis profundi purum
et liquatum, quod sit velut flos quidam ignis intimi nostri
habens cum solstitiali lumine cognationem, solis porro lumen instrumentum animae fore ad visibilium specierum
contemplationem, siquidem ad oculos feratur, quorum levi-
gata soliditas et tersa rotunditas, utpote munita tunicis tex-
tis tenui neruorum subtemine, fert facile obviam lucem.
Medietas vero, in qua constituitur videndi vis, delicati corporis et sincerae propemodumque incorporeae puritatis admittit contemplationis ingressum; causaque principalis videndi lumen est intimum, nec tamen usque quaque perfecta
et sufficiens ad muneris competentis perfunctionem. Opus
est quippe adiumento cognati extimi luminis, maxime quidem solstitialis, alias tamen etiam eorum quae solis lumen
imitantur. Igitur extimum lumen accorporatum lumini quod
ex oculis fluit confirmat illud et facit idoneum obtutibus
fluere proptereaque ducit ex ipsis corporibus quae videntur
colores. Colorem porro proprium esse visus sensum quis nesciat? Flamma est igitur quaedam, inquit, corporum color

doctrine from Plato. For whereas he put forward a complete account and explained the actual cause of seeing as well as other things that follow from and assist the cause, including those without which vision cannot occur, later interpreters after extracting parts of the full theory pronounced on those same parts as though on the whole; and so in their giving voice to truths they make legitimate progress, but since the part is possessed of no completeness they to some extent fall short, as the actual reality will show once Plato's view has been expounded.

244. For Plato holds that a pure and limpid light streams forth from the eyes, which is like the flower, as it were, of our internal fire in having a natural affinity with solar light, and that the light of the Sun is instrumental in the soul's contemplation of visible forms once it reaches the eyes, the smooth solidity and polished roundness of which, owing to the protection received from their outer layers woven in a thin network of nerves, easily receives the incoming light. And the center, where the power of seeing is situated, being of a delicate corporeality, indeed, of a purity that is uncontaminated and practically *in*corporeal, lets the vision in. The primary cause of seeing is the internal light; but it is not in every respect complete and sufficient for the performance of its apportioned task, since assistance is required from cognate external light, above all that of the Sun, but also elsewhere—that of the things that imitate sunlight. Well then, once the external light coalesces with the light flowing from the eyes it strengthens it, makes it fit to flow in acts of seeing, and to that end extracts colors from the bodies actually seen. And who does not know that color is the sense percept proper to sight? *Color*, he says [67c–e], is a particular

infundens superficiem; quae cum erit aequalis oculorum ca-
pacitati, manifesta sunt atque erunt quae videntur, cum vero
minor, clara et candida, ut quae patulus et apertus visus ad-
mittat; si vero maior erit color qui ex corporibus evaporatur
quam est oculorum ambitus, tegitur confunditurque acies et
quae videntur atri coloris videntur.

245. Tribus ergo his concurrentibus visus existit trinaque
est ratio videndi: lumen caloris intimi per oculos means,
quae principalis est causa, lumen extra positum, consangui-
neum lumini nostro, quod simul operatur et adiuvat, lumen
quoque, quod ex corporibus visibilium specierum fluit,
flamma seu color, qui perinde est atque sunt omnia sine quibus propositum opus effici non potest, ut sine ferramentis
quae sunt operi faciendo necessaria; quorum si quid deerit,
impediri visum necesse est.

246. His tam plene tamque diligenter elaboratis iuniores
philosophi, ut non optimi heredes paternum censum in
frusta dissipantes, perfectam atque uberem sententiam in
mutilas opiniunculas cecîderunt. Quare faciendum, ut ad
certam explorationem Platonici dogmatis commentum vetus advocetur medicorum et item physicorum, illustrium
sane virorum, qui ad comprehendendam sanae naturae sollertiam artus humani corporis facta membrorum exectione
rimati sunt, quod existimabant ita demum se suspicionibus
atque opinionibus certiores futuros, si tam rationi visus
quam visui ratio concineret. Demonstranda igitur oculi

form of flame that *suffuses the surface of bodies;* and when it is *equal* to the ocular capacity the objects of vision are and continue to be *conspicuous,* but when it is *smaller* they are clear and bright, being received by vision that is wide open, and if the color emanating from bodies is *greater* than the ocular sphere then the sight is veiled and confused and the objects of vision appear dark in color.

245. Vision results, then, from the concurrence of these three things, and the cause of seeing is threefold: the light of the internal warmth making its way through the eyes, which is the primary cause; the external light descending from the same source as our own, which cooperates with and assists it; and the light that flows from the bodies of visible forms, the flame or color which is just like *all* of the things without which the set task of seeing cannot be accomplished—like without tools that are necessary for performing a task: if any of them is missing, then the vision is necessarily impeded.

246. Despite these so fully and carefully elaborated points, later philosophers, behaving like selfish heirs who vainly dissipate their paternal estate, carved a rich and complete doctrine up into mutilated little opinions. And that is why, in the interests of a secure exploration of the Platonic doctrine, we must ensure that the ancient test conducted by the physicians and natural philosophers, illustrious men to be sure, should be summoned to account: in order to grasp the ingenuity underlying a soundly functioning nature, they surveyed the limbs of the human body by dissecting its parts; for they estimated that in this way, if observation were to harmonize with reason and reason with observation, they would eventually become more secure in their conjectures and opinions. Now, in need of explanation is the nature of

natura est, de qua cum plerique alii tum Alcmaeo Crotoni-
ensis, in physicis exercitatus quique primus exectionem
aggredi est ausus, et Callisthenes, Aristotelis auditor, et
Herophilus multa et praeclara in lucem protulerunt: duas
esse angustas semitas quae a cerebri sede, in qua est sita potestas animae summa et principalis, ad oculorum cavernas
meent naturalem spiritum continentes; quae cum ex uno
initio eademque radice progressae aliquantisper coniunctae
sint in frontis intimis, separatae bivii specie perveniant ad
oculorum concavas sedes, qua superciliorum obliqui tramites porriguntur, sinuataeque illic tunicarum gremio naturalem humorem recipiente globos complent munitos teg-
mine palpebrarum, ex quo appellantur orbes. Porro quod ex
una sede progrediantur luciferae semitae, docet quidem sectio principaliter, nihilo minus tamen intellegitur ex eo quoque, quod uterque oculus moveatur una nec alter sine altero
moveri queat. Oculi porro ipsius continentiam in quattuor
membranis seu tunicis notaverunt disparili soliditate; quarum differentiam proprietatemque si quis persequi velit,
maiorem proposita materia suscipiet laborem.

247. Interim verbis Platonis expositis et quae sit in his
naturalium arcanorum comprehensio atque expressio consideremus. Cum de sensibus loqueretur quos capitis instrumenta esse dixerat, addidit: E quibus primi luciferi oculorum orbes coruscant, et mox, Duae sunt, opinor, virtutes

the eye, concerning which Alcmaeon of Croton, who was thoroughly versed in the workings of nature and first took the bold step of performing dissection, and Aristotle's student Callisthenes, and Herophilus, among numerous others, brought many notable points to light: that there are two narrow paths that lead from the seat of the cerebrum, where the highest and principal power of the soul is situated, to the ocular cavities containing the natural breath; and proceeding from a single starting point and the same root they are conjoined within the recesses of the forehead for a short distance; after separating in the pattern of a forked road they reach the hollow seats of the eyes, along which the paths of the eyebrows stretch obliquely, and swelling up there as the cavity created by the outer layers receives the natural liquid they fill the spheres protected by the covering of the eyelids, that being the reason for their being named orbs. And that these light-bearing paths proceed from a single seat dissection above all teaches us, although it is also deducible from the fact that the two eyes move conjointly, that one cannot move independently of the other. They further observed that the eye itself is contained within four membranes or outer layers of varying firmness; anyone interested in pursuing the distinguishing property of each will be undertaking a task that outruns the scope of our material.

247. After a preliminary exposition of Plato's words, we should consider what comprehension, what expression of the secrets of nature is in them. In addressing the senses which he had said were the *organs* of the head, he added [45b–c]: *And first among them the light-bearing ocular orbs glimmer,* and then, *Fire, I suppose, has two powers, one consuming and*

ignis, altera edax et peremptoria altera mulcebris innoxio lumine. Huic igitur ex qua lux diem inuehens panditur cognatum et familiare corpus oculorum divinae potestates commentae sunt, intimum siquidem nostri corporis ignem, utpote germanum ignis lucidi sereni et defaecati liquoris, per oculos fluere ac demanare voluerunt. Solis et oculorum cognationem scit ab ineunte aetate communis omnium anticipatio, quippe sol mundi oculus appellatur ab omnibus ideoque idem auctor in Politia solem quidem simulacrum esse ait invisibilis dei, oculum vero solis et solstitiale quiddam, ut sit eminens sol intellegibili mundo suus, huic similis in sensili globus iste ignitus lucifer, cuius simulacrum id lumen, quo illustratur visus animalium, id est oculus. Fluere porro visum per oculos consentiunt tam physici quam etiam medici, qui exectis capitis membris, dum scrutantur naturae providam sollertiam, notaverunt ferri bivio tramite ignis liquorem. Ut per leves, inquit, congestosque et tamquam firmiore soliditate probatos orbes luminum, quorum tamen esset angusta medietas subtilior, serenus ignis per eandem flueret medietatem.

248. Quid ergo? Num aliter physici membranis vel etiam tunicis solidis contineri oculorum orbes asseverantes de natura eorum interpretari videntur? Angusta porro illa medietas, quae pervenit usque ad oculorum cavas sedes, quae alia est quam haec per quam fluit ignis serenus? Itaque, inquit, cum diurnum iubar applicat se visus fusioni, tunc nimirum

destructive and the other soothing due to its harmless light. The di-
vine powers, then, devised an ocular body that was cognate with
and related to the power from which the light that ushers in the
day emanates, for they determined that as the sibling of the brightly
shining fire and the unmuddied fluid the fire within our body
should flow and stream through the eyes. A preconception common to all people recognizes from early age the natural affinity between the Sun and eyes, for all refer to the Sun as
the eye of the world. And that is why our author says in the
Republic that the Sun is an image of the invisible god while
the eyes possesses an element of the Sun or solar element; so
that the intelligible world possesses its own sun, the preeminent one, and like unto it is the fiery light-bearing sphere in
the sensible world, whose image is the light by which the vision possessed by living beings is illuminated, i.e., the eye.
And that vision flows through the eyes is a point of agreement among natural philosophers and physicians, who in
scrutinizing the provident ingenuity of nature observed,
based on their dissection of the parts within the head, that
the fiery fluid moves along a double path. *Such,* he says, *that*
the bright fire would flow through the smooth, dense orbs of light,
which had been tested, as it were, for a higher degree of firm solid-
ity but whose narrow center was nevertheless of a subtler consis-
tency, and such that it would flow through that center.

248. Well then, given their assertion that the eyeballs are
contained within membranes or solid outer layers, can the
natural philosophers really be construed as offering some
other interpretation of their nature? And what is that *narrow*
center [45c–e] that reaches as far as the hollow seats of the
eyes other than the one *through* which the *bright fire flows?*
And so, he says, *when daylight makes contact with the stream of*

incurrentia semet invicem duo similia in unius corporis cohaerent speciem, quo concurrunt oculorum acies emicantes
quoque effluentis intimae fusionis acies contiguae imaginis
occursu repercutitur. Evidenter visum fieri dicit quotiens
intimi caloris lumen, quod inoffense per oculos fluit, aliquam visibilem materiam, quam contiguam imaginem appellat, incurrit ibidemque iuxta materiae qualitatem formatum et coloratum; sensus visusque confit ex lumine, qui
contiguae imaginis occursu repercussus reditu facto ad oculorum fores usque ad mentis secreta porrigitur. Atque etiam
diurni iubaris applicatio cum ignis intimi lumine manifestat
sine solis effulsione nihil videri. Denique postquam in noctem, inquit, discesserit cognatus ignis, desertum eius auxilio
lumen intimum remanet otiosum nullam habens cum proximo tunc aere naturae communicationem videreque desinit
factum illecebra somni. Obductis quippe palpebris, quarum
tegmen salubre oculorum auxilium dixit esse, vis illa ignis
intimi coercetur compressaque fundit se per membra, quo
pacto intimorum motuum relaxatur intentio in soporam
quietem minime tunc interpellante mentem visus inquietu-
dine.

II. De Imaginibus

249. Cumque erit, inquit, altior quies crassiore facto
naturali spiritu, nihil aut leve quiddam incertumque et

vision, then on encountering one another the two like entities undoubtedly cohere in the form of a single body where the rays emanating from the eyes meet and the ray of the effluent inner stream rebounds after encountering a contiguous image. His point is evidently that vision occurs when the light of the internal warmth, which flows unimpeded through the eyes, encounters some visible material, which he calls the *contiguous image,* and, depending on the quality of the material, there receives form and color; and from this light visual perception emerges, which *rebounding after encountering a contiguous image* and after returning to the double doors of the eyes extends as far as the hidden depths of the mind. And the *contact of daylight* with the light of the internal fire is further evidence of the fact that nothing is visible in the absence of sunlight. He says, finally: *once the cognate fire has departed at nightfall,* the internal light, *being deprived of its support,* remains otiose, *having at that point no natural means of communication with the surrounding air, and it ceases to see, having come to that by the inducement of sleep.* For *once the eyelids are drawn shut,* whose *salubrious covering* he spoke of as being the *eyes'* protection, then *the power of the internal fire becomes confined and under pressure spreads throughout the limbs,* with the result that the tension accompanying internal movements *relaxes* into a sleepy *rest,* the restlessness of vision then leaving the mind uninterrupted.

II. ON IMAGES

249. And *when,* he says [45e–46a], the *rest* is deeper due to the fact that the natural breath has become denser, then we dream of nothing or of something light, uncertain, and

perfunctorium somniamus; sin erunt insignes reliquiae commotionum animi, cuius modi erunt et quibus in locis, talia visuum simulacra nascentur expressa et ob insigne imaginum diu penes memoriam residentia. Sunt porro reliquiae commotionum vel ex modestis vel ex intemperantibus interdumque sapientibus interdum stolidis cogitationibus, sedatae vel ad iracundiam incitatae, proque locis, ut in capite ubi est sedes domiciliumque rationis vel in corde in quo dominatur virilis ille indignationis vigor vel in iecore subterque; dimensa porro haec omnis regio libidini[s].

250. Et quoniam tractatum incurrimus somniorum, de quo varie senserunt veteres, fiat earum quae in honore sunt opinionum commemoratio. Aristoteles, ut qui dei providentiam usque ad lunae regionem progredi censeat, infra vero neque providentiae scitis regi nec angelorum ope consultisque sustentari nec vero daemonum prospicientiam putet intervenire proptereaque tollat omnem divinationem negetque praenosci futura, unum genus somniorum admittit atque approbat, quod ex his quae vigilantes agimus aut cogitamus residens in memoria movet interpellatque per quietem gestarum deliberatarumque rerum conscias animas. Nec errat; est enim etiam haec progenies somniorum, sed non sola, ut Aristoteles putat; multa quippe incognita inopinataque neque umquam temptata animis somniamus, quotiens provenisse uspiam significantur quae nondum scientiae fama

perfunctory; but if commotions *lingering* within the mind are of special significance, then visual *images corresponding to their mode and locations will arise,* expressly reproduced and residing in *memory* for long periods because of the significance attaching to the images. Moreover, the lingering commotions originate in thoughts, either moderate or immoderate, sometimes wise and sometimes foolish; they are sedate or provoked to irascibility, and respond to their *locations,* e.g., in the head, where the seat and domicile of reason is, or in the heart, where the virile force of indignation dominates, or in the liver and below; the whole of the latter area, moreover, is consigned to lust.

250. And since we are coming now to the treatment of dreams, about which the ancients hold differing opinions, we should review those which carry particular weight. Aristotle, holding the view that divine providence extends to the region of the Moon, and supposing that below it there is no governance by the decrees of providence—no support through the aid and counsel of angels and no intervention on the part of demonic foresight—, and so discounting all divination and claiming that the future is not foreknown, admits with approval a single category of dreams, that which, in stemming from what we do and think while awake and while residing in our memory, stirs our souls, still cognizant of things done and thought, into motion during sleep. He is not wrong, for there is indeed this family of dreams, although not, as he supposes, only this one. In fact, we dream many unknown and unanticipated things, ones that have never occurred to us, whenever things from elsewhere, of which word has not yet brought knowledge, are manifested by signs, or when things yet to be, which have not yet

conciliaverit vel futura portenduntur quae nondum prove-
nerint. Sed hic suo quodam more pleni perfectique dogmatis electo quod visum sit cetera fastidiosa incuria neglegit.

251. Heraclitus vero consentientibus Stoicis rationem
nostram cum divina ratione conectit regente ac moderante
mundana: propter inseparabilem comitatum consciam decreti rationabilis factam quiescentibus animis opere sensuum futura denuntiare, ex quo fieri ut appareant imagines
ignotorum locorum simulacraque hominum tam viventium
quam mortuorum. Idemque asserit divinationis usum et
praemoneri meritos instruentibus divinis potestatibus.

252. Hi quoque parte abutentes sententiae pro solida
perfectaque scientia sunt qui nostrum intellectum et per-
volitare convexa mundi putent miscereque se divinae intellegentiae, quam Graeci noyn vocant, et velut ex maiore
disciplina minusculas scientias mutuatas <ea> quae summa
et eminens imaginetur mens nuntiare mentibus nostris in-
vitante ad coetum animae nocturnae solitudinis opportunitate. Sed cum pleraque non inreligiosa modo verum etiam
impia somniemus, quae imaginari summam eximiamque intellegentiam sive mentem seu providentiam fas non sit putare, falsam esse hanc opinionem hominum liquet.

253. Sed Plato magna diligentia summaque cura discussis
penitus latibulis quaestionis vidit atque assecutus est non

come about, are portended. But having selected what appeared best with his characteristic instinct for a full and complete doctrine, he neglects the other categories with a disdainful lack of interest.

251. Heraclitus, on the other hand, and with him the Stoics, connects our reason with the divine Reason that rules and moderates things in the world: because of the inseparable connection our reason becomes aware of the decree of Reason and with the support of sensory data announces, while our souls are at rest, things to come, with the result that images of unknown places and visual representations of people both living and dead appear. And he asserts the utility of divination, that those deserving of it are advised in advance by the divine powers that instruct.

252. And those who wrongly adopt a partial opinion in place of solid and complete knowledge are the ones who suppose that our intellect wings its way through the vaults of the world and mingles with the divine intelligence, which the Greeks call *nous;* and that when nocturnal solitude furnishes the opportunity by summoning the soul to union the intellect communicates to our minds — as though in discrete bits of knowledge borrowed from a greater store thereof — those things which the highest and preeminent mind has mental images of. But since much of what we dream is not only irreligious but actually impious, and since it is blasphemous to suppose that the highest and noblest intelligence, mind, or providence has mental images of such things, it is obvious that this view held by people is false.

253. Plato, however, after having discussed thoroughly, in great detail and with supreme care, the obscurities of the question, saw and understood that dreams do not stem from

unam somniorum esse genituram; gigni quippe vel ex reliquiis cogitationum et accidentis alicuius rei stimulo, ut in
nono Politiae libro docet oratione tali: Inutiles minimeque
necessariae cupiditates, quae adversantur legibus, videntur
mihi omnium quidem hominum promisce labefactare mentes; quaedam tamen earum tam castigatione legum quam
sobriis et melioribus rectae voluptatibus vel omnino exolescere vel in paucas admodum atque exiles attenuatae reliquias otiosae latere, porro aliae usque ad praecipitem amen-
tiam confirmari, quae se exerunt immanius per quietem,
quotiens ratione sopita, quae est rector mansuetissimus,
cetera pars animae agrestior immani quadam ebrietate luxu-
rians pulsa quiete pergit ad incestas libidines. Tunc quippe
nihil est quod non audeat velut soluta et libera honestatis
verecundiaeque praeceptis; namque maternos (ut putat)
amplexus concubitusque non expavescit nec quemquam
dubitat lacessere vel hominum vel deorum nec ab ulla sibi
videtur caede aut flagitio temperare. Contra cum erit in salubri statu posita casteque cubitum ibit, rationabili quidem
mentis industria vigiliis imperatis; eaque pasta sapienti virtutis indagine atque etiam libidine moderate mansuefacta,
ut neque de inopia queri possit nec expletione nimia grave-
tur ultraque modum maerens vel gestiens tumultuetur
impediatque prudentiam sed pura vitiis ratione opus proprium efficere in ratiocinando atque indagine veritatis insti-
tuat; nihiloque minus iracundia delinita et minime saeviente

a single point of origin, but that they certainly *do* arise out of the residue of our thought processes and the stimulus of a particular chance event, as he explains in the ninth book of the *Republic,* in the following words: "Useless and unnecessary desires that act in opposition to the laws appear to me to undermine the minds of all men indiscriminately; but some of them, when corrected by both the castigation of the laws and sober, better pleasures, either disappear completely or on being reduced to exceedingly faint and weak residues lie hidden and inactive, while others gather strength to the point of headlong madness, raising their heads the more savagely during sleep, when that most gentle driver reason has been rendered dormant and the other, more savage part of the soul by its rioting about in some ferocious orgy drives away sleep and rushes to fulfill its unholy appetites. And then there is nothing it will not dare, having been unleashed, as it were, and freed from the precepts of decency and shame; for it has no fear (so it supposes) of embracing or having intercourse with a mother, it does not shrink from attacking any man or god, nor does it see fit to rein in any form of bloodshed or profligacy. But when it has achieved a healthy disposition and enters chastely into sleep, after the watch has been assigned by the mind's rational diligence; and when it has pastured on the wise pursuit of virtue and become tamed to moderation in its appetite, so that it cannot complain for want and is not burdened by overindulgence or thrown into confusion by inordinate grieving and longing, thereby impeding its wisdom, but determines instead, with its reason pure of vices, to perform its proper task in reasoning and the pursuit of truth; and when it sleeps, after the irascible part too has been soothed

dormiat: tunc certe rationabilis animae pars nullis sibi ob-
strepentibus libidinis aut iracundiae vitiis perveniet ad indaginem veri, quae est sincera prudentia, nec ulla existet species nefaria somniorum. Quippe in his perfecte docuit, quod
perfunctorie posuit in Timaeo.

254. At vero somniorum, quae divina providentia vel caelestium potestatum amore iuxta homines oboriuntur, causam rationemque exposuit in eo libro qui Philosophus inscribitur. Ait enim divinas potestates consulere nobis,
quotiens per quietem ea quae grata sunt deo intimant veris
minimeque fallacibus visis, earumque miram quandam esse
dicit memoriae tenacitatem dignitatique et divinitati congruam sapientiam, quibus cum cogitationes hominum
perspicuae sint, consequenter amorem bonis, odium malis
exhiberi; probationemque affert de exemplis illustribus mu-
tuatam, ut in eo libro quem appellavit Critonem praesagit
Socrates proventum imminentem regente somnii relatione.
Visa est mihi quaedam, inquit, mulier eximia venustate,
etiam candida veste, nomine me appellasse dixisseque illud
Homericum: Tertia luce petes Pthiae praefertilis arva. Rursus in Phaedone: Saepenumero unum et idem mihi somnium adventans in alia atque alia forma iubebat me navare
operam musicae. Id ego nunc usu et necessitate moriendi
admonitus interpretor hactenus, ut hymnum, quem iam
dudum institueram in Apollinem, compleam, ne promissi

and ceases raging: then surely the rational part of the soul, being unobstructed by the failures of its appetite or irascibility, will enter upon the pursuit of truth, or uncontaminated wisdom, and of the types of dreams it has none will prove morally offensive." Clearly, with these words he provided a full explanation of what he laid out cursorily in the *Timaeus*.

254. But in the book entitled *The Philosopher* he set out a causal explanation of the dreams that originate in divine providence and in the favor celestial powers show toward human beings. For he says that the divine powers look after our interests whenever during our sleep they intimate in true and undeceiving visions what pleases god, and he indicates that their memory is possessed of a certain extraordinary tenaciousness and that their wisdom is in conformity with their divine dignity; since human thoughts are clearly seen by them, favor is shown to the good and disapproval to the wicked, as accords with each. And he adduces evidence drawn from illustrious examples, e.g., in the book which he called *Crito* his Socrates has a premonition, through guidance related in a dream, of what is to come. He says: "A certain woman, exceedingly beautiful and in a white gown, appeared before me, addressed me by name, and said in the words of Homer, 'On the third day you will direct your course to the fields of most fertile Phthia.'" Again, in the *Phaedo:* "On numerous occasions one and the same dream, coming before me in different forms, would bid me to devote myself to making music. Having been informed of the inevitable necessity of dying, I now interpret this to mean that I should complete the hymn that I had begun some time ago for Apollo, so that I do not finish this life owing on

debitor et voti reus vitam prius finiam. Musicae quippe consanguineam esse poeticam palam est omnibus. Socratem vero haec evidenter solitum somniare arbitror ex eo, quod tam corporis quam animae puritate totum eius animal vigeret.

255. Denique etiam vigilanti non deerat propitia divinitas quae eiusdem moderaretur actus, ut Plato demonstrat in Euthydemo dicens ita: Est ab ineunte aetate numen mihi comes quoddam idque vox est quae, cum ad animum sensumque meum commeat, significat ab eo quod agere proposui temperandum, hortatur vero ad nullum actum; atque etiam si quis familiatis uti meo consilio volet aliquid acturus, hoc quoque agi prohibet. Quarum quidem rerum et significationum fides certa est; eget enim imbecilla hominum natura praesidio melioris praestantiorisque naturae, ut idem asseruit supra. Vox porro illa quam Socrates sentiebat non erat, opinor, talis quae aere icto sonaret, sed quae ob egregiam castimoniam tersae proptereaque intellegentiori animae praesentiam coetumque solitae divinitatis revelaret, siquidem pura puris contigua fore miscerique fas sit. Atque ut in somnis audire nobis videmur voces sermonumque expressa verba, nec tamen illa vox est sed vocis officium imitans significatio, sic vigilantis Socratis mens praesentiam divinitatis signi perspicui notatione augurabatur. Nec vero dubitare fas est intellegibilem deum pro bonitate naturae suae rebus omnibus consulentem opem generi hominum,

a promise and bound by a vow." That poetry is naturally akin to music is no doubt evident to all; but I think that Socrates's habit of dreaming these things clearly stems from the fact that the whole of his living being throve on a purity of body as well as soul.

255. Finally, even while he was awake there was not lacking a propitious divinity to guide the actions of this same man, as Plato indicates when he says in the *Euthydemus:* "There is a kind of divine power, with me since youth, and it is a voice that on entering my mind and awareness indicates the need to refrain from what I have proposed to do, without urging me toward any course of action; and even if some friend wishes to avail himself of my advice before undertaking something, this too it prevents from happening." And the reliability of these indications is certain, for in its weakness human nature requires the protection of a superior and higher nature, as he also claimed above. Moreover, the voice Socrates repeatedly sensed was, I suppose, not the sort to produce a sound through an impact on the air but rather to reveal to a soul, which by virtue of its exceptional chasteness was pure and therefore of heightened intelligence, the presence and companionship of a familiar divinity, since things pure are permitted contact and intercourse with things pure. And just as we think we hear voices and the articulated words of speech in dreams despite its not being a voice but a message imitating the function of the voice, so in waking hours Socrates's mind would intuit for itself the presence of divinity through observation of a conspicuous sign. But it is blasphemous to doubt the willingness of the intelligible god, who in the goodness of his nature looks after the interests of all things, to confer—in consideration of his own lack

quod nulla esset sibi cum corpore conciliatio, divinarum potestatum interpositione ferre voluisse; quarum quidem beneficia satis clara sunt ex prodigiis et divinatione vel nocturna somniorum vel diurna fama praescia rumores ventilante, medelis quoque aduersum morbos intimatis et prophetarum inspiratione veridica.

256. Multiformis ergo est ratio somniorum, siquidem sunt quae velut percussa gravius verberataque mente vestigiis doloris penitus insignitis per quietem refovent imagines praeteritae consternationis, sunt item quae iuxta cogitationes rationabilis animae partis vel purae atque immunis a perturbatione vel in passionibus positae oboriuntur, nihiloque minus quae divinis potestatibus consulentibus praemonstrantur vel etiam poenae loco ob delictum aliquod formata in atrocem et horridam faciem. Consentit huic Platonico dogmati Hebraica philosophia; appellant quippe illi varie, ut somnium et item visum, tum admonitionem, etiam spectaculum nihiloque minus revelationem: somnium quidem, quod ex reliquiis commotionum animae diximus oboriri, visum vero, quod ex divina virtute legatur, admonitionem, cum angelicae bonitatis consiliis regimur atque admonemur, spectaculum, ut cum vigilantibus offert se videndam caelestis potestas clare iubens aliquid aut prohibens forma et voce mirabili, revelationem, quotiens ignorantibus sortem futuram imminentis exitus secreta panduntur. De somniis satis dictum; sermo nunc ipse considerandus.

257. At vero simulacrorum, inquit, quae in speculis oboriuntur. Docet nunc illam visus rationem, quae intuitio

of connection with body—aid upon the human race through the intervention of the divine powers: their services are abundantly clear from prodigies and divination, whether at night in dreams or by day when a prescient report fans the spread of rumors, also from the remedies intimated for diseases and the truthful inspiration of prophets.

256. Our account, therefore, involves numerous forms of dreams, since there are those that revive in sleep the images of past disturbance when the mind is the more gravely struck and beaten, as it were, by deeply embedded vestiges of grief, and those that arise in connection with the thoughts within the part of the soul that is rational or pure and immune to perturbation or subject to passions, and equally well those revealed in advance by the divine powers that watch over us and, in lieu of punishment for some wrong, assume an atrocious and terrifying form. The Hebrew philosophy is in agreement with this Platonic doctrine, although they employ different terms, such as "dream," "vision," "admonition," "manifestation," and also "revelation": a dream, which we said arises out of vestigial disturbances within the soul; a vision, the kind that is ushered in by a divine power; an admonition, when we are guided and admonished by the counsel of angelic goodness; a manifestation, e.g., when a celestial power makes itself openly visible to us during waking hours, ordering or forbidding something in awe-inspiring form and speech; a revelation, whenever the secrets of a coming event are revealed to those who are ignorant of what the future holds in store. So much for dreams; the text itself must now be considered.

257. He says [46a–b]: *But of the images that appear in mirrors.* He now gives an account of the type of vision called

dicitur, intra speculum vel stagnorum profundum simulacris resultantibus nec tamen eodem quo Aristoteles magisterio. Namque ille censet radii visualis impacti in solidam speculi superficiem proptereaque infracti mucronem ad os reverti obviumque vultui factum vultum suum cernere et in speculo putare sibi vultus apparere simulacrum, at vero Plato pro ingenii prudentiaeque divinitate duum luminum coetum confluentium in tersam speculi et solidam cutem, id est diurni luminis et intimi, quod per oculos fluit, trahentis se-cum de vultu manantem colorem, in speculo corporari colo-ratisque vultus lineamentis et formato ac deliniato colore simulacrum aemulum vultus adumbrari. Sic quippe loquitur: At vero simulacrorum quae in speculis oboriuntur facilis as-secutio est, siquidem utriusque ignis tam intimi quam extra positi concursu, intimi scilicet caloris et extra positi lumi-nis, incidentis in tersam aliquam levemque materiam, hoc est speculum, formatique in multas et varias figuras, quia di-verse formata specula diversas edunt imagines, simulacra, inquit, ex levigati corporis conspectu resultant.

258. Dextrae vero partes quae sunt sinistrae videntur. Agit nunc de immutatione visus; et quia specula quaedam facta sunt ad similitudinem dimidiatae sphaerae concava, si ad eam partem, quae umbonis habet tumorem, contempla-tio dirigatur, dextrae partes sinistrae videbuntur contraque; item oculi dextri contemplatio laevas simulacri partes sinis-trique item acies dextras tangent insolito more. Merito;

reflection, when images are refracted from within a mirror or from beneath the surface of pools. His teaching is not, however, the same as Aristotle's. For the latter holds that the leading edge of a visual ray that has hit the hard surface of a mirror and thus been refracted returns toward the countenance, sees its own face standing opposite itself, and supposes that the facial image is presented to it in the mirror. Plato, however, with his divine combination of ingenuity and wisdom, thinks that the intersection of two sources of light—i.e., daylight and the internal one that draws the color emanating from the body as it flows through the eyes—which are confluent on the smooth, hard surface of the mirror is figured forth in the mirror, and that an image replicating the face takes shape as the facial outlines acquire color and the color acquires shape and outline. Here is how he states it: *But of the images that appear in mirrors the explanation is simple, for when a combination of the two fires, internal and external,* namely, the internal heat and external light, *encounters a polished or smooth material,* i.e., the mirror, *and assumes a variety of different shapes,* for differently formed mirrors give off different images, the *images,* he says, *rebound as a function of our directing our gaze at the smooth body.*

258. *Parts that are on the right appear left* [46b]. He is treating now of the reversal of a visual ray; and since some mirrors are made concave in the manner of a hemisphere, if the gaze is directed toward the part that has the rounded protuberance of the boss on a shield, then the *parts on the right* will *appear left* and vice versa; at the same time, the gaze of the right eye will make contact with the left side of the image and *likewise* the *left* eye's ray with the right side, *against the usual norm.* Rightly so, for given that the visual rays of both

cum enim in directum rigorem utriusque oculi visus ferantur, erat consequens dexterioris visus directione partes dextras tangi sinistrique item sinistras; nunc fit contra velut
circumactis et e diverso consistentibus imaginibus.

259. At vero dextrae corporis partes dextrae ita ut sunt in
speculis quoque sinistraeque item sinistrae videntur. Persequitur aliud duplicis imaginationis genus, quod apparet in
his speculis quae facta sunt ad formam cylindri cavi sive imbricis. Rursum enim cum in directum rigorem utriusque
oculi visus ferantur, dexter visus dextrum latus eminens et
obliquum, sinister etiam sinistrum tale latus incurrant necesse est. Formae tunc in lateribus geminis conglobatae ob
tersam et inclinatam proptereaque lubricam utriusque lateris superficiem labuntur in latera diversa, quae quidem a
dextro visu nascitur, in sinistrum latus, quae vero a sinistro,
similiter in dextrum; quae quia in diversa latera transitum
faciunt et simul e diverso videntur consistere, dextras simulacrorum partes dextris nostris, sinistras item sinistris obvias exhibent. Ceteros errores videndi ab hoc iuniores philosophi mutuati exposuerunt, ita ut supra comprehensum est.

260. Deinde prosequitur: Qui quidem sensus famulantur
actibus opificis dei summam optimamque et primariam
speciem molientis. Quia cum de visu loqueretur, qui est optimus omnium sensuum, corporeis eum nominibus appellaverat modo ignem modo lumen interdum flammam cognominans, ne quis putaret se ita existimare quasi corporeis

eyes travel in a direct line, what followed was that the right side should be brought directly into contact with the right visual ray and likewise the left side with the left one; but now it is reversed, as though the images had been turned round and were standing *opposite* to where they were.

259. [46b] *However, the right-hand parts of the body appear on the right in the mirror, exactly as in reality, and the left-hand ones on the left.* He pursues another kind of double imaging, the kind that appears in mirrors made in the form of a concave cylinder or semicylindrical tile. *For* once again, *given that the visual rays of both eyes travel in a direct line,* the right-hand one necessarily encounters the right side, which protrudes in a slope, and the left-hand one the left side, which is of the same shape. Given the smoothly sloping and hence slippery surface of both sides, the forms on both sides, now *compressed in the shape of balls,* glide to the opposite sides, the one issuing from the right-hand visual ray to the left side and likewise the one issuing from the left-hand one to the right; and since they effect the shift to the opposite sides and simultaneously appear to stand *opposite* to where they were, they display the right-hand parts of their images facing our right-hand ones and likewise the left-hand ones facing our left-hand ones. With this material in hand later philosophers expounded the other visual illusions as interpreted above.

260. He then continues [46c–d]: *And these senses serve the activities of the craftsman god in his striving for the highest, noblest, and primary form.* Since in discussing vision, the noblest of all senses, he referred to it by the names of corporeals, speaking variously of *fire, light,* and *flame* [45b, 67c], and to prevent anyone's supposing that in his estimation the *senses*

opificiis sensus administrentur sine melioris incorporeae potentiae consortio, dicit hos ipsos sensus famulari divinis actibus perinde ut opifici famulantur organa; porro optimum dei opus est id quod intellegit. Sed opinari plerosque dicit, eos videlicet qui existimant nihil esse quod carens corpore quicquam patiatur aut faciat, nihil etiam incorporeum fore cui pareat famuleturque corpus, ut puta mentis intellectui animae naturae, sed ipsa corpora qualitatibus propriis rerum creare diversitatem, frigus quidem terram et aquam, calorem vero ignem et aera, rursus astrictionem quidem et duritiam terram et ignem, relaxationem vero et effusionem aera et aquam; igneamque vim contraria molientem pro corporum diversitate modo astringentem modo relaxantem, ut cum uno et eodem calore limus quidem durescit, cera vero liquescit.

261. Haec porro omnia, inquit, neque sentiunt nec rationem intellectumque in rebus ratione prudentiaque agendis sciunt. Praeclare, siquidem ratiocinari et intellegere non corporis sed animae proprium. Haec porro incorporea, non enim videntur, cum omne corpus sit visibile ac sentiatur; itaque, cum discreta sint corpus et anima diversaque eorum natura sit, dignitas quoque et ordo diversus est. Quotus quisque igitur amator est sapientiae, dabit operam ut prudentis naturae causas prius quam ceteras assequatur. Sunt porro hae: deliberativa et item intellegens animae potentia, quibus deliberat ratiocinatur intellegit. Illas vero, inquit, quae ab aliis motae movent alias, secundas existimandum.

administer to acts of corporeal construction independently of a higher incorporeal power, he says that these *senses* in fact *serve* the divine *activities* in the way that tools *serve a craftsman;* and in the case of god, the *noblest* work is that which he thinks. But he says that most people, namely, those who think that there is nothing incorporeal which is in any way acted upon or acts, further *suppose* that there is no incorporeal such as mind, intellect, soul, or nature for body to be subject to and serve, but that through their proper qualities the bodies themselves create the diversity among things: *cold* creates earth and water, whereas *heat* creates fire and air; again, *constriction* and hardness create earth and fire, whereas *relaxation* and effusion create air and water; and the power of fire gives rise to contraries according to the differences between bodies, alternately causing constriction and relaxation, "as when under one and the same heat clay hardens but wax liquefies."

261. Moreover, all of these, he says [46d–e], *have neither sensation nor knowledge of the reason and understanding involved in performing tasks rationally and wisely.* Obviously, for to reason and understand is a property, not of body, but of soul. These, moreover, are incorporeal; for they are *invisible,* whereas body of every kind is *visible* and sensible; hence, since body and soul are separate and the nature of each is different, different also is their stature and rank. Thus the rare *lover* of wisdom will devote himself to understanding the *causes belonging to the wisest of natures* before understanding others. And they are these: the deliberative as well as intelligent faculty of soul, those by which it deliberates, reasons, and understands. *And,* he says, *those causes which are moved by others and set yet others in motion should be regarded as*

Perspicue patibilem partem rationabilis animae vitiosamque
significat, in qua est impetus; quippe impetus principaliter
quidem ab ea parte animae movetur, quae motu intimo genuinoque ex semet ipsa movetur, ex accidenti vero etiam
desideriis moventibus, ipse autem impetus movet corpus.

262. Itaque principalis animae motus definitur aeterna
substantia semet ipsam movens, hic vero communis, qui
commotus movet, operatio moventis est in eo quod movetur, ut sectio operatio secantis in eo quod secatur. Cuius quidem motus aliquot diversitates sunt, quas demonstravit in
Legibus, octo corporis, animae duas, corporeum motum
locularem vocans, cuius duae sint species, translatio et cir-
cumlatio, item alium, quem appellat qualitatem, aeque in
duplici specie, concretione et discretione, tertium, quem
positum esse dicit in quantitate, habentem item duas species, incrementum et diminutionem, quartum iuxta essentiam, cuius aeque duae species intelleguntur, una generatio,
altera interitus. Animae item duplex motus, unus qui alia
movet, ipse a nullo movetur sed proprio genuinoque motu,
alius qui alia movens ab alio movetur; qui est patibilis habitus animae et aegritudine oppressus.

263. Recte ergo faciet amator sapientiae si cum de his rebus tractandum erit naturalem ordinem servet, ac principe
loco de anima disserat, post demum de corpore; deinde cum
de anima tractabit de illa prius disserat quae tam semet

secondary. He clearly means the part of the rational soul that is subject to the passions and vices, in which impulse resides. For impulse is moved primarily by the part of the soul that moves itself with an innate inner principle of motion, and incidentally by its motive desires; but impulse on its own moves the body.

262. And so the movement pertaining to soul in the primary sense is defined as an eternal self-moving substance, whereas the common movement, which moves on being moved, is the effect of what moves in that which is moved, as cutting is the effect of what cuts on that which is cut. Of the latter movement there are numerous varieties, which he pointed out in the *Laws;* eight pertain to body and two to soul. Corporeal motion he calls locomotion, of which there are two kinds, motion from place to place and circumlation; and another, which he calls quality, is similarly of two kinds as well, aggregation and disaggregation; a third, which he says falls under quantity, likewise has two kinds, increase and diminution; a fourth pertains to substance, of which again there are understood to be two kinds, one generation and the other destruction. The movement of soul is likewise of two kinds, the one which moves other things while itself being moved by nothing except its own innate motion, another which while moving certain things is moved by another, which is the state of soul that is subject to passions and burdened by distress.

263. The lover of wisdom will therefore act rightly to preserve the natural order when treating of these matters: in the first instance, he will *examine* [46e] soul, and body only thereafter; then, in coming to treat of soul he will first discuss that which moves both itself and other things, which

ipsam movet quam cetera, in qua est vis deliberandi et intellegendi; tunc consequenter illam quoque pertractabit
quae ab alia re potiore mota quaedam movet. Id porro
motus genus si quidem pareat intellectui erit aliquatenus
ordinatum, si minus, temere, inquit, et ut libet se exerens
confusa et inordinata quae agit relinquit. Et addit: Nobis
quoque igitur in eundem modum faciendum; ac prius de ea
loquendum natura quae suo motu movetur—haec quidem
praecedit ordine, per quam intelleguntur et sciuntur aeterna
quae sola semperque vera sunt—, tunc demum illa quoque
alia demonstranda quae ad movendum quid motu indiget
alieno. Utrique porro motui sensus necessarii sunt, quoniam
ex his tam cupiditates excitantur improbae quam rerum op-
timarum intellectus et scientia convalescit.

12. Laus Videndi

264. Et de oculorum quidem ministerio satis dictum; nunc
de praecipua operis eorum utilitate dicendum, quae cum in
plerisque rebus tum in obtentu philosophiae clare perspicitur, quo beneficio negat quicquam maius a deo generi esse
humano tributum. Duplex namque totius philosophiae
spectatur officium, consideratio et item actus: consideratio
quidem ob assiduam contemplationem rerum divinarum et
immortalium nominata; actus vero qui iuxta rationabilis
animae deliberationem progreditur in tuendis conservan-
disque rebus mortalibus. Utrique autem officiorum generi

contains the deliberative and intellective faculty; then, next in order, he will come to treat also of that which, while being moved by something more powerful, moves certain others. And if the latter type of motion submits to intellect it will be ordered to some degree, but if not, he says, then in *thoughtlessly and randomly* thrusting ahead it *leaves* everything it does in a *disordered state of confusion*. And he adds, *It is also incumbent upon us, therefore, to proceed accordingly;* and the discussion should first be of that nature which moves itself by virtue of its own motion—in order this takes precedence, and through it are understood and known the eternal things that uniquely, always, and in truth *are*—only then should the others, which require extraneous motion in order to move something, be pointed out as well. The senses, moreover, are necessary for both types of movement, since owing to them knowledge of the highest things is strengthened but immoral desires too are stirred up.

12. IN PRAISE OF VISION

264. [46e–47b] *And concerning the service provided by the eyes enough has been said;* we must now discuss the *particular utility of the work they do,* a utility that is clearly manifested in our acquisition of philosophy, among many other things. And he says that *no benefit greater than this* has been bestowed upon *mankind* by god. For the function of philosophy as a whole is discernibly twofold, consideration and action: consideration, so called because of continuous contemplation of divine and immortal things; and action, which in its oversight and preservation of mortal affairs proceeds according to the deliberation of the rational soul. Now, vision is necessary to

visus est necessarius ac primum considerationi. Dividitur porro haec trifariam, in theologiam et item naturae sciscitationem praestandaeque etiam rationis scientiam. Neque enim quisquam deum quaereret aut ad pietatem aspiraret, quod est theologiae proprium, nec vero id ipsum quod nunc agimus agendum putaret nisi prius caelo sideribusque visis et amore nutrito sciendi rerum causas, eorum etiam quae ortum habent temporarium exordia; haec quippe demum ad naturalem pertinent quaestionem. Quid quod dierum et noctium vice considerata menses et anni et horarum curricula dinumerata sunt numerique ortus et genitura dimensionis intro data? Quod ad tertiam partem philosophiae pertinere perspicuum est.

265. At vero actuosae philosophiae visus quatenus sit utilis et necessarius, docet ita dicens: deum oculos hominibus idcirco dedisse ut mentis providentiaeque circuitus qui fiunt in caelo notantes eorum similes constituerent in suis mentibus, hoc est, motus animi qui deliberationes vocantur quam simillimos instituerent divinae mentis providis motibus placidis tranquillisque perturbatos licet. Quod est morum vitaeque correctio, quae publice privatimque prodest tam ad domesticas quam ad publicas res recte salubriterque administrandas, ex his quippe constat alterum philosophiae genus quod activum vocatur. Id porro dividitur trifariam, in moralem domesticam publicam, quibus omnibus officiis prodest certe usus videndi.

both types of function but to consideration in the first instance. And consideration is divided three ways, into theology, the investigation of nature, and the knowledge of how to employ reasoning. For no one would search for god or aspire to a state of piety, which is the task proper to theology, nor would anyone suppose the very thing we are now doing to be worth doing if he had not first viewed the heaven and stars and nourished a love of knowing both the causes of things and the origins of those that have their coming-to-be in time; and these matters pertain ultimately to the inquiry into nature. And what about the facts that months, years, and hourly rounds are numbered, and that the origin of number and the generation of measurement are introduced in consideration of the alternation between days and nights? And it is obvious that this pertains to the third part of philosophy.

265. But he explains the degree to which vision is useful and necessary to the part of philosophy that concerns action, as follows [47b]: *that god gave eyes to human beings so that by observing the circuits of mind and providence that occur in the heaven* they might establish *ones like them* in *their own minds,* i.e., so that they might make the mental movements *which are called deliberations as like as possible, despite their disturbances, to the provident, calm, and tranquil movements of the divine mind.* And this is the *correction* of one's character and life, which brings public and private advantage for the upright and *beneficial* administration of both domestic and public affairs, since from these the second kind of philosophy consists, the kind that concerns action. And it is divided three ways, into the moral, domestic, and public philosophy, to all of which functions the use of vision undoubtedly proves advantageous.

266. Minora, inquit, alia praetereo, scilicet ea, quae in variis artibus disciplinisque versantur. Neque enim navium regimen neque cultus agrorum nec vero pingendi fingendique sollertia recte sine visu proprium opus efficere posset solaque contemplatio est quae mentes hominum usque ad caeli convexa protelat, proptereaque Anaxagoras cum ab eo quaereretur cur natus esset ostenso caelo sideribusque monstratis respondisse fertur "ad horum omnium contemplationem." At vero Stoici deum visum vocantes quod optimum putabant idem pulchro dei nomine tribuendum esse dixerunt. Theophrastus visus pulchritudinem asserens visum formae nomine appellat quod quorum extincta est acies videndi vultus informes sint et velut in aeterna consternatione. Denique ex oculorum habitu mens atque animus indicatur irascentium maerentium laetantium. Irascentium quidem ut apud Homerum commotae mentis orator:

Stabat acerba tuens defixo lumine terrae

et item:

. . . furor ignea lumina volvit;

maerentium vero ut fert poeta de eo qui iugi fletu oculos amiserat:

. . . maeroreque lumina linquunt,

item apud Ciceronem, "in huius amantissimi sui fratris . . . gremio maerore et lacrimis consenescebat."

266. *I pass over,* he says [47b], *the other minor benefits,* namely, those concerning the various arts and disciplines. For the guidance of ships, the cultivation of fields, and skill in painting and sculpting—without vision, none would be able to effect its proper task, and contemplation alone is what propels the minds of men up to the heavenly vaults, which is why Anaxagoras, on being asked why he had been born, is reported to have pointed to the heaven and stars and said, "for the contemplation of all *them*." The Stoics, for their part, spoke of vision [*thea*] as a god[dess] and maintained that that which they held in the highest esteem should also receive the tribute of being referred to by the noble name "god" [*theos*]. Theophrastus in proclaiming the nobility of vision [*eidon*, "I see"] refers to it by the name "form" [*eidos*] on the grounds that the faces of those whose eyesight has been extinguished are deformed and as though in a state of perpetual consternation. Finally, in the disposition of the eyes the mood and thought of those who are irate, grieving, or happy is indicated. In the case of those who are irate, as with the orator of agitated mind in Homer:

> He would stand, staring bitterly with his eye fixed on the earth,

and again:

> . . . fury makes his fiery eyes roll;

and in the case of those who are grieving, as the poet says of the man who had lost his eyes through constant weeping:

> . . . and his eyes disappear in his grief,

or in Cicero, "in the bosom of this his most loving brother he wasted away in grief and tears."

267. Transit deinde ad alterius sensus examinationem, ait enim: eadem vocis quoque et auditus ratio est ad eosdem usus atque ad plenam vitae hominum instructionem datorum. Sunt igitur principales duo sensus visus et auditus, utrique philosophiam adiuvantes; quorum alter quidem evidentior, utpote qui res ipsas acie sua comprehendat, alter latior, ideo quod etiam de rebus absentibus instruat, modulatus siquidem aer articulatae voci factusque vox et intelligibilis oratio pergit ad intimos sensus audientis intellectui nuntians tam praesentia quam absentia. Idem auditus quod intellectum quoque adiuvet, sic probat: quantumque per vocem utilitatis capitur ex musica, totum hoc constat hominum generi propter harmoniam tributum, quia iuxta rationem harmonicam animam in superioribus aedificaverat naturalemque eius actum rhythmis modisque constare dixerat, sed haec exolescere animae ob consortium corporis necessario obtinente oblivione proptereaque immodulatas fore animas plurimorum. Medelam huius vitii dicit esse in musica positam, non in ea qua vulgus delectatur quaeque ad voluptatem facta excitat vitia non numquam, sed in illa divina, quae numquam a ratione atque intellegentia separetur; hanc enim censet exorbitantes animas a via recta revocare demum ad symphoniam veterem. Optima porro symphonia est in moribus nostris iustitia, virtutum omnium principalis, per quam ceterae quoque virtutes suum munus atque opus exequuntur, ut ratio quidem dux sit, vigor vero intimus, qui

267. He shifts to examination of another sense, saying [47c–d]: *The same account holds also for voice and hearing, which have been given for the same purposes and for the full instruction of human life.* There are, then, two principal senses, vision and hearing, both of them aids to philosophy: one of them the more obviously so, in that by virtue of its proper acuity it is suited to comprehend things in themselves, and the other more subtly so, in that it is suited to provide *instruction* even concerning absent things, since air, when modulated according to the articulation of voice and *becoming* voice or intelligible speech, reaches the inner senses of the listener, announcing to the intellect things present as well as absent. And that this hearing aids intellect too he shows as follows: *and it is clear that as much of the vocal utility as is captured in connection with music has been conferred upon mankind entirely for the sake of harmony.* For in earlier sections he constructed the soul in accordance with harmonic ratio and indicated that its natural activity consists of rhythms and modes, but that the latter fade owing to soul's association with body, as the state of oblivion inevitably takes hold, and that the souls of many are consequently deprived of modulation. The remedy for this defect, he says, is found in music, not the music in which the mob delights and which sometimes gives rise to vices, when performed for the sake of pleasure, but in the divine music that is never disposed to separation from reason and intelligence. For he holds that this is the music that finally calls souls that stray from the right path back to their original state of harmony. And the noblest form of harmony in our character is justice, chief among all the virtues, by way of which the other virtues too execute their task and work, so that reason leads while an inner power resembling

est iracundiae similis, auxiliatorem se rationi volens prae-
beat; porro haec provenire sine modulatione non possunt,
modulatio demum sine symphonia nulla sit, ipsa symphonia
sequitur musicam. Procul dubio musica exornat animam
rationabiliter ad antiquam naturam revocans et efficiens
talem demum, qualem initio deus opifex eam fecerat. Tota
porro musica in voce et auditu et sonis posita est. Utilis ergo
etiam iste sensus est philosophiae totius assecutioni ad no-
tationem intellegibilis rei.

13. De Silva

268. Deinde ait: Nunc quoniam cuncta exceptis admodum
paucis executi sumus, quae providae mentis intellectus instituit, oportet de illis etiam quae necessitas invexit dicere.
Mundi sensilis explanaturus omnem substantiam iure commemorat prope omnia se pertractasse quae provida mens
dei contulerit, efficiens eum ad exemplum et similitudinem
intellegibilis mundi, solumque residuum superesse tractatum, ex quo ea quae necessitas invexit considerentur,
quando providis necessariisque rationibus mundi universitas constare videatur. Necessitatem porro nunc appellat hylen, quam nos Latine silvam possumus nominare, ex
qua est rerum universitas eademque patibilis natura, quippe
subiecta corpori principaliter, in qua qualitates et quantitates et omnia quae accidunt proveniunt; quae cum a natura
propria non recedat, diversis tamen et contrariis speciebus

irascibility willingly offers itself as its supporter. These things, moreover, cannot occur without modulation; but there would ultimately be no modulation without harmony, while harmony itself follows from *music*. Without any doubt, music provides the adornment of reason to the soul by calling it back to its primordial nature and finally rendering it as the craftsman god originally made it. And the whole of music is found in voice, hearing, and sounds. Thus this sense too is useful for the understanding of philosophy as a whole as regards the observation of intelligible reality.

13. ON MATTER

268. He says next [47e]: *Since with very few exceptions we have treated of all that the intellect of the provident mind established, it is necessary now to speak also about the things for which necessity is responsible.* Since he intends to provide a thorough explanation of the sensible world, he rightly draws attention to the fact that he has discussed nearly everything that the *provident mind* of god has conferred by making it after the example and likeness of the intelligible world, and that the only other treatment left is a consideration of the *things for which necessity is responsible,* since the world in its entirety is seen to consist of two explanatory principles, the provident and the necessary. *Necessity,* moreover, is what he uses here to designate *hylê,* which we can call *silva* in Latin: it is the source of the universal array of things and is at the same time passible by nature, being for body the primary substrate in which qualities and quantities and all accidental phenomena occur; although it *does not recede from* the nature *proper to it* [50b], it nevertheless changes in accordance with the

eorum quae intra se recipit formisque variatur. Hanc igitur explanare proposuit dicturus deinceps rationem ob quam necesse fuerit tractatum hunc minime praeteriri.

269. Denique addit: mixta siquidem mundi sensibilis ex necessitatis intellegentiaeque coetu constitit generatio. Quia igitur de mundi generatione tractatur perfecteque id fieri convenit, oportet de utroque genere disseri; ex quo de natura silvae necessarius esse tractatus ostenditur. Mixtam vero generationem dicit esse ideo quod ex diversis elementis initiisque constet, rectecteque ex <necessitatis providentiaeque coetu non ex> necessitate et providentia; non enim ex his mixtus est mundus sed consultis providae mentis et necessitatis rationibus constitit operante quidem providentia et agente, silva vero perpetiente exornationique se facilem praebente, penetratam siquidem eam usque quaque divina mens format plene, non ut artes formam tribuentes in sola superficie sed perinde ut natura atque anima solida corpora permeantes universa vivificant.

270. Dehinc consequenter intellegentiae necessitatisque demonstrat consortium, cum ita dicit: dominante intellectu. Duplex porro est dominatio, altera violentior tyrannicae potentiae similis item alia sanctitatis imperatoriae. Omne porro violentum non diu subiectum conservat sed facile perdit. Omne, inquit, quod rationabiliter et regit et tuetur prodest et melius efficit quod regit. Ut igitur mundus aeternus esset, oportuit silvam ei morigeram parentemque

different, even contrary, species and forms of what it receives within itself. So his intention was to explain this before subsequently discussing the reason why it is necessary that the treatment should not be passed over.

269. Then he adds [47e–48a]: *for the generation of the sensible world consisted of a blended union of necessity and intelligence.* Since, then, the treatment concerns the *generation of the world,* and it is fitting that it be carried out fully, it is necessary that there should be discussion of each kind; and from that the treatment of the nature of matter is shown to be necessary. Now, the reason for his speaking of the *generation* as *blended* is that it consists of diverse elements and origins, and he rightly says that it consists of a *union of necessity* and providence, and not *of necessity* and providence; for the world is not a blend of the latter but consists as a result of the reasoned deliberations of *provident mind* and necessity: providence is the operative agent, while matter is passive and offers itself without resistance for adornment, since the divine mind penetrates and informs it completely and in every quarter—not like the arts, which provide form only superficially, but in the way that nature and soul vivify all solid bodies by permeating them.

270. Moving on from this he demonstrates the union of intelligence and necessity, when he says [48a] *with intellect dominating.* Now, domination is twofold: one form, the more violent one, resembles tyrannical power, and the other imperial sanctity. No violent principle, moreover, sustains for long that which is subject to it, but it easily destroys it. Everything, he says, that rules and protects rationally benefits and improves that over which it rules. For the world to be eternal, then, it was necessary that matter should be

subdi nec adversum exornationem suam resistentem sed ita victam ut maiestati opificis libens cedat pareatque eius sapientiae. Proptereaque dixit: salubri persuasione rigorem necessitatis assidue trahente ad optimos actus. Itaque victa, inquit, et parente providis auctoritatibus necessitate prima rerum mundique exordia constiterunt. Quia est et alia minus consulta parentia quae error et facilitas dicitur; ut sit provida parentia ratione nixa necessitas, et opus dei tale est, ut vi persuadeat vimque inroget persuadentem, hoc est ut persuasio vim et vis adhibeat persuasionem. Id porro perspicitur in aegritudinibus virorum prudentium, cum praebent se medicis urendos ac secandos.

271. Deinde progreditur: Si quis ergo vere iuxtaque meram fidem mundi huius institutionem insinuaturus erit, hunc oportet erraticae quoque causae speciem demonstrare. Rursum alio silvam erroris nomine appellat propter inordinatam eius antiquam iactationem, similiter ut necessitatem, propterea quod non est principalis causa mundi constitutionis in silva, sed necesse fuerit ascisci eam ob substantiam corporalem. Est quippe silva perinde ut sunt ea sine quibus quod institutum est effici non potest.

272. Facto igitur recursu redit ad indaginem initiorum et incipit ex eo tempore quod praecedit ortum generationemque mundi. Quaerit quoque naturam ignis sinceri et

compliant with intellect, allowing itself to be subdued, not resisting the adornment it received but being overcome in such a way as to yield willingly to the majesty of the craftsman and to submit to his wisdom. Which explains why he said: *with salubrious persuasion assiduously drawing the recalcitrance of necessity toward the highest acts. And so,* he continues, *once necessity had been subdued and was obedient to the authority of providence, the first beginnings of things and of the world came to be.* For there is as well another, less deliberate form of obedience, which is known as error and mere diffidence; and so the providential form of obedience is a necessity founded upon reason, and the work of god is such as to persuade through force and to impose a force that persuades, i.e., such that persuasion applies force, and force persuasion. And this is witnessed in the illnesses experienced by wise men when they offer themselves to be cauterized and cut by physicians.

271. He then goes on to say [48a]: *If, then, one is going to explain the establishment of this world truly and with pure intention, then it is necessary for him also to identify a form of errant cause.* Again, he calls matter by another name, *errant motion,* because its turbulence is in origin disordered, just as he calls it *necessity* because, although the principal cause of the constitution of the world is not in matter, it was necessary that matter should be introduced in consideration of corporeal substance. Indeed, matter is like those things in the absence of which the object of one's intentions cannot be effected.

272. *After retracing his steps* [48a–c], then, he returns to an investigation of the first principles and begins with the time that precedes the birth and generation of the world. He seeks out as well the *nature* of pure and unmixed fire, also its

sine permixtione, qualitatem quoque eius et passionem, nec
solius ignis sed ceterorum quoque corporum serenorum nec
ulla contagione interpolatorum; omnes quippe, qui de originibus tractaverunt universae rei, quattuor sunt materias
executi has quae concretione mutua ex maioris atque obtinentis materiae vocabulo cognominatae sunt. Quatenus
porro eaedem materiae et ex quibus antiquioribus substite-
rint, nemo usque adhuc dixerat, sed tamquam scientibus
naturam sinceritatemque earum ignem et aera et aquam et
terram velut elementa mundi sensilis esse dixerunt, quae ne
in syllabarum quidem ordinem locanda sunt. Quia sermonis
elementa litterae sunt, post quas secundi ordinis syllabae,
recte dixit quattuor haec mundana corpora ne in syllabarum
quidem ordinem collocanda. Quippe primum elementum
universae rei silva est informis ac sine qualitate quam, ut sit
mundus, format intellegibilis species; ex quibus, silva videlicet et specie, ignis purus et intellegibilis ceteraeque sincerae
substantiae, [quattuor] e quibus demum hae materiae sensiles, igneae aquatiles terrenae et aereae. Ignis porro purus
et ceterae sincerae intellegibilesque substantiae species
sunt exemplaria corporum, ideae cognominatae; quarum ad
praesens differt examinationem nec quaerit unane sit archetypa species eorum quae sunt communis omnium an innumerabiles et pro rerum existentium numero, quarum coetu
et congregatione concreverit universa moles, an vero idem
unum pariter et multa sint, ut docet in Parmenide. Quae
causa declinandi fuit non laborem sed ne instituto sermoni

quality and *condition,* and not of fire alone but also of other bodies that are undisturbed and unaltered by any contagion. For all those who have treated of the origins of the universe have pursued these four *material elements,* which are named after the material element that obtains the dominant share as concerns their mutual *assemblage.* And to what extent and from which more ancient things the same material elements came to be *no one had yet* said, *but as though speaking to people who knew* their unadulterated nature they claimed that fire, air, water, and earth are the elements, as it were, of the sensible world, although they are *not even* to be placed at the rank of *syllables.* Given that the elements of speech are letters, syllables being second in rank thereafter, he rightly said that these four corporeal elements of the world are *not even* to be placed at the rank of *syllables.* To be sure, the primary element of the universe is matter, deprived of form and quality, which intelligible form informs in order that there may be a world; and from them, namely, matter and form, pure and intelligible fire and the other unadulterated substances arise, and from them finally these sensible material elements with dominant shares of fire, water, earth, and air. And pure fire and the other unadulterated and intelligible forms of substance are for corporeal beings the paradigms, called *ideai.* For the moment he postpones examination of them and does not raise the question of whether there is a single archetypal form common for all of the things that exist, or innumerable ones corresponding to the number of existent entities from whose interaction and aggregation the universal mass coalesced, or indeed the same thing is both one and many, as he teaches in the *Parmenides.* The reason was, *not* to avoid effort, *but* to prevent blending into the *proposed*

minime conveniens tractatus admisceatur, haec quippe naturalis, illa epoptica disputatio est, naturalis quidem ut
imago nutans aliquatenus et in veri simili quadam stabilitate
contenta, epoptica vero quae ex sincerissimae rerum scientiae fonte manat.

273. Deum ergo, inquit, etiam nunc liberatorem invoco ex
turbida et procellosa sermonis iactatione. Laborat omnino
et id agit, ut instituamur ad pietatem venerationemque divinitatis, cuius opem exorat ingrediens procellosum de natura
silvae fretum propter novum atque insolitum etiam tunc
disputationis genus. Rursum ergo ab exordio dicamus, inquit. Merito; iam enim de utraque origine tam exemplari
quam corporea tractaverat concedens sensilem mundum ex
isdem substitisse; quippe id quod gignitur et perit nec vere
semperque est corporea species est. Quae quidem corpora,
cum sola et per se ac sine suscipiente ex eadem essentia essentia esse non possunt (quam modo matrem, alias nutriculam, interdum totius generationis gremium, non numquam
locum appellat quamque iuniores hylen, nos silvam vocamus), ut quod deerat adderet, hunc de silva tractatum initiorum tractatui iungit posterioremque divisionem ait operosius esse ordinandam. Tunc quippe res omnis in duo fuerat
initia divisa, quorum alterum intellegibilis erat species quam
mundi opifex deus mente concepit, eamque idean cognominavit Plato, alterum imago eius, quae natura est corporis.

274. Porro corpora si per se ipsa spectentur perfectam
videbuntur habere substantiam, sed si ad originem eorum

discussion a treatment that would have been out of place. For the disputation here concerns nature, whereas there it is epoptic: "concerns nature," as in the case of a slightly shifting image that is limited to the level of stability associated with a degree of verisimilitude; and "epoptic," in that it flows from the fountainhead of the purest knowledge of reality.

273. *Once again, then,* he says [48d–e], *I invoke god as liberator from the turbulent and stormy agitations of our discussion.* He endeavors to do it entirely so that we may be instructed in piety and veneration for the divinity, whose aid he implores in entering into the *stormy* sea that attaches to the nature of matter owing to a style of *disputation* that was *new and uncommon* even then. Hence he says, *Let us once again take the discussion from the beginning.* Rightly so, for he had already discussed both types of origin, the exemplary and corporeal, allowing that the sensible world has come to be from them; for that which is born and perishes and does not exist in the true sense or forever is the corporeal form. Since these bodies cannot exist on their own, *per se,* or without a substance to engender them from within itself (which he variously calls the *mother, nurse, womb of all generation,* and *Place* [49a–52b], and later thinkers call *hylê,* and we *silva*), in order to supply what was missing he adjoins this discussion of matter to one on first beginnings and says that a second *division* must be provided for *with greater elaboration.* For *then* everything was divided into *two* principles, of which one was the intelligible *form* which the craftsman god of the world conceived in his mind, and Plato gave it the name *idea,* and the other its image, which is the nature of body.

274. Bodies, moreover, if viewed in themselves will appear to possess substance in the full sense, but if you turn

convertis mentis intentionem invenies cuncta et eorum sca-
tebras silvae gremio contineri. Tunc ergo compendio principalibus materiis quattuor sumptis exaedificaverat sermone
mundum. Sed quia erat philosophi proprium cuncta quae
ad causam pertinent summa cura mentis et diligentiore
examine peragrare, ratio porro asserit subiacere corporum
diversitati silvae capacitatem, recte rationabiliterque censuit hanc ipsam rationem trahendam usque ad intellegentiae lucem, difficile opus omnino vel assequi, longe tamen
difficilius declarare ac docere. Talis quippe natura est initiorum quae neque exemplis demonstrari, nondum his quae ad
exemplum comparentur existentibus, possit nec ex praece-
denti ratione aliqua intimari, nihil quippe origine antiquius,
sed obscura quadam luminis praesumptione, non ut quid sit
explices sed contra, sublatis quae sunt singulis, quod solum
remanet ipsum esse quod quaeritur intellegendum relin-
quas, hoc est, ut, universis corporibus quae intra gremium
silvae varie varia formantur mutua ex alio in aliud resolutione singillatim ademptis, solum ipsum vacuum sinum
speculatione mentis imagineris.

275. Qua ratione factum ut, cum nullus eam veterum
dubitet esse, utrum tamen facta an contra infecta sit discep-
tetur. Eorumque ipsorum qui infectam sine generatione

your mind's gaze to their origin you will find that they and their wellsprings are all contained in the womb of matter. Now, at first he constructed the world according to an account which for the sake of brevity assumed the four principal material elements. But since it is the task proper to the philosopher to search, through the highest level of mental care and an exceptionally diligent process of examination, all that pertains to causality, and since reason asserts that a material capacity acts as a substrate for the diversity manifest in corporeal things, he rightly and reasonably determined that this line of reasoning should itself be drawn out into the light of intelligence, and that although the task would prove extremely difficult to grasp, to explain and teach it would nevertheless prove far more difficult. For the nature of first principles is such as to be indemonstrable through examples, since the things that might be furnished by way of example do not exist in advance; nor is it deducible from some antecedent ground, for nothing is prior to an origin, but from an obscure preconception, as it were, of light, and not in the sense that you explain what the thing is but rather that after removing all the things that are you leave only that which remains as the object actually sought to be understood, i.e., in the sense that, after removing one by one all of the corporeal things variously formed within the womb of matter through the varied process of reciprocal analysis from one thing into another, you by mental speculation imagine only the empty womb in itself.

275. This is how it has come to pass that, although none of the ancients doubts that matter exists, there nevertheless is disagreement over the question whether it is created or, on the contrary, uncreated. And of those in fact who have held

posuerunt, plerique continuam et iugem alii vero divisam
putent; rursumque eorum qui dividuam esse censent partim
sine qualitate et informem partim formatam esse pronuntient; hi vero qui iugem continuatamque posuerunt dis-
ceptent inter se de qualitatibus formaque eorum quae ibidem conformantur et omnium quae isdem accidunt, utrum
ex silva proveniant an ex alio potiore numine accommoden-
tur. Quorum breviter perstringentur opiniones.

276. Hebraei silvam generatam esse censent. Quorum
sapientissimus Moyses non humana facundia sed divina, ut
ferunt, inspiratione vegetatus in eo libro qui De Genitura
Mundi censetur ab exordio sic est profatus iuxta interpreta-
tionem septuaginta prudentium, "Initio deus fecit caelum
et terram, terra autem erat invisibilis et incompta," ut vero
ait Acyles, "Caput rerum condidit deus caelum et terram,
terra porro inanis erat et nihil," vel ut Symmachus, "Ab exordio condidit deus caelum et terram, terra porro fuit otiosum
quid confusumque et inordinatum." Sed Origenes asseverat
ita sibi ab Hebraeis esse persuasum quod in aliquantum sit a
vera proprietate derivata interpretatio, fuisse enim in exemplari, "Terra autem stupida quadam erat admiratione." Omnia tamen haec in unum aiunt concurrere, ut et generata sit
ea quae subiecta est universo corpori silva sermonesque ipsos sic interpretantur: Initium minime temporarium dici,
neque enim tempus ullum fuisse ante mundi exornationem
dieique et nocturnas vices quibus temporis spatia dimensa

that it is uncreated and ungenerated most suppose that it is
continuous and constant, and others that it is discrete; of
those in turn who think that it is discrete some claim that it
is without quality or form, while others claim it has form;
and those who have held that it is constant and continuous
disagree with one another about the qualities and shape of
the things that receive form within matter and of all the accidental attributes attaching to them: do they arise out of
matter or adhere to it through the agency of another more
powerful force? Their opinions will be briefly touched upon.

276. The Hebrews think that matter is generated. Moses,
wisest among them, was quickened, they say, by divine inspiration rather than human eloquence. In the book known as
The Generation of the World he began by saying, according
to the translation of the seventy wise men, "In the beginning God made heaven and earth, but the earth was invisible and without order," or as Aquila says, "At the head of
things God fashioned heaven and earth, but the earth was
empty and nothing," or Symmachus, "At the start God fashioned heaven and earth, but the earth was something inert,
confused, and disordered." But Origen claims to have been
persuaded by the Hebrews that the translation deviates
slightly from the true sense, and this on the grounds that
the original had, "but the earth was in a certain state of
dumb admiration." Nevertheless, they say that all of these
versions converge in one respect, that the matter which underlies all corporeal reality was generated, and they interpret the actual words as follows: "Beginning" is not meant in
the temporal sense, for prior to the world's receiving order
there was no time or successions of day and night to measure

sunt; tum initii multas esse significationes, ut "initium sapientiae timorem domini" fore Salomon ait, item "initium
sapientiae cultus dei" nihiloque minus "initium viae opti-
mae iustus actus" atque etiam in praeconio sapientiae caelestis auctor, "initium vitae panis et aqua et tunica," inquit,
"et domus idonea velandis pudendis." Quippe in his non una
initii sed diversa et multiplex habetur significatio. Est tamen unum rerum omnium initium, de quo Salomon in Pro-
verbiis "Creavit me," inquit, "deus progressionis suae semitam, cui nitens efficeret opera divina constituitque ante
ortum mundi terraeque et profundi fundationem, ante tractus fontium aggestionesque montanas," aperte indicans
praeeunte divina sapientia caelum terramque facta eandemque divinam sapientiam fore universitatis primordium. Ex
quo apparet sapientiam factam quidem a deo sed non aliquo
in tempore, neque enim fuerit tempus ullum quo deus fuerit
sine sapientia, quodque deum percipi cogitationibus hominum ante quam sapientiam eius sit necesse ob eminentiam
naturae, quia prius cuius res est, tunc demum ipsa res nosci-
tur. Et de initio quidem sic habendum.

277. Quod autem caelum quamve terram Scriptura loquatur, intellegendum. Qui tumultuario contenti sunt intellectu, caelum hoc quod videmus et terram qua subvehimur
dici putant. Porro qui altius indagantur negant hoc caelum

temporal extension. They then say that "beginning" has multiple significations; for example, Solomon says, "fear of the Lord is the beginning of wisdom," or again, "worship of God is the beginning of wisdom," or similarly, "a just act is the beginning of the noblest way," and in the hymn to wisdom in particular the heavenly author says, "the beginning of life is bread, water, a garment and house suitable to conceal the pudenda." In these passages the signification of "beginning" is clearly understood to be manifold rather than unitary. There is, nevertheless, one beginning of all things, concerning which Solomon says in Proverbs, "God created me as the pathway of his progression, in reliance upon which he might effect his divine works, and he established me before the origin of the world and the earth and the foundation of the deep, before the flowing of springs and the massing of mountains," explicitly indicating that divine wisdom came before heaven and earth were made, and that the same divine wisdom was the primordial origin of the universe. And from this it is clear that wisdom was indeed made by God but not at any point in time, for there was no time when God was without wisdom, and that human thought necessarily perceives God before wisdom owing to the superiority of his nature, since the possessor of a thing is known first, and only then does the thing itself come to be known. And this is how we should take the term "beginning."

277. But we should come to an understanding of the sense in which Scripture speaks of heaven and earth. Those who are content with an unstable understanding think that this heaven which we see and the earth that supports us from below are meant. And those who pursue the question in greater depth say that this heaven was made, not in the

ab initio factum sed secundo die, namque ab initio factum lumen idque "diem" esse cognominatum, hoc vero caelum postea quod deus appellaverit "soliditatem." Tertio deinceps die remotis "aquis apparuit sicca" eique "terrae" nomen impositum ut sit evidens neque hoc caelum cognitum nobis neque hanc in qua sumus terram ab exordio facta sed alia esse antiquiora, intellectu potius quam sensibus haurienda. Aliud ergo verum caelum et aliud quiddam esse soliditatem Scriptura testatur eodemque modo aliud terram et item aliud siccam.

278. Quod ergo illud caelum prius quam cetera deus condidit quamve terram? Philo carentes corpore atque intellegibiles essentias fore censet, ideas et exemplaria tam siccae istius terrae quam soliditatis; denique etiam hominem prius intellegibilem et exemplum archetypum generis humani tunc demum corporeum factum a deo esse dicit. Alii non ita sed scientem prophetam duas esse species rerum omnium, alteram intellegibilem alteram sensibilem, eas virtutes quae utramque naturam circumplexae contineant caelum et terram cognominasse, caelum quidem incorpoream naturam, terram vero quae substantia est corporum, quam Graeci hylen vocant. Astipulantur his ea quae sequuntur, "terra autem erat invisibilis et informis," hoc est silva corporea, vetus mundi substantia, prius quam efficta dei opificis sollertia sumeret formas, etiam tunc decolor et omni carens qualitate; quod vero tale est, invisibile certe habetur et informe; inanis porro et nihil propterea dicta, quia

beginning, but on the second day, for in the beginning light was made, and it was called "day," whereas the heaven which God called the "firmament" was made afterward. Then after the "waters" had been removed "there appeared" on the third day the "dry," and the name "earth" was given to it, so that it is evident that neither this heaven known to us nor this earth on which we exist were created in the beginning but other more ancient ones were, ones that must be absorbed by the intellect rather than the senses. Thus Scripture testifies to the true heaven's being one thing and the firmament something else, and in the same way that earth is one thing and the dry, likewise, another.

278. Which, then, is that heaven which God fashioned before the others, and which earth? Philo thinks that they are incorporeal and intelligible essences, the ideas or exemplars of both this dry earth and the firmament; he goes so far as to say that man too was first made intelligible, in an archetypal exemplar of the human race, and only subsequently made corporeal by God. Others hold a different view, that the Prophet, knowing that there are two forms of all things, one intelligible and the other sensible, called the qualities which embrace and encompass the two natures heaven and earth, and that whereas heaven is an incorporeal nature, earth is that which is the substance of bodies and which the Greeks call *hylê*. They adduce in support of this the following words, "but the earth was invisible and formless," that is, corporeal matter, the ancient substance of the world, prior to being shaped and assuming forms through the skill of God its craftsman, while still colorless and lacking any quality; but that which is in such a state is certainly held to be invisible and deprived of form and is called void

cum sit omnium qualitatum receptrix propriam nullam habet ex natura. Silva ergo, ut quae cuncta quae accidunt recipiat in se, "inanis" appellata e<s>t, ut quae compleri numquam posse videatur, porro quia sit expers omnium, "nihil" dicta. "Otiosa" vero et "indigesta" nuncupatur a Symmacho: quod quidem per se nihil valeat, "otiosa"; quod vero habeat opportunitatem suscipiendi ordinis ab exornante semet deo mundum moliente "indigesta" censetur. "Stupidae" vero ex "admiratione" significatio animae vim quandam similitudinemque declarat, siquidem opificis et auctoritatis sui maiestate capta stuperet. Quod si facta est a deo silva corporea quondam informis, quam Scriptura "terram" vocat, non est, opinor, desperandum incorporei quoque generis fore intellegibilem silvam, quae "caeli" nomine sit nuncupata. Factam vero et ita factam ut sit quae non fuerit sic probant, quod opificibus mortalibus apparata ab aliis opificibus silva praebeatur hisque ipsis natura suppeditet, naturae deus, deo nemo apparaverit, quia nihil deo sit antiquius; ipse igitur silvestres impensas mundi fabricae sufficientes utilesque constituit. Multasque alias probationes afferunt quas singillatim persequi longum est.

279. Restat nunc ut eorum quoque qui generatam esse corpoream silvam negant sententias exequamur; quorum aeque diversae opiniones omnino sunt. Sunt enim qui textum eius et quasi continuationem quandam corpusculis, quae intellegantur potius quam sentiantur, conexis sibi

and nothing in the sense that as the recipient of all qualities it by nature has no quality of its own. Matter, then, being that which receives all incidental attributes in itself, is called "void" in the sense that it appears incapable of ever being filled, and it is called "nothing" because it is devoid of all things. By Symmachus, however, it is called "inert" and "disordered": "inert," in the sense that of itself it is incapable of doing anything; and it is considered "disordered" in that it has the aptitude for receiving order from God, who in building the world adorns it. The phrase, "in a state of dumb admiration," on the other hand, identifies a certain power of or likeness to soul, since it was struck dumb by the majesty of its craftsman and maker. But if a previously formless corporeal matter which Scripture calls "earth" was made by God, then, I suppose, there is no need for despair concerning there having been an intelligible matter of the incorporeal kind as well, which is given the name "heaven." And the view that it was made, and made in such a way that there exists matter which did not exist, they defend as follows: matter is bestowed ready-made upon mortal craftsmen by other craftsmen, and upon the latter by nature, upon nature by God, and upon God by no one, since nothing is prior to God; thus *He* fashioned building materials that were sufficiently and suitably calibrated to the fabrication of the world. And they adduce many other arguments, which to rehearse individually would be a lengthy task.

279. It remains now for us to investigate the views of those who say that corporeal matter is not generated, whose opinions are altogether just as diverse. There are those who assign its texture and a certain continuity, as it were, to interconnected particles which are perceptible to intellect

invicem assignent in aliquo modo positis et aliquatenus figu-
ratis, ut Democrito et Epicuro placet. Addunt alii qualitatem, ut Anaxagoras, sed hic omnium materiarum naturam
proprietatemque in singulis materiis congestam esse censet.
Alii propter exiguitatem individuorum corporum, quorum
numerus in nullo fine sit, subtilitatem silvae contexi putant,
ut Diodorus et non nulli Stoicorum, quorum sit fortuitus
tam coetus quam segregatio. Quas opiniones cum sint omnino sine fine praetereo.

280. Qui tamen providentiae opus silvae quoque constitutionem esse pronuntiaverunt, censent eam una quadam
ab exordio usque ad finem continuatione porrectam, nec tamen omnes eodem modo, aliter enim Pythagoras et item aliter Plato diversoque Aristoteles modo et cum aliquanta differentia Stoici. Sed hi quidem omnes informem eam et sine
ulla qualitate constituunt, alii formam dederunt, ut Thales,
quem ferunt ante omnes naturalia esse secreta rimatum,
cum initium rerum aquam esse dicat, opinor ideo quod
omnem victum quo utuntur quae vivunt humectum vide-
ret; inque eadem sententia Homerus esse invenitur, cum
Oceanum et Tethyn dicat parentes esse geniturae, cumque
iusiurandum deorum constituat aquam, quam quidem ipse
appellat Stygem, antiquitati tribuens reverentiam et iureiu-
rando nihil constituens reverentius. At vero Anaximenes
aera iudicans initium rerum, initium quoque corporum ceterorum et ipsius aquae, non consentit Heraclito caput rerum ignem putanti. Omnes ergo hi qui vel aquae vel aeri vel

rather than sense perception and have a certain position and degree of shape, as Democritus and Epicurus hold. Others, such as Anaxagoras, add quality, although he thinks that the nature and property of matter in all its forms are compounded within each and every kind of matter. Others, such as Diodorus and certain Stoics, hold that the subtle structure of matter is given coherence due to the minuteness of its indivisible particles, which are limitless in number and the coupling or separation of which is a matter of chance. These opinions I pass over, since they are quite endless.

280. Those, however, who proclaimed that even the constitution of matter is the work of providence think that it extends from beginning to end in a kind of unified continuum, but not all view it in the same way, for Pythagoras, Plato, Aristotle, and to a certain extent the Stoics see things differently. All of them, however, establish it as deprived of form and any quality, whereas others granted form, such as Thales, who according to tradition was the first to survey the secrets of nature in saying that water is the beginning of all things—owing, I suppose, to his observation that all food consumed by living creatures is moist. Homer is found to be of the same view when he says that Ocean and Tethys are the parents of generation and establishes water as that by which the gods swear oaths; he himself calls it Styx, of course, in deference to antiquity and showing that there is nothing more worthy of reverence than the swearing of oaths. Anaximenes, on the other hand, in holding that air is the beginning of things, including the other solid bodies and even water, disagrees with Heraclitus, who reckons that fire is the source of things. All of those, then, who attribute

igni tribuunt principatum, in motu positam rerum originem censuerunt.

281. Sunt tamen qui immobilem fore defendant et eandem ex omnibus in unam molem redactam, unum omnia esse censentes immobile sine ortu et sine interitu, ut Xenophanes Melissus Parmenides. Sed Parmenides quidem unum omne perfectum et definitum pronuntiat, Melissus infinitum et indeterminatum.

282. Empedocles varium et multiforme quiddam esse silvam docet quattuor diversis sustentatum radicibus ignis aquae aeris terrae atque ex his fieri corporum modo concretionem modo discretionem; idemque concretionem quidem vocat amicitiam discretionem vero discordiam. Hi sunt, opinor, qui formatam descriptamque qualitatibus et corpus silvam esse pronuntiant.

283. At vero qui detrahunt ei qualitates informemque constituunt et sine consortio corporum solam per semet ipsam mente intuentur, Aristoteles quidem tria initia constituit corporeae rei, silvam speciem carentiam, eaque singula sine duum residuorum conexione considerat, licet profiteatur altera sine alteris esse non posse. Idem sine genitura et sine interitu dicit mundum esse divina providentia perpetuitati propagatum; cuius sententia cum sit praeclara et nobilis et ad Platonici dogmatis considerationem satis accommodata non otiose praetereunda est. Prius tamen exponendus videtur physicorum veterum syllogismus qui asserit nihil eorum quae sunt generatum esse nec periturum fore;

primacy to water, air, or fire held that the origin of things is disposed toward motion.

281. There are, however, those, such as Xenophanes, Melissus, and Parmenides, who defend the view that it is immobile, self-identical, reduced from the multiplicity of things to a unitary mass; they hold that all things are one, immobile, without coming-to-be or passing-away. But whereas Parmenides claims that the one is altogether complete and delimited, Melissus claims that it is unlimited and indeterminate.

282. Empedocles teaches that matter is something variegated and multiform, sustained by the four different roots of fire, water, air, and earth, and that from them there arises an alternation between the concretion and discretion of bodies; he calls concretion Friendship and discretion Discord. These, I suppose, are the ones who proclaim that matter has form, is determined by qualities, and is body.

283. But as to those who strip it of qualities and deprive it of form and mentally conceive of it apart from corporeal contact, alone and *per se:* Aristotle establishes three first principles of corporeal reality, matter, form, and privation, and considers each separately and without connection to the remaining two, although he acknowledges that none is able to exist without the others. He says that the world has by divine providence been made to continue through perpetuity, without coming to be or passing away; and since his view is distinguished, noble, and well suited to the consideration of Platonic doctrine, it should not be casually overlooked. First, however, it seems advisable to expound a syllogism upheld by the ancient natural philosophers, which states that none of the things that exist has been generated

formula syllogismi talis est: Si quid fit id necesse est vel ex eo
fieri quod iam erat vel ex eo quod non est; utrumque autem
impossibile: de existente quidem quia quod iam dudum est
fieri ad praesens non potest (id enim quod gignitur nondum
est); nec vero de non existente quia necesse est ei quod fit
subesse aliquam materiam ex qua fiat: nihil ergo fit. Sed nec
corrumpitur: id enim quod corrumpitur vel in aliquas reliquias vel in nullas dissolvitur; sed neque in aliquas (ut doce-
bitur) neque in nullas: nihil ergo corrumpitur. Ostensum est
porro quod nec fiat quid: neque igitur fit aliquid neque corrumpitur. Quatenus ergo quod est et quod corrumpitur
negamus in nihilum posse dissolvi? Quia quod est et idem
corrumpitur ac perit: si in nullas reliquias dissolvatur, erit
pariter et non erit, quod rationem non habet; rursum si erit
aliquid futurum quod dissolvitur, illud et perit et non perit.

284. Hoc syllogismo veteres physici tollere conabantur
rerum genituram et interitum. Sed Aristoteles dividit syllogismum notata et patefacta duplici significatione nominum,
existentis scilicet et non existentis, item verborum fieri et
corrumpi. Etenim omnia quae fiunt vel secundum naturam
suam fiunt vel ex aliquo accidenti, ut puta si musicus aegro-
tus convalescat: quod quidem ex natura est aegrotat et
convalescit non tamen quia musicus est; ex accidenti porro
quia musicus est, accidit quippe ut musicus esset qui aegritudinem sustineret. Similiter quod corrumpitur: si quid

or will pass away; the syllogism takes the following form: Whatever *comes to be* necessarily comes to be either from that which already was or from that which is not; but neither is possible: not from what exists, since what already exists cannot now come to be (for that which is generated is not yet); nor again from what does not exist, since what comes to be necessarily has some underlying material from which it comes to be: thus nothing comes to be. But neither does it *pass away:* for that which passes away dissolves either into some remaining elements or into none; but neither into some (as will be explained) nor into none: thus nothing passes away. But it has been demonstrated that nothing comes to be: hence nothing either comes to be or passes away. In what sense, then, do we maintain that that which exists and that which passes away is incapable of dissolving into nothing? It is that that which exists also passes away and perishes: if it dissolves into no remaining elements, then it will both be and not be, which makes no sense; conversely, if that which dissolves is going to be something, then it both perishes and does not perish.

284. This is the syllogism by which the ancient natural philosophers tried to remove the coming-to-be and passing-away of things. Aristotle, however, disambiguates the syllogism by observing and drawing out the double signification of the substantives, namely, "existent" and "nonexistent," as also of the verbs to "come to be" and "pass away." For everything that comes to be does so either according to its *nature* or somehow *incidentally*, as, for example, if a musical person who is ill becomes well: his being ill and recovering comes from nature and is unrelated to the fact that he is musical; but his being musical—that it was a *musical* person who

candidum pedalis proceritatis corrumpatur in atrum colorem, secundum naturam quidem et principaliter patitur
immutationem sui, quia est candidum; ex accidenti vero
quia est pedalis modi. Cum igitur dicimus musicum conva-
lescere tunc quod fit ex accidenti fit, quia provenit ut convalescat; porro cum aegrotare eum dicimus secundum naturam patitur. Rursum cum dicimus candidum illud pedalis
mensurae corrumpi, quia convertatur in nigredinem, hoc ex
accidenti dicimus fieri; cum vero candidum cognominamus
naturam eius exprimimus. Si ergo dicimus etiam de non
existente fieri aliquid, dupliciter dicimus non existere: semel
iuxta naturam, quod est impossibile ut, quod nusquam omnino gentium est, ex eo aliquid fiat quod sit; iterum ex accidenti dicimus non existere, cum quod fit aliter se habebit
quam erat antea et cui plus accidit quam a natura tributum
est, ut si ex informi massa aeris simulacrum fiat, informitas
quippe aeris ex natura est, formae vero impressio, quam im-
ponit opifex, de non existente provenit proptereaque ex accidenti dicitur provenire. Fieri tamen potest ut ex eo quoque quod est fiat aliud quod sit sed hoc ex accidenti ut si cui
grammatico proveniat medicinae scientia; nam et hic ex pe-
rito fit alterius quoque disciplinae peritus. Consequenter
igitur etiam corrumpetur aliquid et dissolvetur existens in
aliud existens, sed non principaliter verum ex accidenti ut si

suffered the illness — is incidental. Similarly, passing away: if something white that is a foot in height passes away in the sense that it becomes black in color, then it undergoes a change in itself according to nature and in the primary sense, since it is white; but its measuring a foot is incidental. So when we say that a musical person is recovering, what comes to be does so *incidentally,* since it so happens that *he* recovers; and when we say that he is ill, his suffering is according to *nature.* Again, when we say that this white thing measuring a foot passes away in the sense that it turns black, we say that this comes to be incidentally; but when we call it white we pick out its nature. So if we say even of the nonexistent that something comes to be, we are using "nonexistent" in two senses: in one, according to *nature,* for it is impossible that something that exists should come to be from that which is in no sense whatsoever; in the other, we use "nonexistent" *incidentally,* for what comes to be will be different than it was before, incidentally acquiring something beyond what has been attributed by nature, as when a statue comes to be from a formless mass of bronze, for the lack of form in bronze is a fact of its nature, whereas the form impressed upon it by the artist arises out of the nonexistent and for that reason is said to arise incidentally. At the same time, it is possible for one thing that exists to come to be from another one that does, but in the incidental sense, as when this grammarian acquires a knowledge of medicine; for in this case from one who is skilled there comes to be one who is additionally skilled in a different discipline. It follows, then, that one existent thing will pass away and dissolve into another existent one, not in the primary sense but incidentally, as when someone transfers the shape from a

ex simulacro Liberi patris formam quis transferat in simulacrum Apollinis; videtur enim hoc quoque pacto forma in
aliam speciem demigrare, sed non proprie verum ex accidenti. Similiter poterit existens quid in non existens corrumpi ac resolvi sed non ut ex corruptela plenus afferatur
interitus proveniatque, ut id quod erat nihil omnino neque
uspiam gentium sit.

285. Una igitur haec ratio est iuxta quam posse Aristoteles
putat et fieri aliquid tam de existente quam de minime
existente et interire vel in existens vel in nihilum; alia vero
ratione esse et non esse dicitur quid quotiens, nondum adhibito effectu, esse dicitur quod procul dubio futurum erit (si
adhibeatur effectus). Quae cuncta possibilitate dicuntur
esse praesumpta eorum existentia contemplatione possibili-
tatis, ut cum aes dicimus possibilitate statuam fore cum adhuc metallum sit informe. Est ergo statua et non est, et est
quidem quia potest esse, non est autem quia nondum effectus accessit. Eodemque modo aliquatenus est aliquatenus
non est, et ex eo quod aliquatenus est potest aliquid effici,
nihiloque minus etiam in id quod aliquatenus non est potest
aliquid dissolvi atque interire. Est ergo genitura et interitus.

286. Haec ad praesens visa nobis necessaria fore ad explanationem Aristotelici dogmatis de initiis rerum, in quibus
etiam silva est, praetractari curavimus, sicut eiusdem Aristotelis verba declarant. Ait enim sic: Nobis ergo videbitur
[in]dividua esse silva carentiae, ita ut silva non sit existens
quid sed ex accidenti, carentia vero principaliter et omnino

statue of Father Liber to a statue of Apollo: in this way too the shape appears to shift to another, not in the proper sense but incidentally. Similarly, an existent thing will be able to pass away or dissolve into a nonexistent one, but not such that complete destruction is wrought or results from the passing-away, or such that what existed is in no sense whatsoever.

285. This, then, is one sense in which Aristotle thinks that it is possible for something to come to be from the existent or nonexistent and to pass away into the existent or nonexistent; in another sense, however, something is said to be or not be whenever that which will undoubtedly be (assuming the actuality obtains) is said to be when the actuality has not yet obtained. All of these things are said to exist potentially, in that their existence is presumed in consideration of the potentiality, as when we say that bronze is potentially a statue even though it is still metal deprived of form. Thus it is and is not a statue: it is, in that it is possible for it to be; but it is not, in that the actuality has not yet obtained. Similarly, it to some extent is and is not: something can be produced from that which to some extent is; it can equally well dissolve and pass away into that which to some extent is not. There is, then, generation and destruction.

286. So far we have ensured that these matters should be discussed [on the understanding] that they appear necessary for an explanation of the Aristotelian doctrine of the first principles of reality, among which principles, as Aristotle's own words declare, matter too is included. For here is what he says: "To us, then, matter will appear to be distinct from privation in the sense that matter is something existent only incidentally whereas privation is nothing in the

573

nihil; et silva quidem prope habeat essentiam, carentiae
nulla prorsum <sit> substantia. Et aliis, inquit, videtur carentia et silva unum esse non recte spectantibus, cum idem
breve et grande cognominent duasque res separatim spec-
tandas in unam eandemque rem redigant et unum aliquid
subiacere corporibus putent. Qui etiamsi dividant maius
illud et minus, ut sint duo, aeque ex hac duitate una res significatur alia intermittitur; siquidem silva tamquam mater
corporum formationi adiumento est, carentia vero non
adiuvat formationem sed potius impedit ac renititur, quatenus quia, cum species divina res sit et appetibilis, contraria
est ei carentia; silva vero appetit formam et illustrationem
cupidaque eius est iuxta naturam propriam. Porro carentia
si appetat formam, appetere eam necesse est contrarietatem
suam, et omnis contrarietas interitum affert; minime igitur
interitum suum carentia desiderabit. Nec vero species se ipsam potest cupere, est enim plenum et perfectum bonum, et
omne quod desiderat in indigentia positum est. Sola ergo
silva est quae cupit illustrationem, perinde ut femineus
sexus virilem et deformitas pulchritudinem, ita tamen ut
deformitas silvae non ex natura sed ex accidenti sit. Quae
silva fit et corrumpitur certe, cumque fit est aliquatenus, et
cum dissolvitur non est aliquatenus, corruptelaque eius
propter individuam carentiam provenit. Ipsa vero possibilitate, non natura, immortalis est ac sine generatione, propterea quod necesse erat his quae nascuntur subiacere aliquid
antiquius ex quo fierent atque ad generationem venirent,

primary and absolute sense; and whereas matter has something approaching substance, there is no substance whatsoever of privation. And others," he says, "who take the wrong view think that privation and matter are one thing, for they call the same thing small and big and reduce two things that should be viewed separately to one and the same thing and suppose that a single determinate thing acts as a substrate for bodies. And although they divide it into the greater and smaller, so as to make two, one thing is indicated and another omitted despite the duality; for matter, like a mother, cooperates in the formation of bodies, whereas privation does not cooperate in the formation but rather impedes and resists to the extent that, while form is a divine and desirable thing, privation is contrary to it; but matter seeks form and clarity and by its very nature is desirous of it. Moreover, if privation were to seek form then it must seek its own contrary, and yet all contrariety occasions destruction; privation, then, will not desire its own destruction. At the same time, form cannot desire itself, for it is a full and perfect good, and everything that desires is in a position of need. Hence matter alone desires clarity, as the female sex desires the male and deformity desires beauty, but in such a way that the deformity of matter is not in virtue of its nature, but incidental. And to be sure, matter comes to be and passes away: when it comes to be it to some extent is; when it dissolves it to some extent is not, and its corruption emerges as a result of an inseparable privation. But in pure potentiality, not by nature, it is immortal and not subject to generation, since it was necessary that something prior should act as a substrate for the things that are generated, something from which they might come to be and enter

talis est porro haec natura. Necesse est igitur fuisse silvam
ante quam fieret, siquidem ex ea fiunt cetera, sive quod dissolvitur et perit ad hanc eandem naturam postremo redeat
necesse est; ergo etiam corrupta erit ante corruptelam dissolutionemque.

287. Haec Aristoteles assistens sententiae suae de initiis
rerum deque natura silvae loquitur; sed quia obscurior
sermo est, explanandus videtur. Tres ab eo ponuntur origines universae rei, species silva carentia. Speciem laudat ut
summi dei similem divinitatem pleno perfectoque nixam
bono ideoque appetibilem. Quid est ergo quod "appetit"?
Neque ipsa se, inquit, quia nihil ei deest ad perfectam exornationem et est proprius indigentium appetitus. Nec vero
carentia cupit speciem, "interitum" enim "suum" cuperet,
quippe accessu speciei formaeque tollitur indigentia nec in
habitu proprio perseverat. Superest ergo ut silva cultum or-
natumque desideret, quae deformis est non ex se sed ob indigentiam. Est enim turpitudo silvam cultu formaque indigere, sic quippe erit vidua carens specie perinde ut carens
viro femina. Proptereaque et, inquit, appetit speciem "ut
sexus femineus virilem," quoque sit in aliqua posita "deformitate," formam atque cultum, simul cupiens perire atque
exolescere quod est in semet ex indigentiae vitio, contraria
siquidem haec duo sibi et repugnantia, species et item carentia, quorum quod obtinuerit alterum perimit. Cupiditatem vero negat esse talem qualis animalium sed ut cum quid

into generation, and such is this nature. Matter, therefore, necessarily was before it came to be, for from it all other things come to be, and what dissolves and perishes necessarily returns in the end to this same nature; it will also, therefore, have suffered corruption before its corruption and dissolution."

287. Aristotle makes these points in support of his views on the first principles of reality and the nature of matter; but his language, being rather obscure, seems in need of explanation. He posits three origins for the universe: form, matter, and privation. *Form* he praises on the grounds that it is a divinity, like the highest god, and desirable by virtue of its being supported by the full and perfect good. What, then, is there for it to "seek"? It does not seek itself, he says, since it lacks nothing for its complete adornment, and desire is proper to things that are in need. But neither does *privation* desire form, for it would desire "its own destruction," since through the advent of form and beauty need is done away with and fails to continue in its proper state. It remains, then, that *matter* should desire order and adornment, matter which is deformed not in and of itself but in virtue of its need. For there is an uncomeliness in the fact that matter lacks order and form, for it will in this respect be bereft of form just as a woman who lacks a man is. And so, he says, it desires form "as the female sex desires the male," and it is in a certain state of "deformity," desiring form and order and, at the same time, that the element within it that stems from the defect of its need should perish and fade away; for these two things, form and privation, are contrary to and repel one another, and the one that obtains destroys the other. He says, however, that the desire is not like that in living beings

coeptum atque inchoatum dicitur perfectionem desiderare. Sic, opinor, etiam silva speciem cupit, potest enim eius florere consortio.

288. Ergo iuxta Aristotelem proprie quidem et principaliter existens est species, ex accidenti vero esse dicitur silva, propterea quod natura talis est, ut recipiat formam. Rursum quod minime est proprie quidem et principaliter, carentia, ex accidenti vero silva; patitur quippe id quod vere atque ex natura non est, id est, carentiam. Ergo silva alio quodam genere "est" item alio "non est," et potest aliquid ex ea fieri ut de re non existente, non una tamen sed diversa significatione. Consequenter ergo dicemus malitiam esse atque initium malorum non silvam sed carentiam; haec est enim informitas et nullus cultus et turpitudo silvae, proptereaque etiam maleficentia. Et ideo silvam definit seu potius appellat corpus incorporeum, ut possibilitate quidem sit corpus, effectu vero atque operatione nullum corpus. Haec Aristotelis de silva sententia, nisi quod addit Platonem tria illa nominibus tantum attigisse, effectu autem duo posuisse initia corporeae rei, speciem et minimum grande, quod sit silva. Non ergo tria sed duo haec erunt initia, inquit, species et silva, quam ait ex natura nullam "habere substantiam"; aut si, inquit, "grande" hoc "minimum" carentiam fore intellegendum est, rursum silva praeterita erit et duo videbuntur initia rerum, species atque carentia.

289. Stoici quoque ortum silvae reiciunt, quin potius ipsam et deum duo totius rei sumunt initia, deum ut opificem, silvam ut quae operationi subiciatur; una quidem essentia

but is instead as when something that has been started and begun is said to desire completion. That, I suppose, is just the sense in which matter desires form, for the possibility of its flourishing is in its union with it.

288. According to Aristotle, then, *form* is what exists in the proper and primary sense, whereas matter is said by him to be incidentally, since its nature is such as to receive form. Conversely, *privation* is what in the proper and primary sense is not, whereas *matter* is incidentally, for it suffers that which truly and by nature is not, i.e., privation. *Matter,* then, in a certain respect "is" and in another "is not," and it is possible for something to come to be from it as from a nonexistent thing, not in one and the same sense but in a different one. The result of this, then, is that we will say, not that matter is evil or the source of evil, but that privation is, for it is the lack of form, the want of order, and the uncomeliness of matter, and for that very reason its capacity for evil. And that is why he defines, or rather calls, matter bodiless body: potentially it is indeed body but in effect and actuality it is none. This is Aristotle's view of matter, although he adds that Plato touched upon the three things in name only, having posited in effect two principles of corporeal reality, form and the great-small, or matter. And so, he says, the first principles will not be three but two, form and matter, which he claims "has" no "substance" in virtue of its nature; or if, he says, this "great-small" is to be understood as *privation,* then matter instead will have been overlooked, and the first principles of reality will appear to be two, form and privation.

289. The Stoics too reject the coming-to-be of matter, assuming instead form and god as the principles of all reality, with god as the craftsman and matter as the substrate for his

praeditos, facientem et quod fit ac patitur, corpus esse, diversa vero virtute, quia faciat, deum, quia fiat, silvam fore. Quorum ab re non erit opinionem diligentius explicari. Aiunt enim ut aenea quaeque ex aere sint argenteaque ex argento sic corporeas materias ex silva fore cum isdem, ut aere et argento etiam similibus ceteris; esse enim quasdam magis alias minus silvestres materias aliasque aliis corpulentiores, quarum tamen exordium fore unam quandam antiquiorem communem omnium silvam. Atque ut statua quae cum sit formatum corpus habet tamen subiectam sibi aeris antiquiorem substantiam sic aes informe corpus, compos tamen qualitatis, habere dicunt subiectam praeeuntem substantiam eamque esse corpus cohaerens sine qualitate, patibile totum et commutabile, quod silvam, simul essentiam appellant hactenus definientes: "essentia et silva est quod subiacet corpori cuncto" vel "ex quo cuncta sunt corpora" vel "in quo proveniunt rerum sensibilium commutationes ipso statu proprio manente" item "quod subditum est corporibus qualitates habentibus, ipsum ex natura propria sine qualitate."

290. Plerique tamen silvam separant ab essentia, ut Zeno et Chrysippus. Silvam quippe dicunt esse id quod est sub his omnibus quae habent qualitates, essentiam vero primam rerum omnium silvam vel antiquissimum fundamentum earum, suapte natura sine vultu et informem, ut puta aes aurum ferrum, cetera huius modi silva est eorum quae ex

action. They assume that the maker and that which is made and acted upon are body, being endowed with a single substance, but that in being endowed with different powers one is god by virtue of making and the other matter by virtue of being made. It will not be inapposite to explain their opinion in greater depth. For they say that as particular brazen things consist of bronze and silver ones of silver, so corporeal materials consist of matter in conjunction with these same things, e.g., bronze and silver, and indeed all other such things; for they say that certain substances are more material, others less, and some more corporeal than others, but that their origin nevertheless is a particular, unique matter prior and common to all. And just as a statue which, despite being a body that has received form, has as its substrate a prior substance, i.e., bronze, so they say that the bronze, a formless body which nevertheless possesses a quality, has as its substrate a preexisting substance, and that it is a continuous body lacking quality, completely passible and changeable; and they call this matter, also substance, defining it as follows: "substance, or matter, is that which acts as a substrate to all body," or "of which all bodies consist," or "in which the changes occur in sensible things, although its own state remains," and "what underlies bodies that possess qualities although of its own nature it is without quality."

290. Many, however, such as Zeno and Chrysippus, separate matter from substance. For they say that matter is that which underlies all the things that possess qualities, whereas substance is the primary matter of all things, their most ancient foundation, of its own nature without appearance or form. For example, bronze, gold, iron, and the like are the matter in, but not the substance of, the things that are

isdem fabrefiunt, non tamen essentia; at vero quod tam his quam ceteris ut sint causa est, ipsum esse substantiam.

291. Plerique etiam hoc pacto silvam et substantiam separant, quod asseverant essentiam quidem operis esse fundamentum, ut mundi fore merito dicatur atque existimetur essentia, silvam vero contemplatione opificis dictam, quod eam fingat ac formet.

292. Deinde Zeno hanc ipsam essentiam finitam esse dicit unamque eam communem omnium quae sunt esse substantiam, dividuam quoque et usque quaque mutabilem; partes quippe eius verti sed non interire, ita ut de existentibus consumantur in nihilum. Sed ut innumerabilium diversarum, etiam cerearum, figurarum, sic neque formam neque figuram nec ullam omnino qualitatem propriam fore censet fundamenti rerum omnium silvae, coniunctam tamen esse semper et inseparabiliter cohaerere alicui qualitati; cumque tam sine ortu sit quam sine interitu, quia neque de non existente substitit nec consumetur in nihilum, non deesse ei spiritum ac vigorem ex aeternitate, qui moveat eam rationabiliter totam interdum, non numquam pro portione, quae causa sit tam crebrae tamque vehementis universae rei conversionis; spiritum porro motivum illum fore non naturam sed animam et quidem rationabilem, quae vivificans sensilem mundum exornaverit eum ad hanc qua nunc illustratur venustatem. Quem quidem beatum animal et deum appellant.

293. Ergo corpus universum iuxta Stoicos determinatum est et unum et totum et essentia: totum quidem quia nihil ei partium deest; unum autem quia inseparabiles eius partes

wrought from the very same, but they say that that which is the cause of existence for both them and all other things is itself substance.

291. Many also separate matter and substance in asserting that substance is the foundation of a work, such that the world is rightly said and thought to possess substance, whereas matter is said in consideration of the maker, in that he fashions and forms it.

292. Zeno adds that this substance is itself finite and that it is the one substance common to all of the things that exist, also that it is divisible and susceptible of change in every respect, for its parts change although they do not perish in the sense that they dissolve from their existent state into nothing. Rather, he thinks that it is as in the case of innumerable different forms, including waxen ones: no form, shape, or quality generally is proper to matter, the foundation of all things, although it is always conjoined and inseparably coheres with some quality. And he thinks that since it is equally without origin or end—since it does not come to subsist from a nonexistent or dissolve into nothing—from eternity there is not lacking to it the breath and power to move it rationally, sometimes as a whole, sometimes in part, which is the cause of the frequent and violent process of change in the universe. He thinks, moreover, that this motive breath is not nature but soul, *rational* soul, which in bestowing life adorned the sensible world for the sake of this beauty which now makes it resplendent. And they call the world a blessed living being or god.

293. According to the Stoics, then, the body of the universe is determinate, one, whole, and a substance: whole, in that nothing is lacking to it in the way of parts; one, in that

sunt et invicem sibi cohaerent; essentia vero quia princeps silva est omnium corporum per quam ire dicunt rationem solidam atque universam perinde ut semen per membra genitalia. Quam quidem rationem ipsum fore opificem volunt, cohaerens vero corpus et sine qualitate patibile totum et commutabile silvam sive essentiam; quae vertatur quidem nec intereat tamen neque tota neque partium excidio, ideo quia philosophorum omnium commune dogma est neque quid fieri ex nihilo nec in nihilum interire—licet enim cuncta corpora casu aliquo diffluant, silva tamen semper est et opifex deus, ratio scilicet in qua sit fixum quo quidque tempore tam nascatur quam occidat—proptereaque de existentibus genituram fieri et in existens desinere quod finiatur immortalibus perseverantibus, a quo fit et item ex quo fit quod gignitur.

294. Reprehendunt etiam quod, cum sint in eminenti praestantissimaque et vetere existente alia substantia rerum omnium exempla, mundum sensilem iuxta immortale exemplum a deo factum esse dicat Plato, non enim opus ullo exemplo fuisse quando seminum ratio incurrens aliquam concipientem comprehendentemque naturam totum mundum quaeque in eo sunt enixa sit. Haec Stoici de silva deque initiis rerum partim a Platone usurpantes partim commenti, sic ut facile sit intellegere nullam eos ne suspicari quidem potuisse divinam virtutem substantiamque carentem corpore cunctis corporibus vel etiam seminibus efficaciorem; proptereaque factum ut opiniones incurrerent impias, deum

its parts are inseparable and mutually coherent; and a substance, in that it is the primary matter of all bodies—throughout which, they say, reason runs, solid and universal, like semen on its way through the genital organs. According to them, this reason is the actual craftsman, while matter or substance is coherent body, without quality, passive throughout, and subject to change; it changes but does not perish, either as a whole or through the loss of parts—for it is a doctrine common to all philosophers that nothing arises from nothing or passes away into nothing: although all bodies dissolve owing to some contingent factor, matter nevertheless always is, also the craftsman god, namely, the reason in which is fixed the appointed time for each and every thing to come to birth and pass away. And so they hold that the generation arises out of existent things and that that which is brought to an end passes away into an existent, while the immortal things persevere: that *by* which and that *from* which that which comes into being emerges.

294. They criticize Plato for saying, on the grounds that there are exemplars of all things in the higher, most excellent, ancient, and separately existing substance, that the sensible world was made by god after the pattern of an immortal exemplar. For in their view, there was no need of any exemplar given that the seminal reason, by penetrating the particular nature that receives and enfolds it, gave birth to the whole world and the things in it. This view of matter and the principles of reality the Stoics partly took from Plato and partly devised for themselves, so that it is easy to understand their inability even to intuit a divine power or bodiless substance more efficacious than any bodies or even seeds; and easy to understand their consequently incurring

scilicet hoc esse quod silva sit vel etiam qualitatem inseparabilem deum silvae, eundemque per silvam meare velut semen per membra genitalia, et omnium quae nascuntur tam
originem quam etiam causam fore, non malorum modo sed
turpitudinis quoque et obscenitatis, omniaque agere et pati,
vel pudenda. Cuius opinionis deformitas evidentius detege-
tur exposita Platonis sententia.

295. Nunc iam Pythagoricum dogma recenseatur. Numenius ex Pythagorae magisterio Stoicorum hoc de initiis
dogma refellens Pythagorae dogmate (cui concinere dicit
dogma Platonicum) ait Pythagoram deum quidem singularitatis nomine nominasse, silvam vero duitatis, quam duitatem indeterminatam quidem minime genitam, limitatam
vero generatam esse dicere; hoc est antequam exornaretur
quidem formamque et ordinem nancisceretur, sine ortu et
generatione, exornatam vero atque illustratam a digestore
deo esse generatam; atque ita, quia generationis sit fortuna
posterior, inornatum illud minime generatum aequaevum
deo a quo est ordinatum intellegi debeat, sed non nullos Py-
thagoreos vim sententiae non recte assecutos putasse dici
etiam illam indeterminatam et immensam duitatem, ab
unica singularitate institutam recedente a natura sua singularitate et in duitatis habitum migrante. Non recte, ut quae
erat singularitas esse desineret, quae non erat duitas sub-
sisteret, atque ex deo silva et ex singularitate immensa et

impious opinions, namely, that god is the same as matter or indeed an inseparable quality thereof, that he permeates matter as semen does the genital organs, that he is both the origin and cause of *all* things that come to be, evils, turpitude, and obscenity included, and that he performs and undergoes all manner of things, even shameful ones. The deformity of this opinion is the more evidently revealed once Plato's view has been expounded.

295. This is now the point for examination of the Pythagorean doctrine. Numenius, a follower of Pythagoras's teaching, in refuting with Pythagoras's doctrine (with which he says the Platonic one agrees) this Stoic doctrine of principles, says that Pythagoras referred to god by the name "monad" and to matter by "dyad," and that insofar as it is indeterminate this dyad is ungenerated, whereas insofar as it is determinate it is generated. That is, that prior to being adorned by the reception of form and order it was without birth or generation, but that once adorned and illuminated by the god who gave it order it was generated; and that since the circumstance of generation is a later one, the unadorned and ungenerated should thus be considered coeval with the god by whom it was brought into order, but that some Pythagoreans, in misinterpreting what was meant by this view, thought that the indeterminate and immeasurable dyad was intended as well, that it was produced by the solitary monad as the latter receded from its own natural unity and migrated to the state of the dyad. "Misinterpreting," in the sense that the monad that was would have ceased to be while the dyad that was not would have come to be, and there would have been a conversion, matter from god and the immeasurable and indeterminate dyad from the

indeterminata duitas converteretur, quae opinio ne medi-
ocriter quidem institutis hominibus competit. Denique
Stoicos definitam et limitatam silvam esse natura propria,
Pythagoram vero infinitam et sine limite dicere, cumque illi
quod natura sit immensum non posse ad modum atque ordinem redigi censeant, Pythagoram solius hanc dei fore virtutem ac potentiam asserere, ut quod natura efficere nequeat,
deus facile possit, ut qui sit omni virtute potentior atque
praestantior, et a quo natura ipsa vires mutuetur.

296. Igitur Pythagoras quoque, inquit Numenius, fluidam
et sine qualitate silvam esse censet nec tamen, ut Stoici,
naturae mediae interque bonorum malorumque viciniam,
quod genus illi appellant indifferens, sed plane noxiam;
deum quippe esse, ut etiam Platoni videtur, initium et
causam bonorum, silvam malorum, at vero quod ex specie
silvaque sit, indifferens, non ergo silvam sed mundum ex
speciei bonitate silvaeque malitia temperatum; denique ex
providentia et necessitate progenitum veterum theologorum scitis haberi.

297. Silvam igitur informem et carentem qualitate tam
Stoici quam Pythagoras consentiunt, sed Pythagoras malignam quoque, Stoici nec bonam nec malam. Dehinc tamquam in progressu viae malis aliquot obviis perrogati, unde
igitur mala, perversitatem seminarium malorum [fore] cau-
sati sunt. Nec expediunt adhuc, unde ipsa perversitas, cum
iuxta illos duo sint initia rerum, deus et silva: deus summum

monad—an opinion unsuitable even for men of modest learning. Finally, he says that the Stoics say that matter is defined and limited by its proper nature but that Pythagoras says that it is infinite and limitless, and that, whereas they think that that which is by nature immeasurable cannot be reduced to limit and order, Pythagoras asserts that this is the power and potency that pertains uniquely to god, so that what nature cannot accomplish god can do with ease, being more potent and more excellent than any other power, and the source from which nature acquires its force.

296. Thus Pythagoras too, Numenius says, thinks that matter is fluid and without quality; unlike the Stoics, however, he does not think that it is of a nature intermediate between good and evil, what they call indifferent, but that it is noxious in the full sense of the word. For like Plato, he thinks that god is the source and cause of good, and matter of evil, but that the product of form and matter is indifferent, so that the world, not matter, is a blend of the goodness of form and the maliciousness of matter. Finally, he thinks that according to the pronouncements of the ancient theologians the world is held to be the offspring of providence and necessity.

297. Both the Stoics and Pythagoreans agree, then, that matter is formless and lacks quality, but Pythagoras claims that it is actually evil, and the Stoics that it is neither good nor evil. Consequently, on being asked where, then, the evils originate when a number of them block our progress, as it were, along the way, they pointed to perversity as their root cause. Nor do they go so far as to explain where the perversity originates, since in their view there are two principles of things, God and Matter: God, the highest and preeminent

et praecellens bonum; silva, ut censent, nec bonum nec malum. Sed Pythagoras assistere veritati miris licet et contra
opinionem hominum operantibus asseverationibus non ve-
retur, qui ait existente providentia mala quoque necessario
substitisse, propterea quod silva sit et eadem sit malitia
praedita. Quod si mundus ex silva, certe factus est de
existente olim natura maligna, proptereaque Numenius laudat Heraclitum reprehendentem Homerum, qui optaverit
interitum ac vastitatem malis vitae, quod non intellegeret
mundum sibi deleri placere, siquidem silva, quae malorum
fons est, exterminaretur. Platonemque idem Numenius laudat, quod duas mundi animas autumet, unam beneficentissi-
mam malignam alteram (scilicet silvae), quae, licet incondite
fluctuet, tamen, quia intimo proprioque motu movetur, vi-
vat et anima convegetetur necesse est, lege eorum omnium
quae genuino motu moventur. Quae quidem etiam patibilis
animae partis, in qua est aliquid corpulentum mortaleque et
corporis simile, auctrix est et patrona, sicut rationabilis animae pars auctore utitur ratione ac deo; porro ex deo et silva
factus est iste mundus.

298. Igitur iuxta Platonem mundo bona sua dei tamquam
patris liberalitate collata sunt, mala vero matris silvae vitio
cohaeserunt. Qua ratione intellegi datur Stoicos frustra cau-
sari nescio quam perversitatem, cum quae proveniunt ex
motu stellarum provenire dicantur. Stellae porro corpora

good; and Matter, as they reckon, neither a good nor an evil. But Pythagoras does not hesitate to stand by the truth, although with claims that are paradoxical or contrary to human opinion; and he says that since providence exists it was necessary for evil to have come to be as well, given that Matter exists and is endowed with the same principle of evil. But if the world consists of Matter, then it was surely made from a preexisting evil nature, which is why Numenius praises Heraclitus for criticizing Homer, who longed for an end and the wiping out of life's ills, failing to understand that he would actually be arguing for the destruction of the world if Matter, the source of evil, were to be exterminated. And Numenius also praises Plato for insisting on two world souls, one supremely beneficent and the other (namely, the one pertaining to Matter) malign, which despite its disorderly fluctuation nevertheless necessarily is endowed with life and quickened by soul, since it moves according to an internal and intrinsic principle of motion in conformity with the law governing all things that move according to an innate principle of motion. Matter is what gives rise to and oversees the passible part of soul, which is possessed of a corporeal and mortal element similar to body, just as the rational part of soul has reason and God to give rise to it; and the world came to be from God and Matter.

298. According to Plato, then, the world received its proper goods owing to the liberality of God, its father, as it were, whereas its evils adhered to it owing to the defect of Matter, its mother. And from this reasoning it becomes possible to understand the pointlessness of the Stoics' laying the blame on some perversity or other when the things that happen are claimed to do so because of stellar movement.

sunt ignesque caelites; omnium quippe corporum silva nutrix, ut etiam quae sidereus motus minus utiliter et impros-
pere turbat originem trahere videantur ex silva, in qua est
multa intemperies et improvidus impetus et casus atque ut
libet exagitata praesumptio. Itaque si deus eam correxit, ut
in Timaeo loquitur Plato, redegitque in ordinem ex incon-
dita et turbulenta iactatione, certe confusa haec intemperies eius casu quodam et improspera sorte habebatur nec ex
providentiae consultis salubribus. Ergo iuxta Pythagoram
silvae anima neque sine ulla est substantia, ut plerique arbitrantur, et adversatur providentiae consulta eius impugnare
gestiens malitiae suae viribus. Sed providentia quidem est
dei opus et officium, caeca vero fortuitaque temeritas ex
prosapia silvae, ut sit evidens iuxta Pythagoram dei silvaeque item providentiae fortunaeque coetu cunctae rei
molem esse constructam, sed postquam silvae ornatus accesserit ipsam quidem matrem esse factam corporeorum et
nativorum deorum, fortunam vero eius prosperam esse
magna ex parte non tamen usque quaque, quoniam naturale
vitium limari omnino nequiret.

299. Deus itaque silvam magnifica virtute comebat vitia-
que eius omnifariam corrigebat, non interficiens ne natura
silvestris funditus interiret nec vero permittens porrigi dilatarique passim sed, ut manente natura quae ex incommodo
habitu ad prosperitatem devocari commutarique possit, ordinem inordinatae confusioni, modum immoderationi, et

Moreover, the stars are bodies or celestial fires; and matter is the nurse of all bodies, so that those things too which to no apparent purpose or to ill effect are driven by the stars are seen to originate in matter, which is possessed of much intemperance, an improvident drive, the element of chance, and a randomly motivated determination. So if *god* corrected and, as Plato says in the *Timaeus* [30a], *brought it back to order from* a confused and turbulent *state of agitation,* then surely this its confused intemperance was due to some element of ill-fated chance rather than to the salutary plans of providence. According to Pythagoras, then, soul as it pertains to Matter is not the absence of any being, as many suppose, and it resists providence, struggling through the force of its own malice to impugn its plans. Providence, however, is the work and function of God, whereas blind and fortuitous rashness is the inheritance of Matter, so that according to Pythagoras it is clear that the mass of the universe was constructed through the convergence of God, Matter, providence, and fortune, but that upon receiving order Matter itself became the mother of corporeal and generated gods while the fortune it confers is for the most part prosperous but not entirely so, since the natural defect could not be eliminated altogether.

299. Thus with his magnificent power God set about adorning Matter and correcting its defects in all aspects, neither destroying them to the point of the material nature's entirely perishing nor permitting them to extend and spread everywhere, but on the understanding that there is an enduring nature capable of being recalled and changed from a debased state to one of prosperity, in bringing order to disordered confusion, limit to immoderation, and dignity to

cultum foeditati coniungens totum statum eius illustrando atque exornando convertit. Denique negat inveniri Numenius et recte negat immunem a vitiis usque quaque generatorum fortunam, non in artibus hominum non in natura, non in corporibus animalium nec vero in arboribus aut stirpibus non in frugibus non in aeris serie nec in aquae tractu nec in ipso quidem caelo, ubique miscente se providentiae deterioris naturae quasi quodam piaculo. Idemque, nudam silvae imaginem demonstrare et velut in lucem destituere studens detractis omnibus singillatim corporibus quae gremio eius formas invicem mutuantur et invicem mutant, ipsum illud quod ex egestione vacuatum est animo considerari iubet, eamque silvam et necessitatem cognominat, ex qua et deo mundi machinam constitisse deo persuadente, necessitate obsecundante. Haec est Pythagorae de originibus asseveratio.

300. Superest ipsa nobis ad tractandum Platonis de silva sententia, quam diverse interpretari videntur auditores Platonis. Quippe alii generatam dici ab eo putaverunt verba quaedam potius quam rem secuti, alii vero sine generatione sed anima praeditam, quando ante illustrationem quoque motu instabili atque inordinato dixerit eam fluctuasse (cum motus intimus genuinusque sit viventium proprius); quoque idem saepe alias duas esse mundi animas dixerit, unam malignam ex silva alteram beneficam ex deo; existentibus itaque bonis ac malis, bona quidem ex anima benefica mundo tributa, incommoda porro ex silvestri maligna; cum divina

depravity he altered its state entirely by illuminating and adorning it. Finally, Numenius rightly points out that the lot of generated things is nowhere found to be immune to defects, whether in the devices of men or in nature: animal bodies, trees, plants, fruits, the broad expanses of air and water, and indeed the heaven itself—everywhere a lower nature is expiating its sin, as it were, by intermingling with providence. And in an effort to display a stripped down image of matter and to expose it, so to speak, to the light after having removed one by one all of the corporeal entities that undergo reciprocal changes of form within its womb, he bids us to contemplate the very thing hollowed out by the abstraction, calls it matter and necessity, and says that it is from it and god that the engine of the world has come to be, through god's persuasion and necessity's compliance. This is Pythagoras's claim concerning the first beginnings.

300. It remains for us to treat of Plato's own opinion concerning matter, which Plato's students evidently interpret in different ways. For some, fixing on certain phrases rather than the substance of what he says, have thought that it is said by him to be generated, while others have thought that it is ungenerated but endowed with soul. And the latter on strength of his claim that even prior to its illumination matter was in a state of flux, its movement being unstable and disorderly (for movement is an intrinsic and innate property of living things); also, on strength of his repeated claim in other works that there are two world souls, a malign one originating in matter and a beneficent one originating in god; and that, given therefore that good and evil things exist, good ones accrue to the world owing to the beneficent soul whereas harmful ones do so owing to the material or

sapientia intellegentiaque opificis dei silvae severe atque ef-
ficaciter persuaderet praebere cultui atque exornationi suae
patientiam, patientia vero non nisi animantibus vitaque
fruentibus adhibeatur. Quibus Hebraei concinunt cum dicunt homini quidem a deo datam esse animam ex inspiratione caelesti, quam rationem et animam rationabilem appellant, mutis vero et agrestibus ex silva rationis expertem
iussu dei vivis et animantibus bestiis terrae gremio profusis;
quorum in numero fuerit etiam ille serpens, qui primitias
generis humani malis suasionibus illaqueaverit.

301. Nec desunt qui putent inordinatum illum et tumultuarium motum Platonem non in silva sed in materiis et
corporibus iam notasse quae initia mundi atque elementa
censentur. Quippe si est informis et inordinata, nimirum
etiam immobilis natura sua, nec immobilis modo, verum
etiam incommutabilis (quippe commutationes non silvae
accident sed corporibus in quibus sint qualitates) eodemque
pacto etiam exanimis, quando quidem immobilis. Malitiam
porro aiunt virtutis esse carentiam, ut informitatem in-
opiam intemperantiam, proptereaque virtutibus addita orationis parte negativa contra quam virtutes cognominatas
fore imprudentiam iniustitiam imperitiam. Haec atque
huius modi est dissensio Platonicorum philosophorum.

302. Nos tamen quam ex his putamus potiorem et ad
veritatis examen propensiorem maximeque tanti auctoris

malign soul; and that although the divine wisdom and intelligence of the craftsman god sternly and effectively *persuaded* [48a] matter to submit passively to its ordering and adornment, the passivity pertains only to living beings that partake of life. And with the latter the Hebrews agree when they say that the soul, which they call reason and the rational soul, was given to man by God through his celestial insufflation, and that the irrational soul deriving from matter was given to dumb creatures of the fields, living and animate beasts which by the command of God issued forth from the earth's womb, among them too that serpent who through his malicious persuasion ensnared the firstfruits of humankind.

301. Nor are those lacking who hold that Plato remarked earlier upon the *disorderly and tumultuous motion* [30a] as being, not in matter, but in the material elements and bodies which are considered the first principles and elements of the world. For if matter is without form or order, then it is surely by its nature motionless as well, and not only motionless but unchanging (for change will affect, not matter, but the bodies in which qualities inhere) and by the same reasoning also inanimate in virtue of its being motionless. They claim, moreover, that evil is an absence of power, as in "*de*formity," "*in*capacity," and "*in*temperance," and that "*im*prudence," "*in*justice," and "*in*experience" therefore result from the addition of the negative particle to the correspondingly named virtues. This and the like is a point of dissent among Platonic philosophers.

302. We, however, will pursue from among these the view which we consider the stronger, the one better poised for the test of truth, and the one worthy of the wisdom of so

prudentia dignam exequemur. Est igitur propositarum
quaestionum duplex probatio: altera quae ex antiquioribus
posteriora confirmat, quod est proprium syllogismi, praece-
dunt quippe ordine acceptiones quae elementa vocantur
conclusionem; altera item quae <ex> posterioribus ad praecedentium indaginem gradatim pervenit, quod genus probationis resolutio dicitur. Nos ergo quia de initiis sermo est
quibus antiquius nihil est utemur probationis remediis ex
resolutione manantibus, certum est siquidem apud omnes
vel philosophantes vel qui se non dediderint huic studio esse
in nobis sensus, esse etiam intellectum, et haec esse non eadem sibi; ergo etiam effectus tam sensuum quam intellegentiae, siquidem ipsa genera diversa sint, esse diversos. Quae
cum ita sint, necesse est illa etiam esse quorum sint tam intellectus quam etiam sensus; sunt igitur tam sensilia quam
intellegibilia. Et intellegibilia quidem sunt quae intellectu
comprehenduntur rationabili indagine, sensilia vero quae
inrationabili opinione praesumuntur incerto quodam opinionis eventu. Illa quidem ex aeternitate nec ullum initium
habentia; haec temporaria et ex aliquo initio temporis, a regione nostra primaria, ad naturam versus vero secunda; rursum intellegibilia e regione quidem naturae priora iuxta nos
vero secunda sunt. Quotus quisque igitur in disputatione sic
exordietur ut ab his quae prima sunt ad nos versum ascendat

great an author. Now, there is a twofold method of proof for questions that have been raised for consideration: one method provides confirmation of posterior things on the basis of prior ones, and this is proper to the *syllogism,* for in order the premises, which are called elements, precede the conclusion; and the other is that which on the basis of posterior things reaches the investigation of prior ones by steps, and this kind of proof is called *analysis.* Since, then, the discussion concerns the first principles which are prior to all else, we will avail ourselves of the method of demonstration deriving from analysis. For all, whether they are engaged in philosophy or have not dedicated themselves to its pursuit, hold it as certain that there are in us the senses and also intellect, and that they are not the same as one another; and consequently that since they are themselves different in kind their effects, those of the senses and of intelligence, are different as well. And given that this is so, it is necessary also that there should be those objects of which there are thoughts as also those of which there are sense perceptions; thus there are both sensibles and intelligibles. And intelligibles are what are grasped by the intellect through rational investigation, and sensibles what are perceived in irrational opinion, resulting in a particular uncertainty associated with opinion. The former are in a state of having from eternity no beginning; the latter are in time and stem from a determinate beginning in time, they are primary from our perspective but secondary in the order of nature; conversely, intelligibles are prior from the perspective of nature but secondary with respect to us. To the extent, then, that anyone undertakes a disputation in such a way as to ascend from things which are primary in relation to us to those

ad ea quae sunt a nobis secunda, resolvere dicitur quaestionem, siquidem ab his orsus quae vere non sunt sed imagines potius sunt vere existentium rerum perveniat ad ea
quae vere existentium initia causaeque sunt.

303. Sunt igitur vicina nobis omnia quidem quae sentiuntur, ignis aer aqua terra, aliquanto tamen propiora quae ex
his concreta sunt, rursum magis applicita nobis nostra corpora. Est igitur in corporibus nostris contiguum quiddam,
est etiam solidum, est visibile, est calor. Et contiguum quidem ac solidum nihil erit sine terra; rursum visibile et calidum sine igni esse non poterit; est ergo in nobis terrenum
quiddam et igneum. Est etiam spirabile, siquidem spiritus in
venis quae arteriae dicuntur conditus invenitur; est humectum quoque; quod humectum sine aqua demum esse non
potest, nec vero spiritus sine aere. Quodsi haec omnia partes sunt corporis, necesse est etiam illa fore, quorum haec
partes sunt, ut diximus, id est solidum universumque corpus. Est igitur in solido atque universo corpore tam ignis
quam terra et ceterae materiae; deinde harum ipsarum congrua et moderata concretio, quae constat ex formis et qualitatibus, ignis quidem splendor levitas calor et figura, terrae
vero siccitas gravitas figura; similiter etiam earum materiarum quae inter ignem terramque insertae sunt aliquae sint
naturales proprietates oportet. Si ergo has qualitates et
quantitates, etiam formas figurasve volemus ratione animi
separare, tum demum deliberare, quid sit illud, quod haec
omnia inseparabiliter adhaerens complexumque contineat,

which are at second remove from us, he is said to analyze the question, for beginning with things which are not truly existent but are rather images of truly existent ones he reaches those which are the first principles and causes of truly existent things.

303. Now, near to us are all of the things perceived by the senses—fire, air, water, earth; nearer still, however, are the things composed of them; in yet stricter proximity to us are our bodies. There is, then, in our bodies something tangible, and there is also the solid, the visible, and warmth. And nothing will be tangible and solid without earth; it will be equally incapable of being visible and warm without fire; thus there is in us something earthy and fiery. There is at the same time the breathable, for breath is found deep within the veins which are known as arteries; and there is also the moist; and the moistness is ultimately incapable of existing without water, as breath is without air. But if these are all parts of the body, then, as we have indicated, there must also be the things of which they are parts, i.e., the solid body of the universe. Thus there is in the solid body of the universe fire as well as earth and the other material elements; and there is then a congruous and tempered concretion of these very material elements, a concretion consisting of forms and qualities, brightness, levity, warmth, and shape in the case of fire, and dryness, weight, and shape in that of earth; and determinate natural properties are similarly required in the cases of the material elements situated between fire and earth. If, then, we intend by a process of mental reasoning to separate these qualities and quantities and the forms and shapes and then finally to reflect on what that is which contains them all, embracing and binding them inseparably, we

inveniemus nihil aliud esse quam id quod quaerimus, silvam; inventa igitur est origo silvestris. Et hoc quidem est unum duarum probationum genus, quod resolutio dicitur.

304. Nunc illud aliud consideremus quod compositio cognominatur; sequitur quippe resolutionem compositio et discretionem concretio. Quae igitur modo separare animo videbamur a silva, rursus ei praesentemus ac velut in suum locum reponamus, hoc est genera qualitates figuras, nec inordinate haec ipsa et utcumque sed cum cultu et ordine. Ordo autem sine harmonia esse non potest, harmonia demum analogiae comes est, analogia item cum ratione, et demum ratio comes individua providentiae reperitur; nec vero providentia sine intellectu est, intellectusque sine mente non est. Mens ergo dei modulavit ordinavit excoluit omnem continentiam corporis; inventa ergo est demum opificis divina origo. Operatur porro opifex et exornat omnia iuxta vim rationabilem maiestatemque operum suorum; opera vero eius intellectus eius sunt, qui a Graecis ideae vocantur; porro ideae sunt exempla naturalium rerum. Quo pacto invenitur tertia exemplaris origo rerum. Igitur silvam quidem iuxta legem rationemque dissolutionis invenimus; iuxta compositionis vero praecepta ipsum opificem deum; ex operibus porro dei opificis exemplum.

305. Et quoniam singula haec initia sunt, rursus erit ex integro de initiis disserendum. Est igitur initium primus limes post quem sunt cuncta quae ex eodem sunt limite; et quia

will find that it is nothing other than that which we are seeking, Matter. Thus the material origin has been found. And this is one of the two kinds of proof, and it is called analysis.

304. Let us now consider the other kind, which is called *synthesis;* for synthesis follows analysis, and concretion separation. Let us then reintegrate the things, i.e., the genera, qualities, and shapes, which in our minds we just now imagined ourselves separating from matter, and put them back into their place, as it were, not in a disorderly or haphazard way but with an eye to their pattern and order. Now, order is incapable of existing without harmony, and harmony is ultimately a concomitant of proportion, and proportion is similarly coupled with reason, and reason is ultimately found to be the inseparable concomitant of providence; but providence is not without intellect, nor intellect without mind. Thus the mind of god tempered, ordered, and adorned the whole of the corporeal structure; thus the divine origin arising from the craftsman has at last been found. And the craftsman puts into effect and adorns everything according to his rational power and the majesty of his works; but his works are his thoughts, which by the Greeks are called *ideai;* and the ideas are the exemplars of natural realities. And in this way the third, exemplary origin of things is found. Thus by following the rational law of analysis we have found Matter; and by following the precepts of synthesis we have found the craftsman God himself; and from the works of the craftsman God we have found the Exemplar.

305. And given that these are each principles, it will be necessary to resume once again the discussion of principles. Now, a principle is the first limit after which are all the things that come from that same limit; and since every

omne initium, utpote origo, rerum praecedit ortum, necesse
est eam fore simplicem sine qualitate perpetuam. Si simplex
non erit, perinde erit atque ea quae sunt ex eiusdem substantia nec intererit quicquam inter ipsum initium et cetera
etiamsi antiquitas in tempore constituatur, quando etiam
illa ex aliquo tempore sint quae post initium sunt, et nullam
esse differentiam rationem non habet. Simplex ergo est rerum origo nec habet qualitatem; nam si detur ei qualitas,
erit, opinor, compositum quiddam ex materia et accidenti,
omnia quippe huius generis sunt quae habent qualitatem:
igitur sine qualitate.

306. Aeternum quoque initium esse sic probatur. Nam si
non aeternum, ex aliquo tempore sit necesse est; si hoc ita
erit, causa quoque cur sit praecedat ortum eius necesse est:
ita erit initio aliquid antiquius. Sed hoc absurdum est,
initium initii suspicari: aeterna est igitur origo rerum
eademque immortalis. Nam si occidua, deerit ei condicio
interitus, neque enim in simplex aliquid neque in compositum dissolvetur: in simplex ideo quod sola initia simplicia,
ergo in se dissolvetur et recreabitur potius quam interibit;
neque in compositum quidem, continebitur enim ex compositis, ergo nec dissolvetur, quippe omne compositum ex
simplicium naturarum conexione subsistit; nec vero in nihilum dissolvi potest, nec enim quicquam potest esse quod nihil est. Certe, ut ait Plato, initio perdito nec ipsum ex alio

principle precedes the coming-to-be of things as their origin, it is necessary that it be simple, without quality, and eternal. If it is not simple, then it will be just like the things that are of the same substance as it and there will be no difference between the actual principle and everything else even if its temporal priority should be agreed upon, since things that come after a principle also exist from some determinate point in time; and it makes no sense that there should be no difference. The origin of things is therefore simple and lacking quality; for if it should be given a quality, then, I suppose, it will be a determinate composite of matter and an accidental attribute, since everything that possesses quality is of this sort: therefore it is without quality.

306. That the principle is also eternal is proved as follows. For if it is not eternal, then it necessarily exists from some determinate point in time; but if this is so, then in addition the cause of its existence necessarily precedes its coming-to-be: thus there will be something prior to the principle. But this supposition of a principle of the principle is absurd: therefore the origin of things is eternal and also immortal. For if it is perishable, then it will lack a condition for its perishability, since it will be indissoluble into anything either simple or composite: into anything simple, precisely because principles are uniquely simple, and so it will be dissolved into itself and, rather than perishing, will be recreated; neither will it be dissoluble into a composite, for its coherence will then depend on the elements of composition, and so it will not be dissolved, since every composite consists of a union of simple natures; but neither can it be dissolved into nothing, for that which is nothing is incapable of being anything. To be sure, as Plato says, "if the

quoquam nec ex eodem aliud quicquam recreabitur; quo pacto immortale rerum initium reperitur.

307. Quia igitur quid et cuiusmodi sit initium demonstravimus, consequens erit iam nunc considerare, utrum hoc ignis sit an terra an cetera quae dicuntur elementa. Arbitror quippe non recte horum quid initium putari; haec enim minime simplicia sed ex diversis materiis naturisque concreta sunt corpora; initii porro simplicem esse naturam in superioribus constitit. His ita digestis demonstrandum est duo esse initia rerum et haec contraria sibi invicem. Sic quippe non solus Plato sed antiquiores quoque omnes consentiunt, cum partim calorem et frigus initia constituunt, partim humorem et siccitatem, alii quidem consensum et dissensionem vel unum et item multa, parque et impar, id est singularitatis duitatisque naturam, ut Pythagorae placebat. Quorum omnium sententiae de contrarietate initiorum concinunt sed utrum ea aeterna an temporaria et an incorporea an corporeae molis, quorum alterum ut faciens alterum ut patiens, dissentiunt. Oportet porro initia nec ex aliis rebus originem trahere nec ex se invicem constare, quin potius omnia ex isdem substantiam mutuari. Quod igitur <"ut> faciens" diximus, deus est, quod vero "ut patiens," silva corporea"; sed quia id quod facit aliquid ad exemplum aliquod

principle perishes, then neither will it be recreated from anything else nor will anything else be from it"; and in this way the principle of things is found to be immortal.

307. Since, then, we have demonstrated what and what sort of thing a principle is, the next step will be to consider now whether it is fire, earth, or any of the other things referred to as elements. I think that it is certainly incorrect for any of them to be considered a principle, for they are not in any sense simple bodies but rather ones involving the coalescence of diverse material entities and natures, and it has been established above that a principle is by nature simple. These points having been laid out thus, it needs to be demonstrated that there are two principles of things and that they are contrary to one another. To be sure, whether they posit as principles the hot and cold, the moist and dry, or in other cases concord and discord or the one and many, the equal and odd, i.e., the nature of singularity and duality, as Pythagoras thought, not only Plato but all of the ancients agree on this point. Their opinions are all in accord as concerns the contrariety of principles, but they disagree over the questions of whether the principles are eternal or in time, and whether they are incorporeal or possessed of corporeal mass, one of them with an active function and the other with a passive one. And it is necessary, not that the principles should either take their origin from other realities or arise out of one another, but rather that all things should derive their being from *them*. That which we have referred to as having an active function, then, is god, whereas that which we have referred to as having a passive one is corporeal matter; but since that which acts produces something while looking toward some exemplar, the necessity of

respiciens operatur, tertiae quoque originis intellecta est
necessitas. Sunt igitur initia deus et silva et exemplum, et est
deus quidem origo primaria moliens et posita in actu, silva
vero ex qua prima fit quod gignitur.

308. Nunc iam de silva tractabitur, quam originem fore
rerum consentiunt Pythagorei Platonici Stoici. Nomen vero
ei dederunt auditores Platonis, ipse enim nusquam silvae
nomen ascripsit sed aliis multis ad declarationem naturae
eius convenientibus nuncupamentis usus est, cum animis
nostris intimare vellet intellectum eius utcumque, vel ex
natura propria rei vel ex passionibus commotionibusque
animorum nostrorum: ex natura quidem propria primam
materiam nuncupans et item simile quiddam mollis ceden-
tisque materiae in quam imprimuntur signacula et rerum
receptaculum et interdum matrem atque nutriculam totius
generationis; ex passione vero audientium, cum dicit adulte-
rino quodam intellectu recordandam et contiguam sine tangentium sensu. Omnibus vero supra memoratis communiter
placet silvam esse mutabilem totam et conversibilem sed
conversionem mutationemque eius diverse interpretantur.
Namque alii putant ex sua propria ratione converti et sumere qualitates, cum ex conversione nihil accidat praeter
variam qualitatem; quam quidem qualitatem nihilo minus
esse silvam in alio atque alio habitu. Nobis autem nequaquam placet eandem silvam esse et qualitatem, quippe quarum altera sit quasi quaedam subiecta materia, altera accidens quid eidem materiae. Quae causa est cur silva patibilis

a third origin is understood as well. Thus there are as principles God, Matter, and the Exemplar, and God is the primary motive origin posited in act while Matter is that from which the thing generated first comes to be.

308. There will now be a treatment of matter, which the Pythagoreans, Platonists, and Stoics agree is the origin of things. Plato's students, however, gave it a name, for he himself nowhere ascribed to it the name "matter" but used a number of other terms suitable for picking out its nature when he wanted somehow to instill a conception of it in our minds as based on either the proper nature or our mental modifications and experiences of the thing: as based on the proper nature, when he calls it "prime matter" and something *like the soft and malleable material upon which seal impressions are made,* and the *Receptacle* of things, and in certain passages the *mother* and *nurse* of all generation; and as based on the mental modifications of those who are listening, when he says that it has to be recalled *by means of a certain illegitimate conception* and that it is tangible *without any sense perception on the part of those who touch it* [49a–52b]. And all of those mentioned above share the view that matter is wholly mutable and transformable, although they form different interpretations of its transformation and change. For some think that it is transformed and assumes qualities on the basis of its proper nature, since apart from change in quality there is no accidental change based on transformation, and that the quality is nevertheless *matter* in one or another state. We, however, in no way subscribe to the view that matter is the same as quality, since the former is a sort of material substrate, as it were, and the latter something accidental to the same material. And that is the reason why matter is proved

esse probetur, quippe quae suscipiat diversas qualitates ex immutatione.

309. Fit porro conversio iuxta silvam non ipsa silva perpetiente mutationem, sed earum quae sunt in eadem et continentur ab ea qualitatum. Quippe si ipsa mutabitur, in aliud quiddam convertatur necesse est ac desinat esse silva; quod ratione certe caret. Namque ut cera, quae transfigurata in multas diversasque formas non ipsa vertitur sed figurae, ipsa in propria natura perseverante, cum figurae non sint quod cera est, sic opinor silvam quoque formis figurisque variatam, cum de sua condicione minime recedat, recte patibilem dici.

310. Etiam hoc communiter ab omnibus pronuntiatur, silvam sine qualitate esse ac sine figura et sine specie, non quo sine his umquam esse possit, sed quod haec ex propria natura non habeat nec possideat potius quam comitetur species et qualitates. Denique si mentis consideratione volumus ei haec adimere sine quibus non est, possumus ei non effectu sed possibilitate horum omnium possessionem dare. Possibilitas autem gemina ratione intellegitur: una ut cum dicimus in semine omnem totius corporis perfecti rationem intus latere semenque possibilitate animal esse; altera quod rationem quidem in se futurae generationis nondum habet sed quia tale est natura ut extrinsecus accipere possit rationes formarum et qualitatum possibilitate dicimus fore

to be passible: in virtue of its change it is susceptible of different qualities.

309. Moreover, a material transformation occurs, not because the matter itself undergoes change, but because of a change in the qualities which are in and contained by it. For if it is to be changed in itself, then it has to be transformed into something else and cease to be matter, which clearly makes no sense. For as in the case of wax, which although transfigured into a multiplicity of different shapes is not transformed in itself but the shapes are transformed while it in fact abides in its proper nature (for the shapes are not what the wax is), so I suppose that matter too with its variations in form and shape is rightly said to be passible even though it in no way abandons its proper state.

310. This claim too, that matter is deprived of quality, shape, and form, is common to all, not in the sense that matter can ever exist in the absence of these things, but because it does not have them in virtue of its proper nature and does not possess forms and qualities but instead exists in conjunction with them. Finally, if we are prepared by a process of mental abstraction to remove from matter those things in the absence of which it does not exist, then we are in a position to grant its possession of them all, not actually but potentially. And potentiality is understood in two senses: one, as when we say that the full structure of the whole and complete body lies hidden within the seed and that the seed is the animal in potentiality; the other, as when we say that that which does not yet possess the structure of its future development but by virtue of its being naturally such as to be receptive of extrinsic formal and qualitative structures is potentially that which it is not yet, as in the case of a

quod nondum est, ut aeris ceraeve massa informis ante quam ex arte recipiat formas.

311. Quare si intra silvam ratio formarum et qualitatum latet, ut Stoicis videtur, abundat opificis moderatio, sed opinor silvae opificem necessarium, sicut ipsi etiam Stoici sanciunt. Opifex igitur silvae ut aeris informitati ceraeve formas insigniet atque ita constabit ob necessariam dogmatis rationem.

312. Nihilo minus de aeternitate etiam silvae consentiunt perpetuam fore censentes, quando sit arx et origo rerum; sed utrum limitata, id est determinata, nequaquam consentiunt, quando determinatum quoque magnitudinem habeat necesse est, magnitudo autem est vel lineae vel superficiei vel corporis, quae cuncta proprias figuras habent, sive plana sint seu solida, figura porro species qualitatis est. Quare si est limitata silva, qualitate praedita et figurae compos erit per semet ipsam, quae informis et qualitate carens evidenter ostensa est, ergo infinita quoque et minime terminata. Infinita porro non ut quae immense lateque et insuperabiliter porrecta sunt sed ut quae possunt aliquo limite circumiri nec tamen adhuc mentis consideratione vallata; atque ut sine qualitate sine figura quoque dicimus sic etiam infinitam velut nondum, ante exornationem dumque adhuc silva est, fine circumdatam.

formless mass of bronze or wax before receiving forms because of an artisan's skill.

311. And so if, as the Stoics think, the formal and qualitative structure lies hidden within matter, then the control exercised by a craftsman is superfluous; but I suppose that matter requires a craftsman, as even the Stoics themselves allow. The craftsman, then, will impress the forms upon matter as upon the formlessness of bronze or wax, and this much will be agreed upon because of what the structure of their doctrine requires.

312. They are equally in agreement concerning the eternity of matter too, maintaining that it is eternal on the grounds that it is the pinnacle and origin of reality; but as to the question of whether it is limited, i.e., determinate, they disagree entirely, on the grounds that the determinate must also possess magnitude, but magnitude is associated with the line, plane surface, or body, all of which, whether they be two- or three-dimensional, have their proper shapes, and shape is a species of *quality*. Hence if matter is limited, then it will be endowed with quality and by its very nature possessed of shape; and yet it has clearly been shown to be formless and deprived of quality; thus it is infinite and completely indeterminate. And infinite, not in the way that things of unsurpassably large and broad extension are, but in the manner of things which are subject to being circumscribed by some limit without thereby being walled in by the mind's consideration; and just as we maintain that matter is also deprived of quality and shape, so too we maintain that it is infinite in the sense that it is not, prior to its adornment and for so long as it *is* matter, thereby circumscribed by limit.

313. Eademque nec incrementum nec imminutionem pati dicitur. Merito; fiet enim, ut ex nihilo subsistat aliquid et dissolvatur in nihilum, quod fieri non potest. Quippe quod augetur accessu magnitudinis crescit, et praeter ipsam silvam nihil esse arbitror ex quo fiat accessio vel in quod id quod ex silva defluit inanita silva minuatur.

314. Sunt qui censent eam fundi et item contrahi. Sed neque funditur quid sine humore nec contrahitur sine replicatione. Utrumque autem hoc non caret qualitate, et silva caret qualitate: neque igitur ut fusilis materia porrigitur nec contrahitur ut replicabilis.

315. Sunt item qui putent infinitae sectionis patibilem silvam. Sed omne quod secatur compositum minimeque simplex erit et in aliquo spatio, quod est proprium quantitatis: ergo silva minime secabitur, caret enim quantitate perinde ut qualitate quamvis qualitatem quantitatemque comitetur. Si vero, quia corpora qualitatibus et quantitatibus praedita, quae ab ea continentur, secari queunt, ipsam quoque una cum isdem secari fingamus, non erit omnino abhorrens a ratione vel inconveniens praesumptio.

316. Recta est igitur nostra opinio neque ignem neque terram nec aquam nec spiritum esse silvam sed materiam principalem et corporis primam subiectionem, in qua non qualitas non forma non quantitas non figura sit ex natura

313. Matter is also said to be susceptible of neither increase nor diminution. And rightly so, for otherwise it would turn out that something comes from nothing and is resolved into nothing, which is impossible. For that which is augmented increases by an addition of magnitude, and I suppose that there is nothing apart from matter itself from which the addition might arise or into which a material effluence might by its emptying out of matter produce a state of diminution.

314. There are those who think that it flows and contracts. But nothing either flows without moisture or contracts without folding in on itself. Neither of these, however, is lacking in a quality, and matter *does* lack quality; therefore it neither extends itself in the manner of a fluid material nor contracts in the manner of one that folds in on itself.

315. There are also those who suppose that matter is susceptible of infinite division. But everything that is divisible will be composite and not at all simple, and will be in some space, which is a property of quantity: thus matter will not be at all divisible, for it lacks quantity just as it does quality even though it exists in conjunction with quality and quantity. But if we should suppose, in consideration of the fact that bodies endowed with qualities and quantities which are contained within it are divisible, that it too is divisible along with them, then the supposition will not be altogether unreasonable or inapposite.

316. Our opinion, then, is correct: that matter is, not fire or earth or water or air, but a foundational material and the primary corporeal substrate within which according to its proper nature there is not quality or form or quantity or

propria sed virtute opificis haec ei cuncta conexa sint, ut ex his universo corpori et singillatim perfectio et communiter varietas comparetur.

317. Quod vero sit universi corporis fomes et prima subiectio, facile probatur ex elementorum in se conversione mutua et ex qualitatum inconstanti mutatione. Etenim terra duas habet proprias qualitates, frigus et siccitatem (perinde enim tractemus ad praesens, quasi terra ex aliqua parte in aliud aliquod convertatur elementum). Similiter aqua in duabus qualitatibus invenitur, humoris videlicet et frigoris; et est propria qualitas terrae quidem siccitas, aquae vero humor, communis vero utriusque natura frigoris. Cum igitur terra late fusa convertetur aliquatenus in aquam, tunc siccitas quidem eius mutata erit in humorem, frigus vero quod commune est perseverat in statu proprio, quia neque etiam tunc est in terra nec iam in aqua: in terra quidem propterea quia quod conversum est desinit esse terra; nec vero in aqua, dum enim mutatur adhuc et convertitur neque plene mutatum neque perfecte conversum est ut iam in aquae materiam migrarit. Superest igitur ut sit uspiam frigus, nec enim potest esse sine eo in quo est; hoc porro nihil esse aliud quam silvam ratio testatur.

318. Rursum dicimus aera duas qualitates habere, calorem et humorem; constitit autem aquam quoque in duabus qualitatibus inveniri humoris et frigoris. Erunt ergo et horum propria quae videntur contraria, aquae quidem frigus, aeris

shape, although by virtue of the craftsman these are all connected with it so that from them the body of the universe may acquire both perfection in its individual parts and variety across the whole of them.

317. And that it is the kindling and primary substrate of the corporeal universe is easily proved from the reciprocal change between qualities. For earth has two proper qualities, coldness and dryness (for our treatment shall assume for the moment that earth is in some portion transformable into some other element). Similarly, water is found to consist of two qualities, namely, moistness and coldness; and dryness is the proper quality in the case of earth whereas moistness is the one in the case of water and common to both is the nature associated with coldness. Now, whenever the broad expanse of earth is by degrees transformed into water, then its dryness will be changed into moistness while the coldness common to both abides in its proper state, being at that precise point neither in earth nor yet in water: not in earth, because that which is transformed ceases to be earth; but neither in water, for while still in the process of change and transformation it is neither fully changed nor completely transformed so as already to have migrated to the material state of water. It remains, then, that the coldness must be somewhere, since it is unable to exist without that in which it exists; and reason attests that the latter is precisely matter.

318. Again, we say that air has two qualities, warmth and moistness, and it is agreed that water for its part is found to consist of the two qualities of moistness and coldness. Now, between them there will be properties which are evidently contrary, coldness in the case of water and warmth in that of

vero calor, sed communis his humor. Cum igitur resoluta in vapores aqua aeri quod ex aqua conversum fluxit quaeritur ac vindicatur, tunc, opinor, frigus quidem ad calorem transitum facit, humor porro communis manet neque in aeris nec in aquae gremio, esse tamen eum uspiam necesse est: erit igitur in silva. Eodemque modo ignis duae sunt qualitates, siccitas et calor, aeris vero, ut supra comprehensum est, calor et humor: ergo etiam et horum communis qualitas in calore. Ignis item propria siccitas, aeris humor; ignito ergo aere et aliquatenus converso in naturam ignis humor quidem ad siccitatem facit transitum, calor autem, communis qualitas, neque in igni neque in aere residebit, nec vero nusquam erit: manebit igitur in silva. Ex quo perspicuum est quod in illa corporum mutua permutatione invenitur silva antiquissima et principalis subiectio, perinde ut cera mollis in qua imprimuntur signacula aut ut eorum quae generantur commune omnium receptaculum.

319. Quibus ita decursis sequitur ut an corpus silva sit consideremus. Neque corpus neque incorporeum quiddam posse dici simpliciter puto, sed tam corpus quam incorporeum possibilitate; quippe quod proprie dicitur corpus ex silva constat et qualitate, silva autem nequaquam ex silva constat et qualitate: minime ergo corpus est. Deinde nullum corpus sine qualitate, silva autem per se sine qualitate: non

air, but the moistness is common to both. Thus when water
is resolved into vapor and that portion of the air which in
the process of transformation has flowed out of the water is
searched for and then found, at that instant, I suppose, the
coldness effects the transition to warmth while the moistness, as the common quality, abides in the womb of neither
air nor water, and yet it is necessary that it should be somewhere: it will therefore be in matter. Similarly, fire has two
qualities, dryness and warmth, whereas air has warmth and
moistness, as was made clear earlier: thus between them as
well there is a common quality in the warmth. And the dryness is proper to fire and the moistness to air; thus once the
air has been ignited and by degrees transformed into the nature associated with fire, then the moistness effects the
transition to dryness while the warmth, as the common
quality, will reside in neither fire nor air and yet will not be
nowhere: it will therefore abide in matter. And from this it
is clear that in this reciprocal permutation of bodies matter
is found to be the most ancient and primary substrate, just
like the *soft* wax *upon which seals are impressed* [50b], or the
Receptacle [49a] common to all of the things which are generated.

319. These points have been laid out so as to bring us to
consideration of the question of whether matter is body. I
suppose that it cannot without qualification be said to be
anything which is either a body or an incorporeal but that it
is potentially as much the one as it is the other; for that
which is referred to as body in the proper sense consists of
matter and quality whereas matter in no sense consists of
matter and quality: thus it is not body. Again, no body is
lacking in quality whereas matter per se lacks quality: thus it

igitur corpus est. Quid quod omne corpus habet figuram et silvae iuxta naturam suam nulla figura est: non ergo corpus. Deinde omne corpus finitum ac determinatum est, silva autem infinita et minime determinata: non ergo corpus. Item omne genus corporis sub categoricam redigitur appellationem. Dicimus enim corpus essentiam, utpote quod diversis temporibus contrarias sustineat passiones et in quo alterum ex duobus contrariis inveniatur necesse est. Idem hoc dicimus quantitatem, cum est perfectum longitudinis latitudinis soliditatisque consortio. Nihilo minus corpus quale et qualitate praeditum nuncupamus. Idem hoc ad aliud corpus comparantes maius esse dicimus aut minus vel aequale; quam comparationem Graeci vocant pros ti, quippe maius sine comparatione minoris et aequale sine comparatione alterius aequalis intellegi non potest. Ceteramque significationem de categoriis mutuamur, at enim silvae detrahimus haec omnia quando passionem quoque ipsam quae propria eius videtur adimimus, ideo quod numquam ex propria condicione desciscat sed aliis, id est corporibus, intra eam perpetientibus illa concors perpessionis putetur. Denique passio <eius> eius modi est ut ipsa quidem in nihil aliud convertatur sed quia recipit ea quae mutantur pati aliquid falso putatur. Denique ut deus qui primitus operatur ac facit neque genus est neque ulli subiacet generi sic etiam quod primitus patitur, id est silva, origo altera, neque genus est neque ulli subiacet generi; quapropter cum sit origo nihil

is not body. What of the fact that every body possesses shape and matter by its proper nature possesses no shape: thus it is not body. Again, every body is finite and determinate whereas matter is infinite and indeterminate: thus it is not body. Likewise, body of every kind comes under a predication according to Category. For we say that a body is a Substance, i.e., in the sense that it at different times sustains contrary modifications, one of two contraries necessarily being found in it at any given time. We also say that it is a Quantity, since it is made complete by the convergence of length, width, and depth. We similarly refer to a body as qualified or endowed with a Quality. We also say that it is greater, smaller, or equal when comparing it to another body; and this form of comparison the Greeks refer to as *Pros ti* [Relation], for the greater is intelligible only by comparison with the smaller and the equal by comparison with another equal. And we take the remaining range of predications from the Categories but separate *all* of them from matter by removing the very Passivity which appears to be proper to it, and doing so on the grounds that it never abandons its proper condition yet is believed to undergo a modification sympathetically with the other things, i.e., bodies, that undergo modifications within it. And then, its passivity is such that although it itself is transformable into nothing else it is falsely believed to undergo some form of modification because of its reception of things which undergo change. And then, just as God, who before all else acts and brings into act, is neither a genus nor subject to any genus, so too that which before all else is possible, i.e., Matter, the other principle, is neither a genus nor subject to any genus; and its being a principle explains why nothing is to be

antiquius ea mente concipiendum est. Quae cum ita sint, corpus sentitur, silva sensibilis non est: silva igitur non erit corpus. Eodemque modo silva simplex res est et incomposita, corpus neque simplex et compositum: minime ergo silva corporea.

320. Dico eandem hanc ne incorpoream quidem, quia quidquid incorporeum est nullam condicionem corporis patitur nec corpus umquam fieri potest; at vero silva formata qualitatibus, quantitatibus etiam figurisque et omni cultu convenustata corpus mundusque facta est effectu opificis atque operatione: igitur ne incorporea quidem. Deinde, si corpus est, sensile est; at enim sensile non est: ne corpus quidem igitur erit; si autem incorporeum quiddam erit silva, intellegibilis eius natura est; at intellegibilis non est: ne incorporea quidem. Recte igitur eam simpliciter et ex natura sua neque corpoream neque incorpoream cognominamus sed possibilitate corpus et item possibilitate non corpus.

321. Iam cum omnia quae propositum erat recensere perspicaci consideratione decursa sint iuxta Platonici dogmatis auctoritatem, superest reditum fieri ad orationis ipsius explanationem. Ait ergo: Quam igitur eius vim quamve esse naturam putandum? Vim nunc appellat opportunitatem silvae vultus induendi; etenim tam vultus quam qualitates varias nec non quantitates habet, non effectu sed possibilitate ob inconstantem eorum mutuam ex alio in aliud conversionem. Naturam vero substantiam eius significat, recteque

mentally conceived as prior to it. And bearing all of this in mind, body is sensible whereas matter is not sensible: thus matter will not be body. Similarly, matter is a simple and noncomposite reality whereas body is nonsimple and composite: thus matter is not corporeal.

320. My point is that matter is at the same time not *incorporeal* either, since nothing that is incorporeal is subject to any of the conditions associated with body or is capable of ever becoming a body; but once informed by qualities, quantities, and shapes and once embellished by all manner of adornment, matter was through the act and agency of the craftsman made body and the world: thus it is not incorporeal either. Again, if it is body then it is a sensible; but it is not a sensible: thus it will not be body either; but if matter is to be something *incorporeal* then its nature is intelligible; but it is not intelligible: thus it is not incorporeal either. We are right, then, to speak, without qualification and in consideration of its proper nature, in terms of its being neither corporeal nor incorporeal but both body in potency and nonbody in potency.

321. Given that we have with careful consideration gone through all points proposed for review with an eye to the authority of Plato's doctrine, it remains for us to return now to explication of the text proper. Now, he says [49a]: *What, then, should we suppose it to have by way of force, what by way of a nature?* By *force* he refers here to matter's ability to change its appearance; for in addition to the appearances, it has qualities and indeed quantities which vary, not in act, but potentially, owing to their shifting mutual transformation from one into another. By *nature,* however, he refers to its essence, and he is right to say *should we suppose,* since we are

etiam putandum, non enim possumus certa aliqua comprehensione vel ex sensu cognita vel ex ratione intellecta de veritate eius praesumere; quippe ut somnium, quo magis
contrectare cupimus, hoc impensius imago effugit. Opinor,
inquit, omnium quae gignuntur receptaculum est et quasi
quaedam nutricula. Omnia quae gignuntur et ex aliquo tempore sint necesse est; sunt ergo mortalia immortalium vereque existentium simulacra et imagines, accipiunt autem
substantiam in silva proptereaque et ipsa illic apparent et
silvae nobis iniciunt recordationem. Quam quidem receptaculum eorum appellat, quia non ex gremio silvae generatae
species florescunt (ut putant Stoici) sed extrinsecus obveniunt ut in cera signacula, nutriculam vero ideo quod alienos
fetus velut propriis humeris vehat; quippe nihil his praebet
amplius praeter subiectionem.

322. Deinde progreditur: Atque hoc quod de ea dicitur verum est quidem et dicendum videtur apertius, quia non statim quae vere dicuntur aperte etiam manifesteque dicuntur.
Multae quippe orationes verae quidem sed obscurae; nascitur quippe obscuritas vel dicentis non numquam voluntate
vel audientis vitio vel ex natura rei de qua tractatus est. Iuxta
dicentem fit obscuritas, cum vel studio dataque opera
dogma suum velat auctor, ut fecerunt Aristoteles et Heraclitus, vel ex imbecillitate sermonis, iuxta audientem vero vel
cum inaudita et insolita dicuntur vel cum is qui audit pi-
griore ingenio est ad intellegendum, iuxta rem porro cum

incapable of obtaining any certain grasp of the truth about it as understood on the basis of either sense perception or reason; indeed, it is like the case of a dream: the more we desire to touch it, the more forcibly the image slips away. He says: *It is, I suppose, the Receptacle and a kind of nurse, as it were, of all that comes to be. All that comes to be* necessarily exists as well from some determinate point in time; thus mortal entities are reflections and images of immortal and truly existent ones, but they receive substance in matter and consequently appear as themselves there and conjure up for us a conception of matter. And he refers to it as their *Receptacle,* not in the sense that generated forms grow out of the womb of matter (as the Stoics suppose), but that they supervene from without, as with the seal impressions in wax, and as their *nurse* in the sense that it carries foreign offspring, so to speak, on its own shoulders; for it offers them nothing beyond the substrate.

322. He then continues [49a–b]: *And although this point is truly stated of it and should evidently be stated more plainly,* since points which are truly stated are not thereby plainly and explicitly stated as well. For many modes of discourse are *indeed true* but obscure; for obscurity sometimes arises from the speaker's intention, from a failure on the part of the listener, or from the nature of the subject under consideration. Obscurity arises in connection with the speaker, when an author veils his doctrine either studiously and deliberately, as Aristotle and Heraclitus did, or out of a stylistic fault; or it arises in connection with the listener, when either unheard of and extraordinary subjects are discussed or the listener's gift for comprehension is on the slow side; or it arises in connection with the subject, whenever it is like the very

talis erit qualis est haec ipsa de qua nunc sermo nobis est, ut neque ullo sensu contingi neque intellectu comprehendi queat, utpote carens forma, sine qualitate, sine fine. Sed neque Timaeus, qui disserit, instabilis orator nec audientes tardi; restat, ut res ipsa difficilis et obscura sit. Nec silva quicquam difficilius ad explanandum; ergo cuncta quae de natura eius dicta sunt mera praedita veritate sunt nec tamen aperte dilucideque intimata. Denique praestat causam difficultatis, cum ita dicit: Est tamen arduum eo magis, quod praeconfundi mentis aciem necesse est et aestuare tam de igni quam de ceteris materiis, qui magis aquam iure aquam dici putarique oporteat quam terram, cum nulla sit certa et stabilis proprietas corporum quae cuiusque indicet naturalem proprietatem. Initium quaestionis arripit ex reciproca de alio in aliud elementorum conversione.

323. Principio ut de aqua, cuius modo, inquit, fecimus mentionem, ordiamur: cum astringitur in glaciem, certe saxum terrenaeque soliditatis corpus minimeque fusile apparet. Acriter et nimium vigilanter apparet, quippe non in sua propria natura perseverans aqua solidatur et fit terra; siquidem est humida sed quod [ea quae] subiacet, videlicet silva, contrariam naturam, hoc est siccitatem, suscipiens fit ex conversione terra, mutato repente habitu mutataque condicione apparens quod non erat. Sed aquam in saxum solidari dicit, quia in glacialibus et gelidis locis aqua diu constricta mutatur in saxum, quod crystallus vocatur ab Alpinis gentibus montium Raeticorum. Est quoque in Asia

one we are now discussing, such that owing to its lack of form, quality, and limit it is incapable of being either contacted by any form of sense perception or grasped by the intellect. But the Timaeus who conducts the discussion is not a faltering speaker, and his audience is not sluggish; it remains that the subject itself is difficult and obscure. Nothing is more difficult to explain than matter; thus everything said about its nature is endowed with pure *truth* without thereby being *plainly* or transparently intimated. He then provides the reason for the difficulty, when he says: *the task nevertheless proves the more difficult because of an inevitable confusion and fluctuation in our mental acuity when it comes to fire and the other material elements: given that the bodies possess no certain and stable property to provide indications of the natural property of each, in what sense is it necessary that water should by right be called and thought of as water rather than earth?* He approaches the question beginning with the reciprocal transformation of elements from one into another.

323. *To begin first,* he says [49b], *with what we have just now referred to as water: when it hardens into ice it appears, so we think, to be stone, a body of earthen solidity and not at all liquid.* The word *appears* is used precisely and with particular care, for in departing from its proper nature the water solidifies and becomes earth; for it is moist but its substrate, namely, the matter, in assuming the contrary nature, i.e., dryness, becomes earth through a process of transformation, and with the sudden change of state and condition it *appears* to be what it was not. He says, however, that the water *solidifies* into *stone* because the water in frozen glacial regions changes through an extended process of hardening into a stone called crystal by the Alpine peoples of the Rhaetian mountains.

civitas Tripolis aquis immensum calentibus vaporata, quae cum missa in formulas diversas obriguerit, formatur in uvarum pomorumque aliorum figuras. Idem, quo modo haec fiant, deinceps dicturus erit.

324. Nunc exequitur quod aggressus est et, quia conversam aquam fieri terram dixerat, hanc eandem aquam demum tenuatam in vapores aereae misceri subtilitati docet rursumque ambustum aera converti in ignem. Deinde gyris <et> anfractibus genituram eorum conversionemque procedere admonet, cum ignis a propria subtilitate discedens condicionem aeris accipit, qui densatus primo quidem in nebulas nubesque opimatur, post soluta et liquefacta sagina in pluvias diffluit; ex aqua rursum soliditas et saxa subsistunt. Igitur secundum hanc orbitam rationemque circuitus terra quoque videtur in alia elementa mutari; si enim sola non convertitur, ad postremum omnia terra fient, siquidem cetera in ipsam convertentur, ipsa autem in nihil eorum habebit conversionem. Sed quia probatio consistit in visu et numquam visa est terra in aquam aliamve quam materiam converti, idcirco abstinuit ac refugit terrenae immutationis assertionem ne pugnare adversum sensus videretur.

325. Sumpsit tamen quo perfectius tractaret de mutua elementorum ex alio in aliud conversione. Ait enim: Atque ita circuitu quodam vires fomentaque generationis corporibus invicem sibi mutantibus nec in una eademque forma

There is moreover in Asia a city, Tripolis, which is immersed in vapor because of the extreme heat of its waters; once the water hardens after having been poured into molds of various types it takes on the shape of grapes and other fruits. And he is going to explain next how these things occur.

324. He follows up now on the point taken up for consideration and, based on his observation concerning water's transformation and becoming earth, explains [49c] that after having been thinned out finally into vapors this *same* water blends with the subtle texture of *air* and that under combustion the air in turn converts to *fire*. He then points out that their coming to be and transformation proceeds in a cyclical round, as fire in departing from the subtleness proper to it takes on the condition of air, which through condensation is first fattened up in *vapors and clouds* then flows out in *showers* once the fattening effect has been dissolved and liquefied; from the *water* solidity and stones in turn come to be. Thus according to this cycle and cyclical pattern earth too evidently changes into other elements; for if it alone is untransformed, then everything will eventually become earth, since the other elements will be transformed into it but it will admit of no transformation into any of them. But since proof is based on observation, and earth was never observed to be transformed into water or any other material element, he held back and avoided any assertion concerning the transformation of earth in order not to give the appearance of impugning our sensory experiences.

325. Still, he resumed in order to treat more fully of the mutual transformation of elements from one into another. For he says [49c–e]: *But if the bodies thus borrow the powers and kindling of generation from one another in a sort of cycle and do not*

perseverantibus quae tandem erit certa eorum et a cunctatione semota comprehensio? Nulla certe. Merito; fingamus enim esse hunc ignem sincerum et sine ullius materiae
permixtione, ut putat Heraclitus, vel aquam, ut Thales, vel
aera, ut Anaximenes: haec, inquit, si semper eadem immuta-
bilia censeamus, multos et inextricabiles incurremus errores. Quare non oportet facile de huiusce modi naturis ac-
commodare consensum nec, si veri simile quid videbitur,
statim habere pro certo. Quid est igitur quod errore nos li-
beret? Quoniam est essentia est etiam qualitas, et haec diversa sunt; nam essentia quidem alicuius rei substantia est,
qualitas autem [quae] rebus substantiam habentibus contingit ac provenit. Si observemus, ut semper quotiens naturam
istam penitus introspicimus partemque aliam eius videmus
deficere a se et in aliam materiam migrare, ut puta ignem,
non ut constans aliquid et semper idem certa pronominis
appellatione monstremus dicentes "hoc" vel "illud," haec
quippe pronomina sunt essentiae signa, sed illo magis utamur in demonstratione quod est proprium qualitatis
dicamusque non "hoc" sed potius "tale," nec "illud" sed potius "illius modi" vel "huius modi." Neque enim ignis quam
patitur immutationem iactura est essentiae sed qualitatis.
Cum ignis fit aer, transit in diversam contrariamve materiam, certum est siquidem essentiam nihil in se sibi habere
contrarium sed potius circa eandem essentiam res versari
contrarias; itaque conversio commutatioque fit non essentiae sed qualitatis, in qua et diversitas et contrarietas

remain in one and the same form, what certain and unwavering comprehension of them will there be in the end? Surely none. Rightly so, for let us imagine that there is this fire, pure and lacking in any other material admixture, as Heraclitus supposes, or water, as in the case of Thales, or air, as in that of Anaximenes: if, he says, we think that these things are always the same and unchanging, then we will run into many "inextricable errors." Hence in connection with natures of this sort the facile contrivance of consensus is inappropriate, as will be the automatic taking of any apparent probability as certain. What is there, then, to free us from the error? Given that there is substance there is also quality, and the two are distinct; for a substance is the substance of a particular thing, whereas a quality is contingent and supervenient upon things that have substance. If we are being attentive, as always in cases where we look deep into this nature and see that one part of it abandons itself and migrates to another material element, e.g., fire, then we should not with the use of a definite *pronominal appellative* indicate a thing as though it were constant and always the same by saying *"this"* or *"that,"* for these *pronouns indicate* substance, but should instead *use* the proper *demonstrative* expression for a quality and say, not "this" but rather *"of this sort,"* and not "that" but rather *"of that"* or *"this sort."* For the transformation which fire undergoes involves a loss, not of substance, but of quality. When fire becomes air it shifts to a different or contrary material, for it is certain that the substance has within it nothing contrary to itself but that instead contrary realities come and go in relation to the same substance; thus there does not occur a transformation or change of substance but one of quality, in connection with which both

invenitur. Eadem ratio est ceterorum quoque elementorum, quippe nihil eorum habet essentiam propriam, et nos praesumimus ex consuetudine uti demonstratione pronominum eorum quae sunt essentiae, cum qualitati accommodatis pronominibus utendum potius sit; semper enim et sine intermissione ullius temporis fluunt haec quattuor corpora priusque ex conversione mutantur quam erunt cognominata, more torrentis inrefrenabili quodam impetu proruentis.

326. Itaque, inquit, ignis iste qui velut exudans in aereas auras dissolvitur, cum instabilis mutabilisque sit nec habeat perpetuam proprietatem, non est ignis censendus, sed igneum quiddam, nec quae exhalatis vaporibus in auras aqua vertitur humor est nuncupanda, sed humidum quid; similiter cetera. Et exequitur: At vero id in quo fieri cuncta haec singillatim videntur et demum dissolvi pereuntiaque ad alias transire formas, silvam scilicet, solum illud appellandum puto certo pronomine recteque de eo dici posse "hoc" vel "illud." Merito; sola enim haec, ut cuius nulla qualitas sit nullaque forma, nec in contrarias qualitates nec in diversas formas patitur conversionem, et quia semper eadem manet, certo nomine appellari firme potest. Atque ut omne nubilum naturalis discuteret obscuritatis adhibito splendore illustris exempli iubet concipere animo et infingere cogitatione opificem ex uno eodemque auro innumeras sine intermissione formantem figuras, modo pyramidis et ex ea mox octahedri dictoque citius icosahedri et item cubi

difference and contrariety are found. The same explanation applies to the other elements as well, for none of them has a proper substance, and we assume the *conventional use of the pointing function of pronouns* for what are substances even though it would be preferable to use demonstratives assigned to the quality; for these four bodies are forever in a state of uninterrupted fluctuation, and like a torrent rushing forth under some irresistible impulse they change through a process of transformation before they can be named.

326. And so, he says [49d–50b], since this fire which dissolves *into airy breezes* as though by evaporation is *unstable* and mutable and *does not possess* an enduring property, it should *not* be considered *fire but a fiery something,* nor is the water which through the exhalation of vapors turns into breezes to be referred to as moisture but as something moist, and so on for the others. And he continues: *But I suppose that that in which each of these things appears to arise and subsequently dissolve and by its perishing to shift from one form to another,* namely, matter, *is alone to be indicated by a fixed pronoun, and that "this" or "that" can rightly be predicated of it.* Rightly so, for matter *alone,* being possessed of no quality and no form, undergoes no *transformation* to either *contrary qualities* or different forms, and by virtue of its always remaining the same *can* reliably *be indicated by a fixed name.* And in order to dissipate any cloudiness attaching to this point of natural obscurity, he casts the light of a brilliant illustration upon it and bids us to conceive in our mind and imagine in our thought a craftsman *continuously* fashioning innumerable *figures from one and the same gold,* first the form of a pyramid, immediately thereafter that of an octahedron, and faster than you can say it that of an icosahedron or cube, and so on

species, ceteras item—triangulorum quadratorum hemicy-
cli circuli—tunc, si quis electa qualibet figura quaerat quid
illud sit, aurum esse responderi oportere censet ne (si pyra-
midem esse responsum sit), illa in aliam figuram mox et inter ipsa verba responsionis migrante, qui sic responderit
mentiatur. Eodem igitur modo nec ignem, qui est pyramoides, ignem esse respondebimus sed vel ignitam silvae
partem vel igneam qualitatem, nec octahedrum sed spirabi-
lem silvam, nec icosahedrum nec cubum sed humectam
hanc terrenam illam silvae soliditatem.

327. Nec vero putandum est agere nunc Platonem de nominum proprietate, quin potius dare operam ut assuesca-
mus sinceram silvam, quae concursu variorum corporum tegitur, ab eorundem corporum permixtione sollertia mentis
distinguere. Ait enim: Eadem et consimilis ratio difficultasque in ea <natura> quae cunctas recipit corporum formas
reperitur. Haec quippe minime recedit ex condicione propria; recipit enim cuncta nec ullam de isdem formam trahit.
Ergo formata quidem sunt corpora, silva sine forma. Cumque intra gremium eius formentur, inquit, quae recipiuntur—consequenter supra dictis quae recipiuntur, omnium
quippe eam corporum appellaverat receptaculum—, ipsa
informis manet estque usus eius similis molli cedentique
materiae in qua imprimuntur varia signacula. Perspicuum
est aliqua esse mollia corpora, quae cedentia variorum simulacrorum impressionibus recepta diu conservent imposita

for the rest—triangles, quadrilaterals, a semicircle or circle—, *then if one were to select any figure and ask what* the thing *is,* he thinks that the *reply* must be that it *is gold,* to prevent the respondent from speaking falsely (supposing his response is that it is a pyramid), for the figure is already shifting to another even as he utters the reply. On the same principle, then, our response will be, not that the fire which is pyramidal in form is fire, but either that it is a portion of matter containing fire or that it is a fiery quality, not that the air is an octahedron, but that it is breathable matter, not that the water is an icosahedron or the earth a cube, but that the one is moist matter and the other an earthen solidification of matter.

327. It should not be supposed, however, that Plato is here treating of the property of names but rather that he is concerned with our developing the habit and skill of mentally distinguishing the pure matter hidden beneath the traffic between the various bodies from the intermingling of those same bodies. For he says [50b–c]: *Precisely the same explanation and difficulty is encountered in connection with the nature that is recipient of all bodily* forms, *since it in no way recedes from the condition proper to it; for it receives all things without extracting any form from them.* Thus whereas the bodies have received form, matter is without form. *And although,* he says, *the things received take on form within its womb—things received* follows from what was stated earlier [49a], for he referred to it as the *Receptacle* of all bodies—, *it remains formless in itself, and its behavior is like that of the soft and supple material upon which different seal impressions are stamped.* It is evident that there are certain *soft* bodies which in their *supple* response to the impressions of *different* images preserve for extended

signacula, ut si ceram quis vel plumbum vel argentum con-
signet undique: erit tunc in silvae vicem cera informis et
habebit innumeras formas non suas sed aliunde adhibitas
sibi. Ratione igitur et recte usui silvae corporeae, quae con-
signata est undique corporum formis, natura mollis ceden-
tisque materiae comparatur.

328. Sed de cera quidem etiam in Theaeteto locutus est,
cum diversae hominum memoriae, tenacioris et labidae,
causas exprimeret. Ait esse in hominum ingeniis vim quandam cerae simillimam, quae faciat et acutos ad intellegendum et celeres ad ediscendum, et eosdem subinde oblivio-
sos, item alios quidem tardos ad discendum, verum iugiter
memores, quosdam ita ingeniatos, ut et cito discant et diu
memoria vigeant. Nam quorum in animo cerae illa similitudo, quam Homerum dicit <cor> cognominasse, fluxior
solutiorque erit, facile quidem discunt sed cito amittunt
obsoletis ob nimiam remissionem cerae signaculis. Contra
ingenii mentisque durior cera vix recipit formas quae imprimuntur, sed si umquam receperit, diu conservat operose
impressas figuras, utpote stabili materia locatas. Tertia divinae felicitatis concretio, cum cerae similitudo sic solida est
ut neque respuat formas nec renitatur adversum impres-
sionem signaculorum, nec ita fluxa recipiat sede ut incertae
minimeque visibiles impressiones sint.

periods the imposed *seal impressions* once they have been received; take, for example, the case in which someone makes seal impressions all over wax, lead, or silver: the wax, functioning at that point in the place of matter, will be *formless* and possess innumerable forms which are not its own but have been extrinsically made upon it. With good reason, then, and rightly is the nature of the *soft and supple material* compared in its *behavior* to the corporeal matter that has *bodily forms* stamped all over it.

328. But he also spoke in terms of wax in the *Theaetetus,* when he explained why human beings experience different types of memory, whether more tenacious or fleeting. He says that there is among the native mental abilities possessed by human beings a certain power closely resembling wax which makes some people acute of understanding and quick to learn but then immediately forgetful, others slow to learn but enduring of memory, and some naturally endowed in such a way as to be both quick to learn and enduring of memory. For those individuals in whose minds the wax likeness, which he says Homer referred to as the heart, turns out to be of the more liquid and looser type acquire knowledge readily but lose it quickly because the impressions disappear owing to the extreme suppleness of the wax. By contrast, a harder wax in the mental ability receives the impressed images with difficulty but on having done so preserves the laboriously impressed images for long periods by embedding them in a stable material. The third level of consistency is a matter of divine good luck: the wax likeness is neither so firm as to reject images or to resist the impression of images, nor so fluid a receptive medium as to render the impressions indistinct and hardly visible.

329. Nunc, quoniam informem esse ac sine qualitate silvam manifestaverat, immobilem quoque curat ostendere asserens moveri eam conformarique ab introeuntibus multimodis, cum ipsa ita ut formae sic motus quoque sit expers, sed a speciebus formam habentibus motam varie diverseque formari. Manet ergo haec in tali fortuna et condicione semper, archetypum quoque exemplum manet in substantia propria, idea scilicet cuiusque existens rei natae, similiter deus opifex per aevum manet, sed archetyporum exemplorum simulacra, quae silvae obveniunt, non permanent, namque assidue ac sine intermissione mutantur mortis nascendique perpetua successione ob inexcusabilem naturae cuiusdam necessitatem. Quam ob rem dicta est a Platone silva posita esse ad recipienda rerum signacula. Praeclare posita, quia, cum sit natura immobilis, ingredientium formantiumque eam specierum commeatu movetur et easdem invicem movet species, ut progrediens docebit. Recte itaque, cum eadem sit semper et immutabilis, videtur tamen, inquit, ob specierum multiformium coetum dispariles induere formas; at vero quae obveniunt silvae species et in ea dissolvuntur ac pereunt, aeternarum atque immortalium specierum simulacra sunt, earum videlicet, quas ideas vocamus, formanturque ab isdem miro quodam modo, iuxta memorati videlicet exempli consignationem. Miro autem modo propterea, quod difficile atque inexplicabile est concipere mente, quatenus ex idearum sinceritate nativis vera rebus similitudo proveniat, utrum perinde ut mollibus

329. Having made it evident that matter is formless and without quality, he now undertakes to show that it is also immobile, pointing out [50c] that it is *moved and given form* by all manner of things that *enter it,* although it is *itself* devoid of *movement* just as it is of *form,* but that once moved by forms endowed with form it is given form in various and different ways. Matter, therefore, remains in such a state or condition forever, and the archetypal exemplar too remains in its proper substance, namely, being the idea of each and every reality that comes to be, and the craftsman god similarly remains through eternity, but the images of the archetypal exemplars that engage with matter do not remain, for they forever and continuously change in a perpetual succession of death and birth because of the inescapable necessity attaching to each particular nature. And that is why matter is said by Plato to be *disposed* to receive the impressions of things. *Disposed,* for the obvious reason that, although it is by nature immobile, it is moved by the traffic of the forms that *enter* and shape it and in turn moves those same forms, as he will explain further on. And so, although it is forever the same and immutable, it nevertheless appears, he rightly says, to assume diverse *forms* because of its interaction with multi-shaped forms; but the forms which encounter matter and dissolve and perish in it are *images* of the eternal and immortal forms, namely, those which we call the *ideae,* and are in *some mysterious manner,* namely, in conformity with the impression conferred by the exemplar at issue, *given form by the same.* And in a *mysterious manner,* because to form a mental concept of how a true likeness emerges out of the purity of the ideas in the things that come to be is difficult and *inexplicable,* whether it is as in the case of the *seal impressions in*

materiis signacula, sicut supra dictum est, an ut cum de
exemplo liniamenta in materias tractabiles transferuntur,
quod in pictoria et item fictoria fieri videmus.

330. Quare differt ad praesens tractatum hunc suo reser-
vans loco ac tempori, ac distinguit intellectum imperata
animi conceptione tali ut tria genera nobis occurrant, genera nunc improprie appellans, neque enim silva nec vero
exemplum genera sunt, sed ut appellatio generum significet
primas substantias. Illud quidem, inquit, quod fit et quod
gignitur, generata videlicet species quae in silva subsistit et
ibidem dissolvitur; item aliud in quo gignitur, in quo est ipsa
silva, in hac quippe species dissolubiles substantiam sortiun-
tur; tertium praeterea, ex quo similitudinem trahit mutuaturque quod gignitur, idea scilicet, quae exemplum est rerum omnium quas natura progenuit, hoc est eorum quae
silvae quasi quodam gremio continentur exemplorumque
imagines esse dicuntur. Deinde evidenti quadam comparatione atque exemplo quaestionem revelat. Comparat enim
quod percipit in se species matri, videlicet silvae, haec enim
recipit a natura proditas species; illud vero ex quo similitudo
commeat, patri, hoc est ideae, huius enim similitudinem
memoratae species mutuantur; quod vero ex his duobus est,
proli, generatae scilicet speciei, est enim haec posita inter
naturam vere existentem constantem eandemque semper,
nimirum idean quae intellectus dei aeterni est aeternus, et
[inter] eam naturam quae est quidem sed non eadem semper, id est silvam, quippe haec natura sua nihil est eorum

soft materials, as indicated earlier, or as when outlines are transferred from a model to tractable materials, as we see happening in the cases of painting and sculpture.

330. And so he *momentarily* [50c–d] postpones this treatment, reserving it for the proper place and time, and elaborates on his line of thought in bidding us to form a mental conception such that we are confronted with *three kinds of thing, for the moment* using *kinds,* not in the strict sense, for neither matter nor the exemplar is a genus [kind], but to signify the primary substances. *That,* he says, *which* comes to be or *becomes,* namely, the generated form which both subsists and dissolves in matter; *secondly, that in which it becomes,* the *in-which* being matter itself, for in it the forms which are subject to dissolution acquire substance; *and thirdly, that from which that which becomes draws or obtains its element of likeness,* namely, the idea, which is the exemplar for all things brought forth by nature, i.e., for the things which are contained within the womb, as it were, of matter and are said to be images of the exemplars. He then sheds light on the question by means of an evident *comparison* or illustration of a particular sort. For he compares that which receives the forms within itself to a *mother,* namely, to matter, for it receives the forms brought forth by nature; *and* that *from which the element of likeness* comes to a *father,* i.e., to the idea, for it is from it that the forms under consideration *borrow their element of likeness;* and that which is from the *two* to their *offspring,* namely, to the generated form, for it is situated *between* the *nature* which is truly existent, constant, and forever the same, namely, the idea or eternal intellect of the eternal god, and the *nature* which indeed is but is not forever the same, i.e., matter, for by its nature matter is none of the

quae sunt, cum sit aeterna. Ergo quod inter has duas naturas positum est vere existens non est. Cum enim sit imago vere existentis rei, videtur esse aliquatenus, quia vero non perseverat patiturque immutationem sui, non est existens vere, ut sunt exempla; illa quippe exempla rata et immutabili constantia vigent. Erunt igitur tria haec: quod semper est; item quod semper non est; deinde quod non semper est. Nec vero moveri quemquam oportet, si exempla exemplis non usque quaque similia videbuntur; comparatio enim iuxta similitudinem instituitur, quae similitudo parilitatis disparilitatisque concretio est. Quare si quid in huius modi rebus perfunctoriam similitudinem habere invenietur, amplecti nos oportet intellectus manifestationisque causa.

331. Deinde ait fieri non posse ut una existat facies quae omnes rerum omnium formas vultusque contineat variaque universi corporis undique ora demonstret nisi subiecto prius informi aliquo corporum gremio, perinde ut quae in picturis substernitur infectio decolor ad colorum lumina subvehenda. Nunc praestat causas cur necesse fuerit silvam esse inopem qualitatis. Etenim si erit aliquod opus futurum cui nihil desit ad perfectam atque integram pulchritudinem, praebitum esse debet exemplum iuxta quod fit, nec <tantum> opifex optimus et praestantissimus sed etiam ipsa silva atque materies, ex qua illud opus fieri necesse est. Erit porro materia idonea si habebit opportunitatem facilitatemque formabilem. Habebit autem si erit pura et qualitate

things that are, since it is eternal. Thus that which is situated *between these* two *natures* is not truly existent. For being the image of a truly existent reality it has to some degree the appearance of being, but in its not enduring and its undergoing change within itself it is not truly existent as the exemplars are; for the exemplars thrive on a fixed and immutable constancy. Hence there will be the following three things: that which forever is; that which forever is not; and that which is not forever. And no one should feel disturbed if his illustrations do not turn out to appear similar to their correlates in every respect; for a *comparison* is formed on the basis of *similarity,* but a similarity is the coalescence of sameness and difference. And so whenever in matters of this sort something is found to possess a perfunctory degree of similarity, we ought to embrace it in the interests of our clarity of understanding.

331. He says next [50d–e] that *it is impossible for there to be a single aspect to capture all of the forms and appearances of all things and to display the various appearances throughout the body* of the universe *if a kind of formless womb has not first been provided as a substrate for bodies, like the neutral base which is laid down to support the luminous colors in paintings.* He is here providing the reasons for the necessity of matter's being deprived of quality. For if there is going to be some work which lacks nothing for its perfect and complete beauty, then provisions have to be made for a pattern in conformity with which it is produced, and not only a craftsman of the highest and most exceptional ability but also matter, the material from which that particular work must necessarily be made. Moreover, the material will be suitable provided it has the ability or facility for being formed. And it will have, provided it is pure

omni carens; quippe si habebit propriam qualitatem erit impedimento ceteris qualitatibus genuina qualitas, maxime igitur si erunt variae multiplicesque insigniendae nec multiplices modo sed omnes etiam formae ac figurae. Igitur quia omnes silva recipit figuras, omnes quoque colores et ceteras, quot sunt, qualitates, nihil autem horum habet ipsa ex natura sua, iure eam modo informem modo minime figuratam interdum sine qualitate cognominat, non quo habuerit haec umquam et amiserit sed ut quae potuerit habere, utpote natura praedita splendoris atque ornatus capace, quem ad modum appellatur informe saxum cui nondum accesserit ex artificio forma formari tamen possit.

332. Et concludit asserens omne quod bene atque affabre recepturum erit formas informe esse debere purumque ab his omnibus quae erit recepturum, hoc est, sine figura et sine colore, odore etiam et ceteris quae corporis naturam sequuntur. Etenim si erit, inquit, alicuius eorum quae in se recipit simile receptaculum, cum quid obveniet dissimile his quibus simile est, discordabit, opinor, <vultus eius cum introgressi corporis> vultu nullamque exprimet similitudinem. Quod dicit tale est: si aqua sit universae rei silva sive substantia, ut Thales censet, habebit certe qualitates naturae suae proprias, quae numquam ab ea recedent, sed si necesse sit eam a natura sua declinare aliquatenus et ignescere, suscipiet certe rursum igneas qualitates. Humecta et ignea contrariae sibi sunt, quippe alterius humor et frigus propria sunt, alterius siccitas et calor. Haec ergo, inquit, diversa sibi

and lacking in a quality of any sort; for if it has a proper quality, then the innate quality will act as an impediment to other qualities, especially if the forms and shapes to be imprinted upon it are variegated and manifold, and not just manifold but in fact of every possible type. Since, then, matter receives every possible shape, every possible color, and as many other qualities as there are but of its own nature has none of them itself, he rightly describes it as formless or elsewhere as unshaped or without quality, not in the sense that it once had and then lost these attributes, but that, being endowed with a nature capable of receiving splendor and adornment, it was able to have them, as when a stone which has not yet received form from the skill of an artisan but is nevertheless able to be formed is referred to as formless.

332. And he concludes with the assertion that anything which is going to be receptive of forms in a suitably skillful way has to be without form and free of all the things it is to receive, i.e., to be without shape, color, scent and the other things entailed by the nature of a body. *For,* he says [50e], *if ever the Receptacle is like any of the things it receives within itself, then, I suppose, whenever anything unlike the things it is like appears, its appearance will be out of accord with that of the incoming body and express no likeness to it.* His point is the following: if water is the material substance of the universe, as Thales thinks, then it will surely have proper to its nature qualities which will never recede from it; but if it should be necessary for it to turn away in some respect from its nature and become fire, then it will surely assume in turn the qualities of fire. Moist and fiery natures are *contrary* to one another, moistness and coldness being proper to the one and dryness and heat to the other. Thus these mutually *different* and

et repugnantia non patientur alterius sinceram exprimi qualitatem, cum calor quidem frigus impugnet, siccitas demum
interimat humorem, vel, ut alio utamur exemplo, si sit aliquid candidum, ut psimithium, deinde hoc oporteat trans-
ferri in alium colorem vel diversum, ut ruborem sive pal-
lorem, vel contrarium, ut atrum, tunc candor non patietur
introeuntes colores sinceros perseverare sed permixtione
sui faciet interpolatos.

333. Quid igitur sibi vult, dicet aliquis, ista divisio diversorum colorum et item contrariorum? Quia contraria sunt ea
quae a se plurimum distant, licet sint generis eiusdem, ut
puta candor et item nigredo, quorum genus unum est quod
vocatur color. Sed haec duo plurimum a se distant, candido
enim minimum distat quod dicitur pallidum, aliquanto plus
quod appellatur rubeum, hoc amplius cyaneus color, plurimum vero nigredo, ideoque candidum et item nigrum non
diversa sunt sed contraria, quia intercapedo prolixior. Ergo
contraria separata quidem a se sunt magna quadam separati-
one nec tamen omnino aliena sunt, facit enim ea veluti
cognata et consanguinea genus suum, quod colorem esse
praediximus. Natura vero distant omnino ea quae diversa
dicuntur, ut candor et dulcedo nigredoque et odor; illorum
quippe genus color, horum sucus et vapor propetereaque diversis sensibus comprehenduntur. Ut igitur ea quae subiacet
his omnibus silva possit horum facies sinceras minimeque

repellent things, he says, will not tolerate expression of the pure quality of a counterpart, since heat conflicts with coldness and dryness ultimately destroys moistness; or to use another example, if there is something white, such as ceruse, and it at some point proves necessary for it to be made another color, whether a different one such as red or yellow or the contrary one, in this case black, then at that point the white will not tolerate the colors remaining pure upon entry but will by the admixture of itself cause them to be altered.

333. Well then, someone will say, what does he mean by this division into different and contrary colors? That contraries are those things which are most separated from one another despite their belonging to the same genus, as in the case of white and black, which belong to the genus called color. But the two are most separated from one another, for that which is called yellow is minimally separated from white, that which is called red is slightly more separated, the color blue more so again, and black the most separated, and in this sense white and black are not different but contrary by virtue of a greater degree of separation. Contraries, then, are indeed separated from one another by a certain broad degree of separation and yet are not altogether foreign to one another, for their genus, which as we have already indicated is color, makes them kindred blood relations of a sort. Those things which are said to be different, on the other hand, are by nature completely separated, as in the cases of whiteness and sweetness or blackness and scent; for the first elements belong to the genus color and the second ones to those of fluid and vapor, that being the reason for their being grasped by different sense faculties. In order, then, for the matter which acts as a substrate to all of the above to be

interpolatas ostendere, ipsam necesse est nullas qualitates habere.

334. Id ipsum quod generaliter asseverat nunc specialiter vult probare positis exemplis in usu frequenti: Ut qui odora pigmenta conficiunt non patiuntur esse odoris naturalis ac proprii quod condiunt, quo meracos sincerosque suscipiat sucos odoraminum; vascularii quoque argento informi signa impressuri levigant prius superficiem, ut figurae sincerae imprimantur molli cedentique materiae, ita, inquit, illa etiam quae omnium specierum formas receptura erat pura et sine qualitatibus debuit apparari. Factum vero generatumque et visibile animal vult intellegi sensilem mundum, matremque eius et corporum receptaculum silvam vocat ob rationem supra dictam, sed neque terram hanc neque aquam nec ignem vel aera recte existimari. Haec quippe corpora esse sed eam quae cuncta haec ambiat invisibilem speciem et informem esse capacitatem mira quadam et incomprehensibili ratione inter nullam et aliquam substantiam nec plane intellegibilem <nec plane sensibilem> positam.

335. Haec operosius in Parmenide, cum quaereret quatenus res existentes idearum participarent similitudinem. Etenim est difficilis consideratio propter silvae naturales tenebras, quippe quae subterfugiat non modo sensus omnes sed etiam rationis investigationem intellectusque indaginem. Sive enim per semet ipsam et sine consortio corporum quae recipit spectare curet nihil esse propemodum videtur, seu cum illis confundetur nec naturalem ostendet proprietatem

able to project their aspects as pure and unaltered, it is necessary for it to possess none of their qualities itself.

334. The point which he stated generally he sets out now to demonstrate in a specific way by introducing illustrations of common usage [50e–51a]: *As those who are preparing scented lotions do not allow* the material they *work with* to have a natural *scent* of *its own,* so that it may receive the *scented fluids* undiluted and pure, and the makers of vessels before stamping impressions upon formless silver first *smooth* its surface in order that the figures may be *impressed* in a pure state upon the *soft and supple material,* in the same way, he says, the matter which was to *receive* the shapes of all forms had to be prepared in a *pure* state and without qualities. And by a *made, generated, and visible living being* he intends the sensible world to be understood and for the reason stated earlier calls matter its *mother* and the *Receptacle* of bodies but says that it is *not* right for it to be considered *earth, water, fire, or air.* For he holds that the latter are bodies but that the matter which envelops them all is an *invisible form and formless capacity, situated in some mysterious and incomprehensible way between nonbeing and some sort of being, clearly neither intelligible nor sensible.*

335. These considerations he treated of in greater detail in the *Parmenides,* when he raised the question of the extent to which existent things participate in likeness with the ideas. For the problem is a difficult one owing to the darkness in which matter is by its very nature enshrouded, eluding as it does not only all forms of sense perception but also rational investigation and the intellect's pursuit. For if the concern is to view it on its own and separately from its association with the bodies it receives then it appears to be virtually nothing, or if it is taken in its confused state of conjunction with

estque inter sensum et rationem, neque plane sensile quid
nec omnino rationabile sed motu animi comprehendenda
tali ut qui contigerit eam nihil sentiat et qui rationem eius
animo exercuerit adulterina quadam ratione assecutus esse
videatur. Solum ergo remedium assecutionis id erit, ut putemus ignem esse partem eius quae ignita, aquam vero quae
humectata est, similiter cetera.

336. Quatenus igitur ista natura omnia decem quae sunt
genera complectitur? Essentia est, opinor, cum eam species
coetu proprio esse ac videri aliquid effecerint, vel hominem
vel equum vel quid aliud ex animalibus arboribus stirpibus;
qualitas vero cum aliquam percipit qualitatem calefacta vel
colorata; quantitas cum corporum est augmentis imminutionibusque variata; pros ti cum erit in aliquo habitu et comparatione eminentia sua vel humilitate adversum alterius
eminentiam aestimata; ubi autem cum determinatur et accipit aliquam figuram—sic enim in aliquo esse loco putatur—;
quando cum circumactio mundi incrementa ei temporis de-
derit; positio porro cum ordinaretur inter prima corpora
quae dicuntur elementa, ratiocinantibus nobis terram quidem in medietate mundi sitam, summum autem ignem alta
omnia undique capessentem; habere ut cum dicimus mundum non solum anima sed etiam ratione atque intellegentia

them then it will not reveal a natural property, and is *between*
[51b] sense perception and reason, *clearly* being nothing either *sensible* or wholly rational *but* having to be grasped by a
mental act such that the one who comes into contact with it
perceives nothing and the one who trains his mental powers
of reasoning has the impression of having formed some understanding of it by a *certain illegitimate form of reasoning*
[52b]. The sole solution for the forming of some understanding of it, then, will be this [51b]: that we should think of *fire*
as being the *part of it* that has *become fiery and water* as that
which has *become moist,* and so on for the others.

336. In what sense, then, does this nature embrace the ten
Genera of Being in their entirety? A Substance obtains, I
suppose, when forms have by their proper combination
caused something to be and to be recognizable, whether a
human being, horse, or any other animal, tree, or plant; and
a Quality obtains when matter acquires a determinate quality by being made warm or colored; a Quantity, when it is altered by the growth or diminution characteristic of bodies;
a Relation, whenever it is in a particular state of comparison, its length or shortness being determined relative to the
length of something else; and a Place-Where, when it is delimited and receives a particular shape—for that is the sense
in which it is considered to be in a particular place; a Time-
When, once the circumlation of the world has conferred
the increments of time upon it; and a Position, once it is ordered among the primary bodies called elements, for we
think of earth as being situated at the center of the world
and fire as occupying the upper regions all around it; Having, as when we say that the world is endowed not only with
soul but with reason and intelligence as well; Acting, when

praeditum; facere vero cum eadem silva intra se movet species; pati cum invicem ipsa speciebus semet moventibus commovetur.

337. Deinde progreditur: estne aliquis ignis seorsum positus et incommunicabilis? Nunc iam de his tractare incipit volens ostendere, quod intellegibilis illius ignis sensilis iste ignis simulacrum sit, similiter terra sensilis imago quaedam intellegibilis terrae, sic etiam ceterae species, quodque haec omnia quae videmus aliarum specierum invisibilium simulacra sint, illa item horum invicem exempla. Oportet ergo nos etiam de exemplari breviter quae sunt dicenda disserere. Atque ut de silva diximus, cum de ea tractatum haberemus, esse eam principaliter subiectam rerum naturalium generationi, sic etiam de exemplo dicendum, quod sit species principalis. Omnis quippe materia silvestris opifici subiacet, ut aes statuarum artifici, naupego item ligna, sed haec non primitus subiacent, quia sunt aliarum artium inventa, aes quidem metallicae, ligna vero sectionis sive putationis; his demum subest terra, terrae item silva, silvae nihil, unde recte principalis subiectio est cognominata. Eodem igitur modo etiam in exemplo rerum gemina species consideratur: illa qua exornata silva est, nihiloque minus alia species ad cuius similitudinem illa species facta est quae silvae tributa est; et est imposita quidem silvae species secunda, prima vero illa

the matter causes the forms within itself to move; and Being-Affected, when it is in turn moved by the forms moving within it.

337. He then proceeds [51b]: *Is there some fire which is set apart and incommunicable?* He begins now to treat of these matters for the first time, his intention being to point out that the sensible fire here is a likeness of the intelligible fire beyond, that sensible earth is similarly a particular image of intelligible earth, and so on for the other forms, and that all of these things visible to us are likenesses of other invisible forms, with the latter serving in turn as their exemplars. Thus it behooves us to give a brief explanation of what needs to be said also about the exemplars. And just as in the case of matter we pointed out in the course of our treatment that it is the primary substrate for the generation of natural things, so too in the case of the exemplar it needs to be pointed out that it is the primary form. For every material substance functions as a substrate for the craftsman, e.g., bronze in the case of the artist who produces statues and wood in the case of the shipwright, but the latter do not function as substrates in the primary sense, since they are the products of other arts, mining in the case of bronze and cutting or pruning in that of wood; beneath both there is ultimately earth, and beneath earth matter, but beneath matter nothing, so that it is rightly referred to as the primary substrate. Now, in the case of the exemplar of things too there is similarly a double sense of form to consider: one is that by which matter is adorned, and the other (no less important) the form in the likeness of which the form assigned to matter is made, and the one imposed upon matter is the second form, while the first is that in the likeness of

ad cuius haec secunda similitudinem facta est. Sed nimirum fiet hoc manifestius in aliqua similitudine et comparatione consideratum. Ut enim in simulacro Capitolini Iovis est una species eboris, est item alia quam Apollonius artifex hausit animo, ad quam directa mentis acie speciem eboris poliebat, harum autem duarum specierum altera erit antiquior altera sic etiam species quae silvam exornavit secundae dignitatis est, illa vero alia iuxta quam secunda species absoluta est principalis est species de qua sermo habetur ad praesens.

338. Rursum silvam dicebamus esse inopem qualitatis, dicemus etiam principalem speciem neque qualitate praeditam neque sine qualitate. Siquidem omne praeditum qualitate habeat in se qualitatem necesse est, at vero primaria species non est particeps qualitatis, deest enim natura cui qualitas possit insidere, minime igitur posita est in qualitate; <nec vero caret qualitate,> omnia enim carere dicuntur quae, cum natura talia sint ut habeant, non habent. Ut igitur non dicimus intrepidum lapidem, quia non est natura eius huius modi ut aliquid possit timere, sic ne primaria quidem species qualitate dicetur carere, quia et natura eius aliena est a qualitate et ipsa aliis causa est cur sint praedita qualitate. Atque ut animam neque animatam dicimus nec exanimem—animatam quidem ideo quia anima animae praesidio non eget, exanimem vero quia ipsa causa est ceteris animalibus vitae—, sic silvam quoque neque silvestrem putamus nec silva carere—silvestrem quidem non dicimus quia silvae

which the second is made. But this will undoubtedly become clearer when considered in light of a particular simile or comparison. For just as in the case of the statue of Capitoline Jupiter there is one form in the ivory and another which the artist Apollonius absorbed in his mind and by directing his mental gaze toward it gave polished form to the ivory, and just as one of the two forms will be prior to the other, so too the form which has adorned matter is of secondary rank whereas the other one, that in accordance with which the second form was brought to completion, is the primary form under discussion here.

338. Again, we were pointing out that matter is deprived of quality, and will add that the primary form is neither endowed with quality nor without quality. For everything endowed with a quality necessarily has the quality in it, but the primary form does not participate in a quality, for it lacks a nature in which the quality might inhere and therefore has no qualitative disposition; but neither is it deprived of quality, for all things which are not in a state of possession when they are naturally such as to possess are said to be in a state of deprivation. Hence, just as we do not call a stone intrepid, for its nature is not such as to be capable of fearing anything, so the primary form will not be said to be deprived of quality either, for its nature is alien to quality and it itself is the cause of other things being endowed with quality. And just as we say that soul is neither animate nor inanimate — "animate," because soul does not require the assistance of soul, and "inanimate," because it itself is the cause of life in other living beings —, so too we suppose that matter is neither material nor deprived of matter — ruling out "material," because matter is not requisite to matter, and "deprived of

silva non est necessaria, carere autem silva ideo quod omnia silvestria propter hanc sint materialia. Quae cum ita sint, etiam de principali specie perinde sentiemus, ut neque qualitate praeditam putemus nec carentem qualitate. Rursum silva dicebatur informis, <dicetur etiam principalis species non formata> sed nec informis. Formatum enim quidque compositum sit necesse est ex participante et ex participabili, ut statua, in qua participat quidem aes participatur vero impressa forma, sed species est simplex et incomposita, propterea igitur species negatur esse formata; nec vero minime est formata, nam propter hanc alia quoque omnia quae sunt formata in possessione vultus sunt.

339. Est igitur principalis species, ut cum aliqua dicatur effigie, iuxta nos quidem qui intellectus compotes sumus primum intellegibile, iuxta deum vero perfectus intellectus dei, iuxta silvam modus mensuraque rerum corporearum atque silvestrium, iuxta ipsam vero speciem incorporea substantia causaque eorum omnium quae ex ea similitudinem mutuantur, iuxta mundum vero exemplum sempiternum omnium quae natura progenuit. Atque ut conceptim dicatur, primaria species, quae idea est, substantia definitur carens corpore colore figura, sine tactu, intellectu tamen cum ratione comprehendenda causaque omnium quae ex se similitudinem mutuantur.

340. Quod vero haec sit ex aeternitate, manifestat ipse, cum dicit: Si intellectus itemque vera opinio duae res sunt, necesse est haec ipsa per semet esse, intellectu potius quam sensibus assequenda; sin vero, ut quibusdam videtur, vera

matter," because all material things are material because of it. In light of these considerations we will take precisely the same view of the primary form, supposing it to be neither endowed with quality nor deprived of quality. Again, matter was said to be formless, and the primary form too will be said to be unformed and yet not formless. For every formed thing is necessarily a composite of that which participates and that which is participated in, as in the case of a statue, where the bronze participates and the form impressed upon it is participated in, but the form is simple and noncomposite, and in that sense, therefore, is said to be unformed; but neither is it formless, for because of it all other formed things possess an appearance.

339. To state the point, then, in a kind of broad outline: in relation to us, who possess intellect, the primary Form is the first intelligible; in relation to God, it is his perfect intellect; in relation to Matter, it is the limit and measure of corporeal and material realities; in relation to the Form itself, it is an incorporeal substance and the cause of all the things that *obtain their element of likeness* [50d] from it; and in relation to the world, it is the eternal Exemplar of all the things which nature has brought forth. And to state the point concisely: the primary Form or Idea is definable as a substance which lacks corporeality, color, shape, and tangibility but is nevertheless comprehensible by the intellect in combination with reason and is the cause of all the things that *obtain their element of likeness* from it.

340. That it exists from eternity he himself indicates when he says [51d–52a]: *If intellect and true opinion are two things, then it is necessary that they should exist as those very things in themselves, perceptible by intellect rather than the senses; but if*

opinio ab intellectu nihil differt, omnia quae corpore sentimus certa habenda sunt. Sed opinor duo esse dicendum,
propterea quod utraque magna differentia distent; quippe
quorum alterum doctrina nobis insinuet, alterum persuasionis assumptio, et alterum quidem semper cum ratione vera,
porro sine ulla ratione alterum, item alterum eorum nulla
persuasione transducibile, alterum nutans incertumque
semper et derivabile. Quid quod rectae opinionis omnis
homo particeps, intellectus vero dei proprius et paucorum
admodum lectorum virorum? Quadrifariam dividit intellectus opinionisque differentiam, cum docet alterum eorum, id
est intellectum, provenire ex disciplina, alterum <ex> sola
persuasione, deinde cum asserit alterum cum ratione vera,
porro alterum sine rationis examine. Quid cum dicit <ut>
alterum eorum nulli persuasioni <transducibile sit, alterum
nutans incertumque semper et> derivabile, et ad postremum alterum eorum, id est opinio, in quemvis hominem
cadat, intellectus vero dei solius et paucorum admodum sit
examinatorum virorum? Quod si horum tanta est differentia, eorum etiam quae comitantur alterutrum magnam fore
necesse est distantiam, sunt porro haec intellegibile genus
et item opinabile. Unde recte pronuntiat unam fore speciem
per semetipsam, sine ortu sine occasu, neque quid in se reci-
pientem nec progredientem uspiam, invisibilem insensibi-
lemque. Intellectus <est> species, quae idea dicitur: est igitur exemplum.

341. Nunc vero ut in superioribus dubitat ne forte frustra
praesumatur esse intellegibilem speciem hanc, cuius sint

true opinion is no different from intellect, as some think, then all of the things which we perceive by the body must be considered certain. But I suppose we should maintain that they are two, in that both are separated by a wide range of difference; for instruction instills one of them in us while the acceptance of persuasion instills the other, one is always combined with a true account while the other has none, and one of them is not misled by any persuasion while the other is vacillating, always uncertain, and susceptible to diversion. And what about the fact that every human being has a share in right opinion whereas intellect is proper to god and a few very select men? He differentiates between intellect and opinion with a fourfold division, when he explains that one of them, i.e., intellect, proceeds from *instruction* and the other solely from *persuasion,* and then when he maintains that one of them is *combined with a true account while the other has no* test or *account.* And what about his observation that one of them is *not misled by any persuasion while the other is vacillating and always uncertain and susceptible to diversion,* and finally that one of them, i.e., *opinion,* befalls any *human being* at all whereas *intellect* belongs solely to *god and a few well* tested *men?* But if the *difference* between them is so great, then there must also be a *wide range of separation* between the respective objects of each, for in kind they are intelligible and opinable. And so he rightly speaks of one *form* as being through *itself, without birth or death, receiving nothing within itself,* proceeding nowhere, *invisible and imperceptible.* The form pertains to intellect and is called the *idea:* there is therefore an exemplar.

341. And now, as before, he raises the question [51c–d] whether it is perhaps *idle to suppose the existence of* this *intelligible form that has sensible ones as its images, and whether we are*

imagines sensiles eamque nihil aliud esse quam verba. Id tamen ipsum syllogisticis quoque rationibus explanare non
dubitat; quippe cavens ne vel inexaminatum quicquam re-
linquat vel ad prolixum natura sua tractatum minime pertinens ad quaestionem verborum agmen addat, omnem
dubitationem syllogisticis compendiis dirimit ductu et via
pergens ad syllogismum. Etenim inter intellegentem et item
vere opinantem hoc interest: Quod intellegens fidem rerum
rationis habet indagine comprehensam, confirmata porro
ratio fit intellectus, <cuius> scientia est eademque sapientia;
itaque intellegens ut qui recte sciat quod intellegit neque
veri similibus persuasionibus inductus mutat sententiam et
potest ut scius praestare rationem rei comprehensae. At
vero qui vere opinatur, ut qui sola mentis elegantia nitatur
sine ratione ac disciplina, neque rationem cur ita opinetur
praestare potest et falsis aliquando persuasionibus captus
mutat sententiam nutans et ambiguus, ut quem nulla stabilis
ratio sustentet. Itaque Plato syllogisticae rationis formulam
exprimit talem: si intellectus et vera opinio una res est, omnia quae corpore sentimus certa sunt eritque eorum indubi-
tabilis veritas; si autem vera opinio minus habet atque intellectus, non una atque eadem res est sed duae atque diversae,
et erunt alia quae sentiuntur et alia quae intelleguntur; si

to suppose that it is nothing other than words. But he does not question our explaining that very point with the aid also of syllogistic reasoning; and guarding, as he must, against either *leaving* any point *unexamined* or *adding an irrelevant abundance of words to an inquiry which by its very nature tends toward prolixity,* he *sets* syllogistic *limits* on the whole question by proceeding along a carefully controlled path to his syllogism. For the difference between one who employs *intellect* and one who holds a *true opinion* is the following: The one who employs intellect possesses an assurance about things, one grasped by investigation based on reasoning, and once confirmed his reasoning becomes intellection, which includes knowledge and indeed wisdom; and so by "one who employs intellect" is here meant one who has a correct knowledge of that which he has in his intellect, who is not induced by persuasion based on probability to change his opinion, and who on the basis of his knowledge can render a reasoned account of the matter grasped. By "one who holds a true opinion," on the other hand, is meant one who in the absence of reasoning and instruction relies solely on mental polish without being able to render a reasoned account in support of his opinion, and who when ensnared by false persuasion changes his opinion as the occasion demands, wavering vaguely like one who has no stable reasoning to support him. And so Plato expresses an abbreviated figure of syllogistic reasoning, as follows: *if intellect* and *true opinion* are one thing, then *all of the things which we perceive through the body are certain* and of them there will be undoubtable truth; but if true opinion is inferior to intellect, then it is not one and the same thing as it but they are *two* different things, and there will be some things which are ob-

diversa sunt quae sentiuntur et quae intelleguntur, sint intellegibiles species necesse est, quae ideae nuncupantur; at
enim non omnia quae corpore sentimus vera et certa sunt:
sunt igitur ideae.

342. Sed, opinor, explanari dilatarique oportet quae contracta sunt angustiis syllogismi. Intellectum appellat hoc
loco motum animi comprehendentem; huic comparat opinionem cum in plerisque aliis libris tum evidenter in Politia.
Secat enim intellectum quidem in duo haec, scientiam et recordationem, opinionem vero in alia totidem haec, credulitatem et aestimationem, singulaque haec quattuor convenientibus sibi rebus accommodat: scientiam quidem altis et
sapientia sola percipibilibus rebus, cuius modi sunt deus et
intellectus eius, quas ideas vocamus; recordationem vero rebus deliberativis, hoc est his quae praeceptis artificialibus et
theorematibus percipiuntur; credulitatem porro sensilibus,
scilicet quae oculis auribus ceterisque sensibus comprehenduntur; aestimationem fictis commenticiisque et imaginariis rebus, quae iuxta veros simulata vultus corpora tamen
perfecta et viva non sunt. Quae cuncta dicit per semet esse,
intellectu potius quam sensibus assequenda, quia nihil ex his
quattuor sub sensus nostros venit sed tam scientiam quam
opinionem et ceteras mente discernimus.

343. Sin vero, ut quibusdam videtur, inquit, vera opinio ab
intellectu nihil differt. Merito; multae quippe sectae sunt
philosophorum quas certum est initia rerum putasse corpora; cumque intellegibile genus, id est ideas, paene sub

jects of sense perception and others which are the objects of intellect; but if the objects of sense perception and intellect are different, then there necessarily are intelligible forms, called *ideai;* but not *all of the things which we perceive through the body* are true and *certain:* there are therefore Ideas.

342. But, I suppose, points which have been reduced to the narrow confines of a syllogism require a fuller form of explanation. By intellection he in this passage refers to the movement governing comprehension within the mind; he contrasts opinion with it not only in numerous other books but explicitly in the *Republic.* For he divides intellection into two things, knowledge and discursive reasoning, and opinion into two others, belief and conjecture, and connects each of the four with their corresponding realities: knowledge, with the realities on high, those which are perceptible by wisdom alone, as in the case of god and his acts of intellection, which we call the *ideae;* discursive reasoning, with matters that summon reflection, i.e., those perceived in connection with technical precepts and theorems; belief, with sensible things, namely, those grasped by the eyes, ears, and other sense faculties; and conjecture, with things fabricated and contrived in the imagination, simulations of true appearances but not complete living bodies. And he says [51d] that they all *exist in themselves, perceptible by intellect rather than the senses,* because none of the four comes under our sense faculties but we discern knowledge, opinion, and the others with our mind.

343. *But,* he says [51d–52a], *if true opinion is no different from intellect, as some think.* Rightly so, for there are numerous philosophical schools which certainly hold that bodies are the first principles of reality; and after having virtually

oculos constituisset dicens intellegibilem speciem semotam a sensibus in se ipsa locatam, sine ortu sine occasu, quae nec recipit in se quicquam aliunde nec ipsa procedit ad aliud quicquam, invisibilem insensilem soli mentis intuentis intentioni animadversionique perspicuam, consequenter addidit: porro quod ab hoc secundum est, nativum sensile sustentabile, consistens aliquo in loco et inde rursum cum immutatione atque interitu recedens, sensibus et opinione noscendum. Quo loco vult intellegi secundam speciem, quae nascitur cum opifex concipit animo futuri operis liniamenta effigieque intus locata iuxta eandem format quod aggressus est; id ergo consistere aliquo in loco dicit et inde rursum cum immutatione et interitu recedere. Praeclare; demolitionem quippe statuae formae quoque interitus sequatur necesse est et item ad alterius statuae collocationem revocari ac redire. Sensibus autem noscendam dicit hanc speciem, quia impressa forma operi spectantium oculis videtur, opinione vero noscendam, quia mens opificis non de certo exemplari transfert hanc speciem, sed ex propria mente haustam pro viribus.

344. Tertium genus esse dicit loci. Puto eum dignitatis respectu tertium genus dixisse silvam; quippe secunda species, id est nativa, mutuatur substantiam de specie principali, quae sine ortu est et aeterna, censita ideae nomine, silva demum ex nativa specie sumit substantiam. At vero

brought that which is intelligible in kind, i.e., the ideas, into view by describing the intelligible *form* as *removed from the senses and situated within itself, without birth or death, neither receiving anything external within itself nor itself proceeding toward anything else, invisible, imperceptible, and evident only to the intuiting mind's attention and awareness,* he went on to add, *and second to it, that which is born, perceptible, and sustained, which comes to be in some place and recedes once again with its transformation and passing away, and which is knowable by the senses and opinion.* And in this passage he intends a secondary form to be understood, one that comes to be when a craftsman conceives in his mind the outlines of a future work and, based on the image situated within, accordingly gives form to his endeavor; thus he speaks of its *coming to be in some place and receding once again with its transformation and passing away.* This is particularly lucid, for the demolition of a statue necessarily entails the destruction also of its form, and its being summoned back and returning for the forming of another statue is likewise necessary. And he speaks of this form being *knowable by the senses* because the form stamped upon a work is visible to the eyes of those who gaze upon it, and as *knowable by opinion* because the craftsman's mind transfers the form, not from a fixed exemplar, but in virtue of the its being drawn from one's own mind to the best of one's ability.

344. He says that the *third kind is that of Place* [52a]. My understanding is that by *third kind* he meant matter in virtue of its rank; for the secondary form, i.e., that which is *born,* owes its being to the primary form, which is unborn and eternal, having been assigned the name *idea,* while matter, finally, draws its being from the form that is born. But by *Place* he

locum vocat eam velut regionem quandam suscipientem specierum incorporearum intellegibiliumque simulacra, semper eandem, vel quia sine generatione est et interitu vel quia necesse est eam locum stationemque esse et velut receptaculum corporearum specierum, quae sunt membra mundi, ut videtur prope omnibus, indissolubilis et aeterni; ipsa ergo immortalis est, sed his quae pariuntur in eiusdem gremio datur substantia.

345. Deinde progrediens mira quadam animi conceptione dicit ipsam sine tangentis sensu tangi; quippe omne quod tangitur sensile est et sensibus subiacet, quidquid ergo tangitur sensu sentiatur necesse est. Quo modo igitur possumus dicere tangi aliquid quod ex natura sua minime contiguum est? Vide altitudinem pectoris et ut brevi elocutione suspicionem mentis suae de silva revelaverit: Omne certe quod alicuius simile est ex simili suo recognoscitur; ut igitur certae rei definitaeque certa et definita est comprehensio, sic incertae minimeque definitae incerta et indefinita suspicio sit necesse est. Quia igitur sensus certarum definitarumque rerum sensus est, quippe habentium figuras et qualitates, necesse est etiam comprehensionem earum certam definitamque esse; sed enim silva indefinita res est, utpote informis et figura carens iuxta naturam suam; minime igitur cum

indicates a kind of region, as it were, that receives the images of the incorporeal and intelligible forms and is forever the same, and this in two senses: that it is immune to coming-to-be and *passing away,* and that it is necessary that it should serve as the *Place,* the station or Receptacle, as it were, of the corporeal forms that serve as parts of a world which, as virtually everyone holds, is *indissoluble* [41a] and thus eternal; in itself, then, matter is immortal, but within its womb being is conferred upon the things that are begotten.

345. Then moving on he says, with a certain remarkable conception in mind, that it is *itself tangible independently of any sensory experience on the part of the one who comes into contact with it* [52b]. For everything that is tangible is sensible and comes under the senses, and so whatever is tangible is necessarily perceived in *sensory experience.* How, then, can we claim that something which by its very nature is intangible is tangible? Notice his depth of thought, and the conciseness of expression with which he reveals his mental suspicion concerning matter: without any doubt, everything which resembles something proves knowable in turn because of an element of resemblance with *it;* thus as the comprehension of a certain and definite thing is certain and definite, so the suspicion of an uncertain and indefinite one is necessarily uncertain and indefinite. Given, then, that sense perception is the perception of things that are certain and definite insofar as they possess shapes and qualities, it is necessary that the comprehension of them should be certain and definite as well; but matter is an indefinite thing, being formless and by nature lacking shape; therefore no mental representation of it occurs in conjunction with sense perception; it is

667

sensu eius fit imaginatio; sine sensu igitur. Fit tamen evanida quaedam eius attrectatio sine contagio nec ipsius mage quam eorum quae intra ipsam sunt corporum; quae cum sentiuntur, suspicio nascitur ipsam sentiri, propterea quod ex his speciebus quas recipit formari, cum sit informis, videtur. Itaque sensus quidem specierum in silva constitutarum clarus est ipsius autem silvae quae speciebus subiacet obscurus et consensus potius quam sensus est. Ergo quia silvestria quidem sentiuntur silva vero minime sentitur natura propria sed propter silvestria cum isdem sentiri putatur, fit huiusmodi sensus incertus, praeclareque dictum silvam sine sensu tangentium tangi, quia puro sensu minime sentiatur. Ut si quis dicat tenebras quoque sine sensu videri. Non enim perinde sentit visus hominis tenebras intuentis ut cum solet intueri res coloratas dilucidasque sed contraria passione et amissione atque indigentia eorum omnium quae oculi vident (sunt enim tenebrae decolores et sine claritudinis illustratione), nec potest visus comprehendere aliquam qualitatem tenebrarum sed suspicari quod non sit potius quam quid rerum sit, nihilque videns id ipsum sibi videtur videre quod non videt et videre se aliquid putat cum nihil videat (quis enim visus in tenebris?); sed quia natura oculi haec est ut colores discernat, conans, opinor, discernere naturam decolorem tenebras sentire se suspicatur. Sic igitur etiam

therefore *independent of any sensory experience*. Nevertheless, a certain faint form of contact with it occurs in the absence of touching, less in the case of it than in that of the bodies within it; and when the latter are perceived a suspicion of its being perceived arises owing to the fact that despite its formlessness it appears to be given form because of the forms it receives. And so although perception of the forms found in matter is clear, perception of the matter which actually acts as a substrate to the forms is obscure, being an incidental form of perception rather than perception. Since, then, material things are perceived whereas matter is not perceived in its proper nature but because of the material things is thought to be perceived along with them, there occurs an uncertain perception of the sort described, and his claim that matter is *tangible independently of any sensory experience on the part of those who come into contact with it* is particularly lucid, since matter is imperceptible by pure sense perception. It is as if one were to say that darkness too is visible *independently of any sensory experience*. For the vision of a person who gazes upon darkness is not comparable to his normal experience of gazing upon distinctly colored objects, but owing to a contrary affection, an absence or want of the things which the eyes see (for darkness is colorless and lacks the illumination of light), his vision is in a position, not to comprehend any quality in the darkness, but to suspect the fact of nonbeing but not the existence of any particular reality, and despite seeing nothing he thinks he is actually seeing what he does not see and supposes he is seeing something although he sees nothing (for what vision is there in darkness?); but since the eye is naturally conditioned to discern colors, in his attempt to discern a colorless nature he suspects, I suppose, that he is *seeing* darkness. In some such

silva contigua quidem est quia contingi putatur cum ea quae
principaliter continguntur sub sensus veniant, sed contactus
eius provenit ex accidenti; verum hoc ipsum sine sensu, quia
ipsa per se neque tactu sentitur neque ceteris sensibus.

346. Nec contentus hac tanta diligentia superaddidit notha et adulterina quadam ratiocinatione silvam esse dicens
opinabilem. Filios omnes naturales esse nullus ignorat sed
tam Graeci quam nos legitimos et item praesumptos nominibus discernimus. Legitimos Graeci gnisios vocant, <prae-
sumptos nothous.>

347. [. . .] ut <consonantes> sine vocalibus quidem per se
mutae sunt, mixtae vero vocalibus conferunt aliquid imper-
tiuntque genuinum sonum. Oratio tamen de silva infinitam
eam et incertam esse asserens certa est. Rite igitur notha et
spuria ratiocinatione atque opinione potius quam intellectu
certo comprehendi eam censet Plato, utpote cuius natura
rectae rationis et non recti confusique intellectus praesumatur consortio. Divisa ergo a se sunt tria illa separatimque
examinata: et est idea quidem intellegibilis species, utpote
quae puro intellectu comprehendatur; species vero nativa
opinione percipibilis proptereaque opinabilis; silva porro
neque intellegibile quid neque opinabile, quia neque intellectu neque sensu comprehendatur, verum est suspicabilis,
suspicio autem spuria quaedam ratio est atque adulterina.

way, then, although matter too is tangible in that it is believed to be touched even though the objects of touch in the primary sense come under the senses, in fact our contact with it occurs incidentally; but the experience itself is *independent of any sensory experience* because matter in itself and on its own is imperceptible by either touch or the other senses.

346. Not content with this extraordinary level of precision, he made a further addition, pointing out [52b] that matter is *opinable by a certain* bastard or *illegitimate form of reasoning*. No one is unaware of the fact that all children are products of nature, but like the Greeks we make a nominal distinction between the legitimate and the suppositious. The Greeks refer to the legitimate as *gnêsioi* and to the suppositious as *nothoi*.

347. [. . .] as consonants without vowels are mute in themselves but when combined with vowels confer something and impart a genuine sound. When it comes to matter, however, the statement which asserts that it is infinite and uncertain is certain. Thus Plato is right in thinking that it is comprehensible by a bastard or spurious *form of reasoning* [52b] and by opinion rather than by certain intellection, its nature being suppositionally grasped by the mating of correct reasoning and incorrect or confused intellection. The following three things, then, are distinct and examined separately from one another: the idea is an intelligible form, being comprehensible by pure intellection; the form subject to birth is perceptible by opinion and therefore opinable; matter, being comprehensible by neither intellection nor sense perception, is neither an intelligible nor an opinable but is accessible to suspicion, and suspicion is a *certain* spurious or *illegitimate form of reasoning*.

348. Pergit ulterius insistitque probationi coeptae perfectius ita dicens: Denique cum id animo intuemur, patimur quod somniantes; putamus enim necesse esse ut omne quod est in aliquo sit loco positum regionemque obtineat ullam. Incertam et caligantem animi nostri intentionem, cum silvae naturam consideramus, vanis somniis comparat et opinioni quae ex sensibus nascitur. Etenim cum corpus aliquod videmus aut tangimus, necesse est id a nobis sentiri cum locis suis et regionibus; neque enim sine loco nec vero sine sede sentiri corpus ullum potest. Dicit ergo nos hac opinionis percelebratae consuetudine ita esse imbutos ut, cum res intellegibiles contemplamur animo, putemus eas consistere aliquo in loco ullamve regionem obtinere perinde ut mundi corpus, quod situm est loco quem complet mundana moles habens etiam regionem quae perceptis corporum formis exornata est, videlicet silvam. Cuius partes ex quibus constat quia divisas locis ac regionibus consideramus, putamus omnia quae sunt eodem modo consistere in locis ac regionibus certis. Dehinc denique si quis dicat fore substantiam sine sede ac loco quae neque in terra neque in caelo sit, portento similia dici putamus et res vana mentis opinione conceptas. Iam dudum quippe et ab ineunte aetate praeiudicavimus omne quod sit corpus esse nec quicquam fore quod substantia sensili careat, cognitoribus et velut assertoribus corporum credentes sensibus.

348. He moves ahead and presses for a fuller development of the proof already underway, speaking as follows [52b]: *Finally, when gazing upon it in our mind we experience what those who are dreaming do, for we suppose that everything that exists must necessarily be situated in some place and occupy some region.* He compares the uncertain and murky attention of our mind when reflecting on the nature of matter to empty dreams and the opining that arises out of our sensory experiences. For when we see or touch some body it is *necessary* for it be perceived by us in combination with its *places* and *regions;* for it is impossible for any body to be perceived independently of either its place or its location. Thus he says that we are so imbued with the widespread habit of operating according to opinion that while contemplating intelligible realities *in our mind* we *suppose* that they exist *in some place* or *occupy some region* in the same way that the world body does, it being situated in the place which the world mass fills and the latter in turn occupying a region, namely, matter, which is adorned by the forms of bodies once it receives them. And in reflecting on the distribution of its constitutive parts across places and regions we suppose that all of the things that exist similarly exist in fixed places and regions. And so if someone should *finally* point out the existence of a being which is independent of location and place, one which is *neither on earth nor in heaven,* we suppose that his words portend something fantastic, realities conceived by the mind's empty opining. For in trusting from the earliest phase of life in our senses as the guarantors and claimants, so to speak, for bodies, we have long since formed the presupposition that everything that exists is body and that there is nothing that lacks sensible being.

349. Et concludit: Ob quam depravationem itemque alias consanguineas ne in reputatione quidem et consideratione vere existentis vereque pervigilis naturae mente consistimus propter huiusmodi somnia. Exsomnem pervigilemque naturam nuncupat intellegibile atque incorporeum genus, quod semper idem est principaliterque subsistit, sine ortu sine occasu, minime mutabile, nullam habens cum sensilibus societatem, pura mente percipibile, deum videlicet et cogitationes eius, intellegibiles atque incorporeas species. Has porro esse quidam negant, quod his usu accidit ex alto et profundo sopore. Denique si quis eos ad contemplationem veram minimeque soporatam excitet aeternarum et immortalium rerum, indignantur ac moleste ferunt, similiter ut in Politia illi dediticii perpetuis abditi tenebris speluncae densis umbris opacae. At vero qui se a profunda imperitia vindicant laboriosius licet, ex tenebris ad lumen emergunt et ad scientiae veritatisque claritudinem aspirant nec moleste ferunt excellentes in studiis humanitatis viros dividere ac separare sensilem intellegibilemque naturam, docere etiam ac demonstrare, quod sint rerum initia species archetypae sive quod exempla genuina sint substantia praedita; neque enim ad cuiusquam alterius rei similitudinem facta atque instituta sunt, quia nihil est originibus antiquius. Imagines vero exemplorum, quia iuxta exempla sunt factae, aliunde oportet substantiam mutuentur, ut forma Socratis naturalis existens

349. And he concludes [52a–c]: *And because of this and other related distorting effects arising from such dream states we become mentally unsteady in our reflection on and consideration of the truly existent and truly waking nature.* By the unsleeping or *waking nature* he means that which is intelligible and incorporeal in kind, which is forever the same and subsists in the primary sense, *without birth or death,* is immutable and has no association with sensibles, and is perceptible by pure mind, namely, he means god and his thoughts, the intelligible and incorporeal forms. Now, some claim that the intelligible forms do not exist, and such an attitude usually results from a deep and profound state of slumber. If someone were finally to arouse them to a true and nonslumbering contemplation of eternal and immortal realities, then they become indignant and resentful, as happens in the case of the captives in the *Republic* who are buried away in the perpetual darkness of an opaque, densely shadowed cave. Those, however, who despite the difficulty free themselves from their profound ignorance emerge out of the darkness into the light and aspire to the clarity of knowledge and truth, and they do not resent the fact that men who excel in the civilized pursuits divide and distinguish between sensible and intelligible nature, that they also teach and demonstrate that the archetypal forms are the first principles of reality or that the exemplars are endowed with genuine being, not having been made or established in the likeness of any other reality because nothing is prior to the first principles. But because the images of the exemplars are made after the pattern of the exemplars, it is necessary for them to borrow their being from another source, as the naturally existent figure belonging to Socrates illustrates: it serves as a kind of

comparatione imaginis velut archetypa species est; imago autem ex arte facta et iuxta archetypam speciem effigiata nisi habeat silvam—si quidem erit pictura, colores, si autem fictura, limum vel aes ceteramque huius modi supellectilem—carebit certa perfectione. Igitur, quia sensiles quoque species imagines sunt specierum intellegibilium, sicut saepe iam diximus, et ab intellegibilibus substantiam trahunt, nec substantiam modo sed etiam similitudinem, opus est his, opinor, silva in qua fiant et substantiam sortiantur.

350. Deinde interponit auctoritatem suam dicens: Haec est meae quidem sententiae mens: esse et ante mundi quoque sensilis exornationem fuisse tria haec, existens locum generationem. Suam profitetur sententiam. Merito; nullus quippe veterum etiam tunc tria haec animadverterat, quippe quorum plerique sola opinati sunt esse sensilia, ut Empedocles, alii sola intellegibilia, ut Parmenides; silvam nullus omnino mente conceperat, ut ipse dixit in superioribus. Vult autem intellegi existens quidem idean sive intellegibilem speciem, locum autem silvam, generationem vero quantitates et qualitates et ceteras sensiles conformationes: et existens quidem quia suapte natura sit idemque aliis quoque rebus causa existendi sit; locum vero propterea quod silva receptaculum est corporum et qualitatum ceterorumque sensilium; generationem porro quia haec non diu perseverant in uno statu sed alia ex aliis invicem subrogantur.

archetypal form in relation to its image; but unless the image, made by an artisan's skill and shaped after the pattern of the archetypal form, possesses matter—in the case of a painting, pigments, and in that of a statue, clay, bronze, and other related materials—, it will lack its appointed state of completion. Since, therefore, sensible forms too are images of intelligible forms, as we have repeatedly pointed out earlier, and draw their being from intelligible forms, and not only their being but their element of likeness as well, they require, I suppose, matter in which they may come to be and acquire being.

350. He then interjects his own note of authority, saying [52d]: *The thinking behind my view is then the following: That there are and were even before the adornment of the sensible world these three things, Being, Place, and Becoming.* The *view* he professes is his own. Rightly so, for even by his day none of the ancients had drawn attention to *these three things;* for most of them, Empedocles included, were of the opinion that only sensibles exist, others, including Parmenides, that only intelligibles do; absolutely no one had formed a mental conception of matter, as he himself has pointed out in earlier passages. By *Being* he wants the idea or intelligible form to be understood, by *Place,* matter, and by *Becoming,* quantities, qualities, and other sensible configurations: *Being,* because the intelligible form of its own nature is and is at the same time the cause of being also in other things; *Place,* because matter is the Receptacle of bodies, qualities, and other sensible phenomena; and *Becoming,* because these things do not remain in a fixed state for any period of time but are replaced in succession, one of them by another.

351. Igitur generationis, inquit, nutriculam humectatam modo modo ignitam terraeque item et aeris formas suscipientem. Generationis nutriculam silvam significat, quia quidquid nascitur recursum habet ad materias principales, materiae demum principales huic in acceptum feruntur; est enim earum omnium silva nutrix easdemque gestat. Humectatam modo modo ignitam. Recte; non enim ipsa silva vel humectatur vel ignitur immutationemve patitur ullam; omnino enim est incommutabilis nec declinat a natura sua sed, ut quae recipiat qualitates et quantitates humoris et item caloris, humectari atque igniri putatur. Explanat evidentius cum adiungit: terraeque et item aeris formas suscipientem ceterasque pedissequas passiones perpetientem. Rationabiliter; non enim tantum solent hae qualitates humectari et calefieri sed etiam siccari et frigescere quaeque his similia proveniunt. Ceteras pedissequas passiones perpetientem, ideo quia formatur et figuratur conventu formatorum corporum, nam ipsa ex natura sua impetibilis est nec ullam fert perpessionem.

352. Deinde ait: Quod tamen privatim neque similibus viribus neque exaequatis potentiis instruatur, nihil esse eius aequale. Nunc iam veluti separato opifice deo solam per semet ipsam silvam intuetur duplici consideratione, una nondum susceptis qualitatibus, altera post qualitates. Et ante consortium quidem qualitatum neque stabat, opinor, neque movebatur, erat tamen quaedam in ea naturalis opportunitas ad motus stationisque perceptionem; post qualitatum

351. *And,* he says [52d–e], *that the nurse of Becoming is therefore moistened one moment and made fiery another, and in her taking up the shapes of earth and air.* Nurse of Becoming indicates matter, in that everything that comes to be reverts to the primary material elements and the primary material elements are ultimately credited to matter; for it is the nurse of them all and carries them in her womb. *Is moistened one moment and made fiery another.* Rightly so, for matter itself becomes neither moist nor fiery and undergoes no change; for it is completely unchanging and does not depart from its proper nature but is thought to become moist or fiery because of its receiving the qualities, or quantities, of moisture or heat. He explains the point more explicitly by adding: *and in taking up the shapes of earth and air and undergoing all of their attendant modifications.* With good reason, for not only do the qualities associated with becoming moist or hot regularly arise but those associated with becoming dry, cold, and the like do as well. *Undergoing all of their attendant modifications,* in the sense that it is formed and shaped through the convergence of bodies that have been formed, for in virtue of its proper nature it is itself impassible and intolerant of any modification.

352. He then says [52e]: *But that since on her own she is equipped with powers which are neither alike nor evenly balanced no part of her is in a state of equilibrium.* With the craftsman god momentarily set aside, as it were, he directs his gaze toward matter, alone and in itself, with two considerations in mind: one, its state when qualities have not yet been received; the other, its state after the advent of qualities. Before sharing in qualities it was, I suppose, neither stationary nor in motion, but there was within it a certain natural capacity for the reception of motion and rest; but after

porro consortium exornata et perfectum corpus a deo facta motus stationisque sumpsit officia, quibus diversis temporibus uteretur. Ergo volens motus eius praestare causam dicit silvae primitus corporibus iniectis et ex praeponderatione eorum hinc illinc vergentium substitisse motum, sed incertum adhuc et fluctui similem, cum hinc illinc oppressa modo modo sublevata silvae imbecillitas reciprocaret et iniquus turbulentusque motus per universam eius fluctuaret capacitatem. Ex quo factum ut hunc inordinatum motum intimam silvae propriamque et ex natura eius agitationem plerique esse censerent, qui alienus pulsus est, proptereaque animatam eam vitaeque compotem arbitrarentur. Motus ergo qui in ea fiebat alienus erat; confusio porro motus et inordinatio secundum naturam silvae proveniebat praebentis instabilem tremulamque sedem, ideo: quod privatim neque similibus viribus neque exaequatis potentiis instructa nec quicquam in ea esset aequale quod iactationem praeponderationemque corporum coerceret. Sed ut in stagnis, cum immobilis est aquae superficies, incidente aliqua graviore mole primo nascitur initium motus deinde agitatione facta totius elementi non solum agmen aquae movetur sed illud ipsum quod incidit causamque motus praebuit vicissim movet: sic silva quoque ex initio corporum sumpto motu non solum ipsa omnifariam movetur verum ipsa corpora quae initium motus sunt invicem pellit.

sharing in qualities and once adorned and made a complete body by god it assumed the functions of motion and rest in order to deploy them at different times. With the intention, then, of bringing the cause of its movement into view he says that movement first arose when bodies were cast into matter, i.e., because of the *inclination* caused by their *leaning* one way and another, but that the movement was still indeterminate and similar to that of waves, since in its uncontrolled state the matter alternated between *reciprocal* states of sinking one moment and rising another, now one way, now another, the uneven and turbulent movement causing fluctuations throughout the whole of its capacity. And so it happened that most came to think of this disorderly movement, this foreign *jolting,* as an *agitation* deep within matter and proper to it in virtue of its nature, and consequently judged it to be animate and in possession of life. Now, the movement that arose within it was foreign to it; but the confused lack of order in the movement arose in accordance with the nature of matter, which provided an unstable and tremulous foundation, as he says: *since on its own it was equipped with powers which were neither alike nor evenly balanced* nothing in it was in a *state of equilibrium* to counteract the jostling *inclination* caused by the bodies. But as when the surface of the water in a pond sits motionless but with the impact of a body of some weight there first arises an initial movement; and then once the element as a whole is in a state of agitation the "mass of water" not only is moved but it in turn moves the very thing which by its impact caused the movement: so too matter not only is moved in every imaginable way because of the movement it initially receives from bodies but it *in return* propels the very bodies initiating the movement.

353. Talem porro motum eius significat non ad aliquem usum rerum nascentium fieri sed ad solam conversionem commutationemque corporum, siquidem dicit: Ex quo fluctu turbatas materias in diversa raptari discernique a se, hoc est separari. Quo pacto clare demonstrat non unam esse in silva potentiam opportunitatemque formarum recipiendarum, sed multiformem; nam si una eius esset potentia, unum quiddam semper esset. At nunc, cum in omnes qualitates figurasque vertatur atque omnia fiat, potentias eius necesse est opportunitatesque variae commutationis praenosci mentibus. Deinde manifesto exemplo quod dicit explanat cum separat a se quattuor materias, id est ignem terramque et ceteras, separationis causam docens in fluctu silvae atque agitatione consistere, perinde ut in frumenti purgatione. Novimus enim esse quaedam iam dudum parata, ut solent poetae dicere, arma Cerealia, quibus ea quae messa erunt secernuntur, grana quidem seorsum motu et agitatione, paleae vero aliorsum ex iactatione; et levia quidem volitare gravia vero residere. Sic, inquit, quattuor quoque illa prima corpora velut in Euripo fluctuante iactantur et ad postremum generatim secernuntur, Euripum quidem silvam cognominans secretionem vero sedem elementi cuiusque divina providentia separatam. Quae ordinatio est scilicet ne ex diversorum corporum cohaerentia confusio et inordinatio, quae ante constitutionem mundi fuerat,

353. He means, moreover, that its movement, being such as it is, occurs, not to support things in their coming to be, but only for the process of transformation and change between bodies, for he says [52d–53a]: *And that once thrown into confusion because of this fluctuation the material elements were tossed in different directions and sorted,* i.e., separated, *from one another.* And in this way he shows clearly that the power or capacity within matter for receiving forms is not uniform but multiform; for if its power were uniform, then matter would always be one determinate thing, but given its turning into all qualities and shapes, its becoming all things, it is in fact necessary that its powers or capacities for various types of change be conceptually acknowledged in advance. Then appealing to a concrete illustration he explains his point when he separates the four material elements, i.e., fire, earth, and so on, out from one another, indicating that the cause of the separation arises from the fluctuation and agitation within matter, *as in the cleansing of grain.* For we know that certain "arms of Ceres," as the poets like to say, have been in use for generations to separate that which is going to be harvested, the grain being *concentrated* in one place by a process of moving and shaking and the chaff going in all other directions because of the tossing: that the *light* things fly up while the *heavy* ones settle down. *So,* he says, the *four* primary bodies too are *jostled about as though in the fluctuating Euripus* and eventually *sorted* according to kind, by *Euripus* indicating matter, and by *sorting,* the separate region assigned to each and every element by divine providence. And the ordering is *of course* to prevent the *disordered confusion* which obtained *before* the establishment *of the world* from continuing because of the cohesion of bodies

perseveraret. Hanc ait fortunam mundi fuisse, priusquam exornata silva splendor et pulchritudo proveniret universitati.

354. Sed ubi cuncta, inquit, redigi ad modum placuit. Dei voluntatem significat providam, <cui> complacuisse dicit ignem primo terramque et aera atque aquam continuasse, non talia ut nunc sunt sed eorum exigua vestigia. Quippe vestigium ignis nondum ignis est nec vero ceterorum corporum vestigia ipsa corpora sunt; vestigium quippe potentiam rei, non rem significat multoque etiam minus corpus significatur vestigii nomine; ergo silva etiam vestigium corporis fuit ante mundi exornationem. In eo, inquit, squalore ac deformitate quae apparet in his quibus divina deest prospicientia. Iure meritoque; quid enim divina opera carens pulchrum aut venustate erit praeditum? Apparatus ille igitur erat etiam tunc, elementis confusis incondite, nondum mundus nec claritudo quae ex opportunitate providae ordinationis accessit. Erat igitur subiecta silva cum naturali opportunitate suscipiendae pulchritudinis ac venustatis, erant etiam quattuor corporum potentiae seu vestigia confusa adhuc minimeque ordinata. Haec ergo cum voluit deus disponens et ordinans immortale hoc sensilis mundi animal figuris et qualitatibus convenustavit certis et in aeternum duraturis rationibus. Omnia porro quae fiunt optima divina mente ac voluntate fieri praesumere nos iubet; qua praesumptione nihil esse verius asseverat.

which were different in kind. And he says that this *was* the state *of the world before* splendor and beauty came to the universe by the *adornment* of matter.

354. *But,* he says [53a–b], *after taking the decision to bring everything back within measure.* He means the provident will of god, and says that god *decided first to give binding unity to fire, earth, air, and water, not in their present states but* as faint *traces* thereof. For a trace of fire is not yet fire, nor are traces of other bodies the actual bodies; for *trace* signifies the potency in a thing, not the thing, and a body is even farther removed from being signified by the word *trace;* thus *before the adornment of the world* matter too was a *trace* of body. *Despite the squalor,* he says, *and deformity manifested by things that lack divine oversight.* Rightly so indeed, for in the absence of the divine activity what will be beautiful or endowed with grace? Thus the apparatus existed even at the point when the elements were in a crude state of confusion, but it did not yet exist as the world, nor was there the clarity that came to it on the occasion of the providential ordering. Thus there was matter, along with its natural capacity for receiving beauty and grace, to act as a substrate; and there were the potencies of the four bodies, their confused and still disordered traces. And so in disposing and ordering them at his will god graced this immortal living being that is the sensible world with determinate shapes and qualities and with formative patterns destined to endure unto eternity. Moreover, Plato bids us to hold that all that comes to be comes to be in the *best possible way* because of the divine mind and will, and asserts that there is nothing truer than such a conviction.

355. Nunc iam ordinationem genituramque eorum singillatim demonstrari, inquit, convenit novo quidem et inusitato genere demonstrationis verum vobis qui omnes eruditionis ingenuae vias peragraveritis neque incognito et ex levi
admonitione perspicuo. Demonstraturus ratione substantias quattuor principalium corporum quae censentur elementa ordinationem quidem vocat habitum eorum iuxta se
communicationemque et quasi quandam societatem quae
nascitur iuxta analogiam, quae talis est: "ut hoc iuxta illud
sic illud iuxta aliud"; genituram vero appellat ipsam formam
et effigiem. De quibus secundum geometricam rationem
disputaturus, quae ratio minime nutat semperque certas et
inexpugnabiles affert probationes, novam quidem aliis et in-
cognitam dicit esse hanc eandem rationem ipsis tamen qui
omnes ingenuae eruditionis vias peragraverint neque igno-
tam et ex levi admonitione perspicuam. Etenim qui aderant
omnes erant instructi praecipuis doctrinis, quas ingenuas
disciplinas appellavit propterea quod a pueris aetas illa veluti principiis altioris doctrinae et tamquam gradibus im-
buebatur geometrica musica arithmetica astronomia. De
quibus Cebes pronuntiavit, si quidem philosophiae causa
discantur ut per eas tamquam gradibus ad summum culmen
philosophiae perveniatur, operae pretium fore; si sine philosophia, plenae tamen dignitatis esse fundamenta, imper-

355. *It is appropriate now,* he says [53b–c], *to demonstrate their arrangement and generation individually, and to do so with a mode of demonstration which although new and unfamiliar is not unknown to you, who have traveled all the paths of liberal erudition, and will become clear with gentle reminding.* In preparing for a rational demonstration of the substances of the four primary bodies considered elements he refers, with the word *arrangement,* to their disposition relative to one another, their communication or form of association, as it were, which arises according to a proportion of the following sort: "as this is to that, so that is to something else"; and with *generation* he appeals to their actual shape or appearance. And in preparing to explain them according to geometrical reasoning, the reasoning which does not waver but always furnishes certain and unassailable proofs, he speaks of this same reasoning as being *new* and *unknown* to others but as *not unknown* or as becoming *clear, with gentle reminding,* to those who have *traveled all the paths of liberal erudition.* For all of those who were present had been instructed in the specialized doctrines, which he called the *liberal* disciplines because in those days people were steeped from childhood in geometry, music, arithmetic, and astronomy, the first principles or steps, as it were, of higher doctrine. And concerning these doctrines Cebes stated that if they are learned with philosophy as the goal, so that by passing through them one arrives by steps, as it were, at the highest peak of philosophy, then it will repay the effort; but that if they are learned without regard for philosophy, then they nevertheless serve as the foundation for a fully formed sense of dignity, although the *erudition* is incomplete. Thus Plato is *re-*

fectae licet eruditionis. Hos igitur tamquam exercitatos in geometrica viros admonet, quod sciebant huius modi quaestiones non nisi geometricis probationibus explicari; simul habet exhortationem sermo ad effectionem institutionis ingenuae.

minding these men who had been trained, as it were, in geometry, for they would have known that such questions are explained only by geometrical proofs; at the same time, his words contain an exhortation to the fulfillment of a *liberal* education.

DIAGRAMS

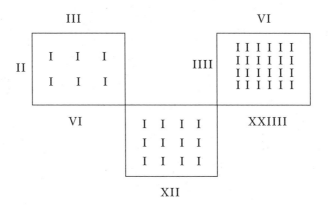

Diagram 1 (chapter 9)

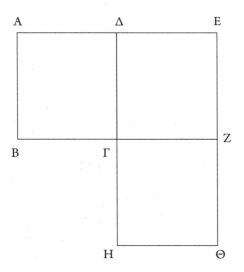

Diagram 2 (chapter 11)

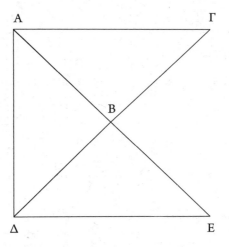

Diagram 3 (chapter 12)

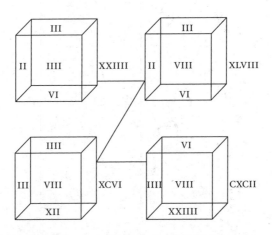

Diagram 4 (chapter 14). Descriptio Solidarum Figurarum
cum Numeris Suis iuxta Arithmeticam Disciplinam

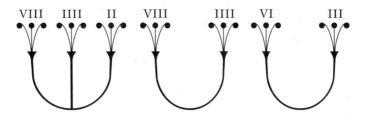

| VIII | IIII | II | VIII | IIII | VI | III |

Diagram 5 (chapter 16).
Continuum Competens
in Tribus Finibus

Distans Competens in Quattuor Finibus

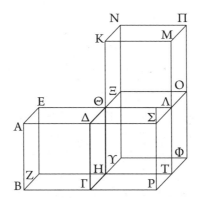

Diagram 6 (chapter 18). Descriptio Parallelepipe-
dorum Duum Distantium, Quae Parallelepipeda
Continuantur ad Unam Soliditatem Insertis Aliis
Duobus iuxta Rationem Continui Competentis,
Quod a Graecis Appellatur Analogia Syneches

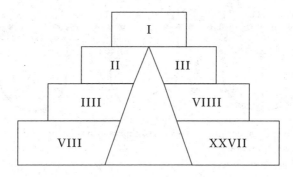

Diagram 7 (chapters 33, 47, 95)

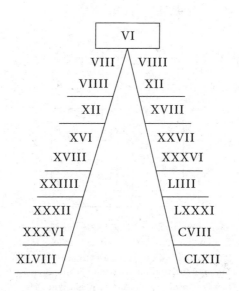

Diagram 8 (chapters 41, 47)

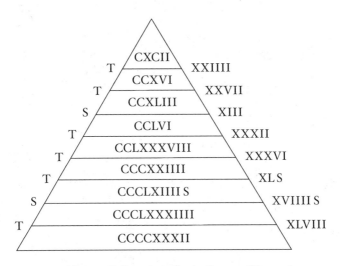

Diagram 9 (chapter 48). Descriptio Tertia, Quae est Harmonica, iuxta Epogdoam Rationem Modulans Utramque Symphoniam Diatessaron et Diapente

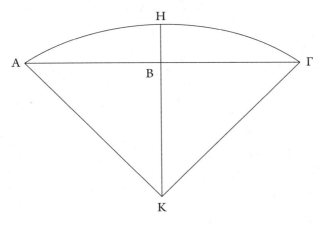

Diagram 10 (chapter 62)

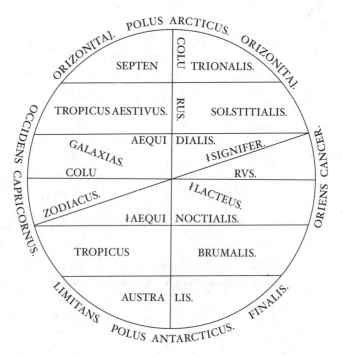

Diagram 11 (chapter 67). **Descriptio Aplanos**

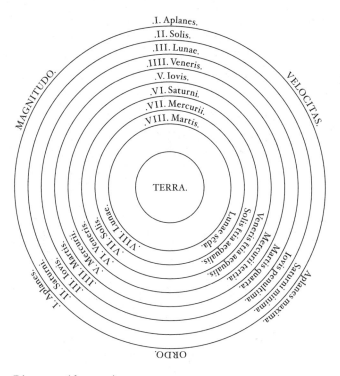

MAGNITUDO.

VELOCITAS.

.I. Aplanes.
.II. Solis.
.III. Lunae.
.IIII. Veneris.
.V. Iovis.
.VI. Saturni.
.VII. Mercurii.
.VIII. Martis.

TERRA.

VIII. Lunae.
VII. Solis.
VI. Veneris.
V. Martis.
IIII. Iovis.
III. Saturni.
II. Aplanes.
.I. Aplanes.

Lunae scda.
Solis tria aequalis.
Veneris tria aequalis.
Mercurii tertia.
Martis quarta.
Iovis penultima.
Saturni penultima.
Aplanes maxima.

ORDO.

Diagram 12 (chapter 73)

Diagram 13 (chapter 78)

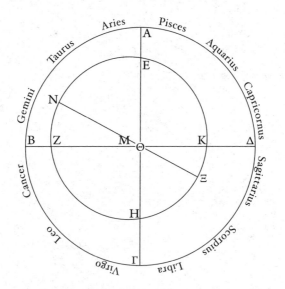

Diagram 14 (chapter 79)

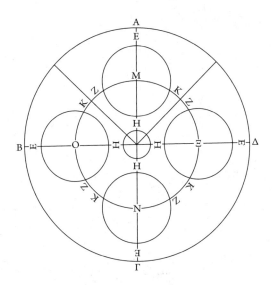

Diagram 15 (chapter 81)

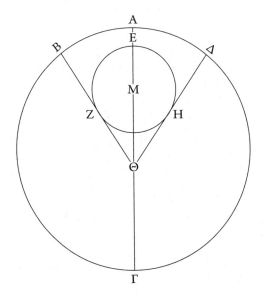

Diagram 16 (chapter 85)

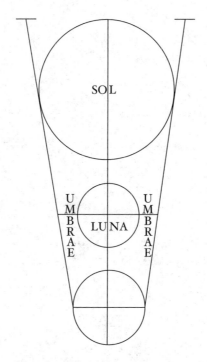

Diagram 17 (chapter 87)

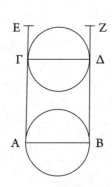

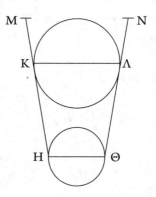

Diagram 18 (chapter 89)

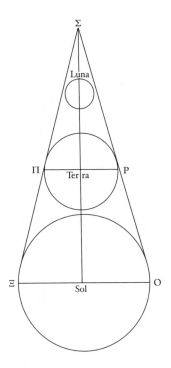

Diagram 19 (chapter 90)

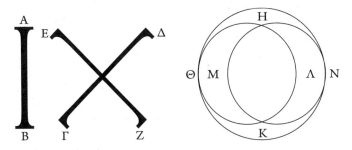

Diagram 20 (chapter 92)

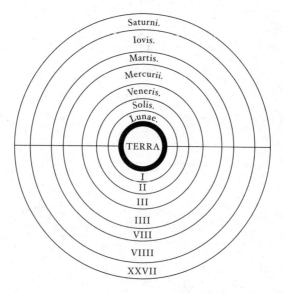

Diagram 21 (chapter 96)

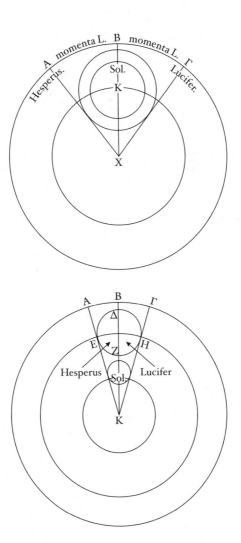

Diagram 22 (chapter III)

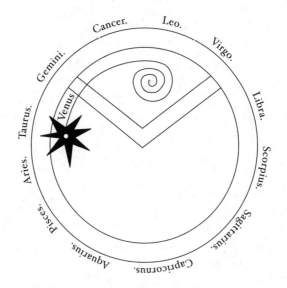

Diagram 23 (chapter 116)

Abbreviations

Aëtius = H. Diels, *Doxographi Graeci* (Berlin, 1879), 273–444

BLL = J. N. Adams, *Bilingualism and the Latin Language* (Cambridge, 2003)

CIL = *Corpus Inscriptionum Latinarum* (Berlin, 1863–)

DK = H. Diels and W. Kranz, *Die Fragmente der Vorsokratiker* (Berlin, 1951–52⁶)

DL = Diogenes Laertius, *The Lives and Doctrines of the Eminent Philosophers*

LD = C. T. Lewis and C. Short, *A Latin Dictionary* (Oxford, 1879)

LS = A. A. Long and D. Sedley, *The Hellenistic Philosophers, I–II* (Cambridge, 1987)

LSS = J. B. Hofmann and A. Szantyr, *Lateinische Syntax und Stilistik* (Munich, 1972²)

NLS = E. C. Woodcock, *A New Latin Syntax* (London, 1959)

OLD = P. G. W. Glare, *Oxford Latin Dictionary* (Oxford, 1982)

PLRE = A. H. M. Jones, J. R. Martindale, and J. Morris, *The Prosopography of the Later Roman Empire I, A.D. 260–395* (Cambridge, 1971); J. R. Martindale, *The Prosopography of the Later Roman Empire II, A.D. 395–527* (Cambridge, 1980)

PW = H. W. Parke and D. E. W. Wormell, *The Delphic Oracle, I–II* (Oxford, 1956)

RE = G. Wissowa et al., eds., *Paulys Real-Encyclopädie der classischen Altertumswissenschaft* (Stuttgart, 1894–1978)

SVF = H. von Arnim and M. Adler, *Stoicorum Veterum Fragmenta, I–IV* (Stuttgart, 1903–24)

TLL = *Thesaurus Linguae Latinae* (Leipzig, 1900–)

Note on the Text

The Latin text printed here follows Bakhouche *(Bk),* revert-
ing occasionally to Waszink 1975 *(Ws)* or Wrobel *(Wr),* and
introducing a number of independent conjectural emenda-
tions *(Mg).* Unless otherwise indicated, the Notes to the
Text are restricted to points of departure from *Bk,* so that
inferences concerning manuscript readings, previous editions, or any modern sources of conjecture should not be
drawn on the basis of silence. For further information concerning this extraordinarily complex textual tradition, readers are advised to consult the magisterial editions of *Bk* and
Ws, along with the commentaries and explanatory notes of
van Winden, den Boeft, and Moreschini.

Calcidius's division of the work into two parts has been
preserved in the manuscripts. The titles of the thirteen tracts
cataloged in 7, however, were reintegrated by *Wr* based on
points of correspondence with the commentary. Similarly,
the chapter divisions go back to *Wr,* but were subsequently
modified by *Ws; Bk* correctly restores *Wr*'s division at 252,
and the present text introduces a further adjustment at 18.

The scientific diagrams have been reprinted from *Ws,*

with one correction (Diagram 19; see Bakhouche, *Calcidius,* 321; Theon, *Exposition,* 196 Hiller). A fully revised series is included as part of the French translation in *Bk,* and it merits careful consideration. See further, B. Eastwood and G. Graßhoff, *Planetary Diagrams for Roman Astronomy in Medieval Europe, ca. 800–1500* (Philadelphia, 2004), 73–115; M. Huglo, "Recherches sur la tradition des diagrammes de Calcidius," *Scriptorium* 62 (2008): 185–230 (and plates).

Dorfbauer suggests that for Greek terms Calcidius employed the original characters, which disappeared in the course of transmission ("Favonius Eulogius," 379 n. 11). That Calcidius used them for the scientific diagrams is certain (11–12, 18), but vestigial Greek appears otherwise to be relatively sparse in the received text. Faint echoes can be heard in variant readings for Ἅιδην (134), *noyn* (176, 252), and (probably) *epilenticus* (231). *Ws* favors transliteration, while *Bk* more readily restores (176, 252, 268, 278, 319, 328, 336, 346); the present text restores only with Ἅιδην, but on the understanding that the question of Calcidius's intentions remains open. Otherwise, the following may be noted: iotacism in *pthongi* (44), *limma* (45, 47), *Pyrois* (66, 70), *poli* (69), *Politia* (73, 95, 136, etc.), *hypolipticas* (74), *conoides* (90), *aides* (134, possibly), and *gnisios* (346); loss of aspiration in *pthongi* (44), *anticthona* (122), *Pthiae* (254), and *Acyles* (276); collapse of *ou* to *o/u* in *aplanos/-us* (see Notes to the Translation, 47c), to *o* in *gnisios* (346), and to *u* in *uranon* and *usian* (98, 129); and smooth breathings in *Osio* (Dedicatory Epistle), *aides* (134, possibly), and *orizonta* (Diagram 11).

Notes to the Text

\< \> = text supplied to correct for a suppositional lacuna

[ ] = text removed to correct for a suppositional interpolation

† † = corrupt text with no conjectural emendation

Timaeus

21d	quod] quid?
23e	(annis) ante *Mg*: post *Bk*
26d	aestima\<s\> *Mg*
27b	(ante) nos *Mg*: hos *Bk*
29a	†operisque sui† *Mg*
35a	[quippe] *Mg*
35b	[gemina natura] *Mg*
37d	animal\<is\> *Mg*
	[id quod est generale animal] *Mg*
38e	cuius *Mg*: quod operis *Bk*
	tempore *Ws*: tempori *Bk* (*see 113, with* Calcidius, *608 n. 429*)
42c	[tamen] *Mg*
44c	iam *Wr Ws*: tam *Bk*
46c	simile *Mg*: similis *Bk*
50a	recteque *Mg*: recte quippe *Bk* (*see 326*)
50b	cylindri ve\<l\> cuiusvis alterius \<quod\> *Mg*: cylindrive cuiusve alterius \<formae\> *Bk*
51d	corpore[a] *Ws*: corporea *Bk* (*see 340–41*)
52b	pervigilis *Ws*: per vigilis *Bk* (*see 349*)
52c	\<rei\> *Mg*

COMMENTARY

5	decem libris omnibus] *interpolation?*
11	ΑΓΘ *Ws*: ΑΓΔ *Bk*
12	Δ *(litterae) Mg*: (Α)Δ *Bk (see critical apparatus)*
16	[quadrato] *Mg (compare 240)*
18	*See Notes to the Translation*
19	ΚΘΛΜΝΞΟΠ *(second occurrence) Ws*: ΚΘΛΜΝΞΥΟΠ *Bk*
22	*(elementum)* quid *Mg*: quod *Bk*
26	*(conditores)* eorum *Mg*: earum *Bk*
28	[idem diversum dividuum] *Mg*: idem diversum \<individuum\> dividuum *Bk*
36	item ut] ita ut? *(compare Notes to the Translation, 46c)*
45	\<adversum tria\> ... [bis] ... [hanc] ... [enim] *Mg* (hanc - τὴν ?)
49	[sibi] *Mg*
57	ut\<pote\> ... [vero] *Mg*
59	item ut] *see note on 36*
64	at *(aequalia) Mg*: et *Bk*
69	[circa illam] *Mg*
73	verticillis *Mg*: verticulis *Bk*
74	aplanos *Mg*: aplanis *Bk*
75	aplanus *Mg*: aplanis *Bk*
81	ΝΞ *Mg*: ΝΖ *Bk*
82	*(ab)* Η *Ws*: Κ *Bk*
	(per) ΞΜ *Ws*: ΝΞ *Bk*
	a Ζ ad Ε *Ws*: a Η ad Ζ *Bk*
85	ΔΑ *Mg*: ΑΔ *Bk*
90	his *(quae) Ws*: omitted *Bk (see critical apparatus)*
91	ut\<pote\> *conjecture J. Stover*
92	aplanus ... aplanus *Mg*: aplanis ... aplanis *Bk*
102	a deo *conjecture J. Stover*: adeo *Bk*
110	Ponticus *Ws*: [Ponticus] *Bk*
118	altititudini altitudo *Mg*: latitudini latitudo *Bk*
130	[id est summus atque imus] ... [scilicet ratione utentibus] *Mg*
144	aplane *Mg*: aplanem *Bk*
162	[ipsorum] *Mg*

164	nisi forte putatur beatus] *interpolation?*
175	es<se>t *Mg*
176	aemula[e] *Mg*
187	<id> est ira *Mg*: ira est *Bk*
188	legi (obsequentes) *Ws*: legis *Bk*
194	[sit] *Mg*
195	[tamen] *see note on 42c*
211	<Quod> *Mg*
219	a[pu]d *Mg*
220	(neque) enim *Mg*: tamen *Bk*
225	[quae in conceptu sunt] *Mg*
228	[alia] *Ws*
231	[habeat] *Mg*: ab ea *Bk*
	<sit> *Mg*
	epilepticus *Wr*: epilenticus *Bk* (*on the confusion of* Π *and* N, *compare R. A. Kaster, ed.,* Macrobius, Saturnalia *[Oxford, 2011], xxxix*)
237	[exordio] *Ws*
239	supra nos erunt ad directum rigorem *Mg*: ad directum rigorem supra nos erunt *Bk*
240	[quadrati] *Mg* (*compare 16, and* turris quadrata, *237*)
249	libidini[s] *Ws*
266	idem (pulchro) *Mg*: id enim *Bk*
272	[quattuor] *Mg*
307	(patiens,) dissentiunt *Mg*: dissentiunt *before* quorum alterum *Bk*
319	<eius> eius modi *Ws*: eius huius modi *Bk*
323	[ea quae] *Ws*
325	[quae] *Ws*
328	<cor> *Ws*: ψυχῆς <κέαρ> *Bk*
330	[inter] *Mg*
340	<ut> . . . <transducibile sit, alterum nutans incertumque semper et> *Mg*
341	Nunc *Mg*: Nec *Bk*
345	(sub sensus) veniant *Wr*: veniunt *Bk*
354	quae (apparet) *Mg*: qui *Bk* (*see 53b*)
355	ignotam . . . perspicuam *Wr*: ignotas . . . perspicuas *Bk*
	Diagram 11 ORIZON[TA] . . . ORIZON[TA] *Mg*

Notes to the Translation

E1   Isocrates, *To Demonicus* 7: The positioning of this reference raises a question of programmatic significance. The task of the previous day's discussion (from Calcidius's perspective, the *Republic*) was to elucidate the relationship between the good of the individual soul and that of the state; it falls to the present discussion (Calcidius's explication of the *Timaeus*) to affirm the rational order of the individual soul as a reflection of the architecture of the universe. The emphasis on virtue, in other words, is consistent with the cosmology, and in that sense Calcidius is true to Plato: for both, the structure of the world informs those of the state and individual soul (6, 95, 202, 233, 267). Given the different educational ideals represented by Plato and Isocrates, however, we may wonder why the work is launched in this way. Of course, Isocrates had found his place in the tradition; but if Calcidius is indeed to be seen as a kind of Socrates in relation to Osius (see note on E4/7), then the reference to Isocrates may contain a hint of the "mirror of princes" genre, which might explain the repeated emphasis on the mathematical sciences and a "liberal" education as the first steps toward Philosophy (see notes on E4/7, 2).

E3   *I suppose:* Latin *opinor,* a distinctive and often slightly clumsy element of Calcidius's prose style, with nearly sixty-five occurrences; in both position (second) and valence (softening effect) it recalls the Greek parenthetic first-person *oimai.*

E4   *You had conceived the hope:* This is the first of four points at which Calcidius expressly addresses his dedicatee Osius. He uses the singular here, in 126, and in 133, but the plural in 4.

E4/7   *all forms of liberal education . . . And so . . . I complied:* Latin *omnibus studiis humanitatis . . . Itaque parui,* vividly echoed at 20a–b *(in studiis humanitatis omnibus . . . Ideoque . . . parui).* This yields the analogy, Osius : Calcidius = Critias : Socrates, with Osius therefore as Calcidius's elder. *Humanitas* targets the Greek notion of *paideia,* or "liberal education," particularly the four mathematical sciences (53c, 2, 32, 55, 128, 168, 264–65, 355); compare Cicero, *In Defense of Archias* 2.3; *Timaeus* 1.1; Aulus Gellius, *Attic Nights* 13.17.1.

E4   *a hitherto unattempted work:* Note the silence concerning Cicero's *Timaeus.*

E5   *whom you regarded as your other you:* Proverbial; compare Aristotle, *Nicomachean Ethics* 1166a31–32, 1170b6–7 ("for the friend is another self"); Cicero, *Laelius* 21.80; Augustine, *Confessions* 4.6.11.

E7   *more obscure than the original itself:* The point is repeated in 4. Plato himself is aware of the impossibility of furnishing an exact account of his subject matter, and so offers a "likely story" instead (29b–d, 48d–50a). Calcidius follows his lead in explaining any apparent obscurity as arising from constraints laid by the highly technical subject matter (1, 274, 322, 355)—while also explaining Aristotle and Heraclitus as cases of *stylistic* obscurity (287, 322). Compare Cicero, *On Ends* 2.5.15; Ps.-Aristotle, *On the World* 396b20.

TIMAEUS

20a   *Timaeus . . . love of wisdom:* The Latin *amor sapientiae* ("love of wisdom") is a loan translation of Greek *philosophia,* used here by Plato and added by Calcidius earlier in the sentence *(philosophiaeque);* with it may be compared "lover of wisdom" *(amator sapientiae,* 261, 263) for "philosopher." "Philosophy" was often associated with the Pythagorean tradition (Nicomachus, *Introduction to Arithmetic* 1.1; Boethius, *On Arithmetic* 1.1; *On Porphy-*

ry's Isagoge, I, 1.3; compare Augustine, *Confessions* 3.4.8), and although Plato does not identify his Timaeus as a Pythagorean, Calcidius takes the connection for granted (6, 50). It is therefore unsurprising that Pythagoras (45), Pythagoreans (35), and Pythagorean doctrine (51) inhabit the commentary as they do from beginning to end (308).

20a–b *all forms of liberal education ... And so I ... complied:* See note on E4/7.

21e *the Saïtic Law:* Latin *lex (Saitica),* understanding Greek *nómos* ("law") rather than *nomós* ("district").

23c *in war and peace:* Latin *belloque et pace,* a connective (*-que et*) that occurs with notable frequency (29a, 31b, 34b–c, 40c, 42e, 45c/e, 46c, 87, 93, 109, 151, 167, 172, 334, 353; compare *-que et item* [53, 55, 183], *-que item et* [52d]). Although the combination has limited attestation for other Latin sources (*-que, LD* IV.1, *OLD* 3.c; Tacitus, *Annals* 4.2.1, 11.24.2), Calcidius's usage may well reflect the direct influence of Greek *te kai* (compare *LSS* §287).

23e *eight thousand years ago:* The received text states (eight thousand years) "later" *(post),* an error attributed by Moreschini to Calcidius (*Calcidio,* 27). The emendation to *ante* presupposes a copying error occasioned by *posteriorem.*

26d *do you think you will be content with:* The received Latin is *fieri ... contentus aestima,* with no hint of an indirect question ("consider *whether* you will be content"). The emendation *aestima<s>* assumes the loss of an *s* between *aestimas* and *Socrates,* and that *fieri contentus aestimas* takes the role of some Greek idiom such as *genêsesthai* (note *fieri - genêsesthon,* 52d) *stergôn oiei / dokeis (soi).* Compare *LSS* §199.I.

27c *Let it be understood ... that:* Latin *Sit ... comprehensum ... ut (dicantur),* with *ut* ("that") evidently functioning as a Greek declarative *hôs,* as also in 110, 179, 228, and 340 (with emendation). Compare *OLD, ut* 41; *LSS* §349.II; Cicero, *Tusculan Disputations* 5.39.113 *(respondisse ut).*

28a *craftsman:* Latin *opifex* - Greek *dêmiourgos.* At 28a–30b Plato describes "the god" as a father, maker, craftsman, builder, and cause, and the world as his work or product (compare *Statesman* 273b–e). The metaphor targets the notion of an artisan

who manipulates materials according to a pattern in order to produce an artifact, and it reflects the fact that the cosmology is a "myth" based on likelihood rather than scientific certitude (see note on E7). Although *opifex* is Calcidius's preferred term (28a, 26), *auctor* (28c, 26), *genitor* (28c, 72), *fabricator* (29a, 17), *deus* (30a, 17), and *creator* (42e, 132) appear in both the translation and the commentary. *Conditor* appears only in the translation (29d), and *architectus* only in the commentary (137); *artifex* is used only of human artisans (23, 337), unlike in Cicero (*Timaeus* 2.6). Doublets are frequent (*opifex deus, conditor deus, auctor deus, opifexque et fabricator, opifex genitorque,* etc.). In the translation, *opifex (deus)* is implicitly associated with the divine *ratio (mens)* and *providentia* (38d, 44c, 45a, 47b), and in the commentary, with the divine *ideae* (260, 273, 304), the Stoic principle of *ratio* (293, compare *SVF* 1.160), and indeed, the God of Genesis (278). See further at notes on 30c, 42e; and for Latin *Demiurgus,* Tertullian, *Against the Valentinians* 15.2–29.3.

28b   *and by this we are assuming:* Latin *et qui,* obscure and deviating from the Greek.

29d   *and yet:* Latin *et tamen,* for Greek *to men oun* (*. . . de [- quidem igitur . . . vero]*), as again at 43d, both evidently reflecting phonetic interference from *men (ta-men).* Compare note on 40a.

30c   *divine providence:* Latin *divinae providentiae,* as again at 44c, in both cases for Greek *pronoia* ("forethought"), a notion that is not central to the *Timaeus* but became so with the Stoics. "Providence" *(providentia)* intrudes upon the Greek at 47b, as "celestial foresight" *(caelestis . . . prospicientia)* does at 44c; similarly, 47b–c ("provident . . . movements of the divine mind"), 47e ("the intellect of the provident mind"), 53b ("divine foresight"). Calcidius, in other words, has a particularly strong conception of divine Providence, treating it as a central metaphysical postulate in 176–77 and 188. See further, Reydams-Schils, "Calcidius on God," 243; Bakhouche, *Calcidius,* 639–40 n. 82.

31b–c   *And since no two things . . . brings this about:* Anacoluthic: the conjunction *quoniamque* ("and since") mistranslates the Greek particle *de* ("but"), and there is no apodotic clause to complete the

thought. Cornford translates the Greek (*Plato's Cosmology*, 44): "But two things alone cannot be satisfactorily united without a third; for there must be some bond between them drawing them together. And of all bonds the best is that which makes itself and the terms it connects a unity in the fullest sense; and it is of the nature of a continued geometrical proportion to effect this most perfectly."

32a   *the material:* Latin *materia* appears frequently in both the translation, where as a non-Platonic concept it intrudes upon the Greek, and the commentary; the alternate, *materies,* appears in 236 and 331. In the singular, *materia* differs from *silva* ("matter," Greek *hylê*) primarily in the sense that it includes the qualities that cause "materials" such as fire, earth, gold, wax, wood, or glass to behave in particular ways, thereby laying certain constraints on the craftsman who shapes or manipulates them (43a, 46a, 50a/c; 7, 76, 236, 242, 248, 305, 314, 324–25, 331; compare Cicero, *In Defense of Milo* 27.74). The plural *materiae,* by contrast, generally signifies the four elements of earth, air, fire, and water (32b, 46d, 48b, 49b, 52e, 23–24, 76, 351), including their constituent qualities (307). Calcidius's usage is however not entirely consistent, and so the expression *prima materia* (not *silva*) occurs in connection with what is essentially an Aristotelian doctrine of prime matter (308 [50c]), while the adjectives *materialis* and *silvestris* ("material") function as strict synonyms (222, 338). See further at notes on 49a, 50d, 7, 222–26.

34b   *even, balanced:* Latin *aequiremum indeclivemque,* for Greek *homalon* ("even"). The metaphor appears to be one of a ship of balanced oarage (even keel), and hence not listing. Unfortunately, we do not know how Calcidius (would have) translated *homalên,* 67b. Compare 93 *(ad indeclivem rotunditatem).*

35a–37a   *Being:* See note on 27.

35b   *of Being, Other, and that which is called the Same:* Latin *ex substantia, diversi, et item eius quod idem vocatur* - Greek *ek te tautou kai thaterou kai tês ousias;* evidently conflating the prepositions *ex* (hence ablative *substantia*) and *ek* (hence genitive *diversi . . . eius*). Compare *BLL* 628–29.

36a–b *called . . . by the Greeks . . . the Greek letter chi:* Again in the lemmata
and citations (47, 52, 58, 92). Timaeus is made to explain to Socrates, Critias, and Hermocrates how Greeks speak and write!
Although the details may be uncertain, Cicero obviously had a
Roman literary frame to provide a context for such observations (*Timaeus* 4.13, 6.17, 7.23, 8.27, 10.35, 11.38). Compare note
on 5.

36b *243:256:* The ratio (256:243) is inverted again in 44, 47, and 50,
but not in 45.

37a *superior to all other intelligibles:* Latin *cunctis intellegibilibus praestantior,* mistaking the partitive genitive *tôn noêtôn (aristê)* for a
comparative, and so translating with the ablative *cunctis intellegibilibus (praestantior).* A related confusion produces precisely
the opposite result in 68. Compare notes on 37d, 286.

37c *When . . . observed that:* Latin *Quam cum . . . animadverteret,* literally, (when he observed) "how," a subtle confusion in the rendering of Greek *hôs (de . . . enoêsen).* Compare note on 27c.

37d *with eternity left untouched and abiding:* Latin *aevo intacto et . . . perseverante,* converting the Greek genitive *menontos aiônos (aiônion
eikona)* to an ablative absolute. Compare notes on 37a, 68, 286.

38c *wandering stars:* Latin *stellae . . . erraticae* (- Greek *planêta,* from
planasthai, "to wander about"); otherwise, Calcidius uses *planes*
or *planeta* (72).

38e *for the task in hand:* Latin *ad id quo de,* the last two words mimicking Greek anastrophe *(hou péri),* and doing so independently of
Plato. Compare *LSS* §114, *Zus.*b.

40a *with stability:* Latin *indeclinabiliter* (- *eukyklon,* "well-rounded"),
evidently roughly synonymous with *indeclivis* ("balanced," 34b,
93).

  and through the same orbit: Latin *perque eandem orbitam,* evidently
taking the wrong cue from the Greek <u>*peri*</u> *tôn autôn* ("concerning the same things"), perhaps because of *peri panta kuklôi ton
ouranon* ("around the whole of the heaven, in a circle") immediately preceding. The same pattern of phonetic interference
(peri - per) is indicated in 85 and 93. Compare 26 *(archê - arx),* 69
(polloi - poli); and note on 29d.

40d *those who are capable of understanding:* Omitting the negative par-

ticle ("incapable"), as also in certain Greek manuscripts, and in 125. See further Taylor, *Commentary,* 243–44.

of the ... divine powers known as demons: Latin *divinarum potestatum quae daemones nuncupantur.* To Plato's "demons," Calcidius adds "divine powers." Compare 44d (235), 45b/d (247), 127, 134, 232, 254; Apuleius, *On the God of Socrates 6.*

40e   *To mistrust:* Literally, "to be mistrusted" *(non credi),* the passive infinitive, possibly mimicking the Greek middle voice; compare (among others) 47a, 48c, 53b, 6, 127, 130, 176, 197, 260, 298.

41a   *O gods, you gods of whom:* Latin *Dii, deorum quorum.* See Taylor, *Commentary,* 248–49; Cornford, *Plato's Cosmology,* 367–70; Bakhouche, *Calcidius,* 613 n. 40.

42a   *desire ... pleasure ... pain ... fear ... irascibility:* Latin *cupido, voluptas, tristitia, metus, iracundia* (~ Greek *erôs, hêdonê, lupê, phobos, thumos).* See notes on 182, 194.

42e   *the creator of things:* Latin *rerum creator,* for Plato's "he who had set all of these things in order" (compare *is ... qui cuncta composuit,* Cicero, *Timaeus* 13.47). The term *creator* appears here (hence in 146) and in 132. Although it recalls the language of the Latin Vulgate (Ecclesiasticus 24:12; 2 Maccabees 7:23), relevant analogues are also found in Cicero *(On Divination* 2.30.64 *[Iliad* 2.324]), Ovid *(Metamorphoses* 8.309), and others. See further at note on 28a.

43a   *and being confined:* Latin *ut (... obligati),* deviating from the original *(hai d' ... endetheisai),* but possibly a Grecism *(hôs);* compare note on 299.

43c   *agitations ... called sensations:* Latin *aestus ... sensus (cognominantur).* The etymology intended by Plato may be *aisthêsis* ("sensation") ~ *aissein* ("to move about rapidly").

43d   *and yet:* Latin *tamen,* for Greek *men (... de [~ quidem ... vero]);* see note on 29d.

43e   *And so there arose:* Latin *Propterea ... existere,* mimicking a Greek clause of natural or anticipated result *(hôste gignesthai),* with no adjustment to the subjunctive mood *(ut existerent).* The problem stems from Calcidius's reorganization of Plato's complex sentence, which itself contains two such clauses *(hôste ... strepsai ... empoiein ... hôste ... pheresthai men [~ quidem feratur] ... de*

pheresthai). Further instances of the consecutive infinitive (and indicative) appear in 215 and 224, possibly also at 51a and in 219. Compare *LSS* §346.I.b–c.

44c   *once the merits . . . have been posited:* Latin *meritis . . . locatis,* not in the Greek but recurring in 151 *(collocati . . . meriti);* compare 153 *(iuxta meritum praecessionis),* 175 *(merita . . . locentur),* 189 *(meritorum collocationem).*

45d   *no natural means of communication:* Latin *nullam . . . naturae communicationem.* "Natural" is a strained rendering of the dative *naturae,* which in turn is a strained rendering of Greek *sumphues* ("naturally united"). At 30d and 44b (possibly also in 130), Calcidius uses the dative *naturae suae* with participial forms of *convenire* and *competere* to translate *kata physin* ("by nature"); here (possibly also in 204) he uses the dative *naturae (suae)* in the manner of a Greek instrumental dative *(têi physei* ("by [their] nature"). Compare *BLL* 498–99.

46c   *(area) and likewise:* Latin *similis . . . ut* ("similar to" - "likewise"), analogous to *aeque ut* (16) or *item ut* (36, 59 [see Notes to the Text]). But *similis* does not construe; the emendation to *simile* assumes that *-lis* has been influenced by the neighboring *(deiect)is.*

47a   *the notion of time:* Latin *temporis recordatio.* At 25e–26a and in 231, *recordatio* expresses the idea of "memory" or "recollection." Here, however, it translates Greek *ennoia* (perhaps also in 321), while in 342 it translates *dianoia;* otherwise, it functions as a synonym of *intellectus,* 83, and *cogitatio,* 101. Hence the term is not exclusively restricted to the notion of memory. Compare Bakhouche, *Calcidius,* 867 n. 1196; 877 n. 1314.

    has informed our inquiry into the nature: Literally, (has instructed the nature's) "being inquired into" *(quaeri);* compare 127 and note on 40e.

47c   *the nonwandering circumlation:* Latin *aplanem . . . circumactionem.* Two manuscripts suggest a Greek form of the adjective *(aplanê),* and *TLL* interprets Calcidius as apparently employing a Greek declension throughout; in fact, however, he uses a hybrid morphology, in the masculine (adjective) and feminine

(adjective, substantive) singular. The nominative is *aplanês* (69, 87), as in Greek; the ablative is of course a Latin form (*aplani*, 73, 92), as is the dative *aplani* (72, 120, assuming no iotacism). Manuscript evidence for the accusative is divided, as here, between Latin *aplanem* (178) and Greek *aplanê* (144); for the genitive, *aplanos* (- Greek *aplanous*) is attested in the title to Diagram II, and either *aplanos* or *aplanus* in 74–75, 92. The Greek forms have been adopted in 74–75, 92, 144.

48c   *to arrive at:* Literally, (its) "being arrived at" (*perveniri*); see note on 40e.

49a   *Receptacle:* Latin *receptaculum* translates Greek *hypodochê*, which appears here and at 51a; *receptaculum* and *receptaculi sinus* render *dechomenon* and *to ekdexomenon* at 50e. Calcidius combines the term with the Aristotelian notion of a substrate, or matter (*silva*), which in 278 is described as a recipient (*receptrix*) of all qualities. See next note.

50d   *a substrate for bodies:* The Latin *subiecto (corporum)* has no counterpart in the Greek but clearly expresses the Aristotelian notion of a material substrate (*hypokeimenon*) for change, a notion that was adapted by the Stoics before being passed back to later Platonists. Expressions involving *subiacere* (and related forms) appear in 268, 274, 286, 289, 308, 316–18, 331 (50d), 333, 337, 345, 354. See further at notes on 32a, 7, 222–26, and previous note; also, Bakhouche, *Calcidius*, 832 n. 843.

51a   *the mother . . . must not be called . . . formless capacity:* Calcidius departs from Plato's syntax and in so doing introduces a construction that does not construe in Latin. Two possible explanations: (1) *Ideoque* ("And so") functions in the manner of Greek *hôste (- dio)*, to introduce a clause of natural result (see note on 43e), perhaps under the influence of *Ex quo fit ut* (*habeat*, 50e); this would assume an ellipsis of *esse* (with *appellandum*) and assimilation to the gender and number of *quicquam*. (2) Calcidius converts the subjunctive *legômen* ("let us call") to the impersonal (active) verbal adjective *lekteon*, which then becomes the Latin gerund *appellandum*. The latter is the more probable explanation: Greek *tên . . . mêtera kai hypodochên mête gên mête aera*

mête pyr mête hydôr [legómen] lekteon mête hosa . . . all' . . . eidos . . . kai . . . pandeches - Latin *matrem . . . receptaculum neque terram neque aquam nec vero ignem vel aera nec quicquam . . . appellandum sed . . . potius speciem . . . et . . . capacitatem.* For related Grecisms, compare *NLS* §204 n. ii; *LSS* §202.C.a.

52c On Calcidius's rendering, see H. Cherniss, *"Timaeus* 52c2–5," *Selected Papers,* ed. L. Tarán (Leiden, 1977), 364 n. 1; Bakhouche, *Calcidius,* 624 n. 263.

53b *to bring everything back:* Literally, (that everything should) "be brought back" *(redigi);* see note on 40e.

gave binding unity: Latin *continuavit,* for Greek *epecheireito kosmeisthai* ("he undertook to set in order"). *Continuari, continuatio,* and *competens continuum* appear with particular frequency in 8–25, which treat of the mathematical bonds that link bodies (particularly the four elements) and geometrical figures together. See further Bakhouche, *Calcidius,* 624–25 n. 272.

to demonstrate their arrangement and generation: Literally, (that their arrangement and generation should) "be demonstrated" *(demonstrari);* see note on 40e.

53c *the paths of liberal erudition:* See note on E4/7.

COMMENTARY

1 *Plato's Timaeus difficult, not because of . . . the obscurity of its language:* See note on E7.

technical reasoning: Latin *artificiosae rationis;* here targeting the mathematical sciences (see next note), but in all instances evoking the sense of an *ars* ("art," "skill" - Greek *technê*). Compare 2, 56, 62, 119, 165, 185, 222, 342.

2 *arithmetic, astronomy, geometry, and music:* The commentary begins and ends with an emphasis on the four mathematical sciences, which in 355 are described as the "liberal" disciplines and first "steps" of a philosophical ascent. They were later christened the *quadruvium,* or "fourfold path," by Boethius (*On Arithmetic* 1.1), who also envisioned them as the foundations of a "liberal" education and philosophical ascent. The Latin term

mathematicus is reserved for astronomy and astrology (73, 79, 86, 124, 157). See note on E4/7.

4   *to satisfy your request:* See note on E4.

an even greater charge of obscurity: See note on E7.

5   *in ten complete books:* Calcidius apparently becomes caught between the dramatic conceit of Socrates's having spoken on the subject (17c–19a) and Plato's actually having written a dialogue "in books" (compare 233). The Latin *res publica* ("state") occurs at 17c, 19b, and here; for the title of Plato's dialogue, however, Calcidius uses only *Politeia* (73, 95, 136, etc.). Is *decem libris omnibus* a later interpolation? Compare note on 36a–b.

6   *justice pertaining to human affairs . . . equity of nature . . . positive . . . natural . . . unwritten:* That the Latin *inscripta* means "unwritten" rather than "inscribed" is evident from context. The *Republic* is concerned with "positive" justice, and the *Timaeus* with the "natural" justice laid up in heaven and serving as its pattern. The "decrees" of the latter are reflected in but ultimately independent of the prohibitions and sanctions provided for by the legislation and conventions of human society; hence the metaphorical "common city or republic . . . of this sensible world." See further at note on E1.

Timaeus of Locri, a follower of Pythagoras's teaching: See note on 20a.

thought there should be an inquiry into: Literally, (desired that it should) "be inquired into" *(inquiri);* see note on 40e.

7   The thirteen thematically defined sections of the commentary are periodically referred to as "treatments" or "tracts," Latin *tractatus* (26, 31, 59, 74, 97, 236, 268–69, 273, 337), a term used also in connection with the subtreatise on fate (142, 190).

On matter: The Latin term *silva* ("matter") and its adjectival form *silvestris* ("material," see next note) are among the most distinctive elements of Calcidius's philosophical vocabulary (van Winden, *Calcidius on Matter,* 31; Moreschini, *Calcidio,* 716 n. 210; Bakhouche, *Calcidius,* 831–32 n. 841, 862 n. 1136). *Silva* translates Greek *hylê* (123, 268, 273, compare 278), the post-Platonic (Aristotelian) origins of which Calcidius acknowledges in 273

and 308; and despite eschewing the term in the translation, Calcidius nevertheless reads the Aristotelian doctrine into the *Timaeus* at numerous point. The historical significance of his usage is tied to the fact that in the longer tradition *hylê* came to be translated by *materia* instead (for example, Philastrius, *Catalog of Heresies* 67.95.1; Victorinus's and Boethius's translations of Porphyry, *Introduction* 3.10, 8.7 [11.12, 15.6 Busse]), which left *silva* to appear strangely outmoded if also brilliantly alluring to medieval writers such as Bernardus Silvestris. *Silva - hylê* may be analogous to *mundus - kosmos* as an instance of loan shift (*BLL* 463). Like *materia, silva* expresses the notion of the wood or material from which things are made, but further targets that of a complete absence of quality; the two conceptions converge in 222, where Calcidius speaks of both "untreated wood" and "formless material" *(intractatum lignum, materia informis)*. See further at notes on 32a, 49a, 50d, 222–26.

On the primary material elements: Latin *De primis materiis silvestribus* (see previous note). The plural *materiae* generally denotes the four material elements of fire, earth, water, and air (see note on 32a) and presumably does so here, assuming title 15 targets 53c–59e or thereabouts (note *et perpessionibus earum,* with *ipsorum elementorum perpessiones,* 48b). It should be noted, however, that the notion of *materia silvestris* recurs in 289 and 337, both times in connection with the higher-order (hylomorphic) "material substances" shaped by artisans (bronze, silver, wood); compare 222 *(silvestris et materialis essentia),* 338 *(silvestria . . . materialia).*

8–25   The first of Calcidius's thirteen thematically defined tracts ("On the Generation of the World"), devoted to demonstrating the necessity of means to bind discrete terms—more precisely, to laying the mathematical groundwork for a demonstration of the necessity of water and air to bind earth and fire. Arithmetic (9–10, 14–15) and geometry (11–12, 16–19) dominate until 19, after which physical (20–22) and metaphysical (23–25) speculation intervenes. Important claims are staked in the final chapters: the world is completely self-contained and *eternal* (of causal or atemporal origins). Calcidius, in other words, inter-

prets Plato's creation narrative metaphorically rather than literally (26, 138, 228). See further, Tarán, "Creation Myth."

16   *we call a proportion and the Greeks an analogia:* This technical application of *competens* appears first in 11 (absent from 31c, 32c).
In 19 and 22 Calcidius moves between the Latin and Greek,
whereas in 21, 304, and 355 he favors the Greek. Attestation
for this usage is rare (*TLL, competens* II.B.2); Cicero translates,
comparatio pro portione, instead (*Timaeus* 4.13).

18   The chapter division has been moved to *Quatenus* on the understanding that the phrase, *Descriptio . . . analogia syneches,* is the
title to Diagram 6 (mentioned at the beginning of the chapter),
which has also been moved. Compare Bakhouche, *Calcidius,*
636 n. 55.

23   *that which is made . . . and coming to be:* Pleonastic, *quae fiunt
quaeque nascuntur facta dissolvantur nata occidant,* and thought
by Waszink (*Timaeus,* note on 73.6–8) to echo the Nicene
Creed *(natum, non factum);* see, however, Moreschini, *Calcidio,*
696 n. 22; Bakhouche, *Calcidius,* 614 n. 43 and 641 n. 85.

challenge to normal human expectations: Latin *quod est praeter opinionem hominum;* compare Aristotle, *On the Heavens* 279b17–21 (on
the *impossibility* of making the generated eternal); and note on
297.

26–39 The second tract, or psychogony ("On the Origin of Soul"), in
which, however, the term *psychogonia* does not actually appear
(compare, however, 95, 208).

26   *the insufflation of soul:* "Insufflation" *(inspiratio)* seems preferable
to "inspiration" here and in 55 and 300 (compare 276): here Calcidius uses *inspiratio* in connection with Plato's account of the
divine construction of soul; in 55 and 300 he uses it in connection with a "Hebrew" doctrine of the divine insufflation of
reason (compare 219). Philastrius, it may be noted, brands the
strict identification of soul with divine insufflation *(inspiratio)*
as heretical (*Catalog of Heresies* 70.98.1).

contriving processes of generation for eternal things: See note on 8–25.
the origin and pinnacle: Latin *origo et arx.* Such doublets are characteristic of Calcidius's style (two further instances in this

chapter). The task to hand is the disambiguation of the term *origo* ("origin"), for which *arx* ("pinnacle") seems a less transparent synonym than *exordium* (39d [118; *caput,* 148]), *initium* (23), or *ortus* (128). The immediately preceding doublet *(auctoritas et origo)* targets a "mortal" sense of the term *origo,* and *arx* is evidently meant to capture its divine or eternal sense (compare 20a, 44e [213, 231], 39). In 312, on the other hand, *arx et origo* appears as a rather flat pleonasm. Unless Calcidius is aiming at an etymological figure, *arx* may reflect phonetic interference from Greek *archê* ("origin," "beginning"). Compare 40a *(peri - per),* 69 *(polloi - poli);* 276 (disambiguation of *initium*); Aristotle, *Metaphysics* 1012b34–13a23 *(archê).*

27–31   These chapters, along with 51–55, may reflect Numenian influence (Moreschini, *Calcidio,* 701 n. 52, 706 n. 105; Bakhouche, *Calcidius,* 647 n. 112, 665 n. 264). For the doctrine of two souls, compare 297, 300.

27   *Substance* [*substantia*] *or . . . Being* [*essentia*]: Compare 53 *(essentia sive substantia).* The Latin *substantia* and *essentia* are semantic calques of the Greek *hypostasis* and *ousia,* respectively (compare *BLL* 461). That Calcidius treats them as synonyms is clear from the shift to *essentia* after the observation concerning Cicero (compare Seneca, *Epistle* 58.6); otherwise, *substantia* occurs with roughly twice the frequency of *essentia.* Given the uncertainties surrounding both Calcidius's own philosophical assumptions and the Greek background(s) against which he worked, there is no consistent or fully satisfactory method of rendering the terms in English. Generally speaking, he uses them interchangeably for the Greek *ousia* (35a–37a, compare 28–30), and in clearly Platonizing contexts it is usually safe to translate with "being" ("Being"). As to Aristotle, in 286 Calcidius translates *ousia* (*Physics* 192a6) with both *essentia* and *substantia* but in 226, 319, and 336 adheres to *essentia* for the first of the ten Categories; in both contexts, "substance" suits well. There is no indication of any sensitivity to the fourth- and fifth-century Trinitarian speculations that occasioned terminological confusion in the West (Augustine, *On the Trinity* 5.8.10; *City of God* 12.2), a point that would be particularly remarkable if

Calcidius's dedicatee Osius was indeed the bishop of Cordoba. See further, C. Markschies, *Ambrosius von Mailand und die Trinitätstheologie. Kirchen- und theologiegeschichtliche Studien zu Antiarianismus und Neunizänismus bei Ambrosius und im latinischen Westen (364–81 n. Chr.)* (Tübingen, 1995), 9–38; B. Inwood, *Seneca. Selected Philosophical Letters* (Oxford, 2007), 113.

29   *the forms conceived in his mind:* See note on 302–4.

      matter . . . fountainhead of bodies: Latin *silvam . . . fons . . . corporum.* Compare "fountainhead . . . of . . . numbers" *(ex . . . numerorum . . . fonte),* 35; "perennial fount of provident intelligence" *(fontis perennis providae intellegentiae),* 39.

31   *as he indicated:* Latin *ut ipse . . . dixit.* The demonstrative *ipse* is otiose insofar as no stress is here laid on what Plato *himself* indicated, and Calcidius clearly does not mean that "the Master hath spoken" (127); related to this weakening of *ipse* is the use of the demonstrative *idem* where context calls for no specification to the effect that the *same* Plato is intended. The two phenomena suggest interference from Greek *autos* (attributive or predicative) combined with confusion arising from the lack of a Latin definite article; hence *idem (ipse) dicit* takes the place of Greek *autos legei,* while *idem (ipse) Plato dicit* takes the place of *ho Platôn legei.* Compare 22c *(ipsumque* [- *kai autos*]), 50a *(de eodem* [- *autou péri*]), 56 *(declarat idem),* 66 *(et ipse* [- *kai autos,* Theon, *Exposition,* 130.16 Hiller], and see note on 70), 98 *(idem prosequitur),* 102 *(ipse explicabit),* 104 *(in isdem = in ipsis),* 107 *(idem Plato dicit),* 108 *(manifestat ipse),* 122 *(idem ait),* 125 *(iste* [- *ho,* Homer]), 127 *(idem locutus),* 129 *(idem Plato dicit),* 192 *(dicit idem Plato),* 200 *(idem asserat),* 206 *(ipse ait),* 213 *(idem auctor appellat),* 220 *(Definit idem . . . ait idem Chrysippus),* 231 *(idem Plato docuit),* 247 *(idem auctor ait),* 251 *(Idemque asserit),* 282 *(idemque vocat),* 297 *(iste mundus),* 299 *(idemque iubet);* also, *LSS* §105.f; *BLL* 518.

32–91   Possibly from 32, but very clearly from 37, Calcidius's text runs parallel with extended passages of Theon of Smyrna's *Exposition of Mathematical Subjects Useful for the Study of Plato;* the parallels effectively end in 91, although there are a few faint points of connection thereafter. Theon indicates his reliance upon

the Peripatetic Adrastus of Aphrodisias, whose lost work, to judge from a remark in Porphyry (*On Ptolemy's Harmonics,* 96.1–2 Düring), was a commentary on the *Timaeus.* Hence the question of Calcidius's source(s) arises, leaving modern commentators divided between Adrastus and Theon. If Calcidius followed Theon, then certain points of confusion are easily explained, for trouble would have been likely to occur wherever he had to reorganize material in order to accommodate the requirements of his own very different work; other points, however, become difficult to explain, especially when he clearly diverges from Theon (compare note on 72).

32   *geometry, arithmetic, and harmonic theory:* See note on E4/7.

33   *this diagram:* The lambda of Crantor (Plutarch, *On the Generation of the Soul in the "Timaeus"* 1027d).

35   *fountainhead . . . of . . . numbers:* See note on 29.
     from them arise numbers and musical intervals in . . . ratios: See note on 40–45.

36–37   Compare Theon, *Exposition,* 103.1–104.19 Hiller; Philo, *On the Creation* 33.99; Martianus Capella, *On the Marriage of Mercury and Philology* 7.738.

38   *secondary . . . tertiary square:* $(1 + 2) + (3 + 4) + (5 + 6) + (7 + 8) = 36$; $1 + (2 + 3) + (4 + 9) + (8 + 27) = 54$.

39   *unity . . . the perennial fount of provident intelligence:* As matter is the "fountainhead" of corporeality (29), so unity is that of provident intelligence.

40–45   The subject of this third tract ("On Harmonic Modulation") was intimated in 35 and is here dealt with in connection with Plato's text. The musical intervals and mathematical ratios can be roughly illustrated with reference to any modern stringed instrument (for the ancient monochord), on which, to take only the four primary consonances, an ascending diatonic octave will be produced by stopping the string halfway from the nut to the bridge ($C - c = 2:1$), a fifth by stopping it a third of the way ($C - G = 3:2$), a fourth by stopping it a quarter of the way ($C - F = 4:3$), and a whole tone by stopping it a ninth of the way ($C - D = 9:8$).

42–46   For the number 16, Calcidius uses the additive forms *sedecim* and

decem et sex; for 18 he uses only *decem et octo,* never the subtrac-
tive *duodeviginti. Decem et sex* and *decem et octo* may be analytical
"translations" of the Greek signs, ις' and ιη'. Compare Diony-
sius Exiguus's translation of the first Canon of the Acts of I
Constantinople (381 CE), *decem et octo (- dekaoktô).*

44   *243:256:* See note on 36b.

45   *a leimma . . . 256:243:* The interval or "remainder" that when compounded with two whole tones completes the tetrachord or
fourth (47–50); confused here with the *diesis,* or minor semitone. See Taylor, *Commentary,* 140–46; Cornford, *Plato's Cosmology,* 71–72; Bakhouche *Calcidius,* 662 n. 238.

    he suspended fixed units of weight from strings: One of two legends
concerning Pythagoras, the other being that of blacksmiths'
hammers producing precise pitches when struck against an-
vils. Compare Theon, *Exposition,* 57.1–58.12 Hiller; Macrobius,
On the Dream of Scipio 2.1.9–14; Boethius, *On Music* 1.10–11.

46–55   The fourth tract ("On Numbers"), continuing with treatment of
the *leimma* (47–50) before returning to the psychogony (51–54),
and with a brief first reflection on Genesis (55).

47   *semitone . . . called a leimma:* See note on 45.

50   *243:256:* See note on 36b.

    Timaeus . . . a follower of Pythagoras's teaching: See note on 20a.

51–55   See note on 27–31.

51   Empedocles, DK 31 B 109.

53   *Being [essentia], or Substance [substantia]:* See note on 27.

54   *of the natural and rational soul:* Latin *naturalis (et rationabilis item
animae). Naturalis* evidently stems from a misreading of Greek
physikê for *phytikê* ("vegetative" - *stirpea,* 31). Compare note on
182.

55   *a sect . . . more holy and wise:* Latin *secta* is the equivalent of Greek
hairesis. Here it targets the notion of a religious "sect," whereas
in 343 it targets that of a philosophical "school"; neither passage coveys any hint of the notion of "heresy," but both reflect
Calcidius's understanding of philosophy as embracing revealed
wisdom, and vice-versa. The Old Testament is a recurrent
point of reference for Calcidius, who elsewhere mentions "the
Hebrews" or "Hebraic philosophy" (130, 132, 171, 219, 256, 276,

300), Moses (154, 276), Solomon (276), Prophets (126 ["Egyptian"], 172, 275 [unspecified], 278), Scripture (277), and Philo (278). On Calcidius's point(s) of contact with the tradition, see Bakhouche, *Calcidius,* 668 n. 290.

the insufflation: See note on 26.

the harmonic, arithmetic, and geometrical ratios: See note on E4/7.

56–97   The fifth tract ("On the Fixed and Wandering Stars"), the longest and most elaborate of those that make up the first part of the commentary. Exegesis of 36b–37c provides the framing (56–58, 92–97), while the middle section (59–91) runs parallel to Theon of Smyrna (*Exposition,* 120.1–98.8 Hiller; see note on 32–91).

57   Plato, *Phaedrus* 245c–246a.

66   *called the horizôn in Greek:* From *horizein,* to "separate," "bound," or "divide"; compare Cicero, *On Divination* 2.44.92; Seneca, *Natural Questions* 5.17.2–3; Theon, *Exposition,* 131.4–9 Hiller.

   the poet: Virgil, *Georgics* 1.243.

68   *smaller than this so-called midzodiacal circle:* Latin *circuli huius ipsius qui inter signa medius vocatur breviores.* At 37a Calcidius converts a Greek partitive genitive to the Latin ablative of comparison; here, by contrast, he *fails* to convert a Greek comparative genitive (*tou dia mesou,* Theon, *Exposition,* 133.24–25 Hiller) to the Latin ablative of comparison (*circulo hoc ipso*). Compare *LSS* §75, *Zus.*e; and notes on 37d, 286.

69   *the poles:* Latin *poli,* evidently for the Greek adjective *polloi* ("many," Theon, *Exposition,* 134.1 Hiller - *multae*), a case of phonetic interference involving iotacism (*-loi* ~ *-li*). Compare notes on 40a (*peri* ~ *per*), 26 (*archê* ~ *arx*); and on iotacism, Note on the Text.

70   *Venus departing:* Latin *Veneris . . . discedens,* a grammatically impossible combination of the genitive and nominative. The mistake is understandable when viewed against its probable Greek background, for in Theon's *ho de tês Aphroditês* ("the X of Venus"), the definite article compensates for the ellipsis of "planet" or "star" (*Exposition,* 137.5 Hiller). Compare 66, where in the face of the same pattern of omission, Calcidius translates *Phae-*

non idemque Saturni ("Phaenon the X of Saturn," see Theon, *Exposition,* 130.22 Hiller), but then follows with two simple genitives *(Phaethon Iovis . . . Lucifer Veneris).* See further at note on 31.

71   *akronychos:* The "peak point" *(akro-)* of the night *(nyx,* compare Theon, *Exposition,* 137.13–15 Hiller).

Dog Star: Sirius.

72   *Moon . . . Mercury . . . Venus . . . Sun . . . Mars . . . Jupiter . . . Saturn:* The "Chaldaean" as opposed to "Egyptian" (73) order (Bakhouche, *Calcidius,* 683–85 nn. 387, 397).

Alexander of Miletus: Alexander Polyhistor (born ca. 110/105 BCE), teacher of Hyginus and author of works on Pythagorean lore and ancient philosophical successions *(RE* 1.2.1451). Theon attributes the same lines to Alexander of Aetolia, a third-century BCE poet and contemporary of Aratus *(Exposition,* 138.19 Hiller). The favored candidate for authorship of the verses appears however to be Alexander of Ephesus, a contemporary of Cicero and author of an astronomical poem in the Pythagorean tradition *(RE* 1.2.1448). If Calcidius followed Theon, then we have to wonder how he arrived at the Milesian attribution; it may be significant that certain manuscripts omit *Milesius.* Compare note on 110.

the Cyllenian: Mercury.

The . . . Cytherean: Venus.

the Mighty in Arms: Mars.

Phaethon's: Jupiter's.

73   *harmonic ratio . . . celestial bodies:* See note on 95–96.

to its flywheels: Assuming Latin *verticillus* rather than *verticula,* and that *fusus* ~ Greek *sphondylos* ("spindle," Plato, *Republic* 616c).

74–75   *of the nonwandering sphere . . . of the aplanês:* See note on 47c.

76   *the ancient verse:* Empedocles, DK 31 B 121.2.

83   *it ignorantly misapprehends:* Latin *sine intellectu et recordatione;* see note on 47a.

84   Aristotle, *On the Heavens* (2.8?), according to Theon *(Exposition,* 178.3 Hiller), although the exposition here is riddled with confusion.

85 *and around this center as its proper axis:* Latin *per (quam medietatem velut axem proprium);* literally, "through" (which center, etc.), a probable point of confusion between Greek *peri* and Latin *per* (note *peri . . . dia,* Theon, *Exposition,* 190.4–6 Hiller). See note on 40a.

91 *So much for these matters . . . let us now come to the text:* Compare 137–38, 321.

92 *of the nonwandering sphere . . . of the aplanês:* See note on 47c.

93 *around which the circle of the meridian revolves:* Latin *per (quam meridialis circulus volvitur);* literally, "through" (which the circle, etc.), a probable point of confusion between Greek *peri* and Latin *per.* See note on 40a.

Homer, *Iliad* 12.239.

95–96 *seven planetary orbits . . . musical intervals:* The numerical series 1, 2, 3, 4, 8, 9, 27 (35b–c) is here aligned with the planetary series Moon, Sun, Venus, Mercury, Mars, Jupiter, Saturn with reference to the harmonic ratios of the octave (2:1), fifth (3:2), fourth (4:3), whole tone (9:8), and octave + fifth (3:1), as follows: **1** (2:1) **2** (3:2) **3** (4:3) **4** (2:1) **8** (9:8) **9** (3:1) **27** = **Moon** (octave) **Sun** (fifth) **Venus** (fourth) **Mercury** (octave) **Mars** (whole tone) **Jupiter** (octave + fifth) **Saturn.** Compare 73, 267.

95 Plato, *Republic* 617b.

The aplanês . . . will be the rational part . . . the planets will be . . . the spirited and appetitive parts: See notes on E1, 182.

98–118 This sixth tract ("On the Heaven") brings the first part of the commentary to a close, and its continuity with what precedes gives the thematic division a certain appearance of artificiality. At 28b Calcidius put *caelum* ("heaven") and *mundus* ("world") into place as renderings of Greek *ouranos* and *kosmos;* 36e now stimulates an effort to focus on the former (98), which, however, has been active since 59.

98 *oranos:* Compare Plato, *Cratylus* 396b–c, with others thereafter (Waszink, *Studien,* 53–57; Moreschini, *Calcidio,* 710–11 n. 152; Bakhouche, *Calcidius,* 705 n. 628). Calcidius's meaning is obscure. The possibilities would appear to be: Greek *horan + anô* ("to gaze on high"); Latin *ora + non* ("nonborder" or "-limit"); or perhaps hybrids compounded from either Greek *horan +*

Latin *non* ("to see-not") or Latin *ora* + Greek *anô* (the "border" or "limit on high"). The second seems particularly improbable, but none is entirely satisfactory. Compare note on *bicori,* 243.

100   Compare Theon, *Exposition,* 187.14–88.7.

101   *of thought and intellection:* Latin *cogitationis recordationisque;* see note on 47a.

107   *our discussion of the natural order:* See note on 127.

110   *Heraclides of Pontus:* Bakhouche detects the misattribution and athetizes *Ponticus* (*Calcidius,* 712–14 n. 691). It has been restored only in consideration of uncertainties attending the source of the error (Calcidius, a later editor or copyist). Compare note on 72.

     showed that: Latin *demonstravit ut (fiat);* see note on 27c.

115   *twenty-nine days:* The inverval here, as opposed to the twenty-seven (and a third) days specified in 70 and 114, is tied to the cycle of lunar phases relative to solar movement along the ecliptic.

119–201   The seventh tract ("On the Four Kinds of Living Beings"), and second longest of the commentary. Broadly speaking, the first part of the commentary was devoted to explanation of the mathematical proportions and means that form the basis for the "bonds" that give unity to the world, from the domain of the four elements to that of the outermost heaven. The second part now proceeds according to a kind of principle of plenitude, on the understanding that the universe must be "full and complete" (119), with no part of it "left deserted" (130). The world, in other words, must now be suitably populated with living beings in every quarter. Hence this tract, especially with its attention to demons and fate, furnishes the linkage between the universe, or Macrocosm (8–118), and mankind, or Microcosm (202–67), which will occupy center stage until the advent of the great treatise on Matter (268–355). It is in five sections:

     1. Exegesis, 40b–d: 119–26
     2. Excursus on demons: 127–36 (40d–e)
     3. Exegesis, 41a–e: 137–41

4. Subtreatise on fate: 142–90 (41d–43a)

5. Exegesis, 42a–e: 191–201

119   *the terrestrial:* Grouping the aerial, aquatic, and earthbound together, as at Ps.-Plato, *Epinomis* 981c–d. Compare 130.

120   *the angelic nature . . . demons:* See 127–36.

       beyond the contemplation of nature: See note on 127.

122   Plato, *Phaedrus* 247a.

123   *guardian and craftsman:* "And craftsman" as in the Greek, but omitted from the continuous translation (40c).

       Hesiod, *Theogony* 116–17.

       hylê . . . silva: See note on 7.

124   *obstacles:* Omitted from the continuous translation (40c).

125–26   *Homer . . . Canicula . . . prophets of the Egyptians . . . Ach: Iliad* 22.26–31.

126   *Homer . . . Egyptian: Iliad* 1.1–7. Traditions that traced Homer back to Thebes in Boeotia would naturally have bred confusion with Thebes in Upper Egypt, especially wherever there was a will to find an inspired "theologian" in Homer; any knowledge of the ancient Alexandrian editions and commentaries would probably have tended to fuel speculation concerning Homer and Egypt as well. For similar reasons, and no doubt also because of the tale of Solon at 21e–25d, Plato himself was believed to have studied in Egypt (Apuleius, *On Plato and His Doctrine* 1.3; DL 3.6–7). On Calcidius and Homer, see R. Lamberton, *Homer the Theologian. Neoplatonist Allegorical Reading and the Growth of the Epic Tradition* (Berkeley, Los Angeles, and London, 1986), 250–56.

       another recorded tale: Matthew 2:1–2, Calcidius's sole express allusion to the New Testament. Although the concluding apostrophe to Osius ("better known to you") implicitly acknowledges the latter's Christianity, Calcidius plays his own cards close to the chest. It is not clear, for example, whether the closing "than to others" (possibly "*the* others," or "the rest") targets Christians, pagans, or both; and "Chaldaean" Magi are no less reminiscent of Numenius (fr. 1a–c des Places) or Porphyry (fr.

324 Smith; *Life of Pythagoras* 6, 11) than of Clement of Alexandria, who similarly traces Homer back to Egypt while also speaking of a circumcised Pythagoras as foreshadowing the Church (*Miscellanies* 1.15.66.1–3). Compare A. Momigliano, *Alien Wisdom. The Limits of Hellenization* (Cambridge, 1975), 142–49; Boys-Stones, *Post-Hellenistic Philosophy*, 105–14, 188–200.

127–36 Calcidius enters into an excursus on the nature of demons (128–36), which is prefaced by a brief exegesis of 40d–e (127). Particularly noteworthy is his use of the Ps.-Platonic *Epinomis*, especially 984b–5c, which he, like others before him, refers to under the title, *The Philosopher* (128, 254). With the *Epinomis*, Calcidius reads the Aristotelian fifth element of ether into Plato's doctrine, which in turn drives his postulation of a fifth class of ethereal beings beyond the four mentioned at 39e–40a (compare 119). Calcidius occasionally departs from both Plato and the *Epinomis*, for example, in positing demonic beings as means analogous to those required to bind the body of the universe together (131). Although such points of divergence are sometimes explained as reflecting Porphyrian influence, there is no firm evidence for the view (Tarán, *Academica*, 159).

127 *epoptic:* Greek *epoptikos*, "of or pertaining to the highest mysteries." The underlying distinction is between what may otherwise be termed "theology," or metaphysics (120, 264), and "natural philosophy," or physics (107, 119, 264), which in 272 are linked with the *Parmenides* and *Timaeus*, respectively. See further van Winden, *Calcidius on Matter*, 44–45; den Boeft, *Calcidius on Demons*, 12; Moreschini, *Calcidio*, 717–18 n. 231; Bakhouche, *Calcidius*, 729–30 n. 51.

these powers . . . thought to be gods: Thought by Moreschini to be an indication of Calcidius's Christianity (*Calcidio*, 718 n. 232). Compare note on 133.

the tradition of Pythagoras's "having pronounced": Cicero, *On the Nature of the Gods* 1.5.10; DL 8.46.

Pythagoras's . . . Orpheus's, Linus's . . . Musaeus's: See note on 143.

128 *a liberal education:* See note on E4/7.

for further inquiry: Literally, "its being (further) inquired into" (*quaeri*); compare 47a and note on 40e.

130   *the extreme limits are filled with living beings befitting their nature:*
The extreme limits, that is, are filled with living beings that are adapted to the nature of the regions so delimited. The phrases, *id est summus atque imus,* and, *scilicet ratione utentibus,* have been athetized as probable glosses. If authentic, the latter would suggest a different sense: "the extreme limits are filled with living beings, namely, rational ones, naturally befitting them." It looks, however, as though *scilicet ratione utentibus* ("namely, rational ones") was later added in order to draw out the implications of *stellis* and *hominibus* ("with stars . . . with human beings"), and *id est summus atque imus* ("i.e., the highest and lowest [limits]") in order to explain *extimi* ("extreme"). See further at note on 45d.

to suppose . . . that human beings: Literally, (that human beings should) "be supposed" (*putari,* note *existimari . . . putare,* before and after); see note on 40e.

the Hebrews: Genesis 1:16–17.

132   *"demons" . . . daêmones:* Plato, *Cratylus,* 398b, with others thereafter (den Boeft, *Calcidius on Demons,* 30; Moreschini, *Calcidio,* 720–21 n. 256; Bakhouche, *Calcidius,* 734 n. 85).

reporting . . . "angels": From Greek *aggellein,* "to announce" or "report."

the creator and preserver of all things: Latin *creator omnium et conservator.* Insofar as Calcidius is focusing on a view presumed to be shared by Hebrews, Greeks, Romans, and barbarians alike, the expression would appear to have no specifically Christian resonance but rather to evoke a more general doctrine of "common notions" or universally received truths. See further at note on 42e; Moreschini, *Calcidio,* 721 n. 261; Bakhouche, *Calcidius,* 735 n. 89.

133   The final passage addressed directly to Osius (see note on E4). Calcidius seeks to allay concerns over the fact that evil as well as good beings belong to the class designated as "angels" (Hebrew usage, 132), that being the point that introduces the parenthetical "as you know perfectly well." He then reverses strategy, in asserting the same point in connection with "demons"

(Greek usage). Hence the first sentence implies a square of opposition:

Angel — — — — — — — — — —Demon
Good — — — — — — — — — — —Evil

with four logical possibilities (good angels, evil angels, good demons, evil demons). Osius "knows perfectly well" that there
are evil as well as holy angels, from which it follows (*igitur*) that
there are good as well as evil demons (compare 135). Calcidius,
in other words, may be appealing to Osius from across the
Hebrew-Greek divide in connection with what is in any case
assumed to be a point of universal agreement (132)—at any
rate, it is a very different emphasis from that expressed by Augustine at *City of God* 10.9 (demons counterfeiting as "angels").
As den Boeft observes, the veil enshrouding Osius's identity is
to some degree lifted here (*Calcidius on Demons,* 34), and something of Calcidius is perhaps revealed as well; see however note
on 127.

pleasure . . . pain . . . repulsion: Latin *voluptas, tristitia, odium.* See
note on 194.

134   *"Hades" . . . aidês:* Plato, *Phaedo* 80d, *Cratylus* 403a, *Gorgias* 493b,
with others thereafter (den Boeft, *Calcidius on Demons,* 37–38;
Bakhouche, *Calcidius,* 737 n. 101). The intended Greek form
(*aidês, haid-, aeid-*) is uncertain.

    Hesiod, *Works and Days* 252–53.

135   *ancients . . . malign soul:* Compare 172, 297.

136   Empedocles, DK 31 B 115.5; Ps.-Pythagoras, *Golden Verses* 70–71;
Plato, *Republic* 615e–16a.

137–38   *So much for the nature of demons . . . the language of the text:* Compare 91, 321.

138   *The conceit of the dialogue . . . a drama:* See note on 8–25.
    an "inevitable decree": See 143–44.

139   *the father . . . not of their being, but of their coming to be:* Compare
"the most eminent living being is that which of itself bestows
being upon all other celestial ones while also cultivating another far more eminent one in whom the origin of things resides," 191.

by which he says the rational power . . . is called: Latin *cognomentum vocat rationis potentiam;* evidently, for *legomenon hêgemonoun* and omitted from the continuous translation (41c). Plato's terminology influenced what the Stoics subsequently labeled the *hêgemonikon,* or commanding faculty of the soul (*SVF* 2.834–49 [LS 53F]), which in turn shaped later Platonist accounts, such as Calicidius's (compare 156, 213, 220). See further, Moreschini, *Calcidio,* 725 n. 302; Bakhouche, *Calcidius,* 743–44 nn. 139–40.

142–90 A subtreatise (*tractatus,* 142, 190) on providence, fate, and free will, occasioned by the laws of destiny laid down at 41e–42d but also fueled by an effort to construct a Platonic refutation of Stoic determinism. Although the ancient Stoa was essentially a faded memory by Calcidius's day, Stoic thought had long since penetrated the main philosophical traditions, by which it was in turn reshaped; it is therefore unsurprising that much of what Calcidius has to say about Stoic doctrines reflects intellectual currents of the second century CE rather than third century BCE. That the problem of fate in particular continued to fascinate is evident from the extant works of Cicero, Alexander of Aphrodisias, St. Augustine, and (much later) Boethius, among others. Caldidius's treatment contains interesting points of correspondence with two works in particular, Ps.-Plutarch, *On Fate,* and Nemesius, *On the Nature of Man.* It is in six sections:

1. Introduction: 142
2. Exegesis, 41d–43a: 143–47
3. Platonic doctrine (1): 148–59
4. Stoic criticisms, Platonic responses: 160–75
5. Platonic doctrine (2): 176–89
6. Conclusion: 190

143–44 Plato, *Phaedrus* 248c; *Republic* 617d. *Scitum inevitabile* ("inevitable decree") translates *thesmos Adrasteias,* the "law of Adrastea," the one from whom "one cannot run." On the order, Atropos—Clotho—Lachesis, see den Boeft, *Calcidius on Fate,* 11–13; Bakhouche, *Calcidius,* 747 n. 164.

143   *not in the tragic style . . . the theologians:* Similarly 296, and Ps.-Plutarch, *On Fate* 568d. Calcidius presumably means figures such as Orpheus, Linus, Musaeus, Homer, Hesiod, Pythagoras, the Chaldaeans, Moses, Solomon, and the Prophets (123, 126–27, 154, 172, 276, 278).

144   *the nonwandering sphere:* See note on 47c.

    providence and fate . . . Chrysippus . . . Cleanthes: SVF 1.551 = 2.933 (LS 54U).

    fate . . . a series of causes: Again in 175; compare SVF 2.917–21 (LS 55J).

146   *the creator of things:* See note on 42e.

147   *fate . . . from providence . . . providence . . . not from fate:* Compare Ps.-Plutarch, *On Fate* 573b; Nemesius, *On the Nature of Man* 38.304; Boethius, *Consolation* 4.6.14.

148   *moral, natural, and logical disputes:* Intimating a traditional division of Philosophy into Ethics, Physics, and Logic. Compare Aristotle, *Topics* 105b20–21; Cicero, *Academica* 1.5.19; Sextus Empiricus, *Against Learned Men* 7.16; DL 1.18, 7.39; and note on 264–65.

149   *an "inevitable decree":* See 143–44.

150   *from some premise . . . according to a premise:* Latin *ex aliqua praecessione . . . secundum praecessionem.* The term *praecessio* ("premise") is difficult, especially given the geometrical analogy, to render in English but has a certain "Stoic coloring" suggesting the first point in a causal chain (Bakhouche, *Calcidius,* 752 n. 195); to complicate matters, the prepositions *ex* ("from") and *secundum* ("according to") appear to be reversed applications of the Greek *kata* ("according to") and *ek* ("from"), respectively, as used by Nemesius, *On the Nature of Man* 38.304 (den Boeft, *Calcidius on Fate,* 27). Like Nemesius, however, Calcidius has both prepositions governing a single term, whereas Ps.-Plutarch pits "from an hypothesis" *(ex hypotheseôs)* against "according to fate" *(kath' heimarmenên, On Fate* 569d–70e). The theory is one of entailment: the law of fate decrees that, if X is chosen (enacted), then Y will inevitably follow. The decree (consequence) is universally applicable but preconditions the premise in no indi-

vidual case; hence the rewards or punishments it entails constitute no violation of human autonomy (179). This holds also in connection with decrees issuing from oracles (153–54, 170–71).

151   *situated in us . . . within our control:* Latin *in nobis posita . . . penes nos* (- Greek *eph' hêmin*); compare Aristotle, *Nicomachean Ethics* 1113b6; *SVF* 2.979 (LS 62G); Cicero, *On Fate* 17.40.

152   *the words of the . . . law:* Plato, *Phaedrus* 248c; compare Ps.-Plutarch, *On Fate* 570a.

153   *the prediction . . . given by Apollo:* Euripides, *Phoenician Women* 18–20 = PW 2.65–66 (148).

154   *Thetis . . . Plato . . . Moses:* Scholium to Homer, *Iliad* 16.37; *Republic* 617e; Genesis 2:17.

155–56   Compare Ps.-Plutarch, *On Fate* 571b–d.

156   *ruling principle . . . assent . . . impulse . . . imagination:* Latin *principale, assensus, appetitus, imaginatio* (- Greek *to hêgemonikon* [see note on 139], *sugkatathesis, hormê, phantasia*). Compare *SVF* 2.836 (LS 53H).

157   *law . . . ordains virtue and forbids its contrary:* Again in 180; compare Cicero, *Laws* 1.6.18; *SVF* 3.314–15.

158   *He says that . . . fortune . . . chance:* A unique glimpse into Calcidius's interaction with an otherwise undetectable source, in that the verb "says" has no stated or implied subject. The thought is Aristotelian (*Physics* 197a36–b22) but almost certainly distilled from or by an intermediary (compare Ps.-Plutarch, *On Fate* 572b–e; Nemesius, *On the Nature of Man* 39.312).

160–75   This section is devoted to silencing the perceived threat of certain Stoic doctrines. It is philosophically one of the most complex sections of the commentary, consisting of a layered assemblage of material drawn from different traditions; and that it is far removed from ancient Stoicism as such is clear, not only from the fact that the Stoics themselves are named only once (165), but that 172–75 anticipate Numenian material that resurfaces toward the end of the commentary, once again on the heels of Stoic doctrine (289–99). For detailed assessments of Calcidius's treatment, see den Boeft, *Calcidius on Fate,* 47–84; Moreschini, *Calcidio,* 731–35 nn. 381–419; Bakhouche, *Calcidius,*

COMMENTARY

759–71 nn. 253–346. Also important are S. Bobzien, *Determinism and Freedom in Stoic Philosophy* (Oxford, 1998); Reydams-Schils, *Demiurge and Providence.*

160   *Aristides:* An Athenian statesman and soldier (born ca. 520 BCE) whose honesty was rewarded with ostracization and, apparently, an impoverished old age (172).

161   Cofated causes and the "lazy argument"; *SVF* 2.956–58 (LS 55S).

164   *apart, perhaps, . . . for being fortunate:* Latin *nisi forte putatur beatus;* awkwardly intrusive, if not an interpolation (compare the "Nisifortinus" glossator, or *i²* hand, of Eriugena's *Periphyseon*).

       and the other virtues: Prudence and courage; Plato, *Laws* 631c–d; *SVF* 3.262–65, 280 (LS 61C–H); Cicero, *On Duties* 1.5.15.

165   *perversion:* Latin *perversio* (- Greek *diastrophê*); otherwise, *perversitas* (175, 297–98), *depravatio* (172), *dementia* (174). Compare *SVF* 3.228–36.

166   *the power to do what they want . . . a royal animal:* Compare Plato, *Gorgias* 466b–e; *SVF* 3.617–22 (LS 67M).

168   *a liberal education:* See note on E4/7.

       Socrates . . . "accompanied . . . by a demon": See note on 255.

169   *as in . . . Apollo's:* Aristotle, *Rhetoric* 1407a38 = PW 2.24 (53).

170   *the oracle:* Herodotus, *Histories* 7.148.3 = PW 2.40 (92).

171   *the Hebrews:* Deuteronomy 6:3, 11:9.

       an "inevitable decree": See 143–44.

172–75 These chapters are closely aligned with 295–99: both sections raise the question of the origin of evil in precisely the same terms (*unde mala,* 174, 297); 174 refutes a view of the "celestial substance" as "degenerating" from its nature and giving rise to evil, while 295 refutes a "Pythagorean" view of unity as "receding" or "migrating" from its nature and generating duality; 172 and 174 tax a view that makes fate or the "celestial substance" indiscriminately good and evil, while 296–97 target a "Stoic" view of matter as indifferent (neither good nor evil); and both sections target a ("Stoic") notion of perversion as explanatory of evil (see note on 165). It seems probable, in other words, that these chapters represent another Numenian attack on a Stoicizing Pythagoreanism of some sort.

743

172 *Aristides . . . Prophets:* For Aristides, see note on 160; for the Prophets, possibly Isaiah and Jeremiah.

173–74 Compare Sextus Empiricus, *Outlines of Pyrrhonism* 3.10–11; Lactantius, *On the Anger of God* 13.19–21 (Epicurus, fr. 374 Usener); Plotinus, *Enneads* 1.8, 2.3; Augustine, *Confessions* 3.7.12, 7.3.4; Boethius, *Consolation* 1.4.30, 4.1.5.

175 *would be iniquitous and indeed libidinous:* The Latin adjectives *(iniquus, libidinosus)* do not agree in gender with the word for "reason" *(ratio),* leaving the verb "be" without an obvious subject. The interpretation offered here is based on two considerations: (1) Calcidius is mounting a counterfactual refutation of the Stoic hypothesis: If (he says) their principle of Reason is indeed the cause of everything, then it is also the cause of evil; but (they would agree) reason cannot be the cause of evil; therefore their principle of Reason is not the cause of everything. The difficulty arises from the manner in which Calcidius lands, immediately before the phrase under consideration, on the rhetorically charged observation that evil is irrational: given the existence of evil, the Stoics would do better to admit that their principle of Reason is *no reason at all.* Hence the emendation to *esset* ("would be"), for *est* ("is"); (2) The understood subject of *esset* is therefore the Stoic principle of Reason, but Calcidius either forgets that Greek *logos* is, unlike Latin *ratio,* masculine in gender or perhaps has in mind a class of Greek adjectives whose masculine and feminine forms are identical in the nominative singular.

 inevitable series of causes: See note on 144.

176–77 The hierarchy articulated here and in 188–89 is essentially tripartite, consisting of God, Mind, and Soul under varying descriptions (Supreme God/Good, Second God, Providence, divine Will, Nous, Intellect, Fate, Second Mind, Third God, World Soul) and entailing a number of lower powers (Souls, Nature, Fortune, Chance, Demons). The terminological fluidity is a reflection of the fact that Calcidius is describing a "cascading view of providence" (Reydams-Schills) rather than articulating a static system of metaphysical hypostases. Points of connection with Numenius, Alcinous, Plutarch, Ps.-Plutarch,

COMMENTARY

and the *Chaldaean Oracles* are suggestive of a "Middle Platonic" orientation of some sort, while the reference to conversion *may* evoke a "Neoplatonic" one (as well). Such classifications are however rather unenlightening in the case of Calcidius, who inhabits a philosophical territory very much his own. See further den Boeft, *Calcidius on Fate*, 85–100, 118–22; Reydams-Schils, "Calcidius on God"; Bakhouche, *Calcidius*, 771–75 nn. 347–69, 781–82 nn. 410–16.

176   the ... Good "beyond all being": Plato, *Republic* 509b.

to say anything further: Literally, (for anything further) "to be said" *(dici)*; see note on 40e.

that Supreme God which the Greeks call Nous: Latin *illum summum ... quem noyn Graeci vocant*. The antecedent of *quem* may how-ever be *providentia*: "ruled by Providence, which is second in preeminence to that Supreme God and which the Greeks call *Nous*." Compare *angelicae naturae quos daemonas vocat*, 120 (as op-posed to *potestatum quae daemones nuncupantur*, 40d).

178   Plato, *Phaedrus* 246e–47a.

179   the law is that: Latin *lex est ut (afficiatur)*; see note on 27c. Note the contrast with constructions involving more explicitly for-mulated limiting or stipulative conditions, as for example in Caesar, *Civil War* 1.32.3 *(latum ... ut ... haberetur)*, or Boethius, *Consolation* 2.m3.17–18 *(positumque lege est ut constet)*.

180   ordaining virtue ... and forbidding its contrary: See note on 157.

182   nourishment ... sense perception ... reason ... cupidity ... irascibility: Latin *nutriri, sentire, ratio, cupiditas, iracundia*, combining two traditional divisions of the soul. One is Aristotelian, targeting the soul's vegetative, sentient, and rational functions (Greek *threptikon, aisthêtikon, [dia]noêtikon, On the Soul* 413b12–13; *Parts of Animals* 641b5–7; Boethius, *On Porphyry's Isagoge*, II 1.1); the other is Platonic, targeting its appetitive, spirited, and ratio-nal elements *(epithumêtikon, thumos, logistikon, Republic* 439d–e). The latter is frequently invoked by Calcidius (95, 183, 187, 223, 225, 229, 233, 249, 267), whose terminology recalls Cicero *(Tus-culan Disputations* 1.10.20) and Apuleius *(On Plato and His Doc-trine* 1.18, 2.6) while anticipating Macrobius *(On the Dream of Scipio* 1.6.42) and Boethius *(Arithmetic* 1.32.1).

745

183   Homer, *Odyssey* 20.17–18; Euripides, *Medea* 1078–79.

184   Terence, *Eunuchus* 46–49.

188–89 See note on 176–77.

189   *Souls that have neglected God's retinue:* Plato, *Phaedrus* 248c.

        by being in accordance with it: Ellipsis of *sunt* after *quae secundum eandem.*

191   *the most eminent living being . . . bestows being:* See note on 139.

194   *pleasure . . . pain . . . desire . . . hope . . . irascibility . . . fear:* Latin *voluptas, dolor, cupiditas, spes, ira(cundia), formido.* Pleasure (Greek *hêdonê*), pain ("distress," *lupê*), hope ("appetite," *epithumia*), and fear *(phobos)* correspond to the four Stoic cardinal passions (*SVF* 3.378–94 [LS 65A]), while desire and irascibility reflect the Platonic tripartite soul (see note on 182). Compare Boethius, *Consolation* 1.m7.25–28.

197   Empedocles, DK 31 B 117, 136–37.

        of abstaining: Literally, (of its) "being abstained" *(abstineri);* see note on 40e.

198   *to its lingering defects:* Latin *ad vitiorum reliquias;* compare 45e *(motuum reliquiis)* and 249 on a similar psychosomatic pathology.

        The prospect of human souls inhabiting animal bodies is ruled out on grounds of the impossibility of their exercising any rightful "return" through repentance. Since the lion and wolf are incapable of moral deliberation, Calcidius is as unwilling to allow human (rational) souls into their bodies as he is to allow unity to "migrate" to duality (295). This contradicts Plato, who grants the possibility of return for those souls "who were once human beings" (*Phaedrus* 249b; compare *Republic* 620d), and raises the question of whether Calcidius restricts the transmigration of human souls to movement between human bodies, as Porphyry does (fr. 300 Smith), or takes a metaphorical view of metempsychosis, as Boethius does (*Consolation* 4.3.15–21). See further *Hermetic Corpus* 10.19; Nemesius, *On the Nature of Man* 2.117–19 (Iamblichus).

200   *in other books:* Compare Ps.-Timaeus of Locri, *On the Soul, World, and Nature* 99d; Plato, *Laws* 904c–e.

202–7   The eighth tract ("On the Origin of Mankind"), emphasizing

the notion of man as Microcosm (202), and with faint indications of a doxographical tradition resembling those at work in other parts of the commentary (203).

202 *the world in miniature:* See note on E1; also, Bakhouche, *Calcidius,* 788–89 n. 479.

203 *Diodorus . . . Axaxagoras . . . Democritus and Leucippus . . . Empedocles . . . the Stoics:* Compare Ps.-Galen, *History of Philosophy* 18; Aëtius 1.3.27; and notes on 279, 282.

204 *dissolution and dissipation for their nature:* Latin *naturae suae dissolutionem dissipationemque;* here taking *suae* as an indirect reflexive referring back to *corporibus,* although Calcidius may be thinking in terms of a Greek instrumental dative *têi physei* ("which . . . by their nature threatened dissolution and dissipation"). See further at note on 45d.

206 Plato, *Laws* 666a.

208–35 The ninth tract ("The Reasons Why a Good Many Human Beings are Wise and the Rest Unwise"), the title of which conceals what is in effect a discussion of the soul, building on the "psychogony" (208) in the first part of the commentary (26–39). The treatment is in three parts:

1. Exegesis, 43e–44e: 208–13
2. Doxographical review of those who hold that soul is:
    a. Corporeal:
        (1) Discrete: 214–17 (Asclepiades, Democritus, Epicurus)
        (2) Continuous: 218–21 (Empedocles, "the Hebrews," Stoics)
    b. Incorporeal: 222–30 (Aristotle, Plato)
3. Exegesis, 44d–45a: 231–35

The method of analysis is clearly related to the one applied in 268–355 (note "those who held that the substance of matter [*silvae*] is discrete," 214), with the Stoics once again as a point of concerted attack.

208–9 Aristotle, *Protrepticus* fr. 17 Ross; *Physics* 184b12–14.

211 *That the one who resists . . . will be crippled:* The received text gives

the sense, "Therefore the one who resists instruction . . . will have a crippled life, [and] it is beyond doubt that the soul of the one who possesses . . . will also be crippled." However, Calcidius is explaining the neglect of either body or soul as the third of three possibilities, that is, as a *single* "certainty" consisting of two parts. The emendation assumes that the words, *ergo . . . procul dubio,* reflect a common Greek idiom (*hoti men oun . . . dêlon* or *phaneron,* "that X is the case . . . is therefore clear"), the first element of which (*Quod - Hoti*) was lost in the course of transmission, and that *procul dubio* governs two constructions at once (*habebit, fore*). Compare 37c (*Quae quidem . . . palam est*); 114 (*Diversa natura quae sit, saepe iam ostensum est in superioribus, quodque motus eius ab occidente ad orientem feratur*).

213   *principle part of the soul . . . hêgemonikon:* See note on 139.

214   *soporific:* - Greek *karôtikos.*

215   *smooth:* Latin *lêves;* but possibly *leves* ("light," "fleet").

      So it happens that . . . we move: A consecutive clause with verbs in the indicative (*spuunt, oscitant*) and infinitive (*recordari, moveri*) moods, and *Unde* ("so it happens that") assuming the role of Greek *hôste.* The result is a hybrid construction mimicking Greek clauses of both actual and natural result (see note on 43e).

218   Empedocles, DK 31 B 105.3, 109.1–2.

219   *"the blood of your brother . . . sons of . . . god":* Genesis 2:7, 4:10, 9:4; Leviticus 17:11; Deuteronomy 12:23; Psalm 81:6; Matthew 5:9; Luke 20:36; John 10:34. Compare notes on 26, 55.

      as they ought to be, such that: Latin *ita . . . ut,* somewhere between a correlative ("as they ought to be") and consecutive construction ("in such a way that," with the infinitive *esse;* see note on 43e).

220   *SVF* 1.138 = 2.879 (LS 53G).

221   *SVF* 2.796.

222–26   The Aristotelian or Peripatetic doctrine of soul (222–24), followed by its Platonic corrective (225–26). Aristotle, *On the Soul* 2.1–2, and Plato, *Phaedrus* 245c–d (compare 57), are central to these chapters, which however draw on an array of material in a manner suggestive of a doxographical tradition, possibly of Peripatetic origin. The discussion begins (222) with a diaeresis

that leads to Aristotle's definition of soul as the "first actuality of a natural body possessed of the capacity for life" (*On the Soul* 412a27–28). Calcidius evinces a harmonizing impulse both here and in 283–88. Aristotle, he claims, got "nearly all points correctly" (225), and his thought is "well suited" to Plato's and so "not to be casually overlooked" (283). In 226, 319, and 336, moreover, he brings the Categories to bear on the problems to hand, using them in 226 to clarify Plato's doctrine while correcting Aristotle's own. Compare notes on E7, 32a.

224   *to such an extent that . . . undergo . . . tolerates:* Latin *usque adeo . . . ut . . . patiantur . . . sustinere,* a consecutive clause with verbs in the subjunctive and infinitive moods, the latter mimicking a Greek clause of natural result (see note on 43e).

226   *as was indicated earlier:* See 40–45.

227   *substance is twofold . . . corporeal . . . incorporeal:* The first bifurcation in the "Porphyrian Tree" (Porphyry, *Introduction* 2.6 [4.21–22 Busse]).

227–28   *it has been demonstrated above . . . the Phaedrus:* See 57.

228   *the craftsman god . . . as it were, fitting it together:* See note on 8–25.

    he does not mean that . . . or that . . . but that: Latin *nec . . . dicit (trahere) nec ut . . . (coeperit) sed quod (habeat);* see note on 27c.

230   *bodily members are . . . assigned:* Latin *membra dimensa sunt,* literally, "measured out" (compare *epitritis . . . dimensis,* 48); compare, however, *membra . . . sunt distributa,* 225.

231   *citadel . . . and palace:* Compare Plato, *Republic* 560b; *Timaeus* 70a, 90a.

231   Plato, *Republic* 533e–34a.

233   Plato, *Republic* 434d–35b, 439d–e; compare Alcinous, *Handbook* 34; and note on E1.

236–48   The tenth tract ("On Vision"), and the first in a series of three devoted to 45b–47d, on the eyes as the first organs of perception fashioned by the lesser deities charged with the formation of mankind. The preeminence of vision is defended on the grounds that it enables the celestial observations that form the basis for our notions of number, time, nature, and philosophy itself; hence the encomium delivered by the twelfth tract. At the end of the series, hearing will emerge as a close second to

vision in that it furnishes the connection to music, which in turn reflects the cosmic harmony governing the movements of the world (267). Chapters 243 and 246 interestingly harken back to a tradition according to which "later interpreters" splintered the unified Truth revealed by Plato (compare note on 249–63).

237   Heraclitus, DK 22 A 16; Stoics, *SVF* 2.863.

the breath, after progressing . . . and gaining . . . once located . . . flows . . . and is broadcast: Violating standard classical syntax, with an identity of subject across the absolute and primary clauses: *Stoici . . . constituunt . . . hoc (spiritu) . . . progresso . . . et . . . opimato . . . (spiritum) locatum fundi . . . dilatarique.* Although consistent with vulgar and late Latin (*LSS* §85.a, *Zus.*β), the construction may also recall certain uses of the Greek genitive absolute.

239   *direct vision . . . reflection . . . transparent vision:* Latin *tuitio* (- *phasis,* "appearance"), *intuitio* (- *emphasis,* "reflection"), *detuitio* (- *paraphrasis,* see 242; Bakhouche, *Calcidius,* 816 n. 716).

240   *will glide crosswise:* See Moreschini, *Calcidio,* 749–50 n. 613; Bakhouche, *Calcidius,* 817 n. 720.

243   *those with double pupils:* Latin *bicori;* otherwise unattested, and presumably an adjectival hybrid (Latin *bi-* + Greek *korê* = "double pupil") related to Greek *dikoros,* which is itself only rarely attested. The translation assumes a triple-termination morphology (*bicorus, -a, -um*) rather than the double termination one indicated by *TLL* (*bicoris, -e);* hence the masculine nominative plural *bicori* (as substantive). Compare note on *oranos,* 98.

the ancients . . . Plato . . . later interpreters . . . extracting parts of the full theory: The thought presumably owes something to Numenius's image of Plato's being torn, like Pentheus, limb from limb by his Hellenistic successors, perhaps also to Clement's image of the one Truth being torn apart by Greek philosophers (Boys-Stones, *Post-Hellenistic Philosophy,* 140, 192–93). It will resurface in Boethius's image of the gown of Philosophy as rent apart by the Hellenistic sects (*Consolation* 1.3.7). Compare 246, 252.

246   *later philosophers . . . carved a . . . complete doctrine up:* See previous
        note; for Alcmaeon, DK 24 A 10. The discussion of medical dis-
        section seems an almost humorous pendant to the image of
        Plato's successors carving his philosophy up into pieces.

247   Plato, *Republic* 508a–d.

249–63 The eleventh tract ("On Images"), with hints of a doxographi-
        cal tradition similar to the one evidently at work in the tenth
        tract, a further reference (252) to the splintering of truth by
        misguided interpreters (see note on 236–48), and a kind of
        minitract (*tractatus,* 250) on dreams. The latter involves a tax-
        onomy (256) that, although much more limited in scope than
        that of Macrobius's *Commentary on the Dream of Scipio* (1.3.1–11),
        is nevertheless of genuine interest. Particularly noteworthy is
        Calcidius's translation of Plato's account of the behavior of the
        unconscious soul during periods of sleep (253).

251   Heraclitus, DK 22 A 20; Stoics, *SVF* 2.1198.

252   *those who wrongly adopt a partial opinion:* See note on 243. The
        metaphor of the winged soul was a commonplace that among
        Platonists owed most to *Phaedrus* 246b–c; Calcidius's target
        here is uncertain. On the chapter division, see Bakhouche, *Cal-
        cidius,* 821 n. 764.

253   Plato, *Republic* 571b–72b.

254   Ps.-Plato, *Epinomis* 984e–85a (see note on 127–36); Plato, *Crito*
        44a–b (Homer, *Iliad* 9.363); *Phaedo* 60e–61b.

255   Plato, *Theages* 128d (not *Euthydemus*); compare *Apology* 31c–d;
        and 168.

257   *reflection:* Latin *intuitio;* see note on 239.

259   *as interpreted above:* See 240.

260   *administer to:* Unless there is a copying error (possibly prompted
        by *famulari . . . famulantur*), the passive *administrentur* here func-
        tions as a deponent or quasi-middle; see note on 40e.
        the noblest work is that which he thinks: See note on 302–4.
        nothing incorporeal . . . acted upon or acts: See note on 319.
        "as when . . . wax liquifies": Virgil, *Eclogue* 8.80–81.

261   *the . . . lover of wisdom:* See note on 20a.

262   Plato, *Laws* 893b–894c.

263   *The lover of wisdom:* See note on 20a.

264–67   The twelfth tract ("In Praise of Vision"), dealing with the function or service provided by vision (264–66), followed by a brief consideration of hearing (267). The section is perhaps of interest chiefly for its taxonomy of the sciences, which throughout the commentary are so closely linked with the theme of a "liberal" education as propaedeutic to the pursuit of philosophy.

264–65   *consideration and action:* The theoretical and practical branches of Philosophy (note the hint of a traditional etymology, "consideration" [*consideratio*] - cognitive alignment [*con-*] with the heavens [*sidera*]). The system mapped out here is essentially Peripatetic and in the West achieved full articulation with Boethius (*On Arithmetic* 1.1; *On Porphyry's Isagoge, I* 1.3; *On the Trinity* 2):

> Philosophy:
>   Practical:
>   Ethics
>   Economics
>   Politics
>   Theoretical:
>   Physics
>   Mathematics
>   Multitude:
>   Arithmetic
>   Music
>   Magnitude:
>   Geometry
>   Astronomy
>   Theology (Metaphysics)

The phrase, "knowledge of how to employ reasoning," targets mathematics but might also be taken as referring to logic, as in a system hinted at in 148 (see further Boethius, *On Porphyry's Isagoge, I* 1.4, *II* 1.3). See further at note on E4/7.

266   Anaxagoras, DK 59 A 1 (DL 2.10); Stoics, *SVF* 2.863 (compare Plutarch, *On Isis and Osiris* 375c); Homer, *Iliad* 3.217, 12.466 (compare Virgil, *Aeneid* 10.447); Cicero, *In Defense of Cluentius*

5.13. The Theophrastus anecdote and third poetic citation (hexameters) are of uncertain origins.

267   *the divine music:* See note on 95–96.

the noblest form of harmony in our character is justice: Possibly, "the noblest form of harmony is justice in our character." The emphasis, however, is on a moral manifestation of cosmic harmony in the human soul (compare note on E1). For "reason" and "irascibility," see note on 182.

268–355 This final tract (*tractatus,* 337), "On Matter," is the longest of all and marks the transition from exploration of the works of Reason to those of Necessity. Its structure is as follows:

I. Exegesis, 47e–52b: 268–75
II. Doxographical review of those who hold that Matter is:
   A. Generated: 276–78 ("the Hebrews," Scripture, Philo)
   B. Ungenerated:
     1. Discrete: 279 (Democritus, Epicurus, Anaxagoras, Diodorus, Stoics)
     2. Continuous:
       a. Possessing form:
         (1) Uniform:
           (a) Mobile: 280 (Thales, Anaximenes, Heraclitus)
           (b) Immobile: 281 (Xenophanes)
             i) Determinate (Parmenides)
             ii) Indeterminate (Melissus)
         (2) Multiform: 282 (Empedocles)
       b. Formless:
         (1) 283–88 (Aristotle)
         (2) 289–94 (Stoics)
         (3) 295–99 (Pythagoras, Numenius)
         (4) 300–20 (Plato)
III. Exegesis, 49a–53c: 321–55

The rigidly dichotomic divisions (mapped out in 275) are designed to reveal pairs of contrarily opposed philosophical positions, and the compression of II.B.1–2.a (279–82) serves to

highlight the fundamental contrast between II.A (276–78), the Biblical doctrine of God as the sole principle of creation, and II.B.2.b (283–320), philosophical doctrines of Matter and God as eternal co-principles. The contrast is further emphasized by the balanced appearances of the Demiurge in 278 and "the Hebrews" in 300. Compare note on 208–35.

268   *hylê . . . silva:* See note on 7.

     the primary substrate: See note on 50d.

270   *Everything . . . that rules . . . over which it rules:* Plato, *Statesman* 297a–b.

272   *"concerns nature" . . . "epoptic":* See note on 127.

273   *new and uncommon . . . from the beginning:* Omitted from the continuous translation (48d–e).

     without a substance to engender them from within itself: Latin *sine suscipiente ex eadem essentia essentia;* literally, "without a substance taking [them] up from the same substance." The translation takes *ex eadem essentia* as standing for *ex se ipsa,* possibly a confused rendering of Greek *ex hautês* (see note on 31). See further Bakhouche, *Calcidius,* 836 n. 882.

     mother, nurse, womb . . . place: Compare 308; Bakhouche, *Calcidius,* 836 n. 883, 862 nn. 1140–44.

     hylê . . . silva: The "later thinkers" are "Plato's students" (308), more precisely, Aristotle (*Physics* 209b11–12; *Metaphysics* 988a7–17). Compare note on 7.

     the intelligible form . . . conceived in his mind: See note on 302–4.

274   *acts as a substrate:* See note on 50d.

     difficult to grasp, to explain and teach . . . far more difficult: See note on E7.

     the varied process of reciprocal analysis from one thing into another: Latin *varia . . . mutua ex alio in aliud resolutione,* with which compare 321–22, *ob inconstantem eorum mutuam ex alio in aliud conversionem . . . ex reciproca de alio in aliud elementorum conversione.* On "analysis" (*resolutio*) as a dialectical method, see 302–3.

276–78   *The Generation of the World:* Genesis 1:1–10. Origen's *Hexapla* was a synoptic compilation of Old Testament versions, in six columns: Hebrew text; Greek transliteration; Greek translations,

of Aquila, Symmachus, the Septuagint (LXX), and Theodotion. Aquila, Symmachus, and Theodotion date to the second century CE. On these chapters, see Köckert, *Christliche Kosmologie,* 229–37; Bakhouche, *Calcidius,* 40–41.

276   *divine inspiration:* See note on 26.

"beginning" has multiple significations: Latin *initium;* compare note on "origin" (*origo*), 26.

Solomon: Proverbs 1:7, 8:22–25, 9:10, 16:7; Ecclesiasticus 29:21.

278   Philo, *On the Creation of the World* 4.15–16, 46.134.

the Greeks call hylê: See note on 7.

God its craftsman . . . its craftsman: See note on 28a.

279   *Democritus and Epicurus . . . Anaxagoras . . . Diodorus . . . Stoics:* Compare Aëtius 1.3.5/18; Aristotle, *Metaphysics* 985b13–15; and note on 203.

280   *Stoics . . . Thales . . . Homer . . . Anaximenes . . . Heraclitus:* SVF 2.321; *Iliad* 14.201, 15.37–38; compare Aristotle, *Metaphysics* 983b18–84a8.

281   *Xenophanes, Melissus, and Parmenides:* Compare Aristotle, *Metaphysics* 984a29–32, 986b10–27.

282   *Empedocles:* Compare Aëtius 1.3.20; and note on 203.

283–88   Aristotle, the first of four philosophers (schools) who maintain that matter is an eternal, formless principle. The section is in two parts, a review of Aristotle's doctrine of matter, form, and privation, to demonstrate the possibility of generation and destruction (283–85), followed by a translation of *Physics* 192a3–34, with commentary (286–88). See further at note on 222–26.

284   *according to its nature . . . somehow incidentally:* Compare Aristotle, *Physics* 191b13–15.

is in no sense whatsoever: Latin *nusquam omnino gentium . . . nihil omnino neque uspiam gentium,* similar to the pleonastic Greek *oudepote oudamêi oudamôs* (Plato, *Phaedo* 78d). (*Gentium* is not a copying error for *genitum*.)

285   *in another sense . . . actuality . . . potentiality:* Compare Aristotle, *Physics* 191b27–29.

286   *matter . . . distinct from privation:* Latin *dividua . . . silva carentiae,* for Greek *hylên kai sterêsin heteron* ("matter and privation [=

something] distinct," 192a3–4), and replacing Aristotle's construction with a (Greek) genitive of difference rather than the
Latin ablative *carentiâ*. Compare notes on 37a/d, 68.

287 *language . . . rather obscure:* See note on E7.

288 *bodiless body:* Compare Aristotle, *On the Soul* 409b21.

289–94 *SVF* 1.86–88, 2.316 (LS 44D–E). The Stoics are somewhat dis-
consolately sandwiched between Aristotle, a philosopher to be
taken seriously (see note on 222–26), and Pythagoras, Numenius, and Plato, the bearers of Truth (295–320). But although
destined to serve as straw men of a sort (294), they are nevertheless essential once again as indirect contributors to the general argument (compare note on 160–75).

289 *god . . . craftsman . . . matter . . . substrate:* Compare Aëtius 1.3.25;
SVF 2.301, 374; LS 28E; and note on 50d.

 lacking quality: Matter as the Passive principle, or unqualified
substance *(to paschon, apoios ousia); SVF* 1.85 = 2.300 (LS 44B).

295–99 Numenius, fr. 52 des Places, closely aligned with 172–75 (which
however do not mention Pythagoras, the Stoics, or Numenius). See van Winden, *Calcidius on Matter,* 103–21; Köckert,
Christliche Kosmologie, 104–17.

295 *some Pythagoreans . . . to the state of the dyad:* Alexander Polyhistor,
Eudorus, Moderatus, and Nicomachus have been suggested,
but the identification remains uncertain (compare Dillon,
Middle Platonists, 126–28, 346–49; Bakhouche, *Calcidius,* 852 n.
1035). The point of Calcidius's criticism is at any rate clear:
unity would have to abandon its nature in order to become duality, thereby forfeiting its existence and status as a principle.

296–97 *the Stoics . . . indifferent . . . neither good nor evil: SVF* 3.117–19
(LS 58A–B); compare Plato, *Gorgias* 467e; Aristotle, *Categories*
12a24.

296 *the ancient theologians:* See note on 143.

297–98 *perversity:* See note on 165.

297 *paradoxical or contrary to human opinion:* Latin *miris . . . et contra
opinionem hominum;* compare Cicero, *Stoic Paradoxes* 4 *(admira-
bilia contraque opinionem omnium . . . paradoxa);* Boethius, *Consolation* 4.2.33, 4.4.10/12 *(mirum);* and note on 23.
Heraclitus, DK 22 A 22.

two world souls: Plato, *Laws* 896d–e. Compare 300 and note on 27–31.

298 *to understand:* Literally, "to be understood" (*intellegi,* note *intellegere,* 294); see note on 40e.

the absence of any being, as many suppose: The doctrine of evil as privation (301) or nonbeing is of course familiar from Plotinus (*Enneads* 1.8.3, 3.2.5), who developed it partly to counter Gnostic dualism (2.9.16–18). Augustine uses it against the Manichees (*Confessions* 3.7.12), and Boethius makes it the focal point of his theodicy (*Consolation* 3.12.29, 4.2.39). Calcidius maintains a distanced stance ("dissent among Platonic Philosophers," 301).

299 *on the understanding that there is an enduring nature:* Latin *ut manente natura,* a clear Grecism *(hôs menousês physeôs),* as noted by Waszink (on *Timaeus,* 301.6), and Bakhouche (*Calcidius,* 856 n. 1075). Compare note on 43a; *LSS* §85, *Zus.γ.*

the devices of men: Latin *artibus hominum;* possibly, "human limbs."

300 *two world souls:* Compare 297 and note on 27–31.

celestial insufflation: See note on 26.

301 *those . . . who hold:* Porphyry, to judge from Philoponus, *On the Eternity of the World* 14.3; the view is revisited in 352. "Disorderly and tumultuous motion" translates *inordinatum . . . et tumultuarium motum,* which in turn renders the Greek, *kinoumenon plêmmelôs kai ataktôs,* more accurately than in the continuous translation (30a). That may be because the phrase appears to have been the one to which Porphyry attached his interpretation (so Philoponus, 5.1344 Scholten).

They claim . . . evil . . . absence of power: See note on 298.

302–4 Calcidius sets out to reveal the three principles of God, Matter, and the Ideas (Forms), as in 307 and 339 (compare Alcinous, *Handbook* 8–10; Apuleius, *On Plato and His Doctrine* 1.5–6). Each of the principles is associated with a dialectical method: in these chapters Matter is said to be discovered by analysis *(resolutio),* and God by synthesis *(compositio);* in 341 the Ideas are discovered by syllogistic *(syllogismus).* Chapter 302 further highlights an Aristotelian distinction between what is prior or more intelligible to us (here, the sensible objects of opinion),

757

as the starting point of investigation, and what is prior or more intelligible by nature (the intelligible objects of intellect), as its end (*Physics* 184a16–23). Some confusion emerges from the facts that syllogistic is contrasted with analysis in 302 but then set aside until 341, leaving the transition to synthesis (the "other" method) in 304 abrupt and unexplained, and that in 303 analysis is essentially treated as a form of mental abstraction. Syllogistic is perhaps postponed on the understanding that, as the thoughts of God (29, 260, 273, 330, 339), the Ideas are embedded within an otherwise irreducible polarity of God and Matter (297, 307). The underlying philosophical point would appear to be that, as Matter is required to receive all forms, so the Ideas are required to produce them. The doctrine of the Ideas as residing within the mind of God is foreign to the *Timaeus* but indisputably in evidence from the time of Philo (*On the Creation* 5.20) and Seneca (*Epistle* 65.7; compare Cicero, *Orator* 3.9–10). See further, Taylor, *Commentary*, 81–82; Cornford, *Plato's Cosmology*, 34–41; van Winden, *Calcidius on Matter*, 128–36; Bakhouche, *Calcidius*, 858–59 n. 1099.

305   *without quality:* See note on 289.

306   Plato, *Phaedrus* 245d.

307   *whether they posit . . . a passive one:* Compare Aristotle, *Physics* 188b27–35, 189b11–16.

         God, Matter, and the Exemplar: See note on 302–4.

308   *nowhere ascribed . . . the name "matter" . . . calls it "prime matter":* The first point is correct (see note on 273), and the second obviously incorrect (Aristotle, *Metaphysics* 1015a7, 1049a25–27). Compare note on 7.

         Receptacle . . . mother . . . nurse: Compare 273.

         some think . . . material substrate: The Stoics (311, 321); see *SVF* 2.309; and notes on 50d, 289.

311   *the Stoics:* See previous note.

312   *pinnacle and origin:* See note on 26.

316   *the primary corporeal substrate:* See note on 50d.

317–18   Compare Aristotle, *On Generation and Corruption* 330a30–31b2.

318   *primary substrate:* See note on 50d.

319   Eight anti-Stoic arguments—supported by Aristotle's *Categories* (see note on 222–26)—for the incorporeality of matter, on the grounds that it is: unconjoined with quality; hence quality-less; hence shapeless; hence indeterminate; hence no instance of a Category of being; hence neither a genus nor under one; imperceptible; noncomposite. The Stoics held that there are two principles, the Active and Passive (see note on 289), and that only body can act or be acted upon (*SVF* 1.90 [LS 45A]).

the very Passivity . . . proper to it: "Passivity" (*passionem*) captures the Aristotelian Category (1b27), and "the very . . . proper to it" (*ipsam . . . propria eius*) the Stoic notion of passivity as the defining property of matter. Hence the removal of the one Aristotelian Category in principle wipes out any Stoic claim in support of the corporeality of matter, and with it the Stoic system of principles generally.

321   *explication of the text proper:* Compare 91, 137–38.

a conception: Latin *recordationem;* see note on 47a.

the Stoics . . . substrate: See notes on 50d, 308.

322   *many modes of discourse . . . obscure:* See note on E7.

323   *its substrate:* See note on 50d.

the Alpine peoples . . . Tripolis: See van Winden, *Calcidius on Matter,* 179.

325   *"inextricable errors":* Virgil, *Aeneid* 6.27.

"of this sort": Omitted from the continuous translation (49e).

328   Plato, *Theaetetus* 194c–d, playing on the Greek for "wax" (*kêros*) and "heart" (*kêr,* Latin *cera, cor*).

329   *disposed:* Latin *posita* (Greek *keitai*), omitted from the continuous translation (50c).

330   *the idea or eternal intellect of the eternal god:* See note on 302–4.

331   *a substrate for bodies:* See note on 50d.

332   *contrary . . . different:* Omitted from the continuous translation (50e).

333   *acts as a substrate:* See note on 50d.

336   *the ten Genera of Being:* See note on 222–26.

337   *the primary substrate . . . material substance:* See notes on 50d, 7.

338   *so the primary form . . . being endowed with quality:* Insofar as the

primary form is not naturally disposed to possess quality, it cannot be *deprived* of it; but insofar as it *confers* quality, it cannot be deprived of it either.

339   *God . . . his perfect intellect . . . Matter . . . Form:* See note on 302–4.

340   *his observation that . . . susceptible to diversion:* The first half of this third "division" evidently dropped out at an early point in the transmission (Bakhouche, *Calcidius,* 876 n. 1306). The phrase has been conjecturally restored in accordance with Calcidius's use of declarative *ut* and the subjunctive (see note on 27c).

341   *an abbreviated figure of syllogistic reasoning:* If (A) intellect and opinion are the same, then (B) sensibles are infallibly perceived [intelligibles]; but if (-A) they are different, then (C) there are separately existing sensibles and intelligibles (Ideas); but (-B) sensibles are not infallibly perceived; [therefore (-A) intellect and opinion are different;] therefore (C) there are separately existing intelligibles (Ideas). Proof of the *existence* of intelligible Ideas depends on the unstated assumption that every mode of cognition corresponds to an existing proper object (Plato, *Republic* 511d–e). See note on 302–4.

342   Plato, *Republic* 533e–34a; for "discursive reasoning" *(recordationem),* see note on 47a.

345   *acts as a substrate:* See note on 50d.

346–47   *suppositious . . . suppositionally grasped:* The Latin *praesumptos* and *praesumatur* are difficult to translate. Insofar as Calcidius sets "suppositious" *(praesumptus)* and its Greek counterpart *(nothos)* in opposition to "legitimate" *(legitimus - gnêsios),* the simplest solution might be to translate with "illegitimate" on the assumption that the change in terminology reflects mere rhetorical variation. The emphasis laid on the notion of suspicion in 345 and 347 suggests, however, that Calcidius is straining for a quasi-legal nuance, perhaps hinting at epistemological "parentage" that is based on mere assumption—and is therefore questionable or *suspicious*—rather than evidence-based certainty.

349   Plato, *Republic* 514a–17a.

352   *this foreign shaking . . . movement . . . foreign to it:* See note on 301. "Most" may be an allusive plural, for Numenius (297), although

Plutarch too acknowledges a principle of motion intrinsic to matter (*On the Generation of the Soul in the "Timaeus"* 1015e).

the "mass of water": Virgil, *Georgics* 1.322.

353   *certain "arms of Ceres":* Virgil, *Aeneid* 1.177.

354   *to act as a substrate:* See note on 50d.

the best possible way: Omitted from the continuous translation (53b).

355   *a proportion of the following sort:* Compare 16.

reasoning . . . new and unknown: See note on E7.

the paths of liberal erudition . . . geometry, music, arithmetic, and as-tronomy, the first . . . steps: The metaphor evokes Greek *methodos,* the "pursuit of a path," or "method." See further at note on E4/7.

Ps.-Cebes, *The Tablet* 13.2; see Moreschini, *Calcidio,* 780 n. 1012.

Bibliography

Editions, Translations, Commentaries

Bakhouche, B., ed. *Calcidius. Commentaire au "Timée" de Platon, I–II*. Paris, 2011.

Boeft, J. den. *Calcidius on Demons (Commentarius Ch. 127–136)*. Leiden, 1977.

———. *Calcidius on Fate, His Doctrine and Sources*. Leiden, 1970.

Moreschini, C. *Calcidio. Commentario al "Timeo" di Platone*. Milan, 2003.

Waszink, J. H., ed. *Timaeus a Calcidio translatus commentarioque instructus*. London and Leiden, 1975².

Winden, J. C. M. van. *Calcidius on Matter, His Doctrine and Sources. A Chapter in the History of Platonism*. Leiden, 1965².

Wrobel, J., ed. *Platonis Timaeus interprete Chalcidio cum eiusdem commentario*. Leipzig, 1876.

Secondary Literature

Baltes, M. *Die Weltentstehung des platonischen "Timaios" nach den antiken Interpreten, I–II*. Leiden, 1976–78.

Boys-Stones, G. R. *Post-Hellenestic Philosophy. A Study of Its Development from the Stoics to Origen*. Oxford, 2001.

Cornford, F. M. *Plato's Cosmology. The "Timaeus" of Plato*. London, 1935.

Dillon, J. *The Middle Platonists. A Study of Platonism 80 B.C. to A.D. 220*. London, 1977.

Dorfbauer, L. J. "Favonius Eulogius, der früheste Leser des Calcidius?" *Hermes* 139 (2011): 376–94.

Dronke, P. *The Spell of Calcidius. Platonic Concepts and Images in the Medieval West*. Florence, 2008.

Dutton, P. E. "Medieval Approaches to Calcidius." In *Plato's "Timaeus" as Cultural Icon*, edited by Reydams-Schils, 183–205.

Gersh, S. *Middle Platonism and Neoplatonism. The Latin Tradition, I–II*. Notre Dame, 1986.

Hoenig, C. *"Timaeus Latinus:* Calcidius and the Creation of the Universe." *Rhizomata* 2 (2014): 80–110.

Jones, R. M. "Chalcidius and Neo-Platonism." *Classical Philology* 13 (1918): 194–208.

Köckert, C. *Christliche Kosmologie und kaiserzeitliche Philosophie. Die Auslegung des Schöpfungsberichtes bei Origenes, Basilius und Gregor von Nyssa vor dem Hintergrund kaiserzeitlicher Timaeus-Interpretationen*. Tübingen, 2009.

Ratkowitsch, C. "Die Timaios-Übersetzung des Chalcidius. Ein Plato Christianus." *Philologus* 140 (1996): 139–62.

Reydams-Schils, G. "Calcidius Christianus? God, Body and Matter." In *Metaphysik und Religion: Zur Signatur des spätantiken Denkens: Akten des Internationalen Kongresses vom 13.–17. März 2001 in Würzburg*, edited by T. Kobusch, M. Erler, and I. Männlein-Robert, 193–211. Munich and Leipzig, 2002.

——. "Calcidius on God." In *Platonic Stoicism—Stoic Platonism. The Dialogue between Platonism and Stoicism in Antiquity*, edited by M. Bonazzi and C. Helmig, 243–58. Leuven, 2007.

——. *Demiurge and Providence. Stoic and Platonist Readings of Plato's "Timaeus"*. Turnhout, 1999.

——. "Meta-Discourse: Plato's "Timaeus" According to Calcidius." *Phronesis* 52 (2007): 301–27.

——, ed. *Plato's "Timaeus" as Cultural Icon*. Notre Dame, 2003.

Tarán, L. *Academica: Plato, Philip of Opus, and the Pseudo-Platonic "Epinomis."* Philadelphia, 1975.

——. "The Creation Myth in Plato's *Timaeus*." In *Essays in Ancient Greek Philosophy I*, edited by J. P. Anton and G. L. Kustas, 372–92. Albany, 1971. Reprinted in *Collected Papers (1962–1999)*. Leiden, Boston, and Cologne, 2001, 303–40.

Taylor, A. E. *A Commentary on Plato's "Timaeus."* Oxford, 1928.

Waszink, J. H. *Studien zum Timaioskommentar des Calcidius I. Die erste Hälfte des Kommentars (mit Ausnahme der Kapitel über die Weltseele)*. Leiden, 1964.

Index

Arabic numbers preceded by an uppercase "E" refer to the Dedicatory Epistle (E1, E2, E3); those followed by lowercase letters, to the *Timaeus* (17a, 17b, 17c); those without letters, to the commentary (1, 2, 3).